Linux Administration Cookbook

Insightful recipes to work with system administration
tasks on Linux

Adam K. Dean

BIRMINGHAM - MUMBAI

Linux Administration Cookbook

Commissioning Editor: Gebin George
Acquisition Editor: Prachi Bisht
Content Development Editor: Deepti Thore
Technical Editor: Sayali Thanekar
Copy Editor: Safis Editing
Project Coordinator: Jagdish Prabhu
Proofreader: Safis Editing
Indexer: Mariammal Chettiyar
Graphics: Jisha Chirayil
Production Coordinator: Arvindkumar Gupta

First published: December 2018

Production reference: 1311218

Published by Packt Publishing Ltd.
Livery Place
35 Livery Street
Birmingham
B3 2PB, UK.

ISBN 978-1-78934-252-9

www.packtpub.com

`mapt.io`

Mapt is an online digital library that gives you full access to over 5,000 books and videos, as well as industry leading tools to help you plan your personal development and advance your career. For more information, please visit our website.

Why subscribe?

- Spend less time learning and more time coding with practical eBooks and Videos from over 4,000 industry professionals

- Improve your learning with Skill Plans built especially for you

- Get a free eBook or video every month

- Mapt is fully searchable

- Copy and paste, print, and bookmark content

Packt.com

Did you know that Packt offers eBook versions of every book published, with PDF and ePub files available? You can upgrade to the eBook version at `www.packt.com` and as a print book customer, you are entitled to a discount on the eBook copy. Get in touch with us at `customercare@packtpub.com` for more details.

At `www.packt.com`, you can also read a collection of free technical articles, sign up for a range of free newsletters, and receive exclusive discounts and offers on Packt books and eBooks.

Contributors

About the author

Adam K. Dean has used Linux since 2005, when he rendered his first computer unbootable during an Ubuntu installation. Undeterred, a subsequent installation was successful, notwithstanding the odd graphical and Wi-Fi issues.

Between bouts of writing about himself in the third person, Adam now runs his own consultancy offering Linux expertise to a range of clients, though he hasn't forgotten his origins, and still occasionally renders computers unbootable.

This book wouldn't have been possible without the cumulative effort of a number of people. With that in mind, I'd like to first thank Lucy, for being supportive and understanding of my seemingly erratic life; Sam and Jon, for their excellent feedback on this book; and Martyn, Daj, AJ, Colin, Lath, Rob, and many others I've met in my career, for shaping the engineer I am.

About the reviewer

Donald Tevault—but you can call him Donnie—got involved with Linux way back in 2006, and has been working with it ever since. He holds the Linux Professional Institute Level 3—security certification, and the GIAC Incident Handler certification. Donnie is a professional Linux trainer, and thanks to the magic of the internet, teaches Linux classes literally the world over from the comfort of his living room.

Sam Norbury is someone who you never find frowning, at best you'll get a non-informative **mmm** from his general direction, which gives nothing away as to the inner-workings of his head, or what he thinks of your latest suggestion. Prized for his Ansible knowledge and patience, he now splits his time between consulting and travelling the world, spreading apathy everywhere he goes.

Jon Nield is a senior engineer who's reputation for calm and methodical problem solving has earned him a reputation as one of the most easy-going and nicest guys in tech. Having worked in the computing and server industry for many years, his expertise in areas such as C, and the underpinnings of the Linux operating system, make him a highly-sought consultant.

Packt is searching for authors like you

Table of Contents

Preface

When it comes to servers, there's no more popular OS than Linux and its family of distributions. No matter which company you work for these days, there's a good chance at least part of their infrastructure runs some flavor of Linux.

Because of this, there's never been a better time to get into Linux system administration and engineering (along with the tangentially related disciplines), though I would say that, of course... being a Linux sysadmin.

This book aims to be your reference and guide for certain common tasks in the Linux world, from the mundane and basic to the fun and complex, though anything can be complex if you try hard enough. I hope that, while reading it, you find something new (preferably a lot of new things) and maybe come across suggestions that you wouldn't have come across otherwise.

We're also going to get practical in our work (because just reading about things is boring), using virtual machines throughout to achieve our intended goals.

Who this book is for

This book is for a mixture of people, from the new and inexperienced, to the old and grumpy (like me).

It aims to teach you the basics of what you need to know to get started, while also introducing some real-world examples and suggesting various tips and tricks that you may not know already.

Even if you've been using Linux for a couple of decades, I hope you'll find something in this book that you didn't know, or find enlightening.

What this book covers

Chapter 1, *Introduction and Environment Setup*, explains how to set up a vanilla environment so that you understand what Vagrant does behind the scenes, and why we do what we do in terms of installation.

Chapter 2, *Remote Administration with SSH*, helps you understand the marvel that is SSH, and how it can make your life not only easier, but significantly better.

Chapter 3, *Networking and Firewalls*, covers a topic I find to be more of a pain than any other, networking and firewalling. We're going to look at the importance of each of these.

Chapter 4, *Services and Daemons*, inspects the nature of daemons, hunting them down, and killing them when they get too power-hungry. Services are also covered in this chapter.

Chapter 5, *Hardware and Disks*, covers the most treacherous part of any system, the hardware. Here, we'll talk about the evils of disks and how you might go about troubleshooting a physical system.

Chapter 6, *Security, Updating, and Package Management*, covers the stuff that makes servers useful. Packages have to get on systems in some way, shape, or form, and here, we'll investigate how they do it!

Chapter 7, *Monitoring and Logging*, explores the two topics most sysadmins groan at, knowing they're important at the same time. We're going to look at why you need both sensible monitoring and robust logging.

Chapter 8, *Permissions, SELinux, and AppArmor*, covers the innate security systems in place on a lot of servers, no matter how painful they might be to use and configure. Here, we'll talk about their importance.

Chapter 9, *Containers and Virtualization*, explores a favorite topic of mine, the segmentation of operating systems and how you might go about accomplishing such an arcane task.

Chapter 10, *Git, Configuration Management, and Infrastructure as Code*, discusses the importance of not losing your configuration when your computer randomly dies, and the ease with which solutions can be spun up and torn down.

Chapter 11, *Web Servers, Databases, and Mail Servers*, looks at some of the core functionality servers can provide, underpinning the majority of what the internet was invented to accomplish: communication.

Chapter 12, *Troubleshooting and Workplace Diplomacy*, expounds some basic troubleshooting techniques, and contains a philosophical discussion on keeping your head in stressful situations. The author is something of an authority on this.

Chapter 13, *BSDs, Solaris, Windows, IaaS and PaaS, and DevOps*, is a fun final chapter on semi-related systems in the Linux world, some of which you'll definitely come across, and some which should have been greater than they turned out to be.

To get the most out of this book

You're going to need a computer. If you intend to work along with the examples, the easiest way to do so is by utilizing Vagrant, which is software for building portable development environments programmatically.

At the start of each chapter with working code, you'll find a Vagrantfile entry. This can be downloaded from the links provided later in this preface, but it can also be typed out if you prefer.

For the best experience, I'd recommend a computer with at least four cores and preferably 8 GB of RAM, though you might be able to tweak each entry for your own purposes.

This book assumes basic knowledge of moving around a Linux filesystem using the command line.

Download the example code files

You can download the example code files for this book from your account at www.packt.com. If you purchased this book elsewhere, you can visit www.packt.com/support and register to have the files emailed directly to you.

You can download the code files by following these steps:

1. Log in or register at www.packt.com.
2. Select the **SUPPORT** tab.
3. Click on **Code Downloads & Errata**.
4. Enter the name of the book in the **Search** box and follow the onscreen instructions.

Once the file is downloaded, please make sure that you unzip or extract the folder using the latest version of:

- WinRAR/7-Zip for Windows
- Zipeg/iZip/UnRarX for Mac
- 7-Zip/PeaZip for Linux

The code bundle for the book is also hosted on GitHub at https://github.com/PacktPublishing/Linux-Administration-Cookbook. In case there's an update to the code, it will be updated on the existing GitHub repository.

We also have other code bundles from our rich catalog of books and videos available at `https://github.com/PacktPublishing/`. Check them out!

Download the color images

We also provide a PDF file that has color images of the screenshots/diagrams used in this book. You can download it here: `https://www.packtpub.com/sites/default/files/downloads/9781789342529_ColorImages.pdf`.

Conventions used

There are a number of text conventions used throughout this book.

`CodeInText`: Indicates code words in text, database table names, folder names, filenames, file extensions, pathnames, dummy URLs, user input, and Twitter handles. Here is an example: "I've put together the following `Vagrantfile` for use in this chapter."

A block of code is set as follows:

```
# -*- mode: ruby -*-
# vi: set ft=ruby :

$provisionScript = <<-SCRIPT
sed -i 's#PasswordAuthentication no#PasswordAuthentication yes#g'
/etc/ssh/sshd_config
systemctl restart sshd
SCRIPT
```

When we wish to draw your attention to a particular part of a code block, the relevant lines or items are set in bold:

```
[vagrant@centos2 ~]$ ip a
<SNIP>
3: eth1: <BROADCAST,MULTICAST,UP,LOWER_UP> mtu 1500 qdisc pfifo_fast
state UP group default qlen 1000
    link/ether 08:00:27:56:c5:a7 brd ff:ff:ff:ff:ff:ff
    inet 192.168.33.11/24 brd 192.168.33.255 scope global
noprefixroute eth1
       valid_lft forever preferred_lft forever
    inet6 fe80::a00:27ff:fe56:c5a7/64 scope link
       valid_lft forever preferred_lft forever
```

Any command-line input or output is written as follows:

```
[vagrant@centos1 ~]$ ssh centos2 -X
```

Bold: Indicates a new term, an important word, or words that you see onscreen. For example, words in menus or dialog boxes appear in the text like this. Here is an example: "The last thing to do from the main screen is set our **INSTALLATION DESTINATION**."

Warnings or important notes appear like this.

Tips and tricks appear like this.

Sections

In this book, you will find several headings that appear frequently (*Getting ready, How to do it..., How it works..., There's more...,* and *See also*).

To give clear instructions on how to complete a recipe, use these sections as follows:

Getting ready

This section tells you what to expect in the recipe and describes how to set up any software or any preliminary settings required for the recipe.

How to do it...

This section contains the steps required to follow the recipe.

How it works...

This section usually consists of a detailed explanation of what happened in the previous section.

There's more…

This section consists of additional information about the recipe in order to make you more knowledgeable about the recipe.

See also

This section provides helpful links to other useful information for the recipe.

Get in touch

Feedback from our readers is always welcome.

General feedback: If you have questions about any aspect of this book, mention the book title in the subject of your message and email us at customercare@packtpub.com.

Errata: Although we have taken every care to ensure the accuracy of our content, mistakes do happen. If you have found a mistake in this book, we would be grateful if you would report this to us. Please visit www.packt.com/submit-errata, selecting your book, clicking on the Errata Submission Form link, and entering the details.

Piracy: If you come across any illegal copies of our works in any form on the Internet, we would be grateful if you would provide us with the location address or website name. Please contact us at copyright@packt.com with a link to the material.

If you are interested in becoming an author: If there is a topic that you have expertise in and you are interested in either writing or contributing to a book, please visit authors.packtpub.com.

Reviews

Please leave a review. Once you have read and used this book, why not leave a review on the site that you purchased it from? Potential readers can then see and use your unbiased opinion to make purchase decisions, we at Packt can understand what you think about our products, and our authors can see your feedback on their book. Thank you!

For more information about Packt, please visit packt.com.

Introduction and Environment Setup

1

In this chapter, we will cover the following recipes:

- Understanding and choosing a distribution
- Installing VirtualBox
- Installing our chosen distribution manually
- Connecting to our **virtual machine** (**VM**)
- Accessing and updating our VM
- Understanding how VMs differ
- Quick `sudo` explanation
- Using Vagrant to automatically provision VMs
- Anecdote (try, try, and try again)

Introduction

Before we get into the nitty-gritty of what distribution (sometimes shortened to "distro") we're going to use, we must first take a rather large step backwards and consider the concept of **Linux** in a somewhat philosophical way.

A good description of "what Linux is" can be hard to pin down, due in no small part to a level of confusion willfully propagated by IT professionals, because it makes them sound much smarter than they actually are when they come to explain it.

Because you're reading this book, I'm going to assume that you know of Linux at a high level; you know that it's an **operating system** (**OS**) like Windows or macOS, that it's not seen much of the limelight, and that it's not generally used on the desktop.

This assessment is both right and wrong, depending on who you're speaking to.

Laid-back **systems administrators (sysadmins)** will lean back further, nod their 80s era mohawk, and agree that Linux is an OS—and a decent one at that. They will then go back to playing with whatever trendy software they're learning this week so that they can try and shoehorn it into the infrastructure next week.

Self-proclaimed graybeards will stop what they're doing, sigh audibly, and pick up their fourth cup of coffee before swiveling around to give you a lecture on the difference between GNU/Linux (or GNU+Linux) and the Linux kernel.

 A kernel is an important part of any complete OS. It's the piece of software that sits between the hardware and the software, performing the grunt work of translating between the two. All operating systems will have a kernel of one sort or other, for example, the macOS kernel is call **XNU**.

The lecture you receive will be tedious, will involve names such as Richard Stallman, Linus Torvalds, and possibly even Andrew Tanenbaum, and may even take upwards of an hour, but the main takeaway will be that Linux is the accepted name of the OS you're learning about, while also being technically incorrect. They will say that Linux is really just the kernel, and everything beyond that is a distribution wrapped atop the GNU tools suite.

It is considered sensible to avoid this debate at all costs.

 For the purposes of this book, when I refer to Linux, I'm talking about the OS as a whole, and when I refer to the **kernel**, I'm really talking about the Linux kernel, the development of which is spearheaded by Linus Torvalds.

Understanding and choosing a distribution

Linux, as hinted at in the preceding section, is fragmented. There's no better way to describe this, due to the sheer number of different **distributions** you can download from a multitude of different vendors. Some of these vendors are for-profit, offering support contracts and SLAs with your purchase of their OS, and some are entirely voluntary, manned by one person in their garage.

There are literally hundreds of distributions to choose from, and each has their advocate-army to tell you why theirs is "the one true distribution" and "there's really no reason to go shopping around for a different one."

 There are also Linux distributions that have been created for specific purposes, such as Red Star OS, the purportedly North Korean Linux distribution.

The truth of the matter is that most businesses use the Linux distribution they do because it was:

- The first one that popped up when the owner Googled **free OS**
- The one the first IT Administrator liked
- The one that offers a contract they can invoke when something breaks

Going through each distribution that's around at the moment would be futile, as they're being created or abandoned on an almost weekly basis. Instead, I'm going to run through a popular selection (in the server space, rather than the desktop), explain some key differences, and then talk about which I'll be using for the rest of this book.

Don't be deterred if the distribution your business uses isn't one we talk about here – most of the tooling is consistent across distributions, and where it differs, documentation exists to help you out.

 If you want to learn more about the various distributions available to you, a site called **DistroWatch** (`https://distrowatch.com/`) has been around for years, and offers a regularly updated list of most Linux distributions, organized by page hit ranking.

Ubuntu

Ubuntu is the first Linux distribution I ever installed, and I'd wager the same could be said for a lot of people who started in Linux around the mid-2000s. It's also the distribution I'm using to write this book.

It has enjoyed consistent mindshare on the desktop, thanks to its decent attempt at marketing (including its position in Google's rankings when searching `Linux`), its perception as **Linux for Human Beings**, and its user-friendliness.

Downstream from Debian, Ubuntu's development is headed by Canonical, and while they started with an emphasis on making a rock-solid desktop OS, they have since moved into the lofty realms of attempting to dominate the server space, and have entered the IoT device market too.

When we say "downstream" in this sense, we mean that Ubuntu shares a lot of its foundation with Debian, except it adds some extra bits and takes some bits out. In the Linux world, there are few **from-scratch** distributions, with most using another distribution as their bedrock.

Known also for its cutesy naming convention (18.04 being Bionic Beaver), the fact Ubuntu was so popular on the desktop meant it was the obvious distribution of choice for sysadmins to install on their servers, reaching for what they were already familiar with.

More recently, it's become increasingly common to find Ubuntu installations when dealing with inherited systems, usually a **long-term support** (**LTS**) release (so that confusion and headaches around OS upgrades can be avoided for a reasonable length of time.)

Ubuntu releases on a six-monthly cycle, with every two years being an LTS release (14.04, 16.04, and 18.04, most recently). Their numbering convention is year-released, followed by month (so April 2018 is 18.04). It is possible to upgrade from version to version of Ubuntu.

Canonical also aren't shy of introducing new technology and software in Ubuntu, even when it diverges from their Debian base. Recent examples of this include the following:

- **Snaps**: A way of distributing distribution-agnostic software
- **Upstart**: A replacement initialization system that was later also replaced by `systemd`
- **Mir**: A display server, which was initially conceived as a way to replace the ageing X Window System

Ubuntu can be downloaded from `https://ubuntu.com`.

Debian

As mentioned previously, Debian (the universal OS) is the basis for a lot of other distributions that came later, but it has consistently been one of the most popular, both on the desktop and on servers. It is still highly likely that you will choose to install Debian yourself, or will inherit a system running this distribution, with its reputation for stability.

Traditionally, the server-space war was fought between two camps, the Debian Druids and the CentOS Cardinals. In more recent years, newcomers have entered the fray (like Ubuntu,) but these two still hold a considerable amount of hardware to ransom.

Releasing every two or three years, the Debian versions are named after Toy Story characters (7—Wheezy, 8—Jessie, 9—Stretch). They have a reputation for being one of the most stable Linux distributions around, with tried and tested versions of software, as well as sensibly backported fixes.

 Backporting is the act of taking a fix from a recent release of software, such as the kernel itself, and incorporating those fixes into the version you're running, recompiling it into a new piece of software. Features are rarely backported, due to features having the potential to introduce more breaking changes into long-term support distributions.

Some criticism is sometimes leveled at Debian because it generally has older versions of packages available in its release version, which may not include all the trendy and cool features a systems administrator wants, or a developer desires. This isn't fair, given that people generally look for stability and security in the server world, over the latest and greatest version of Node.js.

Debian has staunch defenders, and it holds a special place in a lot of hearts, though it's unusual to see it in some Enterprise environments because it's developed by the Debian Project, rather than a traditional company that can offer support contracts. In my anecdotally dismissible experience, I have more often seen Debian in smaller companies who needed a quick solution, and slightly larger companies who still run some legacy systems.

Debian can be downloaded from `https://www.debian.org`.

CentOS – the one we'll mostly be using

The other part of the traditional server-space war, CentOS features its own soldiers and martyrs. It is still widely used, and has a reputation for stability and boredom that rivals Debian's.

The **Community Enterprise Operating System** (**CentOS**) is a freely available and compiled version of the Red Hat Enterprise Linux distribution, which aims to offer functional compatibility, generally replacing the Red Hat logo with the CentOS logo to avoid trademark infringement. (In January of 2014 it was announced that Red Hat was joining forces with CentOS, to help drive and invest in CentOS development.)

Because of its nature, a lot of systems administrators have installed CentOS to better understand the Red Hat world, because (as mentioned previously) Red Hat has a good reputation in Enterprise companies, so it would make sense to install something so strikingly similar.

This installation trend goes both ways. I have seen companies who started out by installing CentOS because it was readily available and allowed them to design their infrastructure easily, utilizing publicly available and free repos, before moving to a RHEL deployment for the finished product.

 Repos is a short form way of saying repositories, which are the common location from which software is installed on a Linux system. Where Windows usually has downloads from websites, and macOS has the App Store, Linux has used software repositories for most of its life, and they have the advantage of being easily searchable with a few keystrokes on the command line.

I have also seen companies who deployed RHEL everywhere, only to realise that they were spending a lot of money, and never invoking the support they'd bought because their operations team was just that good! They would then gradually phase out their Red Hat deployments and move to CentOS, changing very little in the process.

Releases come about every few years, with version 7 being released in 2014, and getting consistent updates since then. However, it should be noted that version 6, which was released in 2011, will be getting maintenance updates until 2020.

 CentOS can be downloaded from `https://centos.org`. We will go through this in the installation section.

Red Hat Enterprise Linux

Red Hat Enterprise Linux, or RHEL as it's more commonly known (because it's a long name), has a very firm footing in Enterprises. It targets the commercial space very well, and as a result it is not uncommon to find yourself on a RHEL box, which you've initially assumed to be a CentOS installation.

What makes RHEL different is the support offered by Red Hat, Inc. and the various services that you can utilize if you've bought an official package.

While Red Hat still offers the source code for their distribution without question (hence CentOS), they sell versions and packages for everything from the desktop up to data centre installations.

There's an adage that states "no one got fired for buying IBM," which is a little dated in this day and age, but I've heard people invoke this philosophy to describe Red Hat on more than one occasion. No one will get fired for buying Red Hat (but you might be asked what the benefits are of paying for something that's available for free under another name.)

 Beautifully, it was announced while I was in the editing stage of this book that IBM have bought Red Hat, bringing my comment above full circle. The universe is great sometimes.

Aside from the support, the business-like attitude that other businesses like, and the contributions back to the community as a whole, Red Hat also offer something which has been variously described as "a waste of time" and "crucial for this role."

Exams are looked at with both affection and derision, depending on who you speak to in the Linux community (as with many things, there's something of a holy war about them). Red Hat offers two of the most popular, and many more to boot. You can study for and become a Red Hat Certified System Administrator, followed by a Red Hat Certified Engineer, which are widely seen as very acceptable qualifications to have.

As a college dropout, I'm quite happy to have an RHCE qualification under my belt.

Some people see these exams as a way of getting past the first line of those hiring (as in the people who scan your CV, and look for badges they recognize). Others see them as proof that you know what you're doing around a Linux system due to the fact that these exams are practical, (meaning they sit you in front of a computer and give you a set of steps to finish.) Some people dismiss exams altogether, although they're usually the ones who've never bothered trying the exam.

 Take a look at `https://www.redhat.com`, taking particular note of the various packages on offer. They do have a developer account too, which gives you access to services you would otherwise pay for (as long as you don't try and sneak them into a production environment!).

Installing VirtualBox

As I said in the previous section, I've chosen to mostly use CentOS for the recipes in this book. Hopefully, this gives you a good baseline for learning about Linux Administration, but also gives you a bit of a head start if you plan on going for any of the Red Hat exams.

Instead of requiring you to have a spare laptop handy, or renting a server somewhere, I'm going to advocate using VMs for testing and running through the examples given.

VMs are exactly as they sound – a way of virtualizing computer hardware on one or a cluster of physical machines, thus allowing you to test, break, and play to your heart's content, without risking rendering your own computer unbootable.

There are many ways of creating a VM: macOS has xhyve, Windows has Hyper-V, and Linux has a native implementation called **Kernel Virtual Machine** (**KVM**).

 KVM (along with libvirt) is the technology that you will come across most often in the Linux virtualization space. It forms the basis of popular technologies, such as Proxmox and OpenStack, while providing near-native speeds.

Another way of creating and managing VMs is a program called VirtualBox, which is now developed by Oracle. The nice thing about this software, and the reason I shall be using it here, is that it's cross-platform, being produced for macOS, Windows, and Linux.

Installing VirtualBox on Ubuntu

I'm using Ubuntu to write this book, so I'll run through the basic way of installing VirtualBox on an Ubuntu desktop.

This will be slightly different to installing it on other distributions, but a good number of them package it for installation, and should provide a guide for installing it.

Command-line installation

Open your Terminal and run the following:

```
$ sudo apt install virtualbox
```

 Using sudo will generally prompt you for your password, and you won't see anything being printed to screen as you type.

You will likely be prompted to confirm installation of VirtualBox and its dependencies (there may be a lot—it's a complex program and if you haven't updated in a while, you may get a few dependency updates too).

Hit *Y* and *Enter* to continue. The following screenshot shows an example of the installation if started from the command line:

```
                          adam@adam-XPS-13-9360: ~
File  Edit  View  Search  Terminal  Help
To run a command as administrator (user "root"), use "sudo <command>".
See "man sudo_root" for details.

adam@adam-XPS-13-9360:~$ sudo apt install virtualbox
[sudo] password for adam:
Reading package lists... Done
Building dependency tree
Reading state information... Done
The following additional packages will be installed:
  build-essential dkms dpkg-dev fakeroot g++ g++-7 gcc gcc-7
  libalgorithm-diff-perl libalgorithm-diff-xs-perl libalgorithm-merge-perl
  libasan4 libatomic1 libc-dev-bin libc6-dev libcilkrts5 libdouble-conversion1
  libfakeroot libgcc-7-dev libgsoap-2.8.60 libitm1 liblsan0 libmpx2
  libqt5core5a libqt5dbus5 libqt5gui5 libqt5network5 libqt5opengl5
  libqt5printsupport5 libqt5svg5 libqt5widgets5 libqt5x11extras5 libquadmath0
  libsdl1.2debian libstdc++-7-dev libtsan0 libubsan0 libvncserver1
  libxcb-xinerama0 linux-libc-dev make manpages-dev qt5-gtk-platformtheme
  qttranslations5-l10n virtualbox-dkms virtualbox-qt
Suggested packages:
  menu debian-keyring g++-multilib g++-7-multilib gcc-7-doc libstdc++6-7-dbg
  gcc-multilib autoconf automake libtool flex bison gcc-doc gcc-7-multilib
  gcc-7-locales libgcc1-dbg libgomp1-dbg libitm1-dbg libatomic1-dbg
  libasan4-dbg liblsan0-dbg libtsan0-dbg libubsan0-dbg libcilkrts5-dbg
  libmpx2-dbg libquadmath0-dbg glibc-doc qt5-image-formats-plugins qtwayland5
  libstdc++-7-doc make-doc vde2 virtualbox-guest-additions-iso
The following NEW packages will be installed
  build-essential dkms dpkg-dev fakeroot g++ g++-7 gcc gcc-7
  libalgorithm-diff-perl libalgorithm-diff-xs-perl libalgorithm-merge-perl
  libasan4 libatomic1 libc-dev-bin libc6-dev libcilkrts5 libdouble-conversion1
  libfakeroot libgcc-7-dev libgsoap-2.8.60 libitm1 liblsan0 libmpx2
  libqt5core5a libqt5dbus5 libqt5gui5 libqt5network5 libqt5opengl5
  libqt5printsupport5 libqt5svg5 libqt5widgets5 libqt5x11extras5 libquadmath0
  libsdl1.2debian libstdc++-7-dev libtsan0 libubsan0 libvncserver1
  libxcb-xinerama0 linux-libc-dev make manpages-dev qt5-gtk-platformtheme
  qttranslations5-l10n virtualbox virtualbox-dkms virtualbox-qt
0 to upgrade, 47 to newly install, 0 to remove and 4 not to upgrade.
Need to get 63.4 MB of archives.
After this operation, 275 MB of additional disk space will be used.
Do you want to continue? [Y/n] Y
```

Once done, you should have a working VirtualBox installation.

Graphical installation

If you'd like, you can also install VirtualBox through Ubuntu software.

Simply search for the software you desire, in this case, **VirtualBox**, and click through to its store page.

Once there, click **Install** and the package will be installed, no Terminal required!

After installation, your screen will change to show **Launch** and **Remove** options.

Installing VirtualBox on macOS

Although I'm using Ubuntu, it's not the end of the world if you're not. macOS is a fine OS too, and handily it supports VirtualBox.

In this recipe, we'll run through a couple of ways of installing VirtualBox in macOS. You'll find that the layout is extremely similar, regardless of the OS you use.

Command-line installation

If you already have the command-line program `brew` installed, then getting VirtualBox is as easy as running the following command:

```
$ brew cask install virtualbox
```

You may be prompted for a superuser password to complete the installation.

Homebrew is available from `https://brew.sh/` and is effectively the package manager that macOS needs, but doesn't have out of the box. I can't readily recommend blindly running scripts from mysterious websites, so be sure you understand what's being done (read the code) before you take the plunge and install brew.

Graphical installation

Oracle also provides an installation image for macOS, if you'd like to install it in the more traditional way.

Simply navigate to `https://www.virtualbox.org/wiki/Downloads` and select the **OS X hosts** option.

This will prompt you to download the installer to your local system, which you can unpack and install.

Running through the installation, you may be prompted for your superuser password.

Installing VirtualBox on Windows

If you're not using a Linux flavor on your computer, and you're not using macOS, it's a good bet that you're running Windows (unless you've delved into FreeBSD on the desktop or similar, in which case I can't help you here—we'd need an entire afternoon).

If using Windows, I can suggest VirtualBox again, due to its cross-OS nature, and it can again be installed from Oracle's site.

Graphical installation

Like the macOS installation, navigate to `https://www.virtualbox.org/wiki/Downloads` and select the **Windows hosts** option:

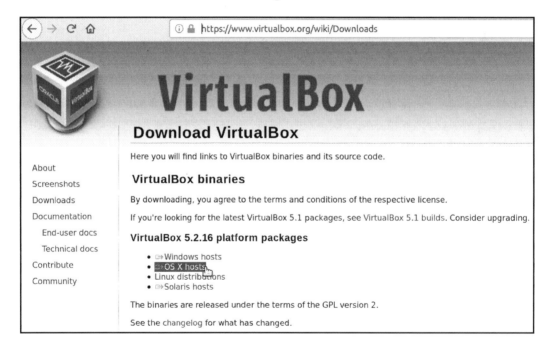

This will download an executable that can be run.

It's worth noting that Windows can complain if you're attempting to run multiple virtualization solutions at once. If you've previously run Hyper-V, or Docker, and you experience issues attempting to start VirtualBox machines, try disabling your other solutions first.

Installing our chosen distribution manually

Phew, that was a journey, and we've not even started properly!

Next, we're going to look at setting up a VM manually. But fear not! We will also be looking at automating this procedure with Vagrant to avoid having to perform repetitive steps in the rest of the book.

 Seriously, if you're already well-versed in installing CentOS, feel free to skip this section entirely. I have provided Vagrantfiles throughout the rest of this book for automating the boxes we're going to work on.

Obtaining our CentOS installation media

The main way Linux distributions are distributed is in the form of ISO images. These images can then be burned onto a DVD as appropriate, or mounted for a VM to boot from.

Head over to `https://centos.org/download/` and have a look at the options on offer.

I'm going to download the **Minimal ISO**, for reasons that will become clear shortly.

Clicking through should bring you to a mirror page:

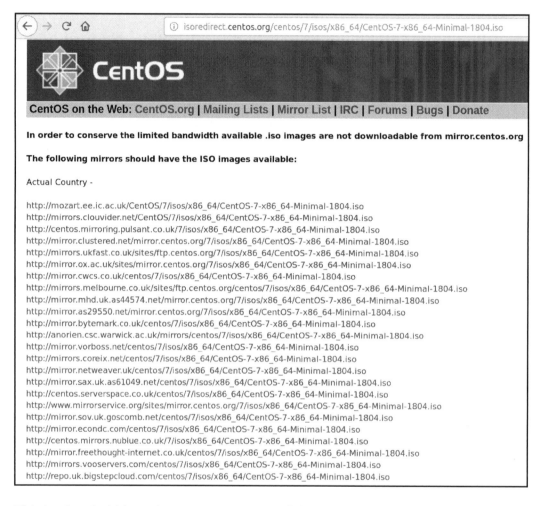

This is a bandwidth-saving measure on part of the CentOS Project by prompting the end user to download from any number of different hosts. They can spread the cost of bandwidth out to volunteers.

What you tend to find is that these providers typically fall into two categories, with exceptions. Generally, the images are provided by universities, or hosting providers. The cynic in me thinks that the hosting providers offer a mirror service as an easy source of marketing, rather than some philanthropic gesture.

Choose a download location near to you, and wait for the download to complete.

You may note that one of the download options is via Torrent. Torrenting is a great way of spreading out the cost of bandwidth to multiple people, and allowing a small piece of the software to be downloaded from multiple locations greatly reduces load on any one source. However, it should be noted that some workplaces watch out for this type of traffic on their networks due to the reputation torrenting has.

Checking the checksum

Once downloaded (which may take a while, since even minimal is large), you will be faced with an ISO image.

On my Ubuntu installation, I can see it in my `Downloads` folder:

```
$ ls ~/Downloads/
CentOS-7-x86_64-Minimal-1804.iso
```

One way to confirm our installation media and ensure that we've downloaded exactly what we expect, is to compare the `Sha256` sum of the downloaded file with a known-good value. This both proves that it's the download we expect it to be, and also checks that no corruption has occurred during the file download.

CentOS provides a release notes page that we can visit to find the `Sha256` sum we're comparing: `https://wiki.centos.org/Manuals/ReleaseNotes`.

Click through to **Release Notes for CentOS 7**, which should bring you to the most recent version of the release notes.

On this page, we can scroll down to **Verifying Downloaded Installation Images**, which will list the current `Sha256` sums for the download images.

Always make sure that the site you're getting your known-good `Sha256` values from is itself legitimate.

In my case, I can see that the `Sha256` value for the file I just downloaded is as follows:

```
714acc0aefb32b7d51b515e25546835e55a90da9fb00417fbee2d03a62801efd
CentOS-7-x86_64-Minimal-1804.iso
```

With this in hand, I can go back to where I listed out the file in my Terminal, and run a basic command to check the `Sha256` value of the downloaded image:

```
$ sha256sum CentOS-7-x86_64-Minimal-1804.iso
714acc0aefb32b7d51b515e25546835e55a90da9fb00417fbee2d03a62801efd
CentOS-7-x86_64-Minimal-1804.iso
```

Comparing the value from the CentOS website with the value from my downloaded image confirms that they are the same.

The media is what we expected!

`Sha256` checks can also be performed on Windows and macOS. On macOS, this is accomplished using built-in tools, though Windows may require other software.

Setting up our VM

Now that we have our media and VirtualBox is installed, it's time to run through manually provisioning (technical term) our machine and installing CentOS.

In this section, we will be provisioning a small VM, but even that will come with the cost of processing power, memory, and disk space. Always ensure that you have the appropriate resources available for the machine you're trying to create. In this case, at least 50 GB of free drive space and a minimum of 8 GB of memory is advisable.

VirtualBox main window

Upon starting, you will be greeted with the VirtualBox main window. At the moment, we're only interested in the **New** button in the top left. You need to click the New button.

Next, you will be prompted to name your VM.

Call your first machine CentOS-1.

Notice how when you name your machine, the **Type** and **Version** automatically detects what you've typed, and reconfigures the selection as appropriate.

In this case, it gives us a **Type** of **Linux**, and a **Version** of **Red Hat (64-bit)**. This is okay because of what we said before about CentOS and Red Hat Enterprise Linux being very close.

Hit **Next.**

 64-bit is the architecture of the OS, though the OS you install must be supported by the CPU you have (most CPUs these days are x86_64.) The common architectures were generally x86 (32-bit) and x86_64 (64-bit) for years, but more recently the x86 variant has been dying off. The most common installations these days are x86_64, though ARM and aarch64 machines are becoming more commonplace. In this book, we will only be using x86_64 machines.

Now, we have to configure the amount of memory to give our machine. If you're constrained by this, you can put it to a lower value than the default of 1024 MB (1 GB), but 1,024 MB is a reasonable place to start, and we can always adjust it later if needed.

Now, we'll be prompted to configure the hard disk for our virtual system.

Leave the default option of **Create a virtual hard disk now** selected, and click **Create.**

You'll be prompted to choose a type. Leave the default selected, that is, **VDI (VirtualBox Disk Image).**

You'll be given the option of provisioning the disk over time (**Dynamically allocated**) or all in one go (**Fixed size**). I tend to leave it as **Dynamically allocated.**

Next, you'll be prompted to choose a location and a size for the disk. I would advise leaving the disk in the default location, and for the moment the default size of 8 GB should be enough disk space to get started.

Hit **Create.**

If everything goes well, you will return to the main window, and a new VM should be listed on the left, in the Powered Off state.

CentOS installation

Now that we have our VM, it's time to install our OS on it.

Clicking **Start** on the top of the main VirtualBox window, with your VM selected, should prompt you to first select a startup disk.

I've navigated to my Downloads folder and chosen the downloaded image from earlier.

Pressing **Start** will boot the machine from our media.

You will be presented with the option screen within the VM, with **Test this media & install CentOS 7** selected by default.

I usually hit the up arrow (within the VM window) to select only **Install CentOS 7** and skip the media check, though you may wish to perform the test.

 If you're using physical media to install a machine (a DVD or CD), it might be a good idea to run a test of the media prior to installation.

Pressing *Enter* will continue the installation.

You will be prompted to choose your language. I choose **English**, because I'm monolingual.

Once done, you will find yourself on the landing page of the most recent CentOS installer:

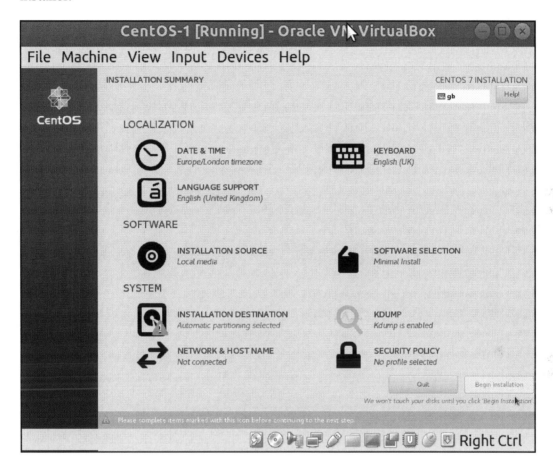

 Note the message at the bottom, suggesting that items marked with the yellow icon need to be completed.

Because our date/time, keyboard, and language are all correct, we'll move on to the next stages, but feel free to correct any of these settings if they're wrong for you.

Notice that under **INSTALLATION SOURCE** we've got **Local media** selected, and under **SOFTWARE SELECTION** we've got **Minimal Install**. This is a product of us selecting the minimal image earlier on, and gives us a good chance to talk about installation over the internet.

First, we need to configure our network. Click on **NETWORK & HOST NAME** to do this.

You should have a single **Ethernet** device, provided as part of the default provisioning step when making our VM.

Toggle the **ON/OFF** toggle to the right of your device name, and check that the network values are populated in a similar way to mine:

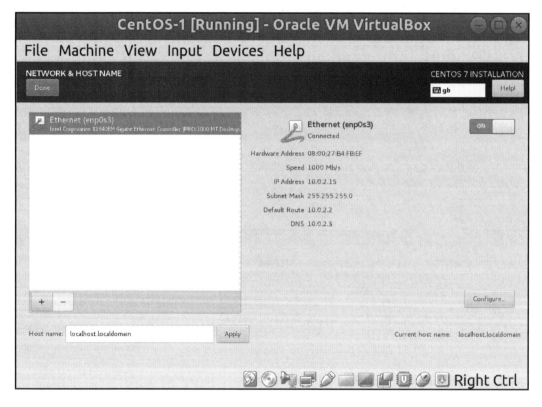

VirtualBox creates a NAT network by default, meaning that your VM doesn't sit on the exact same network as the host computer. Instead, the VM exists in a network by itself, but with a path to the outside world (via your host machine).

Press **Done** in the top left to complete our network setup (for now)!

Back on the main screen, click on **INSTALLATION SOURCE**:

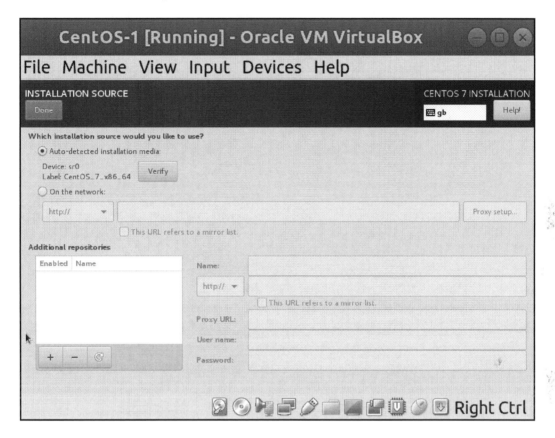

Within this screen, you can see that the auto-detected media is actually our disk image (`sr0` being Linux's denotion of the disc drive).

Change the selected radio button to be **On the network**.

Populate the URL bar with the following:

```
mirror.centos.org/centos/7/os/x86_64/
```

You should end up with the following screenshot:

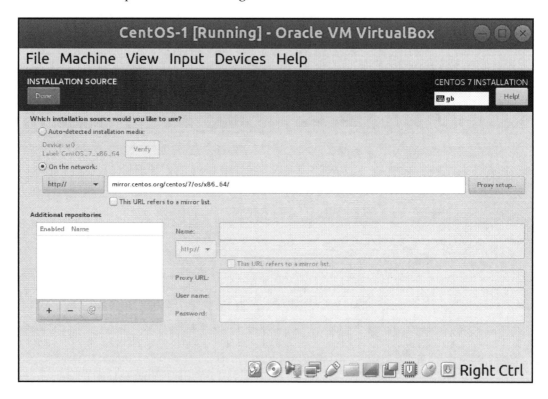

Press **Done** in the top left.

Once you're back on the main screen, it will be indicated that your software source has changed, and you need to verify this by entering the **SOFTWARE SELECTION** window. Proceed with this.

Have a read through the different options, but for now leave **Minimal Install** selected and click **Done**:

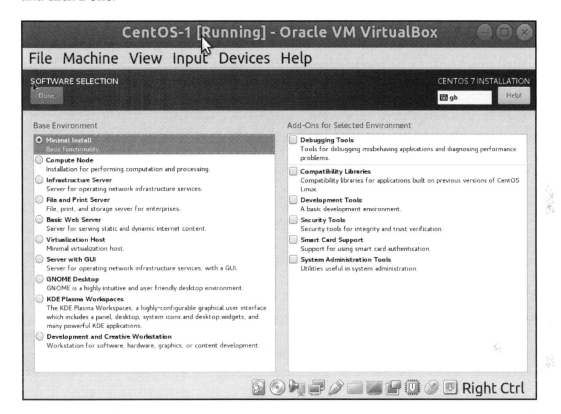

The last thing to do from the main screen is set our **INSTALLATION DESTINATION**. Click through to this screen.

Have a read of the options, but for now we're not going to bother with changing the default partition layout, or encrypting our disk. You should also see that the default selected disk is our 8 GB VirtualBox one.

Click **Done** (you shouldn't have had to make any changes, but the installer makes you enter this screen at the very least):

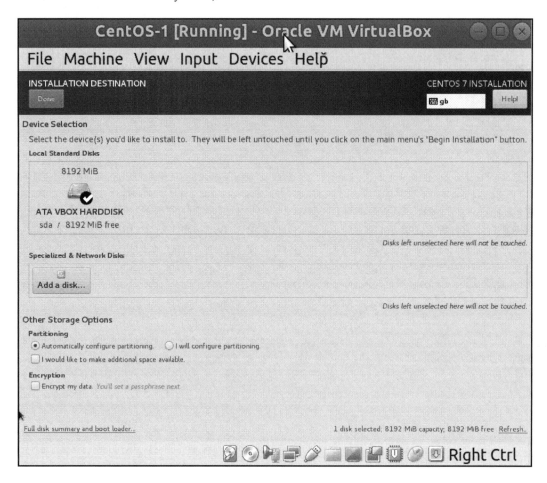

We've finally finished our (fairly basic) configuration. Hit the **Begin Installation** button at the bottom of the main screen.

You'll see the installation begin, and will be given the following screen while you wait:

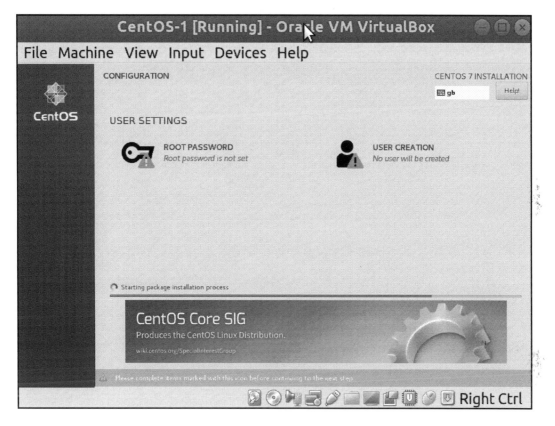

Click on the options at the top in turn, setting a `root` password and creating a user.

The `root` user is akin to the administrator on a Windows system; it's all-powerful and can be dangerous in the wrong hands. Some distributions don't even prompt you to set a root password on installation, making you use your own user and `su` or `sudo` instead.

When making your user, flag them as an administrator too:

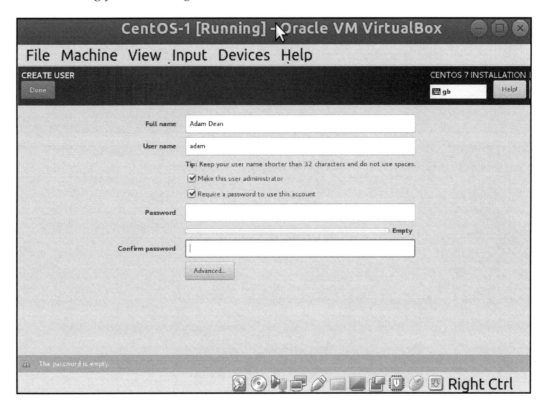

Clicking **Done** will take you back to the installation progress screen, where you may be prompted through the rest of the installation, and eventually get asked to reboot into your freshly installed system.

No sane person should ever have to produce that many screenshots.

Accessing and updating our VM

Now that we have our installed VM, we're going to log in and have a quick poke around.

Logging in from the VirtualBox window

Clicking into our VM, as we did during installation, will allow us to type at the login prompt:

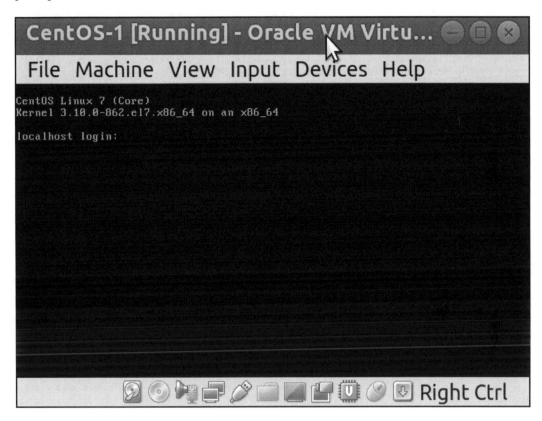

We're going to use the user we created at installation time, rather than root.

Note that you also get a bit of information on login attempts since your last login. In this case, I failed my first attempt at logging in, and it tells me this:

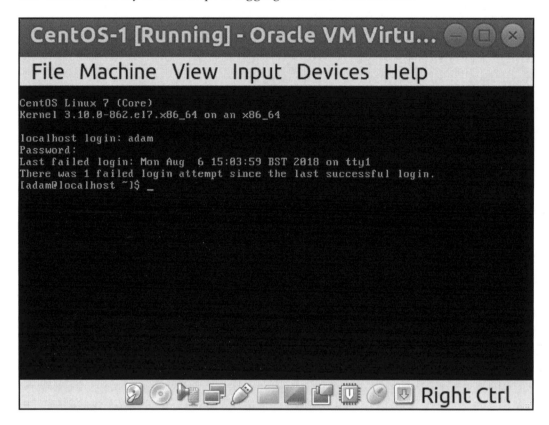

Congratulations – you've installed CentOS!

It's very rare to find a Linux server with a **graphical user interface (GUI)** installed, though it does happen. Of the thousands of servers I've worked with, I can count the number of times I've come across a GUI on one hand. It's usually cause for momentary confusion and distress, before concluding that someone had to have installed the GUI by accident – there can be no other explanation.

Before we go further, we're going to run a quick command to find the IP address of our machine:

```
$ ip a
```

ip a is a shorthand way of typing ip address which we will cover more later.

This gives us a lot of network information, but crucially it gives us the inet address of our network interface, 10.0.2.15:

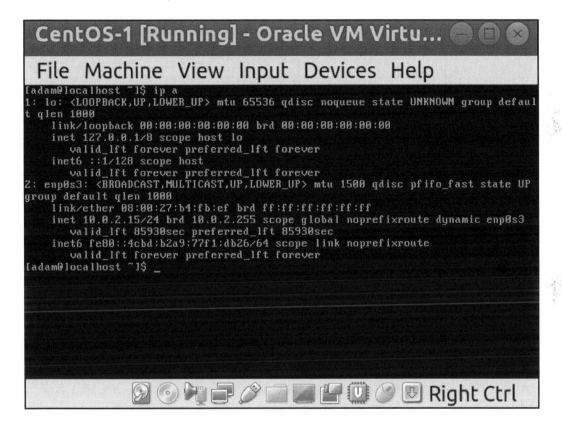

Logging in from the host Terminal

Because using the VirtualBox interface is somewhat cumbersome (making things such as copy and paste tricky), it makes sense that there's a more elegant way to connect and interact with our machine.

Secure Shell (SSH) is the tool we're going to use for this, as it provides a fast and secure way of connecting to remote machines.

Native SSH clients are available for macOS and all Linux distributions. Windows has made some progress in the area too, though I'm to understand that the easiest way of using SSH on Windows is still to download a program called PuTTY.

Think of SSH as a Windows Remote Desktop Protocol. If you're new to this world, only it's generally faster to use, owing to the fact it's not got to stream a graphical connection at you. SSH is entirely text-based.

Using our IP address from a moment ago, we're going to try and SSH to our VM, from our host (the machine you're running VirtualBox on:)

```
$ ssh adam@10.0.2.15
ssh: connect to host 10.0.2.15 port 22: Connection refused
```

Oh no! Something is off!

We haven't connected, and the connection was apparently refused!

Making sure sshd is running

First, we're going to make sure that the server component of sshd is running by logging onto our VM in VirtualBox and running the following:

```
$ sudo systemctl enable sshd
$ sudo systemctl start sshd
```

You should be prompted (at least once) for your user password that we set earlier.

What we're doing is enabling the sshd service to start when the server is booted with the first command, and starting it right now with the second (so that we don't have to reboot the VM).

Making sure that VirtualBox lets us through

Just starting sshd isn't enough to get us connecting to the VM from the host – we also have to set up some **Port Forwarding** for the VirtualBox NAT network.

Port Forwarding is the method of manually specifying how traffic is to traverse a NAT'd network. If you were playing Diablo 2 or Warcraft III in the mid-2000s, you may have had great fun trying to get Port Forwarding working with your home router.

From the main VirtualBox window, highlight your VM and click **Settings** at the
top. Head to the **Network** section and click the arrow by **Advanced** to drop down a
larger section. Click **Port Forwarding**:

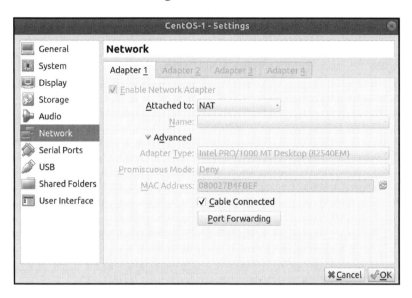

In the new window that's popped up, click to add a new rule on the right, and
populate it with the settings from the following screenshot, substituting your **Guest
IP** if it differs:

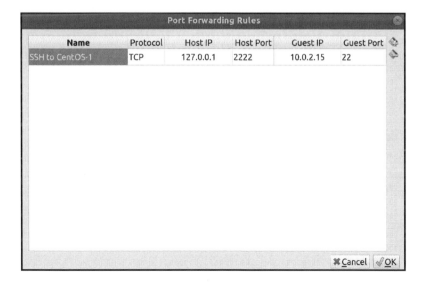

Notice that we're effectively mapping `127.0.0.1:2222` on our host to `10.0.2.15:22` on our guest. We've set it up so that any connection attempt made to the `localhost` address of our host machine, on port `2222`, gets forwarded to the VM on port `22`.

 `2222` in the example given is entirely random – it could be `8222`, `5123`, `2020`, and so on. I chose `2222` for convenience. You shouldn't attempt to use ports lower than `1024` for this sort of thing, as these are restricted to root-only access.

We can now try our SSH command again, tweaked for what we've just set up:

```
$ ssh adam@127.0.0.1 -p2222
The authenticity of host '[127.0.0.1]:2222 ([127.0.0.1]:2222)' can't
be established.
ECDSA key fingerprint is
SHA256:M2mQKN54oJg3B1lsjJGmbfF/G69MN/Jz/koKHSaWAuU.
Are you sure you want to continue connecting (yes/no)? yes
Warning: Permanently added '[127.0.0.1]:2222' (ECDSA) to the list of
known hosts.
adam@127.0.0.1's password:
```

There are some things to break down about this command.

I've specified the username by using `adam@` and I've told SSH to try connecting to the localhost address `127.0.0.1`, along with the port we've chosen, that is, `2222`.

We're presented with the fingerprint of the host, which we'll talk more about later, and which we accept.

We're then prompted to log in, using the password we set up in the VM, for our user:

```
Last login: Mon Aug  6 15:04:26 2018
[adam@localhost ~]$
```

Success!

We can now work on our VM as if it were a real server – just be mindful to make sure that you're on your VM when running any commands.

Updating our VM

Now that we've got access to our machine, we're going to run one command to make sure that we've got the latest version of all the installed software:

```
$ sudo yum update
```

When run, you may be presented with a long list of software to update. Typing *Y* for confirmation and hitting *Enter* will work through the upgrade of this software, as well as any dependent software that's needed. You may also be prompted to accept new or updated GPG keys.

GPG is a book by itself – not an exciting book, but certainly a book.

If you've upgraded software that's constantly running, such as an Apache web server, it can be a good idea to schedule a restart of that service to make sure that the newer version is in use.

As a rule of thumb, the only things that should require a full system reboot after being updated are the kernel and the init (initialization) system. This is a stark difference to Windows, where rebooting seems to be what the OS is designed to do, and actual work is just a by-product.

In my case, my kernel got updated. I'm able to confirm this by doing the following.

First, we list the installed versions of the `kernel` package:

```
$ yum info kernel
Loaded plugins: fastestmirror
Loading mirror speeds from cached hostfile
 * base: repo.uk.bigstepcloud.com
 * extras: mirror.sov.uk.goscomb.net
 * updates: mirrors.melbourne.co.uk
Installed Packages
Name         : kernel
Arch         : x86_64
Version      : 3.10.0
Release      : 862.el7
Size         : 62 M
Repo         : installed
From repo    : anaconda
Summary      : The Linux kernel
```

```
URL          : http://www.kernel.org/
Licence      : GPLv2
Description  : The kernel package contains the Linux kernel (vmlinuz),
the core of any
             : Linux operating system.  The kernel handles the basic
functions
             : of the operating system: memory allocation, process
allocation, device
             : input and output, etc.

Name         : kernel
Arch         : x86_64
Version      : 3.10.0
Release      : 862.9.1.el7
Size         : 62 M
Repo         : installed
From repo    : updates
Summary      : The Linux kernel
URL          : http://www.kernel.org/
Licence      : GPLv2
Description  : The kernel package contains the Linux kernel (vmlinuz),
the core of any
             : Linux operating system.  The kernel handles the basic
functions
             : of the operating system: memory allocation, process
allocation, device
             : input and output, etc.
```

Then, we check the version of the kernel currently in use, using `uname`:

```
$ uname -a
Linux localhost.localdomain 3.10.0-862.el7.x86_64 #1 SMP Fri Apr 20
16:44:24 UTC 2018 x86_64 x86_64 x86_64 GNU/Linux
```

We can see from this that we're running version `3.10.0-862.el7`, but we have `3.10.0-862.9.1.el7` too.

Rebooting the system causes the newer kernel to be selected at boot time, and running `uname` again shows a different result:

```
$ uname -a
Linux localhost.localdomain 3.10.0-862.9.1.el7.x86_64 #1 SMP Mon Jul
16 16:29:36 UTC 2018 x86_64 x86_64 x86_64 GNU/Linux
```

Huzzah – we're running the newer kernel!

Understanding how VMs differ

Earlier, we started talking about VMs and what they are. We're now going to look at a couple of ways of working out if we're in a VM, from inside the machine itself.

I would generally do this if I'd got a new **virtual private server** (**VPS**) from a hosting provider, and wanted to know what software was being used to virtualize my new machine.

dmidecode

One of my favourite tools, dmidecode, can be used to dump a computer's **desktop management interface** (**DMI**) table. In practice, this means that it can be used to find out what kind of hardware you're running in a machine.

This command requires root access, so we'll be using sudo throughout these examples.

First, we're going to list the valid types we can pass to dmidecode:

```
$ dmidecode --type
dmidecode: option '--type' requires an argument
Type number or keyword expected
Valid type keywords are:
  bios
  system
  baseboard
  chassis
  processor
  memory
  cache
  connector
  slot
```

Starting at the top, we're going to use bios and see if it gives us anything useful:

```
$ sudo dmidecode --type bios
# dmidecode 3.0
Getting SMBIOS data from sysfs.
SMBIOS 2.5 present.

Handle 0x0000, DMI type 0, 20 bytes
BIOS Information
 Vendor: innotek GmbH
 Version: VirtualBox
```

```
Release Date: 12/01/2006
Address: 0xE0000
Runtime Size: 128 kB
ROM Size: 128 kB
Characteristics:
ISA is supported
PCI is supported
Boot from CD is supported
Selectable boot is supported
8042 keyboard services are supported (int 9h)
CGA/mono video services are supported (int 10h)
ACPI is supported
```

Instantly, we can see `VirtualBox` next to `Version`, which is a pretty strong hint that we're dealing with a VM.

Next, we will choose something else, `system`:

```
$ sudo dmidecode --type system
# dmidecode 3.0
Getting SMBIOS data from sysfs.
SMBIOS 2.5 present.

Handle 0x0001, DMI type 1, 27 bytes
System Information
    Manufacturer: innotek GmbH
    Product Name: VirtualBox
    Version: 1.2
    Serial Number: 0
    UUID: BDC643B8-8D4D-4288-BDA4-A72F606CD0EA
    Wake-up Type: Power Switch
    SKU Number: Not Specified
    Family: Virtual Machine
```

Again, the `Product Name` seen here is `VirtualBox`, and the `Family` is `Virtual Machine`, both of which are pretty damning pieces of evidence.

Lastly, we're going to look at the `Chassis Information`:

```
$ sudo dmidecode --type chassis
# dmidecode 3.0
Getting SMBIOS data from sysfs.
SMBIOS 2.5 present.

Handle 0x0003, DMI type 3, 13 bytes
Chassis Information
    Manufacturer: Oracle Corporation
    Type: Other
```

```
Lock: Not Present
Version: Not Specified
Serial Number: Not Specified
Asset Tag: Not Specified
Boot-up State: Safe
Power Supply State: Safe
Thermal State: Safe
Security Status: None
```

Oracle corporation is, again, a significant piece of information that leads us to believe we're in a virtualized environment.

If we don't want a lot of other information, we can fine-tune our search using dmidecode's -s option.

Running this option without an argument outputs a list of potential arguments we can use:

```
$ sudo dmidecode -s
dmidecode: option requires an argument -- 's'
String keyword expected
Valid string keywords are:
 bios-vendor
 bios-version
 bios-release-date
 system-manufacturer
 system-product-name
 system-version
 system-serial-number
 system-uuid
 baseboard-manufacturer
 baseboard-product-name
 baseboard-version
 baseboard-serial-number
 baseboard-asset-tag
 chassis-manufacturer
 chassis-type
 chassis-version
 chassis-serial-number
 chassis-asset-tag
 processor-family
 processor-manufacturer
 processor-version
 processor-frequency
```

Here, we can instantly see `bios-version`, and as we know from earlier, it should be `VirtualBox`:

```
$ sudo dmidecode -s bios-version
VirtualBox
```

These types of short-output commands are very useful for scripting, where succinctness is sometimes desirable.

dmidecode is usually installed by default, at least on Ubuntu and CentOS installations.

lshw

Should dmidecode not be available, you can also make use of `lshw`, a command for listing hardware. Again, it makes use of the DMI table on a device.

Very quickly, we can use a format option of `lshw` to show the bus information of a system:

```
$ sudo lshw -businfo
Bus info Device Class Description
=========================================================
 system VirtualBox
 bus VirtualBox
 memory 128KiB BIOS
 memory 1GiB System memory
cpu@0 processor Intel(R) Core(TM) i7-7500U CPU @ 2.70GHz
pci@0000:00:00.0 bridge 440FX - 82441FX PMC [Natoma]
pci@0000:00:01.0 bridge 82371SB PIIX3 ISA [Natoma/Triton II]
pci@0000:00:01.1 scsi1 storage 82371AB/EB/MB PIIX4 IDE
scsi@1:0.0.0 /dev/cdrom disk CD-ROM
pci@0000:00:02.0 display VirtualBox Graphics Adapter
pci@0000:00:03.0 enp0s3 network 82540EM Gigabit Ethernet Controller
pci@0000:00:04.0 generic VirtualBox Guest Service
pci@0000:00:05.0 multimedia 82801AA AC'97 Audio Controller
pci@0000:00:06.0 bus KeyLargo/Intrepid USB
usb@1 usb1 bus OHCI PCI host controller
pci@0000:00:07.0 bridge 82371AB/EB/MB PIIX4 ACPI
pci@0000:00:0d.0 scsi2 storage 82801HM/HEM (ICH8M/ICH8M-E) SATA
Controller [AHCI mode]
scsi@2:0.0.0 /dev/sda disk 8589MB VBOX HARDDISK
scsi@2:0.0.0,1 /dev/sda1 volume 1GiB Linux filesystem partition
```

```
scsi@2:0.0.0,2 /dev/sda2 volume 7167MiB Linux LVM Physical Volume
partition
 input PnP device PNP0303
 input PnP device PNP0f03
```

This gives us information that instantly suggests a VM, such as the system, bus, and display entries.

We also have an easy-to-read breakdown of the classes available, meaning that we can query those directly, starting with `disk` in this example:

```
$ sudo lshw -c disk
  *-cdrom
        description: DVD reader
        product: CD-ROM
        vendor: VBOX
        physical id: 0.0.0
        bus info: scsi@1:0.0.0
        logical name: /dev/cdrom
        logical name: /dev/sr0
        version: 1.0
        capabilities: removable audio dvd
        configuration: ansiversion=5 status=nodisc
  *-disk
        description: ATA Disk
        product: VBOX HARDDISK
        vendor: VirtualBox
        physical id: 0.0.0
        bus info: scsi@2:0.0.0
        logical name: /dev/sda
        version: 1.0
        serial: VB5cbf266c-3015878d
        size: 8GiB (8589MB)
        capabilities: partitioned partitioned:dos
        configuration: ansiversion=5 logicalsectorsize=512
sectorsize=512 signature=000b6a88
```

Alternatively, if we think that's too much information, we could query the system class:

```
$ sudo lshw -c system
localhost.localdomain
 description: Computer
 product: VirtualBox
 vendor: innotek GmbH
 version: 1.2
 serial: 0
 width: 64 bits
```

```
capabilities: smbios-2.5 dmi-2.5 vsyscall32
configuration: family=Virtual Machine uuid=BDC643B8-8D4D-4288-BDA4-
A72F606CD0EA
```

Quick sudo explanation

In the various commands that were given in the preceding recipe, we used sudo repeatedly. This was so that we didn't have to log in as the root user to perform various restricted actions.

 sudo is a contraction of 'superuser do' because sudo used to be used for running commands as the "superuser" only, nowadays you can use it to run commands as various users.

Generally, if you attempt to run a command that you lack permissions to complete successfully, you'll be greeted with an error:

```
$ less /etc/sudoers
/etc/sudoers: Permission denied
```

Here, I tried to have a look at the /etc/sudoers file, which also happens to be the file that determines a user's sudo privileges.

Running this command with sudo is a different story. Instead, it opens the file for me, dropping me into the less pager.

Toward the bottom of this file, we find the following block:

```
## Allows people in group wheel to run all commands
%wheel  ALL=(ALL)       ALL
```

The wheel portion of this block is uncommented, and the text above that tells us what that means.

So, the obvious next question is, am I in the wheel group?

 The term wheel has ancient origins in old-school UNIX installations. These, days it might be called admin or other. CentOS keeps it classic by using wheel.

Thankfully, this is very easy to check – the file in question is always in the same place: /etc/group.

Here, we print the contents of the group file to our screen, and look specifically for wheel.

We see the following layout:

```
group_name:password:GID:user_list
```

We can see that the group_name is wheel, the password is a lower x, which means that shadow passwords are being used, the group ID is 10, and the only user in this group is myself:

```
$ sudo cat /etc/group | grep wheel
wheel:x:10:adam
```

We can even do this with a single word, that being the groups command, which prints the groups that your current user is a member of:

```
$ groups
adam wheel
```

Being granted the ability to run superuser commands with sudo isn't the immediate right of everyone on the system, and it's up to the individual company and administration team to decide how that power is distributed.

There are places where everyone in operations has the power of sudo, and places where one person has that power.

Using Vagrant to automatically provision VMs

Going through the tedium of installing a new VM every time you want to test something new, or create a sandbox to work in, can get old fast.

Because of this, various administrators and developers have come up with solutions that make provisioning a VM (or several) a breeze.

If we take a moment to think about the advantages of this approach, it's easy to highlight just a few benefits of automated VM provisioning:

- It eliminates the time it takes to manually type answers into a VM window.
- It allows for the automated running of software tests in a development environment.
- It allows for the sharing of text files that act as recipes for how to build a VM, rather than the shifting of large VM images from station to station. This is a form of **Infrastructure as Code (IaC)**.

Kickstart

One method of automating the deployment of boxes are kickstart files, which are frequently used in large deployments to automatically answer the questions that the installer asks the user.

If you take a look in the `/root/` folder of a CentOS VM, there's a good chance you'll find a file called `anaconda-ks.cfg`, which is effectively the kickstart file for the manual steps you took when installing the machine (anaconda being the name of the installer).

These files are tweaked, or written from scratch, and then hosted on a web server, on an installation network, ready to be picked up by an unconfigured machine.

Vagrant

Locally, kickstart files aren't really practical, and they're not quick to work with. We need something that can be set up quickly and easily, but which is also very powerful.

Enter `Vagrant`.

Developed by Hashicorp as an open source piece of software, Vagrant can be used for automatically provisioning VMs, and even whole development environments.

Typically, somewhere, you might find a `Vagrantfile` (the name of the core Vagrant... file...) is in a repository of some in-house application.

The developers working on the application pull down the repository to their local machine, and use the Vagrant configuration file to spin up a local development environment, which they can then use to test code changes or feature additions without utilizing expensive development environments.

 Vagrant is available for macOS, Linux, and Windows.

On my Ubuntu host, I install Vagrant like so:

```
$ sudo apt install vagrant
```

There's quite a few dependencies, totalling around 200 MB of used disk space afterwards.

Ubuntu's packages are reasonably up to date, so we get a recent version:

```
$ vagrant --version
Vagrant 2.0.2
```

I'm quite particular about where I keep my files, so I'm going to create a dedicated folder called Vagrant in my home directory, which I'll use for working with my Vagrant VMs:

```
$ ls
 Desktop     Downloads   Pictures   snap        Videos
 Documents   Music       Public     Templates   'VirtualBox VMs'
$ mkdir Vagrant
$ cd Vagrant/
```

Next, we will initialize a new Vagrantfile. The following command will do this automatically:

```
$ vagrant init
$ ls
Vagrantfile
```

Have a look in the Vagrantfile, but don't make any changes yet. You'll see that a lot of the options are listed, but commented out by default. This is a good way of introducing you to what Vagrant is capable of.

Note that, by default, Vagrant will attempt to use a box called `base`, but will also prompt you to look at `https://vagrantcloud.com/search` for other boxes:

```
# Every Vagrant development environment requires a box. You can
search for
# boxes at https://vagrantcloud.com/search.
config.vm.box = "base"
```

Doing a search for CentOS on `vagrantcloud` reveals a nice default box we can use: `https://app.vagrantup.com/centos/boxes/7`.

It also lists the providers that the box can be provisioned under. VirtualBox is one of them, meaning it will work in our installation.

We need to change our `Vagrantfile` to point at this box. From the folder in which your `Vagrantfile` exists, run the following:

```
$ sed -i 's#config.vm.box = "base"#config.vm.box = "centos/7"#g'
Vagrantfile
```

We've just used `sed` (a common tool for editing text on the command line, either in files or on standard out) with the `-i` option, to modify our `Vagrantfile` in-place. Opening the file now will show us that the `base` line has changed to point to `centos/7` instead.

Now, we can provision our VM with another simple command:

```
$ vagrant up
Bringing machine 'default' up with 'virtualbox' provider...
==> default: Box 'centos/7' could not be found. Attempting to find and
install...
    default: Box Provider: virtualbox
    default: Box Version: >= 0
==> default: Loading metadata for box 'centos/7'
    default: URL: https://vagrantcloud.com/centos/7
==> default: Adding box 'centos/7' (v1804.02) for provider: virtualbox
    default: Downloading:
https://vagrantcloud.com/centos/boxes/7/versions/1804.02/providers/vir
tualbox.box
==> default: Successfully added box 'centos/7' (v1804.02) for
'virtualbox'!
<SNIP>
    default: No guest additions were detected on the base box for this
VM! Guest
    default: additions are required for forwarded ports, shared
folders, host only
    default: networking, and more. If SSH fails on this machine,
```

```
please install
    default: the guest additions and repackage the box to continue.
    default:
    default: This is not an error message; everything may continue to
work properly,
    default: in which case you may ignore this message.
==> default: Rsyncing folder: /home/adam/Vagrant/ => /vagrant
```

All being well, your VM image will start to download from `vagrantcloud`, and your box will spin itself up in VirtualBox.

We can even see our VM in the VirtualBox main window:

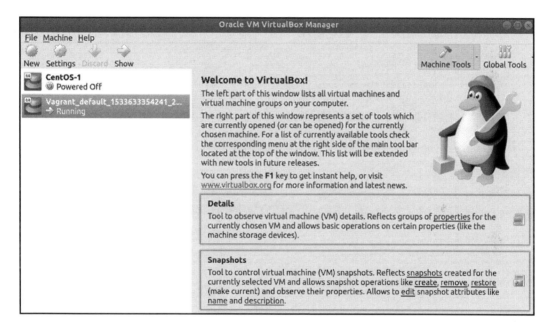

Taking a look under **Settings | Network** and **Port Forwarding** shows how Vagrant also automatically sets up access for the NAT's network, in a very similar way to the manual way we did.

We can also connect to our new VM using a built-in Vagrant shortcut:

```
$ vagrant ssh
Last login: Tue Aug  7 09:16:42 2018 from 10.0.2.2
[vagrant@localhost ~]$
```

This means that we've provisioned and connected to a VM in four commands, in summary:

```
$ vagrant init
$ sed -i 's#config.vm.box = "base"#config.vm.box = "centos/7"#g'
Vagrantfile
$ vagrant up
$ vagrant ssh
[vagrant@localhost ~]$
```

We can also destroy any VMs we create from within the same folder that we ran against our `Vagrantfile` using one command:

```
$ vagrant destroy
```

 I wrote about manually setting up the VM with VirtualBox (and took all those screenshots) first, because it's good to get into the habit of learning about how things are done manually prior to automating the tedious bits. This same rule can be applied to most software, because even when it takes longer, knowing how something works under the hood makes troubleshooting much easier later on.

Anecdote – try, try, and try again

You will find that in your career the concept of holy wars is dominant, and every new generation of technology has its apologists and opponents. This is not least seen in the distribution-wars, which has tribal factions staunchly defending their OS of choice. If you ever find yourself in the position of choosing which distribution to install for a company or project, take into consideration everything you've read here, and do your own reading around before blindly accepting one person's opinion as truth.

That's not to say you should become tribal yourself – I've installed all of the preceding distributions at one time or another, the first of which was Ubuntu.

Back in 2005, I learned about this thing called Linux.

Before then, I'd known Macs my entire life, as it was the brand my dad had decided upon. I'd also cobbled together a single Windows machine for the purpose of playing Diablo, though I can't say I ever enjoyed using the OS itself.

Everything changed when I spotted a computer magazine on holiday, and ended up flipping through the various pages until I landed on a piece about Linux, which captured my imagination immediately. Something different and quirky appealed to my rebellious attitude, and as a result I ended up burning this thing called Ubuntu to a CD (or several).

Back then, Canonical would freely send you Ubuntu CDs if you requested them, but I was impatient, and burning disks was quicker.

I made a backup of everything I cared about on my computer, and set about working my way through my first installation once I'd worked out exactly how to boot from a CD. By all accounts it went well, and though I had to nip to another computer occasionally (no smartphones, remember) to look up what certain options meant, I eventually had a shiny new desktop OS installed.

The trouble started around this time.

My wireless card didn't work, the graphics seemed sluggish, and I ran a single update before rebooting, which landed me not on a desktop, but at a command-line interface.

I had never seen a command-line interface before.

To this day, I have no idea how I ever managed to get a functional OS on that box, and I was forever fighting a program called `NdisWrapper` to get my wireless to work, or installing proprietary (though I didn't know the word at the time) graphics drivers, which would break as soon as you upgraded the kernel (though again, I had no idea that was what was happening at the time).

I somehow plodded along, soon getting bored of Ubuntu when I discovered different distributions, and spending the next few months with a different desktop every week. I distinctly remember running through Ubuntu, Debian, Fedora, OpenSUSE, and a very, very early attempt at installing Gentoo, which I gave up on after about five minutes.

I ended up on forums frequently, painstakingly copying errors into Google to try and find other people who'd had the issues I was experiencing, and often discovering a post where the poster had inconveniently announced they'd **Fixed It!** without actually providing the solution they'd used.

All of this, as irritating as it was to me at the time, was a learning experience, and I think my love of Linux and computing in general can be traced back to the first time I installed Ubuntu. Prior to that date, computers had been games machines and that was it.

Soon, I was using Linux Mint to bypass the school firewall, booting to a Live USB drive, and ignoring all the feeble attempts at blocking that the school IT department had enabled (for some reason, they believed Windows was the only OS in existence). I still don't quite know how this worked, but the point was that it did.

Between bouts of World of Warcraft, Linux was something I tinkered with for years, keeping up on the latest releases and installing other distributions to try ("distribution-hopping" frequently). I broke things, fixed them, got angry with Linux, got angry with computers in general, but on the whole, I slowly improved.

Fast forward a little while and generally bad school results meant I bailed out without finishing college, or going to university. I had very little in the way of qualifications, but still had something of an aptitude for computing. I found and went on a course that lasted a few months and resulted in a couple of noddy Microsoft certifications, but which ultimately meant that I had a sparse CV that I could start submitting to companies.

I was called by and went for an interview with a hosting provider based in Manchester, and met with the man who's now the CTO. The interview was weird, with us variously discussing taking computers apart, a bit of Linux, and a lot of Counter Strike, as it turned out he'd played a lot in years past. I left feeling nervous, but fairly amused at how it had gone.

Upon returning, after being called back in, I was fairly stunned to get offered the job of Data Center Engineer, which while not a Linux-focused position, was more than I could have hoped for given my level of education. It made me incredibly happy to be employable, and I'm forever grateful to that company and interviewer for giving me a chance.

The takeaway I'd like to present from this is that Linux is fairly great – it can give even the most academically illiterate of us a decent career, and it's so vibrant and forever evolving that there's always something new to learn. I've met some great people, and learned some fascinating things on my journey, a lot of which I hope to pass on in these pages.

I hope you find the rest of this book informative, whether you're a newcomer to Linux administration, or you're someone experienced that's just checking for tips and tricks you might not know.

Remote Administration with SSH

2

The following recipes will be covered in this chapter:

- Generating and using key pairs with ssh-keygen
- SSH client arguments and options
- Using a client-side SSH configuration file
- Modifying the server-side SSH configuration file
- Rotating host keys and updating `known_hosts`
- Using local forwarding
- Using remote forwarding
- ProxyJump and bastion hosts
- Using SSH to create a SOCKS Proxy
- Understanding and using SSH agents
- Running multiple SSH servers on one box

Introduction

In the first chapter, we SSH'd to our VM using one command:

```
$ ssh adam@127.0.0.1 -p2222
adam@127.0.0.1's password:
Last login: Mon Aug 6 17:04:31 2018 from gateway
[adam@localhost ~]$
```

In this chapter, we're going to expand on this, looking at making connecting easier with SSH key pairs; running over the security benefits of SSH; making changes to both the client and server side configuration; setting up a port forward and reverse port forward connections; learning about ProxyJump and bastion hosts, as well as setting up a temporary proxy with SSH; and finally, we're going to look at SSH agents and setting up an additional SSH server on our VM.

This chapter assumes that you have a rudimentary understanding of SSH.

Technical requirements

As introduced in the first chapter, we're going to use Vagrant and VirtualBox for all of our work in this chapter and those going forward. This allows us to quickly provision infrastructure for testing, and saves you the manual job of creating multiple VMs each time.

 If you really, really, don't want to use VirtualBox or Vagrant, then you don't have to, and I've tried to keep the examples as generic as possible, but you will probably find it much easier if you do.

I've put together the following Vagrantfile for use in this chapter:

```ruby
# -*- mode: ruby -*-
# vi: set ft=ruby :

$provisionScript = <<-SCRIPT
sed -i 's#PasswordAuthentication no#PasswordAuthentication yes#g'
/etc/ssh/sshd_config
systemctl restart sshd
SCRIPT

Vagrant.configure("2") do |config|
 config.vm.provision "shell",
 inline: $provisionScript

 config.vm.define "centos1" do |centos1|
   centos1.vm.box = "centos/7"
   centos1.vm.network "private_network", ip: "192.168.33.10"
   centos1.vm.hostname = "centos1"
   centos1.vm.box_version = "1804.02"
 end

 config.vm.define "centos2" do |centos2|
```

```
    centos2.vm.box = "centos/7"
    centos2.vm.network "private_network", ip: "192.168.33.11"
    centos2.vm.hostname = "centos2"
    centos2.vm.box_version = "1804.02"
  end

  config.vm.define "centos3" do |centos3|
    centos3.vm.box = "centos/7"
    centos3.vm.network "private_network", ip: "192.168.33.12"
    centos3.vm.hostname = "centos3"
    centos3.vm.box_version = "1804.02"
  end
end
```

 Note something new about this `Vagrantfile`. We've included a provision step, which runs the code assigned to the variable at the top of the file. In this case, we're making some changes to the SSH configuration of the default CentOS image, so our examples work as we expect. We've put all three VMs on their own private network.

It would be advisable to create a folder called `Chapter Two` and copy this code into a file called `Vagrantfile` or if you're using the code from GitHub, navigating into the right folder.

Running `vagrant up` from inside the folder containing your `Vagrantfile` should configure two VMs for testing.

Once provisioned, make sure that you can connect to the first by running the following:

$ vagrant ssh centos1

 Vagrant is great for testing purposes, but you shouldn't use it in a production environment for deploying machines. Some of the decisions that are made are for ease of use (such as those around the default `vagrant` user in our image) and as a result, are not best practices for a secure deployment.

Generating and using key pairs with ssh-keygen

Passwords are great, but they're also terrible.

Most people use weak passwords, and while I hope that's not you, there's always the chance that someone in your team doesn't have the discipline you do, and resorts to `football99` or similar for connecting to your shared remote host.

With password access enabled, anyone might be able to connect to your server from any country by brute-forcing their way into your machine, given enough time and enough processing power.

I say "might" because as long as you use secure passwords of a decent length, passwords can be hard to guess, even with the power of a sun. Consult your company security policy when deciding these things, or read up on the best practices at the time you're writing the policy yourself.

Here's where keys come in.

SSH keys are based on the concept of public key cryptography. They come in two parts: a `public` half, and a `private` half, the public part of which you can place onto servers, and the private part of which you keep about your person, either on your laptop, or maybe a secure USB stick (one that is itself encrypted and password protected).

Despite the obvious suggestion of public and private half, I have frequently seen people misunderstand this concept and share their private half instead of the public one. This generally results in the key being labelled as compromised, and the individual in question being asked to generate a new pair, with a short chat about the definition of `private` and `public` in the meantime.

Once your public half of a key is on your server, you can SSH to your remote host using the local, private half of your key for authentication.

SSH keys can even offer a degree of ease, as most operating systems come with a keychain of some sort that can be automatically unlocked on user-login, and which has the private parts of your key safely stored. SSH'ing to a machine then becomes a trivial affair where you can securely connect without being prompted at all!

We're going to generate an SSH key pair and use that pair to SSH between our machines.

Getting ready

To begin, ensure that you have two VMs configured with a private network between each.

You can use the Vagrantfile in the *Technical requirements* section to accomplish this.

Connect to the first of your machines:

```
$ vagrant ssh centos1
```

Check that the IP address of centos1 is correctly configured, using the command ip a from Chapter 1, *Introduction and Environment Setup*.

We expect it to be 192.168.33.10, under the eth1 device:

```
[vagrant@centos1 ~]$ ip a
<SNIP>
3: eth1: <BROADCAST,MULTICAST,UP,LOWER_UP> mtu 1500 qdisc pfifo_fast
state UP group default qlen 1000
 link/ether 08:00:27:ac:f2:12 brd ff:ff:ff:ff:ff:ff
 inet 192.168.33.10/24 brd 192.168.33.255 scope global noprefixroute
eth1
 valid_lft forever preferred_lft forever
 inet6 fe80::a00:27ff:feac:f212/64 scope link
        valid_lft forever preferred_lft forever
```

You can also use hostname -I to get the IP address of a box, as seen below, but you should note that you won't get an obvious interface designation:

```
$ hostname -I
10.0.2.15 192.168.33.10
```

Check that you can ping the IP address of centos2 from within centos1.

We set the second IP to 192.168.33.11:

```
$ ping 192.168.33.11
PING 192.168.33.11 (192.168.33.11) 56(84) bytes of data.
64 bytes from 192.168.33.11: icmp_seq=1 ttl=64 time=1.17 ms
64 bytes from 192.168.33.11: icmp_seq=2 ttl=64 time=0.997 ms
64 bytes from 192.168.33.11: icmp_seq=3 ttl=64 time=1.18 ms
```

We have network connectivity between our VMs!

If you're unable to ping between machines, start by checking your network settings within VirtualBox, and connect to each of your machines using the `vagrant ssh` command to check the assigned IP address.

How to do it...

We're going to go over the steps to generate and copy a key to a remote host, using two types of key.

First, we're going to generate a more traditional **Rivest-Shamir-Adleman (RSA)** key, and then we're going to generate a newer type of key, the `Ed25519` key.

RSA example

First, we're going to generate our key, confirming the default location in which to save the key, and providing a passphrase when prompted:

```
$ ssh-keygen -b 4096 -C "Example RSA Key"
Generating public/private rsa key pair.
Enter file in which to save the key (/home/vagrant/.ssh/id_rsa):
Enter passphrase (empty for no passphrase):
Enter same passphrase again:
Your identification has been saved in /home/vagrant/.ssh/id_rsa.
Your public key has been saved in /home/vagrant/.ssh/id_rsa.pub.
The key fingerprint is:
SHA256:hAUNhTqXtfnBOkXMuIpxkvtTkM6NYRYxRbT5QWSVbOk Example RSA Key
The key's randomart image is:
+---[RSA 4096]----+
|      =@*=+o.o    |
|      o++=+ =     |
|      o.=+*.o     |
|     * X.+.+.E    |
|     & *S+..      |
|     o = = .      |
|      . . .       |
|        o         |
|        .         |
+----[SHA256]-----+
```

The randomart image in the preceding code is mostly for humans so that keys can be validated by sight. Personally, I've never used it (other than a little further along in this chapter,) but you might.

Next, we're going to copy our newly generated RSA key to `centos2`, providing the password for `centos2` when prompted:

 The default password for the `vagrant` user on these boxes is `vagrant`.

```
$ ssh-copy-id 192.168.33.11
/usr/bin/ssh-copy-id: INFO: Source of key(s) to be installed:
"/home/vagrant/.ssh/id_rsa.pub"
The authenticity of host '192.168.33.11 (192.168.33.11)' can't be
established.
ECDSA key fingerprint is
SHA256:LKhW+WOnW2nxKO/PY5UO/ny3GP6hIs3m/ui6uy+Sj2E.
ECDSA key fingerprint is
MD5:d5:77:4f:38:88:13:e7:f0:27:01:e2:dc:17:66:ed:46.
Are you sure you want to continue connecting (yes/no)? yes
/usr/bin/ssh-copy-id: INFO: attempting to log in with the new key(s),
to filter out any that are already installed
/usr/bin/ssh-copy-id: INFO: 1 key(s) remain to be installed -- if you
are prompted now it is to install the new keys
vagrant@192.168.33.11's password:

Number of key(s) added: 1

Now try logging into the machine, with:   "ssh '192.168.33.11'"
and check to make sure that only the key(s) you wanted were added.
```

Finally, we're going to check that we can access `centos2`, by means of the key we just generated.

We will be prompted for the passphrase we set when the key was generated. Type it in when required:

```
[vagrant@centos1 ~]$ ssh 192.168.33.11
Enter passphrase for key '/home/vagrant/.ssh/id_rsa':
[vagrant@centos2 ~]$
```

Ed25519 example

As with our RSA example, we will start by generating a new key, this time specifying the type as 'ed25519'.

Ed25519 keys are elliptical-curve based and a lot of very clever people believe they offer superior security to RSA. The keys themselves are also much shorter (which we'll touch on later,) meaning if you've ever got to type one out, it's a lot less work. Annoyingly you can't use the public half of an Ed25519 key for encrypting files, as you can with an RSA public half, so there's a trade off but it depends on your needs.

We will again accept the default location for where to save our key, and provide a passphrase:

```
[vagrant@centos1 ~]$ ssh-keygen -t ed25519 -C "Example Ed25519 key"
Generating public/private ed25519 key pair.
Enter file in which to save the key (/home/vagrant/.ssh/id_ed25519):
/home/vagrant/.ssh/id_ed25519 already exists.
Overwrite (y/n)? y
Enter passphrase (empty for no passphrase):
Enter same passphrase again:
Your identification has been saved in /home/vagrant/.ssh/id_ed25519.
Your public key has been saved in /home/vagrant/.ssh/id_ed25519.pub.
The key fingerprint is:
SHA256:nQVR7ZVJMjph093KHB6qLg9Ve87PF4fNnFw8Y5X0kN4 Example Ed25519 key
The key's randomart image is:
+--[ED25519 256]--+
|          o*o+=+=|
|          ..+.B*=|
|          ooB Bo|
|        . +o.B+E|
|        S +.. +==|
|        ..  +.+=|
|        ..   o o|
|        ...    o.|
|        o.     +|
+----[SHA256]-----+
```

We're going to copy our new key over to `centos2`. Note that we're also specifying the `id_ed25519.pub` file as the one to copy over:

 Again, the default password for these boxes is `vagrant`.

```
[vagrant@centos1 ~]$ ssh-copy-id -i .ssh/id_ed25519.pub 192.168.33.11
/usr/bin/ssh-copy-id: INFO: Source of key(s) to be installed:
".ssh/id_ed25519.pub"
/usr/bin/ssh-copy-id: INFO: attempting to log in with the new key(s),
to filter out any that are already installed
/usr/bin/ssh-copy-id: INFO: 1 key(s) remain to be installed -- if you
are prompted now it is to install the new keys
vagrant@192.168.33.11's password:

Number of key(s) added: 1

Now try logging into the machine, with:   "ssh '192.168.33.11'"
and check to make sure that only the key(s) you wanted were added
```

 If you've run this example straight after the one before it, you may be asked for the passphrase to your RSA key, instead of the password to the box itself. This is fine, and it highlights the fact that key-based authentication is attempted first. If this is the case for you, simply provide the passphrase to your RSA key.

Once installed, attempt to SSH to `centos2`, specifying the private half of the `Ed25519` key:

```
[vagrant@centos1 ~]$ ssh 192.168.33.11 -i .ssh/id_ed25519
Enter passphrase for key '.ssh/id_ed25519':
Last login: Wed Aug  8 10:06:33 2018 from 192.168.33.10
[vagrant@centos2 ~]$
```

How it works...

The principle of asynchronous keys and public key cryptography can be awkward for people to get their head around. For the most part, you won't need to worry about the mathematics of key generation—you should just know that you will always end up with two keys, a public one and a private one.

Dimble, an entirely fictional engineer who thinks it's a good idea to store his `private` SSH key on a public `GitLab` server in a repository named `my stuff` is a security risk, because he never owned a dictionary, and believes that the word private means "share it with the world", which it doesn't. He also disabled the passphrase on his `private` key because he didn't like the fact there was an extra step between him and his server. Don't be like Dimble—keep your `private` key safe and secure.

The public and private key files

As hinted at previously, what we've done here is create two files, one half of which can be freely passed around (the public half) and one half of which we keep safe somewhere else (the private half).

By default, these files are located in the home directory of your user, in the hidden `.ssh` folder:

```
[vagrant@centos1 ~]$ pwd
/home/vagrant
[vagrant@centos1 ~]$ ls -a
.  ..  .bash_history  .bash_logout  .bash_profile  .bashrc  .ssh
[vagrant@centos1 ~]$ ls .ssh
authorized_keys  id_ed25519  id_ed25519.pub  id_rsa  id_rsa.pub
known_host
```

The public halves of our keys end in `.pub`, and the private halves don't have a file extension.

Let's take a look at each of the four files:

```
[vagrant@centos1 ~]$ cat .ssh/id_rsa
-----BEGIN RSA PRIVATE KEY-----
Proc-Type: 4,ENCRYPTED
DEK-Info: AES-128-CBC,9AFF0BD949B955DA3595262BB18E5BF7

n1K6zUfhIynq9dwRMAGlMuTU/7Ht3KgBuelsWy3mxJM+NxprFkhAV2cyEVhnJI+5
xgDkx7+6PcGVv/oQAH3pSICefZSJvHvnFLO+M7HKkcmdz9IYXlQC1gkeZwhS6708
<SNIP>
wTXVajpn0anc3TWDw78sZkLmoP5MEs14gJvyegmyLd8qAGvSmfXYNFgYh49hnX9E
vdAmtTJPqglcw0F1JVCOEevIWA/WoIkkTAgLuKvka5ZepKKnScwnRiAhKTVXCN3W
-----END RSA PRIVATE KEY-----
```

The private half of our RSA key is a file that's sensitive, and as we made it `4096` bits when we generated it, this file will be very long (hence my snip).

The public half of our RSA key is the file that's placed on remote machines. It is still affected by the bit-length we specified, though it's nowhere near as lengthy as the private half.

```
[vagrant@centos1 ~]$ cat .ssh/id_rsa.pub
ssh-rsa
AAAAB3NzaC1yc2EAAAADAQABAAACAQCwR6+SAohzU9f1SAha634St1JaBGIZ+k5Rb6T6L4
VqxHIfRwCV+uciXbkTg8+lxiP8whGYEiDxfPveqW1xf87JY1WTT3ZT3gd3pfxY1+IgRB7j
5Ttd2RBCMeMYB9VJWLqib6K9oeHJyGzM39aJqE2AzxKxc+rXeXT16R1Fxs7nDZwS9xV7Da
i9LB/Jez0pT8pLFVD/QRsGw0uMjMMSjmKqxPrDpHzZ3OUymB5AdyVfts4JTZINSrWdejPR
8G93pzH4S8ZYijhgpOnSuoyGhMnwAjwOJyNkkFOT1rKCuzpW33hr2c1pJSBPZTAx2/ZvB1
He2/UweBF2VeQpSruQB7tXkQMeXSQBpe+/zMqOLD82vake3M8mqNpFJoVG3afr9RcCXtqn
7cF3fDEqj7nNk0Em6/9akO2/tK5KInWhyOjKdV41ntB6IVPGJWOUBmnvf9HVpOMa8rxeb3
KpBqnn6z70rjMTKqHmAQ5BeCuVSezTl4xAUP940PbkHSm0mDeWYMi2AgbofKDGBmH/GGUn
3QeahhiLTXGzbIHszbXJdJ5dn3OoWAPovW/gc0CeeHgUV7IwJ6wxVIz8jYKpjtDtIPYDs+
RJMrWo8qPnhHWxA6HVp42eUylh7eazPUzitfZ2SBQHe3ShbBHTh2wHcLcRoVgSMrMJmfQ7
Ibad5ZiWepobJw== Example RSA Key
```

Note that we've also got a comment at the end, `Example RSA Key`, which we specified at generation time. This will usually be the user and machine hostname of the box it's generated on, when no comment is explicitly passed.

```
[vagrant@centos1 ~]$ cat .ssh/id_ed25519
-----BEGIN OPENSSH PRIVATE KEY-----
b3BlbnNzaC1rZXktdjEAAAAACmFlczI1Ni1jYmMAAAAGYmNyeXB0AAAAGAAAABCV2EFqnw
9/2J52LIVBzp50AAAAEAAAAAEAAAAzAAAAC3NzaC11ZDI1NTE5AAAAIEGnqP8zTx50SwjP
+Fe26RdDx2W3/TQ+0ET8ylxfFB+aAAAAoJUzLk7IAaszO2npeAJIgfYmsqWCcgTM+EfF15
3A1iw4PruO+q8b3BxAjFZGK0tjFTSm3rkKtM9+JYTxOI+CSnEyqPnjnCjPODa7aF/X8GBt
RNkSKB1M7aROwpon0Z8UXH+Js8uyNOsKto+DS+BfVSKvshkQ6bNF/5D1U0fQcnRaYnVdyl
mIJUaPLdl/vKLwF+S4OyU87n8racOezjfAOhk=
-----END OPENSSH PRIVATE KEY-----
```

Then, there is our private (sensitive) `Ed25519` key. Note that this file is much shorter than its RSA counterpart, and this is because `Ed25519` keys have a fixed length (this also means that the `-b` flag is ignored at generation time).

```
[vagrant@centos1 ~]$ cat .ssh/id_ed25519.pub
ssh-ed25519
AAAAC3NzaC11ZDI1NTE5AAAAIEGnqP8zTx50SwjP+Fe26RdDx2W3/TQ+0ET8ylxfFB+a
Example Ed25519 key
```

Here, we have our public `Ed25519` file, so short that you could conceivably write it onto a bit of paper and hand it to your colleague to copy onto a server (though they really, really won't thank you for it, and will most likely not offer to make you a cup of tea any time soon).

We also have our comment, `Example Ed25519 key`.

 Obviously, printing the private halves of the keys that I've just generated flies in the face of what I said about passing around private keys, although it's for documentation, and I'm going to destroy these VMs once I'm finished with them, so I felt adding them here for clarity was important. DO NOT USE THESE KEYS.

The authorized_keys file

When you connect to your remote host, SSH validates the key ID you're providing against a list of `authorized_keys`.

In our example, we used the `ssh-copy-id` command to place our key on the remote server. What this actually does is put it in a specific file of the home user you're connecting to.

On our `centos2` host, we can find this file in the user's home directory, under `.ssh`:

```
[vagrant@centos2 ~]$ pwd
/home/vagrant
[vagrant@centos2 ~]$ ls .ssh/
authorized_keys
```

Looking inside this file reveals the following:

```
[vagrant@centos2 ~]$ cat .ssh/authorized_keys
ssh-rsa
AAAAB3NzaC1yc2EAAAADAQABAAABAQDNkm9JCaRa/5gunzDZ8xO2/xwRvUx03pITH6f4aY
ziY/j+7o39XnmNyLRVpvh16u9W75ANJeFpBD7lkevluvaFVRQnZGAhuIdGqLHB1GDnVzkz
cQGUFc/fcAc9rDAFGa0h7+BF18P0jpOMXfHQu8+7+cBjJ6cW+ztKerG2ali/JLtSHFirXa
VTkOKYkwYVfK7z7nmdMsSzgEOsfg5XrylI+ufhGdgWCKtweHsBeAVWjBBbvNaIwgdRVpB1
YmLkLgLN7NxRs53OuejwArLS6tvNS+ZBDiSX+was9gErrhGhZ1mdiOMbd3/oTfFEcOiRNO
v/+7Tk4P8fJbnO1dzM8Gid vagrant
ssh-rsa
AAAAB3NzaC1yc2EAAAADAQABAAACAQCwR6+SAohzU9f1SAha634StlJaBGIZ+k5Rb6T6L4
VqxHIfRwCV+uciXbkTg8+lxiP8whGYEiDxfPveqW1xf87JY1WTT3ZT3gd3pfxY1+IgRB7j
5Ttd2RBCMeMYB9VJWLqib6K9oeHJyGzM39aJqE2AzxKxc+rXeXT16RlFxs7nDZwS9xV7Da
i9LB/Jez0pT8pLFVD/QRsGw0uMjMMSjmKqxPrDpHzZ3OUymB5AdyVfts4JTZINSrWdejPR
8G93pzH4S8ZYijhgpOnSuoyGhMnwAjwOJyNkkFOT1rKCuzpW33hr2c1pJSBPZTAx2/ZvB1
```

```
He2/UweBF2VeQpSruQB7tXkQMeXSQBpe+/zMqOLD82vake3M8mqNpFJoVG3afr9RcCXtqn
7cF3fDEqj7nNk0Em6/9akO2/tK5KInWhyOjKdV41ntB6IVPGJWOUBmnvf9HVpOMa8rxeb3
KpBqnn6z70rjMTKqHmAQ5BeCuVSezT14xAUP940PbkHSm0mDeWYMi2AgbofKDGBmH/GGUn
3QeahhiLTXGzbIHszbXJdJ5dn3OoWAPovW/gcOCeeHgUV7IwJ6wxVIz8jYKpjtDtIPYDs+
RJMrWo8qPnhHWxA6HVp42eUylh7eazPUzitfZ2SBQHe3ShbBHTh2wHcLcRoVgSMrMJmfQ7
Ibad5ZiWepobJw== Example RSA Key
ssh-ed25519
AAAAC3NzaC11ZDI1NTE5AAAAIEGnqP8zTx50SwjP+Fe26RdDx2W3/TQ+0ET8ylxfFB+a
Example Ed25519 key
```

Here, we can see three keys, over three lines.

The first key is as follows:

```
[vagrant@centos2 ~]$ cat .ssh/authorized_keys | head -n1
ssh-rsa
AAAAB3NzaC1yc2EAAAADAQABAAABAQDNkm9JCaRa/5gunzDZ8xO2/xwRvUx03pITH6f4aY
ziY/j+7o39XnmNyLRVpvh16u9W75ANJeFpBD7lkevluvaFVRQnZGAhuIdGqLHBlGDnVzkz
cQGUFc/fcAc9rDAFGa0h7+BF18P0jpOMXfHQu8+7+cBjJ6cW+ztKerG2ali/JLtSHFirXa
VTkOKYkwYVfK7z7nmdMsSzgEOsfg5XrylI+ufhGdgWCKtweHsBeAVWjBBbvNaIwgdRVpB1
YmLkLgLN7NxRs53OuejwArLS6tvNS+ZBDiSX+was9gErrhGhZ1mdiOMbd3/oTfFEcOiRNO
v/+7Tk4P8fJbnO1dzM8Gid vagrant
```

This is the key that Vagrant uses to connect to the VMs. It's not one we created.

The second is as follows:

```
[vagrant@centos2 ~]$ cat .ssh/authorized_keys | head -n2 | tail -n1
ssh-rsa
AAAAB3NzaC1yc2EAAAADAQABAAACAQCwR6+SAohzU9f1SAha634StlJaBGIZ+k5Rb6T6L4
VqxHIfRwCV+uciXbkTg8+lxiP8whGYEiDxfPveqW1xf87JY1WTT3ZT3gd3pfxY1+IgRB7j
5Ttd2RBCMeMYB9VJWLqib6K9oeHJyGzM39aJqE2AzxKxc+rXeXT16R1Fxs7nDZwS9xV7Da
i9LB/Jez0pT8pLFVD/QRsGw0uMjMMSjmKqxPrDpHzZ3OUymB5AdyVfts4JTZINSrWdejPR
8G93pzH4S8ZYijhgpOnSuoyGhMnwAjwOJyNkkFOT1rKCuzpW33hr2c1pJSBPZTAx2/ZvB1
He2/UweBF2VeQpSruQB7tXkQMeXSQBpe+/zMqOLD82vake3M8mqNpFJoVG3afr9RcCXtqn
7cF3fDEqj7nNk0Em6/9akO2/tK5KInWhyOjKdV41ntB6IVPGJWOUBmnvf9HVpOMa8rxeb3
KpBqnn6z70rjMTKqHmAQ5BeCuVSezT14xAUP940PbkHSm0mDeWYMi2AgbofKDGBmH/GGUn
3QeahhiLTXGzbIHszbXJdJ5dn3OoWAPovW/gcOCeeHgUV7IwJ6wxVIz8jYKpjtDtIPYDs+
RJMrWo8qPnhHWxA6HVp42eUylh7eazPUzitfZ2SBQHe3ShbBHTh2wHcLcRoVgSMrMJmfQ7
Ibad5ZiWepobJw== Example RSA Key
```

This is our generated RSA key. Note that it's longer than the Vagrant default, owing to the custom `4096` bit-length that we specified.

Our third key is as follows:

```
[vagrant@centos2 ~]$ cat .ssh/authorized_keys | tail -n1
ssh-ed25519
```

```
AAAAC3NzaC11ZDI1NTE5AAAAIEGnqP8zTx50SwjP+Fe26RdDx2W3/TQ+0ET8ylxfFB+a
Example Ed25519 key
```

This is our `Ed25519` key.

 You could, if you so wished, manually copy public keys into the `authorized_keys` file on the host you're connecting to. The `ssh-copy-id` command we used is simply a convenient way of cutting out a few of the extra steps.

There's more...

SSH is sensitive about the **permissions** that its files have.

You don't want your private key to be readable by any random user who might be on your system, so as a result, plain SSH won't work if it thinks you have bad permissions set.

Generally, this won't be an issue if you've just generated your keys, but if you later move them between computers, you might find that you've spoiled the permissions slightly.

A good rule of thumb is to assume locked-down settings:

```
[vagrant@centos1 ~]$ ls -lha .ssh/
total 28K
drwx------. 2 vagrant vagrant  134 Aug  8 14:05 .
drwx------. 3 vagrant vagrant   95 Aug  8 10:29 ..
-rw-------. 1 vagrant vagrant  389 Aug  7 16:40 authorized_keys
-rw-------. 1 vagrant vagrant  464 Aug  8 10:04 id_ed25519
-rw-r--r--. 1 vagrant vagrant  101 Aug  8 10:04 id_ed25519.pub
-rw-------. 1 vagrant vagrant 3.3K Aug  8 11:15 id_rsa
-rw-r--r--. 1 vagrant vagrant  741 Aug  7 16:43 id_rsa.pub
-rw-r--r--. 1 vagrant vagrant  535 Aug  8 11:39 known_hosts
```

In the above command, we can see that the public and private halves of the keys (id_rsa keys and id_ed25519 keys) have different values.

The public halves of the keys (`*.pub`) have the value `644` (read/write, read, read):

```
-rw-r--r--.
```

The private halved of the keys have the value 600 (read/write, none, none):

```
-rw-------.
```

To passphrase or not to passphrase

While you can generate a key without a passphrase, and there are valid use cases for doing so (for example, in the case of automated deployments), it is considered a best practice to generate your own key with a passphrase.

This does mean that if your key isn't unlocked in your keychain (which itself might be unlocked when you log into your machine), you will be prompted for the passphrase to unlock the key. You might consider this a hassle, but think of it in terms of the security onion (multiple layers of security... it's not a great analogy, unless security makes you cry.) If you lost your private key, the malicious person that picks it up won't be able to use it to access your stuff.

 If you do lose a private key, or leave it on a USB stick on a bus, you should immediately rotate your keys by revoking the old one from any location where the public half is installed, and generating a new pair to use.

Additional flags

When we generated our keys, we also added a couple of flags.

As with any software, checking the manual page for the command you're running can provide a sometimes overwhelming amount of additional detail:

```
$ man ssh-keygen
```

To save a little bit of a headache, I'm going to highlight some options that may be of interest to you, starting with -b:

```
-b bits
```

We used the -b flag to specify a large amount of bits during the generation of our RSA key. The minimum is 1024 and the default is 2048. Your place of business may have requirements on the length of RSA keys.

Next, we have the comment flag:

```
-C comment
```

We used this to add a bit of description to our keys. It might be useful if you use different keys for different things (this is my GitLab key, this is my personal server key, this is my company server key, and so on).

If you do need multiple keys, you may want to pass the name of your new key within the generation command (as opposed to typing it out when prompted):

```
-f filename
```

We also have `-l` to print the fingerprint of a key, and/or the ASCII art if you so wish. This can be very useful for verifying key pairs:

```
-l (or -lv for a pretty picture)
```

If you want to change the passphrase of a private half, but don't want to generate a new key, you can use the `-p` option:

```
-p
```

To specify the type of key you wish to generate, you can use the `-t` option:

```
-t dsa | ecdsa | ed25519 | rsa
```

When choosing the type of key to generate, consider your requirements. RSA is generally the most compatible, but your company may have other policies, or you may have a personal preference.

 I've come across two scenarios where `Ed25519` keys couldn't be used – one was an in-house script that required RSA for encrypting files, and the other was OpenStack, at the time.

Finally, there's good old `-v`, providing verbose output since the early days:

```
-v
```

This can be passed multiple times, that is, `-vvv` is also valid, with each `v` increasing the debug level.

See also

This section deliberately doesn't go into the minutia of SSH key exchange or the different types of key (with the exception of the two used in our example). There are excellent books on SSH that can provide a wealth of information, and the OpenSSH developers themselves are constantly working on improvements to the software. OpenSSH is only one implementation of SSH, but it is by far the most popular. It is the default on every Linux distribution I've used, it's in use on macOS, and it's the standard on the BSDs (especially OpenBSD, where it's developed).

SSH client arguments and options

SSH is a powerful piece of software, as we've already discussed, and while it can be used in a very simple way to enable access to your server, it is also extremely flexible.

In this section, we're going to look at common flags that are used with SSH in environments that may have different requirements.

We will be using the same Vagrant boxes as before.

Getting ready

As with the previous section, confirm that both of your Vagrant boxes are enabled, and connect to the first using the `vagrant` command:

```
$ vagrant ssh centos1
```

How to do it...

We're going to take a look at the basics of SSH first.

SSH using hostnames instead of IPs

In our examples so far, we've been using IP addresses to connect to our remote host.

SSH is also capable of connecting to hostnames.

First, we have to create a quick hosts entry so that we can resolve our name to an IP address:

```
[vagrant@centos1 ~]$ echo "192.168.33.11 centos2" | sudo tee -a
/etc/hosts
```

The preceding code is a quick way to make a remote host resolvable to a name. There's no guarantee that it will stick on some systems, especially those where a third party controls the `hosts` file. In a real-world scenario, it is highly likely you'll have some sort of DNS setup that will make connecting to hostnames easier.

We should now be able to SSH using the host's name:

```
[vagrant@centos1 ~]$ ssh centos2
The authenticity of host 'centos2 (192.168.33.11)' can't be
established.
ECDSA key fingerprint is
SHA256:LKhW+WOnW2nxKO/PY5UO/ny3GP6hIs3m/ui6uy+Sj2E.
ECDSA key fingerprint is
MD5:d5:77:4f:38:88:13:e7:f0:27:01:e2:dc:17:66:ed:46.
Are you sure you want to continue connecting (yes/no)? yes
Warning: Permanently added 'centos2' (ECDSA) to the list of known
hosts.
Enter passphrase for key '/home/vagrant/.ssh/id_rsa':
Last login: Wed Aug 8 11:28:59 2018 from fe80::a00:27ff:fe2a:1652%eth1
[vagrant@centos2 ~]$
```

Note that we once again had to accept the fingerprint of the host we're connecting to.

SSHing to a different user

If the user you're connecting to is different to the one you're using locally (in our examples, it's always vagrant and vagrant), then you can manually specify the username on the command line.

The first way to do this is with the following syntax:

```
[vagrant@centos1 ~]$ ssh vagrant@centos2
```

The second way is with a flag:

```
[vagrant@centos1 ~]$ ssh centos2 -l vagrant
```

SSHing to a different port

If the SSH server you're connecting to is listening on a different port (this is quite common), then you might have to specify the port in question.

The default is 22, but if you've changed this for whatever reason, you could also specify the new port, for example, 2020:

```
[vagrant@centos1 ~]$ ssh centos2 -p2020
```

Note this example won't work right now, because we haven't changed the port the server is listening on.

SSHing to an IPv6 address

IPv6 addresses look a lot more imposing than they really are, and it's advisable that you get to grips with them sooner rather than later (even if people have been predicting the dominance of IPv6 for over a decade now).

For this example, we're going to find the IPv6 address of `centos2` and connect to that.

First, connect to `centos2` and run the `ip a` command:

```
[vagrant@centos2 ~]$ ip a
<SNIP>
3: eth1: <BROADCAST,MULTICAST,UP,LOWER_UP> mtu 1500 qdisc pfifo_fast
state UP group default qlen 1000
    link/ether 08:00:27:56:c5:a7 brd ff:ff:ff:ff:ff:ff
    inet 192.168.33.11/24 brd 192.168.33.255 scope global
noprefixroute eth1
       valid_lft forever preferred_lft forever
    inet6 fe80::a00:27ff:fe56:c5a7/64 scope link
       valid_lft forever preferred_lft forever
```

I've highlighted the IPv6 address in the preceding code.

Back on `centos1`, let's connect using IPv6:

```
[vagrant@centos1 ~]$ ssh fe80::a00:27ff:fe56:c5a7%eth1
Enter passphrase for key '/home/vagrant/.ssh/id_rsa':
Last login: Wed Aug  8 11:44:34 2018 from 192.168.33.10
[vagrant@centos2 ~]$
```

Note that we've had to specify the network interface on the end of our command. This is only necessary in the case of link-local addresses, and shouldn't be necessary for global IPv6 addresses.

A comparison to link-local addresses in the IPv6 world are subnets in the IPv4 world, that is, link-local devices are those that can see each other on a local network, via their link-local addresses (which themselves are generated based on factors like the MAC address of the interface that the address is on). They should always have the link-local prefix (FE80::/10).

SSHing before running a command

While you'll mostly use SSH for connecting to remote boxes, it's also possible to run a command on a remote host without having to linger there.

Here, we're running a command to print the hostname file on the remote box, while staying on centos1:

```
[vagrant@centos1 ~]$ ssh 192.168.33.11 "cat /etc/hostname"
Enter passphrase for key '/home/vagrant/.ssh/id_rsa':
centos2
[vagrant@centos1 ~]$
```

This is especially useful for automation software, or scripts that you want to run locally but which interact with remote machines.

SSH and X11 forwarding

Not generally used these days, but still useful in some select situations, X11 forwarding is the act of running a program on a remote box, and displaying said program on your local machine.

You can set up your session using the following command:

```
[vagrant@centos1 ~]$ ssh centos2 -X
```

There are security implications of working with X11 forwarding. Consult your distribution's manual page for information around this, as the default behavior can differ from distribution to distribution.

Currently, this is only possible with X Window Manager setups, and the more modern Wayland display server protocol doesn't have a similar ability, due in part to wanting to keep things simple.

How it works...

SSH is a large and feature-rich program. When you manipulate how it behaves using flags, you're modifying the default behavior to your own ends.

As with any command, they can be simple:

```
$ ssh 192.168.33.11
```

But they can also be complex:

```
$ ssh -Y -D9999 -J buser@BASTION:22 -L 8888:127.0.0.1:80
myself@centos2 -p4433
```

As an exercise, using the SSH manual page if you need to, see if you can work out what this command will accomplish.

There's more...

SSH escape characters are an important additional element to note.

Occasionally, you can be connected to a system and your connection times out, locking up your session.

This usually manifests in the form of an unblinking and unresponsive Terminal. You generally can't hit *Ctrl + D* to log out, and can't type.

You would instead hit the following keys:

~.

 While the key combination is officially listed as ~ . it actually requires the *Enter* key being pressed first (as in, newline), so it's frequently written as \n~.

This tip is brought to you by an eagle-eyed technical editor!

That's a tilde character (find it on your keyboard, usually using the *Shift* key), followed by a dot.

Your session should immediately disconnect.

Check out the SSH manual page for more escape characters.

See also

Again, there's a lot more to SSH options than I've listed in this recipe, and we've yet to cover a few that have their own sections in the rest of this chapter, but still there's a considerable amount we won't be using here.

Take a look at the manual page for SSH on a boring Tuesday. I did.

Using a client-side SSH configuration file

While it's nice to be able to manipulate SSH using command-line arguments, it's also nice to not have to bother.

If you've got a system you work on day in and day out, it can be beneficial to configure your setup with your typical arguments on a permanent basis. This is where the client-side SSH configuration file comes in.

On our example box, the default `ssh_config` file is located in the `/etc/ssh/` directory. Open this file to have a look if you like, but don't make any changes yet.

Getting ready

As with the previous section, confirm that both of your Vagrant boxes are enabled, and connect to the first using the `vagrant` command:

```
$ vagrant ssh centos1
```

To configure different options for our user, we're going to create an SSH configuration file in our home directory.

This goes in the same place as most of our SSH files, `~/.ssh/`.

Whenever you see a ~ character, think of it as **my home** in your head. Expanded, this location is /home/vagrant/.ssh/.

Create the file, lock down the permissions, and open it in your editor of choice—I'm going to use vi.

Be sure to call it config:

```
[vagrant@centos1 ~]$ touch ~/.ssh/config
[vagrant@centos1 ~]$ chmod 600 ~/.ssh/config
[vagrant@centos1 ~]$ vi ~/.ssh/config
```

How to do it...

Within your config file, create the start of four blocks.

One should be a wildcard block (using *) and the other should be variations on the name CentOS2 (note the capitals):

```
Host * !CentOS2-V6
 IdentityFile ~/.ssh/id_ed25519
 Port 22

Host CentOS2-V4
 Hostname 192.168.33.11
 User vagrant

Host CentOS2-V6
 Hostname fe80::a00:27ff:fe56:c5a7%%eth1
 IdentityFile ~/.ssh/id_rsa
 Port 22
 User vagrant

Host CentOS2-Hostname
 Hostname centos2
 User vagrant
```

Note that in the V6 entry, we actually use two percentage signs, instead of the single one we used on the command line. This is so that SSH doesn't misinterpret what we mean and try to read the entry with a %e value.

Inside these blocks, we've set a few basic options based on what we did previously on the command line.

With these settings in place, we can save and exit our configuration file, and try to connect to our specified hosts.

First, we're going to connect to our other VM on its IPv4 address:

```
[vagrant@centos1 ~]$ ssh CentOS2-V4
Enter passphrase for key '/home/vagrant/.ssh/id_ed25519':
Last login: Wed Aug  8 13:31:41 2018 from
fe80::a00:27ff:fe2a:1652%eth1
[vagrant@centos2 ~]$
```

Next, we're going to use our IPv6 address:

```
[vagrant@centos1 ~]$ ssh CentOS2-V6
Enter passphrase for key '/home/vagrant/.ssh/id_rsa':
Last login: Wed Aug  8 13:34:26 2018 from 192.168.33.10
[vagrant@centos2 ~]$
```

Finally, we're going to resolve the hostname of the host:

```
[vagrant@centos1 ~]$ ssh CentOS2-Hostname
Enter passphrase for key '/home/vagrant/.ssh/id_ed25519':
Last login: Wed Aug  8 13:34:04 2018 from
fe80::a00:27ff:fe2a:1652%eth1
[vagrant@centos2 ~]$
```

 Most systems will also auto complete entries in the SSH config file. Try it out yourself by typing ssh C and hitting *Tab* three times.

How it works...

Starting with the wildcard host entry (Host *), this is a global entry. Settings within this block will apply to all hosts (except CentOS2-V6, which we'll get to soon):

```
Host * !CentOS2-V6
 IdentityFile ~/.ssh/id_ed25519
 Port 22
```

Here, we've said that each and every host in this file will use our `Ed25519` key to connect, and we will always connect on port `22`. This block should be used for global settings in general. You can also omit it entirely if you desire:

```
Host CentOS2-V4
 Hostname 192.168.33.11
 User vagrant
```

In our first specific host block, which we've called `CentOS2-V4`, we specify the IPv4 address of the host, and the user to use.

Connecting to this entry with verbosity turned up looks like this:

```
[vagrant@centos1 ~]$ ssh -v CentOS2-V4
OpenSSH_7.4p1, OpenSSL 1.0.2k-fips  26 Jan 2017
debug1: Reading configuration data /home/vagrant/.ssh/config
debug1: /home/vagrant/.ssh/config line 1: Applying options for *
debug1: /home/vagrant/.ssh/config line 5: Applying options for
CentOS2-V4
debug1: Reading configuration data /etc/ssh/ssh_config
debug1: /etc/ssh/ssh_config line 58: Applying options for *
debug1: Connecting to 192.168.33.11 [192.168.33.11] port 22.
debug1: Connection established.
debug1: identity file /home/vagrant/.ssh/id_ed25519 type 4
<SNIP>
debug1: rekey after 134217728 blocks
debug1: SSH2_MSG_NEWKEYS sent
debug1: expecting SSH2_MSG_NEWKEYS
debug1: SSH2_MSG_NEWKEYS received
debug1: rekey after 134217728 blocks
debug1: SSH2_MSG_EXT_INFO received
debug1: kex_input_ext_info: server-sig-algs=<rsa-sha2-256,rsa-
sha2-512>
debug1: SSH2_MSG_SERVICE_ACCEPT received
debug1: Authentications that can continue: publickey,gssapi-
keyex,gssapi-with-mic,password
debug1: Next authentication method: gssapi-keyex
debug1: No valid Key exchange context
debug1: Next authentication method: gssapi-with-mic
debug1: Unspecified GSS failure.  Minor code may provide more
information
No Kerberos credentials available (default cache:
KEYRING:persistent:1000)

debug1: Unspecified GSS failure.  Minor code may provide more
information
No Kerberos credentials available (default cache:
KEYRING:persistent:1000)
```

```
debug1: Next authentication method: publickey
debug1: Offering ED25519 public key: /home/vagrant/.ssh/id_ed25519
debug1: Server accepts key: pkalg ssh-ed25519 blen 51
Enter passphrase for key '/home/vagrant/.ssh/id_ed25519':
debug1: Authentication succeeded (publickey).
Authenticated to 192.168.33.11 ([192.168.33.11]:22).
debug1: channel 0: new [client-session]
debug1: Requesting no-more-sessions@openssh.com
debug1: Entering interactive session.
debug1: pledge: network
debug1: client_input_global_request: rtype hostkeys-00@openssh.com
want_reply 0
debug1: Sending environment.
debug1: Sending env LANG = en_GB.UTF-8
Last login: Wed Aug  8 13:46:27 2018 from 192.168.33.10
```

Within this blob of noise, we can see some crucial things, emboldened for your convenience.

Firstly, we can see where SSH starts to read the configuration data from our config file. It applies the settings for the wildcard entry, followed by those for this specific host.

Later, we can see the prompt for the Ed25519 key specified in the host wildcard block.

Finally, we can see that our session is authenticated to 192.168.33.11 (or the IPv4 address).

If we now take a look at the CentOS-V6 block, we start to see differences:

```
Host CentOS2-V6
 Hostname fe80::a00:27ff:fe56:c5a7%%eth1
 IdentityFile ~/.ssh/id_rsa
 Port 22
 User vagrant
```

 Again, note the double percentage signs.

First, you'll notice that we've got the port and a different `IdentityFile` entry specified. This is due to the `Host *` block not applying to `CentOS2-V6`, as shown here:

```
Host * !CentOS2-V6
```

This means that no settings from the wildcard block will apply to `CentOS2-V6`.

If we connect to our host, again in a verbose fashion, we see the following:

```
[vagrant@centos1 ~]$ ssh -v CentOS2-V6
OpenSSH_7.4p1, OpenSSL 1.0.2k-fips  26 Jan 2017
debug1: Reading configuration data /home/vagrant/.ssh/config
debug1: /home/vagrant/.ssh/config line 1: Skipping Host block because
of negated match for CentOS2-V6
debug1: /home/vagrant/.ssh/config line 9: Applying options for
CentOS2-V6
debug1: Reading configuration data /etc/ssh/ssh_config
debug1: /etc/ssh/ssh_config line 58: Applying options for *
debug1: Connecting to fe80::a00:27ff:fe56:c5a7%eth1
[fe80::a00:27ff:fe56:c5a7%eth1] port 22.
debug1: Connection established.
debug1: identity file /home/vagrant/.ssh/id_rsa type 1
debug1: key_load_public: No such file or directory
<SNIP>
debug1: Next authentication method: publickey
debug1: Offering RSA public key: /home/vagrant/.ssh/id_rsa
debug1: Server accepts key: pkalg rsa-sha2-512 blen 535
Enter passphrase for key '/home/vagrant/.ssh/id_rsa':
debug1: Authentication succeeded (publickey).
Authenticated to fe80::a00:27ff:fe56:c5a7%eth1
([fe80::a00:27ff:fe56:c5a7%eth1]:22).
debug1: channel 0: new [client-session]
debug1: Requesting no-more-sessions@openssh.com
debug1: Entering interactive session.
debug1: pledge: network
debug1: client_input_global_request: rtype hostkeys-00@openssh.com
want_reply 0
debug1: Sending environment.
debug1: Sending env LANG = en_GB.UTF-8
Last login: Wed Aug  8 13:50:39 2018 from
fe80::a00:27ff:fe2a:1652%eth1
```

What's specifically different are the lines about matching config, which this time inform us that the wildcard block won't be applied because of the negated match for `CentOS2-V6`.

We can also see that `id_rsa` is being used this time instead, and we've specifically connected to the IPv6 address of the host.

Lastly, let's look at `CentOS2-Hostname`:

```
[vagrant@centos1 ~]$ ssh -v CentOS2-Hostname
OpenSSH_7.4p1, OpenSSL 1.0.2k-fips  26 Jan 2017
debug1: Reading configuration data /home/vagrant/.ssh/config
debug1: /home/vagrant/.ssh/config line 1: Applying options for *
debug1: /home/vagrant/.ssh/config line 15: Applying options for
CentOS2-Hostname
debug1: Reading configuration data /etc/ssh/ssh_config
debug1: /etc/ssh/ssh_config line 58: Applying options for *
debug1: Connecting to centos2 [192.168.33.11] port 22.
debug1: Connection established.
debug1: identity file /home/vagrant/.ssh/id_ed25519 type 4
debug1: key_load_public: No such file or directory
debug1: identity file /home/vagrant/.ssh/id_ed25519-cert type -1
debug1: Enabling compatibility mode for protocol 2.0
debug1: Local version string SSH-2.0-OpenSSH_7.4
debug1: Remote protocol version 2.0, remote software version
OpenSSH_7.4
debug1: match: OpenSSH_7.4 pat OpenSSH* compat 0x04000000
debug1: Authenticating to centos2:22 as 'vagrant'
debug1: SSH2_MSG_KEXINIT sent
debug1: SSH2_MSG_KEXINIT received
debug1: kex: algorithm: curve25519-sha256
<SNIP>
debug1: Next authentication method: publickey
debug1: Offering ED25519 public key: /home/vagrant/.ssh/id_ed25519
debug1: Server accepts key: pkalg ssh-ed25519 blen 51
Enter passphrase for key '/home/vagrant/.ssh/id_ed25519':
debug1: Authentication succeeded (publickey).
Authenticated to centos2 ([192.168.33.11]:22).
debug1: channel 0: new [client-session]
debug1: Requesting no-more-sessions@openssh.com
debug1: Entering interactive session.
debug1: pledge: network
debug1: client_input_global_request: rtype hostkeys-00@openssh.com
want_reply 0
debug1: Sending environment.
debug1: Sending env LANG = en_GB.UTF-8
Last login: Wed Aug  8 13:55:20 2018 from
fe80::a00:27ff:fe2a:1652%eth1
```

Again, note the matching of configuration, and the fact that we're connected to the IPv4 address.

We can do one more thing with this, which is up the verbosity on our connection, getting to the next debug level, and hopefully seeing something else of note:

```
[vagrant@centos1 ~]$ ssh -vv CentOS2-Hostname
OpenSSH_7.4p1, OpenSSL 1.0.2k-fips  26 Jan 2017
debug1: Reading configuration data /home/vagrant/.ssh/config
debug1: /home/vagrant/.ssh/config line 1: Applying options for *
debug1: /home/vagrant/.ssh/config line 15: Applying options for
CentOS2-Hostname
debug1: Reading configuration data /etc/ssh/ssh_config
debug1: /etc/ssh/ssh_config line 58: Applying options for *
debug2: resolving "centos2" port 22
debug2: ssh_connect_direct: needpriv 0
debug1: Connecting to centos2 [192.168.33.11] port 22.
debug1: Connection established.
```

Here, we can see the second debug level (debug2) and specifically, we can see the moment centos2 was given in the block and was resolved to an address.

There's more...

You might have noticed that in my examples, I used a mixture of upper and lower characters for my names (for example, CentOS2-V4). I do this because it means that I know when I'm using my SSH config file, and can be sure at a glance that I'm using the settings I configured.

There's nothing stopping you from creating a block like so:

```
Host centos2
  Hostname 192.168.33.11
  User vagrant
```

This is perfectly valid, and the settings will be read as normal.

You can also do clever things such as specific domain matching. If you have to manage two different sets of servers differentiated by their domains, you can do the following:

```
Host *.examplecake.com
  Port 2222
  User Alie

Host *.examplebiscuit.co.uk
  Port 5252
  User Gingerbread
```

Attempting to connect to hosts in either of these domains will result in specific configuration options being used:

```
[vagrant@centos1 ~]$ ssh -v potato.examplecake.com
OpenSSH_7.4p1, OpenSSL 1.0.2k-fips 26 Jan 2017
debug1: Reading configuration data /home/vagrant/.ssh/config
debug1: /home/vagrant/.ssh/config line 1: Applying options for *
debug1: /home/vagrant/.ssh/config line 19: Applying options for
*.examplecake.com
debug1: Reading configuration data /etc/ssh/ssh_config
```

See also

The `ssh_config` manual page is worth a look, even if you only use it to fall asleep.

Modifying the server-side SSH configuration file

For the last few sections, we've been focusing on the client configuration. We've tweaked our connection string on the command line and we've written a configuration file to be read automatically by SSH when connecting to our second host.

In this section, we're going to take a look at the `sshd_config` file, or the server-side of the configuration tango, on our second host.

We're going to make a few example and routine changes to get you familiar with the concept.

Getting ready

Connect to both `centos1` and `centos2`. Doing this from outside (in separate windows, and using `vagrant ssh`) is best:

```
$ vagrant ssh centos1
$ vagrant ssh centos2
```

Place your Terminal windows side by side for easy viewing.

There is a chance that you will break SSH access to your server in this section, which is why I advise using Vagrant for your testing. If you do make a mistake, don't worry – simply destroy your VMs and start again.

How to do it...

On your `centos2` machine, open `/etc/ssh/sshd_config` in your favorite editor.

This file is large, and can seem a little daunting the first time you open it up.

The options listed are most of the settings that the SSH server (`sshd`) will read when it starts up, and apply to your running daemon.

Changing the default port

We're going to start with a simple one, that is, changing the default port on which the SSH daemon runs:

```
# If you want to change the port on a SELinux system, you have to tell
# SELinux about this change.
# semanage port -a -t ssh_port_t -p tcp #PORTNUMBER
#
#Port 22
#AddressFamily any
#ListenAddress 0.0.0.0
#ListenAddress ::
```

Change the preceding code so that the `Port` line is uncommented and now reads `2222`:

```
#
Port 2222
#AddressFamily any
#ListenAddress 0.0.0.0
#ListenAddress ::
```

As the handy note before this block informs us, we also have to modify SELinux so that it's aware that the SSH daemon will be trying to use a different port.

This file suggests that we use `semanage`, so let's do just that.

First, we'll find which package provides semanage:

```
[vagrant@centos2 ~]$ sudo yum whatprovides semanage
Loaded plugins: fastestmirror
Loading mirror speeds from cached hostfile
 * base: mirror.vorboss.net
 * extras: mozart.ee.ic.ac.uk
 * updates: mozart.ee.ic.ac.uk
base/7/x86_64/filelists_db
| 6.9 MB  00:00:01
extras/7/x86_64/filelists_db
| 588 kB  00:00:00
updates/7/x86_64/filelists_db
| 2.4 MB  00:00:00
policycoreutils-python-2.5-22.el7.x86_64 : SELinux policy core python
utilities
Repo        : base
Matched from:
Filename    : /usr/sbin/semanage
```

Then, we'll install it:

```
[vagrant@centos2 ~]$ sudo yum install -y policycoreutils-python
```

Finally, we'll run the recommended command with our new port:

```
[vagrant@centos2 ~]$ sudo semanage port -a -t ssh_port_t -p tcp 2222
```

Once done, we can safely restart the SSH daemon:

```
[vagrant@centos2 ~]$ sudo systemctl restart sshd
```

This shouldn't kick you off the VM, as sshd is designed so that changes won't cause a loss of access, even if those changes will stop you from logging on again (once you've voluntarily disconnected.)

Try logging out now, and then logging back in again.

A forewarning: this should fail!

Fear not! Instead, connect to centos1 on your second Terminal (you should have two connections open to centos1 at this point) and SSH back onto centos2 like so:

```
[vagrant@centos1 ~]$ ssh 192.168.33.11 -p2222
```

Congratulations! SSH is now running on a different port!

You can confirm this from within the OS with the following command (which we'll cover in greater detail later on:)

```
[vagrant@centos2 ~]$ ss -nl sport = :2222
Netid State       Recv-Q Send-Q    Local Address:Port
Peer Address:Port
tcp   LISTEN   0      128                  *:2222
*:*
tcp   LISTEN   0      128                :::2222
:::*
```

Note that in the preceding code, we're printing both the IPv4 and IPv6 values.

Changing the listen address

By default, SSH will listen on all addresses and interfaces:

```
#AddressFamily any
#ListenAddress 0.0.0.0
#ListenAddress ::
```

We're going to change this so that it's listening on only IPv4 and our eth1 address.

Change the preceding options to the following:

```
AddressFamily inet
ListenAddress 192.168.33.11
#ListenAddress ::
```

We've uncommented two of the options and changed their values.

In the preceding block, you may have noticed that ListenAddress :: is also listed. Here, :: is the IPv6 equivalent of 0.0.0.0 in IPv4.

Restart the SSH daemon:

```
[vagrant@centos2 ~]$ sudo systemctl restart sshd
```

Running our `ss` command from before, you may notice that the IPv6 option has disappeared:

```
[vagrant@centos2 ~]$ ss -nl sport = :2222
Netid State       Recv-Q Send-Q    Local Address:Port
Peer Address:Port
tcp   LISTEN   0      128       192.168.33.11:2222
*:*
```

If we now exit our session to `centos2` (using *Ctrl + D*) and try to SSH to the IPv6 link-local address, it will fail:

```
[vagrant@centos1 ~]$ ssh fe80::a00:27ff:fe56:c5a7%eth1 -p2222
ssh: connect to host fe80::a00:27ff:fe56:c5a7%eth1 port 2222:
Connection refused
```

A great success—we've squashed any possibility of trend-setters logging into our server on IPv6!

> On to a serious note for a minute, I've been hearing about the demise of IPv4 and the rise of IPv6 for years, pretty much since I started in computing. In that time, not much has changed, and both carriers and service providers have continued to eke everything they can out of IPv4, even introducing horrible things such as Carrier-grade NAT. I do hope that IPv6 picks up steam, not least because we're effectively out of IPv4 addresses to allocate.

Changing the daemon logging level

There are several levels that SSH can log at, dictated by the `LogLevel` setting:

```
# Logging
#SyslogFacility AUTH
SyslogFacility AUTHPRIV
#LogLevel INFO
```

The possibilities are `QUIET`, `FATAL`, `ERROR`, `INFO`, `VERBOSE`, `DEBUG`, `DEBUG1`, `DEBUG2`, and `DEBUG3`.

> The SSH daemon manual lists the `DEBUG` options as all violating the privacy of users, and therefore it is not recommended that you use them.

We're going to bump this up to VERBOSE:

```
# Logging
#SyslogFacility AUTH
SyslogFacility AUTHPRIV
LogLevel VERBOSE
```

Restart the SSH daemon:

```
[vagrant@centos2 ~]$ sudo systemctl restart sshd
```

Now, let's have a look at what difference that made.

Here's our secure log at INFO level:

```
[vagrant@centos2 ~]$ sudo grep "1137" /var/log/secure
Aug  7 16:40:44 localhost sshd[1137]: Accepted publickey for vagrant
from 10.0.2.2 port 53114 ssh2: RSA
SHA256:1M4RzhMyWuFS/86uPY/ce2prh/dVTHW7iD2RhpquOZA
Aug  7 16:40:45 localhost sshd[1137]: pam_unix(sshd:session): session
opened for user vagrant by (uid=0)
```

And here's our secure log at VERBOSE level:

```
[vagrant@centos2 ~]$ sudo grep "5796" /var/log/secure
Aug  8 15:00:00 localhost sshd[5796]: Connection from 192.168.33.10
port 39258 on 192.168.33.11 port 2222
Aug  8 15:00:00 localhost sshd[5796]: Postponed publickey for vagrant
from 192.168.33.10 port 39258 ssh2 [preauth]
Aug  8 15:00:02 localhost sshd[5796]: Accepted publickey for vagrant
from 192.168.33.10 port 39258 ssh2: ED25519
SHA256:nQVR7ZVJMjph093KHB6qLg9Ve87PF4fNnFw8Y5X0kN4
Aug  8 15:00:03 localhost sshd[5796]: pam_unix(sshd:session): session
opened for user vagrant by (uid=0)
Aug  8 15:00:03 localhost sshd[5796]: User child is on pid 5799
```

Disallowing root login

Some distributions deny root login by default, and this is widely considered a good idea. Here, we have a user (vagrant) that we can use to get around so that we don't need to log in as root.

Find the line with PermitRootLogin:

```
#LoginGraceTime 2m
#PermitRootLogin yes
#StrictModes yes
```

Change it to no:

```
#LoginGraceTime 2m
PermitRootLogin no
#StrictModes yes
```

Restart the SSH daemon:

[vagrant@centos2 ~]$ sudo systemctl restart sshd

 This does not disallow local root login, so in a pinch, you can still connect to a console (or plug a keyboard and mouse into the physical machine) and log in with the root user locally.

Disabling passwords (force key use)

Because we've got our public keys on this host, we no longer need to allow password-based access.

Find the PasswordAuthentication line:

```
#PermitEmptyPasswords no
PasswordAuthentication yes
```

Change this line to no:

```
#PermitEmptyPasswords no
PasswordAuthentication no
```

Restart the SSH daemon:

[vagrant@centos2 ~]$ sudo systemctl restart sshd

 The eagle-eyed among you will have noticed that I already flipped this setting once, in the Vagrantfile at the start of this chapter. This was to allow us to use Vagrant as a learning experience, and we are effectively reversing the reversal right now.

Setting a message of the day (motd)

Providing your PrintMotd setting is set to yes, you can have users see the contents of /etc/motd when they log in.

First, ensure that it is set to `yes` in the SSH daemon config:

```
#PermitTTY yes
PrintMotd yes
#PrintLastLog yes
```

Next, restart the SSH daemon, and then modify the `/etc/motd` file to something sensible. Alternatively, you can use the following command:

```
sudo sh -c 'echo "This is a testing system, how did you get here?" >
/etc/motd'
```

This message will now be printed whenever you log in.

 This feature is usually used by companies to warn bad actors who are attempting to gain access to their systems. Occasionally, it's used by bored system administrators to quote Futurama at you.

The UseDNS setting

The last option I'm going to cover is the `UseDNS` entry, as it's a source of pain for quite a few people:

```
#UseDNS yes
UseDNS no
```

Here, we can see that `UseDNS` has been explicitly set to `no` in our configuration file. This is the default.

When set to `no`, the SSH daemon will not look up the remote host name, and check that the remote IP maps back to the expected IP, based on that host name.

To confuse you further, here's the manual entry of `UseDNS` :

> *"Specifies whether sshd(8) should look up the remote host name, and to check that the resolved host name for the remote IP address maps back to the very same IP address.*
> *If this option is set to no (the default) then only addresses and not host names may be used in ~/.ssh/authorized_keys from and sshd_config Match Host directives."*

What this means is that when `UseDNS` is set to `yes`, and the machine you're connecting from doesn't have a reverse DNS entry set, SSH will try and match the IP it expects with what it's seeing, and likely fail to do so.

In practice, all this means is that if your DNS is broken on the box you're trying to connect to, you have to wait around like a lemon for a bit while the DNS request times out, and eventually let you in. To frustrate matters further, this feature is almost useless out of the box, as highlighted in this mailing list email: `https://lists.centos.org/pipermail/centos-devel/2016-July/014981.html`.

AllowUsers

We've already denied the root user access to our system, but what if we wanted to take this a step further and specify the users we want to grant access to?

For that, we need the `AllowUsers` setting.

This is rarely a default setting, or even commented out in the `sshd_config` file, so we're going to add it to the bottom:

```
#        PermitTTY no
#        ForceCommand cvs server
AllowUsers vagrant
```

Restart the SSH daemon:

```
[vagrant@centos2 ~]$ sudo systemctl restart sshd
```

Now, you've got a system that only the `vagrant` user will be able to SSH to. You can also add multiple names to this list, or even substitute this whitelist for a blacklist, with `DenyUsers`.

If we want, we can work on a group basis (instead of individual usernames) with `AllowGroups` and `DenyGroups`.

How it works...

Now that we've been through and changed a few common settings, we're going to have a quick look at what happens when you restart the SSH daemon.

SSH's `systemd` unit file will look similar to this, though your system may vary:

```
[vagrant@centos2 ~]$ cat /etc/systemd/system/multi-
user.target.wants/sshd.service
[Unit]
Description=OpenSSH server daemon
```

```
Documentation=man:sshd(8) man:sshd_config(5)
After=network.target sshd-keygen.service
Wants=sshd-keygen.service

[Service]
Type=notify
EnvironmentFile=/etc/sysconfig/sshd
ExecStart=/usr/sbin/sshd -D $OPTIONS
ExecReload=/bin/kill -HUP $MAINPID
KillMode=process
Restart=on-failure
RestartSec=42s

[Install]
WantedBy=multi-user.target
```

By default, we can see that the binary used is `/usr/sbin/sshd` with `$OPTIONS` passed from elsewhere (in this case the `EnvironmentFile` value, as listed previously).

Reading the manual for `sshd`, we find the following section:

The `-f config_file` option (`https://man.openbsd.org/sshd`) is described as follows:

> *"Specifies the name of the configuration file. The default is /etc/ssh/sshd_config. sshd refuses to start if there is no configuration file."*

Here, we have the answer of why `sshd_config` is read by default—it's baked in.

There's more...

We've only covered some of the basic options people tend to change when configuring the SSH daemon for their own environment, but most administrators don't bother making any changes at all, leaving whatever the configured defaults are.

See also

To get a better understanding of all the daemon options available to you, read through the `sshd_config` manual page and take a look at the page for the `sshd` executable, too.

Rotating host keys and updating known_hosts

One thing we've not mentioned yet are host keys, and the `known_hosts` file.

This is something that is often overlooked, so I'd like to take a few minutes to go over these otherwise-ignored treasures.

In this section, we will inspect what happens when you first SSH to a new machine, and then we will change the keys of that machine to see what problems this causes us.

Getting ready

Connect to `centos1` and `centos2` in different sessions:

```
$ vagrant ssh centos1
$ vagrant ssh centos2
```

If you're working on a fresh setup, SSH to `centos2` from `centos1` and accept the host key when you're presented with it.

Log back out of `centos2`:

```
[vagrant@centos1 ~]$ ssh 192.168.33.11
The authenticity of host '192.168.33.11 (192.168.33.11)' can't be
established.
ECDSA key fingerprint is
SHA256:D4Tu/OykM/iPayCZ2okG0D2F6J9H5PzTNUuFzhzl/xw.
ECDSA key fingerprint is
MD5:4b:2a:42:77:0e:24:b4:9c:6e:65:69:63:1a:57:e9:4e.
Are you sure you want to continue connecting (yes/no)? yes
Warning: Permanently added '192.168.33.11' (ECDSA) to the list of
known hosts.
vagrant@192.168.33.11's password:
[vagrant@centos2 ~]$ logout
Connection to 192.168.33.11 closed.
[vagrant@centos1 ~]$
```

We've now got an entry in our `known_hosts` file, as shown here:

```
[vagrant@centos1 ~]$ cat .ssh/known_hosts
192.168.33.11 ecdsa-sha2-nistp256
AAAAE2VjZHNhLXNoYTItbmlzdHAyNTYAAAAIbmlzdHAyNTYAAABBBOK52r7ZJ8hwU34Rza
Y3AD7HitT6UP2qBv3WK8lWEELSoeTsmJ4+zO8QiuULp3cCQBKYqi55Z60Vf/hsEMBoULg=
```

Note that this IP and key are found on `centos2`:

```
[vagrant@centos2 ~]$ cat /etc/ssh/ssh_host_ecdsa_key.pub
ecdsa-sha2-nistp256
AAAAE2VjZHNhLXNoYTItbmlzdHAyNTYAAAAIbmlzdHAyNTYAAAABBBOK52r7ZJ8hwU34Rza
Y3AD7HitT6UP2qBv3WK81WEELSoeTsmJ4+zO8QiuULp3cCQBKYqi55Z6OVf/hsEMBoULg=
```

We can prove this easily by having a look at the key's fingerprint on both machines, and comparing the ASCII art.

On `centos2`, this is as follows:

```
[vagrant@centos2 ~]$ ssh-keygen -lv -f /etc/ssh/ssh_host_ecdsa_key.pub
256 SHA256:D4Tu/OykM/iPayCZ2okG0D2F6J9H5PzTNUuFzhzl/xw no comment
(ECDSA)
+---[ECDSA 256]---+
|   . .        o. |
|   . . o.    o.. |
| o . =. .   + o. |
|. o o.+.     B . |
|.  + +..S. o o E.|
|. + +o. oo.  .o|
|.+ o +o ...    o|
|o.o . +*        |
|.    o=*=        |
+----[SHA256]-----+
```

And from the `known_hosts` file on `centos1` is as follows:

```
[vagrant@centos1 ~]$ ssh-keygen -lv -f .ssh/known_hosts
256 SHA256:D4Tu/OykM/iPayCZ2okG0D2F6J9H5PzTNUuFzhzl/xw 192.168.33.11
(ECDSA)
+---[ECDSA 256]---+
|   . .        o. |
|   . . o.    o.. |
| o . =. .   + o. |
|. o o.+.     B . |
|.  + +..S. o o E.|
|. + +o. oo.  .o|
|.+ o +o ...    o|
|o.o . +*        |
|.    o=*=        |
+----[SHA256]-----+
```

That's genuinely the first time I've ever used the -v option to get the ASCII art out of a key for comparison purposes.

How to do it...

Now that we've confirmed our setup, we're going to change the host keys on centos2 and see what happens.

On centos2, run the following:

```
[vagrant@centos2 ~]$ sudo mv /etc/ssh/ssh_host_ecdsa_key*
/home/vagrant/
[vagrant@centos2 ~]$ ls
ssh_host_ecdsa_key   ssh_host_ecdsa_key.pub
```

We've just moved the keys we accepted as gospel on centos1.

Our session stays up because we're already authenticated and connected. If we were to disconnect at this point, we would have to accept a different set of keys (we moved the ECDSA keys, but there's still Ed25519 host keys available, which SSH would pick up instead).

Now, we're going to generate a new set of keys by using the catchall -A flag:

```
[vagrant@centos2 ~]$ sudo ssh-keygen -A
ssh-keygen: generating new host keys: RSA1 DSA ECDSA
```

We can confirm these exist by checking the directory:

```
[vagrant@centos2 ~]$ ls -l /etc/ssh/ssh_host_ecdsa_key*
-rw-------. 1 root root 227 Aug  8 16:30 /etc/ssh/ssh_host_ecdsa_key
-rw-r--r--. 1 root root 174 Aug  8 16:30
/etc/ssh/ssh_host_ecdsa_key.pub
```

Log out of centos2 and try to log back in again:

```
[vagrant@centos1 ~]$ ssh 192.168.33.11
@@@@@@@@@@@@@@@@@@@@@@@@@@@@@@@@@@@@@@@@@@@@@@@@@@@@@@@@@@@
@    WARNING: REMOTE HOST IDENTIFICATION HAS CHANGED!    @
@@@@@@@@@@@@@@@@@@@@@@@@@@@@@@@@@@@@@@@@@@@@@@@@@@@@@@@@@@@
IT IS POSSIBLE THAT SOMEONE IS DOING SOMETHING NASTY!
Someone could be eavesdropping on you right now (man-in-the-middle
attack)!
It is also possible that a host key has just been changed.
The fingerprint for the ECDSA key sent by the remote host is
SHA256:vdJTJW4ewGtOAdQXCXJ+cbjvrNm9787/CQQnCeM9fjc.
Please contact your system administrator.
Add correct host key in /home/vagrant/.ssh/known_hosts to get rid of
this message.
```

```
Offending ECDSA key in /home/vagrant/.ssh/known_hosts:1
ECDSA host key for 192.168.33.11 has changed and you have requested
strict checking.
Host key verification failed.
[vagrant@centos1 ~]$
```

SSH tries to save you from doing something bad. Because it's already aware of the IP you're trying to connect to, and has a `known_hosts` entry for it, it compares the known key it has on file with that of the box.

Since we've just regenerated the keys on the box, we've been presented with a horrible-looking error.

 It's worth getting over the mental block of just scoffing and working around this error. Try to lend yourself five seconds of thought and confirm that the error is expected. Too often, I've seen people immediately grumble when faced with this message and bypass it straight away. If you've already accepted the key on a box once, you shouldn't see a warning about it again, this can mean that the box has been tampered with, or your connection is being "man in the middle'd." Be vigilant!

Clear the old key (the line location of which is emboldened in the preceding code) from our `known_hosts` file:

```
[vagrant@centos1 ~]$ ssh-keygen -R 192.168.33.11
# Host 192.168.33.11 found: line 1
/home/vagrant/.ssh/known_hosts updated.
Original contents retained as /home/vagrant/.ssh/known_hosts.olds
```

You should now be able to SSH to `centos2` again and accept the new key:

```
[vagrant@centos1 ~]$ ssh 192.168.33.11
The authenticity of host '192.168.33.11 (192.168.33.11)' can't be
established.
ECDSA key fingerprint is
SHA256:vdJTJW4ewGtOAdQXCXJ+cbjvrNm9787/CQQnCeM9fjc.
ECDSA key fingerprint is
MD5:c3:be:16:5b:62:7f:4d:9c:0b:15:c0:cd:d6:87:d6:d6.
Are you sure you want to continue connecting (yes/no)? yes
Warning: Permanently added '192.168.33.11' (ECDSA) to the list of
known hosts.
vagrant@192.168.33.11's password:
Last login: Wed Aug  8 16:26:50 2018 from 192.168.33.10
[vagrant@centos2 ~]$
```

How it works...

The `ssh-keygen` command we used is a quick way of placing expected host keys in the default location. Because we'd removed the key we expected to be there, we would have failed to connect to our host, and been prompted with the horrible error we saw previously:

```
<SNIP>
debug1: Server host key: ecdsa-sha2-nistp256
SHA256:zW4PXt4o3VRA/OiePUc4VoxBY50us9vl2vemgcrLduA
debug3: hostkeys_foreach: reading file
"/home/vagrant/.ssh/known_hosts"
debug3: record_hostkey: found key type ECDSA in file
/home/vagrant/.ssh/known_hosts:1
debug3: load_hostkeys: loaded 1 keys from 192.168.33.11
@@@@@@@@@@@@@@@@@@@@@@@@@@@@@@@@@@@@@@@@@@@@@@@@@@@@@@@@@@@@@@@
@    WARNING: REMOTE HOST IDENTIFICATION HAS CHANGED!    @
@@@@@@@@@@@@@@@@@@@@@@@@@@@@@@@@@@@@@@@@@@@@@@@@@@@@@@@@@@@@@@@
IT IS POSSIBLE THAT SOMEONE IS DOING SOMETHING NASTY!
<SNIP>
```

In the preceding snippet, we can see SSH checking our `known_hosts` file, then getting the key from the remote host, and finally throwing a fit.

To reconnect to the host, we simply had to remove the offending entry from the `known_hosts` file on our client-side, and then attempt our connection again.

We used `-R` to remove the offending key, but you can use any method to do so as it's just a text file. If you wish you can even empty the entire `known_hosts` file, but this will also mean you'll have to accept keys for every box you've ever connected to, once again.

There's more...

So, what happens if you remove all the host keys from the server?

This is what you get:

```
[vagrant@centos2 ~]$ sudo rm /etc/ssh/ssh_host_*
[vagrant@centos2 ~]$ logout
Connection to 192.168.33.11 closed.
[vagrant@centos1 ~]$ ssh  192.168.33.11
ssh_exchange_identification: read: Connection reset by peer
```

At this point, you can either re-provision your VM, or log on via the console and generate new keys.

Technical requirements

Confirm that both of your Vagrant boxes are enabled, and connect to both using the `vagrant` command.

If you've previously changed the SSH configuration file, it might be an idea to destroy your boxes and re-provision them first:

```
$ vagrant ssh centos1
$ vagrant ssh centos2
```

Using local forwarding

Local forwarding is the act of mapping local TCP ports or Unix sockets onto remote ports or sockets. It's commonly used when either accessing a system securely (by requiring the user to first SSH to the box, thus encrypting their connection), or for troubleshooting problems.

In this section, we're going to start a small `webserver` on `centos2`, which we're going to connect to from `centos1`, first by connecting to the IP and port directly, and then by a connection to a mapped local port, utilizing port forwarding.

Getting ready

On `centos2`, run the following command:

```
[vagrant@centos2 ~]$ python -m SimpleHTTPServer 8888
Serving HTTP on 0.0.0.0 port 8888 ...
```

You've just created a small, Python-based web server, listening on every address at port `8888`.

You can confirm this by running a `curl` command from `centos1`:

```
[vagrant@centos1 ~]$ curl 192.168.33.11:8888
<!DOCTYPE html PUBLIC "-//W3C//DTD HTML 3.2 Final//EN"><html>
<title>Directory listing for /</title>
```

```
<body>
<h2>Directory listing for /</h2>
<hr>
<ul>
<li><a href=".bash_logout">.bash_logout</a>
<li><a href=".bash_profile">.bash_profile</a>
<li><a href=".bashrc">.bashrc</a>
<li><a href=".ssh/">.ssh/</a>
</ul>
<hr>
</body>
</html>
```

Note the listing of the home directory contents from `centos2`.

On `centos2`, you should see your connection (`200` response):

```
[vagrant@centos2 ~]$ python -m SimpleHTTPServer 8888
Serving HTTP on 0.0.0.0 port 8888 ...
192.168.33.10 - - [09/Aug/2018 10:47:13] "GET / HTTP/1.1" 200 -
```

 Python's built-in web server module is very handy for testing. I used it here because it's available out of the box in our installation, but I wouldn't use it in a production environment, as there are better (and faster) alternatives.

To confirm we've not yet got anything listening locally on port `9999`, perform another `curl` command from `centos1`:

```
[vagrant@centos1 ~]$ curl 127.0.0.1:9999
curl: (7) Failed connect to 127.0.0.1:9999; Connection refused
```

How to do it...

We're going to locally forward connections to the local port `9999` to the remote port `8888`.

On the command line

Run the following from `centos1`:

```
[vagrant@centos1 ~]$ ssh -f -L 9999:127.0.0.1:8888 192.168.33.11 sleep
120
```

You may be prompted for your password (depending on what you've done in terms of key setup) and then be dropped back to the `centos1` prompt.

Our SSH connection will stay up for two minutes.

Now, we run a `curl`, checking that our forwarding is working:

```
[vagrant@centos1 ~]$ curl 127.0.0.1:9999
<!DOCTYPE html PUBLIC "-//W3C//DTD HTML 3.2 Final//EN"><html>
<title>Directory listing for /</title>
<body>
<h2>Directory listing for /</h2>
<hr>
<ul>
<li><a href=".bash_history">.bash_history</a>
<li><a href=".bash_logout">.bash_logout</a>
<li><a href=".bash_profile">.bash_profile</a>
<li><a href=".bashrc">.bashrc</a>
<li><a href=".ssh/">.ssh/</a>
</ul>
<hr>
</body>
</html>
```

Success! Here, we're curling the localhost IP address of `centos1` on our forwarded port and we're getting the directory listing from `centos2`!

Using an SSH config file

If we wanted to create this forwarding setup each time we connected to `centos2`, we can add the option to our SSH configuration file.

Add the emboldened line in the following code:

```
Host * !CentOS2-V6
 IdentityFile ~/.ssh/id_ed25519
 Port 22

Host CentOS2-V4
 Hostname 192.168.33.11
 LocalForward 9999 127.0.0.1:8888
 User vagrant

Host CentOS2-V6
 Hostname fe80::a00:27ff:fe56:c5a7%%eth1
 IdentityFile ~/.ssh/id_rsa
```

```
    Port 22
    User vagrant

Host CentOS2-Hostname
 Hostname centos2
 User vagrant
```

Now, if you SSH to the host specified, you will create a forwarded connection without having to specify it:

```
[vagrant@centos1 ~]$ ssh -f CentOS2-V4 sleep 120
[vagrant@centos1 ~]$ curl 127.0.0.1:9999
<!DOCTYPE html PUBLIC "-//W3C//DTD HTML 3.2 Final//EN"><html>
<title>Directory listing for /</title>
<body>
<h2>Directory listing for /</h2>
<hr>
<ul>
<li><a href=".bash_history">.bash_history</a>
<li><a href=".bash_logout">.bash_logout</a>
<li><a href=".bash_profile">.bash_profile</a>
<li><a href=".bashrc">.bashrc</a>
<li><a href=".ssh/">.ssh/</a>
</ul>
<hr>
</body>
</html>
```

You're not limited to one `LocalForward` entry per host—you can have several.

How it works...

When you use the `-L` flag with SSH, you're specifying that any connection attempts made to the local machine, on the first port listed, are to be forwarded to the remote host and port.

Let's break down the command:

```
[vagrant@centos1 ~]$ ssh -f -L 9999:127.0.0.1:8888 192.168.33.11 sleep
120
```

First, the `-f` and `sleep 120` at the end of the command are a quick way to create a session and background it while we perform our test:

```
-f ... sleep 120
```

In the real world, you're not limited to just one Terminal window, and generally, you'll find yourself opening a session to a remote host in one window while you work in another.

The second part is the interesting bit:

```
-L 9999:127.0.0.1:8888
```

Here, we're saying that local port `9999` should have any connection requests forwarded to the remote host on `127.0.0.1:8888`.

Because of the way we created our web server, the following is also valid syntax:

```
-L 9999:192.168.33.11:8888
```

This is because our remote web server was listening on all addresses, so instead of sending our request to the remote localhost address, we're just using the `eth1` address instead.

I've frequently seen setups where less secure programs are run on the localhost address only, meaning that if you want to access the program, you have to SSH to the remote host first.

You're also not limited to cURL and the command line—you could navigate to `http://127.0.0.1:9999` in your web browser, and it would still work.

There's more...

Tips and tricks for SSH are somewhat endless, but the following can be good to practice.

Watching our SSH session

If you want to see when your SSH tunnel has closed, run the following:

```
[vagrant@centos1 ~]$ ps aux | grep "ssh -f" | grep -v grep
vagrant    3525  0.0  0.2  82796  1196 ?        Ss   11:03   0:00 ssh -
f -L 9999:127.0.0.1:8888 192.168.33.11 sleep 120
```

Upon disconnection, this process will end:

```
[vagrant@centos1 ~]$ ps aux | grep "ssh -f" | grep -v grep
[vagrant@centos1 ~]$
```

Connecting to systems beyond the remote host

`LocalForwarding` can even be used to access hosts that the remote machine can see, but your local one can't.

Consider the following configuration entry:

```
Host *
 IdentityFile ~/.ssh/id_ed25519
 Port 22

Host CentOS2-V4
 Hostname 192.168.33.11
 LocalForward 7777 192.168.33.12:6666
 User vagrant
```

In this example, `centos2` can see the host with the IP `192.168.33.12`, and the server it's got listening on port `6666`.

When we connect to `centos2` and create our tunnel, we can connect locally to `127.0.0.1:7777`, viewing the web server on `192.168.33.12:6666`.

 This is widely used in conjunction with bastion hosts, which we will look at soon.

See also

Forwarding local connection attempts to a remote host can be an extremely useful troubleshooting and access control method.

Take a look at the SSH manual page for more detail and expansion on the options listed in this recipe.

The SSH manual page can be brought up on most Linux systems using the following command:

```
$ man ssh
```

Using remote forwarding

In the previous section, we looked at the ability to forward local connection attempts to a remote machine.

In this section, we're going to look at something very similar: remote forwarding.

With remote forwarding, connection attempts made to a specified address and port on a remote machine are passed back through the SSH tunnel you've set up, and are processed on the local machine (your client).

Start on `centos1`.

> Before we start it's worth noting that remote forwarding is a great way to punch holes out of networks, which means that it can also be a nightmare for security professionals charged with maintaining a network. With great power comes great etc.

Getting ready

Confirm that both of your Vagrant boxes are enabled, and connect to both:

```
$ vagrant ssh centos1
$ vagrant ssh centos2
```

How to do it...

First, we're going to start by using our single command at our prompt, and then we'll look at how to set up the connection every time you SSH to a machine using the SSH config file.

On the command line

On `centos1`, run the following:

```
[vagrant@centos1 ~]$ ssh -R 5353:127.0.0.1:22 192.168.33.11
```

Once connected to `centos2`, run the following:

```
[vagrant@centos2 ~]$ ssh 127.0.0.1 -p5353
```

You will probably be prompted to add a host key, and then be prompted for a password. We're connecting back to centos1, so provide the default Vagrant password.

You should be left at the centos1 command-line prompt:

```
vagrant@127.0.0.1's password:
Last login: Thu Aug  9 12:29:56 2018 from 127.0.0.1
[vagrant@centos1 ~]$
```

Using an SSH config file

As with LocalForward, we can also use an SSH config file for RemoteForward connections, too:

```
Host *
 IdentityFile ~/.ssh/id_ed25519
 Port 22

Host CentOS2-V4
 Hostname 192.168.33.11
 LocalForward 9999 127.0.0.1:8888
 RemoteForward 5353 127.0.0.1:22
 User vagrant
```

Here, you can see the exact setup we used in the command line section, only specified in the config file, so that it's always available without having to type the flags out each time:

```
[vagrant@centos1 ~]$ ssh CentOS2-V4
[vagrant@centos2 ~]$ ssh 127.0.0.1 -p5353
[vagrant@centos1 ~]$
```

How it works...

What we actually do here is... odd:

1. We SSH to centos2, while saying that any connection attempts made to port 5353 on the remote machine (centos2) are to be passed back over the SSH session to our client (centos1).

2. We then run SSH on our remote machine (centos2), specifying the localhost address and the port that we're passing back to centos1, 127.0.0.1:5353.

3. The connection attempt is passed back over our established SSH session to `centos1`, where the SSH server accepts the connection request.

4. As a result, we're locally SSH'ing to `centos1` by specifying the local address and remote forwarded port on `centos2`.

Confused? I was the first time someone explained this to me.

To better understand this, we can use the `w` command.

On `centos1`, this gives us the following:

```
[vagrant@centos1 ~]$ w
 12:47:50 up  2:10,  2 users,  load average: 0.00, 0.02, 0.05
 USER     TTY      FROM             LOGIN@   IDLE   JCPU   PCPU WHAT
 vagrant  pts/0    10.0.2.2         10:38    6.00s  1.07s  0.08s ssh -R
 5353:127.0.0.1:22 192.168.33.
 vagrant  pts/1    127.0.0.1        12:44    6.00s  0.07s  0.05s w
```

Here, we can see our default Vagrant connection (from `10.0.2.2`), but we can also see a local connection.

Apparently, we've SSH'd to our machine from the localhost address (`127.0.0.1`). This is actually the SSH session we established on `centos2` using the following command:

```
[vagrant@centos2 ~]$ ssh 127.0.0.1 -p5353
```

On `centos2`, the `w` command gives us the following:

```
[vagrant@centos2 ~]$ w
 12:48:08 up  2:09,  2 users,  load average: 0.00, 0.01, 0.05
 USER     TTY      FROM             LOGIN@   IDLE   JCPU   PCPU WHAT
 vagrant  pts/0    10.0.2.2         10:43    0.00s  0.92s  0.04s w
 vagrant  pts/1    192.168.33.10    12:44    24.00s 0.07s  0.04s ssh
 127.0.0.1 -p5353
```

Here, we can see our default Vagrant connection (from `10.0.2.2`), but we can also see the remote connection from `centos1` (`192.168.33.10`).

There's more...

It's not just SSH that this can be used with. In the same way, we can forward ports from the remote session to our local machine – we have a wealth of options available to us.

Let's start and background a simple web server on `centos1`:

```
[vagrant@centos1 ~]$ python -m SimpleHTTPServer 8888 &
[1] 6010
```

Now, let's SSH to `centos2`, while stating that any requests made on the remote machine to `127.0.0.1:7777` are passed back along the established SSH session to `centos1`:

```
[vagrant@centos1 ~]$ ssh -R 7777:127.0.0.1:8888 192.168.33.11
```

On `centos2`, we should now be able to `curl 127.0.0.1:7777` and see the contents of Vagrant's home directory on `centos1`:

```
[vagrant@centos2 ~]$ curl 127.0.0.1:7777
127.0.0.1 - - [09/Aug/2018 12:56:43] "GET / HTTP/1.1" 200 -
                                               <!DOCTYPE
html PUBLIC "-//W3C//DTD HTML 3.2 Final//EN"><html>
<title>Directory listing for /</title>
<body>
<h2>Directory listing for /</h2>
<hr>
<ul>
<li><a href=".bash_history">.bash_history</a>
<li><a href=".bash_logout">.bash_logout</a>
<li><a href=".bash_profile">.bash_profile</a>
<li><a href=".bashrc">.bashrc</a>
<li><a href=".ssh/">.ssh/</a>
</ul>
<hr>
</body>
</html>
```

Success!

See also

While it may seem that this has limited uses, as far as nifty tricks go, you might find some curious cases for it in your career.

I have used this on one or two occasions, when DNS has been broken on a remote machine, and I've instead forwarded DNS requests back over an established SSH connection.

ProxyJump and bastion hosts

We're going to take a look at one very new SSH option, a slightly older SSH option, and the concept of bastion hosts (or jump boxes) in this recipe.

We need three machines because we're going to use one machine as the "gateway" to another.

Getting ready

Set up your three VMs, preferably using the `Vagrantfile` at the top of this chapter.

Connect to each box, and then check that from `centos1`, you can ping `centos2` and `centos3`:

```
[vagrant@centos1 ~]$ ping 192.168.33.11
PING 192.168.33.11 (192.168.33.11) 56(84) bytes of data.
64 bytes from 192.168.33.11: icmp_seq=1 ttl=64 time=2.54 ms
64 bytes from 192.168.33.11: icmp_seq=2 ttl=64 time=1.09 ms
64 bytes from 192.168.33.11: icmp_seq=3 ttl=64 time=0.929 ms
^C
--- 192.168.33.11 ping statistics ---
3 packets transmitted, 3 received, 0% packet loss, time 2009ms
rtt min/avg/max/mdev = 0.929/1.524/2.548/0.728 ms
[vagrant@centos1 ~]$ ping 192.168.33.12
PING 192.168.33.12 (192.168.33.12) 56(84) bytes of data.
64 bytes from 192.168.33.12: icmp_seq=1 ttl=64 time=0.743 ms
64 bytes from 192.168.33.12: icmp_seq=2 ttl=64 time=1.15 ms
64 bytes from 192.168.33.12: icmp_seq=3 ttl=64 time=1.12 ms
^C
--- 192.168.33.12 ping statistics ---
3 packets transmitted, 3 received, 0% packet loss, time 2015ms
rtt min/avg/max/mdev = 0.743/1.008/1.157/0.187 ms
```

These are on `192.168.33.11` and `192.168.33.12` if you're using the supplied `Vagrantfile`.

How to do it...

From `centos1`, run the following command:

```
[vagrant@centos1 ~]$ ssh -J vagrant@192.168.33.11:22 192.168.33.12
```

You may be prompted to accept keys and also be asked for your password.

You will find yourself on `centos3`, having jumped through `centos2`:

```
[vagrant@centos3 ~]$
```

Using an SSH config file

The same trick can be used by specifying the `ProxyJump` option in your SSH config file:

```
Host *
 IdentityFile ~/.ssh/id_ed25519
 Port 22

Host CentOS2-V4
 Hostname 192.168.33.11
 User vagrant

Host CentOS3-V4
 Hostname 192.168.33.12
 User vagrant
 ProxyJump CentOS2-V4
```

You can now SSH to `centos3` via `centos2`:

```
[vagrant@centos1 ~]$ ssh CentOS3-V4
vagrant@192.168.33.11's password:
vagrant@192.168.33.12's password:
Last login: Thu Aug  9 14:15:03 2018 from 192.168.33.11
[vagrant@centos3 ~]$
```

How it works...

The `-J` and `ProxyJump` options are a way to connect through a specified host, to a host beyond.

The manual entry from the official manual pages (`https://man.openbsd.org/ssh`) for `-J [user@]host[:port]` is as follows:

Connect to the target host by first making a ssh connection to the jump host described by destination and then establishing a TCP forwarding to the ultimate destination from there. Multiple jump hops may be specified separated by comma characters. This is a shortcut to specify a ProxyJump configuration directive.

The manual entry from `https://man.openbsd.org/ssh_config` for `ProxyJump` is as follows:

> *Specifies one or more jump proxies as either [user@]host[:port] or an ssh URI.*
> *Multiple proxies may be separated by comma characters and will be visited*
> *sequentially. Setting this option will cause ssh(1) to connect to the target host by*
> *first making a ssh(1) connection to the specified ProxyJump host and then*
> *establishing a TCP forwarding to the ultimate target from there.*

If we use the –v flag with SSH, we can see what happens in more detail:

```
[vagrant@centos1 ~]$ ssh -v CentOS3-V4
OpenSSH_7.4p1, OpenSSL 1.0.2k-fips  26 Jan 2017
debug1: Reading configuration data /home/vagrant/.ssh/config
debug1: /home/vagrant/.ssh/config line 1: Applying options for *
debug1: /home/vagrant/.ssh/config line 8: Applying options for
CentOS3-V4
debug1: Reading configuration data /etc/ssh/ssh_config
debug1: /etc/ssh/ssh_config line 58: Applying options for *
debug1: Setting implicit ProxyCommand from ProxyJump: ssh -v -W %h:%p
CentOS2-V4
debug1: Executing proxy command: exec ssh -v -W 192.168.33.12:22
CentOS2-V4
<SNIP>
debug1: permanently_drop_suid: 1000
OpenSSH_7.4p1, OpenSSL 1.0.2k-fips  26 Jan 2017
debug1: Reading configuration data /home/vagrant/.ssh/config
debug1: /home/vagrant/.ssh/config line 1: Applying options for *
debug1: /home/vagrant/.ssh/config line 4: Applying options for
CentOS2-V4
debug1: Reading configuration data /etc/ssh/ssh_config
debug1: /etc/ssh/ssh_config line 58: Applying options for *
debug1: Connecting to 192.168.33.11 [192.168.33.11] port 22.
debug1: Connection established.
debug1: key_load_public: No such file or directory
<SNIP>
debug1: kex_input_ext_info: server-sig-algs=<rsa-sha2-256,rsa-
sha2-512>
debug1: SSH2_MSG_SERVICE_ACCEPT received
debug1: Authentications that can continue: publickey,gssapi-
keyex,gssapi-with-mic,password
debug1: Next authentication method: gssapi-keyex
debug1: No valid Key exchange context
debug1: Next authentication method: gssapi-with-mic
debug1: Unspecified GSS failure.  Minor code may provide more
information
No Kerberos credentials available (default cache:
```

```
KEYRING:persistent:1000)

debug1: Unspecified GSS failure.  Minor code may provide more
information
No Kerberos credentials available (default cache:
KEYRING:persistent:1000)

debug1: Next authentication method: publickey
debug1: Trying private key: /home/vagrant/.ssh/id_rsa
debug1: Trying private key: /home/vagrant/.ssh/id_dsa
debug1: Trying private key: /home/vagrant/.ssh/id_ecdsa
debug1: Trying private key: /home/vagrant/.ssh/id_ed25519
debug1: Next authentication method: password
vagrant@192.168.33.11's password:
debug1: Authentication succeeded (password).
Authenticated to 192.168.33.11 ([192.168.33.11]:22).
debug1: channel_connect_stdio_fwd 192.168.33.12:22
debug1: channel 0: new [stdio-forward]
debug1: getpeername failed: Bad file descriptor
debug1: Requesting no-more-sessions@openssh.com
debug1: Entering interactive session.
debug1: pledge: network
debug1: client_input_global_request: rtype hostkeys-00@openssh.com
want_reply 0
debug1: Remote protocol version 2.0, remote software version
OpenSSH_7.4
debug1: match: OpenSSH_7.4 pat OpenSSH* compat 0x04000000
debug1: Authenticating to 192.168.33.12:22 as 'vagrant'
debug1: SSH2_MSG_KEXINIT sent
debug1: SSH2_MSG_KEXINIT received
debug1: kex: algorithm: curve25519-sha256
debug1: kex: host key algorithm: ecdsa-sha2-nistp256
debug1: kex: server->client cipher: chacha20-poly1305@openssh.com MAC:
<implicit> compression: none
debug1: kex: client->server cipher: chacha20-poly1305@openssh.com MAC:
<implicit> compression: none
debug1: kex: curve25519-sha256 need=64 dh_need=64
debug1: kex: curve25519-sha256 need=64 dh_need=64
debug1: expecting SSH2_MSG_KEX_ECDH_REPLY
<SNIP>
vagrant@192.168.33.12's password:
debug1: Authentication succeeded (password).
Authenticated to 192.168.33.12 (via proxy).
debug1: channel 0: new [client-session]
debug1: Requesting no-more-sessions@openssh.com
debug1: Entering interactive session.
debug1: pledge: proc
debug1: client_input_global_request: rtype hostkeys-00@openssh.com
```

```
want_reply 0
debug1: Sending environment.
debug1: Sending env LANG = en_GB.UTF-8
Last login: Thu Aug  9 14:22:08 2018 from 192.168.33.11
[vagrant@centos3 ~]$
```

Emboldened in the preceding output, we can see the key steps that take place during the connection sequence:

1. SSH reads the configuration for the host we're connecting to.
2. SSH realises it has to use a `ProxyJump` host to access the specifed box.
3. SSH translates the `ProxyJump` option into the equivalent `ProxyCommand` entry.
4. SSH reads the configuration for the `ProxyJump` host.
5. SSH connects and authenticates against the `ProxyJump` host.
6. SSH uses its established connection to the `ProxyJump` to connect to the destination host.
7. SSH notes that it's authenticated to the destination host (via proxy).

There's more...

Now that you know the basics of `ProxyJump`, let's take a look at some scenarios you may find useful.

More than once, using `ProxyJump` in the following ways listed has saved me literally milliseconds of time!

Multiple hosts

While the example given previously is relatively simple, it's worth noting that you can do some pretty complex things with `ProxyJump`.

You can list hosts, as the manual page suggests, and you can also chain hosts, as follows:

```
Host *
 Port 22

Host CentOS2-V4
 Hostname 192.168.33.11
 User vagrant
```

```
Host CentOS3-V4
 Hostname 192.168.33.12
 User vagrant
 ProxyJump CentOS2-V4

Host CentOS4-V4
 Hostname 192.168.33.14
 User vagrant
 ProxyJump CentOS3-V4
```

The advantage of `ProxyJump` itself should be obvious: using this technique, you can create a setup where it only takes one command from your local machine to access a remote and otherwise inaccessible box.

Generally, you might use `ProxyJump` in an environment with one ingress server.

 `ProxyJump` also makes forwarding ports easier. If you add a `LocalForward` line to `CentOS4-V4` in the preceding code, SSH will take care of handling the traffic through the `ProxyJump` hosts, too! This can be especially handy as it stops you having to forward ports manually, potentially through several hosts.

ProxyCommand

What we saw in our debug message was SSH translating the fairly simple `ProxyJump` entry into a `ProxyCommand` line.

`ProxyCommand` is the more traditional way of setting up this kind of forwarding, but not only is it syntactically more irritating, it's also messy.

Consider the following example:

```
Host *
 Port 22

Host CentOS2-V4
 Hostname 192.168.33.11
 User vagrant

Host CentOS3-V4
 Hostname 192.168.33.12
 User vagrant
 ProxyCommand ssh -v -W %h:%p CentOS2-V4
```

Looks more awkward, doesn't it? But it works in the same way.

This can be useful on older distributions, which maybe haven't received the `ProxyJump` feature yet.

> If you ever forget the syntax for `ProxyCommand` and you have a box around that supports `ProxyJump`, remember that the `ProxyCommand` syntax is printed for you in the `SSH -v` debug we created before.

Bastion hosts

All of this is great, but why would you need this if you're managing servers? Especially servers you control...

Consider your environment.

In the office, you might have access to every machine the company has under its dominion, because you're sat on a LAN segment that has unfettered access to every other network segment.

Remotely, you might have a VPN machine on the border of your network, to which you need to initially establish a connection before you're able to SSH to other machines.

Bastion hosts are something you might consider, and they can be used in conjunction with a VPN.

You, as the system administrator, can decide that you'd like a single point of ingress for people SSH'ing to machines to easily log traffic and maybe manage keys – perhaps because you're just vindictive and want everyone's config file to be that much longer?

Work with your network team, consult your company's policies, and design a network that you can easily maintain, and that others won't mind using.

> Your company may have specific security policies in place that limit what you're allowed to do. Remember, it's not about what you *can* do, it's about what you should do. No one will congratulate you for being clever when you're being marched out of the office for bypassing security. By all means highlight security problems when you see them, just don't exploit them.

Using SSH to create a SOCKS Proxy

SSH is great.

I never get tired of talking about how great it is, and it would be remiss of me to not mention one of its best features: the ability to quickly and easily set up a SOCKS proxy.

In the previous sections, we forwarded individual ports, but what if we were using a bastion host to connect to a slew of different websites within a network? Would you like to add tens of lines to your SSH config file? Or manually type out each port and mapping every time?

I didn't think so.

That's where the `-D` flag comes in.

See `-D [bind_address:]port` in the SSH manual page (`https://man.openbsd.org/ssh`):

> *Specifies a local "dynamic" application-level port forwarding. This works by allocating a socket to listen to port on the local side, optionally bound to the specified bind_address. Whenever a connection is made to this port, the connection is forwarded over the secure channel, and the application protocol is then used to determine where to connect to from the remote machine. Currently the SOCKS4 and SOCKS5 protocols are supported, and ssh will act as a SOCKS server. Only root can forward privileged ports. Dynamic port forwardings can also be specified in the configuration file.*
> *IPv6 addresses can be specified by enclosing the address in square brackets. Only the superuser can forward privileged ports. By default, the local port is bound in accordance with the GatewayPorts setting. However, an explicit bind_address may be used to bind the connection to a specific address. The bind_address of "localhost" indicates that the listening port be bound for local use only, while an empty address or '*' indicates that the port should be available from all interfaces.*

What this means is that with a single command, you can set up a connection that you can then forward traffic through (from a web browser, or other applications that support `SOCKS` proxies). You don't have to punch holes through firewalls, and you don't have to manually map ports.

SOCKS itself is an internet protocol, and quite an old one at that, though we still actively use SOCKS5, which was approved by the Internet Engineering Task Force in 1996! It's like any other proxy server, allowing you to exchange packets over a connection; in this case, our SSH tunnel. Applications may choose to natively support SOCKS proxies or not, but a lot of commons ones will (Firefox, for example).

Let's get started.

Getting ready

For this section, we're going to be using centos1 and centos2.

Make sure that you have a connection open to both machines:

```
$ vagrant ssh centos1
$ vagrant ssh centos2
```

On centos2, let's set up our small web server again:

```
[vagrant@centos2 ~]$ python -m SimpleHTTPServer 8888 &
[1] 7687
```

How to do it...

Connect to centos1, where we'll first set up our SOCKS proxy using just one command, and then look at how to start the proxy each time we SSH to the box.

On the command line

Let's establish our SSH session and disconnect from the established session at the same time:

```
[vagrant@centos1 ~]$ ssh -f -D9999 192.168.33.11 sleep 120
vagrant@192.168.33.11's password:
[vagrant@centos1 ~]$
```

Once established (until the sleep runs out), we can use our proxy to query anything and everything that centos2 can see via the SSH session.

Let's check out our web server on `centos2`, from `centos1`:

```
[vagrant@centos1 ~]$ all_proxy="socks5://127.0.0.1:9999" curl
127.0.0.1:8888
<!DOCTYPE html PUBLIC "-//W3C//DTD HTML 3.2 Final//EN"><html>
<title>Directory listing for /</title>
<body>
<h2>Directory listing for /</h2>
<hr>
<ul>
<li><a href=".bash_history">.bash_history</a>
<li><a href=".bash_logout">.bash_logout</a>
<li><a href=".bash_profile">.bash_profile</a>
<li><a href=".bashrc">.bashrc</a>
<li><a href=".lesshst">.lesshst</a>
<li><a href=".mysql_history">.mysql_history</a>
<li><a href=".ssh/">.ssh/</a>
</ul>
<hr>
</body>
</html>
[vagrant@centos1 ~]$
```

Brilliant! We've run a cURL against a localhost address, but by passing it through the proxy, our request has been run against `centos2` instead!

Using an SSH config file

The same can be accomplished, as shown previously, by using an SSH config file:

```
Host *
 Port 22

Host CentOS2-V4
 Hostname 192.168.33.11
 User vagrant
 DynamicForward 9999
```

We can now be confident our proxy will be available each time we connect:

```
[vagrant@centos1 ~]$ ssh -f CentOS2-V4 sleep 120
```

And again, look at the contents of the web server:

```
[vagrant@centos1 ~]$ all_proxy="socks5://127.0.0.1:9999" curl
127.0.0.1:8888
<!DOCTYPE html PUBLIC "-//W3C//DTD HTML 3.2 Final//EN"><html>
```

```
<title>Directory listing for /</title>
<body>
<h2>Directory listing for /</h2>
<hr>
<ul>
<li><a href=".bash_history">.bash_history</a>
<li><a href=".bash_logout">.bash_logout</a>
<li><a href=".bash_profile">.bash_profile</a>
<li><a href=".bashrc">.bashrc</a>
<li><a href=".lesshst">.lesshst</a>
<li><a href=".mysql_history">.mysql_history</a>
<li><a href=".ssh/">.ssh/</a>
</ul>
<hr>
</body>
</html>
```

Just to prove we were really using our proxy, let's try the `curl` command without an established session (you will have to wait for SSH to time out, or kill the process if it's not already died):

```
[vagrant@centos1 ~]$ all_proxy="socks5://127.0.0.1:9999" curl
127.0.0.1:8888
curl: (7) Failed connect to 127.0.0.1:9999; Connection refused
```

How it works...

When you add the -D option to SSH, or add the `DynamicForward` option to your SSH config file, you're telling SSH that you want to specify a port on your `local` side that will forward any requests received to it over your SSH connection.

Let's break down our commands:

```
[vagrant@centos1 ~]$ ssh -f -D9999 192.168.33.11 sleep 120
```

First, as we did previously, we've used -f and sleep to keep a connection open, while dropping us back to the `centos1` prompt once a connection is established:

```
-f ... sleep 120
```

We've also specified our -D option, with a randomly chosen port:

```
-D9999
```

I use 9999 through force of habit, but occasionally I mix it up a bit by using 7777, or even 6666 if I'm feeling really wild. You may use whichever port you wish (above 1024, as those below this can only be used by root.)

Once we're established, we use the following command to check our proxy is available for use:

```
[vagrant@centos1 ~]$ all_proxy="socks5://127.0.0.1:9999" curl
127.0.0.1:8888
```

Breaking this down into its two parts, we start with the variable we're setting for just this run:

```
all_proxy="socks5://127.0.0.1:9999"
```

cURL uses `all_proxy` as a way of setting the SOCKS proxy for its run.

In your browser, you may find the option to set a SOCKS server under settings, and in some other applications, SOCKS proxies can be configured when required. Gnome's network manager looks like this:

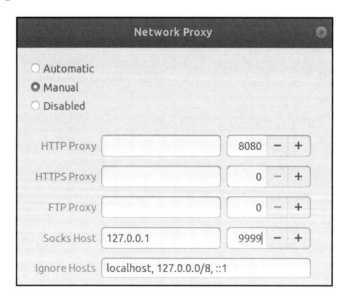

The other part of our command is `curl`:

```
curl 127.0.0.1:8888
```

With our `all_proxy` setting, cURL knows to use the SOCKS proxy on port `9999` for its connections, meaning that when we query `127.0.0.1:8888`, we're sending that request over our SSH session to resolve on `centos2`.

Neat!

There's more...

If you want to take it one step further, have a look at using `tcpdump` on your remote side to check out traffic traversing your network:

```
[vagrant@centos2 ~]$ sudo tcpdump port 8888 -ilo -n
```

You should see traffic come through:

```
<SNIP>
15:18:48.991652 IP 127.0.0.1.54454 > 127.0.0.1.ddi-tcp-1: Flags [F.],
seq 79, ack 618, win 700, options [nop,nop,TS val 16534669 ecr
16534658], length 0
15:18:48.991677 IP 127.0.0.1.ddi-tcp-1 > 127.0.0.1.54454: Flags [.],
ack 80, win 683, options [nop,nop,TS val 16534669 ecr 16534669],
length 0
<SNIP>
```

Understanding and using SSH agents

One thing we touched on briefly was the concept of an SSH agent.

When you SSH to a server (after setting up a key) and you're prompted for a passphrase, what you're actually doing is decrypting the private key part of your public-private key pair (the `id_rsa` file by default), so that it can be used to verify that you are who you say you are against the remote host. It can get tedious to do this each time you SSH to a server, especially if you're managing hundreds or thousands of constantly changing boxes.

That's where SSH agents come in. They're somewhere for your now-decrypted private key to live, once you've given it the passphrase, for the duration of your session.

Once you've got your private key loaded into your agent, the agent is then responsible for presenting the key to any servers you connect to, without you having to type your passphrase again, saving valuable seconds and finger strain.

Most desktop Linux distributions will start an SSH agent of some sort within your user session, sometimes unlocking your private keys when you log in to your user account.

macOS has a specific SSH config file option for `UseKeychain` (`https://developer.apple.com/library/archive/technotes/tn2449/_index.html`):

> *"On macOS, specifies whether the system should search for passphrases in the user's keychain when attempting to use a particular key. When the passphrase is provided by the user, this option also specifies whether the passphrase should be stored into the keychain once it has been verified to be correct. The argument must be "yes" or "no". The default is "no"."*

If you're running macOS on your desktop, you might consider this option.

On my Ubuntu laptop installation, looking for a running agent reveals this:

```
$ env | grep SSH
SSH_AUTH_SOCK=/run/user/1000/keyring/ssh
SSH_AGENT_PID=1542
```

Looking for this process ID shows me what's running as my `ssh-agent`:

```
adam 1542 0.0 0.0 11304 320 ? Ss Aug04 0:02 /usr/bin/ssh-agent
/usr/bin/im-launch env GNOME_SHELL_SESSION_MODE=ubuntu gnome-session -
-session=ubuntu
```

In this section, we're going to start an SSH agent on `centos1` and load a key into it.

Getting ready

As with the previous section, confirm that both of your Vagrant boxes are enabled and connect to the first using the `vagrant` command:

```
$ vagrant ssh centos1
```

Ensure you have an SSH key available on `centos1`. Re-read the previous section on generating an SSH key if you need to:

```
[vagrant@centos1 ~]$ ls .ssh/
authorized_keys  config  id_ed25519  id_ed25519.pub  known_hosts
```

Copy your key to `centos2` if you haven't already, accepting the host key if you need to:

```
[vagrant@centos1 ~]$ ssh-copy-id 192.168.33.11
/usr/bin/ssh-copy-id: INFO: Source of key(s) to be installed:
"/home/vagrant/.ssh/id_ed25519.pub"
/usr/bin/ssh-copy-id: INFO: attempting to log in with the new key(s),
to filter out any that are already installed
/usr/bin/ssh-copy-id: INFO: 1 key(s) remain to be installed -- if you
are prompted now it is to install the new keys
vagrant@192.168.33.11's password:

Number of key(s) added: 1

Now try logging into the machine, with:   "ssh '192.168.33.11'"
and check to make sure that only the key(s) you wanted were added.

[vagrant@centos1 ~]$
```

Check that attempting to log into `centos2` prompts you for your key passphrase:

```
[vagrant@centos1 ~]$ ssh 192.168.33.11
Enter passphrase for key '/home/vagrant/.ssh/id_ed25519':
```

Make sure you're on `centos1` to begin.

How to do it...

Start by running the `ssh-agent` command:

```
[vagrant@centos1 ~]$ ssh-agent
SSH_AUTH_SOCK=/tmp/ssh-9On2mDhHTL8T/agent.6693; export SSH_AUTH_SOCK;
SSH_AGENT_PID=6694; export SSH_AGENT_PID;
echo Agent pid 6694;
```

You can see it's printed several environment variables and the process ID it's running on.

We can confirm this is the case:

```
[vagrant@centos1 ~]$ pidof ssh-agent
6694
```

Copy the various variables that have been provided for you and paste them into the same window:

```
[vagrant@centos1 ~]$ SSH_AUTH_SOCK=/tmp/ssh-9On2mDhHTL8T/agent.6693;
export SSH_AUTH_SOCK;
[vagrant@centos1 ~]$ SSH_AGENT_PID=6694; export SSH_AGENT_PID;
[vagrant@centos1 ~]$
```

Now, run the ssh-add command and fill in your key's passphrase when prompted:

```
[vagrant@centos1 ~]$ ssh-add
Enter passphrase for /home/vagrant/.ssh/id_ed25519:
Identity added: /home/vagrant/.ssh/id_ed25519 (vagrant@centos1)
[vagrant@centos1 ~]$
```

You can see that it informs you that it's added your identity.

SSH to centos2, and prepare to be amazed when you're not prompted for your passphrase:

```
[vagrant@centos1 ~]$ ssh 192.168.33.11
Last login: Thu Aug 9 15:36:02 2018 from 192.168.33.10
[vagrant@centos2 ~]$
```

You may think that you don't mind typing in your passphrase once or twice a day, and you'd be fine to think that, but if you're logging into a machine that infrequently, you're probably a very lucky system administrator. Where SSH agents excel is when you want to log into tens or hundreds of machines, or even if you're using a ProxyJump box, and don't feel like typing your passphrase any more times than is necessary.

To kill a running agent, use -k:

```
[vagrant@centos1 ~]$ ssh-agent -k
unset SSH_AUTH_SOCK;
unset SSH_AGENT_PID;
echo Agent pid 6694 killed;
```

I have seen cases where companies don't like the use of SSH agents, and mandate passwords or passphrases each time. Check you're not violating some obscure security policy to make your life easier.

Then, run the suggested unset commands to remove the variables we set before:

```
[vagrant@centos1 ~]$ unset SSH_AUTH_SOCK;
[vagrant@centos1 ~]$ unset SSH_AGENT_PID;
```

 Simply logging out of your session won't stop the `ssh-agent` program from running. Be mindful of this if you choose to use it. Likewise, you shouldn't run an agent on a remote host shared between multiple people – it's best kept to your personal machine. If you plan on using an SSH agent, read up on current security practices.

How it works...

When we initially run `ssh-agent`, the agent itself is started in the background, and we're given the necessary environment variables for SSH. After they're set, running SSH will cause it to read these variables.

If we add a couple of `-vv` flags to SSH, we can see it find our key in the agent:

```
debug2: key: /home/vagrant/.ssh/id_ed25519 (0x55b11351c410), agent
```

Without the agent loaded, but with the key present, it looks like this:

```
debug2: key: /home/vagrant/.ssh/id_ed25519 (0x55dea5015410)
```

The SSH environment variables are also read by `ssh-add`, which we used to add our key to the agent. To quote the manual page:

"The authentication agent must be running and the SSH_AUTH_SOCK environment variable must contain the name of its socket for ssh-add to work."

When you've got one key or more in an agent, SSH will try to use these keys to authenticate against remote hosts, removing the need to type your password each time.

There's more...

If you want to add the agent start command to a script (say `.bashrc`), you may want to automatically evaluate the environment variables given to you. `ssh-agent` assumes you're starting it this way.

In the manual page for `ssh-agent`, you even get this tip.

> *"There are two main ways to get an agent set up: The first is that the agent starts a new sub-command into which some environment variables are exported, eg ssh-agent xterm &. The second is that the agent prints the needed shell commands (either sh(1) or csh(1) syntax can be generated) which can be evaluated in the calling shell, eg eval 'ssh-agent -s' for Bourne-type shells such as sh(1) or ksh(1) and eval 'ssh-agent -c' for csh(1) and derivatives."*

In practice, this means that it's easiest to start the agent like so:

```
[vagrant@centos1 ~]$ eval $(ssh-agent)
Agent pid 6896
```

Here, we're using a Bash sub-shell to start and read the agent's output.

ssh-add

`ssh-add` has a few decent options available, some of which are handy to know about.

`-l` will allow you to see loaded identities, along with their fingerprints:

```
[vagrant@centos1 ~]$ ssh-add -l
256 SHA256:P7FdkmbQQFoy37avbKBfzMpEhVUaBY0Tl jwYJyNxzUI vagrant@centos1
(ED25519)
```

`-D` will allow you to remove all identities (and `-d` can be used to remove specific ones):

```
[vagrant@centos1 ~]$ ssh-add -D
All identities removed.
```

`-x` will lock an agent, while `-X` will unlock it:

```
[vagrant@centos1 ~]$ ssh-add -l
256 SHA256:P7FdkmbQQFoy37avbKBfzMpEhVUaBY0Tl jwYJyNxzUI vagrant@centos1
(ED25519)
[vagrant@centos1 ~]$ ssh-add -x
Enter lock password:
Again:
Agent locked.
[vagrant@centos1 ~]$ ssh-add -l
The agent has no identities.
[vagrant@centos1 ~]$ ssh-add -X
Enter lock password:
Agent unlocked.
```

```
[vagrant@centos1 ~]$ ssh-add -l
256 SHA256:P7FdkmbQQFoy37avbKBfzMpEhVUaBY0TljwYJyJyNxzUI vagrant@centos1
(ED25519)
```

AddKeysToAgent

When using an agent, you might like the SSH config file option `AddKeysToAgent`, which will automatically add used keys to your `ssh-agent` for future use.

Consider the following; we're starting with no keys in our agent:

```
[vagrant@centos1 ~]$ ssh CentOS2-V4
Enter passphrase for key '/home/vagrant/.ssh/id_ed25519':
Last login: Thu Aug  9 15:58:01 2018 from 192.168.33.10
[vagrant@centos2 ~]$ logout
Connection to 192.168.33.11 closed.
[vagrant@centos1 ~]$ ssh CentOS2-V4
Last login: Thu Aug  9 16:12:04 2018 from 192.168.33.10
[vagrant@centos2 ~]$
```

Note that the first time, we're prompted for our key's passphrase. The second time, we're not.

It is now loaded into our agent:

```
[vagrant@centos1 ~]$ ssh-add -l
256 SHA256:P7FdkmbQQFoy37avbKBfzMpEhVUaBY0TljwYJyJyNxzUI vagrant@centos1
(ED25519)
```

This is all handled by one config option:

```
[vagrant@centos1 ~]$ cat .ssh/config
Host *
 Port 22
 AddKeysToAgent yes
```

See also

There are other SSH agents, other than the default one supplied with OpenSSH (which we used here.) There are also some systems that use more pieces (such as PAM on most desktop distributions.) Have a read around and see if you can work out how your distro of choice does things.

Running multiple SSH servers on one box

Sometimes, it can be a requirement to run multiple SSH servers on one box. You may want to use one for regular, day-to-day activities, and the other server for backups or automation.

In this case, it's perfectly possible to run two distinct versions of the SSH server at once.

We're going to use `centos2` for this, setting up a secondary SSH server on port `2020`.

Getting ready

If you haven't already, I would advise destroying your previous Vagrant boxes and deploying new ones for this.

Once new boxes are created, connect to both:

```
$ vagrant ssh centos1
$ vagrant ssh centos2
```

Install `policycoreutils-python` on `centos2`, for `semanage` later:

```
[vagrant@centos2 ~]$ sudo yum -y install policycoreutils-python
```

How to do it...

First, we're going to make a copy of our initial configuration file:

```
[vagrant@centos2 ~]$ sudo cp /etc/ssh/sshd_config
/etc/ssh/sshd_config_2020
```

Then, we're going to make a couple of changes:

```
[vagrant@centos2 ~]$ sudo sed -i 's#\#Port 22#Port 2020#g'
/etc/ssh/sshd_config_2020
[vagrant@centos2 ~]$ sudo sed -i 's#\#PidFile
/var/run/sshd.pid#PidFile /var/run/sshd_2020.pid#g'
/etc/ssh/sshd_config_2020
```

Now, we're going to copy our `systemd` unit file:

```
[vagrant@centos2 ~]$ sudo cp /usr/lib/systemd/system/sshd.service
/etc/systemd/system/sshd_2020.service
```

Then, we're going to make some changes here:

```
[vagrant@centos2 ~]$ sudo sed -i 's#OpenSSH server daemon#OpenSSH
server daemon on port 2020#g' /etc/systemd/system/sshd_2020.service
[vagrant@centos2 ~]$ sudo sed -i
's#EnvironmentFile=/etc/sysconfig/sshd#EnvironmentFile=/etc/sysconfig/
sshd_2020#g' /etc/systemd/system/sshd_2020.service
```

Copy the old environment file to a new one:

```
[vagrant@centos2 ~]$ sudo cp /etc/sysconfig/sshd
/etc/sysconfig/sshd_2020
```

Then, point this environment file to our new configuration file:

```
[vagrant@centos2 ~]$ sudo sed -i 's#OPTIONS="-u0"#OPTIONS="-u0 -f
/etc/ssh/sshd_config_2020"#g' /etc/sysconfig/sshd_2020
```

Tell SELinux we're going to be running an SSH daemon on 2020:

```
[vagrant@centos2 ~]$ sudo semanage port -a -t ssh_port_t -p tcp 2020
```

Tell systemd we've made changes:

```
[vagrant@centos2 ~]$ sudo systemctl daemon-reload
```

Start and enable our second server:

```
[vagrant@centos2 ~]$ sudo systemctl enable sshd_2020
Created symlink from /etc/systemd/system/multi-
user.target.wants/sshd_2020.service to
/etc/systemd/system/sshd_2020.service.
[vagrant@centos2 ~]$ sudo systemctl start sshd_2020
```

Check it's running by SSH'ing from centos1:

```
[vagrant@centos1 ~]$ ssh 192.168.33.11
The authenticity of host '192.168.33.11 (192.168.33.11)' can't be
established.
ECDSA key fingerprint is
SHA256:I67oI3+08lhdO2ibnoC+z2hzYtvfi9NQAmGxyzxjsI8.
ECDSA key fingerprint is
MD5:03:68:ed:a2:b5:5d:57:88:61:4e:86:28:c3:75:28:fa.
Are you sure you want to continue connecting (yes/no)? yes
Warning: Permanently added '192.168.33.11' (ECDSA) to the list of
known hosts.
vagrant@192.168.33.11's password:
Last login: Thu Aug  9 16:24:50 2018 from 10.0.2.2
[vagrant@centos2 ~]$ logout
```

```
Connection to 192.168.33.11 closed.
[vagrant@centos1 ~]$ ssh 192.168.33.11 -p2020
vagrant@192.168.33.11's password:
Last login: Thu Aug  9 16:40:55 2018 from 192.168.33.10
[vagrant@centos2 ~]$
```

 Remember when we were looking at host keys before? What we can see in the preceding code is that both the port 22 server and 2020 server are sharing host keys, as we were only asked to accept them once.

How it works...

All we've done here is duplicate a few files and made some sensible changes to ensure that the two processes don't interact with each other very much.

First, we created the following file:

/etc/ssh/sshd_config_2020

We then ran a couple of sed commands to change some values. Specifically, we modified the port the server would listen on, and the process ID file it would use (the PID modification is frequently overlooked).

Next, we copied the systemd unit file that comes with the OpenSSH server package on CentOS, tweaking it slightly by changing the description and pointing it to a different environment file.

 We put the resulting unit file (sshd_2020.service) in a different location to the original to differentiate it from a supplied default.

We copied the environment file and made a modification to pass a new option to the SSH daemon when it's started. This new option was a different configuration file (the one we started off making):

OPTIONS="-u0 -f /etc/ssh/sshd_config_2020"

We then updated our SELinux policy to make it aware of the new server's intentions, reloaded systemd's running configuration, and both enabled and started our server.

Your milage may vary in terms of the standard location for configuration and environment files. This can change between major distro releases, and some settings frequently differ between different distributions.

There's more...

If you're interested in seeing both servers running, there's a few methods of doing so.

On centos2, start with ss:

```
[vagrant@centos2 ~]$ sudo ss -tna -4
State          Recv-Q Send-Q      Local Address:Port
Peer Address:Port
LISTEN         0      128                  *:2020
*:*
LISTEN         0      128                  *:111
*:*
LISTEN         0      128                  *:22
*:*
LISTEN         0      100         127.0.0.1:25
*:*
ESTAB          0      0           10.0.2.15:22
10.0.2.2:59594
```

We can also use systemd's built-in commands:

```
[vagrant@centos2 ~]$ PAGER= systemctl | grep sshd
  sshd.service
loaded active running    OpenSSH server daemon
  sshd_2020.service
loaded active running    OpenSSH server daemon on port 2020
```

And lastly, we can use good old ps:

```
[vagrant@centos2 ~]$ ps aux | grep sshd
root       856  0.0  0.8 112796   4288 ?        Ss   16:52   0:00
/usr/sbin/sshd -D -u0 -f /etc/ssh/sshd_config_2020
root       858  0.0  0.8 112796   4292 ?        Ss   16:52   0:00
/usr/sbin/sshd -D -u0
```

Summary

While I've spent this chapter describing some brilliant things that SSH is capable of and singing its praises throughout, it's worth highlighting that it's still software, and it's also constantly evolving. Because it's software, it can have bugs and unexpected behavior, though the developers behind it are some of the best, what with it being part of the OpenBSD suite of software.

If you take anything away from this chapter, make it the following:

- Use key-based authentication
- Disable root login over SSH
- Use a local SSH config file for connecting to remote machines

I'd highly recommend signing up to the various SSH mailing lists if you're a bit sad like I am, and keeping an eye out for new features that might capture your imagination. `ProxyJump` hasn't been around for long, and it's very handy.

I do recall instances that SSH wound me up in some form or other, such as the time I spent a long hour or two bashing my head against a desk, trying to work out why SSH just wouldn't read a private RSA file, only to discover that it needed the public half to be in the same folder too, on the local machine. That's a considerable amount of time I won't get back, but it's a mistake I won't make twice.

That said, I can also share many more instances where SSH has downright impressed me, and made my life easier. It's basically the Swiss Army knife of system administration, and not just because it's usually the way you connect to a box.

People use SSH for administration, transferring backups, moving files between boxes, automation using tools such as Ansible, wrapping other connections inside, and much more.

 I once saw an implementation of OpenSSH atop Windows, because the people running the Windows servers were Unix people, and distrusted RDP. They used to SSH to the box, local forwarding the RDP session on `127.0.0.1:3389` and connecting to RDP through the SSH session... it was slow...

It's solid, secure, and a pleasure to use. It works on Linux, macOS, the BSDs, Solaris, and even Windows!

Here's a big thanks to SSH, and OpenSSH specifically.

 Some things we didn't discuss in this chapter were ciphers, message integrity codes, key exchange algorithms, and so on. Primarily, this is because these subjects are nearly a book in themselves, and are definitely out of scope for what we're doing here. I generally trust the maintainers of the various packages to choose sensible defaults, but there's no harm in reading up on security independently, should you feel compelled.

3
Networking and Firewalls

The following recipes will be covered in this chapter:

- Determining our network configuration
- More examples of using the IP suite
- Adding and configuring network interfaces
- Modern domain name resolution on Linux
- Configuring NTP and the problems we face
- Listing firewall rules on the command line
- Adding firewall rules on the command line
- Determining the running services and ports in use
- Debugging with `iftop`
- Round-up-firewalls and networks

Introduction

Now that we know the ins and outs of SSH and connecting to our machines, whether it be the local VMs or remote servers, we're going to take a look at the most obvious part of the security onion (the firewall) and the Linux network stack in general.

Traditionally, firewall administration was handled by the `iptables` and associated commands, and indeed you'll be hard pressed to find system administrators who don't instantly install the `iptables` suite of tools on every server they find (that doesn't have it installed already).

On modern installations, `firewall-cmd` (CentOS) and `ufw` (Ubuntu) can be found installed in place of, or in addition to, traditional tools. These are an attempt to make the firewall process a more painless experience, though purists will defend `iptables` to the death.

No matter the user space (the name given to programs that operate outside the kernel, at the user level) tool used, all of the changes we make are being made using the Netfilter kernel framework. Indeed, a replacement for `iptables` and Netfilter, called `nft`, has been available in the kernel for some time, though it's not widely used at the moment.

 `iptables` is something of a catchall name, at least informally. Technically, `iptables` is used for IPv4, ip6tables is used for IPv6, ebtables is used for Ethernet frames, and arptables is used for ARP.

Alongside our journey into the confusing world of firewalls, we're going to create a network interface and configure it with both static and dynamic IP allocation.

Technical requirements

We're again going to use Vagrant and VirtualBox for our work. We'll configure three virtual machines.

I've put together the following `Vagrantfile` for use in this chapter:

```ruby
# -*- mode: ruby -*-
# vi: set ft=ruby :

$provisionScript = <<-SCRIPT
sed -i 's#PasswordAuthentication no#PasswordAuthentication yes#g'
/etc/ssh/sshd_config
systemctl restart sshd
SCRIPT

Vagrant.configure("2") do |config|

  config.vm.provision "shell",
  inline: $provisionScript

  config.vm.define "centos1" do |centos1|
    centos1.vm.box = "centos/7"
    centos1.vm.network "private_network", ip: "192.168.33.10"
    centos1.vm.network "private_network", ip: "192.168.44.10",
auto_config: false
    centos1.vm.hostname = "centos1"
    centos1.vm.box_version = "1804.02"
  end
```

```
config.vm.define "centos2" do |centos2|
  centos2.vm.box = "centos/7"
  centos2.vm.network "private_network", ip: "192.168.33.11"
  centos2.vm.network "private_network", ip: "192.168.44.11",
auto_config: false
  centos2.vm.hostname = "centos2"
  centos2.vm.box_version = "1804.02"
end

config.vm.define "ubuntu1" do |ubuntu1|
  ubuntu1.vm.box = "ubuntu/bionic64"
  ubuntu1.vm.hostname = "ubuntu1"
  ubuntu1.vm.box_version = "20180927.0.0"
end

end
```

It would be advisable to create a folder called `Chapter Three` and copy this code into a file called `Vagrantfile`. Running `vagrant up` from inside the folder containing your `Vagrantfile` should configure two VMs for testing. Once provisioned, make sure that you can connect to the first by running the following command:

$ vagrant ssh centos1

For this section, ensure that your `centos1` VM is running, and connect to it. This section assumes you know networking at a basic level, in the sense that you understand the differences between a static and dynamic IP address, and you know roughly how public and private IP addresses differ.

Determining our network configuration

If you ever find yourself working with physical equipment in a data center, you may wind up plonked in front of a box at some point, with only a username and password. You will have to use these credentials to discover the box's IP information so that another individual in an ivory tower somewhere can connect to it remotely.

 The individual in the ivory tower will sometimes be paid better than you for lounging around in a chair all day pressing a keyboard. My advice is to not dwell on this, or you'll end up bitter and grumpy ahead of your years.

Getting ready

Connect to `centos1` if you haven't already.

```
$ vagrant ssh centos1
```

For the purposes of demonstration, ensure that `ifconfig` is installed too:

```
$ sudo yum install net-tools
```

How to do it...

In this short section, we're going to discover what IP address our box has, what network it's on, and we're going to learn how it's configured in the way it is.

Discerning the IP

On a modern box, this is done with `ip`, which we'll go into greater depth with later:

```
$ ip address show
```

 You can shorten `ip` commands to make them quicker to type (as we did in the previous chapter,) but in the preceding code I've used the full expression as it better expresses what we're doing.

This command will give you information about all the interfaces on your system. In the case of our VMs, it looks like this:

```
1: lo: <LOOPBACK,UP,LOWER_UP> mtu 65536 qdisc noqueue state UNKNOWN
group default qlen 1000
    link/loopback 00:00:00:00:00:00 brd 00:00:00:00:00:00
    inet 127.0.0.1/8 scope host lo
       valid_lft forever preferred_lft forever
    inet6 ::1/128 scope host
       valid_lft forever preferred_lft forever
2: eth0: <BROADCAST,MULTICAST,UP,LOWER_UP> mtu 1500 qdisc pfifo_fast
state UP group default qlen 1000
    link/ether 52:54:00:c9:c7:04 brd ff:ff:ff:ff:ff:ff
    inet 10.0.2.15/24 brd 10.0.2.255 scope global noprefixroute
dynamic eth0
       valid_lft 85733sec preferred_lft 85733sec
    inet6 fe80::5054:ff:fec9:c704/64 scope link
       valid_lft forever preferred_lft forever
```

```
3: eth1: <BROADCAST,MULTICAST,UP,LOWER_UP> mtu 1500 qdisc pfifo_fast
state UP group default qlen 1000
    link/ether 08:00:27:4b:03:de brd ff:ff:ff:ff:ff:ff
    inet 192.168.33.10/24 brd 192.168.33.255 scope global
noprefixroute eth1
       valid_lft forever preferred_lft forever
    inet6 fe80::a00:27ff:fe4b:3de/64 scope link
       valid_lft forever preferred_lft forever
4: eth2: <BROADCAST,MULTICAST,UP,LOWER_UP> mtu 1500 qdisc pfifo_fast
state UP group default qlen 1000
    link/ether 08:00:27:50:a5:cb brd ff:ff:ff:ff:ff:ff
```

We know `lo` is the loopback address, which will always have the `127.0.0.1/8`
setup, or some other address in that range.

If you know the device you want explicitly, you can also specify it. In the following
code, we've done this with `eth1`:

```
$ ip address show dev eth1
```

Within the printed block, we're looking for the IPv4 address, which is listed as being
in the `inet` family:

```
3: eth1: <BROADCAST,MULTICAST,UP,LOWER_UP> mtu 1500 qdisc pfifo_fast
state UP group default qlen 1000
    link/ether 08:00:27:0d:d9:0c brd ff:ff:ff:ff:ff:ff
    inet 192.168.33.10/24 brd 192.168.33.255 scope global
noprefixroute eth1
       valid_lft forever preferred_lft forever
    inet6 fe80::a00:27ff:fe0d:d90c/64 scope link
       valid_lft forever preferred_lft forever
```

We have the IP, `192.168.33.10`, and we know the subnet it's in, `/24`
(`255.255.255.0`).

If you're a bit lazier and want to save on eye movement, you could use something like
the following in a scrip to get this information:

```
$ ip address show dev eth1 | grep "inet " | awk '{ print $2 }'
192.168.33.10/24
```

The preceding code is one of many, many ways in which you could write a one-liner to generate the output you desire. Linux is flexible, and you might choose to reach the same output in a completely different way. It doesn't overly matter how you do it, but if it's something you plan on sharing, doing it in a succinct and readable style is often best.

Discerning the IP (deprecated method)

On older systems, or those managed by stick-in-the-mud admins, you might also use `ifconfig` to find the IP and subnet.

Simply running `ifconfig` will print all relevant information:

```
$ ifconfig
eth0: flags=4163<UP,BROADCAST,RUNNING,MULTICAST> mtu 1500
  inet 10.0.2.15 netmask 255.255.255.0 broadcast 10.0.2.255
  inet6 fe80::5054:ff:fec9:c704 prefixlen 64 scopeid 0x20<link>
  ether 52:54:00:c9:c7:04 txqueuelen 1000 (Ethernet)
  RX packets 14404 bytes 12885029 (12.2 MiB)
  RX errors 0 dropped 0 overruns 0 frame 0
  TX packets 5672 bytes 409079 (399.4 KiB)
  TX errors 0 dropped 0 overruns 0 carrier 0 collisions 0

eth1: flags=4163<UP,BROADCAST,RUNNING,MULTICAST> mtu 1500
  inet 192.168.33.10 netmask 255.255.255.0 broadcast 192.168.33.255
  inet6 fe80::a00:27ff:fe4b:3de prefixlen 64 scopeid 0x20<link>
  ether 08:00:27:4b:03:de txqueuelen 1000 (Ethernet)
  RX packets 8 bytes 3164 (3.0 KiB)
  RX errors 0 dropped 0 overruns 0 frame 0
  TX packets 17 bytes 1906 (1.8 KiB)
  TX errors 0 dropped 0 overruns 0 carrier 0 collisions 0

eth2: flags=4163<UP,BROADCAST,RUNNING,MULTICAST> mtu 1500
  ether 08:00:27:50:a5:cb txqueuelen 1000 (Ethernet)
  RX packets 43 bytes 14706 (14.3 KiB)
  RX errors 0 dropped 0 overruns 0 frame 0
  TX packets 112 bytes 19336 (18.8 KiB)
  TX errors 0 dropped 0 overruns 0 carrier 0 collisions 0

lo: flags=73<UP,LOOPBACK,RUNNING> mtu 65536
  inet 127.0.0.1 netmask 255.0.0.0
  inet6 ::1 prefixlen 128 scopeid 0x10<host>
  loop txqueuelen 1000 (Local Loopback)
  RX packets 0 bytes 0 (0.0 B)
  RX errors 0 dropped 0 overruns 0 frame 0
```

```
TX packets 0 bytes 0 (0.0 B)
TX errors 0 dropped 0 overruns 0 carrier 0 collisions 0
```

As with IP, it's trivial to dump the information about a specific interface.

As we can see in the following code, we're looking again at the specifics of `eth1`:

```
$ ifconfig eth1
eth1: flags=4163<UP,BROADCAST,RUNNING,MULTICAST>  mtu 1500
        inet 192.168.33.10  netmask 255.255.255.0  broadcast
192.168.33.255
        inet6 fe80::a00:27ff:fe0d:d90c  prefixlen 64  scopeid
0x20<link>
        ether 08:00:27:0d:d9:0c  txqueuelen 1000  (Ethernet)
        RX packets 24  bytes 4268 (4.1 KiB)
        RX errors 0  dropped 0  overruns 0  frame 0
        TX packets 20  bytes 2116 (2.0 KiB)
        TX errors 0  dropped 0 overruns 0  carrier 0  collisions 0
```

I use the word deprecated for this, but that's generally only true for the Linux world. In the BSDs and macOS, `ifconfig` is still very much the only show in town, and it's still being actively improved and maintained.

Discerning the gateway address

Once we have the IP address of the box and the subnet, we might want to know which device our machine is using to talk to the outside world.

This is the `default` route that traffic takes out of your box.

Using the `ip` command, this is easy to discover:

```
$ ip route
default via 10.0.2.2 dev eth0 proto dhcp metric 102
10.0.2.0/24 dev eth0 proto kernel scope link src 10.0.2.15 metric 102
192.168.33.0/24 dev eth1 proto kernel scope link src 192.168.33.10
metric 100
```

Note the `default via` section.

Discerning the gateway address (deprecated method)

With net-tools installed, we can also use the `route` command to find our default route out:

```
$ route
Kernel IP routing table
Destination     Gateway         Genmask         Flags Metric Ref
Use Iface
default         gateway         0.0.0.0         UG    102    0
0 eth0
10.0.2.0        0.0.0.0         255.255.255.0   U     102    0
0 eth0
192.168.33.0    0.0.0.0         255.255.255.0   U     100    0
0 eth1
```

How it works...

When you use `ip` or `ifconfig`, you're querying the network devices that the kernel is aware of, and which it's currently managing the traffic for.

 If you don't see your network device in the list output by either of the common commands, it's likely that your kernel doesn't have a driver for the device in question. This is rare these days, but can happen for custom networking gear, whereupon the vendor should supply a kernel module for use with it.

`ip` itself is more than just one command: it's a suite, meaning that when we used the `ip address` command here, we were only using a subsection of the tools available to us.

When you use `ip route` or the `route` command, you're actually querying the distribution's routing table.

There's more...

Knowing the basics of how your network is configured is great, but that's usually only step one.

Here, I'll cover some rudimentary network troubleshooting.

Checking connectivity

Just knowing what device our box is using as its gateway is one thing, but actually being able to reach it is another thing entirely.

If you're standing before a box, there's a good chance you've been summoned to try and work out what's not working. Trying to ping the gateway is a good first step:

```
$ ping 10.0.2.2
PING 10.0.2.2 (10.0.2.2) 56(84) bytes of data.
64 bytes from 10.0.2.2: icmp_seq=1 ttl=64 time=0.768 ms
64 bytes from 10.0.2.2: icmp_seq=2 ttl=64 time=0.333 ms
64 bytes from 10.0.2.2: icmp_seq=3 ttl=64 time=0.637 ms
```

Here, our gateway device responded, but if yours doesn't, or you get Destination Host Unreachable, then there's a good chance something is going wrong (or you've been given duff information by your colleague in the ivory tower—always check this first).

In the following code, we're checking the status of the interface itself, again using the ip command:

```
$ ip address show dev eth0
2: eth0: <BROADCAST,MULTICAST,UP,LOWER_UP> mtu 1500 qdisc pfifo_fast
state UP group default qlen 1000
```

You may be interested to know why we have three UP values here.

The initial UP value inside the chevrons is if the interface is physically up. The LOWER_UP value, also inside the chevrons, is shown if a cable is physically connected and up. The state UP value outside the chevrons is if the interface is administratively up, which can be changed to DOWN through software.

Checking what route our box will take

It's also possible that connectivity might be failing because your box is trying to talk out of the wrong interface. We can check this with ip again.

First, let's look at which route we're going to take when communicating with the wider world.

In the following code, we're checking how our box would attempt to talk to the device with the IP 1.1.1.1. It shows us that we would go to this IP via the gateway address, 10.0.2.2, and our eth0 interface:

```
$ ip route get 1.1.1.1
1.1.1.1 via 10.0.2.2 dev eth0 src 10.0.2.15
    cache
```

Now, let's see what route we'll take if we're communicating with our gateway. Here, we can see a direct connection (no via) also going out of eth0:

```
$ ip route get 10.0.2.2
10.0.2.2 dev eth0 src 10.0.2.15
    cache
```

So far, so good, but what about if we want to talk to the other VM on our private network?

```
$ ip route get 192.168.33.11
192.168.33.11 dev eth1 src 192.168.33.10
    cache
```

eth1 would be used, which makes perfect sense given it's on the same network.

Hang on a moment—our own IP is in this subnet too, so what happens if we try to communicate with ourselves?

```
$ ip route get 192.168.33.10
local 192.168.33.10 dev lo src 192.168.33.10
 cache <local>
```

Ah! Clever! We're still using the loopback address (dev lo) to talk to our local IP address, because Linux knows that this IP is ours.

As with the preceding example, Linux occasionally does things that might surprise you, especially if you're coming from a Windows or BSD administration world. Take the lo interface—it's not just 127.0.0.1, but the entire /8 range. You can ping anywhere from 127.0.0.1 to 127.255.255.254 on a typical Linux system, and get a response from your local machine.

You can even ping 127.1 and get a legitimate response, but I'll leave it as an exercise for the reader to determine why this might be.

See also

Take a look at the `ip` and `ip-address` manual pages.

 Personally, I would focus on learning about the `ip` suite, instead of the old net-tools, because if you're trying to work on a networking problem, there's a good chance you won't be able to install net-tools in a pinch.

More examples of using the ip suite

We're going to use `ip` from here on out due to its modern nature.

This section assumes that you know networking at a basic level, in the sense that you understand the differences between a static and dynamic IP address, and know roughly how public and private IP addresses differ.

Getting ready

In this section, we're going to make a few changes to our networking. If at any point you find yourself kicked out of your VM, remember *The Hitchhiker's Guide to the Galaxy* and don't panic—simply destroy your VMs and start again.

Begin on the `centos1` command line.

```
$ vagrant ssh centos1
```

How to do it...

In this section, we're going to use the `ip suite` to change some basic elements of our networking stack, such as adding another IP address, or shutting down an interface entirely.

Adding and removing an IP against an interface

This can be accomplished with the `ip address` command, but does require root.

In this example, I chose another IP in the `192.168.33.0/24` subnet, which I know isn't in use:

> In the real world, it's good practice to ping an IP first, even if you believe it's free to use.

```
$ sudo ip address add 192.168.33.22/24 dev eth1
```

Checking our `eth1` interface, we can now see the secondary IP:

```
3: eth1: <BROADCAST,MULTICAST,UP,LOWER_UP> mtu 1500 qdisc pfifo_fast
state UP group default qlen 1000
    link/ether 08:00:27:0d:d9:0c brd ff:ff:ff:ff:ff:ff
    inet 192.168.33.10/24 brd 192.168.33.255 scope global
noprefixroute eth1
        valid_lft forever preferred_lft forever
    inet 192.168.33.22/24 scope global secondary eth1
        valid_lft forever preferred_lft forever
    inet6 fe80::a00:27ff:fe0d:d90c/64 scope link
        valid_lft forever preferred_lft forever
```

> Upon a reboot, this change will be lost. We will talk about adding IP information permanently in the section titled 'Adding and configuring network interfaces'.

If we want to remove an IP, we again use `ip`, this time replacing the `add` instruction with a `del` instruction:

```
$ sudo ip address del 192.168.33.22/24 dev eth1
```

Shutting down and bringing up an interface administratively

To work with the interface itself, we need to use another element of the `ip` suite, this being `ip link`. Note again the use of `sudo`:

```
$ sudo ip link set eth1 down
```

Checking our interfaces, we can see that the interface is in the `DOWN` state:

```
3: eth1: <BROADCAST,MULTICAST> mtu 1500 qdisc pfifo_fast state DOWN
group default qlen 1000
```

```
     link/ether 08:00:27:0d:d9:0c brd ff:ff:ff:ff:ff:ff
     inet 192.168.33.10/24 brd 192.168.33.255 scope global
noprefixroute eth1
       valid_lft forever preferred_lft forever
```

You will find yourself unable to ping this host from `centos2`.

To bring an interface back up, simply run the following:

```
$ sudo ip link set eth1 up
```

Note that if you add another IP to an interface on a temporary basis before bringing an interface down and up, your temporary additional IP will not be remembered.

Adding a new route to our routing table

If we're working in a network with non-obvious destinations, we might need to add a specific route to our setup.

This is generally seen in cluster scenarios and setups where a route may be accessible via another channel, but may not be advertised by that same channel.

In the following code, we're going to tell our VM that if it wants to talk to any address on the `172.16.0.0/12` network, it must send traffic via `eth1` and gateway `192.168.33.11` (which is our `centos2` VM):

```
$ sudo ip route add 172.16.0.0/12 via 192.168.33.11 dev eth1
```

Checking our routing table, we can see if our route is in place:

```
$ ip route
default via 10.0.2.2 dev eth0 proto dhcp metric 100
10.0.2.0/24 dev eth0 proto kernel scope link src 10.0.2.15 metric 100
172.16.0.0/12 via 192.168.33.11 dev eth1
192.168.33.0/24 dev eth1 proto kernel scope link src 192.168.33.10
metric 101
```

How it works...

Again, we're using the `ip suite` to interact with the various network elements of our machine. Frequently, these commands can be used for troubleshooting and testing of environmental changes, prior to your making those changes permanent.

In the adding or removing of IP addresses to interfaces, you can create a situation where an interface has multiple IP addresses for use with different applications.

> Before the days of SNI, it wasn't uncommon to see multiple IP addresses in use on web servers so that each HTTPS site could have its own IP assignment.

In the shutting down or bringing up of network interfaces, we're first telling our system to administratively down an interface, rather than physically unplugging an Ethernet cable. If you down an interface, then check your `/var/log/messages` file—you should see something like the following:

```
Aug 12 12:38:09 centos1 NetworkManager[566]: <info>  [1534077489.1507]
device (eth1): state change: activated -> unavailable (reason
'carrier-changed', sys-iface-state: 'managed')
Aug 12 12:38:09 centos1 dbus[545]: [system] Activating via systemd:
service name='org.freedesktop.nm_dispatcher' unit='dbus-
org.freedesktop.nm-dispatcher.service'
Aug 12 12:38:09 centos1 systemd: Starting Network Manager Script
Dispatcher Service...
Aug 12 12:38:09 centos1 dbus[545]: [system] Successfully activated
service 'org.freedesktop.nm_dispatcher'
Aug 12 12:38:09 centos1 systemd: Started Network Manager Script
Dispatcher Service.
Aug 12 12:38:09 centos1 nm-dispatcher: req:1 'down' [eth1]: new
request (3 scripts)
Aug 12 12:38:09 centos1 nm-dispatcher: req:1 'down' [eth1]: start
running ordered scripts...
```

Here, we can see the network manager running through a series of steps, upon its realization that the device's state has changed.

> Network manager dispatcher is the service that controls what happens when an interfaces goes down or comes up. Take a look in `/etc/NetworkManager/dispatcher.d/` if you're interested in learning more.

Lastly, when we added a route to our routing table, we were telling the kernel's underlying routing subsystem to send packets for the network 172.16.0.0/12 through our eth1 interface, with a gateway address of 192.168.33.11.

 I have frequently found myself modifying the routing table of devices, though most of that was done for cluster setups in phone PBX environments. It may not be something you do day-to-day, but it's worth knowing!

There's more...

If you want to see our routed traffic that's hitting centos2, log onto your second VM and make sure that tcpdump is installed:

```
$ sudo yum install -y tcpdump
```

Next, ensure that your extra route from the before is in place on centos1, and start a ping going to any address in the range:

```
$ ping 172.16.0.3
PING 172.16.0.3 (172.16.0.3) 56(84) bytes of data.
```

Back on centos2, start tcpdump against our eth1 interface:

```
$ sudo tcpdump -i eth1
```

You should start to see ICMP echo requests from centos1, without a response:

```
12:48:26.735055 IP 192.168.33.10 > 172.16.0.3: ICMP echo request, id
1696, seq 1, length 64
12:48:27.736195 IP 192.168.33.10 > 172.16.0.3: ICMP echo request, id
1696, seq 2, length 64
12:48:28.738030 IP 192.168.33.10 > 172.16.0.3: ICMP echo request, id
1696, seq 3, length 64
12:48:29.743270 IP 192.168.33.10 > 172.16.0.3: ICMP echo request, id
1696, seq 4, length 64
12:48:30.747098 IP 192.168.33.10 > 172.16.0.3: ICMP echo request, id
1696, seq 5, length 64
12:48:31.750916 IP 192.168.33.10 > 172.16.0.3: ICMP echo request, id
1696, seq 6, length 64
12:48:32.752634 IP 192.168.33.10 > 172.16.0.3: ICMP echo request, id
1696, seq 7, length 64
```

Back on `centos1`, stop your `ping` (*Ctrl + C*) and note the packets transmitted and packets lost:

```
--- 172.16.0.3 ping statistics ---
8 packets transmitted, 0 received, 100% packet loss, time 7019ms
```

Because we had nowhere for `centos2` to route our packet to, and `centos2` isn't actually set up as a router, the packets simply went unanswered, and `centos1` remained friendless—poor `centos1`.

See also

If you're interested in using Linux as a router, this is perfectly possible with a sysctl change and potentially a bit of **masquerading** on the part of the firewall. While out of scope for this book, it is something you may find yourself needing in the future.

Adding and configuring network interfaces

In this section, we're going to look at how multiple network interfaces may be configured in a system, and we will discuss how this might be utilized in the real world (such as for backup traffic).

Getting ready

We're going to use our second network, which is new to this chapter. If you're using the `Vagrantfile` from before, you're already set up with this network. If you're running your own system, add another NIC to each of your virtual machines on the same network.

Use Vagrant to connect to `centos1`.

```
$ vagrant ssh centos1
```

Check that the `eth2` interface is available to you. It should look similar to the following:

```
$ ip link show eth2
4: eth2: <BROADCAST,MULTICAST,UP,LOWER_UP> mtu 1500 qdisc pfifo_fast
state UP mode DEFAULT group default qlen 1000
    link/ether 08:00:27:7d:f3:6b brd ff:ff:ff:ff:ff:ff
```

How to do it...

We will look at adding network information permanently using configuration files so that our configuration isn't lost following a reboot (as would be the case if we used the `ip suite` and temporary allocation).

Configuring a new interface

Start by creating a configuration file for `eth2`:

```
$ sudo touch /etc/sysconfig/network-scripts/ifcfg-eth2
```

Next, populate it using the following:

```
$ sudo tee /etc/sysconfig/network-scripts/ifcfg-eth2 << HERE
BOOTPROTO=none
ONBOOT=yes
IPADDR=192.168.44.10
NETMASK=255.255.255.0
DEVICE=eth2
PEERDNS=no
HERE
```

 The `tee` command is used here. It enables reading from standard input and outputting to a destination of our choosing, in this case, a file.

Now, restart your interface as an individual:

```
$ sudo ifdown eth2
$ sudo ifup eth2
```

Alternatively, restart networking in general:

```
$ sudo systemctl restart network
```

 It's generally a good rule of thumb to be the least disruptive when working with components that make up a greater whole. Even in a `dev` environment, it's a good habit to get into.

How it works...

All we've done here is created an interface script that your system can use to correctly configure an interface at boot time.

Let's go through the options we added to our file.

```
BOOTPROTO=none
```

This setting stands for `boot-time protocol` and we've set it to `none` instead of `dhcp` or `bootp`.

In a DHCP environment, you want an address to be assigned automatically by your DHCP server. Here, we're setting a static address, so we state the following.

```
ONBOOT=yes
```

This one might seem obvious, but the default behaviour of an interface is to not initialize at boot. With this setting, we ensure that the network interface is brought up with the system.

```
IPADDR=192.168.44.10
NETMASK=255.255.255.0
```

Somewhat self-explanatory, but these options are the IP address and the subnet mask of the network we're configuring. Here, I chose another `/24` network, a few octets above our `eth1` configuration.

```
DEVICE=eth2
```

This option is used to specify which hardware interface our configuration will apply to. It's worth noting that these interface names can be both generic (`eth0`, `eth1`, and so on) and network card name-specific (they might not always be `eth<something>`).

```
PEERDNS=no
```

Defaulting to `yes` in a DHCP environment, this option ensures that our system doesn't try to modify `/etc/resolv.conf` when the interface is brought up.

There's more...

The Ethernet interface configuration file (`ifcfg-eth2`) has a few other options that can be taken into account when setting up your network. Check whether it's possible to make a configuration change for your desired outcome, prior to wrapping networking in any scripts.

Interface bonds can also be created and configured in interface configuration files for use when a machine has two physical connections to the same destination to protect against either failure of the interface or cable.

> I have seen exactly one bad `Cat-5e` cable in the entirety of my professional life—cables are physical, and don't spontaneously break.

One thing we didn't do was specify that the interface in question wasn't to be managed by a network manager (the network management daemon).

You can see which interfaces are and aren't being managed by the network manager using the simple `nmcli device` command:

```
$ nmcli device
DEVICE    TYPE        STATE        CONNECTION
eth0      ethernet    connected    System eth0
eth1      ethernet    connected    System eth1
eth2      ethernet    connected    System eth2
lo        loopback    unmanaged    --
```

We can change this, if we'd rather the network manager does not interfere, by adding a configuration option to our `ifcfg-eth2` file:

```
BOOTPROTO=none
ONBOOT=yes
IPADDR=192.168.44.10
NETMASK=255.255.255.0
DEVICE=eth2
PEERDNS=no
NM_CONTROLLED=no
```

Now, go down and up your interface once more:

```
$ sudo ifdown eth2
$ sudo ifup eth2
```

Then, check out `nmcli` once again, this time taking note of the `unmanaged` status:

```
$ nmcli device
DEVICE   TYPE       STATE       CONNECTION
eth0     ethernet   connected   System eth0
eth1     ethernet   connected   System eth1
eth2     ethernet   unmanaged   --
lo       loopback   unmanaged   --
```

If you're curious, take a look at the `nmtui` command for an interactive way to configure network interfaces that the network manager is aware of.

See also

Have a think about where it might be useful for additional networks to be in place. A good and common example is for backup networks, where companies will set up a dedicated network that's specifically for backup traffic.

Backups range in size, but can easily be gigabytes and even terabytes sometimes, so it makes sense to give them an entirely independent network of their own.

 You can also manage traffic priority with things such as **Quality of Service (QoS)** settings on larger and enterprise networks. This can be a valid solution if you would rather deal with the software administration overhead of dealing with such scenarios. Generally, I'm a fan of simple, and though it definitely costs more to have physical equipment, it's less to manage in the long run.

Modern domain name resolution on Linux

In this section, we're going to look at domain name resolution, and specifically the software installed on a typical CentOS box that enables the lookup of addresses when presented with a domain.

We'll look at `/etc/resolv.conf` and domain name resolution methods on current generation Linux systems (such as network manager). We're going to test the connection to our DNS server, and run DNS queries to see if it's working.

This section assumes a basic understanding of domain names and IP addresses.

Getting ready

Connect to `centos1` and check that your domain resolution is already working by pinging an address.

I'm in the UK, so I default to using the BBC for my tests:

```
$ ping bbc.co.uk
PING bbc.co.uk (151.101.0.81) 56(84) bytes of data.
64 bytes from 151.101.0.81 (151.101.0.81): icmp_seq=1 ttl=63 time=30.4
ms
```

If yours isn't working for whatever reason, destroy and recreate your VMs.

Once you're sure you can ping a domain, install dig (and the myriad of other tools that come along with this package):

```
$ sudo yum install -y bind-utils
```

How to do it...

Here, we're going to run through some basic troubleshooting steps, designed to help you determine where a problem might be.

Querying a domain

To query a domain name on Linux, `dig` can be used:

```
$ dig bbc.co.uk

; <<>> DiG 9.9.4-RedHat-9.9.4-61.el7 <<>> bbc.co.uk
;; global options: +cmd
;; Got answer:
;; ->>HEADER<<- opcode: QUERY, status: NOERROR, id: 6288
;; flags: qr rd ra; QUERY: 1, ANSWER: 4, AUTHORITY: 0, ADDITIONAL: 1

;; OPT PSEUDOSECTION:
; EDNS: version: 0, flags:; udp: 65494
;; QUESTION SECTION:
;bbc.co.uk.                    IN      A
```

```
;; ANSWER SECTION:
bbc.co.uk.        227    IN    A    151.101.0.81
bbc.co.uk.        227    IN    A    151.101.64.81
bbc.co.uk.        227    IN    A    151.101.128.81
bbc.co.uk.        227    IN    A    151.101.192.81

;; Query time: 24 msec
;; SERVER: 10.0.2.3#53(10.0.2.3)
;; WHEN: Sun Aug 12 14:20:28 UTC 2018
;; MSG SIZE  rcvd: 102
```

Here, we can see that the server being used for domain resolution (emboldened) is 10.0.2.3, which just so happens to be VirtualBox providing a resolution service.

We also see the ANSWER SECTION which, as the name might suggest, is the answer to our query. We can reach bbc.co.uk at any of those addresses (currently).

Checking the domain resolution settings

The source of truth when it comes to DNS configuration on a system is generally the resolver file, /etc/resolv.conf, although increasingly this file isn't used directly, and is instead managed by external programs.

In the case of CentOS, the resolv.conf file is managed by our friend network manager, and on other systems, it might be systemd-resolved.

Have a look at your resolv.conf file:

```
$ cat /etc/resolv.conf
# Generated by NetworkManager
search discworld
nameserver 10.0.2.3
```

 search in the previous code is the search list for hostname lookup. It's generated by looking at the domain the box is sitting on. nameserver is the value of our DNS resolver, in this case, the VirtualBox default.

This tells us that the network manager is the program that's populated our file.

We can then use `nmcli` to list the DNS server it knows about:

```
$ nmcli -f ipv4.dns,ipv4.ignore-auto-dns connection show System\ eth0
ipv4.dns:                          --
ipv4.ignore-auto-dns:              no
```

With the preceding code, we're using `nmcli` with two filters,
`ipv4.dns` and `ipv4.ignore-auto-dns`, to check our default interface
(the `eth0` system, in this case).

The value of `ipv4.dns` isn't set, meaning that it's unlikely to be reading the value
from a configuration directive on the interface.

The value of `ipv4.ignore-auto-dns` is set, and we can tell from the `no` value that
we're not ignoring the auto DNS allocation from the DHCP server.

Changing the domain resolution settings

To use a DNS server of our choosing, we should use `nmcli`.

In the following code, we're setting our own DNS server value (`1.1.1.1`) and we're
flipping the truth value of `ipv4.ignore-auto-dns` from `no` to `yes`:

```
$ sudo nmcli connection modify System\ eth0 ipv4.dns "1.1.1.1"
ipv4.ignore-auto-dns "yes"
```

Note how both of these fields can be modified on one line.

Reload the interface configuration using the following:

```
$ sudo nmcli connection up System\ eth0
```

Look in `/etc/resolv.conf` for good measure, just to check:

```
$ cat /etc/resolv.conf
# Generated by NetworkManager
nameserver 1.1.1.1
```

Then, run `dig`:

```
$ dig bbc.co.uk

; <<>> DiG 9.9.4-RedHat-9.9.4-61.el7 <<>> bbc.co.uk
;; global options: +cmd
;; Got answer:
;; ->>HEADER<<- opcode: QUERY, status: NOERROR, id: 10132
```

```
;; flags: qr rd ra; QUERY: 1, ANSWER: 4, AUTHORITY: 0, ADDITIONAL: 1

;; OPT PSEUDOSECTION:
; EDNS: version: 0, flags:; udp: 1452
;; QUESTION SECTION:
;bbc.co.uk.                IN    A

;; ANSWER SECTION:
bbc.co.uk.         210     IN    A    151.101.0.81
bbc.co.uk.         210     IN    A    151.101.64.81
bbc.co.uk.         210     IN    A    151.101.128.81
bbc.co.uk.         210     IN    A    151.101.192.81

;; Query time: 23 msec
;; SERVER: 1.1.1.1#53(1.1.1.1)
;; WHEN: Sun Aug 12 14:46:05 UTC 2018
;; MSG SIZE  rcvd: 102
```

1.1.1.1 is a new and trendy DNS service from Cloudflare and APNIC. This isn't an endorsement, it's just really easy to remember.

How it works...

When you request the destination of a domain on your system, what you're actually doing is sending a request to your configured resolver, which returns the address it (or further upstream systems) knows about.

In our case, we can see this request happening by connecting two Terminals to centos1.

On our first Terminal, we're going to install and start tcpdump on eth1:

```
$ sudo yum install tcpdump -y
$ sudo tcpdump -i eth0 -n port 53
```

Once set up, hop to a second connection and run your dig against the BBC (or whichever British broadcaster of choice you've gone with):

```
$ dig bbc.co.uk
```

Flip back to your first window, and you should see the results of your request:

```
14:58:50.303421 IP 10.0.2.15.51686 > 1.1.1.1.domain: 19866+ [1au] A?
bbc.co.uk. (38)
14:58:50.331999 IP 1.1.1.1.domain > 10.0.2.15.51686: 19866 4/0/1 A
151.101.0.81, A 151.101.64.81, A 151.101.128.81, A 151.101.192.81
(102)
```

We asked our name server what address `bbc.co.uk` lived at, and in the response, we got a few IP addresses to connect to. Neat, huh?

There's more...

This section obviously made changes using network manager, but that's not to say this is the only way. It's possible to stop the network manager from hijacking and trying to control your DNS.

It's possible to set `dns=none` in the `main` section of the `NetworkManager.conf` file, as detailed in its man page:

> "`none`: NetworkManager *will not modify* `resolv.conf`. *This implies rc-manager unmanaged*"

Seen in the configuration file at `/etc/NetworkManager/NetworkManager.conf`, it would look like this:

```
[main]
#plugins=ifcfg-rh,ibft
dns=none
```

Restarting `NetworkManager` at this point would stop it from trying to modify `/etc/resolv.conf` in the future.

This can be useful if you want something else to manage your system's DNS, even if it's just a script you've written to plonk your DNS servers in `/etc/resolv.conf`.

 It's possible to not use `NetworkManager` at all, disabling it as a daemon and doing everything in the old script fashion. In fact, it's really easy, but in my opinion it's worth getting to grips with how things are done by default these days.

DNS is usually done in pairs, and it's a good idea to have a backup DNS server in case the first one goes to pot. Strange things can start to happen when your DNS fails.

See also

We actually used `nmcli` here to make changes to configuration files. We can physically see those changes by looking at the `eth0` configuration file before and after our DNS changing command.

Before looks like this:

```
$ cat /etc/sysconfig/network-scripts/ifcfg-eth0
DEVICE="eth0"
BOOTPROTO="dhcp"
ONBOOT="yes"
TYPE="Ethernet"
PERSISTENT_DHCLIENT="yes"
```

While after is a bit more verbose:

```
$ cat /etc/sysconfig/network-scripts/ifcfg-eth0
DEVICE=eth0
BOOTPROTO=dhcp
ONBOOT=yes
TYPE=Ethernet
PERSISTENT_DHCLIENT="yes"
PROXY_METHOD=none
BROWSER_ONLY=no
DNS1=1.1.1.1
DEFROUTE=yes
PEERDNS=no
IPV4_FAILURE_FATAL=no
IPV6INIT=no
NAME="System eth0"
UUID=5fb06bd0-0bb0-7ffb-45f1-d6edd65f3e03
```

One thing we didn't cover is IPv6, but the principles are the same as IPv4.

Take a look at how IPv6 servers are configured, and how they end up in `/etc/resolv.conf`.

Configuring NTP and the problems we face

In this section, we're going to look at the **network time protocol** (**NTP**), and the default setup for a typical installation.

This section assumes a basic understanding of time.

Depending on how much Pratchett you read, your understanding of time may or may not be linear.

We're going to look at a few things. First, we're going to look at what NTP is, what software we use to set it up, and how to test whether your system is using it.

Starting at the top, NTP runs on port `123`, and it's the protocol that's used for keeping time in computer systems in sync. This is generally important because we want things like log-timestamps to be consistent between machines, transactions between boxes to have the correct time on both sides, and things like authentication to actually work.

Really though, misconfigured or incorrect time on a system can present a host of problems, not all of them obvious. If you ever find yourself using the phrase "this makes no sense," check the date information on your box, as a good portion of the time it'll be wrong. Funnily, a lot of systems depend on time being correct to work.

Getting ready

We're going to use `centos1` and `centos2`. `centos1` is going to act as our client, and `centos2` is going to act as our server. For this section, ensure that you have a connection open to both machines.

Again, if not already available, install `tcpdump` on both boxes:

```
$ sudo yum install -y tcpdump
$ sudo yum install -y tcpdump
```

How to do it...

The `NTP client/server` on CentOS and other systems is `chrony` these days, replacing the more traditional NTP implementations.

There's two main components, `chronyc` (the command-line tool) and `chronyd` (the daemon, which itself can act as a client or server).

Checking if NTP is running

First, a basic check is to confirm the date is what you expect it to be, with the `date` command:

```
$ date
Mon 13 Aug 10:05:31 UTC 2018
```

Note that the preceding date information is set to **universal time coordinated** (**UTC**). This is increasingly being used as distributed computing takes hold. Servers don't have to be locked to one geographical region, and if you've got a thousand boxes over multiple geographical locations, you might choose to unify their time and manage specific differences in other software instead (such as a web app being responsible for writing the timestamp for the location its user is located at, for example).

To check whether `chronyd` itself is running, use `systemctl`:

```
$ systemctl status chronyd
● chronyd.service - NTP client/server
   Loaded: loaded (/usr/lib/systemd/system/chronyd.service; enabled;
vendor preset: enabled)
   Active: active (running) since Mon 2018-08-13 07:20:48 UTC; 2h
43min ago
     Docs: man:chronyd(8)
           man:chrony.conf(5)
  Process: 576 ExecStartPost=/usr/libexec/chrony-helper update-daemon
(code=exited, status=0/SUCCESS)
  Process: 556 ExecStart=/usr/sbin/chronyd $OPTIONS (code=exited,
status=0/SUCCESS)
 Main PID: 570 (chronyd)
   CGroup: /system.slice/chronyd.service
           └─570 /usr/sbin/chronyd
```

Checking if NTP traffic is flowing

To confirm that NTP traffic is actually flowing, the catchall method is to check the port with `tcpdump`. NTP uses `port 123`, which is very easy to remember (there may be a quiz on this).

We know that default traffic should use `eth0` for communication, so that's what we'll specify:

```
$ sudo tcpdump port 123 -i eth0
```

Soon, you should see your client trying to talk to upstream servers, asking for time information:

```
10:07:33.229507 IP centos1.37284 > ntp3.wirehive.net.ntp: NTPv4,
Client, length 48
10:07:33.266188 IP ntp3.wirehive.net.ntp > centos1.37284: NTPv4,
Server, length 48
10:07:39.411433 IP centos1.49376 > 5751b502.skybroadband.com.ntp:
NTPv4, Client, length 48
10:07:39.453834 IP 5751b502.skybroadband.com.ntp > centos1.49376:
NTPv4, Server, length 48
```

If you've not got `tcpdump` installed, you can also use `chronyc`.

Let's see what servers we're talking to by using the `chronyc sources` command:

```
$ chronyc sources
210 Number of sources = 4
MS Name/IP address         Stratum Poll Reach LastRx Last sample
===============================================================================
^* 85.199.214.100               1   6   377     18   +266us[ +309us]
+/-  7548us
^- clocka.ntpjs.org             2   6   377     17   -126us[ -126us]
+/-    37ms
^- linnaeus.inf.ed.ac.uk        3   6   377     17    -80us[  -80us]
+/-    74ms
^+ 85.199.214.101               1   6   377     17   +166us[ +166us]
+/-  7583us
```

We can get more granular information on the status of our client too by looking at the details it knows about from its last sync. In the following example, we can see that our time is very far off what's expected:

```
$ chronyc tracking
Reference ID    : 5751B502 (5751b502.skybroadband.com)
Stratum         : 3
Ref time (UTC)  : Mon Aug 13 17:39:17 2018
System time     : 26450.427734375 seconds slow of NTP time
Last offset     : -0.000067056 seconds
RMS offset      : 777.442565918 seconds
Frequency       : 1.700 ppm slow
Residual freq   : -0.120 ppm
Skew            : 3.203 ppm
Root delay      : 0.052811030 seconds
Root dispersion : 0.006966238 seconds
Update interval : 60.0 seconds
Leap status     : Normal
```

Assuming that your time isn't ridiculously far out, the output may look as follows. Here, the amount of time difference between upstream and us is negligible:

```
$ chronyc tracking
Reference ID    : 55C7D666 (85.199.214.102)
Stratum         : 2
Ref time (UTC)  : Sun Aug 19 10:55:55 2018
System time     : 0.000031875 seconds slow of NTP time
Last offset     : -0.000032510 seconds
RMS offset      : 0.003755528 seconds
Frequency       : 6.102 ppm slow
Residual freq   : -0.009 ppm
Skew            : 3.659 ppm
Root delay      : 0.014116751 seconds
Root dispersion : 0.000280226 seconds
Update interval : 64.4 seconds
Leap status     : Normal
```

Enabling an NTP client

Assuming that your system isn't using `chronyd`, and its date is sliding constantly, you can enable it manually.

The configuration file for `chronyd` is located at `/etc/chrony.conf`. The following is the default configuration file, with the commented out sections removed:

```
server 0.centos.pool.ntp.org iburst
server 1.centos.pool.ntp.org iburst
server 2.centos.pool.ntp.org iburst
server 3.centos.pool.ntp.org iburst

driftfile /var/lib/chrony/drift

makestep 1.0 3

rtcsync

logdir /var/log/chrony
```

Once in place, if it's not already in place and running, `systemd` is used to maintain the service:

```
$ sudo systemctl enable chronyd
$ sudo systemctl start chronyd
```

Do check that a rogue admin hasn't taken it upon themselves to install `openntpd`, or a different daemon, to try and manage NTP. You can check this by using the preceding `tcpdump` commands, or seeing if anything is running on `port 123`.

Enabling an NTP server

Maybe the network you're managing is very restricted, and it takes ages to get network changes done. In this case, you might have a pool of servers that are designated as NTP providers for the rest of your estate.

In this case, you will need to configure `chronyd` to allow connections from other clients. We'll use `centos2` for the server.

On `centos2`, add a line to the bottom of our `chrony.conf` file to allow access from our `eth1` network (`192.168.33.0`):

```
$ sudo tee --append /etc/chrony.conf << HERE
allow 192.168.33.0/24
HERE
```

Restart `chronyd` with the new changes:

```
$ sudo systemctl restart chronyd
```

Now, on the system that's to be the client, `centos1`, perform the following steps.

First, modify our `chrony.conf` file by commenting out the existing server lines:

```
$ sudo sed -i 's/server/#server/g' /etc/chrony.conf
```

Next, add the required configuration directives for pointing to `centos2`:

```
$ sudo tee --append /etc/chrony.conf << HERE
server 192.168.33.11 iburst
allow 192.168.33.11
HERE
```

Restart `chronyd` on `centos1`:

```
$ sudo systemctl restart chronyd
```

You now have a server configured, and a client connected to it.

How it works...

NTP works in a client-server fashion, in which the client device (`centos1`, in our case) asks the server device (`centos2`) for an accurate time reading, which it then applies to the local machine.

When we wanted to make our own server, it was relatively trivial. On the server side, we only needed the line stipulating which clients could sync with `centos2`:

```
allow 192.168.33.0/24
```

On the client side, we needed to first remove the servers it was talking to (using `sed` to comment out the default pool lines), and then we added our new source-of-time as our configured server by using the following configuration lines:

```
server 192.168.33.11 iburst
allow 192.168.33.11
```

The server option is the address (or DNS name, if configured) of our source-of-truth. The `iburst` option simply makes the first few requests faster so that the sync can happen quicker after starting.

If we start `tcpdump` running on `centos2`, after it's been configured as a server, and then restart `chronyd` on `centos1`, we should see traffic flowing:

```
$ sudo tcpdump port 123 -i eth1
tcpdump: verbose output suppressed, use -v or -vv for full protocol
decode
listening on eth1, link-type EN10MB (Ethernet), capture size 262144
bytes
11:35:51.370634 IP 192.168.33.10.44912 > centos2.ntp: NTPv4, Client,
length 48
11:35:51.370965 IP centos2.ntp > 192.168.33.10.44912: NTPv4, Server,
length 48
11:35:53.394843 IP 192.168.33.10.52976 > centos2.ntp: NTPv4, Client,
length 48
11:35:53.395162 IP centos2.ntp > 192.168.33.10.52976: NTPv4, Server,
length 48
11:35:55.414496 IP 192.168.33.10.42977 > centos2.ntp: NTPv4, Client,
length 48
11:35:55.414659 IP centos2.ntp > 192.168.33.10.42977: NTPv4, Server,
length 48
11:35:57.437187 IP 192.168.33.10.45651 > centos2.ntp: NTPv4, Client,
length 48
11:35:57.437539 IP centos2.ntp > 192.168.33.10.45651: NTPv4, Server,
length 48
```

We can see our client machine (`.10`) requesting time from `centos2`, and then `centos2` responding on the next line.

> This also works to highlight the `iburst` option in action. Note the two-second differences between packet communication.

If we now take another look at `chronyc tracking` on the client, we should see normal details:

```
$ chronyc tracking
Reference ID    : C0A8210B (192.168.33.11)
Stratum         : 3
Ref time (UTC)  : Sun Aug 19 11:37:01 2018
System time     : 0.000000264 seconds fast of NTP time
Last offset     : -0.000468330 seconds
RMS offset      : 0.000468330 seconds
Frequency       : 6.604 ppm slow
Residual freq   : -5.715 ppm
Skew            : 7.044 ppm
Root delay      : 0.016203152 seconds
Root dispersion : 0.000595987 seconds
Update interval : 64.2 seconds
Leap status     : Normal
```

The preceding code may take a second to populate. If you're particularly quick off the mark, try again in a few seconds.

You can again use the `chronyc sources` command to check that the client is talking to the right server:

```
$ sudo chronyc sources
210 Number of sources = 1
MS Name/IP address         Stratum Poll Reach LastRx Last sample
===============================================================================
^* 192.168.33.11             2   6   377   48    +53us[ +106us]
+/- 7783us
```

There's more...

Sometimes, your time is out of sync, and it isn't automatically fixing itself. This can happen if your time is simply too far away from what it should be, as most systems refuse to do sudden and abrupt jerks.

This can be resolved by using another `chrony` command:

```
$ sudo chronyc makestep
200 OK
```

Be wary, though—this command can have unexpected side effects. Sometimes, programs detect sudden jerks, and will forcibly kill themselves to avoid issues.

If you want to tell how busy your server is, you can also use `serverstats` on the command line:

```
$ sudo chronyc serverstats
NTP packets received       : 8
NTP packets dropped        : 0
Command packets received   : 1
Command packets dropped    : 0
Client log records dropped : 0
```

See also

Chrony is actually a much more in-depth program than we've discussed here, and we barely mentioned its command-line utility (`chronyc`), which can be used to make all sorts of changes on the fly.

Check out the documentation pages for Chrony:

`https://chrony.tuxfamily.org/documentation.html`

It's also a good idea to have a think about how you're going to set up an NTP pool, if you find yourself in an environment requiring one. Generally, it's a rule of thumb that you configure multiple potential servers, instead of just one (that might skew or break). Three is better than one or two (two is quite bad, as you don't have an agreement on what the correct time is.)

Listing firewall rules on the command line

Here, we're going to use both the newer method, `firewall-cmd` & `ufw`, for listing firewall rules, along with the older (but still popular) method, `iptables`. We're going to go into the basics of other tables within firewalls, and the storage location for rules.

Getting ready

Connect to your `centos1` VM (and `ubuntu1`, if desired).

Enable and start `firewalld` for later examples:

```
$ sudo systemctl enable --now firewalld
```

How to do it...

While most of this book can be generalized to multiple distributions, firewalls are one area that can differ.

In the CentOS family of distributions, `firewall-cmd` is the common way to interact with firewalls.

In the Ubuntu family, `ufw` is used instead.

Generally, `iptables` should work across distributions, for the foreseeable future at least.

iptables

Typically, you want to check the running configuration of a firewall on a box. To do this, you might use `iptables -L`:

```
$ sudo iptables -L
Chain INPUT (policy ACCEPT)
target prot opt source destination
ACCEPT all -- anywhere anywhere ctstate RELATED,ESTABLISHED
ACCEPT all -- anywhere anywhere
INPUT_direct all -- anywhere anywhere
INPUT_ZONES_SOURCE all -- anywhere anywhere
INPUT_ZONES all -- anywhere anywhere
DROP all -- anywhere anywhere ctstate INVALID
REJECT all -- anywhere anywhere reject-with icmp-host-prohibited

Chain FORWARD (policy ACCEPT)
target prot opt source destination
ACCEPT all -- anywhere anywhere ctstate RELATED,ESTABLISHED
ACCEPT all -- anywhere anywhere
FORWARD_direct all -- anywhere anywhere
FORWARD_IN_ZONES_SOURCE all -- anywhere anywhere
FORWARD_IN_ZONES all -- anywhere anywhere
```

```
FORWARD_OUT_ZONES_SOURCE all -- anywhere anywhere
FORWARD_OUT_ZONES all -- anywhere anywhere
DROP all -- anywhere anywhere ctstate INVALID
REJECT all -- anywhere anywhere reject-with icmp-host-prohibited
<SNIP>
Chain FWDO_public (3 references)
target prot opt source destination
FWDO_public_log all -- anywhere anywhere
FWDO_public_deny all -- anywhere anywhere
FWDO_public_allow all -- anywhere anywhere

Chain FWDO_public_allow (1 references)
target prot opt source destination
<SNIP>
```

By default, the -L option lists all chains within the default table (filter being the default). There are five tables out of the box:

- raw
- filter
- mangle
- security
- nat

We may want to list rules in the nat table, in which case this can be specified with the -t option:

```
$ sudo iptables -t nat -L
Chain PREROUTING (policy ACCEPT)
target prot opt source destination
PREROUTING_direct all -- anywhere anywhere
PREROUTING_ZONES_SOURCE all -- anywhere anywhere
PREROUTING_ZONES all -- anywhere anywhere

Chain INPUT (policy ACCEPT)
target prot opt source destination

Chain OUTPUT (policy ACCEPT)
target prot opt source destination
OUTPUT_direct all -- anywhere anywhere

Chain POSTROUTING (policy ACCEPT)
target prot opt source destination
POSTROUTING_direct all -- anywhere anywhere
POSTROUTING_ZONES_SOURCE all -- anywhere anywhere
POSTROUTING_ZONES all -- anywhere anywhere
```

```
Chain OUTPUT_direct (1 references)
target prot opt source destination

Chain POSTROUTING_ZONES (1 references)
target prot opt source destination
POST_public all -- anywhere anywhere [goto]
POST_public all -- anywhere anywhere [goto]
POST_public all -- anywhere anywhere [goto]
POST_public all -- anywhere anywhere [goto]

Chain POSTROUTING_ZONES_SOURCE (1 references)
target prot opt source destination

Chain POSTROUTING_direct (1 references)
target prot opt source destination
<SNIP>
Chain PRE_public_log (1 references)
target prot opt source destination
```

A different method, and one that I tend to use first, is to print the rules on the command line, instead of listing them (this is a subtle difference). This is done with the -S option:

```
$ sudo iptables -S
-P INPUT ACCEPT
-P FORWARD ACCEPT
-P OUTPUT ACCEPT
-N FORWARD_IN_ZONES
-N FORWARD_IN_ZONES_SOURCE
-N FORWARD_OUT_ZONES
-N FORWARD_OUT_ZONES_SOURCE
-N FORWARD_direct
-N FWDI_public
-N FWDI_public_allow
-N FWDI_public_deny
-N FWDI_public_log
-N FWDO_public
-N FWDO_public_allow
-N FWDO_public_deny
-N FWDO_public_log
-N INPUT_ZONES
-N INPUT_ZONES_SOURCE
-N INPUT_direct
-N IN_public
-N IN_public_allow
-N IN_public_deny
-N IN_public_log
-N OUTPUT_direct
```

```
-A INPUT -m conntrack --ctstate RELATED,ESTABLISHED -j ACCEPT
-A INPUT -i lo -j ACCEPT
-A INPUT -j INPUT_direct
-A INPUT -j INPUT_ZONES_SOURCE
-A INPUT -j INPUT_ZONES
-A INPUT -m conntrack --ctstate INVALID -j DROP
-A INPUT -j REJECT --reject-with icmp-host-prohibited
-A FORWARD -m conntrack --ctstate RELATED,ESTABLISHED -j ACCEPT
-A FORWARD -i lo -j ACCEPT
-A FORWARD -j FORWARD_direct
-A FORWARD -j FORWARD_IN_ZONES_SOURCE
-A FORWARD -j FORWARD_IN_ZONES
-A FORWARD -j FORWARD_OUT_ZONES_SOURCE
-A FORWARD -j FORWARD_OUT_ZONES
-A FORWARD -m conntrack --ctstate INVALID -j DROP
-A FORWARD -j REJECT --reject-with icmp-host-prohibited
-A OUTPUT -j OUTPUT_direct
-A FORWARD_IN_ZONES -i eth2 -g FWDI_public
-A FORWARD_IN_ZONES -i eth1 -g FWDI_public
-A FORWARD_IN_ZONES -i eth0 -g FWDI_public
-A FORWARD_IN_ZONES -g FWDI_public
-A FORWARD_OUT_ZONES -o eth2 -g FWDO_public
-A FORWARD_OUT_ZONES -o eth1 -g FWDO_public
-A FORWARD_OUT_ZONES -o eth0 -g FWDO_public
-A FORWARD_OUT_ZONES -g FWDO_public
-A FWDI_public -j FWDI_public_log
-A FWDI_public -j FWDI_public_deny
-A FWDI_public -j FWDI_public_allow
-A FWDI_public -p icmp -j ACCEPT
-A FWDO_public -j FWDO_public_log
-A FWDO_public -j FWDO_public_deny
-A FWDO_public -j FWDO_public_allow
-A INPUT_ZONES -i eth2 -g IN_public
-A INPUT_ZONES -i eth1 -g IN_public
-A INPUT_ZONES -i eth0 -g IN_public
-A INPUT_ZONES -g IN_public
-A IN_public -j IN_public_log
-A IN_public -j IN_public_deny
-A IN_public -j IN_public_allow
-A IN_public -p icmp -j ACCEPT
-A IN_public_allow -p tcp -m tcp --dport 22 -m conntrack --ctstate NEW
-j ACCEPT
```

The reason why this method is nicer is that it shows you the syntax used to generate the rule in question. In a tense scenario, this type of knowledge can save time and stress.

firewall-cmd

Firewalld (the daemon controlled by `firewall-cmd`) introduces the concept of zones to the Linux firewall.

Zones are assigned to specific interfaces, with specific rules configured per zone.

You can list the currently configured zones using `firewall-cmd`, too:

```
$ sudo firewall-cmd --get-zones
block dmz drop external home internal public trusted work
```

To check which zone we're actively using, and on which interface, we use `--get-active-zones`.

In the following code, we can see that `eth0` and `eth1` are using the `public` zone:

```
$ firewall-cmd --get-active-zones
public
  interfaces: eth0 eth1
```

 eth2 is also under the `public` zone, but the interface is unconfigured, thus, inactive.

Because `eth0` is active under `public`, let's list the details of the `public` zone:

```
$ sudo firewall-cmd --list-all --zone public
public (active)
  target: default
  icmp-block-inversion: no
  interfaces: eth0 eth1 eth2
  sources:
  services: ssh dhcpv6-client
  ports:
  protocols:
  masquerade: no
  forward-ports:
  source-ports:
  icmp-blocks:
  rich rules:
```

Here, we can see that the services this zone is aware of are `ssh` and `dhcpv6-client`.

We can specifically list the services of a zone using `--list-services`:

```
$ sudo firewall-cmd --zone public --list-services
ssh dhcpv6-client
```

If we want information about exactly what that service allows, we can use `--info-service`.

In the following code, we're looking at `ssh`, discovering that it allows port `22/tcp` through:

```
$ sudo firewall-cmd --info-service ssh
ssh
  ports: 22/tcp
  protocols:
  source-ports:
  modules:
  destination:
```

ufw

In your Ubuntu VM, `ufw` probably won't be enabled by default. We will enable it, but first we're going to add a rule to make sure that we can get back in once the firewall is up:

```
vagrant@ubuntu1:~$ sudo ufw allow ssh/tcp
Rule added
Rule added (v6)
```

You can enable it with the following command:

```
vagrant@ubuntu1:~$ sudo ufw enable
Command may disrupt existing ssh connections. Proceed with operation
(y|n)? y
Firewall is active and enabled on system startup
```

We can now see the status of our firewall by using the `status verbose` option:

```
vagrant@ubuntu1:~$ sudo ufw status verbose
Status: active
Logging: on (low)
Default: deny (incoming), allow (outgoing), disabled (routed)
New profiles: skip

To                         Action      From
--                         ------      ----
```

```
22/tcp                          ALLOW IN    Anywhere
22/tcp (v6)                     ALLOW IN    Anywhere (v6)
```

The firewall is active, and there's a `22/tcp` allow rule to allow us in.

How it works...

All of the preceding examples interact with the kernel's Netfilter framework—they just do the same thing using different tools.

When you list rules on the command line, you're querying what the kernel knows to be the security rules for a box.

The reason you can list rules with both the `iptables` and `firewall-cmd` commands (in the case of CentOS) is because they're only acting as userland frontends.

UFW is the same, just in the Ubuntu world.

This is the reason you find a lot of setup scripts in the wild that will remove extra firewall tools, such as `firewalld`, and that simply use the `iptables` suite to manage the firewall.

There's more...

If you do find yourself on a box that has `firewall-cmd` installed, but not the `iptables` userland tool, you might find which package it's in with `yum`:

```
$ yum whatprovides iptables
```

In this case, `iptables` is the package you want to install, if you're something of a purist.

See also

Though not yet installed by default, you may want to look into the `nft` and `nftables` systems.

`nftables` is a replacement for the existing kernel framework, and `nft` is the accompanying command-line tool.

Adding and removing firewall rules on the command line

In this section, we're going to look at adding and removing example rules from our firewall setup.

Getting ready

Ensure that `firewalld` is installed and started on `centos1`:

```
$ sudo systemctl enable --now firewalld
```

Once done, start a Python web server in the background:

```
$ python -m SimpleHTTPServer &> /dev/null &
[1] 2732
```

This should start a web server on port `8000`.

Connect to `centos2` and try to `curl` your `centos1` box on port `8000`. It should fail:

```
$ curl 192.168.33.10:8000
curl: (7) Failed connect to 192.168.33.10:8000; No route to host
```

If you want to work through the Ubuntu examples at the same time, log in to your Ubuntu box.

How to do it...

We're going to use `firewall-cmd`, `iptables`, and `ufw` to adjust our firewall.

firewall-cmd

Our web server is listening on all interfaces (the default) and we're going to allow connections to it through `eth1`.

We know that `eth1` is in the default (`public`) zone, thanks to the previous section:

```
$ sudo firewall-cmd --zone public --list-all
public (active)
  target: default
```

```
icmp-block-inversion: no
interfaces: eth0 eth1
sources:
services: ssh dhcpv6-client
ports:
protocols:
masquerade: no
forward-ports:
source-ports:
icmp-blocks:
rich rules:
```

This means that we have to add another port allowance to our zone, enabling connections to 8000/tcp.

In the following code, we're adding to our firewall configuration, but we're not modifying the running config—we're adding the permanent option so that the rule is loaded on a firewall reload:

```
$ sudo firewall-cmd --permanent --zone=public --add-port 8000/tcp
```

Now, we need to run the command again, without the permanent option. So that our running configuration is modified:

```
$ sudo firewall-cmd --zone=public --add-port 8000/tcp
```

Running the --list-all option will now show your added port:

```
$ sudo firewall-cmd --zone public --list-all
public (active)
  target: default
  icmp-block-inversion: no
  interfaces: eth0 eth1 eth2
  sources:
  services: ssh dhcpv6-client
  ports: 8000/tcp
  protocols:
  masquerade: no
  forward-ports:
  source-ports:
  icmp-blocks:
  rich rules:
```

You should be able to curl centos1 on 8000/tcp from centos2:

```
$ curl 192.168.33.10:8000
<!DOCTYPE html PUBLIC "-//W3C//DTD HTML 3.2 Final//EN"><html>
<title>Directory listing for /</title>
```

```
<body>
<h2>Directory listing for /</h2>
<hr>
<ul>
<li><a href=".bash_history">.bash_history</a>
<li><a href=".bash_logout">.bash_logout</a>
<li><a href=".bash_profile">.bash_profile</a>
<li><a href=".bashrc">.bashrc</a>
<li><a href=".ssh/">.ssh/</a>
</ul>
<hr>
</body>
</html>
```

 If you find it easier, you can also modify the running config primarily, and then when you're happy with it, apply the rules using the `--runtime-to-permanent` option. The choice is yours.

To reverse this addition, you would swap the `add-port` for a `remove-port`, like so:

```
$ sudo firewall-cmd --zone=public --remove-port 8000/tcp
success
```

iptables

To perform the same action in `iptables`, we must first ensure that `firewalld` doesn't interfere.

Start by disabling and stopping `firewalld`:

```
$ sudo systemctl disable --now firewalld
```

You should now have an empty `iptables` configuration, as can be seen with `iptables -S`:

```
$ sudo iptables -S
-P INPUT ACCEPT
-P FORWARD ACCEPT
-P OUTPUT ACCEPT
```

Because we've got an empty rule list, we're going to start by adding some basic rules.

First, we're going to block `centos2` and anything else on our `eth1` network from SSHing to `centos1`:

```
$ sudo iptables -A INPUT -i eth1 -p tcp -m tcp --dport 22 -j DROP
```

Next, we're going to allow only incoming SSH connections from 10.0.2.0/24 sources:

```
$ sudo iptables -A INPUT -s 10.0.2.0/24 -p tcp -m tcp --dport 22 -j
ACCEPT
```

Finally, we're going to change the default incoming policy from ACCEPT to DROP:

```
$ sudo iptables -P INPUT DROP
```

Because we've changed the default policy, we also need to ensure that RELATED and ESTABLISHED connections are permitted (those connections we've initiated from our box). This makes our firewall "stateful" or aware of the state:

```
$ sudo iptables -A INPUT -m conntrack --ctstate RELATED,ESTABLISHED -j
ACCEPT
```

Running iptables -S will display your rules:

```
$ sudo iptables -S
-P INPUT DROP
-P FORWARD ACCEPT
-P OUTPUT ACCEPT
-A INPUT -i eth1 -p tcp -m tcp --dport 22 -j DROP
-A INPUT -s 10.0.2.0/24 -p tcp -m tcp --dport 22 -j ACCEPT
-A INPUT -m conntrack --ctstate RELATED,ESTABLISHED -j ACCEPT
```

Our configuration here is somewhat redundant, because while it serves to show the flexibility of iptables rules, the default traffic rule is a -P INPUT DROP, meaning that if traffic isn't accepted by any of our other rules, it won't be let in. Our eth1 DROP line is therefore pointless.

ufw

Prior to working with ufw in the previous section, we had to add this allow rule to let SSH traffic in, once the firewall was enabled:

```
vagrant@ubuntu1:~$ sudo ufw allow ssh/tcp
Rule added
Rule added (v6)
```

The default `ufw` profile has incoming connections denied, as we can see in the following code:

```
vagrant@ubuntu1:~$ sudo ufw status verbose
Status: active
Logging: on (low)
Default: deny (incoming), allow (outgoing), disabled (routed)
New profiles: skip
```

Because of this, if we wanted to access a web server hosted on our Ubuntu box, we'd need a new rule.

Previously, we used the service name (`ssh`), so this time we're going to specifically allow a port (`80`, the default HTTP port) from our VirtualBox network:

```
vagrant@ubuntu1:~$ sudo ufw allow from 10.0.2.0/24 to any port 80
proto tcp
Rule added
```

We can see this rule in action by using the `status` option:

```
vagrant@ubuntu1:~$ sudo ufw status
Status: active

To                      Action      From
--                      ------      ----
22/tcp                  ALLOW       Anywhere
80/tcp                  ALLOW       10.0.2.0/24
22/tcp (v6)             ALLOW       Anywhere (v6)
```

Deleting with `ufw` is simple—just prefix your original rule (be it `allow` or `deny`) with the word `delete`:

```
vagrant@ubuntu1:~$ sudo ufw delete allow from 10.0.2.0/24 to any port
80 proto tcp
Rule deleted
```

How it works...

Each of these examples are used to manipulate the running firewall configuration on your box. When you use the userland tools, as with the querying examples in the last section, you're actually modifying the Netfilter framework of the kernel.

Personally, I find it easiest to understand what's going on by using the `iptables` command, though you may find yourself more comfortable with an alternative.

As we saw in the last section, if you enable `firewalld` or `ufw`, you will also find that your default `iptables` rules change. Without `firewalld` or `ufw` enabled, the out-of-the-box `iptables` configuration will be much simpler, as we can see in the following lines:

```
$ sudo iptables -S
-P INPUT ACCEPT
-P FORWARD ACCEPT
-P OUTPUT ACCEPT
```

Whenever we modified our firewall, our changes were instantly applied.

Breaking this down, if we go back to our `iptables` example, we can step through what we did:

```
$ sudo iptables -A INPUT -s 10.0.2.0/24 -p tcp -m tcp --dport 22 -j
ACCEPT
```

Here, we modify `iptables` using the `iptables` userland tool:

```
$ sudo iptables
```

We then `append` a rule to our `INPUT` chain (a chain resides within a table):

```
-A INPUT
```

We set the source of traffic as our VirtualBox subnet:

```
-s 10.0.2.0/24
```

We specify the protocol and use the extended match feature:

```
-p tcp -m tcp
```

We say that the destination port should be `22` (the SSH port):

```
--dport 22
```

Finally, we say that we should `ACCEPT` this traffic:

```
-j ACCEPT
```

There's more...

If you make changes with `firewall-cmd` or `ufw`, you can generally save the running config to the persistent config at the same time.

With `iptables`, we want to use `iptables-save` to modify our saved configuration, and ensure that it starts at boot:

```
$ sudo iptables-save
# Generated by iptables-save v1.4.21 on Sun Aug 19 15:04:14 2018
*filter
:INPUT DROP [0:0]
:FORWARD ACCEPT [0:0]
:OUTPUT ACCEPT [3:236]
-A INPUT -i eth1 -p tcp -m tcp --dport 22 -j DROP
-A INPUT -s 10.0.2.0/24 -p tcp -m tcp --dport 22 -j ACCEPT
-A INPUT -m conntrack --ctstate RELATED,ESTABLISHED -j ACCEPT
COMMIT
# Completed on Sun Aug 19 15:04:14 2018
```

This is all fine and dandy, except it's printed the configuration to standard out instead of saving it somewhere. Let's fix that by redirecting it to the default `iptables` config location:

```
$ sudo iptables-save | sudo tee /etc/sysconfig/iptables
```

Now, to properly start this at boot, we need the `iptables-services` package, which includes things such as the `systemd` unit files:

```
$ sudo yum install -y iptables-services
```

We can now enable `iptables` to start at boot:

```
$ sudo systemctl enable iptables
```

Run the `systemctl restart` command for `iptables` and ensure your configuration is correct:

```
$ sudo service iptables restart
Redirecting to /bin/systemctl restart iptables.service
$ sudo iptables -S
-P INPUT DROP
-P FORWARD ACCEPT
-P OUTPUT ACCEPT
-A INPUT -i eth1 -p tcp -m tcp --dport 22 -j DROP
-A INPUT -s 10.0.2.0/24 -p tcp -m tcp --dport 22 -j ACCEPT
-A INPUT -m conntrack --ctstate RELATED,ESTABLISHED -j ACCEPT
```

 Firewalls can be as complex or as simple as you need them to be. It's a good idea to start simple and make them more complex as you go.

There's also the `iptables -F` option, which we didn't cover in this section.

`-F` means flush, and it can be incredibly handy in certain situations for flushing your firewall back to its default configuration.

However, it's worth noting that if you have your default INPUT policy set to DROP incoming traffic, then flushing any rules that otherwise allow you access will render your session unusable.

My default policy is DROP:

```
$ sudo iptables -S
-P INPUT DROP
-P FORWARD ACCEPT
-P OUTPUT ACCEPT
-A INPUT -i eth1 -p tcp -m tcp --dport 22 -j DROP
-A INPUT -s 10.0.2.0/24 -p tcp -m tcp --dport 22 -j ACCEPT
-A INPUT -m conntrack --ctstate RELATED,ESTABLISHED -j ACCEPT
```

If I now flush my rules, my session locks up:

```
$ sudo iptables -F
$
```

We would now need to get to the console of the box and reinstate the rules that allowed us access. Most of the time, this is simply a case of running the `start` command of the firewall.

Determining the running services and ports in use

In this section, we're going to use only our `centos1` VM, as we determine the ports in use on our box, and the services behind them.

Getting ready

Connect to your `centos1` VM.

You should also install the `lsof` package for some of the examples that we will be looking at:

```
$ sudo yum install -y lsof
```

How to do it...

When determining what's running on a server, you usually want to know if anything is listening on for connections and on what ports.

Out of the box, **socket statistics (ss)** is usually available. The older program, netstat, might be installed sometimes too, though it won't be covered here.

A good first step is to run ss -tua, which will list all TCP and UDP sockets:

```
$ ss -tua
Netid   State       Recv-Q Send-Q
Local Address:Port
Peer Address:Port
udp     UNCONN      0      0
127.0.0.1:323
*:*
udp     UNCONN      0      0
*:bootpc
*:*
udp     UNCONN      0      0
*:bootpc
*:*
udp     UNCONN      0      0
*:sunrpc
*:*
udp     UNCONN      0      0
*:ntp
*:*
udp     UNCONN      0      0
*:728
*:*
udp     UNCONN      0      0
::1:323
:::*
udp     UNCONN      0      0
:::sunrpc
:::*
udp     UNCONN      0      0
:::728
:::*
tcp     LISTEN      0      5
*:irdmi
*:*
tcp     LISTEN      0      128
*:sunrpc
*:*
```

```
tcp     LISTEN    0      128
*:ssh
*:*
tcp     LISTEN    0      100
127.0.0.1:smtp
*:*
tcp     ESTAB     0      0
10.0.2.15:ssh
10.0.2.2:36116
tcp     LISTEN    0      128
:::sunrpc
:::*
tcp     LISTEN    0      128
:::ssh
:::*
tcp     LISTEN    0      100
::1:smtp
:::*
```

If we want to list only to ESTAB (established) connections, we can filter down using the state directive:

```
$ ss -tua state established
Netid   Recv-Q Send-Q                            Local
Address:Port
Peer Address:Port
tcp     0      0
10.0.2.15:ssh
10.0.2.2:36116
```

Here, we can see my SSH session from the host machine.

Say we now want to list all sockets that are listening for TCP connections:

```
$ ss -tl
State       Recv-Q Send-Q                         Local
Address:Port
Peer Address:Port
LISTEN      0      5
*:irdmi
*:*
LISTEN      0      128
*:sunrpc
*:*
LISTEN      0      128
*:ssh
*:*
LISTEN      0      100
```

```
127.0.0.1:smtp
*:*
LISTEN      0       128
:::sunrpc
:::*
LISTEN      0       128
:::ssh
:::*
LISTEN      0       100
::1:smtp
:::*
```

Alternatively, we can do this for the UDP:

```
$ ss -ul
State       Recv-Q Send-Q                                          Local
Address:Port
Peer Address:Port
UNCONN      0       0
127.0.0.1:323
*:*
UNCONN      0       0
*:bootpc
*:*
UNCONN      0       0
*:sunrpc
*:*
UNCONN      0       0
*:ntp
*:*
UNCONN      0       0
*:728
*:*
UNCONN      0       0
::1:323
:::*
UNCONN      0       0
:::sunrpc
:::*
UNCONN      0       0
:::728
:::*
```

This is enough to give us a good overview of the services running, but it doesn't let us know the ports.

`ss` will check against a known services list to determine the name to display. In this example, we deliberately chose to list the listening ports, filtering out everything but port 22, and we can see that `ssh` has been chosen:

```
$ ss -l sport = :22
Netid  State      Recv-Q Send-Q
Local Address:Port
Peer Address:Port
tcp    LISTEN     0      128
*:ssh
*:*
tcp    LISTEN     0      128
:::ssh
:::*
```

 `::` is the IPv6 loopback denotion, which is why it shows up here next to one of the SSH entries.

We can check the system's `services` list to see what it thinks `ssh` should be using:

```
$ grep "^ssh " /etc/services
ssh             22/tcp                    # The Secure Shell
(SSH) Protocol
ssh             22/udp                    # The Secure Shell
(SSH) Protocol
ssh             22/sctp         # SSH
```

How it works...

`ss` is a quick way of determining the sockets that a system is currently using, and it's not limited to TCP or UDP, as it's also able to display Unix domain sockets (`-x`).

In this example, we've queried the system to find out which ports are in use, and `ss` has performed some resolution work to determine what services those ports are likely to be used by.

This is not a guarantee, however. For example, if you start a Python web server on `2222`, it would list the following:

```
$ ss -l sport = :2222
Netid  State      Recv-Q Send-Q
Local Address:Port
Peer Address:Port
```

```
tcp     LISTEN     0     5
*:EtherNet/IP-1
*:*
```

This is simply because as far as /etc/services is concerned, this port is used by EtherNet/IP-1:

```
$ grep "^EtherNet" /etc/services
EtherNet/IP-1    2222/tcp   EtherNet-IP-1 # EtherNet/IP I/O
EtherNet/IP-1    2222/udp   EtherNet-IP-1 # EtherNet/IP I/O
EtherNet/IP-2    44818/tcp  EtherNet-IP-2  # EtherNet/IP messaging
EtherNet/IP-2    44818/udp  EtherNet-IP-2  # EtherNet/IP messaging
```

There's more...

An arguably better way of determining which process is using which port is to use the lsof command. I say arguably because it's not usually installed by default, though it is extremely handy and powerful.

If we use lsof and check for commands using port 22, we get the following list:

```
$ sudo lsof -i :22
COMMAND    PID     USER    FD     TYPE DEVICE SIZE/OFF NODE NAME
sshd       877     root    3u     IPv4  17409      0t0  TCP *:ssh (LISTEN)
sshd       877     root    4u     IPv6  17479      0t0  TCP *:ssh (LISTEN)
sshd       4262    root    3u     IPv4  43232      0t0  TCP
centos1:ssh->gateway:36116 (ESTABLISHED)
sshd       4265 vagrant    3u     IPv4  43232      0t0  TCP
centos1:ssh->gateway:36116 (ESTABLISHED)
```

If you don't want to print hostnames (centos1 in the above example) and port names (ssh above) you can use the following extra flags instead (P & n:)

```
$ sudo lsof -Pni :22
COMMAND PID USER FD TYPE DEVICE SIZE/OFF NODE NAME
sshd 3454 root 3u IPv4 26892 0t0 TCP *:22 (LISTEN)
sshd 3454 root 4u IPv6 26894 0t0 TCP *:22 (LISTEN)
sshd 3457 root 3u IPv4 26951 0t0 TCP 10.0.2.15:22->10.0.2.2:33066
(ESTABLISHED)
sshd 3460 vagrant 3u IPv4 26951 0t0 TCP 10.0.2.15:22->10.0.2.2:33066
(ESTABLISHED)
```

If we have our Python web server enabled on 2222, we get this:

```
$ sudo lsof -i :2222
COMMAND  PID    USER    FD    TYPE DEVICE SIZE/OFF NODE NAME
python  4542 vagrant    3u   IPv4  45493      0t0  TCP *:EtherNet/IP-1
(LISTEN)
```

Notice that while the NAME is still listed as EtherNet, we know it's Python because the COMMAND is listed as such.

Because we also have PID (4542), we can get the full command easily:

```
$ ps aux | grep 4542
vagrant   4542  0.0  2.0  97820 10136 pts/2    S    15:39   0:00
python -m SimpleHTTPServer 2222
```

Debugging with iftop

In this section, we're going to look at a member of the top family (which is quite extensive, featuring atop, iotop, htop, and so on), which is specifically geared toward network traffic statistics and debugging.

iftop is both handy and very readable.

Getting ready

For this section, we're going to use centos1 and centos2, connect to both in separate windows.

Make sure that you install iftop on centos2 prior to starting. This comes from the **Extra Packages for Enterprise Linux (EPEL)** repository, so we have to install that first:

```
$ sudo yum install -y epel-release
$ sudo yum install -y iftop
```

Start iftop on centos2:

```
$ sudo iftop -i eth1
```

How to do it...

Once you've started `iftop` on `centos2`, switch to `centos1` and run an `ssh` command to generate some network traffic to `centos2`:

```
$ ssh 192.168.33.11
The authenticity of host '192.168.33.11 (192.168.33.11)' can't be
established.
ECDSA key fingerprint is
SHA256:GwCeJ/ObTsyKxMxzazTaYvvyY3SFgxPl6ucjPDGwmao.
ECDSA key fingerprint is
MD5:0d:41:ad:71:67:07:35:d4:59:07:de:41:bf:a4:b4:93.
Are you sure you want to continue connecting (yes/no)? yes
Warning: Permanently added '192.168.33.11' (ECDSA) to the list of
known hosts.
vagrant@192.168.33.11's password:
Last login: Sun Aug 19 15:04:49 2018 from 10.0.2.2
$
```

Back on `centos2`, you should see a brief entry in your network screen that shows activity:

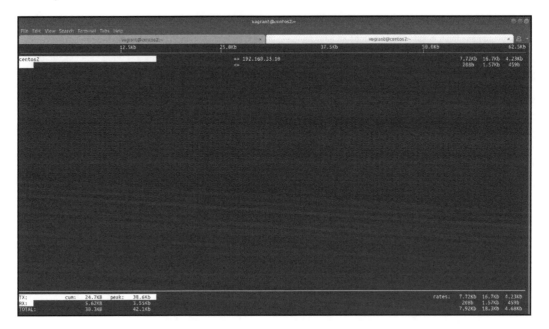

In my `ssh` session on `centos1` (which is now connected to `centos2`), I've started `top` to generate a stream of traffic.

At the bottom of your window, you will see the following values:

- `TX`
- `RX`
- `TOTAL`:

These values are total traffic transferred, received, and total.

To the right we have the rates averaged over 2, 10, and 40 seconds.

Clicking back to `centos1` and stopping, then starting `top`, will cause the `RX` values to rise, as you've sent keystrokes over the connection.

At the top of the window, you can see a visual representation of the traffic:

This displays traffic sent back to `192.168.33.10` (`centos1`) and the traffic received in a somewhat readable format.

The scale for the transfer rate is at the top, and varies depending on quantity.

 In a real-world scenario, this type of information can be invaluable, as it offers an at-a-glance way of seeing who might be hammering your server.

If we swap to watching `eth0` traffic, then restart `chronyd`, we can see more servers being connected to:

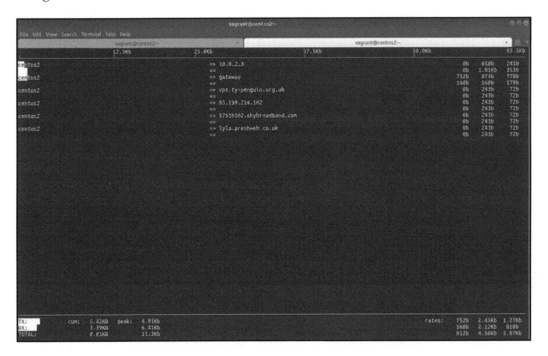

How it works...

Like `tcpdump`, `iftop` listens to the traffic on the interface you specify, or the default if you don't specify one.

It then prints the bandwidth usage by the host, giving a good visual representation of the network on your box.

There's more...

`iftop` offers a lot of options, and a peruse of the manual page is worth considering. Simple things like using `-n` to disable hostname lookups can be handy, or changing how the bandwidth rates are displayed.

You can even print a text-only version to `stdout` using the `-t` flag:

```
$ sudo iftop -i eth1 -t
interface: eth1
IP address is: 192.168.33.11
MAC address is: 08:00:27:f1:e9:56
Listening on eth1
   # Host name (port/service if enabled)              last 2s   last 10s
last 40s cumulative
----------------------------------------------------------------------
-----------------------
   1 centos2                                  =>        35.7Kb     35.7Kb
35.7Kb      8.91KB
     192.168.33.10                            <=          416b       416b
416b        104B
----------------------------------------------------------------------
-----------------------
Total send rate:                                       35.7Kb     35.7Kb
35.7Kb
Total receive rate:                                      416b       416b
416b
Total send and receive rate:                           36.1Kb     36.1Kb
36.1Kb
----------------------------------------------------------------------
-----------------------
Peak rate (sent/received/total):                       35.7Kb       416b
36.1Kb
Cumulative (sent/received/total):                      8.91KB       104B
9.02KB
======================================================================
=======================
```

Summary

In this chapter, we took a look at networking and firewalls in the Linux world. I hope it didn't hurt your head too much, because it certainly causes me some pain.

As I alluded to earlier, networking and firewall configuration can be as complex or as simple as you want it to be, and in the ever-growing world of single-use servers, we're seeing simpler and simpler configurations in the wild.

Where you tend to find problems are around the concepts of multiple networks and multi-homed servers, because flat network structures are a lot easier to understand for the average person (myself included).

You also don't have to do everything with Linux.

Yes, Linux can act as a border firewall for an estate, but you could also use *F5* devices, or Check Point boxes.

Yes, Linux can act as a router, but you're much more likely to see a Cisco or a Juniper device in the network cabinet.

These solutions have their positives, as well as their negatives.

A simple positive is that a purpose-built appliance is generally very good at the thing it was purpose-built for, and the tools to manage it are pretty much uniform in their approach (rather than the sometimes-mash we get in the Linux world).

An obvious negative is that it either means you have to learn the technology stack of the device you're incorporating into your network, or you have to hire a purpose-built-person to manage the solution for you, costing time and money.

Networking seems to be something that you either like or dislike, and I fall firmly in the latter camp. In theory, networks and firewalls "just work" once they're set up, but in practice that means the edge case problems are much more difficult to track down and correct when they do, inevitably, happen.

One final thing to mention—because I guarantee you'll have to deal with it at some point in your professional career—is the problem of locking yourself out.

It happens.

When it does, don't beat yourself up about it. Literally every engineer I've ever worked with has locked themselves out of a box once, either through a misconfigured firewall rule, or a silly mistake such as changing the SSH port without first updating the SELinux configuration.

If you lock yourself out and you have access to a console, either a remote Keyboard Video Mouse system or something like a cloud provider's web-based Terminal, you're usually fine—it just means logging in and correcting your mistake.

If you lock yourself out and the system is on the other side of the city, or country, you've got two options:

1. Hop into your car and resign yourself to a long drive there and back.
2. Contact the remote engineer and prostrate yourself before them, admitting your error and begging them to find a crash cart to resolve your mishap.

If you choose option two, buying them a beverage of their choice the next time you meet is more than agreeable.

 I have been both the remote engineer tasked with fixing someone else's mistake, and the person making the mistake. As I said, it happens to us all.

Services and Daemons

4

The following topics will be covered in this chapter:

- Determining running services
- Listing installed services
- Starting and stopping services
- Changing which services start and stop at boot
- Common services you might expect to see
- Understanding service unit files
- Customizing systemd unit files
- Testing running services
- Writing a basic unit file
- Working with systemd timers (and cron)
- Other `init` systems

Introduction

systemd (stylized lowercase) is a hydra.

In the old world, we had one piece of software for each little thing we wanted to do on a system. Time was handled by NTP, devices were handled by `udev`, and init was generally handled by `SysV Init`.

In the new world, we have systemd:

- System clock management can be handled by `systemd-timesyncd`.
- `udev` was merged into the systemd code base, forming `systemd-udevd`.
- Process initialization is handled by the core of systemd itself.

The list goes on.

Generally, systemd has been adopting other projects, or writing the same functionality into implementations of their own (such as systemd-timesyncd which is an NTP replacement.) However, the systemd suite is also modular, meaning that distributions can broadly choose which bits to adopt and use.

For us, the important job that systemd does is replace the traditional init system on distributions (CentOS, Debian, and Ubuntu all use systemd now). This means that first and foremost, systemd manages services and daemons on your box.

 systemd is the first process, meaning it will often be assigned the first **process ID (PID)**. All other processes have systemd as a parent.

In this chapter, we're going to work with the init component of systemd, learn about unit files, and determining the running state of our system.

Previously, this chapter could have been much longer. Prior to systemd dominating each and every mainstream distribution, fragmentation existed. Canonical wrote something called Upstart for Ubuntu (which was temporarily adopted by Red Hat), and more traditional distributions had a hard time letting go of the `SysV` init style of daemon management. Even today, you'll find systems that use older implementations in the wild:

- CentOS adopted systemd with version 7
- Ubuntu adopted systemd with 15.04
- Debian adopted systemd with Jessie (8)

 If Canonical wrote Upstart, you might be wondering why they went with systemd in the end. This was mainly due to Debian adopting systemd, after something of a civil war internally, and Ubuntu conceding that they would have an easier time of it if they remained aligned with their upstream distribution. The war was not without bitter battles on both sides and some ripples can still be felt.

Technical requirements

For this chapter, a different `Vagrantfile` is needed.

Feel free to use the following example if required—be sure to `destroy` any previous boxes to free up resources:

```ruby
# -*- mode: ruby -*-
# vi: set ft=ruby :

Vagrant.configure("2") do |config|

  config.vm.define "centos1" do |centos1|
    centos1.vm.box = "centos/7"
    centos1.vm.network "private_network", ip: "192.168.33.10"
    centos1.vm.hostname = "centos1"
    centos1.vm.box_version = "1804.02"
  end

  config.vm.define "centos6" do |centos6|
    centos6.vm.box = "centos/6"
  end

  config.vm.define "debian7" do |debian7|
    debian7.vm.box = "debian/wheezy64"
  end

end
```

Determining running services

Whenever you get to a box, especially one you're unsure of (that's been tucked in the back of a cupboard somewhere blinking to itself), it's a good idea to find out what software is running on it.

On modern systems (2013-ish plus), this is accomplished with the `systemctl` command.

`systemctl` is the main control mechanism for any systemd system—literally "system control". Think of it as the human frontend to your initialization software (the first software to run on your box, which manages all others), allowing you to modify and investigate the running state of your computer.

Not only that, in the Unix/Linux world everything is a file; your network connections are a file, your programs are a file, your devices are a file, and because of this you can control everything, just by modifying files.

But that gets tedious fast.

`systemctl` saves you the headache of manually shuffling files around your system by wrapping functionality in simple commands and printing the results in a human-readable way.

How to do it...

At the command line, type the following:

```
$ systemctl
```

You should be dropped into a list of systemd units; this is a good initial overview of every unit systemd is aware of, but it's very noisy (as seen in the following screenshot) and what we specifically want to see are daemons (because of our gothic streak):

Services and daemons are somewhat interchangeable in Linux land; for example, systemd refers to daemons as `service` files. This doesn't stop some people from getting passionately angry about "proper usage".

Try the following:

```
$ systemctl list-units --type service
```

You should be given a list of services and their statuses.

This view is better, but it also shows failed and exited services, for example, on our Vagrant instance, we should see the following:

```
UNIT                                          LOAD   ACTIVE SUB     DESCRIPTION
auditd.service                                loaded active running Security Auditing Service
chronyd.service                               loaded active running NTP client/server
crond.service                                 loaded active running Command Scheduler
dbus.service                                  loaded active running D-Bus System Message Bus
getty@tty1.service                            loaded active running Getty on tty1
gssproxy.service                              loaded active running GSSAPI Proxy Daemon
kmod-static-nodes.service                     loaded active exited  Create list of required static device
lvm2-lvmetad.service                          loaded active running LVM2 metadata daemon
lvm2-monitor.service                          loaded active exited  Monitoring of LVM2 mirrors, snapshots
lvm2-pvscan@8:3.service                        loaded active exited  LVM2 PV scan on device 8:3
network.service                               loaded active exited  LSB: Bring up/down networking
NetworkManager-wait-online.service            loaded failed failed  Network Manager Wait Online
NetworkManager.service                        loaded active running Network Manager
polkit.service                                loaded active running Authorization Manager
postfix.service                               loaded active running Postfix Mail Transport Agent
rhel-dmesg.service                            loaded active exited  Dump dmesg to /var/log/dmesg
rhel-domainname.service                       loaded active exited  Read and set NIS domainname from /etc/
rhel-readonly.service                         loaded active exited  Configure read-only root support
rpcbind.service                               loaded active running RPC bind service
rsyslog.service                               loaded active running System Logging Service
selinux-policy-migrate-local-changes@targeted.service loaded failed failed  Migrate local SELinux policy changes f
sshd.service                                  loaded active running OpenSSH server daemon
systemd-hostnamed.service                     loaded active running Hostname Service
systemd-hwdb-update.service                   loaded active exited  Rebuild Hardware Database
systemd-journal-catalog-update.service        loaded active exited  Rebuild Journal Catalog
systemd-journal-flush.service                 loaded active exited  Flush Journal to Persistent Storage
systemd-journald.service                      loaded active running Journal Service
systemd-logind.service                        loaded active running Login Service
systemd-machine-id-commit.service             loaded active exited  Commit a transient machine-id on disk
systemd-random-seed.service                   loaded active exited  Load/Save Random Seed
systemd-remount-fs.service                    loaded active exited  Remount Root and Kernel File Systems
systemd-sysctl.service                        loaded active exited  Apply Kernel Variables
systemd-tmpfiles-setup-dev.service            loaded active exited  Create Static Device Nodes in /dev
systemd-tmpfiles-setup.service                loaded active exited  Create Volatile Files and Directories
systemd-udev-trigger.service                  loaded active exited  udev Coldplug all Devices
systemd-udevd.service                         loaded active running udev Kernel Device Manager
systemd-update-done.service                   loaded active exited  Update is Completed
systemd-update-utmp.service                   loaded active exited  Update UTMP about System Boot/Shutdown
systemd-user-sessions.service                 loaded active exited  Permit User Sessions
systemd-vconsole-setup.service                loaded active exited  Setup Virtual Console
tuned.service                                 loaded active running Dynamic System Tuning Daemon

LOAD   = Reflects whether the unit definition was properly loaded.
ACTIVE = The high-level unit activation state, i.e. generalization of SUB.
SUB    = The low-level unit activation state, values depend on unit type.

41 loaded units listed. Pass --all to see loaded but inactive units, too.
To show all installed unit files use 'systemctl list-unit-files'.
```

If I want to exclude these, I can use the following command:

```
$ systemctl list-units --type service --state running
```

Now we get a much more condensed list, with 17 items in total:

UNIT	LOAD	ACTIVE	SUB	DESCRIPTION
auditd.service	loaded	active	running	Security Auditing Service
chronyd.service	loaded	active	running	NTP client/server
crond.service	loaded	active	running	Command Scheduler
dbus.service	loaded	active	running	D-Bus System Message Bus
getty@tty1.service	loaded	active	running	Getty on tty1

```
gssproxy.service          loaded active running GSSAPI Proxy Daemon
lvm2-lvmetad.service      loaded active running LVM2 metadata daemon
NetworkManager.service    loaded active running Network Manager
polkit.service            loaded active running Authorization Manager
postfix.service           loaded active running Postfix Mail Transport
Agent
rpcbind.service           loaded active running RPC bind service
rsyslog.service           loaded active running System Logging Service
sshd.service              loaded active running OpenSSH server daemon
systemd-journald.service  loaded active running Journal Service
systemd-logind.service    loaded active running Login Service
systemd-udevd.service     loaded active running udev Kernel Device
Manager
tuned.service             loaded active running Dynamic System Tuning
Daemon

LOAD   = Reflects whether the unit definition was properly loaded.
ACTIVE = The high-level unit activation state, i.e. generalization of
SUB.
SUB    = The low-level unit activation state, values depend on unit
type.

17 loaded units listed. Pass --all to see loaded but inactive units,
too.
To show all installed unit files use 'systemctl list-unit-files'.
```

 You can get rid of the helpful-but-noisy header and footer notes with the `--no-legend` option to `systemctl`.

How it works...

In this section, we're using the `systemctl` command to query systemd.

We'll get gradually more granular with our requests, until we've eventually built a query that shows us only what we want to see, that being services that are running right-this-second.

There's an argument to be made for using `pipes` and `grep` to accomplish what you want and, depending on your preference, you may find one of these two commands neater than the other, though they accomplish roughly the same thing:

```
$ systemctl --no-pager | grep service | grep running | column -t
```

In the previous, we're first printing the default "all" list from `systemctl`, then we're passing it through `grep` a couple of times to filter what we want, and finally we're displaying it in a mostly-readable fashion with a column.

```
$ systemctl list-units --type service --state running --no-legend
```

Here, we're using one command to get a slightly prettier output than the previous, and we're only using one command to do it.

There's more...

As with services that're loaded and running, you may be interested in services that have loaded, done whatever job they were intended for, and then exited:

```
$ systemctl list-units --type service --state exited
```

Or perhaps you're interested in services that have failed? Try the following:

```
$ systemctl list-units --type service --state failed
```

Lastly, systemd will use a pager by default to display results, which while human-friendly, isn't great for scripts. To simply print the output of your command to `stdout`, add `--no-pager` to your command.

See also

Typically, querying the init system is the best way to determine what services are running on a box, though if you're running something outside of init, such as a background task started by `cron`, you might have better look with `ps` or `top`, which we'll cover later.

Listing installed services

In this section, we're going to look at how to list services that are installed, but will never run on your host, generally because they're not enabled to do so.

Getting ready

Connect to your `centos1` VM.

```
$ vagrant ssh centos1
```

How to do it...

Run the following as your user:

```
$ systemctl list-unit-files --type service
```

By default, you'll be dropped into a typically long list of services. A lot of these will be listed as `static`, some will be `enabled`, and others will be `disabled`.

As far as systemd is concerned, this is a list of all services it knows about on your system.

How it works...

We are again querying systemd using `systemctl`, only this time instead of printing running services, we're getting everything that the init system is aware of.

Service files, and indeed all other types of unit file, generally exist in `/usr/lib/systemd/system`. From this location, files are symlinked into the `runlevel` directories at `/etc/systemd/system/`.

As seen in the following, we're going to `ls` this directory:

```
$ ls -la /etc/systemd/system
total 8
drwxr-xr-x. 13 root root 4096 May 12 2018 .
drwxr-xr-x. 4 root root 151 May 12 2018 ..
drwxr-xr-x. 2 root root 32 May 12 2018 basic.target.wants
lrwxrwxrwx. 1 root root 46 May 12 2018 dbus-
org.freedesktop.NetworkManager.service ->
/usr/lib/systemd/system/NetworkManager.service
lrwxrwxrwx. 1 root root 57 May 12 2018 dbus-org.freedesktop.nm-
dispatcher.service -> /usr/lib/systemd/system/NetworkManager-
dispatcher.service
lrwxrwxrwx. 1 root root 37 May 12 2018 default.target ->
/lib/systemd/system/multi-user.target
drwxr-xr-x. 2 root root 87 May 12 2018 default.target.wants
```

```
drwxr-xr-x. 2 root root 38 May 12 2018 dev-virtio\x2dports-
org.qemu.guest_agent.0.device.wants
drwxr-xr-x. 2 root root 32 May 12 2018 getty.target.wants
drwxr-xr-x. 2 root root 35 May 12 2018 local-fs.target.wants
drwxr-xr-x. 2 root root 4096 May 12 2018 multi-user.target.wants
drwxr-xr-x. 2 root root 48 May 12 2018 network-online.target.wants
drwxr-xr-x. 2 root root 31 May 12 2018 remote-fs.target.wants
drwxr-xr-x. 2 root root 51 May 12 2018 sockets.target.wants
drwxr-xr-x. 2 root root 217 May 12 2018 sysinit.target.wants
drwxr-xr-x. 2 root root 44 May 12 2018 system-update.target.wants
```

Note we have a few `targets`, which are basically the different runlevels of a system; most of the day-to-day services you'll interact with live in `multi-user.target.wants`, which are basically the services required for a multi-user session (the typical mode of operation).

Running `ls` again in this sub-directory reveals the symlinks mentioned earlier and their location on disk:

```
$ ls -la /etc/systemd/system/multi-user.target.wants/
total 8
drwxr-xr-x. 2 root root 4096 May 12 2018 .
drwxr-xr-x. 13 root root 4096 May 12 2018 ..
lrwxrwxrwx. 1 root root 38 May 12 2018 auditd.service ->
/usr/lib/systemd/system/auditd.service
lrwxrwxrwx. 1 root root 39 May 12 2018 chronyd.service ->
/usr/lib/systemd/system/chronyd.service
lrwxrwxrwx. 1 root root 37 May 12 2018 crond.service ->
/usr/lib/systemd/system/crond.service
lrwxrwxrwx. 1 root root 42 May 12 2018 irqbalance.service ->
/usr/lib/systemd/system/irqbalance.service
lrwxrwxrwx. 1 root root 46 May 12 2018 NetworkManager.service ->
/usr/lib/systemd/system/NetworkManager.service
lrwxrwxrwx. 1 root root 41 May 12 2018 nfs-client.target ->
/usr/lib/systemd/system/nfs-client.target
lrwxrwxrwx. 1 root root 39 May 12 2018 postfix.service ->
/usr/lib/systemd/system/postfix.service
lrwxrwxrwx. 1 root root 40 May 12 2018 remote-fs.target ->
/usr/lib/systemd/system/remote-fs.target
lrwxrwxrwx. 1 root root 46 May 12 2018 rhel-configure.service ->
...
```

These services are all `enabled` to start in a multi-user session.

There's more...

The concept of `enabled` and `disabled` is relatively easy to understand, those states being that the service will either try to run or it won't.

`static` is something different; this is the terminology used when a unit file exists, isn't enabled, but has no ability to become enabled, owing to a missing `[Install]` section of its unit file.

We can list these services with the following line:

```
$ systemctl --no-pager list-unit-files --type service --state static
```

Taking a service at random (`sshd-keygen`), we can have a look at its service file like so:

```
$ systemctl cat sshd-keygen.service
```

> Using systemctl's `cat` option is great, as it also shows you the location of the unit file in question.

We get the following:

```
# /usr/lib/systemd/system/sshd-keygen.service
[Unit]
Description=OpenSSH Server Key Generation
ConditionFileNotEmpty=|!/etc/ssh/ssh_host_rsa_key
ConditionFileNotEmpty=|!/etc/ssh/ssh_host_ecdsa_key
ConditionFileNotEmpty=|!/etc/ssh/ssh_host_ed25519_key
PartOf=sshd.service sshd.socket

[Service]
ExecStart=/usr/sbin/sshd-keygen
Type=oneshot
RemainAfterExit=yes
```

From this file, we can see it has a `PartOf` definition, suggesting it's run as part of the `sshd` service.

Taking a look at that service (again using systemctl `cat`) reveals the following:

```
# /usr/lib/systemd/system/sshd.service
[Unit]
Description=OpenSSH server daemon
```

```
Documentation=man:sshd(8) man:sshd_config(5)
After=network.target sshd-keygen.service
Wants=sshd-keygen.service

[Service]
Type=notify
EnvironmentFile=/etc/sysconfig/sshd
ExecStart=/usr/sbin/sshd -D $OPTIONS
ExecReload=/bin/kill -HUP $MAINPID
KillMode=process
Restart=on-failure
RestartSec=42s

[Install]
WantedBy=multi-user.target
```

We can see the `Wants` section here, suggesting `sshd-keygen` is run when `sshd` starts.

This explains why it doesn't have to be enabled on its own.

See also

As with most components on a Linux system, the `systemctl` command has a man page.

In this man page, you'll find a table titled `is-enabled output` where you can learn more about the different terminology printed with your status commands.

We have one service of the `indirect` state, which the table lists as having the following meaning:

> *"The unit file itself is not enabled, but it has a non-empty Also= setting in the [Install] unit file section, listing other unit files that might be enabled, or it has an alias under a different name through a symlink that is not specified in Also=. For template unit file, an instance different than the one specified in DefaultInstance= is enabled."*

Starting and stopping services

In this section, we're going to look at the trivial-but-important aspect of starting and stopping services.

Imagine a world without the ability to automatically start daemons when a box boots; you'd have to manually go in and start your services with every reboot, being careful to ensure you start your services in the appropriate way each time.

That world, like one dominated by the Stargate Replicators, isn't one in which I'd want to live.

How to do it...

We're going to use postfix in this example, as it's a service that won't be doing much of anything on our VM.

 postfix is a **Mail Transport Agent** (**MTA**) typically installed on CentOS boxes. Even if your box isn't handling email, processes might use it to email you warning about failures and things of that ilk.

Stopping our service

Run the following (using sudo):

```
$ sudo systemctl stop postfix
$
```

Note the distinct lack of output confirming or denying what you've typed has worked.

Starting our service

As with stopping our service, starting it again is trivial:

```
$ sudo systemctl start postfix
$
```

Note again the confusing silence.

 Silence upon command completion isn't unique to systemd, and it's actually something of a philosophy in the Unix and Unix-like world. If a command has done what it's supposed to, the user doesn't need to be told.

How it works...

When you instruct systemd to start or stop a unit, what you're actually doing is running the `ExecStart` or `ExecStop` portions of its unit file.

Taking `postfix` as our example, its unit file looks like this:

```
# /usr/lib/systemd/system/postfix.service
[Unit]
Description=Postfix Mail Transport Agent
After=syslog.target network.target
Conflicts=sendmail.service exim.service

[Service]
Type=forking
PIDFile=/var/spool/postfix/pid/master.pid
EnvironmentFile=-/etc/sysconfig/network
ExecStartPre=-/usr/libexec/postfix/aliasesdb
ExecStartPre=-/usr/libexec/postfix/chroot-update
ExecStart=/usr/sbin/postfix start
ExecReload=/usr/sbin/postfix reload
ExecStop=/usr/sbin/postfix stop

[Install]
WantedBy=multi-user.target
```

Here we can see that, when we issue a `systemctl start postfix` command, it's literally running the `postfix` binary with the `start` option. The opposite is true for `stop`.

We also have some `ExecStartPre` lines, which are commands executed before the main `ExecStart` command is run.

There's more...

Without `sudo`, you may be prompted to authenticate as `root`; in order that the command might be run as `root`, I typically see this dialogue when I forget to `sudo` first:

```
==== AUTHENTICATING FOR org.freedesktop.systemd1.manage-units ===
Authentication is required to manage system services or units.
Authenticating as: root
Password:
```

You can also confirm whether a service is started or stopped quickly with the `status` argument:

```
$ systemctl status postfix
● postfix.service - Postfix Mail Transport Agent
   Loaded: loaded (/usr/lib/systemd/system/postfix.service; enabled;
vendor preset: disabled)
   Active: inactive (dead) since Sun 2018-08-26 13:43:46 UTC; 2min 56s
ago
```

See also

For more on the `ExecStart` and `ExecStop` options of the unit file you're reading, check out the specific `systemd.service` man page on the subject.

There's also various other options that aren't `start` and `stop`, including `reload-or-try-restart` just to confuse matters. See the `systemctl` command for these options.

Changing which services start and stop at boot

In the CentOS world, installing a new service doesn't immediately start and enable it, though it does in the Debian world (a default that, again, has its advocates and disparagers).

In this example, we're going to enable a new service and reboot our VM, checking what happens when it comes up.

Getting ready

Connect to your `centos1` VM. Install `httpd` (Apache) for these examples:

```
$ sudo yum install -y httpd
```

How to do it...

First, let's see if we actually have a unit file for httpd:

```
$ systemctl cat httpd
# /usr/lib/systemd/system/httpd.service
[Unit]
Description=The Apache HTTP Server
After=network.target remote-fs.target nss-lookup.target
Documentation=man:httpd(8)
Documentation=man:apachectl(8)

[Service]
Type=notify
EnvironmentFile=/etc/sysconfig/httpd
ExecStart=/usr/sbin/httpd $OPTIONS -DFOREGROUND
ExecReload=/usr/sbin/httpd $OPTIONS -k graceful
ExecStop=/bin/kill -WINCH ${MAINPID}
# We want systemd to give httpd some time to finish gracefully, but
still want
# it to kill httpd after TimeoutStopSec if something went wrong during
the
# graceful stop. Normally, Systemd sends SIGTERM signal right after
the
# ExecStop, which would kill httpd. We are sending useless SIGCONT
here to give
# httpd time to finish.
KillSignal=SIGCONT
PrivateTmp=true

[Install]
WantedBy=multi-user.target
```

We have one, and now we need to see what state it's currently in:

```
$ systemctl status httpd
```

Our output lists the service as inactive and disabled.

Enabling our service

If we just want to start our service, we could run the command listed in the previous section, but this wouldn't enable the service at boot.

To enable our service, we run `enable`, surprisingly:

```
$ sudo systemctl enable httpd
Created symlink from /etc/systemd/system/multi-
user.target.wants/httpd.service to
/usr/lib/systemd/system/httpd.service.
```

Note that, for some reason, we do get output while enabling services.

Reboot your box and see whether `httpd` started on boot by using the `systemctl status` command.

Disabling our service

Now we've got `httpd` enabled, we're going to disable it again, because that's just the sort of people we are:

```
$ sudo systemctl disable httpd
Removed symlink /etc/systemd/system/multi-
user.target.wants/httpd.service.
```

How it works...

Seen in the output when we're disabling and enabling our services, what we're actually doing is creating a `symlink` from the default location of our `httpd` unit file, to the `multi-user.target.wants` directory, mentioned previously.

On boot, systemd will check this directory at the appropriate time and start the services it finds there.

There's more...

Starting and enabling services at the same time is perfectly possible and is definitely preferable to rebooting a box to change a service's state.

This can be done easily by inserting `--now` to our `enable` command:

```
$ systemctl enable --now httpd
```

Effectively, we've run the following on one line:

```
$ systemctl enable httpd
$ systemctl start httpd
```

See also

The systemd concept of `targets` is similar in nature to the old-school `runlevel` that you may or may not be familiar with. It's not a direct comparison, as systemd can activate multiple targets at the same time, whereas runlevels were singular. The `multi-user.target` is roughly equivalent to runlevels 2, 3, and 4.

See the `systemd.target` man page for more information.

Common services you might expect to see

In this section, we're going to run down a list of common services you might expect to see on a given box. This list won't be comprehensive, as what services are there by default can change, even between distribution releases.

How to do it...

List out the services on our system, even those that are static and disabled:

```
$ systemctl list-unit-files --type service
```

Scroll through the list, searching with / if you're using the default pager (less).

auditd.service

Starting at the top, we have `auditd.service`, "the Linux audit daemon". Used to write the audit records of your system, you'll find the fruit of its work in the `/var/log/audit/` directory.

chronyd.service

As discussed when we talked about time on our system, `chronyd` is responsible for keeping your system clock correct. I would expect to see this, or `ntpd`, running on most servers in the wild.

crond.service

Not to be confused with `chronyd`, `crond` is the daemon responsible for making sure that scheduled commands are run when they're supposed to be.

lvm2-*.service

The collection of `lvm2` service files are used to maintain and monitor **Logical Volume Manager (LVM)** setups. Most servers you'll come across will probably be using LVM for their filesystem and volume management needs.

NetworkManager.service

We've covered networks to death, but it's useful to know that the `NetworkManager.service` file is one of the annoying few with uppercase letters.

This fact has caught me out on more than one occasion.

nfs.service

Typically installed, the `nfs` suite of services are for management of **Network File System (NFS)** devices.

NFS is still in wide use and is very well maintained by distribution producers, meaning even if you don't use it, it'll probably be there.

postfix.service

A typical MTA, `postfix` is the default you'll see on Red Hat, CentOS, and Fedora systems. On others, it might be the Exim mail server. We'll be going over these briefly later.

rsyslog.service

Either `rsyslog` or `syslog-ng` will probably be installed on your server, at least for the foreseeable future. These are the system log daemons, responsible for writing logs to text files in `/var/log` (usually). They've got a competitor in `binary-log-loving journald`, which we'll come to later.

sshd.service

I should hope to see `sshd.service` running on any system I'm connected to, otherwise I have no idea what baffling method I've used to connect.

systemd-journald.service

The competitor to `syslog` mentioned previously, `journald` is the logging daemon managed by systemd, and which can be queried using an array of syntactical soup on the command line.

systemd-logind.service

Another from `systemd` Borg, `logind` manages user logins to the systems of which you're an administrator.

How it works...

These services, and any others you might be running on your machine, make up what is effectively the OS you're running.

If you're like me, you may find yourself playing around with this list in your spare time, trying to figure out which bits you can disable, and still have a functioning system at the end.

My advice would generally be to leave the defaults as they are, because you never know what random job is cleaning a temporary directory for you without you even realizing it.

Default services are frequently disabled as part of **hardening** tasks; if you ever find yourself having to harden a system, the usual rules apply. Look into what the current best practices are, and see if your vendor has a ready-made guide.

There's more...

We can use handy tools such as `systemd-analyze` to see how long our system took to boot:

```
$ systemd-analyze
Startup finished in 253ms (kernel) + 933ms (initrd) + 6.873s
(userspace) = 8.060s
```

8 seconds isn't bad, excluding the time it takes VirtualBox to initialize our VM and the time it takes the kernel to start (5 seconds on the Grub boot menu).

You can even run this command with `blame` tacked on the end, to see what process is taking your precious seconds from you:

```
$ systemd-analyze blame
  3.811s NetworkManager-wait-online.service
  806ms tuned.service
  680ms postfix.service
  490ms lvm2-monitor.service
  ...
```

See also

Check out other systems for what services they start by default. For example, Ubuntu on the desktop might not start `auditd`, but it will probably have `gdm` to ensure a Gnome login window when you boot your machine.

Understanding service unit files

We now have a good idea of where to find service unit files, as well as how to enable and disable services.

Previously, we touched on a couple of the entries within a unit file, though we haven't gone into much depth on these options or where to find more information and alternative entries you might want to use.

How to do it...

We're going to use sshd.service as an example here, not just because it's a service file you might see a lot, but because it has a good mixture of default entries.

cat our chosen service:

```
$ systemctl cat sshd.service
# /usr/lib/systemd/system/sshd.service
[Unit]
Description=OpenSSH server daemon
Documentation=man:sshd(8) man:sshd_config(5)
After=network.target sshd-keygen.service
Wants=sshd-keygen.service

[Service]
Type=notify
EnvironmentFile=/etc/sysconfig/sshd
ExecStart=/usr/sbin/sshd -D $OPTIONS
ExecReload=/bin/kill -HUP $MAINPID
KillMode=process
Restart=on-failure
RestartSec=42s

[Install]
WantedBy=multi-user.target
```

To understand this file, we have to break it down into its component parts.

Sort of the Main section of the unit file, [Unit] is the area for generic entries, not specific to the Service type:

```
[Unit]
```

For the description, we have a short and snappy entry that can be understood at a glance:

```
Description=OpenSSH server daemon
```

We also have a handy line, detailing the appropriate URI location to peruse if you get stuck. Here we have `man:` as the URI, but it could be `https://` or even `info:::`

> **Documentation=man:sshd(8) man:sshd_config(5)**

`info:` refers to information pages, like man pages, but more widely ridiculed. `After=` (and `Before=`) is a space-separated list of unit names, which stipulates the services that need to start after (or before) this one. Here the network needs to be started, and `ssh-keygen` needs to run prior to `sshd` starting:

> **After=network.target sshd-keygen.service**

We dissected `Wants=` earlier, but to flesh it out a bit, you'll commonly see `Wants=` in unit files, listing services which it would be nice to trigger, prior to this service starting:

> **Wants=sshd-keygen.service**

> `Wants=` is a less-mandated version of `Requires=`. If a `Wants=` service fails to start, the parent service will still give it a try, if a `Requires=` service fails, the parent doesn't either.

Specific to unit files of the `service` type, the `[Service]` block is specific to service options, perhaps obviously:

> **[Service]**

The process start up type, `notify` here means systemd expects the daemon to send a notification message once it's finished starting up. Only when this notification is received will systemd continue starting services that depend on this one:

> **Type=notify**

Used to point the service to the file that contains its environment variables, for `sshd` this contains one option on our box, `OPTIONS="-u0"`:

> **EnvironmentFile=/etc/sysconfig/sshd**

The crux of what's run when the service is started, `ExecStart` gives us the command that's run. Note also the `$OPTIONS` value, read from the file stipulated on the `EnvironmentFile` line:

> **ExecStart=/usr/sbin/sshd -D $OPTIONS**

This section tells systemd what should be run if the `systemctl reload` `sshd` command is run. Specifically, we're sending the `HUP` (hangup) signal to the `sshd` PID:

ExecReload=/bin/kill -HUP $MAINPID

This directive specifies how processes of the unit's own creation are to be killed. `process` here means only the main process itself is killed by systemd:

KillMode=process

> Here, `KillMode` is being used, but `ExecStop` isn't. This is because `ExecStop` is optional, and generally only used if the init daemon has a specific cleanup job to do.

Our `Restart` option tells systemd how the process is to be restarted. `on-failure` used here means `sshd` will be restarted on an unclean exit code, an unclean signal, a timeout, or if the watchdog timeout for a service is breached:

Restart=on-failure

`RestartSec` is the specified time to take before restarting the `sshd` service, following the `Restart=` criteria being met. I'd imagine it's `42` seconds here because the author of the unit file is a fan of Douglas Adams:

RestartSec=42s

Install is another generic section, such as `[Unit]`. This section holds the installation information for the unit file, meaning it's read by the enable and disable directives when run:

[Install]

The only directive here is that this service is `WantedBy` the multi-user target, meaning that, in multi-user mode, `sshd` will be started:

WantedBy=multi-user.target

How it works...

When a service file is interacted with by systemd, the section of the file it reads determines its actions.

If starting a service, `ExecStart` would be read—if stopping, `ExecStop`.

There's more...

Several options are available to the writer of a unit file and more are being added with every systemd release. There's a good chance that the operation you want to accomplish can be achieved with a unit file entry.

 Despite the overwhelming array of options available to unit file authors, you still get people who insist on writing a bash script to do everything, and simply referring to this in a four-line unit file. It's possible, but it's not neat.

See also

If you have a free afternoon, give the `systemd.service` and `systemd.unit` manual pages a read; they're both lengthy and a good sedative in lieu of sleeping tablets.

Customizing systemd unit files

In this section, we're going to look at ways we can modify systemd unit files.

There's an important note to make here, which is that, while you can absolutely modify configuration files as they're delivered, there's no guarantee that your changes will be persistent across updates of your system. Package managers might take offence to your mangling of their service files, and simply replace them without warning.

The correct way to modify the actions of systemd unit files is to write a whole other file with your changes included.

systemd's method for doing this is called a snippet.

How to do it...

systemd has a built-in way of generating the required override file we need.

Create the directory and file for the `sshd.service` unit using the following command:

```
$ sudo systemctl edit sshd.service
```

You will be placed in an empty file, but one that exists within a new directory, namely `/etc/systemd/system/sshd.service.d/override.conf`.

Copy the following into our empty file:

```
[Unit]
Description=OpenSSH server daemon slightly modified
Documentation=man:ssh-additional
Requires=sshd-keygen.service

[Service]
Environment=OPTIONS="-u0"
ExecStart=
ExecStart=/usr/sbin/sshd -4 -D $OPTIONS
RestartSec=10s
```

When we save and exit the file, an implicit `systemctl daemon-reload` is run, meaning that when we run a `systemctl restart sshd`, our new settings are enabled.

How it works...

We said our `edit` command created a new directory and file, in which override commands can be placed; you can now visit this by changing to it:

```
$ cd /etc/systemd/system/sshd.service.d/
$ ls
override.conf
```

Within our override file, our new entries are stored. These entries generally complement those in the primary configuration file.

Breaking our new configuration down, we have the following:

```
[Unit]
Description=OpenSSH server daemon slightly modified
Documentation=man:ssh-additional
Requires=sshd-keygen.service
```

Here we've added a short description of what the file is, showing it's slightly modified. There's a fake manual page entry, which we've suggested might be a good place for documentation when we get around to writing it. We also changed the service so that it now requires `sshd-keygen`, instead of just wanting it.

Now, we change the service section:

```
[Service]
EnvironmentFile=
Environment=OPTIONS="-u0"
ExecStart=
ExecStart=/usr/sbin/sshd -4 -D $OPTIONS
RestartSec=10s
```

Here we're adding our `Environment` directive, instead of using an `EnvironmentFile` (which we've blanked).

We're blanking `ExecStart` too, and passing in our own (which we've added `-4`) to.

And because we're boring, we've decided we want `sshd` to restart in 10 seconds, instead of `42`.

There's more...

It's not always obvious which values can be stacked atop one another, and which have to be blanked out first.

To test whether your configuration is being loaded correctly, use `systemctl show` `sshd` to read the running configuration of your service.

Within the output, I find the following line (`Documentation` can stack, so our new entry just gets added to the end.):

```
Documentation=man:sshd(8) man:sshd_config(5) man:ssh-additional
```

`Description` is overwritten, as you can only have one entry, so ours takes precedence:

```
Description=OpenSSH server daemon slightly modified
```

There's no `EnvironmentFile` option, and the only entry is our `Environment` line:

```
Environment=OPTIONS="-u0"
```

There's only one `ExecStart` line, and it's ours as we blanked the original:

```
ExecStart={ path=/usr/sbin/sshd ; argv[]=/usr/sbin/sshd -4 -D $OPTIONS
...
```

See also

There's another method to making your own unit file changes, but it's messier. Effectively, you write a complete unit file, changing the options you want, and you place your new file in /etc/systemd/system/ before re-enabling the service. The reason this works is because /etc/systemd/system/ has a higher precedence than /usr/lib/systemd/system/ though you've now burdened yourself with management of the whole service definition, instead of just the bits you want to change.

Testing running services

In this section, we're going to look at three ways we can see whether a service is actually running, once we've issued a `start` command.

We'll start with the built-in systemd way (`systemctl`) before moving to a generic way (`ps`) and finally a simple way (`telnet`).

Getting ready

Connect to your `centos1` VM. Install and start `httpd` if it's not already started.

We'll also install `telnet` for some basic port checking:

```
$ sudo yum install -y httpd telnet
$ sudo systemctl enable --now httpd
```

How to do it...

With systemd's built-in tool, we can check the status with the `status` option:

```
[vagrant@centos1 ~]$ systemctl status httpd
● httpd.service - The Apache HTTP Server
   Loaded: loaded (/usr/lib/systemd/system/httpd.service; enabled;
vendor preset: disabled)
   Active: active (running) since Sun 2018-08-26 16:15:50 UTC; 5min
ago
     Docs: man:httpd(8)
           man:apachectl(8)
 Main PID: 3578 (httpd)
   Status: "Total requests: 0; Current requests/sec: 0; Current
traffic:  0 B/sec"
   CGroup: /system.slice/httpd.service
           ├─3578 /usr/sbin/httpd -DFOREGROUND
           ├─3579 /usr/sbin/httpd -DFOREGROUND
           ├─3580 /usr/sbin/httpd -DFOREGROUND
           ├─3581 /usr/sbin/httpd -DFOREGROUND
           ├─3582 /usr/sbin/httpd -DFOREGROUND
           └─3583 /usr/sbin/httpd -DFOREGROUND
```

This is a good indication that things are fine, because systemd believes them to be. We can also use the `ps` tool to try and determine whether our process has started:

```
[vagrant@centos1 ~]$ ps aux | grep httpd
root      3578  0.0  1.0 224020  4996 ?        Ss   16:15   0:00
/usr/sbin/httpd -DFOREGROUND
apache    3579  0.0  0.5 224020  2948 ?        S    16:15   0:00
/usr/sbin/httpd -DFOREGROUND
apache    3580  0.0  0.5 224020  2948 ?        S    16:15   0:00
/usr/sbin/httpd -DFOREGROUND
apache    3581  0.0  0.5 224020  2948 ?        S    16:15   0:00
/usr/sbin/httpd -DFOREGROUND
apache    3582  0.0  0.5 224020  2948 ?        S    16:15   0:00
/usr/sbin/httpd -DFOREGROUND
apache    3583  0.0  0.5 224020  2948 ?        S    16:15   0:00
/usr/sbin/httpd -DFOREGROUND
```

Here I use the `aux` option, partly this is because I can reliably do the same thing on my BSD systems, and partly it's because the person I first watched use `ps` used those flags, so it stuck with me.

We can see `httpd` running with a few processes.

Alternatively, we could try connecting to the port locally with `telnet`:

```
[vagrant@centos1 ~]$ telnet 127.0.0.1 80
Trying 127.0.0.1...
Connected to 127.0.0.1.
Escape character is '^]'.
```

Though if your web server isn't running on localhost, or `80`, this test is somewhat pointless and will fail.

How it works...

We've covered three ways of checking whether a service is running. The first, and arguably most robust, is to see whether the init system believes the service is up.

Our `systemctl` command reported an active, running state and gave us a time that the service had started.

Next, we queried the system's process list to see whether we could find our server; this works well as it could be the case that a misconfigured service file starts your service, but isn't then aware of its state, hence believing it to be dead.

Lastly, we used `telnet` to try and connect to the port we thought the service might be running on; this is the least intelligent way to check whether a service is running locally, as it requires you to know specifics and `telnet` is rarely installed by default.

There's more...

To get information about open sockets on a system, you would use `ss`; see the earlier section on `ss` for details on what commands you might use to determine used ports.

Writing a basic unit file

In this section, we're going to put together a unit file of our own. We're also going to choose a location to save it and we're going to reboot our system to check if it works.

How to do it...

We're going to again use Python's built-in web server, starting an instance using a small unit file.

First, create the directory in which we're going to store our unit file:

```
$ sudo mkdir -p /usr/local/lib/systemd/system
```

Next, we're going to echo the following into a file called `pythonWebServer.service`:

```
$ sudo tee /usr/local/lib/systemd/system/pythonWebServer.service <<
HERE
[Unit]
Description=Python Web Server Example

[Service]
ExecStart=/usr/bin/python2.7 -m SimpleHTTPServer

[Install]
WantedBy=multi-user.target
HERE
```

 This unit file is for demonstration purposes only, and should **absolutely not** be used in production.

Now we can enable and start it:

```
$ sudo systemctl enable --now pythonWebServer
Created symlink from /etc/systemd/system/multi-
user.target.wants/pythonWebServer.service to
/usr/local/lib/systemd/system/pythonWebServer.service.
```

Check it's running with the `status` command:

```
$ systemctl status pythonWebServer.service
● pythonWebServer.service - Python Web Server Example
   Loaded: loaded
(/usr/local/lib/systemd/system/pythonWebServer.service; enabled;
vendor preset: disabled)
   Active: active (running) since Sun 2018-08-26 16:43:55 UTC; 1s ago
 Main PID: 3746 (python2.7)
   CGroup: /system.slice/pythonWebServer.service
           └─3746 /usr/bin/python2.7 -m SimpleHTTPServer
```

How it works...

All we've done here is create a local unit file for systemd to read and load.

In order to understand our path choice, try running the following on your system, and see what's returned:

```
$ systemctl --no-pager show --property=UnitPath
```

One of the options should be `/usr/local/lib/systemd/system`, which doesn't exist at first, but does when we create it.

It's a good idea to use a path like this because, not only is there a good chance it's empty, meaning you can logically separate your unit files from others, it's also uncluttered (unlike the `/etc/systemd/system/` directory).

We then placed a small example unit file in this directory, featuring the bare minimum to make a functioning service file.

Once written, it's a simple case of enabling and starting our service.

There's more...

There're a couple of problems with what we've done here.

The first is that we've created a very static service file, which we can only change by manipulating it directly. The second issue is that we've made a web server that, by default, will list the contents of the root of our server, which I highly doubt you want:

```
$ curl localhost:8000
<!DOCTYPE html PUBLIC "-//W3C//DTD HTML 3.2 Final//EN"><html>
<title>Directory listing for /</title>
<body>
<h2>Directory listing for /</h2>
<hr>
<ul>
<li><a href="bin/">bin@</a>
<li><a href="boot/">boot/</a>
<li><a href="dev/">dev/</a>
<li><a href="etc/">etc/</a>
<li><a href="home/">home/</a>
<li><a href="lib/">lib@</a>
<li><a href="lib64/">lib64@</a>
<li><a href="media/">media/</a>
<li><a href="mnt/">mnt/</a>
```

```
<li><a href="opt/">opt/</a>
<li><a href="proc/">proc/</a>
<li><a href="root/">root/</a>
<li><a href="run/">run/</a>
<li><a href="sbin/">sbin@</a>
<li><a href="srv/">srv/</a>
<li><a href="sys/">sys/</a>
<li><a href="tmp/">tmp/</a>
<li><a href="usr/">usr/</a>
<li><a href="vagrant/">vagrant/</a>
<li><a href="var/">var/</a>
</ul>
<hr>
</body>
</html>
```

Let's address both of these issues, using what we've learned so far.

Open your new systemd unit file for editing, in your editor of choice, and populate it with a few more options:

```
[Unit]
Description=Python Web Server Example
Documentation=man:python(1)
ConditionFileNotEmpty=/var/www/html/index.html
After=network.target

[Service]
Type=simple
EnvironmentFile=/etc/sysconfig/pythonWebServer
ExecStart=/usr/bin/python2.7 -m SimpleHTTPServer $PORT
Restart=always
WorkingDirectory=/var/www/html/

[Install]
WantedBy=multi-user.target
```

Note some we've used previously, and some new ones such as `WorkingDIrectory=`.

Next, populate `/var/www/html/index.html`:

```
$ sudo tee /var/www/html/index.html << HERE
This is a python web server.
Running at the behest of systemd.
Isn't that neat?
HERE
```

And add an entry to our environment file:

```
$ sudo tee /etc/sysconfig/pythonWebServer <<HERE
PORT="8000"
HERE
```

Reload systemd's configuration:

```
$ sudo systemctl daemon-reload
```

And test with `curl`:

```
$ curl localhost:8000
This is a python web server.
Running at the behest of systemd.
Isn't that neat?
```

See also

There are so many different configuration options for systemd unit files; we've not really scratched the surface here, and it could absolutely constitute a book in itself.

Read the relevant man pages, have a go at writing your own unit files, and report back with your findings, you brave explorer.

Working with systemd timers (and cron)

The new kids on the block, and another component that systemd brought into its gargantuan self, are systemd timers. Timers are another type of unit, only one that acts as the instruction for when another unit is to trigger.

In the old world, you'd control periodic events on a system with `cron`, and this is still widely used, but increasingly systemd timers are stealing that mantle away.

 I say *new* but new is relative. Basically something can be in systemd for years before it finally trickles into Debian or CentOS. If you want the latest and greatest, run something like Fedora on a laptop.

In this section, we're going to look at existing `cron` and timer entries on our system, before converting our Python server into a timer-triggered service.

How to do it...

First, we're going to list existing periodic jobs on the system.

systemd timers

Starting with systemd timers, we're going to list what exists on our box by default:

```
$ systemctl --no-pager list-timers --all
NEXT                            LEFT      LAST
PASSED     UNIT                           ACTIVATES
Mon 2018-08-27 17:39:37 UTC  23h left  Sun 2018-08-26 17:39:37 UTC
52min ago systemd-tmpfiles-clean.timer systemd-tmpfiles-clean.service
n/a                            n/a       n/a                          n/a
systemd-readahead-done.timer systemd-readahead-done.service

2 timers listed.
```

Within this output, we can see two timers. The first is `systemd-tmpfiles-clean.timer` and its action is to trigger `systemd-tmpfiles-clean.service`.

Running `systemctl cat` against this file shows us its timer configuration:

```
# /usr/lib/systemd/system/systemd-tmpfiles-clean.timer
#  This file is part of systemd.
#
#  systemd is free software; you can redistribute it and/or modify it
#  under the terms of the GNU Lesser General Public License as published by
#  the Free Software Foundation; either version 2.1 of the License, or
#  (at your option) any later version.

[Unit]
Description=Daily Cleanup of Temporary Directories
Documentation=man:tmpfiles.d(5) man:systemd-tmpfiles(8)

[Timer]
OnBootSec=15min
OnUnitActiveSec=1d
```

Looking at the service file reveals what's actually run:

```
# /usr/lib/systemd/system/systemd-tmpfiles-clean.service
#  This file is part of systemd.
#
#  systemd is free software; you can redistribute it and/or modify it
```

```
#  under the terms of the GNU Lesser General Public License as
published by
#  the Free Software Foundation; either version 2.1 of the License, or
#  (at your option) any later version.

[Unit]
Description=Cleanup of Temporary Directories
Documentation=man:tmpfiles.d(5) man:systemd-tmpfiles(8)
DefaultDependencies=no
Conflicts=shutdown.target
After=systemd-readahead-collect.service systemd-readahead-
replay.service local-fs.target time-sync.target
Before=shutdown.target

[Service]
Type=oneshot
ExecStart=/usr/bin/systemd-tmpfiles --clean
IOSchedulingClass=idle
```

Note that it's a `oneshot` service, meaning it's expected to exit after running.

From the previous information, we can tell when our timer has last run and when it's next due to.

 The second timer we can see, `systemd-readahead-done.timer` and its companion service file, aren't active. This is denoted by the `n/a` details in the various time fields. This service is used in non-virtualized systems to log disk boot patterns, attempting to speed up subsequent boots.

This makes timers much easier to read and work out when they last ran, compared to `cron`.

cron

I'm not aware of an easy way to list information from `cron`; if you know of one, please write to me and blow my mind.

`cron`, as we said previously, is a daemon for executing commands on a schedule. It's still in wide use and there's many systems out there with a hybrid systemd timers/`cron` setup.

By default, `cron` features the following directories in `/etc/`:

```
cron.d/        cron.daily/   cron.hourly/  cron.monthly/ cron.weekly/
```

Within `cron.d`, we can see a single file named `0hourly`, the contents of which are copied in the following:

```
cat 0hourly
# Run the hourly jobs
SHELL=/bin/bash
PATH=/sbin:/bin:/usr/sbin:/usr/bin
MAILTO=root
01 * * * * root run-parts /etc/cron.hourly
```

And within the `/etc/cron.hourly` directory, we have only `0anacron`:

```
#!/bin/sh
# Check whether 0anacron was run today already
if test -r /var/spool/anacron/cron.daily; then
    day=`cat /var/spool/anacron/cron.daily`
fi
if [ `date +%Y%m%d` = "$day" ]; then
    exit 0;
fi

# Do not run jobs when on battery power
if test -x /usr/bin/on_ac_power; then
    /usr/bin/on_ac_power >/dev/null 2>&1
    if test $? -eq 1; then
    exit 0
    fi
fi
/usr/sbin/anacron -s
```

Readable, this is not.

At a glance, it's awkward and fiddly to work out what jobs are running periodically through `cron`, and you'll always get that one bodge-job that someone's written, without any logging, that they forget about.

Chances are good you'll have `cron` screw you over at one point in your life, at least until it goes away forever, so if you ever get unexpected behavior on your system, stop and have a quick look through the `cron` directories for some indication of foul play.

You can get the specific `cron` logs from `journalctl` easily enough:

```
$ sudo journalctl -u crond
-- Logs begin at Sun 2018-08-26 17:24:36 UTC, end at Sun 2018-08-26
19:18:33 UTC
Aug 26 17:24:39 centos1 systemd[1]: Started Command Scheduler.
Aug 26 17:24:39 centos1 systemd[1]: Starting Command Scheduler...
Aug 26 17:24:39 centos1 crond[579]: (CRON) INFO (RANDOM_DELAY will be
scaled wit
Aug 26 17:24:40 centos1 crond[579]: (CRON) INFO (running with inotify
support)
```

How it works...

systemd timers are great; they also work very well, primarily because they're inherently tied to the init and unit system that they're managing the time triggers for.

In a perfect world, I'd love to see all of the `cron` entries featured in CentOS and Debian completely removed within their next release. The truth of the matter is `cron` will probably be around for a long time, and systems such as FreeBSD will use it long after the heat-death of the universe.

When we list timers, we're checking what systemd is aware of in terms of units it has to trigger.

When we're sifting through `cron` logs and subdirectories, we're banging our heads against a metaphorical desk in a vain effort to find that vague one-liner that's constantly touching the file we're trying to delete.

There's more...

We're going to write our own timer unit, using the Python unit file from the last example.

I would recommend starting by disabling the service if you've still got it running or destroying the VM and writing it again, referring to the last section if necessary.

Let's start by adjusting our `pythonWebServer.service` file so that it looks like the following:

```
[Unit]
Description=Python Web Server Example
Documentation=man:python(1)
```

```
ConditionFileNotEmpty=/var/www/html/index.html

[Service]
Type=simple
EnvironmentFile=/etc/sysconfig/pythonWebServer
ExecStart=/usr/bin/python2.7 -m SimpleHTTPServer $PORT
WorkingDirectory=/var/www/html/
```

Specifically, we've removed a few lines. Note the complete removal of the [Install] section, as it's not needed when the timer is controlling the startup.

 In the real world, this wouldn't be something permanent such as a web server, it would usually be something small, such as a script to open a web page on a wallboard somewhere or send a request to the coffee machine to make you a latte.

Next, we're going to write a timer file, putting it in the exact same place as our service file:

```
$ sudo tee /usr/local/lib/systemd/system/pythonWebServer.timer << HERE
[Unit]
Description=Start python web server after a pause

[Timer]
OnBootSec=20s

[Install]
WantedBy=timers.target
HERE
```

Afterwards, we're going to reload systemd and enable the timer, but not the service:

```
$ sudo systemctl daemon-reload
$ sudo systemctl enable pythonWebServer.timer
Created symlink from
/etc/systemd/system/timers.target.wants/pythonWebServer.timer to
/usr/local/lib/systemd/system/pythonWebServer.timer.
```

Note the creation of symlink.

Let's reboot our box and see what happens. If you're quick, and you manage to run systemctl list-timers before your ten seconds are up, you might see something like the following:

```
$ systemctl --no-pager list-timers
NEXT                         LEFT        LAST PASSED UNIT
ACTIVATES
```

```
Sun 2018-08-26 19:43:48 UTC  9s left    n/a  n/a
pythonWebServer.timer        pythonWebServer.service
Sun 2018-08-26 19:58:28 UTC  14min left n/a  n/a    systemd-tmpfiles-
clean.timer systemd-tmpfiles-clean.service

2 timers listed.
Pass --all to see loaded but inactive timers, too.
```

Running it again will show that the job has passed:

```
$ systemctl --no-pager list-timers
NEXT                        LEFT       LAST
PASSED UNIT                            ACTIVATES
Sun 2018-08-26 19:43:48 UTC  10s ago    Sun 2018-08-26 19:43:56 UTC
3s ago pythonWebServer.timer           pythonWebServer.service
Sun 2018-08-26 19:58:28 UTC  14min left n/a
n/a     systemd-tmpfiles-clean.timer systemd-tmpfiles-clean.service

2 timers listed.
Pass --all to see loaded but inactive timers, too.
```

A quick `curl` will confirm our service is up:

```
$ curl localhost:8000
This is a python web server.
Running at the behest of systemd.
Isn't that neat?
```

See also

You can check the status of a systemd timer in the same way as any other unit.

Seen in the following is the output and command used to check the status of our `pythonWebServer.timer`:

```
$ systemctl status pythonWebServer.timer
● pythonWebServer.timer - Start python web server after a pause
   Loaded: loaded
(/usr/local/lib/systemd/system/pythonWebServer.timer; enabled; vendor
preset: disabled)
   Active: active (running) since Sun 2018-08-26 19:43:30 UTC; 56s ago
```

Other init systems

systemd might be the dominant init system in the Linux world, but there are others that you'll still come across. At the time of writing, CentOS 6 is very much alive and kicking, with its upstart core.

That's without going into the nitty-gritty of what the BSDs use and macOS to boot (which I actually quite like).

 I have seen some absolutely ancient Debian installations in my time, some of which went out of support half a decade or longer ago. I once worked out that a box I was SSH'd into, could legally drive.

Getting ready

Connect to both of your other VMs:

```
$ vagrant ssh centos6
$ vagrant ssh debian7
```

How to do it…

We have two systems at play; CentOS 6 uses Upstart, and Debian 7 uses SysV init.

CentOS 6 and Upstart

In the old world, `systemctl` won't work:

```
$ systemctl
-bash: systemctl: command not found
```

What's also slightly annoying is that there's no `upstart` command.

Instead, `Upstart` is skinned to look like a typical `init` system. The main page even lists it as such:

> *"init: Upstart process management daemon"*

Instead of `systemctl`, we use `service --status-all`:

```
$ service --status-all
```

This gives you output similar to the following:

```
smartd is stopped
openssh-daemon (pid  1526) is running...
tuned (pid  1705) is running...
```

Confusingly, the service name might not be what you see. Take `sshd` as an example. The previous command might lead you to believe that the daemon on this system is called `openssh-daemon`, but that's incorrect; it's really `sshd` again:

```
$ sudo service openssh-daemon
openssh-daemon: unrecognized service
$ sudo service sshd status
openssh-daemon (pid  1526) is running...
```

Confused? I was the first time I saw this.

The other way to interact with services is to call them directly (as they're just a script really):

```
$ sudo /etc/init.d/sshd status
openssh-daemon (pid  4725) is running...
```

Starting and stopping is very similar, but one thing that will catch you out is that traditional `init` systems put the control command at the end of the line (unlike systemd):

```
$ sudo service sshd stop
Stopping sshd:                                          [  OK  ]
$ sudo service sshd start
Starting sshd:                                          [  OK  ]
```

Note the `stop` and `start` tacked on the end.

Disabling and enabling services is different too; on old CentOS systems, `chkconfig` was your best friend:

```
$ chkconfig --list sshd
sshd              0:off   1:off   2:on    3:on    4:on    5:on
6:off
```

Note the concept of runlevels still existing, and that `sshd` starts in 2, 3, and 4.

We can disable this service with another `chkconfig` command:

```
$ sudo chkconfig sshd off
$  chkconfig --list sshd
```

```
sshd                0:off    1:off    2:off    3:off    4:off    5:off
6:off
```

And we enable it using `on`:

```
$ sudo chkconfig sshd on
$ chkconfig --list sshd
sshd                0:off    1:off    2:on    3:on    4:on    5:on
6:off
```

Because we're working with runlevels, you can head to the `rc*.d` directories. Specifically, we're going to drop into `rc3.d` for runlevel 3:

```
$ pwd
/etc/rc3.d
$ runlevel
N 3
```

Within this directory, we're again dealing with symlinks. You'll find a list of all jobs run at entry to runlevel 3.

One will be `sshd` (assuming you've not disabled it in the last step):

```
$ ls -l | grep ssh
lrwxrwxrwx. 1 root root 14 Aug 26 20:13 S55sshd -> ../init.d/sshd
```

Debian 7 and SysV init

Unlike CentOS 6, Debian 7 uses an older `init` system, its manual page lists it like so:

"init, telinit: process control initialization"

Again, we're dealing with PID 1 on the system—that much hasn't changed, only now processes are primarily controlled by the `/etc/inittab` file.

Runlevels are again a major player, though we use a different command to discover where we are (as a regular user, `root` still has access to the `runlevel` command, if you want to use it):

```
$ who -r
         run-level 2  2018-08-26 19:54                    last=S
```

As with `upstart`, the actual destination of our service files is the `/etc/init.d/` directory:

```
$ ls | grep ssh
ssh
```

This means that, like `Upstart`, we can manually interact with our service scripts:

```
$ /etc/init.d/ssh status
[ ok ] sshd is running.
```

The tool we used previously (`chkconfig`) can be installed on Debian 7, but by default we use a tool called `update-rc.d` to control starting and stopping services at boot:

```
$ sudo update-rc.d ssh disable
update-rc.d: using dependency based boot sequencing
```

If you really want to use `chkconfig`, I won't shout at you:

```
vagrant@wheezy:~$ sudo chkconfig ssh off
vagrant@wheezy:~$ sudo chkconfig ssh
ssh   off
vagrant@wheezy:~$ sudo chkconfig ssh on
vagrant@wheezy:~$ sudo chkconfig ssh
ssh   on
```

How it works...

Both `Upstart` and traditional `init` systems rely on the `/etc/init.d/` directory and then the various `rc` directories to instruct them what to start at which runlevel:

```
rc0.d/ rc1.d/ rc2.d/ rc3.d/ rc4.d/ rc5.d/ rc6.d/ rcS.d/
```

Looking at Debian's `inittab` we can see the default `runlevel` as configured:

```
# The default runlevel.
id:2:initdefault:
```

So, we know we'll likely end up at runlevel 2, meaning we can check the services that start at that runlevel.

The same can be said for `Upstart`, and on our CentOS system, we can see the default is set to 3:

```
id:3:initdefault:
```

Though it must be said, this is literally the only function that `inittab` serves on Upstart systems.

There's more...

Honestly, there's a lot more to `Upstart`, and more to traditional `init` systems too, but I would suggest that if you're going to be working with Linux and modern systems, you should make learning systemd a priority.

If you're working on BSD systems, read up on their own `init` systems and how they differ.

If you're working with old servers that you're unlikely to be allowed to turn off any time soon, I'm sorry.

See also

There's good documentation on `Upstart` at `http://upstart.ubuntu.com/cookbook/`.

There're also good accounts, if you can find them from the corners of the internet, detailing the events of the Debian Technical Committee vote on their new `init` system.

Round-up – services and daemons

This section turned out a lot longer than I'd expected it to, but at the same time, I'm glad that Ubuntu, CentOS, Red Hat, and Debian now share a single `init` system.

Had I been writing this book four years ago, I might well have given up at the start of this section and gone climbing instead.

That said, it's over, and I hope you learned something about how systemd works in the last few pages.

One last thing to note is that, despite systemd being in all the big players now, it still has its critics, and you'll definitely come across the odd grumpy sysadmin who can't let go of his bash-script driven systems. My advice in these cases is to smile and nod; it's not worth it to get too involved—that or suggest they might like to give FreeBSD a go instead?

I have mixed memories of SysV and Upstart systems, most of them revolving around hacking default bash scripts just to get dependencies working correctly with each other. I do get slightly nostalgic when I log on to a system, discover it's running Fedora Core 3, and I'm forced to remember everything I thought I'd forgotten about SysV init.

systemd is here to stay, and I personally can't wait to see what it sucks into its heaving mass next.

People might draw the line at `systemd-kerneld` though.

Hardware and Disks **5**

The following topics will be covered in this chapter:

- Determining hardware
- Testing hardware
- The role of the kernel
- Disk configuration on Linux
- The filesystem hierarchy
- Configuring a blank disk and mounting it
- Re-configuring a disk using LVM
- Using `systemd-mount` and `fstab`
- Disk encryption and working with encryption at rest
- Current filesystem formats
- Upcoming filesystem formats

Introduction

Your hardware doesn't care for you, like you might care for it.

Hardware is fickle, temperamental, unpredictable, and moody; disks, the rebellious teenager of the hardware family, take this to the next level.

You will find yourself confused at some point in your career, baffled as to why seemingly unrelated errors are occurring in disparate parts of your system. Your SSH daemon might be randomly dying at odd points in a transfer, NTP might be drifting, your database might be locking up, and all the while you're tearing your hair out trying to find the cause.

Hardware is usually the answer to these random issues (when it's not time, as we discussed previously). A bad stick of memory can fail in weird and wonderful ways, while a disk occasionally going read-only can mean sporadic and nighttime-disrupting events that can be tempting to resolve with a particularly heavy hammer.

> If you don't want to use the phrase "hit it with a hammer" in front of your boss, the accepted nomenclature is "percussive maintenance."

When hardware goes bad, there's no recourse other than to replace it. Gone are the days when we'd solder and fix components ourselves, as it's simply not a viable solution, nor is it cost-effective.

At some point, you'll discover yourself crouched over an open server in a data center, scratching your head at the rows of DIMMs and a RAID10 array of disks, trying to determine which one is faulty so that you can swap it out and place the old one in a grinder, for your own peace of mind.

> We spell storage disks such as hard drives with a k, and optical-type discs with a c.

In this chapter, we'll look at ways of identifying specific hardware, as well as some simple troubleshooting steps for finding bad memory. Coupled with this, we'll work through adding new disks to systems and how you might configure them once installed.

Technical requirements

For this chapter, we're going to use the following Vagrantfile, featuring two additional disks:

```ruby
# -*- mode: ruby -*-
# vi: set ft=ruby :

Vagrant.configure("2") do |config|

  config.vm.define "centos1" do |centos1|
    centos1.vm.box = "centos/7"
    centos1.vm.box_version = "1804.02"
    centos1.vm.provider "virtualbox" do |vbcustom|
```

```
    unless File.exist?('centos1.additional.vdi')
      vbcustom.customize ['createhd', '--filename',
'centos1.additional.vdi', '--size', 2 * 1024]
    end
    vbcustom.customize ['storageattach', :id, '--storagectl', 'IDE',
'--port', 0, '--device', 1, '--type', 'hdd', '--medium',
'centos1.additional.vdi']

    unless File.exist?('centos1.additional2.vdi')
      vbcustom.customize ['createhd', '--filename',
'centos1.additional2.vdi', '--size', 2 * 1024]
    end
    vbcustom.customize ['storageattach', :id, '--storagectl', 'IDE',
'--port', 1, '--device', 1, '--type', 'hdd', '--medium',
'centos1.additional2.vdi']

    end
  end

end
```

 The extra disks defined here will be created in the local directory you're running Vagrant from, make sure you have enough space.

Determining hardware

In the first chapter, we used `dmidecode` and other tooling to work out if we were in a VM or not; here, we're going to go a bit further and try to determine what hardware we might be running in a system, from the disk IDs to the type of graphics card in use.

Getting ready

Connect to your Vagrant VM and install some of the extra tools we're going to use:

```
$ vagrant ssh
$ sudo yum install -y pciutils usbutils
```

How to do it...

We're going to pick through a few different methods for determining the hardware a system is running; even if you don't have access to the internet, you should be able to determine some basic information using default tools.

lspci

The tool we installed from the `pciutils` suite, `lspci`, is a good way to list your collective PCI devices, without a lot of extra noise.

If we just run `lspci`, we get a list of devices and their IDs:

```
00:00.0 Host bridge: Intel Corporation 440FX - 82441FX PMC [Natoma]
(rev 02)
00:01.0 ISA bridge: Intel Corporation 82371SB PIIX3 ISA [Natoma/Triton
II]
00:01.1 IDE interface: Intel Corporation 82371AB/EB/MB PIIX4 IDE (rev
01)
00:02.0 VGA compatible controller: InnoTek Systemberatung GmbH
VirtualBox Graphics Adapter
00:03.0 Ethernet controller: Intel Corporation 82540EM Gigabit
Ethernet Controller (rev 02)
00:04.0 System peripheral: InnoTek Systemberatung GmbH VirtualBox
Guest Service
00:05.0 Multimedia audio controller: Intel Corporation 82801AA AC'97
Audio Controller (rev 01)
00:07.0 Bridge: Intel Corporation 82371AB/EB/MB PIIX4 ACPI (rev 08)
```

What we can see in the previous list are the devices in our system. They've actually had their numeric IDs translated into a human-readable format.

If you want to list the IDs alone, you can use the `-n` flag:

```
$ lspci -n
00:00.0 0600: 8086:1237 (rev 02)
00:01.0 0601: 8086:7000
00:01.1 0101: 8086:7111 (rev 01)
00:02.0 0300: 80ee:beef
00:03.0 0200: 8086:100e (rev 02)
00:04.0 0880: 80ee:cafe
00:05.0 0401: 8086:2415 (rev 01)
00:07.0 0680: 8086:7113 (rev 08)
```

Or if you want both, use -nn:

```
$ lspci -nn
00:00.0 Host bridge [0600]: Intel Corporation 440FX - 82441FX PMC
[Natoma] [8086:1237] (rev 02)
00:01.0 ISA bridge [0601]: Intel Corporation 82371SB PIIX3 ISA
[Natoma/Triton II] [8086:7000]
00:01.1 IDE interface [0101]: Intel Corporation 82371AB/EB/MB PIIX4
IDE [8086:7111] (rev 01)
00:02.0 VGA compatible controller [0300]: InnoTek Systemberatung GmbH
VirtualBox Graphics Adapter [80ee:beef]
00:03.0 Ethernet controller [0200]: Intel Corporation 82540EM Gigabit
Ethernet Controller [8086:100e] (rev 02)
00:04.0 System peripheral [0880]: InnoTek Systemberatung GmbH
VirtualBox Guest Service [80ee:cafe]
00:05.0 Multimedia audio controller [0401]: Intel Corporation 82801AA
AC'97 Audio Controller [8086:2415] (rev 01)
00:07.0 Bridge [0680]: Intel Corporation 82371AB/EB/MB PIIX4 ACPI
[8086:7113] (rev 08)
```

In this list, we can see a few friendly descriptions to help us—things such as `Ethernet controller`, `VGA compatible controller`, and `IDE interface`, to name a few.

At a glance, you should get a good understanding of which device does what, thanks to the hard work of the people who keep the `PCI ID` repository up to date: `http://pci-ids.ucw.cz/`.

Even better than listing the devices in our system, we can also list the kernel drive that's handling the device with -k.

In the following snippet, we can see that the Ethernet controller is being managed by the kernel driver, `e1000`:

```
$ lspci -k
00:00.0 Host bridge: Intel Corporation 440FX - 82441FX PMC [Natoma]
(rev 02)
00:01.0 ISA bridge: Intel Corporation 82371SB PIIX3 ISA [Natoma/Triton
II]
00:01.1 IDE interface: Intel Corporation 82371AB/EB/MB PIIX4 IDE (rev
01)
     Kernel driver in use: ata_piix
     Kernel modules: ata_piix, pata_acpi, ata_generic
00:02.0 VGA compatible controller: InnoTek Systemberatung GmbH
VirtualBox Graphics Adapter
00:03.0 Ethernet controller: Intel Corporation 82540EM Gigabit
Ethernet Controller (rev 02)
```

```
        Subsystem: Intel Corporation PRO/1000 MT Desktop Adapter
        Kernel driver in use: e1000
        Kernel modules: e1000
00:04.0 System peripheral: InnoTek Systemberatung GmbH VirtualBox
Guest Service
00:05.0 Multimedia audio controller: Intel Corporation 82801AA AC'97
Audio Controller (rev 01)
        Subsystem: Intel Corporation Device 0000
        Kernel driver in use: snd_intel8x0
        Kernel modules: snd_intel8x0
00:07.0 Bridge: Intel Corporation 82371AB/EB/MB PIIX4 ACPI (rev 08)
        Kernel driver in use: piix4_smbus
        Kernel modules: i2c_piix4
```

The name of the kernel driver and the actual hardware won't always be obvious, which is what makes tools such as lspci so handy.

In modern machines, you might see more than one PCI bus, with devices connected to it; it just so happens that our VM only utilizes one bus for all of its devices.

This means that the tree view is very flat:

```
$ lspci -t
-[0000:00]-+-00.0
           +-01.0
           +-01.1
           +-02.0
           +-03.0
           +-04.0
           +-05.0
           \-07.0
```

However, when we run lspci against a physical machine (in this case, my laptop), the tree view can have more branches:

```
$ lspci -t
-[0000:00]-+-00.0
           +-02.0
           +-04.0
           +-14.0
           +-14.2
           +-15.0
           +-15.1
           +-16.0
           +-1c.0-[01-39]----00.0-[02-39]--+-00.0-[03]--
```

```
|                                      +-01.0-[04-38]--
|                                      \-02.0-[39]----00.0
+-1c.4-[3a]----00.0
+-1c.5-[3b]----00.0
+-1d.0-[3c]----00.0
+-1f.0
+-1f.2
+-1f.3
\-1f.4
```

If you can't see a device you know to be there (a graphics card say), it could be a few things: maybe the device is disabled in the BIOS or the card itself is dead. Try some basic troubleshooting such as checking the BIOS/UEFI configuration or flipping the card to a different slot.

There's also `lsusb` for USB devices. This can be handy if you're using something like a USB Ethernet device. In the following example, you can see that the box I'm connected to (a Raspberry Pi) has its network port on the USB bus:

```
$ lsusb
Bus 001 Device 003: ID 0424:ec00 Standard Microsystems Corp.
SMSC9512/9514 Fast Ethernet Adapter
```

lshw

A particularly useful program, `lshw` has the built-in ability to output your hardware tree as JSON, XML, HTML, and presumably more as they're developed.

By default, the output of `lshw` is very verbose, but should look something like the following:

```
$ sudo lshw
localhost.localdomain
    description: Computer
    product: VirtualBox
    vendor: innotek GmbH
    version: 1.2
    serial: 0
    width: 64 bits
    capabilities: smbios-2.5 dmi-2.5 vsyscall32
<SNIP>
      *-pnp00:00
            product: PnP device PNP0303
            physical id: 3
            capabilities: pnp
```

```
            configuration: driver=i8042 kbd
    *-pnp00:01
            product: PnP device PNP0f03
            physical id: 4
            capabilities: pnp
            configuration: driver=i8042 aux
```

I tend to find that at-a-glance solutions can work better a lot of the time. So, with that in mind, let's take a look at the -short option's output:

```
$ sudo lshw -short
H/W path              Device     Class        Description
==========================================================
                                 system       VirtualBox
/0                               bus          VirtualBox
/0/0                             memory       128KiB BIOS
/0/1                             memory       512MiB System memory
/0/2                             processor    Intel(R) Core(TM) i7-7500U
CPU @ 2.70GHz
/0/100                           bridge       440FX - 82441FX PMC
[Natoma]
/0/100/1                         bridge       82371SB PIIX3 ISA
[Natoma/Triton II]
/0/100/1.1            scsi0      storage      82371AB/EB/MB PIIX4 IDE
/0/100/1.1/0.0.0     /dev/sda   disk         42GB VBOX HARDDISK
/0/100/1.1/0.0.0/1   /dev/sda1  volume       1MiB Linux filesystem
partition
/0/100/1.1/0.0.0/2              volume       1GiB Linux filesystem
partition
/0/100/1.1/0.0.0/3   /dev/sda3  volume       38GiB Linux LVM Physical
Volume partition
/0/100/1.1/0          /dev/sdb   disk         2147MB VBOX HARDDISK
/0/100/1.1/1          /dev/sdc   disk         2147MB VBOX HARDDISK
/0/100/2                         display      VirtualBox Graphics Adapter
/0/100/3             eth0        network      82540EM Gigabit Ethernet
Controller
/0/100/4                         generic      VirtualBox Guest Service
/0/100/5                         multimedia   82801AA AC'97 Audio
Controller
/0/100/7                         bridge       82371AB/EB/MB PIIX4 ACPI
/0/3                             input        PnP device PNP0303
/0/4                             input        PnP device PNP0f03
```

This is much easier to read and means that, at a glance, you can see that the system has three disks, one network device, and 512MiB of system memory.

As we saw in `Chapter 1`, *Introduction and Environment Setup*, you can also select a `class` output with `-c`, shown again here with our network device:

```
$ sudo lshw -c network
  *-network
       description: Ethernet interface
       product: 82540EM Gigabit Ethernet Controller
       vendor: Intel Corporation
       physical id: 3
       bus info: pci@0000:00:03.0
       logical name: eth0
       version: 02
       serial: 52:54:00:c9:c7:04
       size: 1Gbit/s
       capacity: 1Gbit/s
       width: 32 bits
       clock: 66MHz
       capabilities: pm pcix bus_master cap_list ethernet physical tp
10bt 10bt-fd 100bt 100bt-fd 1000bt-fd autonegotiation
       configuration: autonegotiation=on broadcast=yes driver=e1000
driverversion=7.3.21-k8-NAPI duplex=full ip=10.0.2.15 latency=64
link=yes mingnt=255 multicast=yes port=twisted pair speed=1Gbit/s
       resources: irq:19 memory:f0000000-f001ffff ioport:d010(size=8)
```

From this output, we can see a lot of pertinent information, such as the capacity of the network device (`1Gbit/s`), as well as the capabilities of the device.

We can even see its specific configuration, which is useful for potential changes you might want to make.

If you want to see the actual numeric IDs, you can add `-numeric` to your command:

```
$ sudo lshw -c network -numeric
  *-network
       description: Ethernet interface
       product: 82540EM Gigabit Ethernet Controller [8086:100E]
       vendor: Intel Corporation [8086]
       physical id: 3
       bus info: pci@0000:00:03.0
       logical name: eth0
       version: 02
       serial: 52:54:00:c9:c7:04
       size: 1Gbit/s
       capacity: 1Gbit/s
       width: 32 bits
       clock: 66MHz
       capabilities: pm pcix bus_master cap_list ethernet physical tp
```

```
10bt 10bt-fd 100bt 100bt-fd 1000bt-fd autonegotiation
        configuration: autonegotiation=on broadcast=yes driver=e1000
driverversion=7.3.21-k8-NAPI duplex=full ip=10.0.2.15 latency=64
link=yes mingnt=255 multicast=yes port=twisted pair speed=1Gbit/s
        resources: irq:19 memory:f0000000-f001ffff ioport:d010(size=8)
```

/proc

/proc is the **process information pseudo-filesystem** found on most Linux systems (but not the BSDs).

It is the readable interface-to-kernel data structure, with some files that are writable, allowing for on-the-fly changes to be made to your running kernel.

Some useful files within this directory are the likes of /proc/cpuinfo, which, when queried, gives you all of the information the kernel knows about your CPU:

```
$ cat /proc/cpuinfo
processor     : 0
vendor_id     : GenuineIntel
cpu family    : 6
model         : 142
model name    : Intel(R) Core(TM) i7-7500U CPU @ 2.70GHz
stepping      : 9
cpu MHz       : 2904.000
cache size    : 4096 KB
physical id   : 0
siblings      : 1
core id       : 0
cpu cores     : 1
apicid        : 0
initial apicid    : 0
fpu           : yes
fpu_exception     : yes
cpuid level   : 22
wp            : yes
flags         : fpu vme de pse tsc msr pae mce cx8 apic sep mtrr pge
mca cmov pat pse36 clflush mmx fxsr sse sse2 syscall nx rdtscp lm
constant_tsc rep_good nopl xtopology nonstop_tsc pni pclmulqdq monitor
ssse3 cx16 pcid sse4_1 sse4_2 x2apic movbe popcnt aes xsave avx rdrand
hypervisor lahf_lm abm 3dnowprefetch fsgsbase avx2 invpcid rdseed
clflushopt
bogomips      : 5808.00
clflush size      : 64
cache_alignment   : 64
```

```
address sizes    : 39 bits physical, 48 bits virtual
power management:
```

It also gives you a processor number, meaning that if you want a quick count of processors in your system (being used), you can list them with a short command and some piping.

Here, we're dumping the file, looking for the word `processor`, and then counting the lines. It's not the most foolproof system, but it's handy in a pinch:

```
$ grep -c "processor" /proc/cpuinfo
1
```

Another handy file to be aware of is `/proc/meminfo` for a complete dump of everything the system knows about your memory:

```
$ cat /proc/meminfo
MemTotal:        499428 kB
MemFree:          66164 kB
MemAvailable:    397320 kB
Buffers:           2140 kB
Cached:          324952 kB
SwapCached:           0 kB
Active:          222104 kB
Inactive:        142044 kB
Active(anon):     12764 kB
Inactive(anon):   28916 kB
Active(file):    209340 kB
Inactive(file):  113128 kB
Unevictable:          0 kB
Mlocked:              0 kB
SwapTotal:      1572860 kB
SwapFree:       1572860 kB
Dirty:                0 kB
Writeback:            0 kB
AnonPages:        37100 kB
Mapped:           22844 kB
Shmem:             4624 kB
Slab:             44216 kB
SReclaimable:     21800 kB
SUnreclaim:       22416 kB
KernelStack:       1728 kB
PageTables:        4200 kB
NFS_Unstable:         0 kB
Bounce:               0 kB
WritebackTmp:         0 kB
CommitLimit:    1822572 kB
Committed_AS:    302040 kB
```

```
VmallocTotal:     34359738367 kB
VmallocUsed:             4744 kB
VmallocChunk:     34359730812 kB
HardwareCorrupted:          0 kB
AnonHugePages:              0 kB
CmaTotal:                   0 kB
CmaFree:                    0 kB
HugePages_Total:            0
HugePages_Free:             0
HugePages_Rsvd:             0
HugePages_Surp:             0
Hugepagesize:            2048 kB
DirectMap4k:            49088 kB
DirectMap2M:           475136 kB
```

The /proc filesystem is pretty sprawling and vast; check out the manual page for proc if you get a spare moment—you won't regret it in a hurry (you might regret it later).

/sys

/sys or sysfs is a filesystem for exporting kernel objects (according to its manual page), which means it's another filesystem for accessing kernel information (like /proc).

It can be very useful in scripts for doing things such as listing discovered block devices:

```
$ ls -l /sys/block
total 0
lrwxrwxrwx. 1 root root 0 Sep  2 12:29 dm-0 ->
../devices/virtual/block/dm-0
lrwxrwxrwx. 1 root root 0 Sep  2 12:29 dm-1 ->
../devices/virtual/block/dm-1
lrwxrwxrwx. 1 root root 0 Sep  2 12:29 sda ->
../devices/pci0000:00/0000:00:01.1/ata1/host0/target0:0:0/0:0:0:0/bloc
k/sda
lrwxrwxrwx. 1 root root 0 Sep  2 12:29 sdb ->
../devices/pci0000:00/0000:00:01.1/ata1/host0/target0:0:1/0:0:1:0/bloc
k/sdb
lrwxrwxrwx. 1 root root 0 Sep  2 12:29 sdc ->
../devices/pci0000:00/0000:00:01.1/ata2/host1/target1:0:1/1:0:1:0/bloc
k/sdc
```

It can also be useful for finding the device IDs of an individual component (if you don't have `lshw` or `lspci` handy, for example).

In the following example, I've listed the vendor and device IDs of the `eth0` device:

```
$ cat /sys/class/net/eth0/device/vendor
0x8086
$ cat /sys/class/net/eth0/device/device
0x100e
```

With this information, I can check the details against a list of devices. I chose to check out the `PCI ID` repository, where I learned that the vendor ID belongs to the Intel Corporation and the device ID translates to 82540EM Gigabit Ethernet Controller.

There's a lot more to `/sys` outside the hardware realm, and it can be a good idea to research the filesystem in more depth. The manual page (5) for `sysfs` is a debatable must.

dmesg (and the kernel logs)

`dmesg` is a way to print or control the kernel ring buffer according to its manual but, to you and me, it's a great way to quickly see if your hardware was detected by the kernel as it's initialized.

Running `dmesg` will print to `stdout`, so it's handy to pipe it into `less`:

```
$ dmesg | less
```

Once done, you should be able to search for specific strings. Continuing with our theme, we're going to look for `Intel` and see what's loaded:

```
[    2.221242] e1000: Intel(R) PRO/1000 Network Driver - version
7.3.21-k8-NAPI
```

If we look for `ATA`, we can also see our disks being detected:

```
[ 0.940242] ata2.01: ATA-6: VBOX HARDDISK, 1.0, max UDMA/133
[ 0.940248] ata2.01: 4194304 sectors, multi 128: LBA
[ 0.940807] ata1.00: ATA-6: VBOX HARDDISK, 1.0, max UDMA/133
[ 0.940810] ata1.00: 83886080 sectors, multi 128: LBA
[ 0.940815] ata1.01: ATA-6: VBOX HARDDISK, 1.0, max UDMA/133
[ 0.940817] ata1.01: 4194304 sectors, multi 128: LBA
```

There's even a $-T$ option, to give you human-readable timestamps, which can be especially useful, as shown in the following against our IDE (PATA) controllers:

```
[Sun Sep 2 12:29:08 2018] ata1: PATA max UDMA/33 cmd 0x1f0 ctl 0x3f6
bmdma 0xd000 irq 14
[Sun Sep 2 12:29:08 2018] ata2: PATA max UDMA/33 cmd 0x170 ctl 0x376
bmdma 0xd008 irq 15
```

dmidecode

Another noisy-but-favorite tool from Chapter 1, *Introduction and Environment setup*, dmidecode decodes the DMI table.

We used it to check for virtual hardware initially, but on a non-virtual machine, it can be more useful.

Compare the following -t processor dumps:

```
$ sudo dmidecode -t processor
# dmidecode 3.0
Getting SMBIOS data from sysfs.
SMBIOS 2.5 present.
```

Note the stark emptiness on our virtual machine, compared with the example from my laptop:

```
$ sudo dmidecode -t processor
# dmidecode 3.1
Getting SMBIOS data from sysfs.
SMBIOS 3.0.0 present.

Handle 0x003F, DMI type 4, 48 bytes
Processor Information
    Socket Designation: U3E1
    Type: Central Processor
    Family: Core i7
    Manufacturer: Intel(R) Corporation
    ID: E9 06 08 00 FF FB EB BF
    Signature: Type 0, Family 6, Model 142, Stepping 9
    Flags:
<SNIP>
    Core Count: 2
    Core Enabled: 2
    Thread Count: 4
    Characteristics:
        64-bit capable
```

```
Multi-Core
Hardware Thread
Execute Protection
Enhanced Virtualization
Power/Performance Control
```

What this serves to show is that, in some scenarios, more information might be gleaned from a physical machine than a virtual one.

The same can be said in reverse: if someone is doing everything in their power to obfuscate what hardware is running from you, firstly you should suspect you're running on a VM, and then secondly you should wonder why they're going to such great lengths to hide that fact.

/dev

If I had to choose a favorite `pseudo-filesystems`, I would be one odd individual, but if you forced me, it would probably be `/dev`.

This isn't because of some love for the word `dev` or some affinity for its overuse, but rather because I find myself inside it so often.

As with all of the `pseudo-filesystems`, they're transient and temporary (`tmpfs`). Don't do as I once saw a colleague do and store things in them, because the moment you reboot your box: poof, your files are gone.

On the surface, `/dev` looks messy:

```
$ ls /dev/
autofs          hugepages       port     shm        tty18   tty33
tty49   tty7    vcs6
block           hwrng           ppp      snapshot   tty19   tty34
tty5    tty8    vcsa
bsg             initctl         ptmx     snd        tty2    tty35
tty50   tty9    vcsa1
btrfs-control   input           pts      stderr     tty20   tty36
tty51   ttyS0   vcsa2
char            kmsg            random   stdin      tty21   tty37
tty52   ttyS1   vcsa3
console         log             raw      stdout     tty22   tty38
tty53   ttyS2   vcsa4
core            loop-control    rtc      tty        tty23   tty39
tty54   ttyS3   vcsa5
```

cpu	mapper	rtc0	tty0	tty24	tty4
tty55	uhid	vcsa6			
cpu_dma_latency	mcelog	sda	tty1	tty25	tty40
tty56	uinput	vfio			
crash	mem	sda1	tty10	tty26	tty41
tty57	urandom	vga_arbiter			
disk	mqueue	sda2	tty11	tty27	tty42
tty58	usbmon0	vhci			
dm-0	net	sda3	tty12	tty28	tty43
tty59	vcs	vhost-net			
dm-1	network_latency	sdb	tty13	tty29	tty44
tty6	vcs1	VolGroup00			
fd	network_throughput	sdc	tty14	tty3	tty45
tty60	vcs2	zero			
full	null	sg0	tty15	tty30	tty46
tty61	vcs3				
fuse	nvram	sg1	tty16	tty31	tty47
tty62	vcs4				
hpet	oldmem	sg2	tty17	tty32	tty48
tty63	vcs5				

However, when you know the know, you'll find it invaluable.

Let's ls the /dev/disk/ directory:

```
$ ls /dev/disk/
by-id  by-path  by-uuid
```

Intriguing options—I do like those!

Choosing the by-id option shows us all our disk devices, by-id:

```
$ ls /dev/disk/by-id/
ata-VBOX_HARDDISK_VB4eceb5be-efcdfb56
ata-VBOX_HARDDISK_VB804908ad-25f1585c
ata-VBOX_HARDDISK_VBcf466104-c1479f0d
ata-VBOX_HARDDISK_VBcf466104-c1479f0d-part1
ata-VBOX_HARDDISK_VBcf466104-c1479f0d-part2
ata-VBOX_HARDDISK_VBcf466104-c1479f0d-part3
dm-name-VolGroup00-LogVol00
dm-name-VolGroup00-LogVol01
dm-uuid-LVM-
SA8LTUF2yzFEV1RdgThw0ZiRxhyHFKuUIAjIC6ScnMtvH67BTyTN31hd82bgDSzd
dm-uuid-LVM-
SA8LTUF2yzFEV1RdgThw0ZiRxhyHFKuUj6b8IVKEw37bTwOqy81Ud3juFCSJBg12
lvm-pv-uuid-vrrtbx-g480-HcJI-5wLn-4aOf-Olld-rC03AY

$ ls /dev/disk/by-path/
```

```
pci-0000:00:01.1-ata-1.0          pci-0000:00:01.1-ata-1.0-part2
pci-0000:00:01.1-ata-1.1
pci-0000:00:01.1-ata-1.0-part1  pci-0000:00:01.1-ata-1.0-part3
pci-0000:00:01.1-ata-2.1
```

The following is my absolute favorite, `by-uuid`:

```
$ ls /dev/disk/by-uuid/
570897ca-e759-4c81-90cf-389da6eee4cc   c39c5bed-f37c-4263-bee8-
aeb6a6659d7b
b60e9498-0baa-4d9f-90aa-069048217fee
```

The main reason I like these is because these entries are actually symlinks to the device they're named for:

```
$ ls -l /dev/disk/by-uuid/
total 0
lrwxrwxrwx. 1 root root 10 Sep  2 12:29 570897ca-
e759-4c81-90cf-389da6eee4cc -> ../../sda2
lrwxrwxrwx. 1 root root 10 Sep  2 12:29
b60e9498-0baa-4d9f-90aa-069048217fee -> ../../dm-0
lrwxrwxrwx. 1 root root 10 Sep  2 12:29 c39c5bed-f37c-4263-bee8-
aeb6a6659d7b -> ../../dm-1
```

Because of this, I now know that my `sda2` partition has a UUID of `570897ca-e759-4c81-90cf-389da6eee4cc` that can be used for various tasks.

The most obvious use of the UUID is in most systems' `fstab` files:

```
$ cat /etc/fstab

#
# /etc/fstab
# Created by anaconda on Sat May 12 18:50:26 2018
#
# Accessible filesystems, by reference, are maintained under
'/dev/disk'
# See man pages fstab(5), findfs(8), mount(8) and/or blkid(8) for more
info
#
/dev/mapper/VolGroup00-LogVol00 /                       xfs
defaults        0 0
UUID=570897ca-e759-4c81-90cf-389da6eee4cc /boot                       xfs
defaults        0 0
/dev/mapper/VolGroup00-LogVol01 swap                       swap
defaults        0 0
```

So, marrying the two pieces of information up, we now have the actual device designation (sda2) of our fstab UUID entry!

 The reason UUIDs are used is because device designation can change, historically more so than now. On one boot, your /boot filesystem might be denoted as sda2, then on another a different device might be found first, and suddenly /boot is sdb2, breaking fstab.

How it works...

What we're mostly doing here is checking what the kernel is aware of in terms of devices connected to your system.

PCI devices, as well as USB devices, have denotions that are the same across all operating systems (you'll see the same Hex values on Windows, Mac, and BSD). This allows for the kernel to choose and load the appropriate bit of code, written to interact with that same device.

It's rare, but it can happen that one module supersedes an older one or two drivers can both be used with the same hardware; in this case, it's useful to know your hardware device IDs and the bit of kernel code that's running against them.

 If you use Linux on the desktop, and use an Nvidia or AMD GPU, there's a high chance you'll be interacting with drivers and what the kernel loads, as there's both closed source and open source versions to pick from.

Testing hardware

In this section, we'll discuss methods for testing potentially faulty hardware by looking at SMART and disk-testing software, as well as physically troubleshooting RAM issues.

 Working with disks can be exceptionally risky, and you should always make sure that you have working backups before you start anything that might be hazardous to your data.

Getting ready

Here, we're mostly going to be using the Vagrant box we've created, but you may also want to take a look at Memtest86+ from `http://www.memtest.org/`, which I mention for memory testing.

Connect to your VM and install `smartmontools`:

```
$ vagrant ssh
$ sudo yum install -y smartmontools hdparm
```

You might also want to download the latest Memtest86+ ISO.

How to do it...

We'll start by looking at disk health.

Self-monitoring, analysis, and reporting technology (SMART)

Firstly, it's a good idea to make sure that `smartd` is running on whichever system you want to query:

```
$ sudo systemctl enable smartd
```

`smartd` is the monitoring daemon for SMART; the daemon attempts to enable monitoring on compatibly `ATA` devices when it starts and, by default, polls the `ATA` devices every 30 minutes.

By default, errors detected by `smartd` as part of its periodic work are logged using the `SYSLOG` interface. It can also email out to an administrator if configured to do so.

Once enabled, disks can then be queried with the `smartctl` tool:

```
$ sudo smartctl -a /dev/sda
```

Note the use of `sudo` and the denoting of a disk device.

Sadly, because we're in a VirtualBox VM, this won't give us anything useful:

```
smartctl 6.5 2016-05-07 r4318 [x86_64-linux-3.10.0-862.2.3.el7.x86_64]
(local build)
Copyright (C) 2002-16, Bruce Allen, Christian Franke,
www.smartmontools.org

=== START OF INFORMATION SECTION ===
Device Model: VBOX HARDDISK
Serial Number: VBcf466104-c1479f0d
Firmware Version: 1.0
User Capacity: 42,949,672,960 bytes [42.9 GB]
Sector Size: 512 bytes logical/physical
Device is: Not in smartctl database [for details use: -P showall]
ATA Version is: ATA/ATAPI-6 published, ANSI INCITS 361-2002
Local Time is: Sun Sep 2 14:18:30 2018 UTC
SMART support is: Unavailable - device lacks SMART capability.

A mandatory SMART command failed: exiting. To continue, add one or
more '-T permissive' options.
```

However, if you tried this on a physical machine, results differ and more information can be gleaned.

hdparm

It's possible that your disks are reporting back fine to your SMART commands, but you're still seeing some form of slowdown or other issues.

You can benchmark a disk's read with the `hdparm` tool (available in the default repositories).

We can test the speeds of our disk using the following:

```
$ sudo hdparm -tT /dev/sda
```

The manual page for `hdparm` suggests doing these tests two or three times for average results and running them on otherwise inactive systems.

Your mileage may vary, but the results from my system look like this:

```
/dev/sda:
  Timing cached reads:    13158 MB in  1.99 seconds = 6597.20 MB/sec
  Timing buffered disk reads: 2714 MB in  3.00 seconds = 903.83 MB/sec
```

Partly, we have a problem here, because what we're actually doing is reading from the kernel's page cache. We can bypass this using the `--direct` option, which reads directly from the drive into buffers of `hdparm`:

```
$ sudo hdparm -tT --direct /dev/sda
```

These results are more raw disk read performance:

```
/dev/sda:
  Timing O_DIRECT cached reads:    2416 MB in  2.00 seconds = 1208.08
MB/sec
  Timing O_DIRECT disk reads: 3648 MB in  3.00 seconds = 1215.78 MB/sec
```

Memory testing

Memory is a little easier to test, though the most thorough way of checking every inch of your DIMMs is to take the box offline for a few hours while you run Memtest86+.

Programs such as **memtester** also exist, which can be executed on a running system. The problem with these types of test is that they won't test memory already in use by the system, and they can end up fighting processes such as the **Out Of Memory (OOM)** killer.

If you have the ISO image from the Memtest86+ website, you can attach it to your VM and boot into the program (completely independently of CentOS).

It will look something like this:

Any errors will show up in the bottom half of the screen, and you'll know you have bad memory.

I used to let Memtest86+ do five passes over the memory I was testing when I used it every night during my data center days.

If you find that your system won't boot at all, but you suspect memory problems, it can be a good idea to test in a binary fashion. By this, I mean that if your server has 128 sticks of memory (not uncommon), you should remove 64 of them and test the remaining batch. If your server boots, you know your faulty stick is somewhere in the 64 you removed. If your server doesn't boot, your faulty stick is somewhere in the batch that you left inside.

Repeat this technique, halving the memory you check each time, until you're down to two DIMMs, one of which you know to be faulty, and then test each in turn.

Testing in the previous fashion may sound obvious, but at two o'clock in the morning, when you can't think straight, having read these words might save your sanity.

How it works...

SMART reads information by querying the /dev/ device you target and displaying what it's learned about a SMART-compatible device.

When we're using hdparm, we're actually running tests regardless of our filesystem, because the program reads from the disk directly—because of this, real-world speed may be different.

There's more...

I didn't include testing graphics cards and things of that nature in this section because it's usually quite easy to tell when a graphics card is on the way out (graphical glitches, random lines, and occasional beeps).

I also didn't mention physical RAID cards, because there's such an abundance that it would be impossible to list a coherent method for all of them. The best advice I can give for physical RAID cards is to check out the manufacturer's details on testing.

We didn't cover write tests for disks, partly because it's usually pretty obvious to tell disk issues from read tests alone, and partly because a lot of the methods of testing writes can be destructive if done incorrectly.

The role of the kernel

We're going to watch the kernel running through its startup process, as well as look at which modules have been loaded by the time we get to the OS.

Getting ready

For this section, ensure your VM is up and running, as we're going to talk about hardware initialization:

```
$ vagrant ssh
```

Connect to your VM. If you've just come off the previous section, you may want to destroy and recreate your VM to ensure a vanilla experience.

How to do it...

First, we're going to watch our system boot.

Start by disabling the `quiet` option in our boot configuration so that we can actually see information on our VM display:

```
$ sudo sed -i 's/ quiet//g' /etc/sysconfig/grub
```

Now, we need to generate a new `grub` configuration file, as we've made a change:

```
$ sudo grub2-mkconfig | sudo tee /boot/grub2/grub.cfg
```

 The previous code is a good example of what you would do if someone asked you to make a `grub` configuration change, a surprisingly common action.

Now, bring up the VirtualBox main window, and double-click your VM so, you can see the black console:

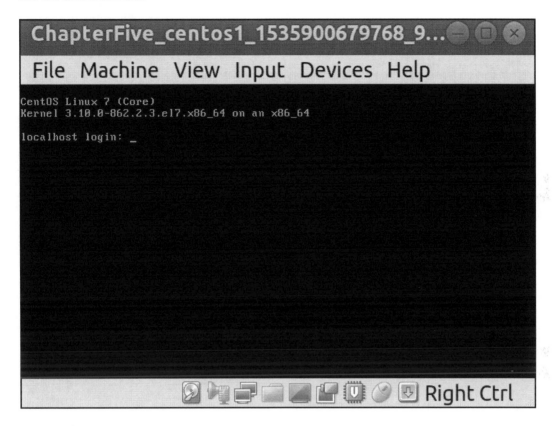

Bring up your Terminal connection so that you can see both and reboot your VM with the `reboot` command:

```
$ sudo reboot
```

Keep your eyes on the VirtualBox window; you should see something like the following screenshot:

Did you note that scrolling information? It probably flew by too fast for you to read, but it's your system working through initializing itself.

You can close your VirtualBox window now and continue in the Terminal.

If you're interested in reading back through what you just saw, you might remember the dmesg command we used previously; everything you've just seen is available to view.

Now that we're in a running system again, we can see which modules the kernel has loaded to deal with our hardware:

```
$ lsmod
Module                   Size   Used by
sunrpc                  353310  1
intel_powerclamp         14419  0
```

```
iosf_mbi                      14990  0
crc32_pclmul                  13133  0
ghash_clmulni_intel           13273  0
snd_intel8x0                  38199  0
ppdev                         17671  0
snd_ac97_codec               130556  1 snd_intel8x0
ac97_bus                      12730  1 snd_ac97_codec
aesni_intel                  189415  0
snd_pcm                      101643  2 snd_ac97_codec,snd_intel8x0
snd_timer                     29810  1 snd_pcm
lrw                           13286  1 aesni_intel
pcspkr                        12718  0
sg                            40721  0
gf128mul                      15139  1 lrw
e1000                        137574  0
glue_helper                   13990  1 aesni_intel
ablk_helper                   13597  1 aesni_intel
snd                           79215  4
snd_ac97_codec,snd_intel8x0,snd_timer,snd_pcm
cryptd                        20511  3
ghash_clmulni_intel,aesni_intel,ablk_helper
i2c_piix4                     22401  0
soundcore                     15047  1 snd
i2c_core                      63151  1 i2c_piix4
parport_pc                    28205  0
parport                       46395  2 ppdev,parport_pc
video                         24538  0
ip_tables                     27126  0
xfs                         1003971  2
libcrc32c                     12644  1 xfs
sd_mod                        46322  3
crc_t10dif                    12912  1 sd_mod
crct10dif_generic             12647  0
ata_generic                   12923  0
pata_acpi                     13053  0
ata_piix                      35052  2
libata                       242992  3 pata_acpi,ata_generic,ata_piix
crct10dif_pclmul              14307  1
crct10dif_common              12595  3
crct10dif_pclmul,crct10dif_generic,crc_t10dif
crc32c_intel                  22094  1
serio_raw                     13434  0
dm_mirror                     22289  0
dm_region_hash                20813  1 dm_mirror
dm_log                        18411  2 dm_region_hash,dm_mirror
dm_mod                       123941  8 dm_log,dm_mirror
```

That's a lot of modules!

As I mentioned previously, some of these modules will be obvious, and more still won't be.

An obvious one from that list might be e1000 because we already know that's our network module from an earlier section.

We can get specific information about a module using modinfo:

```
$ modinfo e1000
filename:
/lib/modules/3.10.0-862.2.3.el7.x86_64/kernel/drivers/net/ethernet/int
el/e1000/e1000.ko.xz
version:        7.3.21-k8-NAPI
license:        GPL
description:    Intel(R) PRO/1000 Network Driver
author:         Intel Corporation, <linux.nics@intel.com>
retpoline:      Y
rhelversion:    7.5
srcversion:     04454A212DD89712602561D
alias:          pci:v00008086d00002E6Esv*sd*bc*sc*i*
alias:          pci:v00008086d000010B5sv*sd*bc*sc*i*
alias:          pci:v00008086d00001099sv*sd*bc*sc*i*
<SNIP>
alias:          pci:v00008086d00001000sv*sd*bc*sc*i*
depends:
intree:         Y
vermagic:       3.10.0-862.2.3.el7.x86_64 SMP mod_unload modversions
signer:         CentOS Linux kernel signing key
sig_key:
66:6E:F0:31:93:3F:51:27:06:23:72:83:2C:E9:BA:8A:49:00:5C:8F
sig_hashalgo:   sha256
parm:           TxDescriptors:Number of transmit descriptors (array of
int)
parm:           RxDescriptors:Number of receive descriptors (array of
int)
parm:           Speed:Speed setting (array of int)
parm:           Duplex:Duplex setting (array of int)
parm:           AutoNeg:Advertised auto-negotiation setting (array of
int)
parm:           FlowControl:Flow Control setting (array of int)
parm:           XsumRX:Disable or enable Receive Checksum offload
(array of int)
parm:           TxIntDelay:Transmit Interrupt Delay (array of int)
parm:           TxAbsIntDelay:Transmit Absolute Interrupt Delay (array
of int)
parm:           RxIntDelay:Receive Interrupt Delay (array of int)
parm:           RxAbsIntDelay:Receive Absolute Interrupt Delay (array
of int)
```

```
parm:              InterruptThrottleRate:Interrupt Throttling Rate (array
of int)
parm:              SmartPowerDownEnable:Enable PHY smart power down
(array of int)
parm:              copybreak:Maximum size of packet that is copied to a
new buffer on receive (uint)
parm:              debug:Debug level (0=none,...,16=all) (int)
```

The preceding code not only gives us the version of the module and the license, but the author and their information for contacting purposes (usually bug reports).

If you try to remove a module that's in use, you won't be allowed, as seen in the following `modprobe` example:

```
$ sudo modprobe -r libata
modprobe: FATAL: Module libata is in use.
```

Similarly, if you want to load a new module (maybe because you want to test it), you can again use `modprobe`:

```
$ sudo modprobe nf_tables
```

We can then see our loaded module:

```
$ lsmod | grep nf_
nf_tables              74179  0
nfnetlink              14490  1 nf_tables
```

Loading a module on boot is a different matter, as it requires a configuration file if not built in to the kernel (and kernel options are usually generic so that vendors can cover as many bases as possible without causing problems).

To ensure `nf_tables` starts with the rest of our kernel, run the following:

```
$ echo "nf_tables" | sudo tee /etc/modules-load.d/nftables.conf
```

Reboot and use `lsmod` to see whether your module has loaded.

How it works...

When your system boots, several things happen in sequence, and these vary slightly depending on trivial differences (such as which bootloader you're using, though mostly it's Grub these days).

One of these things is that the kernel extracts itself and loads, before handing over control to the `init` system (`systemd`).

While the kernel is loading, it also detects hardware in the system and adds the appropriate module to its running state so that hardware can be correctly interacted with and managed.

When we list modules with `lsmod`, we're actually just printing `/proc/modules` in a more readable format.

There's more...

You can dynamically load and unload modules, as well as manually blacklist certain ones from loading at all.

This can come in handy if you have a particular piece of hardware that's faulty, and/or causes a Kernel Panic (the kernel ceasing to function entirely and crashing).

To blacklist a module, it's simply a case of adding it to a blacklist in `/etc/modprobe.d/`:

```
$ echo "blacklist e1000" | sudo tee -a /etc/modprobe.d/blacklist.conf
```

> In the previous example, I blacklisted `e1000`. Clearly, this is going to cause me problems as it means my network card won't have appropriate drivers at boot, but it made the system more secure!

Disk configuration on Linux

In this section, we're going to look at the out-of-the-box configuration of the disks in our VM and discuss the differences between `vda`, `sda`, `hda`, and `nvme`. We're also going to investigate the difference between disks, virtual disks, partitions, and filesystems.

Getting ready

Here, we're going to be using the Vagrant box we created at the beginning of this chapter.

Ensure your `centos1` VM is up and connect to it:

```
$ vagrant ssh centos1
```

Check that your VM has the appropriate packages for this section installed.

```
$ sudo yum install lvm2 -y
```

How to do it...

We'll start by looking at the physical disks in our system and work out how they relate to what we can see with the `df` command.

Listing disks with lsblk

As part of your base system, a program called `lsblk` should be installed.

Running this program gives you a human-readable tree view of our system's block devices, their logical separations, and their mount points:

```
$ lsblk
NAME                 MAJ:MIN RM  SIZE RO TYPE MOUNTPOINT
sda                    8:0    0   40G  0 disk
├─sda1                 8:1    0    1M  0 part
├─sda2                 8:2    0    1G  0 part /boot
└─sda3                 8:3    0   39G  0 part
  ├─VolGroup00-LogVol00
                      253:0    0 37.5G  0 lvm  /
  └─VolGroup00-LogVol01
                      253:1    0  1.5G  0 lvm  [SWAP]
sdb                    8:16   0    2G  0 disk
sdc                    8:32   0    2G  0 disk
```

A block device is basically a layer of abstraction atop a storage medium; character (raw) devices allow direct access to the storage medium, but may have restrictions applied that are abstracted away by using a block device instead.

In the previous example, we have our physical disks:

- sda
- sdb
- sdc

We then have our partitions:

- `sda1`
- `sda2`
- `sda3`

We have our volume group:

- `VolGroup00`

We have logical volumes atop our singular volume group:

- `LogVol00`
- `LogVol01`

Finally, we have our mount points:

- `/boot`
- `/`
- `[SWAP]`

Listing mount points with df

Now that we know the rough disk layout of our system, we might want to know all of the other mount points, too. This is easily achieved with a program called `df`:

```
$ df
Filesystem 1K-blocks Used Available Use% Mounted on
/dev/mapper/VolGroup00-LogVol00 39269648 849960 38419688 3% /
devtmpfs 239968 0 239968 0% /dev
tmpfs 249712 0 249712 0% /dev/shm
tmpfs 249712 4572 245140 2% /run
tmpfs 249712 0 249712 0% /sys/fs/cgroup
/dev/sda2 1038336 64076 974260 7% /boot
tmpfs 49944 0 49944 0% /run/user/1000
```

For better, human-readable output, we can use `-h`:

```
$ df -h
Filesystem                        Size  Used Avail Use% Mounted on
/dev/mapper/VolGroup00-LogVol00    38G  831M   37G   3% /
devtmpfs                          235M     0  235M   0% /dev
tmpfs                             244M     0  244M   0% /dev/shm
tmpfs                             244M  4.5M  240M   2% /run
```

```
tmpfs                          244M    0   244M   0% /sys/fs/cgroup
/dev/sda2                     1014M   63M  952M   7% /boot
tmpfs                           49M    0    49M   0% /run/user/1000
```

Here, we can see the mount points we already know about from the previous section, those being / and /boot.

We can also see other mount points, specifically those tagged with the devtmpfs and tmpfs filesystems.

These mount points are mounted atop RAM disks—a concept that's been around for years, but which we still use because RAM is just so damn quick (considerably faster than SSDs at the moment).

 Temporary directories are those that contain files we don't care about preserving across reboots (for the most part).

Mostly, the mount points you will be concerned with day-to-day are those that contain non-transient files.

Listing filesystems with df

As well as knowing which of your disks is mounted where, you might also want to know which filesystem is being used atop the chunk of space; this is done with the -T flag:

```
$ df -T
Filesystem                    Type      1K-blocks    Used Available
Use% Mounted on
/dev/mapper/VolGroup00-LogVol00 xfs      39269648  849924  38419724
3% /
devtmpfs                      devtmpfs    239968       0    239968
0% /dev
tmpfs                         tmpfs       249712       0    249712
0% /dev/shm
tmpfs                         tmpfs       249712    4572    245140
2% /run
tmpfs                         tmpfs       249712       0    249712
0% /sys/fs/cgroup
/dev/sda2                     xfs        1038336   64076    974260
7% /boot
tmpfs                         tmpfs        49944       0     49944
0% /run/user/1000
```

Here, we can easily see that our slash-root mount point (/) and boot mount point are formatted as XFS.

 CentOS and Red Hat prefer to use XFS at present, but it's not uncommon to come across systems using ext4, ext3, ext2, btrfs, and zfs, to name a few. Functionally, there are differences, but for day-to-day activities, they all handle writing and reading files, which is the important bit.

Listing logical volume manager disks, volume groups, and logical volumes

If you're using LVM (which we are by default, and which a lot of systems do), you may want to know the layout of your disks that are being handled by LVM.

Physical disks

To start, we need to know which physical volumes LVM is aware of; this is accomplished with pvs or pvdisplay:

```
$ sudo pvs
 PV VG Fmt Attr PSize PFree
 /dev/sda3 VolGroup00 lvm2 a-- <38.97g 0
$ sudo pvdisplay
 --- Physical volume ---
 PV Name /dev/sda3
 VG Name VolGroup00
 PV Size <39.00 GiB / not usable 30.00 MiB
 Allocatable yes (but full)
 PE Size 32.00 MiB
 Total PE 1247
 Free PE 0
 Allocated PE 1247
 PV UUID vrrtbx-g480-HcJI-5wLn-4aOf-Olld-rC03AY
```

Note how sudo pvs is a more traditional, unix-y output, whereas the second is more intended for human parsing.

Here, we can see that the only physical device LVM is aware of is the sda3 partition atop the sda device.

A physical volume in LVM land can be either an entire device (sda) or a partition on that device (sda3). Generally, which one is used is down to the system administrator's personal preference, as there are both pros and cons to both methods. Personally, I prefer to give the whole device to LVM and let it do all of the work, removing a layer of abstraction, but I've known people who swear by carving up the disk into partitions before LVM even gets a say.

Volume groups

You can have more than one physical volume grouped together in a volume group; later, this allows for flexibility in terms of the logical volumes that sit on top.

You will get a printout when using pvs and pvdisplay that tells you the volume group that the disk is a part of, but if you want to only list the volume group information, vgs and vgdisplay can be used:

```
$ sudo vgs
  VG           #PV #LV #SN Attr   VSize    VFree
  VolGroup00   1   2   0 wz--n- <38.97g    0
$ sudo vgdisplay
  --- Volume group ---
  VG Name               VolGroup00
  System ID
  Format                lvm2
  Metadata Areas        1
  Metadata Sequence No  3
  VG Access             read/write
  VG Status             resizable
  MAX LV                0
  Cur LV                2
  Open LV               2
  Max PV                0
  Cur PV                1
  Act PV                1
  VG Size               <38.97 GiB
  PE Size               32.00 MiB
  Total PE              1247
  Alloc PE / Size       1247 / <38.97 GiB
  Free  PE / Size       0 / 0
  VG UUID               SA8LTU-F2yz-FEV1-RdgT-hw0Z-iRxh-yHFKuU
```

Here, we can see that there are two logical volumes atop this volume group.

Logical volumes

Finally, in the LVM stack, we have the logical volumes. These are the logical devices that the filesystems get applied to, and which can then be mounted at a point on your system.

Have you worked out the logic behind the command naming?

For this section, we will use `lvs` and `lvdisplay`:

```
$ sudo lvs
  LV        VG           Attr       LSize    Pool Origin Data%  Meta%
Move Log Cpy%Sync Convert
  LogVol00 VolGroup00 -wi-ao---- <37.47g
  LogVol01 VolGroup00 -wi-ao----   1.50g
$ sudo lvdisplay
  --- Logical volume ---
  LV Path                /dev/VolGroup00/LogVol00
  LV Name                LogVol00
  VG Name                VolGroup00
  LV UUID                j6b8IV-KEw3-7bTw-Oqy8-1Ud3-juFC-SJBg12
  LV Write Access        read/write
  LV Creation host, time localhost.localdomain, 2018-05-12 18:50:24
+0000
  LV Status              available
  # open                 1
  LV Size                <37.47 GiB
  Current LE             1199
  Segments               1
  Allocation             inherit
  Read ahead sectors     auto
  - currently set to     8192
  Block device           253:0
  --- Logical volume ---
  LV Path                /dev/VolGroup00/LogVol01
  LV Name                LogVol01
  VG Name                VolGroup00
  LV UUID                IAjIC6-ScnM-tvH6-7BTy-TN31-hd82-bgDSzd
  LV Write Access        read/write
  LV Creation host, time localhost.localdomain, 2018-05-12 18:50:25
+0000
  LV Status              available
  # open                 2
  LV Size                1.50 GiB
  Current LE             48
  Segments               1
  Allocation             inherit
  Read ahead sectors     auto
```

```
- currently set to      8192
Block device           253:1
```

There are two logical volumes!

We know that one of them is sitting under our slash-root and, thanks to `lsblk` earlier, we know that the second is providing our swap space.

Listing swap

Swap is special, and it's more like extended, slow, and somewhat annoying memory than it is disk space.

Swap is used when your system's RAM is full, and the kernel starts to offload infrequently accessed memory onto the disk, where it can be read back at a much slower rate.

 Is it time for another holy war? I think it is! Some systems administrators swear by swap and will always make sure their system has at least a few megabytes of space to swap into, even if they've got 256 GB of RAM; other systems administrators say that, if you're using that much RAM and still swapping, you need more RAM. Smile and nod if you're not the person making the decision about whether or not to even have swap—it's not worth it.

We can list what swap our system is using with `swapon`, like so:

```
$ swapon --show
NAME        TYPE       SIZE USED PRIO
/dev/dm-1 partition 1.5G    0B    -1
```

Here, we can see our one swap device is `/dev/dm-1`, but we think it's an LVM device? That can't be right.

But it can!

Logical volumes are actually mapped; `dm-1` is a low-level representation of our logical volume. Running `ls -l` on our logical volume device proves the following:

```
$ ls -l /dev/mapper/VolGroup00-LogVol01
lrwxrwxrwx. 1 root root 7 Sep  9 09:13 /dev/mapper/VolGroup00-LogVol01
-> ../dm-1
```

Our device is actually linked and mapped to `dm-1`, which is why it's listed as it is in our `swapon` command.

How it works...

Physically, you have a disk.

This disk can be a hard disk drive (the old-school spinning platter type) or a solid state drive of some sort, be it `NVMe` on an M.2 connector or generic SATA.

Whatever the type of disk, you want to use it for storage.

To store data on the disk, it needs to have some things. First, it needs to be readable by the OS; this bit is handled by the kernel. If the kernel determines the disk to be an IDE drive (uncommon), it'll probably show as an `hda` device.

If the disk is SATA or SCSI, it might show up as an `sda` device. If it's a virtio virtual disk, and shows as such to the virtual machine, it will be listed as `vda`.

The disk lettering is sequential, which is why our three disks show up as `sda`, `sdb`, and `sdc`.

 This lettering doesn't have to be consistent; the disks are assigned their denotion at boot-time, meaning your computer can come up with its first disk as `sdb` one day and `sda` another, because of various factors. The way around this is to use disk UUIDs (seen in `fstab` earlier) or labels.

Secondly, after the operating system recognizes that a disk exists, it has to check for partitions and filesystems. Partitions are a segment of a disk, and filesystems are the recipe for how files are read and written to the drive.

In this section, we started out with `lsblk`, which we used to query the `sysfs` filesystem and the `udev` database, before displaying it in a human-readable way. Generally, this is my first stop when trying to determine what a system looks like.

After that, we had a look at mount points and filesystems.

Mount points are the area of the Linux hierarchy to which disks are assigned. Unlike Windows, where the structure starts at the disk, on Linux, the structure is set and the disks fit in (flipping the Windows model on its head).

It's a little hard to visualize the Linux hierarchy of mount points and filesystems, but the important thing to remember is that everything starts at root (that is, slash-root or /) and builds from there. You could have one disk, with one partition, and put slash-root on that partition, hence making the simplest system possible. Or, you could put your home directories (/home) on a physical disk of its own, but it would still exist as /home, one step above slash-root.

 Imagine the logical layout of the Linux hierarchy as the absolute, with the disks almost an irrelevant piece of the puzzle. If you really felt like it, you could mount a bit of the filesystem at /home/me/favourite_things/pokemon/absol, entirely on one disk.

Filesystems are a bit more obvious and generally static (unless you're a system administrator who really wants to live on the wild side). Once you've carved out a section of disk that you want to use (say to mount /home on), you decide on a filesystem.

It's best to go with a typical one in a work environment, something like XFS or ext4, rather than an experimental one, like btrfs.

At the end of your storage-creating adventure, you've got a disk, with a partition, which has the ext4 filesystem atop, and which you've mounted at /home.

There's more...

...There's so much more!

The world of filesystems is an ever-evolving and ever-changing one. You'd have thought that, by now, we'd have data storage licked, but you would be wrong.

There are some filesystems that are better suited for thousands of small files (for example, databases) and some that are better suited for massive blocks of files (such as VM disks). Which one you choose to use is up to you.

There are de-duplicating, snapshotting, and even self-healing (apparently) filesystems.

FreeBSD swears by ZFS, which is also shipped in Ubuntu in the Linux world. OpenSUSE favors btrfs for a lot of its new installations, and some distributions keep with the classics, shipping the ext family for familiarity reasons.

Whichever you decide to use, be sure to keep backups—backups are important.

The filesystem hierarchy

In this section, we'll discuss `hier` and `man hier` as a way of determining what your filesystem's different names mean.

When you look at your system, you might question why certain folders are named in the way they are:

```
$ ls
bin    dev   home   lib64   mnt   proc   run    srv   tmp   vagrant
boot   etc   lib    media   opt   root   sbin   sys   usr   var
```

What's `sbin` or `opt`?

You might also be curious as to know why there's a folder called `root` when we're supposed to be in the root of the system, `/`:

```
[vagrant@localhost /]$ pwd
/
```

The filesystem hierarchy has the answers you want!

Getting ready

This section is going to use our lone VM.

If not already connected, connect to your VM.

We're also going to directly reference a man page, so ensure that your man pages are installed with the following:

```
$ sudo yum reinstall -y man-db man-pages
```

How to do it...

To discern how your distribution maintainer thinks the distribution filesystem should look, run `man hier`:

```
$ man hier
```

The manual page should open in your default pager (usually `less`) and can be navigated as such.

What you should see is something akin to the following—a list of paths, with a description next to each of them:

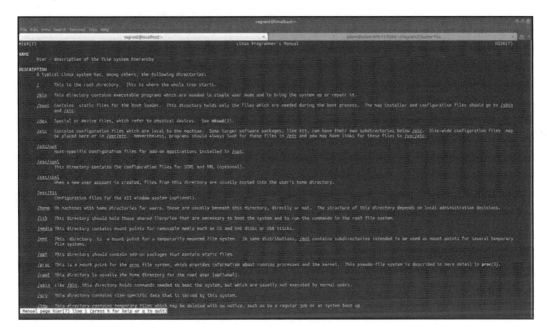

Linux Manual Hier Page

How it works...

This manual page is important, and there's no guarantee that it'll be consistent across the systems that you manage (that is, Debian and CentOS might look distinctly unfamiliar).

What it should be is the distribution maintainer's understanding of where specific files go on this distribution. So, according to this manual page, that is the following:

> *"/bin This directory contains executable programs which are needed in single user mode and to bring the system up or repair it."*

That one is fairly obvious, but what if we want a directory for add-on packages? `hier` for CentOS has you covered:

"/opt   This directory should contain add-on packages that contain static files."

How about if you see a path, and you're not sure what it's for, such as /usr/games? See the following:

" /usr/games Binaries for games and educational programs (optional)."

Curiously, one directory that's omitted from the CentOS-supplied `hier` manual is /srv, and it's one I use quite frequently.

Taken from the Ubuntu `hier` manual, we can see its definition:

"/srv   This directory contains site-specific data that is served by this system."

This is a good example of how different systems might put files in different places, and it's a good place to clear up confusion:

"   /   This is the root directory. This is where the whole tree starts.

<SNIP>

/root This directory is usually the home directory for the root user (optional)."

There's more...

At the bottom of your system's `hier` manual, you might see a reference to The Filesystem Hierarchy Standard, available at http://www.pathname.com/fhs/. This standard is, according to the manual, as follows:

"The filesystem standard has been designed to be used by Unix distribution developers, package developers, and system implementors. However, it is primarily intended to be a reference and is not a tutorial on how to manage a Unix filesystem or directory hierarchy."

This in itself isn't very helpful because it effectively says "*these are more guidelines than rules*", a la *Pirates of the Caribbean.*

Basically, use `man hier` as a good rule of thumb for working out how a system is laid out, but don't assume some narcissistic system administrator hasn't come along and put Terraform in /usr/local/sbin just to be awkward.

Configuring a blank disk and mounting it

In this section, we'll use CLI tools to partition and format one of our disks (without LVM), talking about GPT and MBR while we do so. We'll then mount our disk at /home on our system.

Getting ready

If you're using the supplied Vagrantfile for this chapter, you'll have a system with two blank disks connected. If you're using your own solution, now would be the time to add a couple of blank disks.

Connect to your VM and ensure you can see /dev/sdb; if you can't, double check your Vagrant setup:

```
$ ls -l /dev/sd*
brw-rw----. 1 root disk 8,  0 Sep  9 15:27 /dev/sda
brw-rw----. 1 root disk 8,  1 Sep  9 15:27 /dev/sda1
brw-rw----. 1 root disk 8,  2 Sep  9 15:27 /dev/sda2
brw-rw----. 1 root disk 8,  3 Sep  9 15:27 /dev/sda3
brw-rw----. 1 root disk 8, 16 Sep  9 15:27 /dev/sdb
brw-rw----. 1 root disk 8, 32 Sep  9 15:27 /dev/sdc
```

How to do it...

First, we need to partition our disk. Here, we're going to create two partitions of half the disk each.

Start by using fdisk against /dev/sdb:

```
$ fdisk /dev/sdb
```

You'll be dropped into a different shell, that of fdisk.

First, we will create GPT disklabel by typing g:

```
Command (m for help): g
Building a new GPT disklabel (GUID: DE706D04-7069-456C-B8C4-
C3E405D18A06)
```

Next, we will create a new partition, with a partition number of 1, a first sector of 2048, and of the size 1 GB.

We do this by pressing n and *Enter*, accepting the defaults of the first two prompts (by pressing *Enter* without input) and typing +1G when prompted for Last sector:

```
Command (m for help): n
Partition number (1-128, default 1):
First sector (2048-4194270, default 2048):
Last sector, +sectors or +size{K,M,G,T,P} (2048-4194270, default
4194270): +1G
Created partition 1
```

Next, we use n again to create a second partition although this time we're going to accept the defaults each time (hit *Enter* thrice) because we want to use the rest of the disk:

```
Command (m for help): n
Partition number (2-128, default 2):
First sector (2099200-4194270, default 2099200):
Last sector, +sectors or +size{K,M,G,T,P} (2099200-4194270, default
4194270):
Created partition 2
```

Now, we've got our partitions laid out as we want, we need to write the table to the disk and exist fdisk. Do this with w:

```
Command (m for help): w
The partition table has been altered!

Calling ioctl() to re-read partition table.
Syncing disks.
```

These days, systems are pretty good about automatically re-reading the partition table changes of a device, though occasionally you might still need to run partprobe to inform your kernel of any changes manually.

Running lsblk should now show our new partitions:

```
$ lsblk
<SNIP>
sdb                    8:16  0    2G  0 disk
├─sdb1                 8:17  0    1G  0 part
└─sdb2                 8:18  0 1023M  0 part
<SNIP>
```

Now that we have two partitions, we're going to format them with a filesystem.

For the sake of this tutorial, we're going to format one as ext4, and one as XFS:

```
$ sudo mkfs.ext4 /dev/sdb1
mke2fs 1.42.9 (28-Dec-2013)
Filesystem label=
OS type: Linux
<SNIP>
```

You will be presented with various bits of information, but hopefully the format should be done quickly.

For partition two, we're going to use just the mkfs command, which lacks the implied type of using mkfs.ext4:

```
$ sudo mkfs -t xfs /dev/sdb2
meta-data=/dev/sdb2              isize=512    agcount=4, agsize=65471
blks
         =                       sectsz=512   attr=2, projid32bit=1
<SNIP>
```

We can use a new tool here (blkid) to print the UUID and TYPE of these partitions:

```
$ sudo blkid /dev/sdb1
/dev/sdb1: UUID="4fba66a8-4be9-4835-b393-72db4bb74c0a" TYPE="ext4"
PARTUUID="c517d14f-0c9d-42cc-863c-8a6985a272c1"
$ sudo blkid /dev/sdb2
/dev/sdb2: UUID="44a4b4e1-bf8b-4ec0-8485-d544a0333b00" TYPE="xfs"
PARTUUID="671f397a-3e33-46b8-831d-2d87ca3d170d"
```

It looks good!

Finally, it's a good practice to copy over files from the location you're hoping to mount atop, prior to replacing it with your new filesystem.

If we look at /home at the moment, it looks like this:

```
$ ls /home
vagrant
```

If we mount one of our filesystems at /home and ls again, it looks like this:

```
$ ls /home
lost+found
```

Our Vagrant user's home folder has vanished!

The `lost+found` folder is a function of `fsck` (the filesystem repair utility) and is the dumping ground for pieces of files that it can't make head nor tail of.

This is because we mounted a system over the top of the old location; if we unmount this new filesystem and `ls` the directory again, it looks like this:

```
$ ls /home
vagrant
```

So, what we really need to do is copy over all existing data (preserving ownership and rights) before writing atop it.

Start by creating a folder in `/mnt` (a standard place to do such things), mounting our new filesystem, and copying the data over:

```
$ sudo mkdir /mnt/home2
$ sudo mount /dev/sdb1 /mnt/home2
$ sudo cp -rp --preserve=all /home/* /mnt/home2/
```

In the previous, we used `-r` to recursively copy and `--preserve=all` to preserve things such as the SELinux context of the files, alongside the ownership and timestamps.

Check your results by confirming the Vagrant user's SSH `authorized_keys` file still has the permissions, `-rw-------`:

```
$ ls -lha /mnt/home2/vagrant/.ssh/authorized_keys
-rw-------. 1 vagrant vagrant 389 Sep  9 15:28
/mnt/home2/vagrant/.ssh/authorized_keys
```

Now, `umount` the filesystem from our temporary location and mount it over the top of the previous `/home`, making sure we're not in `/home` first (by moving to a different directory):

```
$ cd /
$ sudo umount /mnt/home2/
$ sudo mount /dev/sdb1 /home
```

We move to the root of the filesystem (`/`) on purpose, to avoid the device being busy and causing complications, though this is more of an issue when trying to unmount a filesystem that you're still sitting in.

Running `df` should now show your newly mounted partition:

```
$ df
<SNIP>
/dev/sdb1                    999320    2576    927932    1% /home
```

 On a reboot, this change will not be preserved. Later, we'll look at making this change permanent with `fstab` and `systemd-mountd`.

How it works...

When we carved our physical device (`sdb`) into two partitions, we created them using `fdisk`.

First, though, we had to give the disk a partition table, where it could store the information about the partitions we're creating.

The classic partition table is called **Master Boot Record** (**MBR**) and the new-school one is called **GUID Partition Table** (**GPT**).

You may still see MBR systems floating around, but GPT is objectively better to use these days, allowing for things such as more than four primary partitions (which MBR is limited to).

You can view the partitions on a disk by again loading `fdisk` and passing `p` on the command line:

```
Command (m for help): p

Disk /dev/sdb: 2147 MB, 2147483648 bytes, 4194304 sectors
Units = sectors of 1 * 512 = 512 bytes
Sector size (logical/physical): 512 bytes / 512 bytes
I/O size (minimum/optimal): 512 bytes / 512 bytes
Disk label type: gpt
Disk identifier: DE706D04-7069-456C-B8C4-C3E405D18A06


#        Start          End    Size  Type            Name
1         2048      2099199      1G  Linux filesyste
2      2099200      4194270   1023M  Linux filesyste
```

These logical spaces can then have a filesystem applied atop them, so that when your OS tries to write files to the disk, the disk knows a way to store the data.

Once done, the disk can then be mounted anywhere in the Linux filesystem hierarchy, replacing any path you care to.

This works because Linux doesn't care how many disks are attached to your system, or what type of disk they are; all it cares about are the mount points.

There's more...

One thing to be aware of is that there are different partition system IDs available for different partition types.

The list of Linux ones that are available on CentOS is as follows:

```
  19 Linux swap                    0657FD6D-
A4AB-43C4-84E5-0933C84B4F4F
  20 Linux filesystem
0FC63DAF-8483-4772-8E79-3D69D8477DE4
  21 Linux server data
3B8F8425-20E0-4F3B-907F-1A25A76F98E8
  22 Linux root (x86)             44479540-F297-41B2-9AF7-
D131D5F0458A
  23 Linux root (ARM)             69DAD710-2CE4-4E3C-
B16C-21A1D49ABED3
  24 Linux root (x86-64)          4F68BCE3-E8CD-4DB1-96E7-
FBCAF984B709
  25 Linux root (ARM-64)          B921B045-1DF0-41C3-
AF44-4C6F280D3FAE
  26 Linux root   (IA-64)          993D8D3D-
F80E-4225-855A-9DAF8ED7EA97
  27 Linux reserved               8DA63339-0007-60C0-
C436-083AC8230908
  28 Linux home                   933AC7E1-2EB4-4F13-
B844-0E14E2AEF915
  29 Linux RAID                   A19D880F-05FC-4D3B-
A006-743F0F84911E
  30 Linux extended boot          BC13C2FF-59E6-4262-A352-
B275FD6F7172
  31 Linux LVM                    E6D6D379-F507-44C2-
A23C-238F2A3DF928
```

These IDs are more informative than anything else these days, though historically, they might be used for informing a system of specific methods required for reading and writing data.

For example, if a partition is labelled correctly on an OpenBSD system and then the drive it's on is plugged into a Linux system, the Linux system should read the ID and realize what it is, preferably not touching the data inside.

Re-configuring a disk using LVM

We're going to format the second disk in our system, and this time we'll use LVM to do so. We'll use the various LVM tools (`lvs`, `pvs`, and `vgs`) to accomplish this, before giving the new logical volume we create a filesystem and mounting it somewhere on our system.

Getting ready

For this section, we're going to use the second disk in our system (it will probably be `sdc` on yours).

Connect to your `centos1` VM and check that another disk is available to work with.

If you've come straight from the last section, your `lsblk` might look like the following:

```
$ lsblk
NAME                       MAJ:MIN RM   SIZE RO TYPE MOUNTPOINT
sda                          8:0    0    40G  0 disk
├─sda1                       8:1    0     1M  0 part
├─sda2                       8:2    0     1G  0 part /boot
└─sda3                       8:3    0    39G  0 part
  ├─VolGroup00-LogVol00    253:0    0  37.5G  0 lvm  /
  └─VolGroup00-LogVol01    253:1    0   1.5G  0 lvm  [SWAP]
sdb                          8:16   0     2G  0 disk
├─sdb1                       8:17   0     1G  0 part /mnt/home2
└─sdb2                       8:18   0  1023M  0 part
sdc                          8:32   0     2G  0 disk
```

We're going to use `sdc` here.

How to do it...

As I mentioned previously, some people like to first create a partition on their drive before introducing it to the LVM lifestyle.

We'll do that here, but only because I'll end up having a fight with one of my technical authors if I don't.

For an added bit of novelty, we're going to use `fdisk` without dropping into the command's shell to hammer home the fact that there are several ways of doing the same thing in Linux:

```
$ printf "g\nn\n\n\n\nt\n31\nw\n" | sudo fdisk /dev/sdc
```

We also set our partition's system ID to be 31—that is, Linux LVM.

To take it one step further, we're going to apply a partition label to our partition, giving it a friendly name:

```
$ sudo parted /dev/sdc name 1 "MostlyHarmless"
```

PartLabels are insanely useful, though next to no-one uses them! They're also only available for GPT disks. They basically mean you can reference a partition by name, instead of number or partition UUID. If you ever find yourself using ZFS on a USB hard drive, I might have just saved you an aneurysm.

Now that we have a partition, let's present it to LVM. First, we have to make LVM aware of it, using `pvcreate`:

```
$ sudo pvcreate /dev/disk/by-partlabel/MostlyHarmless
  Physical volume "/dev/disk/by-partlabel/MostlyHarmless" successfully
created.
```

Once done, a `pvs` command will list our new physical device:

```
$ sudo pvs
  PV          VG          Fmt  Attr PSize   PFree
  /dev/sda3   VolGroup00  lvm2 a--  <38.97g      0
  /dev/sdc1               lvm2 ---   <2.00g <2.00g
```

Adding it to a volume group is step two, which involves creating the volume group too (or we could add it to `VolGroup00`, but for now we'll make a new one):

```
$ sudo vgcreate VolGroup01 /dev/disk/by-partlabel/MostlyHarmless
  Volume group "VolGroup01" successfully created
```

Finally, we're going to create a logical volume within this group, though for novelty we're not going to use all of the available space in the volume group:

```
$ sudo lvcreate -l 50%FREE -n Home3 VolGroup01
  Logical volume "Home3" created.
```

Note that now listing our logical volumes with `lvs` shows our new one, which is using 50% of the `VolGroup01` space:

```
$ sudo lvs
  LV        VG         Attr       LSize     Pool Origin Data%  Meta%
Move Log Cpy%Sync Convert
  LogVol00 VolGroup00 -wi-ao---- <37.47g
  LogVol01 VolGroup00 -wi-ao----   1.50g
  Home3    VolGroup01 -wi-a----- 1020.00m
```

Logical volumes can be many things and have various uses. What we have created here is a simple linear volume, suitable for day-to-day tasks, but lacking things such as redundancy.

We now have a disk that we can place a filesystem atop, before mounting it somewhere on our VM.

To make a filesystem, we again use `mkfs`:

```
$ sudo mkfs.btrfs /dev/mapper/VolGroup01-Home3
btrfs-progs v4.9.1
See http://btrfs.wiki.kernel.org for more information.

Label:              (null)
UUID:               7bf4939e-196a-47cf-9326-1408cdf920ac
Node size:          16384
Sector size:        4096
Filesystem size:    1020.00MiB
Block group profiles:
  Data:             single          8.00MiB
  Metadata:         DUP            51.00MiB
  System:           DUP             8.00MiB
SSD detected:       no
Incompat features:  extref, skinny-metadata
Number of devices:  1
Devices:
   ID        SIZE  PATH
    1  1020.00MiB  /dev/mapper/VolGroup01-Home3
```

And again, we can `mount` it (creating a mount point first):

```
$ sudo mkdir /mnt/home3
$ sudo mount /dev/mapper/VolGroup01-Home3 /mnt/home3
```

`lsblk` can confirm our new setup:

```
sdc                        8:32   0    2G  0 disk
 └─sdc1                     8:33   0    2G  0 part
    └─VolGroup01-Home3    253:2    0 1020M  0 lvm   /mnt/home3
```

How it works...

What we have created are layers:

- We have our physical disk (`sdc`)
- We have a partition atop our physical disk (`sdc1`)
- We have our volume group, with our physical volume inside (`VolGroup01`)
- We have our logical volume, atop our volume group (`Home3`)
- We have our filesystem, atop our logical volume, which we then mounted at `/mnt/home3`

This means that we have complexity, but we also have flexibility.

What we have done is create a virtual block device, in the form of our logical volume. This logical volume will have data written to it and, in turn, will apply that data to a physical volume in the volume group, based on decisions by the kernel.

There's more...

When we created the logical volume, we simply specified that the new device should use 50% of the available space, but we could have also suggested a specific size in absolute values (for example, 1G).

You might be asking why you would use LVM, if we effectively got to the same position we were in when we simply placed a filesystem atop a disk partition. The answer is: flexibility.

In LVM-land, you can grow volume groups by adding more physical disks to them, you can move data from one physical disk to another (in a running system), and you can even shift all data off a drive, before removing that drive in a hotplug (or hot unplug) fashion. This relies on your filesystem supporting such changes, but modern ones will (allowing you to grow and shrink them on the fly).

As an example of the previous, let's extend our logical volume to use all of the available space of the volume group:

```
$ sudo lvextend -l +100%FREE VolGroup01/Home3
  Size of logical volume VolGroup01/Home3 changed from 1.00 GiB (256
extents) to <2.00 GiB (511 extents).
  Logical volume VolGroup01/Home3 successfully resized.
```

Note the + symbol in front of the `100%` section. This suggests to `lvextend` that you want to add the new size onto the old; it's necessary to use all 2G of the disk to do so.

Once extended, we still have to grow our filesystem to fit the available space:

```
$ df -h /dev/mapper/VolGroup01-Home3
Filesystem                        Size  Used Avail Use% Mounted on
/dev/mapper/VolGroup01-Home3 1020M    17M  901M   2% /mnt/home3
```

To do this, we need to use a `btrfs` command:

```
$ sudo btrfs filesystem resize max /mnt/home3
Resize '/mnt/home3' of 'max'
```

And now, we should have our space:

```
$ df -h /dev/mapper/VolGroup01-Home3
Filesystem                        Size  Used Avail Use% Mounted on
/dev/mapper/VolGroup01-Home3  2.0G    17M  1.9G   1% /mnt/home3
```

This is just one example of the flexibility in LVM, and it offers a boatload more functionality on top. It even enables easier migration of data, as you can easily import pools onto other systems.

It does have its trade-offs, though. For example, I was recently trying to get a VM booting as quickly as I could (for testing purposes) and ended up disregarding LVM as it was quicker to directly access the disks at boot time (in OS, it's not different, but for my environment, it was booting speed that mattered).

Using systemd-mount and fstab

In this section, we'll learn about making sure that our newly configured disks appear on boot and how to run a test to see if it'll come up at boot time.

For this, we'll use the traditional method of adding a disk to the `fstab` file, and we'll also use `systemd-mount`.

You could use the following to directly reconfigure `/dev/sdb` as a single partition, formatted to `ext4`:

```
$ printf "g\nn\n\n\n\nw\n" | sudo fdisk /dev/sdb && sudo mkfs.ext4
/dev/sdb1
```

Getting ready

In this section, we're going to use both our `sdb` and `sdc` drives.

If you have rebuilt your VM, have a go at the previous sections to end up with a drive that has a simple filesystem atop a partition and one atop a LVM logical volume.

Reboot your VM so that you're at a point where you have partitioned drives, but they're unmounted.

It should look something like the following:

```
$ lsblk
NAME                        MAJ:MIN RM  SIZE RO TYPE MOUNTPOINT
sda                          8:0    0    40G  0 disk
├─sda1                       8:1    0     1M  0 part
├─sda2                       8:2    0     1G  0 part /boot
└─sda3                       8:3    0    39G  0 part
  ├─VolGroup00-LogVol00 253:0    0  37.5G  0 lvm  /
  └─VolGroup00-LogVol01 253:1    0   1.5G  0 lvm  [SWAP]
sdb                          8:16   0     2G  0 disk
└─sdb1                       8:17   0     2G  0 part
sdc                          8:32   0     2G  0 disk
└─sdc1                       8:33   0     2G  0 part
  └─VolGroup01-Home3    253:2    0     2G  0 lvm
```

(Note the lack of mount points by `sdb1` and `VolGroup01-Home3`).

How to do it...

We're going to start with the traditional `fstab` approach.

fstab

Our `fstab` currently looks like this:

```
$ cat /etc/fstab

#
# /etc/fstab
# Created by anaconda on Sat May 12 18:50:26 2018
#
# Accessible filesystems, by reference, are maintained under
'/dev/disk'
# See man pages fstab(5), findfs(8), mount(8) and/or blkid(8) for more
info
#
/dev/mapper/VolGroup00-LogVol00 /                    xfs
defaults        0 0
UUID=570897ca-e759-4c81-90cf-389da6eee4cc /boot                  xfs
defaults        0 0
/dev/mapper/VolGroup00-LogVol01 swap                  swap
defaults        0 0
```

We're going to add another line to the bottom, prompting our /dev/sdb1 partition to mount as /home. First, we're going to get the partition's UUID, because we do not want our sdb device to suddenly come up as sdc and break our boot:

```
$ ls -l /dev/disk/by-uuid/ | grep sdb
lrwxrwxrwx. 1 root root 10 Sep 15 06:45 10572fe4-5f65-4df0-9e69-
dcd885e9f01e -> ../../sdb1
```

Cool—now that we have that (10572fe4-5f65-4df0-9e69-dcd885e9f01e), we can add it:

```
$ echo "UUID=10572fe4-5f65-4df0-9e69-dcd885e9f01e /opt ext4 defaults 0
0" | sudo tee -a /etc/fstab
```

What we're doing here is telling `fstab` where our partition is (UUID), we're telling it where to mount the partition (`/opt`), and we're giving it the filesystem format so that it knows how to mount it (`ext4`). Then, we're telling it to use the default mount options (`defaults`), which are good enough for most use cases; we're specifying that the filesystem doesn't need to be dumped (0), and that we do not want to run any checks on it at boot (0) though in the real world, you might want to enable this.

Note that we can mount `fstab` immediately with `mount`:

```
$ sudo mount -a
$ df -h /opt
Filesystem      Size  Used Avail Use% Mounted on
/dev/sdb1       2.0G  6.0M  1.9G   1% /opt
```

Any errors will be immediately obvious, as `mount` will refuse to work.

Running `mount -a` prior to rebooting is preferable to having your system stall and become unable to boot—take it from experience.

systemd-mount

If you want to be new and trendy, you might want to use `systemd-mount` instead of the decrepit (emphasis mine) `fstab`.

First, create our `local` unit directory if it doesn't already exist from our previous chapters:

```
$ sudo mkdir -p /usr/local/lib/systemd/system
```

Then, populate a new file with the following:

```
$ sudo tee /usr/local/lib/systemd/system/srv.mount << HERE
[Unit]
Description=Mounting our logical volume as srv

[Mount]
What=/dev/mapper/VolGroup01-Home3
Where=/srv
Type=btrfs
Options=defaults
```

```
[Install]
WantedBy=multi-user.target
HERE
```

Now, we can start and `enable` our `mount`:

```
$ sudo systemctl enable --now srv.mount
Created symlink from /etc/systemd/system/multi-
user.target.wants/srv.mount to
/usr/local/lib/systemd/system/srv.mount.
```

At the end of this section, and after a reboot, your `lsblk` printout should look like the following:

```
sdb                         8:16   0    2G  0 disk
└─sdb1                        8:17  0     2G  0 part /opt
sdc                         8:32   0    2G  0 disk
└─sdc1                        8:33  0     2G  0 part
  └─VolGroup01-Home3      253:2   0     2G  0 lvm  /srv
```

How it works...

On `systemd` systems, it's generally the case that `fstab` is managed by `systemd` anyway.

What's actually happening when a system boots is that the `systemd-fstab-generator` reads the `/etc/fstab` file, and translates what it finds there into `systemd` units. This is the reason you can list mounts with `systemctl`:

```
$ systemctl list-units *.mount --no-legend
-.mount                         loaded active mounted /
boot.mount                      loaded active mounted /boot
dev-hugepages.mount             loaded active mounted Huge Pages File
System
dev-mqueue.mount                loaded active mounted POSIX Message Queue
File System
opt.mount                       loaded active mounted /opt
run-user-1000.mount             loaded active mounted /run/user/1000
srv.mount                       loaded active mounted Mounting our
logical volume asrv
sys-kernel-config.mount         loaded active mounted Configuration File
System
sys-kernel-debug.mount          loaded active mounted Debug File System
var-lib-nfs-rpc_pipefs.mount loaded active mounted RPC Pipe File
System
```

And this is why we can see the details of a partition with `systemctl cat`:

```
$ systemctl cat boot.mount
# /run/systemd/generator/boot.mount
# Automatically generated by systemd-fstab-generator

[Unit]
SourcePath=/etc/fstab
Documentation=man:fstab(5) man:systemd-fstab-generator(8)
Before=local-fs.target

[Mount]
What=/dev/disk/by-uuid/570897ca-e759-4c81-90cf-389da6eee4cc
Where=/boot
Type=xfs
```

This does beg the question of why you would want to use `fstab` at all, if you have the option to use `systemd` entirely, and the simple answer is: tradition. At the moment, people expect `fstab` to be the place they go to find `mount` information but, in the future, this might change.

There's more...

If your system does fail to boot, following a change to `fstab` or one to your `systemd-mount` files, then the next step (beyond panic) is to log in to the console of your server. In this case, we do this by connecting to the VirtualBox window and connecting to the graphical representation of our console session, before booting into single user mode.

You would then remove the offending line from your configuration and reboot your system once more.

I've caused a system to get stuck at boot more times than I can count, and historically this hasn't been a problem, for the reasons I mentioned previously. However, in modern cloud environments, you might not always get a console (at the time of writing, Azure has only just implemented this feature) so ensuring your `fstab` entries are correct, prior to rebooting, is a good idea!

The `systemd.mount` man page is a good place to look for the mount options that `systemd` understands.

See also

`fstab` has been around in one form or another since 4.0 BSD, released in 1980. Obviously, back then, it didn't use `systemd`, but then, 4.0 BSD did not do much of anything.

I would look at the history of the `fstab` file, if you're into that sort of thing, and there's nothing good on TV.

`_netdev` is something else to be aware of, and I'll mention it here because it's routinely saved my bacon. It's an option that can be added to mount points (like defaults) and it tells `systemd` that the filesystem is dependent on your network being up. For NFS and iSCSI environments, this is probably a must.

Disk encryption and working with encryption at rest

Here, we're going to take a look at using `dm-crypt` to encrypt our disk so that the data on the device is safe when removed from a machine. We'll touch on file encryption locally, too.

Getting ready

In this section, we're going to use both our `sdb` drives.

If you have rebuilt your VM, have a go at the previous sections to end up with a drive that has a simple filesystem atop a partition.

On your VM, first, make sure that any `fstab` entries you've added are removed; for me, this was a case of running the following `sed` command:

```
$ sudo sed -i 's#UUID=10572fe4-5f65-4df0-9e69-dcd885e9f01e /opt ext4
defaults 0 0##g' /etc/fstab
```

I then rebooted my system to ensure that `/opt` was not mounted at boot, and finally I regenerated the first partition on my disk:

```
$ printf "g\nn\n\n\n\nw\n" | sudo fdisk /dev/sdb
```

Again, your mileage may vary, but what you want to end up with is a disk that has one partition on it, unformatted for now.

We'll also need to install the appropriate tools for this section:

```
$ sudo yum install -y cryptsetup
```

How to do it...

First, it's recommended that you fill your drive with random data, prior to creating an encrypted partition on top of it; this is so that data that wasn't encrypted can't be recovered later.

I'm going to accomplish this with shred:

```
$ sudo shred -v -n1 /dev/sdb1
shred: /dev/sdb1: pass 1/1 (random)...
shred: /dev/sdb1: pass 1/1 (random)...1.6GiB/2.0GiB 82%
shred: /dev/sdb1: pass 1/1 (random)...2.0GiB/2.0GiB 100%
```

Now that we've filled our drive with random data, we have to format our partition as a **Linux Unified Key Setup** (**LUKS**), an encryption specification:

```
$ sudo cryptsetup luksFormat /dev/sdb1

WARNING!
========
This will overwrite data on /dev/sdb1 irrevocably.

Are you sure? (Type uppercase yes): YES
Enter passphrase:
Verify passphrase:
```

As you can see, there are some sanity-check elements, such as getting you to type all uppercase YES before you're prompted for a password. The password has some requirements, such as being a minimum of 12 characters and not being based on a dictionary word.

We've created an encrypted partition, which we now need to open before we can work with it:

```
$ sudo cryptsetup luksOpen /dev/sdb1 encrypted-opt
Enter passphrase for /dev/sdb1:
```

Using `lsblk`, you should now see the crypt device:

```
sdb                      8:16  0    2G  0 disk
└─sdb1                   8:17  0    2G  0 part
  └─encrypted-opt      253:3   0    2G  0 crypt
```

So, what do we do with it? We format it with the following:

```
$ sudo mkfs.btrfs /dev/mapper/encrypted-opt
```

 You may have noticed that I'm using `btrfs` a lot here; this isn't because of some misplaced allegiance to a filesystem format that can't even do RAID correctly, instead it's because when I type, I read what I'm typing in my head, and it's easier to think "*butter fs*" than it is "*ext*". So now you know; you're welcome.

It's time to mount it:

```
$ sudo mount /dev/mapper/encrypted-opt /opt
```

Congratulations! Your encrypted disk will now function as any other would, and you can be safe in the knowledge that, if someone steals your hard drive, its contents are locked behind encryption and a password. We can see our setup with `lsblk`:

```
sdb                      8:16  0    2G  0 disk
└─sdb1                   8:17  0    2G  0 part
  └─encrypted-opt      253:3   0    2G  0 crypt /opt
```

To close an encrypted volume, the filesystem first has to be unmounted:

```
$ sudo umount /opt
```

Now, you run `cryptsetup` again, only with `luksClose` this time:

```
$ sudo cryptsetup luksClose encrypted-opt
```

But what if we want to mount our disk on boot?

Well, first, you should question doing this and consider the ramifications. The purpose of encryption is to protect data, and if you set up a disk to come up automatically, you're nullifying your security (assuming an entire box has been taken, and not just the sole hard drive).

However, there's an argument to be made that encrypting a drive but having an "unlock key" automatically unlock and mount it is still useful if your drive dies and you want to send it back to the drive manufacturer for a replacement. Without the key, even if they could read the data off the platters, all they get is jumbled noise.

With that in mind, let's mount `/dev/sdb1` at boot.

We need the UUID of the encrypted disk; for this, we use `luksUUID` to make life easy:

```
$ sudo cryptsetup luksUUID /dev/sdb1
8d58f0ec-98f1-4cf8-a78d-3cb6a4643350
```

First, place an entry into `/etc/crypttab`:

```
$ echo "encrypted-opt UUID=8d58f0ec-98f1-4cf8-a78d-3cb6a4643350
/cryptfile" | sudo tee -a /etc/crypttab
```

Second, we need to add our `fstab` entry for our disk:

```
$ echo "/dev/mapper/encrypted-opt /opt btrfs defaults 0 0" | sudo tee
-a /etc/fstab
```

 As we saw previously, this could also be its own `systemd` unit file if you so wish.

Third, create a keyfile to use, with a suitably complex key:

```
$ echo "SuperSecretKeyPhrase" | sudo tee -a /cryptfile
```

Now, add this key to our encrypted partition. When prompted for any existing passphrase, give the one you gave when first creating the drive:

```
$ sudo cryptsetup luksAddKey /dev/sdb1 /cryptfile
Enter any existing passphrase:
```

At this point, you can reboot your VM and, hopefully (keep an eye on the console in VirtualBox), it'll come up seamlessly.

It's worth noting that the encrypted volume can now be opened using either your passphrase or the keyfile (shown as follows):

```
$ sudo cryptsetup luksOpen /dev/sdb1 encrypted-opt -d /cryptfile
```

How it works...

What we've done here is simply created an encrypted volume; it's yet another logical disk, that the system can treat as any other storage medium once it's been unlocked.

`cryptsetup` is the key component used here, and it couldn't be described better than by its own manual page.

> *cryptsetup is used to conveniently setup dm-crypt managed device-mapper mappings. These include plain dm-crypt volumes and LUKS volumes. The difference is that LUKS uses a metadata header and can hence offer more features than plain dm-crypt. On the other hand, the header is visible and vulnerable to damage.*

With `cryptsetup`, we started by formatting the partition we'd set up and setting an initial passphrase. This was the `luksFormat` element. Once done, our LUKS partition could then be opened, which is the process of passing our assigned passphrase to the device, for it to then set up a device mapping automatically. We were then able to format our mapped device with a useful filesystem for using natively (`btrfs` again) and mount it.

Most of the work you do with LUKS devices will be done using `cryptsetup` (at least on servers).

There's more...

By default, if you try to mount a filesystem on an encrypted drive, without knowing or caring that it's LUKS encrypted, you'll get a descriptive message that should give you a hint:

```
$ sudo mount /dev/sdb1 /opt
mount: unknown filesystem type 'crypto_LUKS'
```

At this point, you know you need to run `luksOpen` on the drive first, and you might find that you've long since forgotten the password and the data on the disk has effectively gone to silicon-heaven (or silicon-purgatory).

In this section, we mounted our drive using a keyfile on the root partition; if instead you add a line with `none` in it to `crypttab` and then add the entry to `fstab`, you will get prompted for a password at boot:

```
$ echo "encrypted-opt /dev/sdb1 none" | sudo tee -a /etc/crypttab
$ echo "/dev/mapper/encrypted-opt /opt btrfs defaults 0 0" | sudo tee
-a /etc/fstab
$ sudo reboot
```

Now, you need to go to your console and put in your LUKS password, as we can see in the following screenshot:

This has to be done from the console, as SSH won't be up yet. Obviously, in a cloud environment or a physical server build, this can be tricky.

See also

If you've been following along, you might be asking what `systemd` does with `crypttab`, if it translates `fstab` into `systemd` units.

The answer is that it does something very similar, in fact, using a similarly named program at boot-time: `systemd-cryptsetup-generator`.

We can actually see what happened to our encrypted device at boot by catting the automatically generated file:

```
$ systemctl cat systemd-cryptsetup@encrypted\\x2dopt.service
# /run/systemd/generator/systemd-cryptsetup@encrypted\x2dopt.service
# Automatically generated by systemd-cryptsetup-generator

[Unit]
Description=Cryptography Setup for %I
Documentation=man:crypttab(5) man:systemd-cryptsetup-generator(8)
man:systemd-cryptsetup@.service(8)
SourcePath=/etc/crypttab
DefaultDependencies=no
Conflicts=umount.target
IgnoreOnIsolate=true
After=systemd-readahead-collect.service systemd-readahead-
replay.service
After=cryptsetup-pre.target
Before=cryptsetup.target
RequiresMountsFor=/cryptfile
BindsTo=dev-disk-
by\x2duuid-8d58f0ec\x2d98f1\x2d4cf8\x2da78d\x2d3cb6a4643350.device
After=dev-disk-
by\x2duuid-8d58f0ec\x2d98f1\x2d4cf8\x2da78d\x2d3cb6a4643350.device
Before=umount.target

[Service]
Type=oneshot
RemainAfterExit=yes
TimeoutSec=0
ExecStart=/usr/lib/systemd/systemd-cryptsetup attach 'encrypted-opt'
'/dev/disk/by-uuid/8d58f0ec-98f1-4cf8-a78d-3cb6a4643350' '/cryptfile'
''
ExecStop=/usr/lib/systemd/systemd-cryptsetup detach 'encrypted-opt'
```

You can see the `attach` command being run at the bottom.

Current filesystem formats

There're a lot of filesystem formats out there—some are more popular than others; some are used for very specific tasks; some are the darlings of certain operating systems; and others simply should have gone away years ago.

In the Windows world, we typically see NTFS, but FAT32, exFAT, and even FAT16 in some cases are still options.

More recently, Apple has dropped the ageing HFS+ and moved full-steam toward APFS as its filesystem of the future.

FreeBSD defaults to either ZFS (if you've got the RAM for it) or UFS (if you haven't).

OpenBSD—well, OpenBSD uses FFS, which is exactly as good as it sounds.

 Fast File System (FFS) is pretty much UFS.

Linux is a whole other kettle of fish because, not only does it do all of the filesystems listed previously, to a greater or lesser degree, it also has hundreds of others to pick from.

Now, we're going to see what we have available to us on our VM.

Getting ready

For this section, you'll just need access to your VM and possibly the internet as a whole.

Connect to your Vagrant box; this section is purely informational, so don't worry about what state it's in for now.

How to do it...

Listing systems you can create is relatively easy, as you can tab mkfs a couple of times to get a list of established aliases:

```
$ mkfs
mkfs            mkfs.cramfs   mkfs.ext3    mkfs.minix
mkfs.btrfs      mkfs.ext2     mkfs.ext4    mkfs.xfs
```

Your distribution may have others available, though not installed by default.

For example, if I want to manage DOS filesystems, I can install dosfstools:

```
$ sudo yum install dosfstools -y
```

I've suddenly got the `msdos`, `vfat`, and `fat` options:

```
$ mkfs
mkfs           mkfs.cramfs  mkfs.ext3   mkfs.fat    mkfs.msdos
mkfs.xfs
mkfs.btrfs     mkfs.ext2    mkfs.ext4   mkfs.minix  mkfs.vfat
```

You can also list the filesystems your kernel is capable of interacting with by using your current kernel's module directory:

```
$ ls /lib/modules/3.10.0-862.2.3.el7.x86_64/kernel/fs
binfmt_misc.ko.xz  cifs      ext4      gfs2   mbcache.ko.xz  nls
udf
btrfs              cramfs    fat       isofs  nfs            overlayfs
xfs
cachefiles         dlm       fscache   jbd2   nfs_common     pstore
ceph               exofs     fuse      lockd  nfsd           squashfs
```

Note that the likes of `ext3` might be managed by an `ext4` module of yours, so just because `ext3` isn't listed doesn't mean you can't mount, read, and write to an `ext3` drive.

How it works...

Realistically, it doesn't work.

In a perfect world, we would have one filesystem that worked across each OS and was suited for every task, but the truth of the matter is that there's always going to be some filesystems that are better at some jobs than others.

At the time of writing, Red Hat defaults to using XFS as its filesystem of choice, a journaling filesystem that was created in 1993. Before that, the default was the `ext` family of filesystems, which some distributions (such as Debian) continue to use.

OpenSUSE likes `btrfs` at the minute, though how much that's likely to change is anyone's guess, especially as the likes of Red Hat have just decided against including it in future versions.

This is also all before getting on to **Filesystem in Userspace** (FUSE), which is capable of bringing a host of other (userspace) filesystems into the mix.

For now, just be safe in the knowledge that XFS and `ext4` will likely be around for a while, and they're a solid choice for any system as long as your needs aren't too bespoke. You may need to get a storage engineer in if you're planning on doing things such as investigating which filesystem will be best for your new, bespoke, database.

My recommendation is to go with whatever is in use by default.

Upcoming filesystem formats

We've discussed the old favorites, such as XFS and `ext4`, but we've only touched on the likes of ZFS and novelty filesystems such as `btrfs`.

On top of the regular I-need-a-filesystem-for-my-disk filesystems, there're others such as LizardFS and SSHFS, which are worth a mention.

Getting ready

For this section, you'll again need access to your VM and the internet as a whole.

Connect to your VM, but also have a web browser handy.

How to do it...

Starting out simple-ish, let's talk about ZFS.

Less of a traditional filesystem than others, ZFS has recently been mainstreamed on Linux by being bundled into Ubuntu (which caused a lot of arguing and even some claims that Canonical were willfully breaking GPL compliance), and it's causing a bit of a stir.

For years, ZFS was the main reason people installed FreeBSD (don't email me), and it's the backbone filesystem for systems based on Solaris or OpenSolaris. It works differently to XFS or ext4 and is arguably closer to the LVM world.

Disks are placed into VDEVs, which is the bit that handles the mirroring or RAID-ing of drives. These VDEVs then form the basis for zpools, which are storage pools that datasets then sit atop (datasets are more like traditional partitions—kinda).

ZFS on Linux is the project behind putting ZFS on Linux, and I would advise checking them out.

After ZFS, you've got things such as distributed filesystems, which you might mount on your local system using FUSE. LizardFS is one such filesystem.

You use LizardFS if you want distributed and redundant storage, which can be accessed over a network and mounted locally. You can do clever things such as store multiple copies of data and even have multi-master setups of the controller node so that you have some redundancy in the event of hardware failure (because hardware does fail).

If all of that was over your head, don't panic: it was over my head for the longest time too, but it's pretty nifty software and worth a weekend to get to grips with.

SSHFS is another FUSE filesystem, only this time it's a bit of software that's used to mount remote systems directories locally so that you can mangle and mess with them to your heart's content, without being on the command line of the remote box.

How it works...

Again, it generally doesn't work.

Filesystems are a deep and interesting topic, for a very dedicated and specific kind of people. I've met storage engineers who could talk for hours about the different filesystems on offer and why you shouldn't bother using `ext2` as a `/boot` partition these days, simply because the trade-offs aren't there, or who drone on about the selective merit of using **just a bunch of disk (JBOD)** deployments versus traditional SANs.

Once again, I'll point out that there are use cases for every type of filesystem on offer, even WikipediaFS, and that's okay! Just be safe in the knowledge that the options are there, if you need them.

Round-up – hardware and disks

Most of this chapter, quite unintentionally, turned into a breakdown of disks and filesystems. This is because, traditionally, disks were the most likely thing to go wrong in your system. Recently, disks don't die anywhere near as much, because the advent of cheap and commercially available SSDs has removed the "spinning rust" from a lot of systems.

That said, data can, and will, randomly disappear from your life.

Backup! Backup! Backup!

It doesn't matter how many times I say it—some of you will still read those words and think "*yeah, I should do that*" with no intention of ever bothering to set something up. For your own systems, that's your choice, but you might at least consider it for those boxes you manage, as it'll only make your life easier (and you the hero) when you break out the backups after a catastrophic failure that threatens to cost your employer millions.

 It should go without saying, but you should make a point of testing your backups frequently, or you will enter the faith-based backups situation, and that is not somewhere you want to be.

Filesystems are also getting more confusing and feature-rich. If you compare something like `ext2` with `btrfs`, you'll find a wealth of tricks and clever things that are designed to make your life easier in the long term, but in the short term can leave you with a bewildering array of options.

People also do silly things in this world, such as deploy RAID5 `btrfs` solutions in live environments, without doing basic write-hole checks to ensure they won't get any data loss if a disk goes pop (for the full story behind this, do an internet search for "`btrfs` raid lol" and you'll probably get some meaningful results).

On the whole, just remember that hardware is out to get you, and you may find some dark amusement in that knowledge the next time you're sat in a data center at four in the morning, holding a hard drive up to your ear to listen for the telltale sound of clicking, as a mechanical head tries and fails to correctly read that one important payroll database.

6
Security, Updating, and Package Management

The following topics will be covered in this chapter:

- Checking package versions
- Checking the OS version
- Checking for updates
- Automating updates
- Checking mailing lists and errata pages
- Using snaps
- Using Flatpak
- Using Pip, RubyGems, and other package managers
- Dependency hell (a quick word)
- Compiling from sources
- Adding additional repositories

Introduction

Your system will be in a perfect state once (maybe twice) in its lifetime.

The first time that it's perfect, unsullied, and unsoiled, is when it's installed (providing that you've ticked the box to update the packages during installation). Your system will never again be in such a pristine condition, because it has not had dirty human hands meddling with its innards.

The second time it's perfect is when it's turned off for the last time, with a job well done, and with a visit to the scrap factory well earned (or, in the case of cloud computing, a quick ethereal jaunt to silicon heaven).

In this section, you'll learn about different sources of packages, how to go about finding and installing new software, and the importance of keeping your systems secure and up to date (lest you end up as a headline on The Register).

It's not the most fun element of the job, and you might find yourself banging your head against the nearest wall several times, but if you get it right, you'll find you have to deal with considerably fewer problems caused by mismatched software in your infrastructure.

The best installations that I've come across automatically rebuild their images periodically, then roll them out across the infrastructure in a consistent and testable way. That takes time to accomplish, and here, we will look at the building blocks to get you started.

Technical requirements

This chapter will deal with disparate package managers and multiple ways of doing the same thing (which pretty much sums up Linux in general).

Because of that, we're going to use three different boxes in our `Vagrantfile`, as follows:

```ruby
# -*- mode: ruby -*-
# vi: set ft=ruby :

Vagrant.configure("2") do |config|

  config.vm.define "centos7" do |centos7|
    centos7.vm.box = "centos/7"
    centos7.vm.box_version = "1804.02"
  end

  config.vm.define "debian9" do |debian9|
    debian9.vm.box = "debian/stretch64"
    debian9.vm.box_version = "9.5.0"
  end

  config.vm.define "ubuntu1804" do |ubuntu1804|
    ubuntu1804.vm.box = "ubuntu/bionic64"
    ubuntu1804.vm.box_version = "20180927.0.0"
  end

end
```

Spinning up these boxes (with `vagrant up`) will provide you with a CentOS installation, a Debian installation, and an Ubuntu installation:

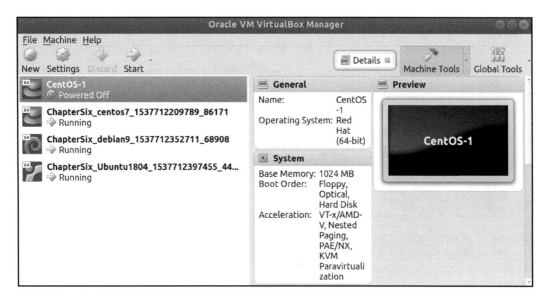

We're going to be using each of these at one point or other.

Checking package versions

In this section, we'll look at listing the packages installed on our systems, and getting the version numbers of those packages.

This will generally be useful if you hear about the latest vulnerability that signals the end of the world, and you are shouted at by your boss to fix it, fix it, fix it.

 There are a considerable number of vulnerabilities out there; it just so happens that a few of the bigger ones bleed through to the mainstream media on occasion. These are arguably the most dangerous, as they make people panic, and if there's one thing worse than a bad situation, it's being in a bad situation while everyone around you is losing their heads.

You should also generally keep your systems up to date, because it's a lot more awkward to jump several version releases (when you inevitably do have to upgrade) than to change things incrementally.

Getting ready

Ensure that all of your boxes are spun up, and try to connect to the first two (CentOS and Debian):

```
$ vagrant ssh centos7
$ vagrant ssh debian9
```

In your Debian box, be sure to install `aptitude`, as it's one of the frontends that we'll be using later in this section; while it is installed by default on some distributions, this Debian installation isn't one of them:

```
$ sudo apt install aptitude
```

How to do it...

The method is similar for each OS, but we're going to take them in turn.

CentOS

CentOS (and Red Hat) have two package managers, with another soon to be added to the equation.

Starting at the top, we have **RPM Package Manager** (**RPM** is a recursive acronym), which is the underpinning of package management in Red Hat based systems. It is what you might consider to be a raw package manager, in the sense that it is primordial, and you probably won't be using it directly day to day.

RPM does the following four things:

- Select
- Query
- Verify
- Install

These options have arguments, and the one that I find myself using the most often is query.

To list all installed packages on your system, use -qa, as follows:

```
$ rpm -qa
kernel-tools-libs-3.10.0-862.2.3.el7.x86_64
```

```
grub2-common-2.02-0.65.el7.centos.2.noarch
dmidecode-3.0-5.el7.x86_64
grub2-pc-modules-2.02-0.65.el7.centos.2.noarch
firewalld-filesystem-0.4.4.4-14.el7.noarch
<SNIP>
gssproxy-0.7.0-17.el7.x86_64
dbus-glib-0.100-7.el7.x86_64
python-slip-dbus-0.4.0-4.el7.noarch
python-pyudev-0.15-9.el7.noarch
plymouth-scripts-0.8.9-0.31.20140113.el7.centos.x86_64
```

To list a specific package, you can name it (without the full version information), as follows:

```
$ rpm -q dmidecode
dmidecode-3.0-5.el7.x86_64
```

To get information on the package, you can use -i:

```
$ rpm -qi dmidecode
Name         : dmidecode
Epoch        : 1
Version      : 3.0
Release      : 5.el7
Architecture : x86_64
Install Date : Sat 12 May 2018 18:52:07 UTC
Group        : System Environment/Base
Size         : 247119
License      : GPLv2+
Signature    : RSA/SHA256, Thu 10 Aug 2017 15:38:00 UTC, Key ID
24c6a8a7f4a80eb5
Source RPM   : dmidecode-3.0-5.el7.src.rpm
Build Date   : Thu 03 Aug 2017 23:53:58 UTC
Build Host   : c1bm.rdu2.centos.org
Relocations  : (not relocatable)
Packager     : CentOS BuildSystem <http://bugs.centos.org>
Vendor       : CentOS
URL          : http://www.nongnu.org/dmidecode/
Summary      : Tool to analyse BIOS DMI data
Description  :
dmidecode reports information about x86 & ia64 hardware as described
in the
system BIOS according to the SMBIOS/DMI standard. This information
typically includes system manufacturer, model name, serial number,
BIOS version, asset tag as well as a lot of other details of varying
level of interest and reliability depending on the manufacturer.

This will often include usage status for the CPU sockets, expansion
```

```
slots (e.g. AGP, PCI, ISA) and memory module slots, and the list of
I/O ports (e.g. serial, parallel, USB).
```

One trick that I find useful is to output specific information in a pseudo-YAML fashion. This can be handy for logging the versions of packages, and can be accomplished with the `--queryformat` option:

```
$ rpm -q --queryformat "---\nName: %{NAME}\n  Version: %{VERSION}\n
Release: %{RELEASE}\n" dmidecode
---
Name: dmidecode
  Version: 3.0
  Release: 5.el7
```

I joke about how RPM is old hat, but there are a considerable number of areas in which it excels, and in a lot of cases it's much quicker to run a package query using the `rpm` command than any of its available frontends, meaning that it is great for scripts. Just be aware that using both RPM and YUM together (to install things) can cause problems.

If you want to use something a bit more recent, the current incarnation of the nice frontend to RPM is called **Yellowdog Updater Modified** (**YUM**), and was originally developed for Yellow Dog Linux.

YUM is generally used because it handles dependency resolution (automatic downloading and installing of dependent packages) as well as installation from configured remote repositories.

Those of you that had a Playstation 3 in the mid-2000s might be interested to know that Yellow Dog was targeted to run on those consoles, during the brief period that Sony allowed for the installation of third-party operating systems alongside its own Orbis OS (based on FreeBSD.)

To list all installed packages with YUM, use `list installed`:

```
$ yum list installed
Loaded plugins: fastestmirror
Loading mirror speeds from cached hostfile
 * base: mirror.vorboss.net
 * extras: mirror.econdc.com
 * updates: mirror.cwcs.co.uk
Installed Packages
GeoIP.x86_64
```

```
1.5.0-11.el7
@anaconda
NetworkManager.x86_64
1:1.10.2-13.el7
@anaconda
NetworkManager-libnm.x86_64
1:1.10.2-13.el7
@anaconda
NetworkManager-team.x86_64
1:1.10.2-13.el7
@anaconda
NetworkManager-tui.x86_64
1:1.10.2-13.el7
@anaconda
<SNIP>
yum-plugin-fastestmirror.noarch
1.1.31-45.el7
@anaconda
yum-utils.noarch
1.1.31-45.el7
@anaconda
zlib.x86_64
1.2.7-17.el7
@anaconda
```

You can also use yum to query individual pieces of information, just like we did with RPM, as follows:

```
$ yum info zlib
Loaded plugins: fastestmirror
Loading mirror speeds from cached hostfile
 * base: mirror.vorboss.net
 * extras: mirror.econdc.com
 * updates: mirror.cwcs.co.uk
Installed Packages
Name        : zlib
Arch        : x86_64
Version     : 1.2.7
Release     : 17.el7
Size        : 181 k
Repo        : installed
From repo   : anaconda
Summary     : The compression and decompression library
URL         : http://www.zlib.net/
Licence     : zlib and Boost
Description : Zlib is a general-purpose, patent-free, lossless data
compression
            : library which is used by many different programs.
```

```
Available Packages
Name        : zlib
Arch        : i686
Version     : 1.2.7
Release     : 17.el7
Size        : 91 k
Repo        : base/7/x86_64
Summary     : The compression and decompression library
URL         : http://www.zlib.net/
Licence     : zlib and Boost
Description : Zlib is a general-purpose, patent-free, lossless data
compression
            : library which is used by many different programs.
```

Note that we also get the available packages by default, and those of you with sharp eyes will have noticed that the only difference between these two packages is the fact that the available one is the 32-bit version.

 DNF (which doesn't stand for did not finish) is the newest of the frontend package managers to take on the task of unifying Red Hat installations. It has been the default in Fedora (a good distribution, and also Red Hat's testing ground) for a while, which means that there is a good chance it'll make it into the next version of CentOS and Red Hat itself. For the most part, it's a drop-in replacement, with a couple of newer features to justify its existence.

Debian

Under the hood, Debian uses the dpkg package manager to install and manage packages. There are also various frontends available, such as apt and aptitude, which make management more user friendly.

Starting with the basics, you can use dpkg-query to query installed packages on a system:

```
$ dpkg-query -W
adduser      3.115
apt      1.4.8
apt-listchanges      3.10
apt-utils      1.4.8
base-files      9.9+deb9u5
base-passwd      3.5.43
bash      4.4-5
<SNIP>
xauth      1:1.0.9-1+b2
```

```
xdg-user-dirs     0.15-2+b1
xkb-data    2.19-1+deb9u1
xml-core     0.17
xxd     2:8.0.0197-4+deb9u1
xz-utils     5.2.2-1.2+b1
zlib1g:amd64     1:1.2.8.dfsg-5
```

You'll no doubt notice that by default, the packages and versions are separated by a tab character. Personally, I think this is hideous (because two spaces are the superior option), but thankfully, we can customize the output by using showformat:

```
$ dpkg-query -W --showformat='${Package} - ${Version}\n'
adduser - 3.115
apt - 1.4.8
apt-listchanges - 3.10
apt-utils - 1.4.8
base-files - 9.9+deb9u5
base-passwd - 3.5.43
<SNIP>
xml-core - 0.17
xxd - 2:8.0.0197-4+deb9u1
xz-utils - 5.2.2-1.2+b1
zlib1g - 1:1.2.8.dfsg-5
```

This can be especially handy for scripts!

On top of dpkg-query, we have apt:

```
$ apt list --installed
Listing... Done
adduser/stable,now 3.115 all [installed]
apt/stable,now 1.4.8 amd64 [installed]
apt-listchanges/stable,now 3.10 all [installed]
apt-utils/stable,now 1.4.8 amd64 [installed]
<SNIP>
xdg-user-dirs/stable,now 0.15-2+b1 amd64 [installed,automatic]
xkb-data/stable,now 2.19-1+deb9u1 all [installed,automatic]
xml-core/stable,now 0.17 all [installed,automatic]
xxd/stable,now 2:8.0.0197-4+deb9u1 amd64 [installed]
xz-utils/stable,now 5.2.2-1.2+b1 amd64 [installed]
zlib1g/stable,now 1:1.2.8.dfsg-5 amd64 [installed]
```

This default output might be preferable to you.

apt is the newer way of interacting with packages on your system, though the traditionalists among you (or those that have learned from traditionalists) might be more familiar with the apt-get and apt-cache suite of tools.

Lastly for this section, there's `aptitude`.

 Aptitude is the first package manager that I can remember using, and I also remember it being a pain to use, because occasionally, it would drop me into a TUI (textual or text-based user interface), and I wouldn't know what was happening.

It's possible to use `aptitude` on the command line, as follows:

```
$ aptitude search  ~i --display-format '%p%v'
adduser
3.115
apt
1.4.8
apt-listchanges
3.10
apt-utils
1.4.8
aptitude
0.8.7-1
aptitude-common
0.8.7-1
base-files
9.9+deb9u5
base-passwd
3.5.43
<SNIP>
xdg-user-dirs
0.15-2+b1
xkb-data
2.19-1+deb9u1
xml-core
0.17
xxd
2:8.0.0197-4+d
xz-utils
5.2.2-1.2+b1
zlib1g
1:1.2.8.dfsg-5
```

It's also possible to type `aptitude` on its own, and get dropped into the TUI:

This interface can be navigated either via the arrow keys on your keyboard, or by using your mouse.

Right off the bat, however, we can see the listed Security Updates and Installed Packages, which make up the 369 packages that we get on the command line:

```
$ aptitude search  ~i --display-format '%p%v'  | wc -l
369
```

We can double-click and drill down into the `aptitude` interface.

In the following screenshot, I've shown the two kernels installed in our VM (`4.9.0-6` and `4.9.0-7`):

```
                                                          vagrant@stretch: ~                                  ⊜ ⊜ ⊗
File Edit View Search Terminal Help
Actions  Undo  Package  Resolver  Search  Options  Views  Help
C-T: Menu  ?: Help  q: Quit  u: Update  g: Preview/Download/Install/Remove Pkgs
aptitude 0.8.7 @ stretch
--\ Security Updates (15)
  --\ kernel       Kernel and kernel modules (2)
    --\ main       The main Debian archive (2)
i A  linux-image-4.9.0-7-amd64                                          4.9.110-1      4.9.110-3+deb9
i    linux-image-amd64                                                  4.9+80+deb9u5  4.9+80+deb9u6
  --- libs         Collections of software routines (2)
  --- net          Programs to connect to and provide various services (3)
  --- python       Python programming language and libraries (0)
--\ Installed Packages (354)
  --- Tasks        Packages which set up your computer to perform a particular task (2)
  --- admin        Administrative utilities (install software, manage users, etc) (42)
  --- devel        Utilities and programs for software development (1)
  --- doc          Documentation and specialized programs for viewing documentation (4)
  --- editors      Text editors and word processors (5)
  --- interpreters Interpreters for interpreted languages (1)
  --\ kernel       Kernel and kernel modules (3)
    --\ main       The main Debian archive (3)
i A  firmware-linux-free                                                3.4            3.4
i A  linux-base                                                         4.5            4.5
i A  linux-image-4.9.0-6-amd64                                          4.9.88-1+deb9u 4.9.88-1+deb9u
  --- libs         Collections of software routines (160)
Security updates for these packages are available from security.debian.org (or mirrors).

This group contains 15 packages.
```

 You might also notice `linux-image-amd64`, which is a meta-package, as opposed to a package in its own right.

We can look for these kernels on the command line, too:

```
$ aptitude search  '~i linux-image' --display-format '%p%v'
linux-image-4.9.0-6-amd64
4.9.88-1+deb9u
linux-image-4.9.0-7-amd64
4.9.110-1
linux-image-amd64
4.9+80+deb9u5
```

How it works...

What you're effectively doing (in both cases) is querying the package database on your system.

On your CentOS system, RPM and YUM are both looking inside `/var/lib/rpm` in order to determine the state of your system.

Similarly, on your Debian system, your package state is held within /var/lib/dpkg.

It is advisable to not mess with these folders outside of the applications that are used to manage them, as modifying the nature of the packages installed on your system (outside of a package manager) can cause odd, and sometimes destructive, behavior.

There's more...

Remember that you don't have to use the system's package manager to list versions; if you would rather trust the output of the application itself, most applications have some variation of the -v, --version standard.

bash, for example, is as follows:

```
$ bash --version
GNU bash, version 4.2.46(2)-release (x86_64-redhat-linux-gnu)
Copyright (C) 2011 Free Software Foundation, Inc.
License GPLv3+: GNU GPL version 3 or later
<http://gnu.org/licenses/gpl.html>

This is free software; you are free to change and redistribute it.
There is NO WARRANTY, to the extent permitted by law.
```

The following shows the code for ssh, which uses -V (uppercase):

```
$ ssh -V
OpenSSH_7.4p1, OpenSSL 1.0.2k-fips  26 Jan 2017
```

And, just to be awkward, Vagrant uses -v (lowercase):

```
$ vagrant -v
Vagrant 2.0.2
```

 You may have noticed the distinct lack of Ubuntu in the preceding examples; this is because anything that works on a Debian system is extremely likely to work on an Ubuntu system.

Checking the OS version

We will be using the same Vagrantfile that was used in the previous section.

In this section, we're going to list the canonical version of our operating system, as well as the kernel version.

We will also take a look at the concept of LSB compliance.

How to do it...

We'll break this section into the different operating systems.

CentOS

We can determine the version of our CentOS installation by printing the contents of the centos-release file, as follows:

```
$ cat /etc/centos-release
CentOS Linux release 7.5.1804 (Core)
```

Here's a fun fact (among a certain type of people): if you cat the contents of redhat-release on your box, you'll get the same information, due to the fact that CentOS and Red Hat systems are so closely aligned:

```
$ cat /etc/redhat-release
CentOS Linux release 7.5.1804 (Core)
```

 cat (derived from concatenate) is a program that was historically used to print the contents of multiple files to standard out.

Likewise, system-release is a symbolic link to centos-release:

```
$ cat /etc/system-release
CentOS Linux release 7.5.1804 (Core)
```

If you wanted more detailed information, you could even print the contents of the `os-release` file:

```
$ cat /etc/os-release
NAME="CentOS Linux"
VERSION="7 (Core)"
ID="centos"
ID_LIKE="rhel fedora"
VERSION_ID="7"
PRETTY_NAME="CentOS Linux 7 (Core)"
ANSI_COLOR="0;31"
CPE_NAME="cpe:/o:centos:centos:7"
HOME_URL="https://www.centos.org/"
BUG_REPORT_URL="https://bugs.centos.org/"

CENTOS_MANTISBT_PROJECT="CentOS-7"
CENTOS_MANTISBT_PROJECT_VERSION="7"
REDHAT_SUPPORT_PRODUCT="centos"
REDHAT_SUPPORT_PRODUCT_VERSION="7"
```

These commands tell you the release of your operating system; what they don't provide you with is the kernel release, which is separate (think back to Chapter 1, *Introduction and Environment Setup*).

To determine the kernel release, one might query `dmesg`, as follows:

```
$ dmesg | grep "Linux version"
[    0.000000] Linux version 3.10.0-862.2.3.el7.x86_64
(builder@kbuilder.dev.centos.org) (gcc version 4.8.5 20150623 (Red Hat
4.8.5-28) (GCC) ) #1 SMP Wed May 9 18:05:47 UTC 2018
```

Alternatively, for a command that doesn't rely on a log file, you might run `uname` with `-a`, in order to print all information about the system:

```
$ uname -a
Linux localhost.localdomain 3.10.0-862.2.3.el7.x86_64 #1 SMP Wed May 9
18:05:47 UTC 2018 x86_64 x86_64 x86_64 GNU/Linux
```

For just the kernel release information, use `-r`, as follows:

```
$ uname -r
3.10.0-862.2.3.el7.x86_64
```

 `uname` is definitely not a Linux-specific command; it'll work on most Unix and Unix-like derivatives. Take a look at what it prints out on your FreeBSD or OpenBSD systems (or your macOS box, if you're not that sad).

You can also use YUM, as listed previously:

```
$ yum -q info installed kernel
Installed Packages
Name        : kernel
Arch        : x86_64
Version     : 3.10.0
Release     : 862.2.3.el7
Size        : 62 M
Repo        : installed
From repo   : koji-override-1
Summary     : The Linux kernel
URL         : http://www.kernel.org/
Licence     : GPLv2
Description : The kernel package contains the Linux kernel (vmlinuz),
the core of any
            : Linux operating system.  The kernel handles the basic
functions
            : of the operating system: memory allocation, process
allocation, device
            : input and output, etc.
```

If you are a real rebel, you can even take a look at what kernels you have installed in `/boot`:

```
$ ls -l /boot
total 25980
-rw-r--r--. 1 root root    147823 May  9 18:19
config-3.10.0-862.2.3.el7.x86_64
drwxr-xr-x. 3 root root        17 May 12 18:50 efi
drwxr-xr-x. 2 root root        27 May 12 18:51 grub
drwx------. 5 root root        97 May 12 18:54 grub2
-rw-------. 1 root root 16506787 May 12 18:55
initramfs-3.10.0-862.2.3.el7.x86_64.img
-rw-r--r--. 1 root root    304926 May  9 18:21
symvers-3.10.0-862.2.3.el7.x86_64.gz
-rw-------. 1 root root   3409102 May  9 18:19
System.map-3.10.0-862.2.3.el7.x86_64
-rwxr-xr-x. 1 root root 6225056 May 9 18:19
vmlinuz-3.10.0-862.2.3.el7.x86_64
```

There's a good chance that the most recent version (emboldened in the preceding code) is the one that you're running, though this doesn't always ring true.

Debian

Things are much the same in the Debian world, although there are fewer OS version files to be worried about.

In Debian, we can look at the contents of /etc/debian_version for the version that we are running:

```
$ cat /etc/debian_version
9.5
```

Or, we can look in /etc/os-release, like with CentOS:

```
$ cat /etc/os-release
PRETTY_NAME="Debian GNU/Linux 9 (stretch)"
NAME="Debian GNU/Linux"
VERSION_ID="9"
VERSION="9 (stretch)"
ID=debian
HOME_URL="https://www.debian.org/"
SUPPORT_URL="https://www.debian.org/support"
BUG_REPORT_URL="https://bugs.debian.org/"
```

Also like in CentOS, we can grep the dmesg log for the version of our kernel:

```
$ sudo dmesg | grep "Linux version"
[    0.000000] Linux version 4.9.0-7-amd64 (debian-
kernel@lists.debian.org) (gcc version 6.3.0 20170516 (Debian
6.3.0-18+deb9u1) ) #1 SMP Debian 4.9.110-1 (2018-07-05)
```

Or, we could use uname, as follows:

```
$ uname -r
4.9.0-7-amd64
```

Yes, Debian has a much more recent version of the kernel at the time of writing this book; this is a mixture of CentOS backporting fixes and features into their older kernels (literally taking improvements from upstream and applying them to older releases,) and the Debian distribution having a much shorter release cycle.

You can list the installed versions by using any of the methods listed previously; the following is the `dpkg-query` example:

```
$ dpkg-query -W linux-image*
linux-image-4.9.0-6-amd64     4.9.88-1+deb9u1
linux-image-4.9.0-7-amd64     4.9.110-1
linux-image-amd64     4.9+80+deb9u5
```

There's also the trusty old /boot, as follows:

```
$ ls -l /boot
total 50264
-rw-r--r-- 1 root root   186567 May  7 22:38 config-4.9.0-6-amd64
-rw-r--r-- 1 root root   186568 Jul  5 01:29 config-4.9.0-7-amd64
drwxr-xr-x 5 root root     4096 Jul 17 01:50 grub
-rw-r--r-- 1 root root 18117609 Jul 17 01:48 initrd.img-4.9.0-6-amd64
-rw-r--r-- 1 root root 18125878 Jul 17 01:50 initrd.img-4.9.0-7-amd64
-rw-r--r-- 1 root root  3190138 May  7 22:38 System.map-4.9.0-6-amd64
-rw-r--r-- 1 root root  3192069 Jul  5 01:29 System.map-4.9.0-7-amd64
-rw-r--r-- 1 root root  4224800 May  7 22:38 vmlinuz-4.9.0-6-amd64
-rw-r--r-- 1 root root  4224800 Jul  5 01:29 vmlinuz-4.9.0-7-amd64
```

Ubuntu

Like all good distributions, Ubuntu also lets you `cat` a file to get information; but, unlike some others, it also tells you when you log in (by default).

SSHing to our Ubuntu box should print something like the following:

```
$ vagrant ssh ubuntu1804
Welcome to Ubuntu 18.04.1 LTS (GNU/Linux 4.15.0-34-generic x86_64)

 * Documentation:  https://help.ubuntu.com
 * Management:     https://landscape.canonical.com
 * Support:        https://ubuntu.com/advantage

  System information as of Sun Sep 30 14:55:26 UTC 2018

  System load:  0.0              Processes:           95
  Usage of /:   9.8% of 9.63GB   Users logged in:     0
  Memory usage: 12%              IP address for enp0s3: 10.0.2.15
  Swap usage:   0%

 * Read about Ubuntu updates for L1 Terminal Fault Vulnerabilities
(L1TF).
   - https://ubu.one/L1TF
```

```
  *  Having fun with some surprising Linux desktop apps... Alan keeps
     the family entertained over the summer/winter holidays.
     - https://bit.ly/top_10_entertainment_apps

  *  Want to make a highly secure kiosk, smart display or touchscreen?
     Here's a step-by-step tutorial for a rainy weekend, or a startup.
     - https://bit.ly/secure-kiosk

    Get cloud support with Ubuntu Advantage Cloud Guest:
      http://www.ubuntu.com/business/services/cloud


 0 packages can be updated.
 0 updates are security updates.


 Last login: Sun Sep 30 14:15:35 2018 from 10.0.2.2
```

Note the emboldened line, which tells you right when you log in what version of Ubuntu you are running.

This **message of the day (MOTD)** is actually built from several files; the header is `00-header`:

$ cat /etc/update-motd.d/00-header

Within this file are some lines, as follows:

```
[ -r /etc/lsb-release ] && . /etc/lsb-release

if [ -z "$DISTRIB_DESCRIPTION" ] && [ -x /usr/bin/lsb_release ]; then
    # Fall back to using the very slow lsb_release utility
    DISTRIB_DESCRIPTION=$(lsb_release -s -d)
fi

printf "Welcome to %s (%s %s %s)\n" "$DISTRIB_DESCRIPTION" "$(uname -
o)" "$(uname -r)" "$(uname -m)"
```

Here, we can check to see whether the `lsb-release` file exists (and is readable) before it's sourced (`. /etc/lsb-release`) for the version.

Then, we have an `if` statement, which says that if the `DISTRIB_DESCRIPTION` variable is empty, and the `lsb_release` binary is executable, we fall back to using that utility to determine the release version (`lsb_release -s -d`).

We then print the output, which is what we saw at the top of the login message.

Failing the MOTD, we can `cat /etc/lsb-release` ourselves, using the following command:

```
$ cat /etc/lsb-release
DISTRIB_ID=Ubuntu
DISTRIB_RELEASE=18.04
DISTRIB_CODENAME=bionic
DISTRIB_DESCRIPTION="Ubuntu 18.04.1 LTS"
```

Or, we can use `os-release` again, as follows:

```
$ cat /etc/os-release
NAME="Ubuntu"
VERSION="18.04.1 LTS (Bionic Beaver)"
ID=ubuntu
ID_LIKE=debian
PRETTY_NAME="Ubuntu 18.04.1 LTS"
VERSION_ID="18.04"
HOME_URL="https://www.ubuntu.com/"
SUPPORT_URL="https://help.ubuntu.com/"
BUG_REPORT_URL="https://bugs.launchpad.net/ubuntu/"
PRIVACY_POLICY_URL="https://www.ubuntu.com/legal/terms-and-policies/pr
ivacy-policy"
VERSION_CODENAME=bionic
UBUNTU_CODENAME=bionic
```

For the kernel, it's much the same as the previous actions; check the `uname`, as follows:

```
$ uname -r
4.15.0-34-generic
```

Check the installed versions, as follows:

```
$ dpkg-query -W  linux-image*
linux-image
linux-image-4.15.0-34-generic      4.15.0-34.37
linux-image-unsigned-4.15.0-34-generic
linux-image-virtual     4.15.0.34.36
```

Or, take a look at `/boot`, as follows:

```
$ ls -l /boot
total 32720
-rw------- 1 root root  4044038 Aug 27 14:45 System.map-4.15.0-34-
generic
-rw-r--r-- 1 root root  1537610 Aug 27 14:45 abi-4.15.0-34-generic
-rw-r--r-- 1 root root   216905 Aug 27 14:45 config-4.15.0-34-generic
```

```
drwxr-xr-x 5 root root     4096 Sep 21 12:13 grub
-rw-r--r-- 1 root root 19423451 Sep 21 12:00 initrd.img-4.15.0-34-
generic
-rw-r--r-- 1 root root        0 Aug 27 14:45 retpoline-4.15.0-34-
generic
-rw------- 1 root root  8269560 Aug 27 15:06 vmlinuz-4.15.0-34-generic
```

> The `vmlinuz` object, as seen previously, is the compressed
> executable of the Linux kernel.

How it works...

When you are querying these files, you are asking the OS what version it thinks it is.

This is useful in everything from security to writing scripts. Not only do you want to know when the version of an OS you're running is insecure, you might also want to add a sanity check to the top of any scripts, to ensure they're only run on systems they're designed for, that is, you can write a script for CentOS systems, and step one can be to "check we're actually being executed on a CentOS system."

`uname` (Unix name) is more interesting, because instead of querying files for the OS version, what we were actually doing was querying the running kernel for its information.

`uname` uses the `uname` system call (confused yet?), which is not only POSIX-compliant, but has roots that go all the way back to the 1970s and PWB/Unix.

There's more...

You might have noticed the Ubuntu usage of `lsb_release` to grab its OS version; the same can be done on `CentOS`, but first, `lsb_release` needs to be installed:

```
$ sudo yum install redhat-lsb-core
```

Now, we can run the same command that Ubuntu uses in order to get OS information:

```
$ lsb_release -s -d
"CentOS Linux release 7.5.1804 (Core) "
```

The same can be done on `Debian`, without having to install anything by default:

```
$ lsb_release -s -d
Debian GNU/Linux 9.5 (stretch)
```

Linux Standard Base (**LSB**) is basically a standard that multiple distributions sign up to. It specifies a **Filesystem Hierarchy Standard** (**FHS**), as well as various other components of a Linux system.

 The LSB also suggests the package format of RPM, although Debian and Ubuntu obviously don't use this by default, opting for `.deb` instead. To get around this, Debian offers the `alien` package, which is used to transform `.rpm` files into `.deb` files prior to installation. It is something of a dirty hack, and it doesn't guarantee compliance; it is more a sort of courtesy nod.

See also...

Take a look at the old Unix programs and conventions, and you'll be surprised by how many of them have survived till the modern day.

GNU is not Unix, though, so why do Linux systems also have `uname`? The answer is, because it's Unix-like, and a lot of the commands and conventions pioneered by Unix were rewritten by the GNU operating system and free software movement, for the convenience of familiarity.

Checking for updates

In this section, we will use the `Vagrantfile` that was used in part of the first section. Now that we know the versions of software associated with our system (packages, OS, and kernel), we're going to look at what updates are available to us, and how we might install them.

We will check for both specific package updates and updates to all packages.

How to do it...

In this section, we're going to drop into our `CentOS` and `Debian` boxes, skipping Ubuntu, as the same rules from Debian will apply.

We are going to use the kernel throughout these examples, although any package on your system can be substituted.

CentOS

In `CentOS`, the easiest way to check for updates to a package is with YUM, as follows:

```
$ yum -q info kernel
Installed Packages
Name : kernel
Arch : x86_64
Version : 3.10.0
Release : 862.2.3.el7
Size : 62 M
Repo : installed
From repo : koji-override-1
Summary : The Linux kernel
URL : http://www.kernel.org/
Licence : GPLv2
Description : The kernel package contains the Linux kernel (vmlinuz),
the core of any
 : Linux operating system. The kernel handles the basic functions
 : of the operating system: memory allocation, process allocation,
device
 : input and output, etc.

Available Packages
Name : kernel
Arch : x86_64
Version : 3.10.0
Release : 862.14.4.el7
Size : 46 M
Repo : updates/7/x86_64
Summary : The Linux kernel
URL : http://www.kernel.org/
Licence : GPLv2
Description : The kernel package contains the Linux kernel (vmlinuz),
the core of any
 : Linux operating system. The kernel handles the basic functions
 : of the operating system: memory allocation, process allocation,
device
```

```
: input and output, etc.
```

Note that we are not limiting the output to installed packages; instead, we are checking what we have installed, and what is available.

The output tells us that while the version number has not changed, the release of the kernel has been updated, and is available from the `updates/7/x86_64` repo.

To update our kernel, we would simply run a `yum upgrade` command, as follows:

```
$ sudo yum upgrade -y kernel
```

 We've previously mentioned the list of packages-that-will-change when running YUM commands. With '-y' we auto-accept these changes, but if you're unsure, it's a good idea to omit the '-y' flag and sanity-check manually by reading the presented list.

So, specific packages are pretty simple, but how do we check all installed packages on our system?

With YUM, of course!

We can use either `update` or `upgrade`, which are basically the same on modern installations:

```
$ sudo yum upgrade
```

 Using `upgrade` (rather than `update`) should technically be different, as it also uses logic to obsolete and replace obsoleted programs, but because this is behavior that most people desire, `obsoletes=1` is also set in `yum.conf`, making `update` and `upgrade` functionally the same by default.

Our preceding command should result in a screen like the following:

```
                                              vagrant@localhost:~                                    ● ● ●
File  Edit  View  Search  Terminal  Help
iptables                          x86_64        1.4.21-24.1.el7_5                    updates      432 k
kernel-tools                      x86_64        3.10.0-862.14.4.el7                  updates      6.3 M
kernel-tools-libs                 x86_64        3.10.0-862.14.4.el7                  updates      6.2 M
kpartx                            x86_64        0.4.9-119.el7_5.1                    updates       76 k
libblkid                          x86_64        2.23.2-52.el7_5.1                    updates      178 k
libcom_err                        x86_64        1.42.9-12.el7_5                      updates       41 k
libgcc                            x86_64        4.8.5-28.el7_5.1                     updates      101 k
libgomp                           x86_64        4.8.5-28.el7_5.1                     updates      156 k
libmount                          x86_64        2.23.2-52.el7_5.1                    updates      180 k
libss                             x86_64        1.42.9-12.el7_5                      updates       45 k
libstdc++                         x86_64        4.8.5-28.el7_5.1                     updates      303 k
libuuid                           x86_64        2.23.2-52.el7_5.1                    updates       81 k
linux-firmware                    noarch        20180220-62.2.git6d51311.el7_5      updates       57 M
mariadb-libs                      x86_64        1:5.5.60-1.el7_5                     updates      758 k
nspr                              x86_64        4.19.0-1.el7_5                       updates      127 k
nss                               x86_64        3.36.0-7.el7_5                       updates      835 k
nss-softokn                       x86_64        3.36.0-5.el7_5                       updates      315 k
nss-softokn-freebl                x86_64        3.36.0-5.el7_5                       updates      222 k
nss-sysinit                       x86_64        3.36.0-7.el7_5                       updates       62 k
nss-tools                         x86_64        3.36.0-7.el7_5                       updates      515 k
nss-util                          x86_64        3.36.0-1.el7_5                       updates       78 k
openldap                          x86_64        2.4.44-15.el7_5                      updates      355 k
procps-ng                         x86_64        3.3.10-17.el7_5.2                    updates      290 k
python                            x86_64        2.7.5-69.el7_5                       updates       93 k
python-firewall                   noarch        0.4.4.4-15.el7_5                     updates      328 k
python-libs                       x86_64        2.7.5-69.el7_5                       updates      5.6 M
python-perf                       x86_64        3.10.0-862.14.4.el7                  updates      6.3 M
qemu-guest-agent                  x86_64        10:2.8.0-2.el7_5.1                   updates      150 k
rsyslog                           x86_64        8.24.0-16.el7_5.4                    updates      607 k
selinux-policy                    noarch        3.13.1-192.el7_5.6                   updates      453 k
selinux-policy-targeted           noarch        3.13.1-192.el7_5.6                   updates      6.6 M
sudo                              x86_64        1.8.19p2-14.el7_5                    updates      1.1 M
systemd                           x86_64        219-57.el7_5.3                       updates      5.0 M
systemd-libs                      x86_64        219-57.el7_5.3                       updates      402 k
systemd-sysv                      x86_64        219-57.el7_5.3                       updates       80 k
tuned                             noarch        2.9.0-1.el7_5.2                      updates      244 k
util-linux                        x86_64        2.23.2-52.el7_5.1                    updates      2.0 M
yum-plugin-fastestmirror          noarch        1.1.31-46.el7_5                      updates       33 k
yum-utils                         noarch        1.1.31-46.el7_5                      updates      120 k

Transaction Summary
================================================================================================
Install    1 Package
Upgrade   60 Packages

Total download size: 164 M
Is this ok [y/d/N]:
```

Note that without flags added to the command, the update will stop here, with a prompt for you to choose y/d/N (with N being the default).

If you are ready to upgrade, passing y to this command will update and install the preceding packages.

If you are not ready to upgrade, passing d will only download the packages.

As we've said before, typically, the only programs that require a reboot to update are the kernel and systemd (the init system), as these are the soul of your installation, and you're basically killing the old program to make way for the new (which will be selected by default on most systems, following an upgrade).

Running our `yum info` command will now show two installed kernels, and no available ones, as follows:

```
$ yum -q info kernel
Installed Packages
Name        : kernel
Arch        : x86_64
Version     : 3.10.0
Release     : 862.2.3.el7
Size        : 62 M
Repo        : installed
From repo   : koji-override-1
Summary     : The Linux kernel
URL         : http://www.kernel.org/
Licence     : GPLv2
Description : The kernel package contains the Linux kernel (vmlinuz),
the core of any
            : Linux operating system.  The kernel handles the basic
functions
            : of the operating system: memory allocation, process
allocation, device
            : input and output, etc.

Name        : kernel
Arch        : x86_64
Version     : 3.10.0
Release     : 862.14.4.el7
Size        : 62 M
Repo        : installed
From repo   : updates
Summary     : The Linux kernel
URL         : http://www.kernel.org/
Licence     : GPLv2
Description : The kernel package contains the Linux kernel (vmlinuz),
the core of any
            : Linux operating system.  The kernel handles the basic
functions
            : of the operating system: memory allocation, process
allocation, device
            : input and output, etc.
```

Debian

On Debian, we're going to use `apt`, which is the newest and, in my opinion, friendliest tool.

Unlike YUM, we can easily and independently update the list of available packages:

```
$ sudo apt update
Ign:1 http://deb.debian.org/debian stretch InRelease
Hit:2 http://deb.debian.org/debian stretch Release
Hit:4 http://security.debian.org/debian-security stretch/updates
InRelease
Reading package lists... Done
Building dependency tree
Reading state information... Done
15 packages can be upgraded. Run 'apt list --upgradable' to see them.
```

Note that it only updates its list, not the programs themselves.

Now, we can look for specific information by using the suggested command:

```
$ apt list --upgradable linux-image*
Listing... Done
linux-image-4.9.0-7-amd64/stable 4.9.110-3+deb9u2 amd64 [upgradable
from: 4.9.110-1]
linux-image-amd64/stable 4.9+80+deb9u6 amd64 [upgradable from:
4.9+80+deb9u5]
```

Without adding the `regex-matched` package on the end, this command will list all packages that are `upgradable`:

```
$ apt list --upgradable
Listing... Done
libcurl3-gnutls/stable 7.52.1-5+deb9u7 amd64 [upgradable from:
7.52.1-5+deb9u6]
libfuse2/stable 2.9.7-1+deb9u1 amd64 [upgradable from: 2.9.7-1]
libpython2.7-minimal/stable 2.7.13-2+deb9u3 amd64 [upgradable from:
2.7.13-2+deb9u2]
libpython2.7-stdlib/stable 2.7.13-2+deb9u3 amd64 [upgradable from:
2.7.13-2+deb9u2]
libpython3.5-minimal/stable 3.5.3-1+deb9u1 amd64 [upgradable from:
3.5.3-1]
libpython3.5-stdlib/stable 3.5.3-1+deb9u1 amd64 [upgradable from:
3.5.3-1]
linux-image-4.9.0-7-amd64/stable 4.9.110-3+deb9u2 amd64 [upgradable
from: 4.9.110-1]
linux-image-amd64/stable 4.9+80+deb9u6 amd64 [upgradable from:
4.9+80+deb9u5]
openssh-client/stable 1:7.4p1-10+deb9u4 amd64 [upgradable from:
1:7.4p1-10+deb9u3]
openssh-server/stable 1:7.4p1-10+deb9u4 amd64 [upgradable from:
1:7.4p1-10+deb9u3]
openssh-sftp-server/stable 1:7.4p1-10+deb9u4 amd64 [upgradable from:
```

```
1:7.4p1-10+deb9u3]
python2.7/stable 2.7.13-2+deb9u3 amd64 [upgradable from:
2.7.13-2+deb9u2]
python2.7-minimal/stable 2.7.13-2+deb9u3 amd64 [upgradable from:
2.7.13-2+deb9u2]
python3.5/stable 3.5.3-1+deb9u1 amd64 [upgradable from: 3.5.3-1]
python3.5-minimal/stable 3.5.3-1+deb9u1 amd64 [upgradable from:
3.5.3-1]
```

As with YUM, we can upgrade a single package by using `apt`:

```
$ sudo apt install linux-image-amd64
Reading package lists... Done
Building dependency tree
Reading state information... Done
The following additional packages will be installed:
  linux-image-4.9.0-8-amd64
Suggested packages:
  linux-doc-4.9 debian-kernel-handbook
The following NEW packages will be installed:
  linux-image-4.9.0-8-amd64
The following packages will be upgraded:
  linux-image-amd64
1 upgraded, 1 newly installed, 0 to remove and 14 not upgraded.
Need to get 39.1 MB of archives.
After this operation, 193 MB of additional disk space will be used.
Do you want to continue? [Y/n]
```

Note that we specifically use the `install` option instead of `upgrade`, as `upgrade` would try to do all packages, instead of just `linux-image-amd64`.

If we wanted to upgrade everything, we would use `upgrade` or `full-upgrade`:

```
$ sudo apt full-upgrade
Reading package lists... Done
Building dependency tree
Reading state information... Done
Calculating upgrade... Done
The following NEW packages will be installed:
  linux-image-4.9.0-8-amd64
The following packages will be upgraded:
  libcurl3-gnutls libfuse2 libpython2.7-minimal libpython2.7-stdlib
libpython3.5-minimal libpython3.5-stdlib linux-image-4.9.0-7-amd64
linux-image-amd64 openssh-client
  openssh-server openssh-sftp-server python2.7 python2.7-minimal
python3.5 python3.5-minimal
15 upgraded, 1 newly installed, 0 to remove and 0 not upgraded.
Need to get 88.3 MB of archives.
```

```
After this operation, 193 MB of additional disk space will be used.
Do you want to continue? [Y/n]
```

The reason that I used `full-upgrade` is because using only `upgrade` can result in packages not being upgraded (if that upgrade requires the removal of another package).

 There may be moments when `upgrade` is preferable to `full-upgrade`, so I would advocate checking the output of your `upgrade` command prior to confirming that it is what you want to do.

How it works...

When you run the preceding package manager commands, what you are doing is querying whichever upstream servers they're configured to talk to, and asking if there are any newer versions of the installed packages available.

Configured repositories are in `/etc/yum.repos.d/` on `CentOS` and `/etc/apt/sources.list.d` (or `sources.list.conf`).

If there are newer versions of your software available, you have the option to install or download for later. Generally, it's a good idea to ensure that all your software is kept up to date, but this is especially true for public-facing services, such as web servers and SSH daemons.

There's more...

Some popular and tricky software exists outside the realm of sense (as far as this opinionated author is concerned).

Of particular note are the Hashicorp suite of tools, which check to see if there's a new version of themselves available when invoked. This means that when you run `Terraform`, there is a chance that it will inform you that it is out of date, and you should download a newer version:

```
$ terraform --version
Terraform v0.11.7

Your version of Terraform is out of date! The latest version
is 0.11.8. You can update by downloading from
www.terraform.io/downloads.html
```

The package maintainers for distributions usually do not keep on top of this, through no fault of their own, and quite a few won't even bother to package software that does this at the moment. What this means is that frequently people will instead add Terraform, Packer, and other pieces of cool software outside of their package manager, doubling the number of package management systems you need to keep track of (one being your system's, and the other being you).

Automating updates

In this section, we will use the `Vagrantfile` that was used in part of the first section.

Something of a slur, "automatic updating" is a sticky subject for a lot of system administrators, because historically, it was frequently the case that updates would brick a system.

This is less and less likely these days, and there are ways you can automate updates on your boxes without worry (though I still wouldn't do this in production, personally).

We will also discuss programmatically rebuilding systems.

How to do it...

Jump into each of your boxes in turn, in this section.

It is important to note that you might not want to automatically install updates at all, especially if you are in an environment where machines are periodically destroyed and rebuilt.

There might also be in-house procedures that tie your hands, meaning that whatever you are technically capable of doing, bureaucracy can always get in the way.

CentOS

On `CentOS` systems, we have a handy tool called `yum-cron`:

```
$ sudo yum install yum-cron -y
```

It comes with two configuration files, located in `/etc/yum/`.

By default, the `/etc/yum/yum-cron.conf` file will be used, and it has a random sleep inside it that we are going to disable:

```
$ sudo sed -i "s/random_sleep = 360/random_sleep = 0/g" /etc/yum/yum-cron.conf
```

Now, this means that when `yum-cron` is called, it will automatically run, applying the default settings of `yum-cron.conf`:

```
$ sudo yum-cron
$
```

If there are no updates, `yum-cron` will not show any output (as seen previously).

If there are updates, by default, you will get a notification that they have downloaded successfully:

```
                                                                        vagrant@localhost:~                              
File  Edit  View  Search  Terminal  Help
initscripts                x86_64  9.49.41-1.el7_5.2              updates  437 k
iptables                   x86_64  1.4.21-24.1.el7_5             updates  432 k
kernel-tools               x86_64  3.10.0-862.14.4.el7           updates  6.3 M
kernel-tools-libs          x86_64  3.10.0-862.14.4.el7           updates  6.2 M
kpartx                     x86_64  0.4.9-119.el7_5.1             updates   76 k
libblkid                   x86_64  2.23.2-52.el7_5.1             updates  178 k
libcom_err                 x86_64  1.42.9-12.el7_5               updates   41 k
libgcc                     x86_64  4.8.5-28.el7_5.1              updates  101 k
libgomp                    x86_64  4.8.5-28.el7_5.1              updates  156 k
libmount                   x86_64  2.23.2-52.el7_5.1             updates  180 k
libss                      x86_64  1.42.9-12.el7_5               updates   45 k
libstdc++                  x86_64  4.8.5-28.el7_5.1              updates  303 k
libuuid                    x86_64  2.23.2-52.el7_5.1             updates   81 k
linux-firmware             noarch  20180220-62.2.git6d51311.el7_5  updates   57 M
mariadb-libs               x86_64  1:5.5.60-1.el7_5              updates  758 k
nspr                       x86_64  4.19.0-1.el7_5                updates  127 k
nss                        x86_64  3.36.0-7.el7_5                updates  835 k
nss-softokn                x86_64  3.36.0-5.el7_5                updates  315 k
nss-softokn-freebl         x86_64  3.36.0-5.el7_5                updates  222 k
nss-sysinit                x86_64  3.36.0-7.el7_5                updates   62 k
nss-tools                  x86_64  3.36.0-7.el7_5                updates  515 k
nss-util                   x86_64  3.36.0-1.el7_5                updates   78 k
openldap                   x86_64  2.4.44-15.el7_5               updates  355 k
procps-ng                  x86_64  3.3.10-17.el7_5.2             updates  290 k
python                     x86_64  2.7.5-69.el7_5                updates   93 k
python-firewall            noarch  0.4.4.4-15.el7_5              updates  328 k
python-libs                x86_64  2.7.5-69.el7_5                updates  5.6 M
python-perf                x86_64  3.10.0-862.14.4.el7           updates  6.3 M
qemu-guest-agent           x86_64  10:2.8.0-2.el7_5.1            updates  150 k
rsyslog                    x86_64  8.24.0-16.el7_5.4             updates  607 k
selinux-policy             noarch  3.13.1-192.el7_5.6            updates  453 k
selinux-policy-targeted    noarch  3.13.1-192.el7_5.6            updates  6.6 M
sudo                       x86_64  1.8.19p2-14.el7_5             updates  1.1 M
systemd                    x86_64  219-57.el7_5.3                updates  5.0 M
systemd-libs               x86_64  219-57.el7_5.3                updates  402 k
systemd-sysv               x86_64  219-57.el7_5.3                updates   80 k
tuned                      noarch  2.9.0-1.el7_5.2               updates  244 k
util-linux                 x86_64  2.23.2-52.el7_5.1             updates  2.0 M
yum-plugin-fastestmirror   noarch  1.1.31-46.el7_5              updates   33 k
yum-utils                  noarch  1.1.31-46.el7_5              updates  120 k

Transaction Summary
================================================================================
Install   1 Package
Upgrade  60 Packages
Updates downloaded successfully.
[vagrant@localhost ~]$
```

If you wanted to apply the updates automatically, that would involve another config file change, as follows:

```
$ sudo sed -i "s/apply_updates = no/apply_updates = yes/g"
/etc/yum/yum-cron.conf
```

Running `yum-cron` again will apply the downloaded updates:

```
                                                                        vagrant@localhost:~
File  Edit  View  Search  Terminal  Help
initscripts              x86_64 9.49.41-1.el7_5.2           updates 437 k
iptables                 x86_64 1.4.21-24.1.el7_5           updates 432 k
kernel-tools             x86_64 3.10.0-862.14.4.el7         updates 6.3 M
kernel-tools-libs        x86_64 3.10.0-862.14.4.el7         updates 6.2 M
kpartx                   x86_64 0.4.9-119.el7_5.1           updates  76 k
libblkid                 x86_64 2.23.2-52.el7_5.1           updates 178 k
libcom_err               x86_64 1.42.9-12.el7_5             updates  41 k
libgcc                   x86_64 4.8.5-28.el7_5.1            updates 101 k
libgomp                  x86_64 4.8.5-28.el7_5.1            updates 156 k
libmount                 x86_64 2.23.2-52.el7_5.1           updates 180 k
libss                    x86_64 1.42.9-12.el7_5             updates  45 k
libstdc++                x86_64 4.8.5-28.el7_5.1            updates 303 k
libuuid                  x86_64 2.23.2-52.el7_5.1           updates  81 k
linux-firmware           noarch 20180220-62.2.git6d51311.el7_5 updates  57 M
mariadb-libs             x86_64 1:5.5.60-1.el7_5            updates 758 k
nspr                     x86_64 4.19.0-1.el7_5              updates 127 k
nss                      x86_64 3.36.0-7.el7_5              updates 835 k
nss-softokn              x86_64 3.36.0-5.el7_5              updates 315 k
nss-softokn-freebl       x86_64 3.36.0-5.el7_5              updates 222 k
nss-sysinit              x86_64 3.36.0-7.el7_5              updates  62 k
nss-tools                x86_64 3.36.0-7.el7_5              updates 515 k
nss-util                 x86_64 3.36.0-1.el7_5              updates  78 k
openldap                 x86_64 2.4.44-15.el7_5             updates 355 k
procps-ng                x86_64 3.3.10-17.el7_5.2           updates 290 k
python                   x86_64 2.7.5-69.el7_5              updates  93 k
python-firewall          noarch 0.4.4.4-15.el7_5           updates 328 k
python-libs              x86_64 2.7.5-69.el7_5              updates 5.6 M
python-perf              x86_64 3.10.0-862.14.4.el7         updates 6.3 M
qemu-guest-agent         x86_64 10:2.8.0-2.el7_5.1          updates 150 k
rsyslog                  x86_64 8.24.0-16.el7_5.4           updates 607 k
selinux-policy           noarch 3.13.1-192.el7_5.6          updates 453 k
selinux-policy-targeted  noarch 3.13.1-192.el7_5.6          updates 6.6 M
sudo                     x86_64 1.8.19p2-14.el7_5           updates 1.1 M
systemd                  x86_64 219-57.el7_5.3              updates 5.0 M
systemd-libs             x86_64 219-57.el7_5.3              updates 402 k
systemd-sysv             x86_64 219-57.el7_5.3              updates  80 k
tuned                    noarch 2.9.0-1.el7_5.2             updates 244 k
util-linux               x86_64 2.23.2-52.el7_5.1           updates 2.0 M
yum-plugin-fastestmirror noarch 1.1.31-46.el7_5             updates  33 k
yum-utils                noarch 1.1.31-46.el7_5             updates 120 k

Transaction Summary
================================================================================
Install   1 Package
Upgrade  60 Packages
The updates were successfully applied
[vagrant@localhost ~]$
```

We have mentioned previously (but it is worth saying again) that this does not necessarily mean that services will instantly be fixed, or will have new features.

That is where the command `needs-restarting` comes in.

You can also run this with a timer (or `cron`, if you must) to list processes that need restarting after they've been updated, or a component they utilize has:

```
$ sudo needs-restarting
2617 : /usr/lib/systemd/systemd-udevd
1082 : qmgr -l -t unix -u
603 : /usr/sbin/crond -n
609 : /sbin/agetty --noclear tty1 linux
574 : /usr/sbin/chronyd
397 : /usr/lib/systemd/systemd-journald
851 : /usr/sbin/sshd -D -u0
1070 : /usr/libexec/postfix/master -w
1 : /usr/lib/systemd/systemd --system --deserialize 21
2155 : sshd: vagrant [priv]
<SNIP>
```

If you would like nicer output, you can specify services, as follows:

```
$ sudo needs-restarting -s
rpcbind.service
chronyd.service
systemd-logind.service
NetworkManager.service
postfix.service
dbus.service
getty@tty1.service
crond.service
lvm2-lvmetad.service
sshd.service
gssproxy.service
systemd-udevd.service
systemd-journald.service
polkit.service
```

Or only if a reboot is needed, use the following command:

```
$ sudo needs-restarting -r
Core libraries or services have been updated:
  kernel -> 3.10.0-862.14.4.el7
  systemd -> 219-57.el7_5.3
  linux-firmware -> 20180220-62.2.git6d51311.el7_5

Reboot is required to ensure that your system benefits from these
updates.

More information:
https://access.redhat.com/solutions/27943
```

A really simple way of starting `yum-cron` is with the following line:

```
$ sudo systemctl enable --now yum-cron
```

Debian

In the Debian (and Ubuntu) world, we use a package called `unattended-upgrades`. It's been around for quite a while, and is usually the option people go with for automatically updating their Debian-based distributions.

Jump into your stretch box and run a quick `install` of the package, as follows:

```
$ sudo apt install unattended-upgrades
```

If you now `ls` the `/etc/apt/apt.conf.d/` directory, you will see a couple of new files:

```
$ ls -l /etc/apt/apt.conf.d/
total 44
-rw-r--r-- 1 root root   49 Jul 17 01:48 00aptitude
-rw-r--r-- 1 root root   82 Jul 17 01:46 00CDMountPoint
-rw-r--r-- 1 root root   40 Jul 17 01:46 00trustcdrom
-rw-r--r-- 1 root root  769 Sep 13  2017 01autoremove
-r--r--r-- 1 root root 1768 Jul 17 01:49 01autoremove-kernels
-rw-r--r-- 1 root root   80 Dec 11  2016 20auto-upgrades
-rw-r--r-- 1 root root  202 Apr 10  2017 20listchanges
-rw-r--r-- 1 root root 4259 Oct  1 16:49 50unattended-upgrades
-rw-r--r-- 1 root root  182 May 21  2017 70debconf
-rw-r--r-- 1 root root   27 Jul 17 01:49 99translations
```

These are the crux of the `unattended-upgrades` package.

If we take a look at the block in the `50unattended-upgrades` configuration file that handles which updates to pull in, we will see the following:

```
Unattended-Upgrade::Origins-Pattern {
  // Codename based matching:
  // This will follow the migration of a release through different
  // archives (e.g. from testing to stable and later oldstable).
  // "o=Debian,n=jessie";
  // "o=Debian,n=jessie-updates";
  // "o=Debian,n=jessie-proposed-updates";
  // "o=Debian,n=jessie,l=Debian-Security";

  // Archive or Suite based matching:
  // Note that this will silently match a different release after
  // migration to the specified archive (e.g. testing becomes the
  // new stable).
  // "o=Debian,a=stable";
  // "o=Debian,a=stable-updates";
  // "o=Debian,a=proposed-updates";
  "origin=Debian,codename=${distro_codename},label=Debian-Security";
};
```

Note that the only uncommented line is the bottom one (before the closing brace).

We are going to uncomment the lines that precede it, as follows:

```
$ sudo sed -i 's/\/\/       "o=Debian,a=stable";/
"o=Debian,a=stable";/g' /etc/apt/apt.conf.d/50unattended-upgrades
$ sudo sed -i 's/\/\/       "o=Debian,a=stable-updates";/
"o=Debian,a=stable-updates";/g' /etc/apt/apt.conf.d/50unattended-
upgrades
$ sudo sed -i 's/\/\/       "o=Debian,a=proposed-updates";/
"o=Debian,a=proposed-updates";/g' /etc/apt/apt.conf.d/50unattended-
upgrades
```

You can run and test your configuration by starting the command in debug mode:

```
$ sudo unattended-upgrade -d
```

It might look something like the following:

Noticed how the upgrades were actually installed, and a log file was created.

How it works...

`yum-cron` is actually just an easy way to use YUM from within a cron job (which we mentioned disparagingly earlier, while discussing `systemd` timers). Because of this, you would find it easy to incorporate into a custom timer (see earlier chapters) or a cron job that might run nightly.

In general, you could apply all updates to a development environment nightly, and then potentially stagger updates to other (higher) environments throughout the week, upgrading production to the next Tuesday. That is entirely up to you, as the all-powerful sysadmin.

If you have taken the suggestion of enabling `yum-cron` as a service, you should now find that the following file exists:

```
$ ls /var/lock/subsys/yum-cron
/var/lock/subsys/yum-cron
```

This enables the two `cron` jobs, as follows:

```
$ ls /etc/cron.daily/0yum-daily.cron
/etc/cron.daily/0yum-daily.cron
$ ls /etc/cron.hourly/0yum-hourly.cron
/etc/cron.hourly/0yum-hourly.cron
```

These will use the configuration files that we mentioned.

In the case of Debian's `unattended-upgrades`, and as with most modern systems, `systemd` is used to run this job daily.

List your `systemd` timers, as follows:

```
$ sudo systemctl list-timers
NEXT                            LEFT         LAST
PASSED      UNIT                             ACTIVATES
Mon 2018-10-01 20:34:32 GMT  3h 16min left Mon 2018-10-01 16:48:00 GMT
30min ago apt-daily.timer               apt-daily.service
Tue 2018-10-02 06:56:19 GMT  13h left      Mon 2018-10-01 16:48:00 GMT
30min ago apt-daily-upgrade.timer        apt-daily-upgrade.service
Tue 2018-10-02 17:03:03 GMT  23h left      Mon 2018-10-01 17:03:03 GMT
15min ago systemd-tmpfiles-clean.timer systemd-tmpfiles-clean.service

3 timers listed.
Pass --all to see loaded but inactive timers, too.
```

Note the two `apt` jobs, the first of which runs the following:

```
[Service]
Type=oneshot
ExecStart=/usr/lib/apt/apt.systemd.daily update
```

The second one runs the following:

```
[Service]
Type=oneshot
ExecStart=/usr/lib/apt/apt.systemd.daily install
KillMode=process
TimeoutStopSec=900
```

There's more...

Like unattended upgrades on Debian, `yum-cron` has the ability to work through only specific types of upgrades. By default, this is set to `default`, as seen in the following snippet, which is why we didn't modify it earlier:

```
$ cat /etc/yum/yum-cron.conf
[commands]
#  What kind of update to use:
# default                            = yum upgrade
# security                           = yum --security upgrade
# security-severity:Critical         = yum --sec-severity=Critical
upgrade
# minimal                            = yum --bugfix update-minimal
# minimal-security                   = yum --security update-minimal
# minimal-security-severity:Critical =  --sec-severity=Critical
update-minimal
update_cmd = default
```

There's nothing stopping you from changing this, perhaps specifying that only security upgrades should be applied automatically?

Automatic provisioning

In the prelude I suggested that we would touch on this, and it is definitely worth discussing.

Once, it was the case that physical machines roamed the earth, preying on unsuspecting sysadmins that dared to enter their swamps and server cages.

Nowadays, servers still exist, but they have been given a more tech-unfriendly and media-savvy name, becoming colloquially known as the **cloud**, and being made transparent enough that sysadmins no longer know whether their favorite hipster distribution is running on a Dell, HPE, or IBM machine.

This has given rise to transient servers, or servers that periodically cease to exist in the evening, only to be born anew the next morning.

Aside from giving you an existential crisis about whether or not you cease to exist when you go to sleep for the night, this might start to give you ideas about never updating your machines, instead simply ensuring that they come back up with all updates already applied.

The notion of automatically provisioning your infrastructure on a schedule is gaining traction, and what it boils down to is creating an image programmatically (with a program such as Packer) before uploading and/or moving it to a different portion of your virtual infrastructure, where another program (Terraform) can use the new image to spin up a lot of shiny new boxes.

Obviously, this works all the way up to a production network without issues, because there are no customers around on your `dev` instances (I hope—I really, really hope). It does present a problem in production, but then you start to think about wild and crazy things such as blue/green deployments.

Checking mailing lists and errata pages

Outside of our systems, we will take a look at where you go for news on how your operating systems are performing, in general. Are they healthy? Do they need some space? Are they going to implode pretty soon?

It's good practice to get into this habit, because occasionally, system and behavioral changes may require manual intervention on the part of the sysadmin, even if you automate all of your other problems away.

Servers – who needs them?

Getting ready

In this section, we will be using our VMs a bit, and the almighty internet.

How to do it...

We're going to take a look at our VMs a little bit, but we are mostly going to be focusing on online locations for news.

There are various methods and places that you might go for information, so let's work through some of the more popular ones.

Package changelogs

If you want information about a package, one thing that you might like is the changelog, accessible from your system with a simple RPM command.

First, find the package you want to check; we're going to grab the most recently installed kernel:

```
$ rpm -q kernel --last
kernel-3.10.0-862.14.4.el7.x86_64          Sun 30 Sep 2018 16:40:08
UTC
kernel-3.10.0-862.2.3.el7.x86_64           Sat 12 May 2018 18:51:56
UTC
```

Now, open the changelog for that kernel (it's long):

```
$ rpm -q --changelog kernel-3.10.0-862.14.4.el7.x86_64 | less
```

You will get something like the following:

This can be a good way to check for specific changes, but it can also sometimes be a bit tricky (depending on the nature of the log).

To show that it's available for other packages, too, here's `lsof`, which is a lot more sparse:

Under Debian and Ubuntu, we can use `apt` to accomplish the same thing, as follows:

```
$ apt changelog linux-image-amd64
```

Admittedly, the output isn't as verbose, as shown in the following screenshot:

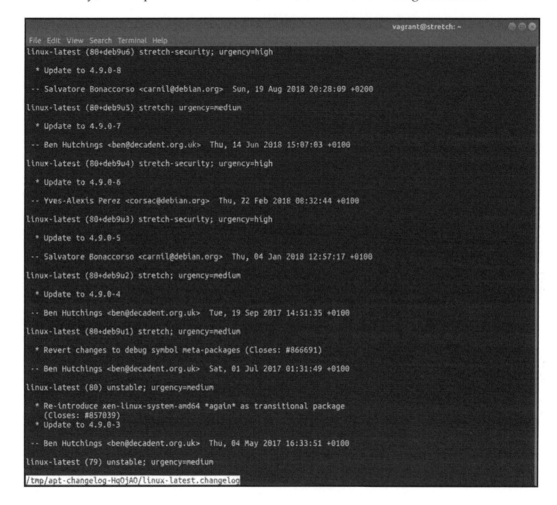

Official sources and mailing Lists

Red Hat, through the goodness of their collective hearts, provide a page to reference for errata and update news: `https://access.redhat.com/security/updates/advisory`

There are some important and very helpful links on this page, such as a link to the Red Hat **Common Vulnerabilities and Exposures (CVE)** database: `https://access.redhat.com/security/security-updates/#/cve`

If you have a Red Hat login, there's also a link to their own errata page on the customer portal.

Mailing lists are a big part of this world, with some going back several decades, and you, too, can receive far too much email (most of which you'll never read)!

Most of the big projects have mailing lists (sometimes several of them), and it would be next to pointless to subscribe to all of them (for example, why sign up to the PowerPC mailing list for the kernel, when you got rid of your New World Macintosh in the mid 2000s?)

Select the ones that interest you, and that might be useful for administration. Security lists are generally a good place to start:

- Red Hat maintains a few at the following at `https://www.redhat.com/ mailman/listinfo`.
- CentOS has their own mailing list at `https://lists.centos.org/mailman/ listinfo/`.
- Debian have their mailing list at `https://lists.debian.org/`. (It includes handy documentation on which lists you might find useful.)
- And, of course, Ubuntu has their list at `https://lists.ubuntu.com/`. (It is also nicely formatted, such as Debian.)

Good lists to sign up to include announcement lists; for example, the `CentOS-announce` list covers general and security information.

Included on the official sources list should be the various publicly viewable source trees of projects, and their associated *Issues* sections (in places such as GitHub). Be sure to keep an eye on any pet projects that you like the look of, or those that might underpin your infrastructure (Terraform, and suchlike).

Other sources

BBC, HackerNews, The Register, and Reddit have all previously informed me of problems that I should have been aware of before reading about them on the front page of popular news sites; don't underestimate the mainstream media when it comes to wanting to drum up panic.

How it works...

These projects are public, and those involved are well aware of the stakes when there's a problem. One only has to take a look at the panic caused when big vulnerabilities are revealed to appreciate why notification avenues are so widely used and appreciated.

If a project had no means of communicating critical problems with its users, it would very quickly find itself inundated with concerned individuals, just wanting to know that the software they're using is being kept up to date.

All that we can do in this fight against security issues and breaking changes is keep informed, and act swiftly when we need to.

There's more...

There is a lot more, really; check for blogs, such as CentOS (`https://blog.centos.org/`), and individual mailing lists for other packages and projects.

OpenSSL, for example, is a good one to keep an eye on (`https://www.openssl.org/community/mailinglists.html`), and I don't say that for any particular heart-health-related reason.

A big one is the kernel mailing list selection, viewable through `https://lkml.org/`; here, kernel news is generally broken first.

Using snaps

In this section, we're going to use our Ubuntu VM.

Snaps (by Canonical) are one of two new kids in the neighborhood. They are a method for packaging software in a universal fashion, so that one package can be deployed to any OS that supports snaps.

At the time of writing this book, Ubuntu probably has the best support for snaps, but Canonical proudly lists installation instructions for quite a few distributions on their website (despite the fact that three of these are just downstream Ubuntu distros), `https://docs.snapcraft.io/core/install`.

I am usually pretty harsh on Canonical, so let me just say that I applaud this effort. It has been true for a while that the disparate packaging methods on Linux are one of the many reasons that some developers stay away, and anything that aims to close that gap is a welcome addition to the community.

How to do it...

Jump onto the Ubuntu machine we created earlier, as follows:

```
$ vagrant ssh ubuntu1804
```

On our VM, the `snapd` service will already be started and running (or it should be; check with `systemctl`).

Searching out snaps

To search for snaps, we use the `snap` command-line utility. In this example, I am going to look for another Canonical product (`lxd`):

```
$ snap search lxd
Name              Version      Publisher        Notes    Summary
lxd-demo-server   0+git.f3532e3  stgraber        -        Online software
demo sessions using LXD
lxd               3.5          canonical        -        System
container manager and API
nova              ocata        james-page       -        OpenStack
Compute Service (nova)
satellite         0.1.2        alanzanattadev   -        Advanced
scalable Open source intelligence platform
nova-hypervisor   ocata        james-page       -        OpenStack
Compute Service - KVM Hypervisor (nova)
```

We get a few results, variously published by Canonical and a few other names.

It's not limited to daemons either; in the following code I'm searching for the `aws-cli` tool:

```
$ snap search aws-cli
Name     Version  Publisher  Notes    Summary
aws-cli  1.15.71  aws√       classic  Universal Command Line Interface
for Amazon Web Services
```

Note the tick next to the publisher's name; this means that the package is from a verified account (in this case, Amazon Web Services).

Installing snaps

The snap that we want has the name `lxd`, making our installation easy:

```
$ sudo snap install lxd
```

You will see a progress bar similar to the following:

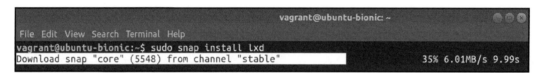

Once finished, you will have the `lxd` container manager installed from a snap.

Listing installed snaps

We can list our installed snaps with `snap list`, as follows:

```
$ snap list
Name    Version     Rev    Tracking   Publisher    Notes
core    16-2.35.2   5548   stable     canonical√   core
lxd     3.5         8959   stable     canonical√   -
```

Interacting with daemon snaps

Because LXD is a daemon, we can enable it by using the `snap` command-line tool again; first, we should check the active state of our service, as follows:

```
$ sudo snap services
Service Startup Current
lxd.activate enabled inactive
lxd.daemon enabled inactive
```

It is inactive, but we can activate it (we have the technology), as follows:

```
$ sudo snap start lxd
Started.
```

Checking the services again, we can see it has started:

```
$ sudo snap services
Service         Startup   Current
lxd.activate    enabled   inactive
lxd.daemon      enabled   active
```

> Under `systemd`, the service is called `snap.lxd.daemon.service`, if you want to use traditional tools to check its status.

To prove that it has started and that we can interact with the daemon, we can use the bundled `lxc` package, as follows:

```
$ lxd.lxc list
Error: Get http://unix.socket/1.0: dial unix
/var/snap/lxd/common/lxd/unix.socket: connect: permission denied
```

You can see that it tries to communicate with the socket; and, while it has given us a permission denied error in the preceding snippet, this does serve to highlight that the socket exists in the `/var/snap/` directory.

Let's try again, with `sudo`:

```
$ sudo lxd.lxc list
+------+-------+------+------+------+-----------+
| NAME | STATE | IPV4 | IPV6 | TYPE | SNAPSHOTS |
+------+-------+------+------+------+-----------+
```

Awesome!

Removing snaps

Finally, we can use our tool to remove `lxd` without prejudice:

```
$ sudo snap remove lxd
lxd removed
```

How it works...

Snaps work like any other package manager, installing and managing packages brought in from a repository on your system.

You'll also have noticed the core installation on our list of installed snaps; this is effectively the base platform that snaps work on top of.

snapd is the daemon that underpins snaps; it's the environment that manages the installed snaps, dealing with installs, updates, and deletion of old versions.

When you install a snap, what you actually download is a read-only squashfs file that lives in /var/lib/snapd/snaps/:

```
$ ls
core_5548.snap  lxd_8959.snap  partial
```

The numbers are snap revision numbers.

When these squashfs images are mounted by snapd, you can see them personified as loop devices with df:

```
$ df -h | grep loop
/dev/loop0 67M 67M 0 100% /snap/lxd/8959
/dev/loop1 88M 88M 0 100% /snap/core/5548
```

You can also see the specific mount information with mount:

```
$ mount | grep snap
/var/lib/snapd/snaps/lxd_8959.snap on /snap/lxd/8959 type squashfs
(ro,nodev,relatime,x-gdu.hide)
/var/lib/snapd/snaps/core_5548.snap on /snap/core/5548 type squashfs
(ro,nodev,relatime,x-gdu.hide)
tmpfs on /run/snapd/ns type tmpfs
(rw,nosuid,noexec,relatime,size=100896k,mode=755)
nsfs on /run/snapd/ns/lxd.mnt type nsfs (rw)
```

Note that we can navigate into the locations where these snaps are mounted, as follows:

```
$ cd /snap/lxd/8959/bin/
```

However, because the filesystem is read only, we cannot write anything inside of it:

```
$ touch test
touch: cannot touch 'test': Read-only file system
```

Neat, right?

We can use our snaps without calling the binaries directly, because of various `snap` entries in our `$PATH`:

```
$ echo $PATH
/usr/local/sbin:/usr/local/bin:/usr/sbin:/usr/bin:/sbin:/bin:/usr/game
s:/usr/local/games:/snap/bin:/snap/bin:/var/lib/snapd/snap/bin:/snap/b
in:/var/lib/snapd/snap/bin
```

 The `PATH` is the list of defined locations where your shell will look for binaries; when you run `ls`, you're locating is the binary somewhere within your `PATH`.

Snaps are also self-contained, meaning that libraries and runtimes are bundled into the package (which makes portability between distributions easy).

There's more...

If you want detailed information about a snap, there's also the `snap info` command.

The following is the output when the command is run against the `lxd` package:

```
$ snap info lxd
name:      lxd
summary:   System container manager and API
publisher: Canonical√
contact:   https://github.com/lxc/lxd/issues
license:   unset
description: |
  LXD is a container manager for system containers.
  It offers a REST API to remotely manage containers over the network,
using an image based workflow
  and with support for live migration.
  Images are available for all Ubuntu releases and architectures as
well as for a wide number of
  other Linux distributions.
  LXD containers are lightweight, secure by default and a great
alternative to virtual machines.
```

```
commands:
  - lxd.benchmark
  - lxd.buginfo
  - lxd.check-kernel
  - lxd.lxc
  - lxd
  - lxd.migrate
services:
  lxd.activate: oneshot, enabled, inactive
  lxd.daemon:   simple, enabled, inactive
snap-id:       J60k4JY0HppjwOjW8dZdYc8obXKxujRu
tracking:      stable
refresh-date: today at 16:44 UTC
channels:
  stable:          3.5          (8959)  69MB  -
  candidate:       3.5          (8959)  69MB  -
  beta:            ↑
  edge:            git-47f0414  (8984)  69MB  -
  3.0/stable:      3.0.2        (8715)  65MB  -
  3.0/candidate:   3.0.2        (8715)  65MB  -
  3.0/beta:        ↑
  3.0/edge:        git-d1a5b4d  (8957)  65MB  -
  2.0/stable:      2.0.11       (8023)  28MB  -
  2.0/candidate:   2.0.11       (8023)  28MB  -
  2.0/beta:        ↑
  2.0/edge:        git-92a4fdc  (8000)  26MB  -
installed:         3.5          (8959)  69MB  -
```

This should tell you most of what you need to know about any particular snap.

See also...

You don't have to search for snaps on the command line, if you live in the 21st century.

You can also use the `snapcraft.io` website at `https://snapcraft.io/`:

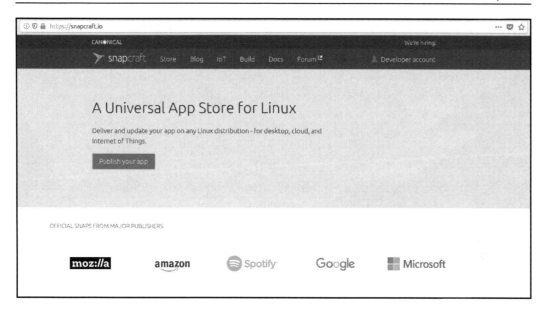

In the **Store** section, you will find a visual search, which can help you to find what you are after in a friendly, click-button fashion. In the following screenshot, I've searched for `aws`:

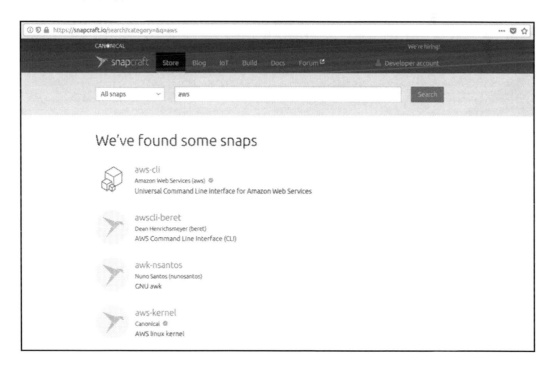

Using Flatpak

Flatpak (by Alex Larsson and the Flatpak team) is the second in the trendy clique of complete-solution package managers. It is also a good way of packaging software so that one package can be deployed to any OS that supports Flatpak installations. Sound familiar?

Really, though, we are also getting into conflicting technology development (yet again) and holy wars (yet again).

To kick things off, I should point out that Flatpak really does emphasize desktop applications over server applications, from their complex run commands to the fact that they are mostly graphical tools. Snaps are definitely more of a mixture between the two worlds.

 Obviously if you want to install a GUI on your server, there's nothing stopping you, you could even use VNC for management! However, it's not really done, like fish fingers and custard.

Getting ready

In this section, we will continue to use our Ubuntu VM (mostly because it's the one I still have open, after having written the last section).

There's no reason why we couldn't use our Debian or CentOS box, instead; a host of other distributions are also supported, including (but not limited to) the following:

- Arch
- Fedora
- Gentoo
- Solus
- Alpine
- openSUSE

To set up our VM for Flatpak, we have to install it, although it is available in the default repositories (potentially after an upgrade, depending on when you're reading this; if you're reading this prior to 2017, I'm impressed by your temporal-displacement abilities, but you should know that the future is dark and full of lemons):

```
$ sudo apt update && sudo apt upgrade -y
$ sudo apt install flatpak -y
```

Next, we need to enable the remote `flathub` repo from `https://flathub.org`:

```
$ sudo flatpak remote-add --if-not-exists flathub
https://flathub.org/repo/flathub.flatpakrepo
```

Now, we can install stuff!

How to do it...

For the purposes of this section, I've chosen the relatively lightweight `vim` package to install from Flathub.

Searching for a package

First, let's look for the package:

```
$ sudo flatpak search vim
Application ID          Version     Branch Remotes Description
org.vim.Vim            v8.1.0443 stable flathub Edit text files
net.mediaarea.AVIMetaEdit 1.0.2     stable flathub Embed, validate,
and export AVI files metadata
org.gnome.Devhelp                  stable flathub A developer tool
for browsing and searching API documentation
org.openshot.OpenShot    2.4.3     stable flathub An easy to use,
quick to learn, and surprisingly powerful video editor
org.gnome.Builder        3.30.1    stable flathub An IDE for GNOME
```

Again, we have a few results, but the top one is what we're after.

Installing our package

We can install the package with a small command, as follows:

```
$ flatpak install flathub org.vim.Vim -y
```

This can take quite some time to download, and it takes up more space than you might expect (despite being a relatively lightweight package).

Running our package

Once the installation is complete, you can run your new version of Vim:

```
$ flatpak run org.vim.Vim
```

The package identifier is in three parts: usually org/com.<company or team>.<app name>.

It's not the prettiest command, but it will drop you into the tried and true text editor, as follows:

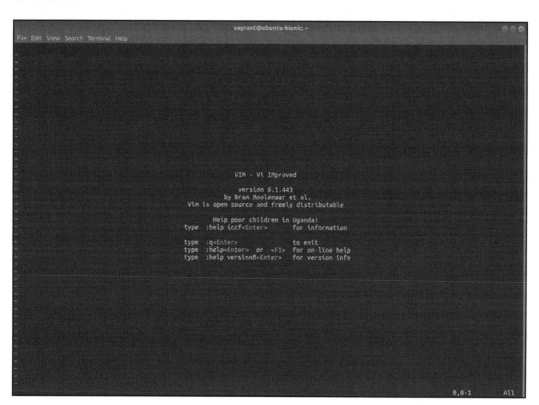

If we look at the versions of the Flatpak installation and the native `Vim` install, we can see the difference:

```
$ flatpak run org.vim.Vim --version | head -n3
VIM - Vi IMproved 8.1 (2018 May 18, compiled Oct  1 2018 10:15:08)
Included patches: 1-443
Compiled by buildbot
$ vim --version | head -n3
VIM - Vi IMproved 8.0 (2016 Sep 12, compiled Apr 10 2018 21:31:58)
Included patches: 1-1453
Modified by pkg-vim-maintainers@lists.alioth.debian.org
```

Listing installed packages

Now that we have something to actually show, we can list our installed `flatpak` packages:

```
$ flatpak list
Ref                                         Options
org.vim.Vim/x86_64/stable                   system,current
org.freedesktop.Platform.ffmpeg/x86_64/1.6  system,runtime
org.freedesktop.Platform/x86_64/1.6         system,runtime
```

Note that it also tells us that the package is a `system` package, rather than a per-user package.

User installations

Flatpak also has the concept of local user installations, meaning that we can install our packages as our user, too:

```
$ flatpak --user remote-add --if-not-exists flathub
https://flathub.org/repo/flathub.flatpakrepo
$ flatpak --user install flathub org.vim.Vim -y
```

Removing packages

When you inevitably get bored with `Vim` and go back to using `ed` for your day to day editing needs (because `ed` is the standard text editor), you can remove your package easily, as follows:

```
$ sudo flatpak uninstall org.vim.Vim --user -y
```

Here, we're specifically removing the user-installed version; the system one will remain.

How it works...

When you install a package using Flatpak, it ends up in one of two places:

- System packages end up in `/var/lib/flatpak`.
- User packages end up in `~/.local/share/flatpak/`.

Looking into these locations, we can find an `app` directory, and within that, our package:

```
$ pwd
/home/vagrant/.local/share/flatpak/app
$ ls
org.vim.Vim
```

Within this directory, there are yet more layers, which house the current version of your package and the various binary files.

Packages are built atop runtimes, like those that you saw when you listed installed packages earlier. These runtimes are distribution agnostic, meaning that they can be installed on all of the Ubuntu, CentOS, and Fedora systems of the world.

If there is something additional required for an application to function, such as a specific library, you can bundle that in your package, too.

There's more...

At the time of writing this book, there are `585` packages available to install from `flathub`, with the number growing every day:

```
$ flatpak remote-ls flathub | wc -l
585
```

You can also update your applications with one command, as follows:

```
$ flatpak update
Looking for updates...
```

See also...

For those of you that hate `Vim` with a passion, despite its obvious superiority, Flathub has you covered:

```
$ flatpak search emacs
Application ID      Version Branch Remotes Description
org.gnu.emacs       26.1    stable flathub An extensible text editor
org.gnome.Devhelp           stable flathub A developer tool for browsing
and searching API documentation
```

There are many more packages available, but, as I've said previously, you are actually unlikely to find yourself using Flatpak on a server, simply because it's a desktop-focused endeavor.

On your own computer, though, snaps and Flatpak packages can be installed side by side.

I once tried to use `Solus` as my daily driver, but wanted to ensure that I did nothing out of the ordinary with my installation. At the time, `Solus` had its own packages, snap support, and Flatpak support. This actually resulted in me using specific snaps for managing a Kubernetes setup, Flatpak to install `Slack`, and the system's own package manager for everything else; it was a bit of a mess by the end, but a consistent mess!

Using Pip, RubyGems, and other package managers

Aside from YUM, Apt, snaps, and Flatpak, there are a host of other package management systems. Pip and RubyGems are programming-language related methods of distributing packages to systems; there are more than these two, but they're by far the most popular right now.

Pip installs packages (Pip) is included by default in recent Python installations. Gem is just a play on the fact that it is for packaging Ruby elements; it, too, is included in recent Ruby installations.

We're going to touch on installing software using these package managers.

Getting ready

In this section, we will continue to use our Ubuntu VM.

Install Pip and RubyGems on your Ubuntu machine (Python will already be installed, but it's a separate package for Pip in this instance), as follows:

```
$ sudo apt update && sudo apt upgrade -y
$ sudo apt install libgmp3-dev make gcc ruby ruby-dev python3-
setuptools -y
```

> Python2 and Python3 are both widely used, although these days, you really shouldn't be writing anything new in Python2 (which will be going out of support in 2020).

We now want to install `pip`, using the `easy_install3` script:

```
$ sudo python3 /usr/lib/python3/dist-packages/easy_install.py pip
```

> There is a way to install `python3-pip` using `apt`, but this version will be frequently out of date, and the whole point of using Pip is that you get the latest version of everything; hence why we use `easy_install`. Together with that, if you try to upgrade the system-installed version of Pip, it might very well work, but you'll be changing system-controlled packages outside of the system-method-of-control... phew.

How to do it...

We will now run through some basic things that you might do with each of these package managers.

Pip

Starting with Pip, you can check which version you're running with the `--version` argument:

```
$ pip3 --version
pip 18.1 from /usr/local/lib/python3.6/dist-packages/pip-18.1-
py3.6.egg/pip (python 3.6)
```

You can list which packages you have installed (and their versions) with `list`, as follows:

```
$ pip3 list
Package             Version
------------------- ---------
asn1crypto          0.24.0
attrs               17.4.0
Automat             0.6.0
blinker             1.4
certifi             2018.1.18
chardet             3.0.4
click               6.7
cloud-init          18.3
colorama            0.3.7
```

You can search for the package that you want; here, I'm checking for Ansible:

```
$ pip3 search ansible
ovirt-ansible (0.3.2) - oVirt Ansible utility
polemarch-ansible (1.0.5) - Wrapper for Ansible cli.
kapellmeister-ansible (0.1.0) - Ansible Playbook manager.
ansible-alicloud (1.5.0) - Ansible provider for Alicloud.
ansible-kernel (0.8.0) - An Ansible kernel for Jupyter
ansible-roles (0.1.4) - Manage ansible roles.
ansible-shell (0.0.5) - Interactive shell for ansible
ansible-toolkit (1.3.2) - The missing Ansible tools
ansible-toolset (0.7.0) - Useful Ansible toolset
. . .
```

There are a lot of packages in the **Python package index (PyPI)**, so you might get a lot of results from your search; this is where learning some `regex` and invoking `grep` can be useful.

Once it's located, we can also install our package, as follows:

```
$ pip3 install ansible --user
```

Note the lack of `sudo`; this is because we want to install it as our user, meaning that the package ends up in a `.local` directory in our home directory (~):

```
$ ls .local/bin/
ansible             ansible-connection  ansible-doc      ansible-inventory
ansible-pull        easy_install
ansible-config      ansible-console     ansible-galaxy   ansible-playbook
ansible-vault       easy_install-3.6
```

By default, the `.local/bin` directory is in our PATH (if we log out and back in):

```
$ echo $PATH
/home/vagrant/.local/bin:/usr/local/sbin:/usr/local/bin:/usr/sbin:/usr
/bin:/sbin:/bin:/usr/games:/usr/local/games:/snap/bin
```

This means that we can just run `ansible` from our shell:

```
$ ansible --version
ansible 2.7.0
  config file = None
  configured module search path =
['/home/vagrant/.ansible/plugins/modules',
'/usr/share/ansible/plugins/modules']
  ansible python module location =
/home/vagrant/.local/lib/python3.6/site-packages/ansible
  executable location = /home/vagrant/.local/bin/ansible
  python version = 3.6.6 (default, Sep 12 2018, 18:26:19) [GCC 8.0.1
20180414 (experimental) [trunk revision 259383]]
```

After our package has been installed, we may find that we actually need an older version; thankfully, Pip lets you specify this easily, as follows:

```
$ pip3 install ansible==2.5.0 --user
```

And, at a later date, if we decide that we need the latest version (because the old playbook has finally been updated to work without deprecated features), we can upgrade, as follows:

```
$ pip3 install ansible --upgrade --user
```

RubyGems

Like Pip, we can check which version of RubyGems we have installed with a simple `gem` command:

```
$ gem --version
2.7.6
```

To list the installed gems, we can use `list`, funnily enough:

```
$ gem list

*** LOCAL GEMS ***

bigdecimal (default: 1.3.4)
cmath (default: 1.0.0)
```

```
csv (default: 1.0.0)
date (default: 1.0.0)
dbm (default: 1.0.0)
did_you_mean (1.2.0)
...
```

If we want to search for a package, we use gem search (we also have the --exact option in RubyGems, which Pip lacks):

```
$ gem search -e chef

*** REMOTE GEMS ***

chef (14.5.33 ruby universal-mingw32, 12.3.0 x86-mingw32)
```

We can also install (as a user) with gem install:

```
$ gem install chef --user-install
```

Note that by default, the .local gem installation location will not be in your PATH, but we can call it with its full path from our home directory (to be added to our PATH at a later date):

```
$ ~/.gem/ruby/2.5.0/bin/chef-client --version
Chef: 14.5.33
```

As with Pip, we can install other versions of packages:

```
$ gem install chef -v14.2.0 --user-install
$ ~/.gem/ruby/2.5.0/gems/chef-14.2.0/bin/chef-client --version
Chef: 14.2.0
```

Note that we used a different path here, dropping into the /gems/ portion of the installation directory to call the package by its version.

If you go to uninstall the package, you now get a choice, as follows:

```
$ gem uninstall chef

Select gem to uninstall:
 1. chef-14.2.0
 2. chef-14.5.33
 3. All versions
>
```

Choose to uninstall 14.5.33 (option 2).

We now have one version of `chef` installed, as follows:

```
$ gem list -e chef

*** LOCAL GEMS ***

chef (14.2.0)
```

Also like with Pip, we can upgrade this, as follows:

```
$ gem update chef --user-install
$ gem list -e chef

*** LOCAL GEMS ***

chef (14.5.33, 14.2.0)
```

Note how it also leaves the old version installed, by default.

How it works...

Pip and RubyGems try to be relatively self-contained, but they're still package managers, meaning that all they're effectively doing is querying an upstream repository for a package, and then downloading it onto your system.

When you update your PATH to update whichever binary location the new executables live in, you're able to run the packages that you've just installed.

There's more...

Pip and RubyGems are huge topics, with a large ethereal-blog-post potential for each, so it makes sense that there is a lot more to them that we have not covered. A couple of the more obvious things to mention will be covered in the following sections.

When to use programming-language package managers

So, here is the thing.

Ansible and Chef are available in the Ubuntu repositories, carefully tailored and packaged for Ubuntu systems the world over.

So, why would I use Pip to install it instead?

It's simple; at the time of writing, the Ansible version in the Ubuntu repositories is 2.5.1, and the version in the PyPI repository is 2.7.0, which is quite a significant bump.

If you want the latest and greatest features of a program, or newer libraries than your distribution ships, you may very well find yourself tempted to install outside of Apt, and that's not necessarily a problem. The problem is remembering how all these packages are installed, and making sure that you know how to keep each up to date.

--user/ --system (pip) and --user-install (gem)

As with Flatpak, we have the option to install packages on either a user level or system-wide. For the examples used, I chose to install things locally, meaning that the packages will generally only be available to my user by default.

```
$ pip3 install ansible==2.5.0 --user
```

Python virtualenv

Python has an inherent problem – conflicting package versions – and because of this, virtualenv is a thing. Effectively, virtualenv is a way to segregate installs so that they don't conflict, and you can (potentially) easily install multiple versions of the same package.

One use case for this might be Molecule, a testing framework designed for Ansible roles. Versions 1 and 2 of Molecule are incompatible with each other, but you could definitely have some Ansible roles in your infrastructure written for version 1 (which no one is going to update any time soon, because there's more pressing issues... there's always more pressing issues.) We have virtualenv though, so we can install both Molecule 1 and Molecule 2 without worrying about them conflicting.

See also

As with any other package manager, Pip and RubyGems manage packages.

Some of you will have spotted a problem with this, and it is one that people rarely realize can be an issue. If you have multiple package managers on a system, each maintaining its own packages and adjusting your PATH, you can end up with packages installed from the system's package manager and those installed from third-party package managers conflicting.

In some cases, you will get name clashes.

I once saw an instance of the Puppet binary `factor` conflicting with another binary of the exact same name, causing strange and wonderful problems on a machine – that was fun.

Dependency hell (a quick word)

We will now take a trip down memory lane; specifically, the author is going to curl up into a ball for a couple of hours while he recalls hours of yelling at servers for being dumb.

Dependency hell is the notion that a package can have dependencies on things that either conflict with other versions of dependent packages or libraries that you have installed, or can try to use incompatible versions, for whatever reason.

In the case of Python and Pip, we've already discussed the concept of virtualenv, but historically, this has also been a problem in other package managers, too. RPM-based distributions are notorious for these issues, developing the term **RPM Hell** to specifically reference their problems.

You can also get into a situation where there are a few options for dependencies when installing software; programs like Apt attempt to mitigate this by presenting several options to the user, and asking them to select which one they want to use.

Getting ready

In this section, we're only going to run a couple of commands on our VMs, in order to look at the output.

Jump into your Debian 9 box and ensure Pip is installed and up to date:

```
$ vagrant ssh debian9
$ sudo apt install gcc python3-dev python3-setuptools -y
$ sudo easy_install3 pip
$ pip --version
pip 18.1 from /usr/local/lib/python3.5/dist-packages/pip-18.1-
py3.5.egg/pip (python 3.5)
```

Now, jump into our Ubuntu box and install `pip` by using `apt`:

```
$ sudo apt update
$ sudo apt install python3-pip -y
```

Check the `version`, as follows:

```
$ pip3 --version
pip 9.0.1 from /usr/lib/python3/dist-packages (python 3.6)
```

Then, `upgrade` it (only on the Ubuntu box), as follows:

```
$ pip3 install pip --upgrade
```

Log out (an important step) and check the `version` again:

```
$ pip3 --version
pip 18.1 from /home/vagrant/.local/lib/python3.6/site-packages/pip
(python 3.6)
```

How to do it...

To visualize what dependency problems can look like, take a look at the following.

System-installed and third-party installed versions of Pip

In our Ubuntu box, we installed `pip` by using the system package manager (`apt`) only to then use Pip to upgrade itself.

This means that `apt` thinks the package looks like this:

```
$ apt list python3-pip -a
Listing... Done
python3-pip/bionic-updates,now 9.0.1-2.3~ubuntu1 all [installed]
```

Our local session thinks that `pip` looks like this:

```
$ pip3 --version
pip 18.1 from /home/vagrant/.local/lib/python3.6/site-packages/pip
(python 3.6)
```

This is a problem, as future packages could rely on Pip 9 and expect it to be installed correctly on the box, despite the different versions.

In this case, what we've actually done is use the system-installed version of Pip to install and upgraded the version locally; hence, the reason that the version string comes from our `.local` directory, but it's still not an ideal scenario.

Dependency problems in conflicting Pip packages

To better understand why virtualenv is a thing, we can look at an installation of Molecule.

In your Debian instance, install the Molecule testing framework (specifically, `2.15.0`):

```
$ pip install molecule==2.15.0 --user
```

All being well, the installation should go fine, and you'll be able to check your Molecule version:

```
$ .local/bin/molecule --version
molecule, version 2.15.0
```

However, we're now going to use `install ansible-lint` (the latest version, at the time of writing this book):

```
$ pip install ansible-lint==3.4.23 --user
```

Our installation works, but in the middle of it, we get a nasty warning:

```
molecule 2.15.0 has requirement ansible-lint==3.4.21, but you'll have
ansible-lint 3.4.23 which is incompatible.
```

If we check the installed `version`, `ansible-lint` looks good:

```
$ .local/bin/ansible-lint --version
ansible-lint 3.4.23
```

However, if we run our Molecule installation again, we get informed that it has helpfully downgraded `ansible-lint` for us:

```
Installing collected packages: ansible-lint
  Found existing installation: ansible-lint 3.4.23
    Uninstalling ansible-lint-3.4.23:
      Successfully uninstalled ansible-lint-3.4.23
  Running setup.py install for ansible-lint ... done
Successfully installed ansible-lint-3.4.21
```

This is obviously an easy example to show you, as there are only two packages involved; imagine how hectic and stressful this could get with five, ten, or even twenty packages managed by Pip.

Apt's conflict solution

The following is an example of Apt detecting dependency problems and refusing to carry on with an installation:

```
$ sudo apt install postfix exim4-base
Reading package lists... Done
Building dependency tree
Reading state information... Done
Some packages could not be installed. This may mean that you have
requested an impossible situation or if you are using the unstable
distribution that some required packages have not yet been created
or been moved out of Incoming.
The following information may help to resolve the situation:

The following packages have unmet dependencies:
 exim4-base : Depends: exim4-config (>= 4.82) but it is not going to
be installed or
                        exim4-config-2
E: Unable to correct problems, you have held broken packages.
```

Note that if you then install `postfix` by itself and attempt to install `exim`, you will be given the following result:

```
$ sudo apt install exim4-base
Reading package lists... Done
Building dependency tree
Reading state information... Done
The following packages were automatically installed and are no longer
required:
  postfix-sqlite ssl-cert
Use 'sudo apt autoremove' to remove them.
The following additional packages will be installed:
  exim4-config exim4-daemon-light guile-2.0-libs libgsasl7
libkyotocabinet16v5 libltdl7 liblzo2-2
  libmailutils5 libmariadbclient18 libntlm0 libpython2.7 libpython2.7-
minimal libpython2.7-stdlib
  mailutils mailutils-common mysql-common psmisc python2.7 python2.7-
minimal
Suggested packages:
  eximon4 exim4-doc-html | exim4-doc-info spf-tools-perl swaks
mailutils-mh mailutils-doc
```

```
    python2.7-doc binfmt-support
The following packages will be REMOVED:
  postfix
The following NEW packages will be installed:
  exim4-base exim4-config exim4-daemon-light guile-2.0-libs libgsasl7
libkyotocabinet16v5 libltdl7
  liblzo2-2 libmailutils5 libmariadbclient18 libntlm0 libpython2.7
mailutils mailutils-common
  mysql-common psmisc
The following packages will be upgraded:
  libpython2.7-minimal libpython2.7-stdlib python2.7 python2.7-minimal
4 upgraded, 16 newly installed, 1 to remove and 7 not upgraded.
Need to get 13.2 MB of archives.
After this operation, 27.5 MB of additional disk space will be used.
Do you want to continue? [Y/n]
```

The line that tells you that postfix will be ripped out of your system if you proceed is in bold.

Potential solutions

In spite of these annoying (and sometimes tedious) problems, there are some solutions to these issues.

We have already mentioned virtualenv, and now, we're going to mention it again, just to hammer the point home. Go out and seek knowledge on it, as it could save you a severe headache in the future.

Docker is another potential solution, and although the idea of jailing applications into their own little environments is nothing new (see Solaris Zones and FreeBSD jails), Docker provides a quick and simple interface to utilize Linux kernel features for segregating apps and dependencies.

Multiple VMs might also be your way forward. It used to be the case that we needed to buy one, two, or maybe three servers, and use multiple packages on each server; nowadays, that isn't as true, and, while you might still have a handful of physical boxes, you're much more likely to be using VMs on each, which provide a great way to completely segregate whole operating systems.

How it works...

Package management works because diligent people make it work. Dependency problems are still an issue, even though they're mostly transparent to the user these days. It becomes more of an issue with the more packages that you support, meaning that Debian, with its thousands of packages, has a tough job of making sure each will always work, or that conflict is detected before it causes issues.

Let's give a shout out to the hardworking package maintainers in each distribution, and thank them for their tireless efforts in ensuring that our systems don't try to install packages and libraries that are incompatible with each other.

If you ever have to make a package of your own, best of luck to you!

Compiling from source

"Oh, it's Linux; call me when you've finished recompiling your kernel!" This is a statement from every uninformed techy ever.

Packages aren't the only way to install software on your system; if you have the source code (the recipe for the software that you want to install), you can compile the program yourself, in your own way!

It's not done very frequently these days, outside of in-house software, as compiling software can be a time-consuming and resource-intensive task. The likes of the Gentoo users of the world might like it, and there are arguments that it can speed up and slim down installations, but these are generally negligible benefits on modern hardware.

Getting ready

Here, we're going to grab the source code of `htop`, a popular and interactive process monitor.

> This isn't a sales pitch, but I do happen to like `htop`, and I make a point of installing it on my personal systems, as well as systems I manage, when I get the chance.

You will need access to the GitHub page of the source code, at `https://github.com/hishamhm/htop`.

You will also be using your CentOS VM.

Log in to your CentOS VM and install `unzip` and `wget`, as follows:

```
$ vagrant ssh centos7
$ sudo yum install unzip wget -y
```

Navigate to `/usr/local/src`, the place where we will put source code for locally installed software, by convention:

```
$ cd /usr/local/src
```

Download the most recent version of the `htop` repository (here, I use `https`):

```
$ sudo wget https://github.com/hishamhm/htop/archive/master.zip
```

How to do it...

You should now have a `master.zip` file in your directory:

```
$ ls -lha
total 248K
drwxr-xr-x.  2 root root   24 Oct  7 03:34 .
drwxr-xr-x. 12 root root  131 May 12 18:50 ..
-rw-r--r--.  1 root root 248K Oct  7 03:34 master.zip
```

We need to `unzip` this, change the ownership for convenience, and jump inside:

```
$ sudo unzip master.zip
$ sudo chown -R vagrant:vagrant htop-master/
$ cd htop-master
```

Inside this directory, you'll find a whole host of files, mostly of the `C` variety, but with a few others here and there. One file you'll almost always find in a source directory is a README, which is an excellent place to start:

```
$ less README
```

READMEs are always different, but I've yet to find a serious project where they aren't good. See the following example:

This file will tell you, in a few words, any dependencies that you need to install, and then the appropriate method for installing the package itself.

As we downloaded the sources, we need the `autogen.sh` line from the preceding screenshot. If we attempt to run the script, we will be given an error:

```
$ ./autogen.sh
./autogen.sh: line 3: autoreconf: command not found
```

This is because the `autoconf` package isn't installed; proceed to do so, then try the script again:

```
$ sudo yum install autoconf -y
$ ./autogen.sh
Can't exec "aclocal": No such file or directory at
/usr/share/autoconf/Autom4te/FileUtils.pm line 326.
autoreconf: failed to run aclocal: No such file or directory
```

Another `yum` that tells us the `automake` package isn't installed, so let's install it!

```
$ sudo yum install automake -y
$ ./autogen.sh
configure.ac:23: installing './compile'
configure.ac:16: installing './config.guess'
configure.ac:16: installing './config.sub'
configure.ac:18: installing './install-sh'
configure.ac:18: installing './missing'
Makefile.am: installing './INSTALL'
Makefile.am: installing './depcomp
```

Good! This time, it worked.

The README suggested checking out the INSTALL file; so, let's take a look at that next:

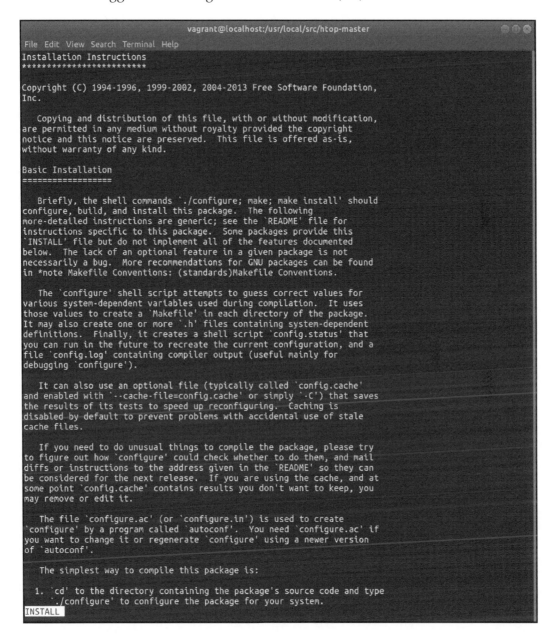

```
                    vagrant@localhost:/usr/local/src/htop-master
File  Edit  View  Search  Terminal  Help
Installation Instructions
*************************

Copyright (C) 1994-1996, 1999-2002, 2004-2013 Free Software Foundation,
Inc.

   Copying and distribution of this file, with or without modification,
are permitted in any medium without royalty provided the copyright
notice and this notice are preserved.  This file is offered as-is,
without warranty of any kind.

Basic Installation
==================

   Briefly, the shell commands `./configure; make; make install' should
configure, build, and install this package.  The following
more-detailed instructions are generic; see the `README' file for
instructions specific to this package.  Some packages provide this
`INSTALL' file but do not implement all of the features documented
below.  The lack of an optional feature in a given package is not
necessarily a bug.  More recommendations for GNU packages can be found
in *note Makefile Conventions: (standards)Makefile Conventions.

   The `configure' shell script attempts to guess correct values for
various system-dependent variables used during compilation.  It uses
those values to create a `Makefile' in each directory of the package.
It may also create one or more `.h' files containing system-dependent
definitions.  Finally, it creates a shell script `config.status' that
you can run in the future to recreate the current configuration, and a
file `config.log' containing compiler output (useful mainly for
debugging `configure').

   It can also use an optional file (typically called `config.cache'
and enabled with `--cache-file=config.cache' or simply `-C') that saves
the results of its tests to speed up reconfiguring.  Caching is
disabled by default to prevent problems with accidental use of stale
cache files.

   If you need to do unusual things to compile the package, please try
to figure out how `configure' could check whether to do them, and mail
diffs or instructions to the address given in the `README' so they can
be considered for the next release.  If you are using the cache, and at
some point `config.cache' contains results you don't want to keep, you
may remove or edit it.

   The file `configure.ac' (or `configure.in') is used to create
`configure' by a program called `autoconf'.  You need `configure.ac' if
you want to change it or regenerate `configure' using a newer version
of `autoconf'.

   The simplest way to compile this package is:

  1. `cd' to the directory containing the package's source code and type
     `./configure' to configure the package for your system.
INSTALL
```

In quite a few words, this gives us the installation process for most packages packaged in this way.

Back in the README file, we're going to try the next bit of the installation step, as follows:

```
$ ./configure
checking build system type... x86_64-unknown-linux-gnu
checking host system type... x86_64-unknown-linux-gnu
checking target system type... x86_64-unknown-linux-gnu
checking for a BSD-compatible install... /usr/bin/install -c
checking whether build environment is sane... yes
checking for a thread-safe mkdir -p... /usr/bin/mkdir -p
checking for gawk... gawk
checking whether make sets $(MAKE)... yes
checking whether make supports nested variables... yes
checking for gcc... no
checking for cc... no
checking for cl.exe... no
configure: error: in `/usr/local/src/htop-master':
configure: error: no acceptable C compiler found in $PATH
See `config.log' for more details
```

We have something else missing; in this case, the error is telling us that a C compiler wasn't found.

The default C compiler in most systems is GCC, but there are others that may or may not work (such as musl):

```
$ sudo yum install gcc -y
$ ./configure
<SNIP>
checking for strdup... yes
checking whether gcc -std=c99 option works... yes
checking if compiler supports -Wextra... yes
checking for addnwstr in -lncursesw6... no
checking for addnwstr in -lncursesw... no
checking for addnwstr in -lncurses... no
configure: error: You may want to use --disable-unicode or install
libncursesw.
```

We can go further now, but as the script checks for requirements, we can see that we can't find a libncursesw installation.

It gives us two options: disabling unicode, or installing libncursesw. For completeness, let's install the ncurses-devel package:

```
$ sudo yum install ncurses-devel -y
$ ./configure
<SNIP>
checking that generated files are newer than configure... done
configure: creating ./config.status
config.status: creating Makefile
config.status: creating htop.1
config.status: creating config.h
config.status: executing depfiles commands
```

Now, we get to the end of the configuration script with no more errors. Hurrah!

Lastly, we make the package, which is the actual step that compiles the source code into usable programs:

```
$ make
```

It can be noisy, as shown in the following screenshot:

In our directory, we now have an htop binary, as follows:

```
$ ls -lah htop
-rwxrwxr-x. 1 vagrant vagrant 756K Oct  7 03:51 htop
```

Give it a whirl:

```
$ ./htop --version
htop 2.2.0 - (C) 2004-2018 Hisham Muhammad
Released under the GNU GPL.
```

Lastly, we need to install the program to its appropriate locations; this is done with the make install command. This does need sudo, as we're moving things out of our local folder and into the rest of the filesystem:

```
$ sudo make install
make  install-am
make[1]: Entering directory `/usr/local/src/htop-master'
make[2]: Entering directory `/usr/local/src/htop-master'
 /usr/bin/mkdir -p '/usr/local/bin'
  /usr/bin/install -c htop '/usr/local/bin'
 /usr/bin/mkdir -p '/usr/local/share/applications'
 /usr/bin/install -c -m 644 htop.desktop
'/usr/local/share/applications'
 /usr/bin/mkdir -p '/usr/local/share/man/man1'
 /usr/bin/install -c -m 644 htop.1 '/usr/local/share/man/man1'
 /usr/bin/mkdir -p '/usr/local/share/pixmaps'
 /usr/bin/install -c -m 644 htop.png '/usr/local/share/pixmaps'
make[2]: Leaving directory `/usr/local/src/htop-master'
make[1]: Leaving directory `/usr/local/src/htop-master'
```

Now, we can run a whereis and find out its installed location (although we can also see it in the preceding code snippet):

```
$ whereis htop
htop: /usr/local/bin/htop
```

How it works...

For most Linux programs (certainly of the C variety), this pattern is fairly standard. Copy down the source code, configure it with its defaults (or make any changes that you want), compile the software, and install it variously on the filesystem.

The INSTALL file provides a good overview of the different steps, but in short, they look like this:

- configure: Creates a Makefile that contains system-specific options, based on your environment. These can be quite long; the htop file comes out at 1,422 lines.
- make: This is invoked to correctly compile any source code that needs it, creating binaries and supplementing files that might be needed.
- make install: This puts the files into their appropriate places.

Easy, right?

There's more...

Things like the kernel can be compiled too, but will take much longer given the sheer number of parts and subsystems that have to be accounted for. Long compile-times are the main reason people and projects have defaulted to using pre-compiled binary blobs these days (because few people want to wait around for their code to compile, unless they're deliberately trying to avoid work.)

Even Gentoo, which is famous for allowing customizability (at the expense of installation time), has precompiled binaries that you can install for the larger programs, if you don't want to sit around for a week waiting for your code to compile.

There's also cross-compiling, which is the act of compiling software for different architectures. For example, I may want to compile htop for aarch64 hardware on my x86_64 VM, because it's got 32 cores and my aarch64 board is a Raspberry Pi 3.

See also...

There are other ways to compile software, depending on the language used. Go, for example, will have you go get the package source code that you want to compile, but it uses the make command to perform the actual build, whereas the Rust programming language uses a tool called cargo.

Technical requirements

In this section, we will use all three of our virtual machines, adding additional repositories to each. This is to showcase how the different package management systems do things differently.

Adding additional repositories

There are default repositories installed when your system is created; there are also wilder and more out-there repositories that may contain that one piece of software that you really need (or can't be bothered to compile yourself).

Some common repositories are as follows:

- EPEL
- RPMfusion
- Remi
- ZFS, on Linux

Here, we will look at adding additional repositories, and the ramifications of doing so.

Getting ready

You can go through this section in any order, but it's probably sensible to start at the start, and finish at the finish.

How to do it...

Log in to your VM. We're going to start with CentOS. To begin, let's take a look at the default repositories that we have to play with, using the yum repolist command:

```
$ yum repolist
Loaded plugins: fastestmirror
Loading mirror speeds from cached hostfile
 * base: mirrors.melbourne.co.uk
 * extras: repo.uk.bigstepcloud.com
 * updates: centos.mirroring.pulsant.co.uk
repo id                                 repo name
```

```
status
base/7/x86_64                                    CentOS-7 - Base
9,911
extras/7/x86_64                                  CentOS-7 - Extras
432
updates/7/x86_64                                 CentOS-7 - Updates
1,540
repolist: 11,883
```

We see three repositories enabled by default, `Base`, `Extras`, and `Updates`.

CentOS – Adding the EPEL repository with epel-release

Extra Packages for Enterprise Linux (**EPEL**) is one of the more popular additional repositories in the CentOS/Red Hat space.

Because of this, it actually has a very easy method for installation, from the given repositories:

```
$ sudo yum install epel-release -y
```

Looking in our `repo` directory, you'll now see two new files:

```
$ ls -lha /etc/yum.repos.d/epel*
-rw-r--r--. 1 root root  951 Oct  2 2017 /etc/yum.repos.d/epel.repo
-rw-r--r--. 1 root root 1.1K Oct  2 2017 /etc/yum.repos.d/epel-
testing.repo
```

And `yum repolist` will show it, too:

```
$ yum repolist
Loaded plugins: fastestmirror
Loading mirror speeds from cached hostfile
epel/x86_64/metalink
|  31 kB  00:00:00
 * base: mirrors.melbourne.co.uk
 * epel: anorien.csc.warwick.ac.uk
 * extras: mirrors.melbourne.co.uk
 * updates: anorien.csc.warwick.ac.uk
epel
| 3.2 kB  00:00:00
(1/3): epel/x86_64/group_gz
|  88 kB  00:00:00
(2/3): epel/x86_64/updateinfo
| 948 kB  00:00:00
```

```
(3/3): epel/x86_64/primary
| 3.6 MB  00:00:01
epel
12721/12721
repo id                          repo name
status
base/7/x86_64                    CentOS-7 - Base
9,911
epel/x86_64                      Extra Packages for Enterprise Linux 7
- x86_64                 12,721
extras/7/x86_64                  CentOS-7 - Extras
432
updates/7/x86_64                 CentOS-7 - Updates
1,540
repolist: 24,604
```

Note that `epel-testing` isn't listed; this is because it's disabled, by default.

We can use this repository to search for packages that might not be in the defaults (such as `htop`, for example):

```
$ yum whatprovides htop
Loaded plugins: fastestmirror
Loading mirror speeds from cached hostfile
 * base: mirrors.melbourne.co.uk
 * epel: mirror.bytemark.co.uk
 * extras: mirrors.melbourne.co.uk
 * updates: centos.mirroring.pulsant.co.uk
htop-2.2.0-1.el7.x86_64 : Interactive process viewer
Repo        : epel
```

CentOS – Adding the ELRepo repository by file

As suggested in the previous section, all that the package installation did was add appropriate GPG keys and the YUM configuration files for additional repositories; there's nothing stopping you from doing the same thing manually.

ELRepo is a popular repo, mostly due to the fact that it offers more up-to-date versions of the Linux kernel, for those people who like the layout and style of CentOS but who really want the latest drivers and features that the kernel can offer.

First, we need to import the repository's public key, like so:

```
$ sudo rpm --import https://www.elrepo.org/RPM-GPG-KEY-elrepo.org
```

It's a good idea to make sure that the key you're installing is legitimate; there are various ways of doing this, including checking that TLS certificates are legitimate, comparing it with other systems, or ringing up the owner of the key and pestering them until they read the whole thing out to you.

At this point, we can either download and `yum install` the `rpm` file from the `elrepo` site, or we download it ourselves and extract the contents, so that we can take a look at what it does:

```
$ wget
https://www.elrepo.org/elrepo-release-7.0-3.el7.elrepo.noarch.rpm
$ rpm2cpio elrepo-release-7.0-3.el7.elrepo.noarch.rpm | cpio -id
```

The `rpm2cpio` command does what it suggests, and allows us to use `cpio` to extract the archive.

If we now `cat` the directory that we've just unarchived, we can see the file that it's going to drop into our system:

```
$ cat etc/yum.repos.d/elrepo.repo
### Name: ELRepo.org Community Enterprise Linux Repository for el7
### URL: http://elrepo.org/

[elrepo]
name=ELRepo.org Community Enterprise Linux Repository - el7
baseurl=http://elrepo.org/linux/elrepo/el7/$basearch/
    http://mirrors.coreix.net/elrepo/elrepo/el7/$basearch/
    http://mirror.rackspace.com/elrepo/elrepo/el7/$basearch/
    http://repos.lax-noc.com/elrepo/elrepo/el7/$basearch/
    http://mirror.ventraip.net.au/elrepo/elrepo/el7/$basearch/
mirrorlist=http://mirrors.elrepo.org/mirrors-elrepo.el7
enabled=1
gpgcheck=1
gpgkey=file:///etc/pki/rpm-gpg/RPM-GPG-KEY-elrepo.org
protect=0
. . .
```

There's more, as there are multiple repo designations in this file. Let's just copy the `elrepo` block and output it to a file of our own making, like so:

```
$ cat <<HERE | sudo tee /etc/yum.repos.d/elrepocustom.repo
[elrepo]
name=ELRepo.org Community Enterprise Linux Repository - el7
```

```
baseurl=http://elrepo.org/linux/elrepo/el7/$basearch/
    http://mirrors.coreix.net/elrepo/elrepo/el7/$basearch/
    http://mirror.rackspace.com/elrepo/elrepo/el7/$basearch/
    http://repos.lax-noc.com/elrepo/elrepo/el7/$basearch/
    http://mirror.ventraip.net.au/elrepo/elrepo/el7/$basearch/
mirrorlist=http://mirrors.elrepo.org/mirrors-elrepo.el7
enabled=1
gpgcheck=1
gpgkey=file:///etc/pki/rpm-gpg/RPM-GPG-KEY-elrepo.org
protect=0
HERE
```

Note that the repo has `enabled=1` set, meaning that we can now just run a `yum update` to make sure that our system is synced and aware of the upstream repository (although if we wanted to permanently disable this repo, we could change it to a `0`, and `yum` would ignore it):

```
$ sudo yum update
```

Now, if we want to, we can also list all of the packages in the repo that we've just added:

```
$ yum list available --disablerepo=* --enablerepo=elrepo
Loaded plugins: fastestmirror
Loading mirror speeds from cached hostfile
 * elrepo: www.jules.fm
Available Packages
CAENVMELib.x86_64                           2.50-2.el7.elrepo
elrepo
VirtualGL.x86_64                            2.3.3-4.el7.elrepo
elrepo
VirtualGL-devel.x86_64                      2.3.3-4.el7.elrepo
elrepo
VirtualGL-libs.i686                         2.3.3-4.el7.elrepo
elrepo
bumblebee.x86_64                            3.2.1-10.el7.elrepo
elrepo
bumblebee-selinux.x86_64                    1.0-1.el7.elrepo
elrepo
drbd84-utils.x86_64                         9.3.1-1.el7.elrepo
elrepo
...
```

Debian – Adding additional repositories

Debian is famous for having a shed-load of packages available to the end users. If you can think of a package, there's a good chance that it's available for installation out of the box, or that someone somewhere is working on how to maintain the package for you.

 FreeBSD is probably the only OS that springs to mind that might have more packages available in its base installation.

Because of this famous fact, there's a good chance that you'll never need to install additional repositories, but never say never (despite me just doing so).

A good place to look for some unofficial repositories is the maintained unofficial page at `https://wiki.debian.org/DebianRepository/Unofficial`.

Here, we can find various repositories, including one for Google Chrome, which we'll add.

First, we will look at the default `sources.list` file that's shipped with our image:

```
$ cat /etc/apt/sources.list
#

# deb cdrom:[Debian GNU/Linux 9.4.0 _Stretch_ – Official amd64 NETINST
20180310-11:21]/ stretch main

#deb cdrom:[Debian GNU/Linux 9.4.0 _Stretch_ – Official amd64 NETINST
20180310-11:21]/ stretch main

deb http://deb.debian.org/debian stretch main
deb-src http://deb.debian.org/debian stretch main

deb http://security.debian.org/debian-security stretch/updates main
deb-src http://security.debian.org/debian-security stretch/updates
main
```

It looks fairly sparse, with only the `stretch main` and `stretch/updates main` repositories enabled.

As with YUM, we need to make sure that we have a legitimate GPG key in place; Google's is installed like so:

```
$ wget https://dl.google.com/linux/linux_signing_key.pub
$ sudo apt-key add linux_signing_key.pub
OK
```

Now, we need to add the repository – in this case, Google Chrome:

```
$ cat <<HERE | sudo tee -a /etc/apt/sources.list
deb http://dl.google.com/linux/chrome/deb/ stable main
HERE
```

Run `sudo apt update` to make sure that your list of available packages is up to date:

```
$ sudo apt update
Ign:1 http://deb.debian.org/debian stretch InRelease
Hit:2 http://deb.debian.org/debian stretch Release
Hit:4 http://security.debian.org/debian-security stretch/updates
InRelease
Ign:5 http://dl.google.com/linux/chrome/deb stable InRelease
Get:6 http://dl.google.com/linux/chrome/deb stable Release [1,189 B]
Get:7 http://dl.google.com/linux/chrome/deb stable Release.gpg [819 B]
Get:8 http://dl.google.com/linux/chrome/deb stable/main amd64 Packages
[1,381 B]
Fetched 3,389 B in 1s (2,285 B/s)
Reading package lists... Done
Building dependency tree
Reading state information... Done
11 packages can be upgraded. Run 'apt list --upgradable' to see them.
```

Then, do a search for Chrome:

```
$ sudo apt search google-chrome
Sorting... Done
Full Text Search... Done
google-chrome-beta/stable 70.0.3538.45-1 amd64
  The web browser from Google

google-chrome-stable/stable 69.0.3497.100-1 amd64
  The web browser from Google

google-chrome-unstable/stable 71.0.3569.0-1 amd64
  The web browser from Google
```

Voilà!

This is not a Chrome advertisement, either, and actually, the open source version of Chrome (Chromium) is already available in the default repositories. I would probably advise installing that, instead.

Mostly, you'll probably be adding the `contrib` repository, which contains non-free software:

```
deb http://ftp.debian.org/debian stable main contrib non-free
```

Ubuntu – Adding PPAs

Interestingly, this is one significant place in which the Ubuntu and Debian worlds differ. In Ubuntu-land, there's the concept of **Personal Package Archives (PPAs)**, which can be used to install third-party software.

You can install regular repositories, too, but PPAs are arguably a little more targeted. Do bear in mind that there's very little stopping anyone from creating a PPA, so make sure to follow due diligence before adding just anything.

PPAs can be searched out on the Canonical site, at `https://launchpad.net/ubuntu/+ppas`.

We'll add the LibreOffice Fresh PPA, as an example:

```
$ sudo add-apt-repository ppa:libreoffice/ppa
```

You may be prompted to accept the additional repository, simply by pressing *Enter*.

The repository configuration that you just added is in the `apt sources.list.d` directory:

```
$ cat /etc/apt/sources.list.d/libreoffice-ubuntu-ppa-bionic.list
deb http://ppa.launchpad.net/libreoffice/ppa/ubuntu bionic main
# deb-src http://ppa.launchpad.net/libreoffice/ppa/ubuntu bionic main
```

This means that you can now install the bleeding edge version of LibreOffice! You'll be the cool kid of the word processing world at last.

How it works...

Repositories are generally just places that house packages you might want to install. There's nothing special about them, as they're generally web servers that react as any might, serving you the contents (package) when you request it.

Adding additional repositories is a fairly common sysadmin activity, usually because you're adding your in-house proxy (commonly Artifactory at the moment,) or your developers really need the latest version of NodeJS.

Whatever the reason for adding repositories, just remember that basic security goes a long way (you are, after all, trusting the upstream not to have anything malicious in it), and appreciate that you can create problems for yourself if the repository disappears (which has happened, and will continue to happen).

Roundup – security, updating, and package management

It's easy to forget about updates. It's comforting to get a system to a stable state, where no matter how much it's hammered, it's going to continue to chug along, doing what you've told it to do, and nothing more. What's uncomfortable is the idea of breaking that perfect peace, and that's where updates come in.

Software doesn't stand still; there are features being developed, security holes being patched, and tougher encryption methods being implemented, and all of these need to be accounted for by you, the sysadmin.

Package maintainers can do a lot, and they do, but it's up to you to make sure that what you're updating is tested, that it won't break anything else in your environment, and that those developers that were using an exploit to get their code to work on your platform have been thoroughly reprimanded.

At the end of the day, things are likely to go wrong, but that's why development and testing environments should exist.

Yes, it was nerve-wracking to perform an update in the past, and that's why we came in on weekends and did updates in the middle of the night, when no one would notice if it broke for a bit. Those breakages can still happen, but now, we've learned from them; we have warnings and erratas and the general public will understand if your site has to go offline for a couple of hours to make sure that their credit card information doesn't get leaked, thanks to a malicious exploit.

At the end of the day, software is stupid, and it's put together by humans, who are fallible. Keep your systems up to date, make sure that you check your sources (in other words, don't install random executables from untraveled corners of the internet), and make sure that you let your superiors know that yes, you might have to take the website offline for a little bit, or shut down their phone system, but it's better than appearing on the front page of the BBC website the next day.

Of course, if you're really interested in the intricacies of how a distribution is built, how the packages all fit together, and why they're built or installed in the way that they are, then there are tools out there that can help you to learn.

Linux from Scratch is one such tool, effectively a book on the ins and outs of building your own version of Linux. It's not for beginners, and it can be frustrating at times (or slightly outdated, as software evolves), but it's a great way to learn why things are the way they are, and I'd encourage everyone to perform the Linux from scratch installation at least once in their professional careers.

Monitoring and Logging 7

This chapter will cover the following topics:

- Reading local logs
- Using `journalctl` on `systemd` systems
- Centralizing logging
- Local resource measuring tools
- Local monitoring tools
- Remote monitoring tools
- Centralizing logging with the Elastic Stack

Introduction

Servers are all well and good when they work, but we don't live in a perfect world, and it's perfectly possible that problems can occur (either through bad code, created by humans, or mismanagement, introduced by humans).

In theory, it would be great to simply install the program you want, set it running, and forget about it, but this is the real world, not some fantasy land where everything goes 100 percent right 100 percent of the time. This is where logging and monitoring shine.

Logging is there so that when something does, inevitably, go wrong, you don't have to keep your program in a broken state while you try and work out what's broken (though, on odd occasions, this might be precisely what you have to do; more about that later). You can bring your system back online, and start to parse the log files to find out precisely why your web server suddenly started replacing all images on your website with pictures of puppies.

Monitoring is the secondary component in keeping your life simple. There to ensure you have a smooth experience when using your software, and keeping tabs on the resource allocation on your systems, monitoring can detect issues before a human being even wakes up in the morning (actually this happens frequently; don't expect a normal sleep pattern if you are on call).

Both of these systems combined can make you appear godlike to those who are watching your every move; like Morpheus, you can feel your watch vibrate with a notification in a meeting, informing you that the company website is under heavy load and about to crash, and calmly inform those talking nonsense around you that you feel a disturbance in the force, before excusing yourself to fix the issue before the customers notice.

Come to think of it, good logging and monitoring can result in your job appearing pointless—what's that Futurama quote?

> *"When you do things right, people won't be sure you've done anything at all." –*
> *Sentient gas cloud*

Technical requirements

In this chapter, we're going to use two CentOS boxes and two Debian boxes but, again, the principles we discuss will be fairly universal in nature.

The following `Vagrantfile` should be enough to get you started:

```ruby
# -*- mode: ruby -*-
# vi: set ft=ruby :

Vagrant.configure("2") do |config|

  config.vm.define "centos1" do |centos1|
  centos1.vm.box = "centos/7"
  centos1.vm.box_version = "1804.02"
  centos1.vm.network "private_network", ip: "192.168.33.10"
  centos1.vm.hostname = "centos1"
  centos1.vm.provider "virtualbox" do |centos1p|
  centos1p.memory = 2048
  centos1p.cpus = 2
  end
  end

  config.vm.define "centos2" do |centos2|
  centos2.vm.box = "centos/7"
```

```
centos2.vm.box_version = "1804.02"
centos2.vm.network "private_network", ip: "192.168.33.11"
centos2.vm.hostname = "centos2"
end

config.vm.define "debian1" do |debian1|
debian1.vm.box = "debian/stretch64"
debian1.vm.box_version = "9.5.0"
debian1.vm.network "private_network", ip: "192.168.33.12"
debian1.vm.hostname = "debian1"
debian1.vm.provider "virtualbox" do |debian1p|
debian1p.cpus = 1
end
end

config.vm.define "debian2" do |debian2|
debian2.vm.box = "debian/stretch64"
debian2.vm.box_version = "9.5.0"
debian2.vm.network "private_network", ip: "192.168.33.13"
debian2.vm.hostname = "debian2"
debian2.vm.provider "virtualbox" do |debian2p|
debian2p.cpus = 1
end
end

end
```

Reading local logs

In this section, we're going to look at the default place for logging on our machines.

Logging is great— it can tell you variously how healthy your system is, how busy it is, who's trying to attack it, and who's successfully gained access in the last few minutes.

It's fairly standardized these days, unless you're working with a Java application, and if you've got the patience to read through a log file, you might want to give *War and Peace* a shot afterward.

Getting ready

Log on to your `centos1` VM:

```
$ vagrant ssh centos1
```

How to do it...

Hier manual pages tell us that if we want to find miscellaneous log files, we should start by looking in `/var/log/`:

> */var/log*
>   *Miscellaneous log files.*

Navigating to `/var/log` and listing its contents shows us that this is the case:

```
$ cd /var/log
$ ls -l
total 156
drwxr-xr-x. 2 root   root         219 May 12 18:55 anaconda
drwx------. 2 root   root          23 Oct  9 16:55 audit
-rw-------. 1 root   root           6 Oct  9 16:55 boot.log
-rw-------. 1 root   utmp           0 May 12 18:51 btmp
drwxr-xr-x. 2 chrony chrony         6 Apr 12 17:37 chrony
-rw-------. 1 root   root         807 Oct  9 17:01 cron
-rw-r--r--. 1 root   root       28601 Oct  9 16:55 dmesg
-rw-r--r--. 1 root   root         193 May 12 18:51 grubby_prune_debug
-rw-r--r--. 1 root   root      292292 Oct  9 17:21 lastlog
-rw-------. 1 root   root         198 Oct  9 16:55 maillog
-rw-------. 1 root   root       91769 Oct  9 17:23 messages
drwxr-xr-x. 2 root   root           6 Aug  4  2017 qemu-ga
drwxr-xr-x. 2 root   root           6 May 12 18:55 rhsm
-rw-------. 1 root   root        2925 Oct  9 17:21 secure
-rw-------. 1 root   root           0 May 12 18:52 spooler
-rw-------. 1 root   root           0 May 12 18:50 tallylog
drwxr-xr-x. 2 root   root          23 Oct  9 16:55 tuned
-rw-rw-r--. 1 root   utmp        1920 Oct  9 17:21 wtmp
```

On CentOS systems, the main log file is the `messages` log; under Debian and Ubuntu, this is called `syslog`, but it's effectively the same thing.

Having a look at the last few lines of this log file should show you various output from some of the programs running on your system:

```
$ sudo tail -10 messages
Dec 28 18:37:18 localhost nm-dispatcher: req:11 'connectivity-change':
start running ordered scripts...
Dec 28 18:37:22 localhost systemd-logind: New session 3 of user
vagrant.
Dec 28 18:37:22 localhost systemd: Started Session 3 of user vagrant.
Dec 28 18:37:22 localhost systemd: Starting Session 3 of user vagrant.
Dec 28 18:38:13 localhost chronyd[567]: Selected source 95.215.175.2
Dec 28 18:39:18 localhost chronyd[567]: Selected source 178.79.155.116
Dec 28 18:39:35 localhost systemd-logind: Removed session 2.
Dec 28 18:39:46 localhost systemd: Started Session 4 of user vagrant.
Dec 28 18:39:46 localhost systemd-logind: New session 4 of user
vagrant.
Dec 28 18:39:46 localhost systemd: Starting Session 4 of user vagrant.
```

Here, we can see `chronyd` complaining a bit, and we can see the point at which I logged in, and `systemd` was kind enough to create me a session.

You can also see the secure log, for the likes of `sshd`, `sudo`, and `PAM`:

```
$ sudo tail -5 secure
Dec 28 18:39:46 localhost sshd[3379]: Accepted publickey for vagrant
from 10.0.2.2 port 44394 ssh2: RSA
SHA256:7EOuFLwMurYJNPkZ3e+rZvez1FxmGD9ZNpEq6H+wmSA
Dec 28 18:39:46 localhost sshd[3379]: pam_unix(sshd:session): session
opened for user vagrant by (uid=0)
Dec 28 18:39:55 localhost sudo: vagrant : TTY=pts/0 ; PWD=/var/log ;
USER=root ; COMMAND=/bin/tail -10 messages
Dec 28 18:40:19 localhost sudo: vagrant : TTY=pts/0 ; PWD=/var/log ;
USER=root ; COMMAND=/bin/tail -10 secure
Dec 28 18:40:37 localhost sudo: vagrant : TTY=pts/0 ; PWD=/var/log ;
USER=root ; COMMAND=/bin/tail -5 secure
```

And files such as the `cron` log for `cron`:

```
$ sudo cat cron
Dec 28 18:36:57 localhost crond[612]: (CRON) INFO (RANDOM_DELAY will
be scaled with factor 89% if used.)
Dec 28 18:36:58 localhost crond[612]: (CRON) INFO (running with
inotify support)
```

As these files are just text, you can manipulate them using any of the standard tools at your disposal.

I might want to grep out mentions of vagrant from the messages log, and then only print the month, timestamp, and the program doing the logging:

```
$ sudo grep "vagrant." messages | cut -d" " -f 1,3,5
Dec 18:37:07 systemd:
Dec 18:37:07 systemd:
Dec 18:37:07 systemd:
Dec 18:37:07 systemd-logind:
Dec 18:37:07 systemd:
```

Why you'd want to do this I don't know, but people have weird hobbies.

So that log files don't get too big and become a real pain to even open (really, a million lines is too many), we also have logrotate, which periodically runs to swap out the old files for new ones to be written to.

Here, I force logrotate to run, so we can see the output:

```
$ sudo logrotate -f /etc/logrotate.conf
$ ls -lh
total 168K
drwxr-xr-x. 2 root   root   219 May 12 18:55 anaconda
drwx------. 2 root   root    23 Oct  9 16:55 audit
-rw-------. 1 root   root     0 Oct  9 17:35 boot.log
-rw-------. 1 root   root     6 Oct  9 17:35 boot.log-20181009
-rw-------. 1 root   utmp     0 Oct  9 17:35 btmp
-rw-------. 1 root   utmp     0 May 12 18:51 btmp-20181009
drwxr-xr-x. 2 chrony chrony   6 Apr 12 17:37 chrony
-rw-------. 1 root   root     0 Oct  9 17:35 cron
-rw-------. 1 root   root   807 Oct  9 17:01 cron-20181009
-rw-r--r--. 1 root   root   28K Oct  9 16:55 dmesg
-rw-r--r--. 1 root   root   193 May 12 18:51 grubby_prune_debug
-rw-r--r--. 1 root   root   286K Oct  9 17:28 lastlog
-rw-------. 1 root   root     0 Oct  9 17:35 maillog
-rw-------. 1 root   root   198 Oct  9 16:55 maillog-20181009
-rw-------. 1 root   root   145 Oct  9 17:35 messages
-rw-------. 1 root   root   90K Oct  9 17:28 messages-20181009
drwxr-xr-x. 2 root   root     6 Aug  4 2017 qemu-ga
drwxr-xr-x. 2 root   root     6 May 12 18:55 rhsm
-rw-------. 1 root   root     0 Oct  9 17:35 secure
-rw-------. 1 root   root   5.3K Oct  9 17:35 secure-20181009
-rw-------. 1 root   root     0 Oct  9 17:35 spooler
-rw-------. 1 root   root     0 May 12 18:52 spooler-20181009
-rw-------. 1 root   root     0 May 12 18:50 tallylog
drwxr-xr-x. 2 root   root    23 Oct  9 16:55 tuned
-rw-rw-r--. 1 root   utmp     0 Oct  9 17:35 wtmp
-rw-rw-r--. 1 root   utmp   1.9K Oct  9 17:21 wtmp-20181009
```

Note how the old files have been moved and date stamped, and the new ones have been given the same name.

Using `cat` on the messages file now will show one line, telling us that the `rsyslogd` daemon was `HUPed`:

```
$ sudo cat messages
Dec 28 18:41:38 centos1 rsyslogd: [origin software="rsyslogd"
swVersion="8.24.0" x-pid="898" x-info="http://www.rsyslog.com"]
rsyslogd was HUPed
```

 Personally, I think it should be HUP'd, but I can see the argument for `HUPed`.

How it works...

The daemon logging to text files is `rsyslogd` (on some older systems, it might be `syslog-ng`).

This reliable and extended syslogd program writes messages that it reads from one of two locations, `imuxsock` (old) and `imjournal` (new); this comes directly from the `syslog(3)` syscall man page:

syslog() and vsyslog()
syslog() generates a log message, which will be distributed by syslogd(8).

Note that `syslogd` (referenced here) is an old program, superseded by `rsyslogd`.

If there's more than one entry of the same name, in the man pages, you can specify the section by using the number. In this case, it would be `man 3 syslog` on the command line.

`rsyslogd` configuration resides at `/etc/rsyslog.conf` and gives us the first bit of information on how specific logs are written where. This is the RULES section:

```
#### RULES ####

# Log all kernel messages to the console.
# Logging much else clutters up the screen.
#kern.*                                                 /dev/console

# Log anything (except mail) of level info or higher.
# Don't log private authentication messages!
*.info;mail.none;authpriv.none;cron.none
/var/log/messages

# The authpriv file has restricted access.
authpriv.*
/var/log/secure

# Log all the mail messages in one place.
mail.*                                                  -
/var/log/maillog


# Log cron stuff
cron.*                                                  /var/log/cron

# Everybody gets emergency messages
*.emerg                                                 :omusrmsg:*

# Save news errors of level crit and higher in a special file.
uucp,news.crit
/var/log/spooler

# Save boot messages also to boot.log
local7.*
/var/log/boot.log
```

This shows us the various rules that are applied when certain messages hit the log location: if they're mail messages, they go to `/var/log/maillog`; if they're anything that's not mail (of `info` level or higher), `authpriv`, or `cron`, they go to `/var/log/messages`.

The `logger` command can be used to write to the log directly, and can be very handy for testing purposes and shell scripts, to show how this works:

```
$ logger "So long, and thanks for all the fish."
$ sudo tail -1 /var/log/messages
Oct 9 18:03:03 centos1 vagrant: So long, and thanks for all the fish.
```

The `logger` command also lets you specify the facility, and the level of the log:

```
$ logger -p cron.err "I'M A PARADOXICAL LOG MESSAGE."
$ sudo tail -3 /var/log/cron
Oct   9 18:07:01 centos1 anacron[3373]: Job `cron.weekly' started
Oct   9 18:07:01 centos1 anacron[3373]: Job `cron.weekly' terminated
Oct   9 18:07:23 centos1 vagrant: I'M A PARADOXICAL LOG MESSAGE.
```

This seems noisy, so let's create a dedicated log file for `cron` error messages.

We need a rule, placed in the `rsyslog.d` directory for such things:

```
$ cat <<HERE | sudo tee /etc/rsyslog.d/cronerr.conf
cron.err
/var/log/cron.err
HERE
```

Now, we restart `rsyslog`, and send our `logger` message again:

```
$ sudo systemctl restart rsyslog
$ logger -p cron.err "I'M A PARADOXICAL LOG MESSAGE."
$ sudo cat /var/log/cron.err
Oct   9 18:17:32 centos1 vagrant: I'M A PARADOXICAL LOG MESSAGE.
```

This is much cleaner; our custom rule looks good!

Log levels are one of the following, and there's only loosely defined guidelines for when the different levels are used, though generally it's considered good manners not to log trivial events as critical problems:

0	*emerg*
1	*alert*
2	*crit*
3	*err*
4	*warning*
5	*notice*
6	*info*
7	*debug*

The numbers are the numerical designation of the individual levels.

There's more...

When we rotated the logs, and HUPed the syslog daemon, we actually ran this script in logrotate:

```
$ cat /etc/logrotate.d/syslog
/var/log/cron
/var/log/maillog
/var/log/messages
/var/log/secure
/var/log/spooler
{
 missingok
 sharedscripts
 postrotate
    /bin/kill -HUP `cat /var/run/syslogd.pid 2> /dev/null` 2>
/dev/null || true
    endscript
}
```

Of course, there's no reason an application has to use the syslog(3) call to log messages, and it could just as easily write a stream of text to /tmp, but that's entirely up to the application developer in question.

All you need to know as an admin is that most logs will probably end up in text format in /var/log, and you can generally configure log file locations on a program-by-program basis.

Happy logging!

Using journalctl on systemd systems

Modern Linux distributions don't just rely on `syslog` files; in fact, they don't need to rely on `syslog` at all. Debian, Ubuntu, and CentOS all have `systemd` as an init system, and bundled with `systemd` is a service called `journald` (`systemd-journald.service`).

This service acts as the journaling solution for your system, and utilizes binary logs instead of text-based logs.

 While it's possible to ignore `syslog` entirely, and just use `journald`, a lot of systems now use both, to make the transition from one format to another easier. If you're using something like Arch or Gentoo, you may decide to dismiss `syslog` solutions entirely, in favour of `journald` alone.

Getting ready

For this section, we can use the `Vagrantfile` from the first section.

We will only be using `centos1`.

SSH to `centos1`:

```
$ vagrant ssh centos1
```

How to do it...

As mentioned earlier, journald utilizes a binary logging format, meaning it can't be opened with traditional text parsers and editors. Instead, we use the `journalctl` command to read logs.

Simply running the following opens your log:

```
$ sudo journalctl
```

The output for the preceding command is shown here:

This is familiar to anyone who's looked as a regular old `syslog` file; note that the format is the same by default.

It is quite noisy though, and on a busy system we might not want to see everything historic.

Maybe we want to just watch the log as it's written? If this is true, we can follow it with `-f`:

```
$ sudo journalctl -f
-- Logs begin at Tue 2018-10-09 18:43:07 UTC. --
Oct 10 17:07:03 centos1 chronyd[554]: System clock was stepped by
80625.148375 seconds
Oct 10 17:07:03 centos1 systemd[1]: Time has been changed
Oct 10 17:07:25 centos1 sshd[1106]: Accepted publickey for vagrant
from 10.0.2.2 port 55300 ssh2: RSA
SHA256:TTGYuhFa756sxR2rbliMhNqgbggAjFNERKg9htsdvSw
Oct 10 17:07:26 centos1 systemd[1]: Created slice User Slice of
vagrant.
Oct 10 17:07:26 centos1 systemd[1]: Starting User Slice of vagrant.
Oct 10 17:07:26 centos1 systemd[1]: Started Session 1 of user vagrant.
Oct 10 17:07:26 centos1 systemd-logind[545]: New session 1 of user
vagrant.
```

```
Oct 10 17:07:26 centos1 sshd[1106]: pam_unix(sshd:session): session
opened for user vagrant by (uid=0)
Oct 10 17:07:26 centos1 systemd[1]: Starting Session 1 of user
vagrant.
Oct 10 17:07:28 centos1 sudo[1131]:  vagrant : TTY=pts/0 ;
PWD=/home/vagrant ; USER=root ; COMMAND=/bin/journalctl -f
```

Whenever a log message is written, it will appear before you, streamed (use *Ctrl + C* to quit out).

We can specifically look at `kernel` logs (as if we were running `dmesg`) with the `-k` flag:

```
$ sudo journalctl -k --no-pager | head -n8
-- Logs begin at Tue 2018-10-09 18:43:07 UTC, end at Wed 2018-10-10
17:09:08 UTC. --
Oct 09 18:43:07 localhost.localdomain kernel: Initializing cgroup
subsys cpuset
Oct 09 18:43:07 localhost.localdomain kernel: Initializing cgroup
subsys cpu
Oct 09 18:43:07 localhost.localdomain kernel: Initializing cgroup
subsys cpuacct
Oct 09 18:43:07 localhost.localdomain kernel: Linux version
3.10.0-862.2.3.el7.x86_64 (builder@kbuilder.dev.centos.org) (gcc
version 4.8.5 20150623 (Red Hat 4.8.5-28) (GCC) ) #1 SMP Wed May 9
18:05:47 UTC 2018
Oct 09 18:43:07 localhost.localdomain kernel: Command line:
BOOT_IMAGE=/vmlinuz-3.10.0-862.2.3.el7.x86_64
root=/dev/mapper/VolGroup00-LogVol00 ro no_timer_check console=tty0
console=ttyS0,115200n8 net.ifnames=0 biosdevname=0 elevator=noop
crashkernel=auto rd.lvm.lv=VolGroup00/LogVol00
rd.lvm.lv=VolGroup00/LogVol01 rhgb quiet
Oct 09 18:43:07 localhost.localdomain kernel: e820: BIOS-provided
physical RAM map:
Oct 09 18:43:07 localhost.localdomain kernel: BIOS-e820: [mem
0x0000000000000000-0x000000000009fbff] usable
```

Note that here, I've disabled the pager (in the exact same way it's done in `systemctl-land`), and I've only dumped the first eight lines of the log, as the `kernel` is quite noisy, especially at boot.

This also serves to show that the logs can still be manipulated on the command line; you've just got to query them first (adding a bit of overhead).

That's not to say you have to use `journalctl` and a combination of other commands; there's a good chance you can get what you need with `journalctl` alone. Here, I choose a very specific time range to query the logs for:

```
$ sudo journalctl --since=17:07 --until=17:09
-- Logs begin at Tue 2018-10-09 18:43:07 UTC, end at Wed 2018-10-10
17:12:51 UTC. --
Oct 09 18:43:18 centos1 chronyd[554]: Selected source 188.114.116.1
Oct 09 18:43:18 centos1 chronyd[554]: System clock wrong by
80625.148375 seconds, adjustment started
Oct 10 17:07:03 centos1 chronyd[554]: System clock was stepped by
80625.148375 seconds
Oct 10 17:07:03 centos1 systemd[1]: Time has been changed
Oct 10 17:07:25 centos1 sshd[1106]: Accepted publickey for vagrant
from 10.0.2.2 port 55300 ssh2: RSA
SHA256:TTGYuhFa756sxR2rbliMhNqgbggAjFNERKg9htsdvSw
Oct 10 17:07:26 centos1 systemd[1]: Created slice User Slice of
vagrant.
Oct 10 17:07:26 centos1 systemd[1]: Starting User Slice of vagrant.
Oct 10 17:07:26 centos1 systemd[1]: Started Session 1 of user vagrant.
Oct 10 17:07:26 centos1 systemd-logind[545]: New session 1 of user
vagrant.
Oct 10 17:07:26 centos1 sshd[1106]: pam_unix(sshd:session): session
opened for user vagrant by (uid=0)
Oct 10 17:07:26 centos1 systemd[1]: Starting Session 1 of user
vagrant.
Oct 10 17:07:28 centos1 sudo[1131]:  vagrant : TTY=pts/0 ;
PWD=/home/vagrant ; USER=root ; COMMAND=/bin/journalctl -f
Oct 10 17:08:08 centos1 chronyd[554]: Selected source 194.80.204.184
Oct 10 17:08:41 centos1 sudo[1145]:  vagrant : TTY=pts/0 ;
PWD=/home/vagrant ; USER=root ; COMMAND=/bin/journalctl -k
Oct 10 17:08:52 centos1 sudo[1148]:  vagrant : TTY=pts/0 ;
PWD=/home/vagrant ; USER=root ; COMMAND=/bin/journalctl -k
```

In 2 minutes, we get 15 lines of log, but this is much easier to sift through and digest (assuming the time is correct on your box of course!)

These timestamps are just examples; you could use a full date (`--since="2018-10-10 17:07:00"`) or even relative statements (`--since=yesterday --until=now`).

If it's not a range of time you're after, but rather the logs of a specific `systemd unit`, `journalctl` also has you covered:

```
$ sudo journalctl -u chronyd
-- Logs begin at Tue 2018-10-09 18:43:07 UTC, end at Wed 2018-10-10
```

```
17:18:58 UTC. --
Oct 09 18:43:09 centos1 systemd[1]: Starting NTP client/server...
Oct 09 18:43:09 centos1 chronyd[554]: chronyd version 3.2 starting
(+CMDMON +NTP +REFCLOCK +RTC +PRIVDROP +SCFILTER +SECHASH +SIGND
+ASYNCDNS +IPV6 +DEBUG)
Oct 09 18:43:09 centos1 chronyd[554]: Frequency -3.308 +/- 6.027 ppm
read from /var/lib/chrony/drift
Oct 09 18:43:09 centos1 systemd[1]: Started NTP client/server.
Oct 09 18:43:18 centos1 chronyd[554]: Selected source 188.114.116.1
Oct 09 18:43:18 centos1 chronyd[554]: System clock wrong by
80625.148375 seconds, adjustment started
Oct 10 17:07:03 centos1 chronyd[554]: System clock was stepped by
80625.148375 seconds
Oct 10 17:08:08 centos1 chronyd[554]: Selected source 194.80.204.184
```

Here, I used the `-u` (unit) flag to only look at logs from `chronyd`, minimizing the amount of output I have to deal with.

What we also get in the preceding example are the `systemd` logs that interact with the `chronyd` unit. But if we only want logs from the `chronyd` binary, we can do that too:

```
$ sudo journalctl /usr/sbin/chronyd
-- Logs begin at Tue 2018-10-09 18:43:07 UTC, end at Wed 2018-10-10
17:21:08 UTC. --
Oct 09 18:43:09 centos1 chronyd[554]: chronyd version 3.2 starting
(+CMDMON +NTP +REFCLOCK +RTC +PRIVDROP +SCFILTER +SECHASH +SIGND
+ASYNCDNS +IPV6 +DEBUG)
Oct 09 18:43:09 centos1 chronyd[554]: Frequency -3.308 +/- 6.027 ppm
read from /var/lib/chrony/drift
Oct 09 18:43:18 centos1 chronyd[554]: Selected source 188.114.116.1
Oct 09 18:43:18 centos1 chronyd[554]: System clock wrong by
80625.148375 seconds, adjustment started
Oct 10 17:07:03 centos1 chronyd[554]: System clock was stepped by
80625.148375 seconds
Oct 10 17:08:08 centos1 chronyd[554]: Selected source 194.80.204.184
```

Seriously, how cool is that?

But wait, there's more!

The `journald` command can be more powerful still, as it has the concept of message explanations, or message context if you prefer. Some log lines can be output in a more verbose fashion (with `-x`) to better understand what's happening.

Take the following two examples using the `sshd` unit, with and without the `-x` flag:

```
$ sudo journalctl -u sshd
-- Logs begin at Tue 2018-10-09 18:43:07 UTC, end at Wed 2018-10-10
17:25:46 UTC. --
Oct 09 18:43:14 centos1 systemd[1]: Starting OpenSSH server daemon...
Oct 09 18:43:14 centos1 sshd[853]: Server listening on 0.0.0.0 port
22.
Oct 09 18:43:14 centos1 sshd[853]: Server listening on :: port 22.
Oct 09 18:43:14 centos1 systemd[1]: Started OpenSSH server daemon.
Oct 10 17:07:25 centos1 sshd[1106]: Accepted publickey for vagrant
from 10.0.2.2 port 55300 ssh2: RSA
SHA256:TTGYuhFa756sxR2rbliMhNqgbggAjFNERKg9htsdvSw
$ sudo journalctl -u sshd -x
-- Logs begin at Tue 2018-10-09 18:43:07 UTC, end at Wed 2018-10-10
17:26:04 UTC. --
Oct 09 18:43:14 centos1 systemd[1]: Starting OpenSSH server daemon...
-- Subject: Unit sshd.service has begun start-up
-- Defined-By: systemd
-- Support:
http://lists.freedesktop.org/mailman/listinfo/systemd-devel
--
-- Unit sshd.service has begun starting up.
Oct 09 18:43:14 centos1 sshd[853]: Server listening on 0.0.0.0 port
22.
Oct 09 18:43:14 centos1 sshd[853]: Server listening on :: port 22.
Oct 09 18:43:14 centos1 systemd[1]: Started OpenSSH server daemon.
-- Subject: Unit sshd.service has finished start-up
-- Defined-By: systemd
-- Support:
http://lists.freedesktop.org/mailman/listinfo/systemd-devel
--
-- Unit sshd.service has finished starting up.
--
-- The start-up result is done.
Oct 10 17:07:25 centos1 sshd[1106]: Accepted publickey for vagrant
from 10.0.2.2 port 55300 ssh2: RSA
SHA256:TTGYuhFa756sxR2rbliMhNqgbggAjFNERKg9htsdvSw
```

Note that the `systemd` specific lines suddenly have a lot more context.

We've covered some good basics, but `journalctl` can still be more complex. After passing options to the output, we can add specific matches to our statements (in the format `FIELD=VALUE`).

Looking at SSH, we can see this in action:

```
$ sudo journalctl --since=yesterday _SYSTEMD_UNIT=sshd.service
_PID=853
-- Logs begin at Tue 2018-10-09 18:43:07 UTC, end at Wed 2018-10-10
17:31:48 UTC. --
Oct 09 18:43:14 centos1 sshd[853]: Server listening on 0.0.0.0 port
22.
Oct 09 18:43:14 centos1 sshd[853]: Server listening on :: port 22.
```

Here, we've said that we want all the messages from yesterday, generated by the systemd sshd unit, but only those from PID 853 (which happens to be the server daemon PID on this box).

For more on matches, take a look at the systemd.journal-fields man page.

Lastly, as with syslog, we can specify the priority of messages we want to see. Here, we're looking at the entire log, but we're only after err level messages:

```
$ sudo journalctl -p err
-- Logs begin at Tue 2018-10-09 18:43:07 UTC, end at Wed 2018-10-10
17:55:48 UTC. --
Oct 09 18:43:09 centos1 systemd[504]: Failed at step STDIN spawning
/usr/libexec/selinux/selinux-policy-migrate-local-changes.sh:
Inappropriate ioctl for device
Oct 09 18:43:09 centos1 systemd[1]: Failed to start Migrate local
SELinux policy changes from the old store structure to the new
structure.
Oct 09 18:43:14 centos1 rsyslogd[857]: imjournal: loaded invalid
cursor, seeking to the head of journal  [v8.24.0 try
http://www.rsyslog.com/e/2027 ]
```

How it works...

Configured in /etc/systemd/journald.conf, journald is a great piece of software but, at least on CentOS 7, it's something of a second class citizen, with syslog still being the primary method of keeping an eye on logs for a lot of people.

Logs aren't persisted through reboots (more on this later) so it's only good for querying the state of a system since boot (which can also be enough, 9 times out of 10).

The file, as we said, is in binary format, and journald pulls in various sources to create its log journals:

- Kernel log messages (`/dev/kmsg`)
- Simple log messages (the `syslog` `libc` call mentioned previously)
- Structured journal log messages from the Journal API (imported into `rsyslog` with the `imjournal` module)
- The `stdout` and `stderr` of service unit files
- Audit records from the kernel audit subsystem

Like `syslog`, this means `logger` can be used to show we can still populate the log manually, here showing only those messages received from the `syslog` transport mechanism:

```
$ logger -p cron.err "I'M ANOTHER PARADOXICAL LOG MESSAGE."
$ sudo journalctl -p err _TRANSPORT=syslog --since 18:00
-- Logs begin at Tue 2018-10-09 18:43:07 UTC, end at Wed 2018-10-10
18:11:15 UTC. --
Oct 10 18:08:18 centos1 vagrant[1736]: I'M ANOTHER PARADOXICAL LOG
MESSAGE.
```

In the future, there's a good chance that `syslog` will be dropped and `journald` will become the new norm, but given how long `syslog` as a concept has been around for, it'll be a very long time before that becomes the case.

The fact `journald` logs in a binary way is something of a point of contention for a lot of traditionalists but, like Columbus, it didn't arrive on the scene first, it's just the one that got all the attention. Those of you who've ever used OpenBSD, and its firewall `pf`, will perhaps find the notion of binary logging a comfort.

There's more...

One thing to be aware of is the space that the journal log will use. The size limitations are governed by options in `journald.conf`.

The options `SystemMaxUse` and `RuntimeMaxUse` govern the maximum disk space the journal can use; these default to 10% of the size of the filesystem, with a cap of 4 GB.

The `SystemKeepFree` and `RuntimeKeepFree` options govern how much disk space `journald` leaves free for other uses; these default to 15% of the size of the filesystem, and are also capped to 4 GB.

There are various scenarios governing size but, basically, `journald` will try its hardest not to be the reason your filesystem fills up, and it's that sort of attention to detail that makes me love it.

See also

On our CentOS system, the log file is transient, being lost upon reboot. While it's live, it exists in `/run/log/journal/`:

```
$ ls /run/log/journal/
4eabd6271dbf4ed0bc608378f4311df8
$ sudo ls -lh /run/log/journal/4eabd6271dbf4ed0bc608378f4311df8/
total 4.0M
-rwxr-x---+ 1 root systemd-journal 4.0M Oct  9 18:43 system.journal
```

> We could actually change this behavior quite easily, by adding a `/var/log/` directory specifically for the journal, and using a one-liner to change the permissions: `sudo systemd-tmpfiles --create --prefix /var/log/journal`

You can also list the boots `journalctl` is aware of from the command line:

```
$ sudo journalctl --list-boots
 0 b4c3669c7a9841ba841c330a75125e35 Tue 2018-10-09 18:43:07 UTC—Wed
2018-10-10 18:13:27 UTC
```

Centralizing logging

You don't want to log on to each and every box in your estate to check logs, you just don't. In this age of the cloud and automatically provisioned infrastructure, it's a lot more faff than it's worth, and it's a great case for centralizing your logs in one (redundant) location.

Being data, our logs can be manipulated and moved relatively easily. Both `rsyslog` and `journald` have the capability to do this, and, in this section, we're going to be streaming our logs around the place, showcasing how useful this can be.

Everything we cover here will be natively possible in the respective programs; this is different to some of the centralized logging solutions that are provided by software such as the Elastic Stack.

 For the purpose of these examples, we're not utilizing TLS, meaning logs will be streamed in a plain format. I would advise against doing this sort of thing in production, without investing in HTTPS setups or tunneled solutions.

Getting ready

For this section, we can use the `Vagrantfile` from the first section.

We will be using `centos1` and `centos2` for the first part, and then `debian1` and `debian2` for the second part, sending logs from one box to the other.

Open two Terminals and connect to both `centos1` and `centos2`; install `tcpdump` on both boxes:

```
$ vagrant ssh centos1
$ sudo yum install tcpdump -y

$ vagrant ssh centos2
$ sudo yum install tcpdump -y
```

For part two (`journald`), connect to both `debian1` and `debian2`, and install `tcpdump` and `systemd-journal-remote` on both boxes:

```
$ vagrant ssh debian1
$ sudo apt install tcpdump systemd-journal-remote -y

$ vagrant ssh debian2
$ sudo apt install tcpdump systemd-journal-remote -y
```

How to do it...

We'll go through both of the logging daemons in turn, starting with `rsyslog` and then doing the same basic thing with `journald`.

Remote logging with rsyslog – UDP example

In order to enable logging to a remote machine with `rsyslog`, you need to enable both streaming to a remote location on your client, and receiving on your server.

For this, `centos1` will be our client, and `centos2` will be our server.

On `centos1` first:

```
$ sudo sed -i 's/#*.* @@remote-host:514/*.* @192.168.33.11/g'
/etc/rsyslog.conf
$ sudo systemctl restart rsyslog
```

Now on `centos2`:

```
$ sudo sed -i 's/#$ModLoad imudp/$ModLoad imudp/g' /etc/rsyslog.conf
$ sudo sed -i 's/#$UDPServerRun 514/$UDPServerRun 514/g'
/etc/rsyslog.conf
$ sudo systemctl restart rsyslog
```

We can check this is working immediately with `tcpdump` on our `centos2` VM; start it using the following command:

```
$ sudo tcpdump port 514 -i eth1
```

Now, generate a message on `centos1` to send; here, we're spoofing a `syslog.info` message:

```
$ logger -p syslog.info "I'm a regular info message."
```

On `centos2`, you should see something like the following:

And, of course, in the `/var/log/messages` file where our log line will end up, you will see the following:

```
$ sudo tail -3 /var/log/messages
Oct 11 18:35:45 centos2 kernel: device eth1 entered promiscuous mode
Oct 11 18:35:48 centos1 vagrant: I'm a regular info message.
Oct 11 18:36:23 centos2 kernel: device eth1 left promiscuous mode
```

Here, we can also see `eth1` being put in promiscuous mode by `tcpdump`, prior to and after us delivering our `syslog` message.

Remote logging with rsyslog – TCP example

The previous example covered UDP, which is simply a stream of information with no confirmation that the server on the other side received the noise. With a TCP connection, the `syslog` servers communicate with each other to establish a connection first.

On your `centos1` machine, replace the single @ sign in your destination address with two @@ signs:

```
$ sudo sed -i 's/*.* @192.168.33.11/*.* @@192.168.33.11/g'
/etc/rsyslog.conf
$ sudo systemctl restart rsyslog
```

Our client is now set, but no logs can be sent until the connection is established.

On `centos2`, let's set the `rsyslog` server to receive TCP connections and data:

```
$ sudo sed -i 's/#$ModLoad imtcp/$ModLoad imtcp/g' /etc/rsyslog.conf
$ sudo sed -i 's/#$InputTCPServerRun 514/$InputTCPServerRun 514/g'
/etc/rsyslog.conf
$ sudo systemctl restart rsyslog
```

 An `rsyslog` server can listen on UDP and TCP at the same time.

Let's test it out! On `centos2`, set up your `tcpdump` again:

```
$ sudo tcpdump port 514 -i eth1
```

And send a log message from `centos1`:

```
$ logger -p syslog.err "I'm a confusing error message."
```

Your `tcpdump` output should look similar to the following:

And, again, your messages file should have the new alert:

```
$ sudo tail -3 /var/log/messages
Oct 11 18:39:09 centos1 vagrant: I'm a confusing error message.
Oct 11 18:39:15 centos2 kernel: device eth1 left promiscuous mode
Oct 11 18:39:27 centos1 systemd-logind: Removed session 3.
```

Remote logging with journald

The `systemd-journal-remote` command allows you to receive journal messages over a network. Sadly, it's a fairly recent addition to the `systemd` suite, and isn't yet available on CentOS systems.

On your first Debian system (`debian1`), set up your remote upload location:

```
$ sudo sed -i 's/# URL=/URL=http:\/\/192.168.33.13/g'
/etc/systemd/journal-upload.conf
```

On your second box (`debian2`), start by editing the listening service, using `systemctl edit`:

```
$ sudo systemctl edit systemd-journal-remote
```

When presented with the empty editor, add the following three lines:

```
[Service]
ExecStart=
ExecStart=/lib/systemd/systemd-journal-remote --listen-http=-3 --
output=/var/log/journal/remote
```

It should look something like the following:

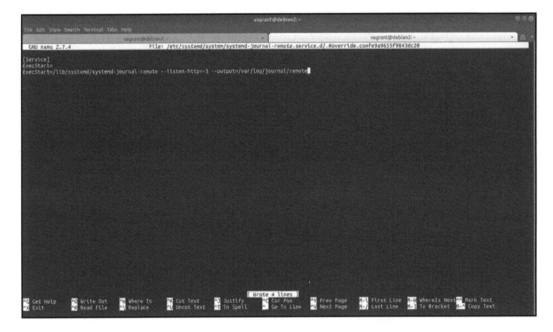

Save and exit (*Ctrl + O, Enter, Ctrl + X*).

Now you need to make the remote folder location, and make sure it has the appropriate permissions, before finally restarting the service:

```
$ sudo mkdir -p /var/log/journal/remote
$ sudo chown systemd-journal-remote /var/log/journal/remote
$ sudo systemctl restart systemd-journal-remote
```

And don't forget to start the service on debian1:

```
$ sudo systemctl restart systemd-journal-upload
```

Give it a test by following your log on debian2:

```
$ sudo journalctl -D /var/log/journal/remote/ -f
```

It can also be tested by using our trusty logger command on debian1:

```
$ logger -p syslog.err "Debian1 logs, on Debian2!"
```

With any luck, you'll see the following:

How it works...

What we're effectively doing is opening up a listener for logs in both the `syslog` and `journald` solutions. A network port is opened on our boxes, and the daemon is aware of a source of data that it might be forced to read from. In the case of `syslog`, we had to enable specific modules in the `rsyslog` daemon to make this happen; `systemd` and `journald` required specific packages.

Obviously, journald's implementation appears a bit clunkier, but that's mostly because it's newer.

Fundamentally, we're just dealing with streaming log data, and neither `syslog` nor `journald` care where that data comes from, as long as it's in a format that they can understand.

There's more...

Time is very important when centralizing logging. Think about how confusing it can be to look in a log file that features multiple hosts, and discover interspersed time jumps.

It can also make log parsing hard, as we can use specific timestamps to properly arrange data, and we could miss something critical if our remote box has the wrong time.

TLS and secure transport are also something to think about, as mentioned in the introduction to this section. You can configure `systemd-journal-remote` to listen on HTTPS, instead of HTTP, as long as you sort your certificates properly.

For syslog, TLS and encryption can be a bit trickier, but there are more solutions to consider, such as streaming log data over an SSH tunnel, or using a program such as `spipe` to offload the heavy work of TLS.

Local resource measuring tools

Occasionally, it can be incredibly handy to know what a box is doing right this second. Usually, this will be during a debugging session, when you're trying to work out why the website is responding an order of magnitude slower, or why it's taking 5 minutes to type your SSH command on a remote session.

Here, local resource monitors come in handy. We've already touched on these briefly, but this section will look at them in slightly more detail, and will cover some of the more obscure tools that you might find useful when remotely connected to your server.

We're going to look at the classics of `free` and `top`, before moving on to the more recent additions, such as `netdata` and `htop`.

Getting ready

For this section, we're going to use our `centos1` and `debian1` VMs.

All of the programs we look at will be universally available in one form or another.

SSH to your `centos1` VM, and ensure that the EPEL repository is enabled:

```
$ vagrant ssh centos1
$ sudo yum install epel-release -y
$ sudo yum install htop -y
```

SSH to your `debian1` VM, very specifically, forwarding port `19999` to your local machine (more on this later):

```
$ vagrant ssh debian1 -- -L 127.0.0.1:19999:127.0.0.1:19999
```

How to do it...

As with most of what we look at, there are classic examples of software that has been kicking around in one form or another since roughly the 1970s, back when most programs had names of two or three characters (ls, cp, mv). One of these is `top` and another is `free`, both of which still have their place.

Then there are the more modern, slick, and beautiful programs. Gone are the monochrome CRT-designed applications, and, in their place, are Terminal applications that even support 256 colours!

Finally, there's NetData, which I touch on here because it's making quite the storm in the world of local administration.

top

An old friend, and guaranteed to be installed on any Unix or Unix-like system, top is your immediate window into what your system thinks it's doing:

```
$ top
```

The output for the preceding command is shown as follows:

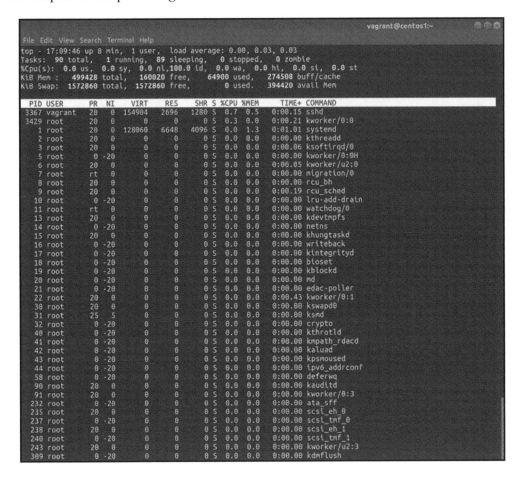

Right from the start, we can see several things:

- The time in the top left, and how long the box has been up – 17:09:46 up 8 min
- The number of users logged in – 1 user
- The load average – 0.00, 0.03, 0.03
- The number of running, sleeping, and so on tasks
- CPU usage information
- Volatile memory information (RAM)
- SWAP information (disk memory)

Breaking these down, let's look at some in more detail:

- **Load average**: In detail, the load average is the load of the system over the last 1, 5, and 15 minutes. This load average is a display of processes running, or those waiting for resources such as CPU time or disk I/O.

 The disk I/O element is important, as it's something that's pretty Linux-specific and that a lot of people forget. You can have a system that's completely free of load on the CPU, and yet has high load average values; this can be an indication that you need to upgrade that old and creaking HDD into a shiny new NVMe drive.

- **Tasks**: Basically, you can think of tasks as the number of processes that are running now, or that are in the sleeping/zombie/stopped state on your system. It's the same number you'd get with `ps aux`.

- **%CPU**: It's best to defer to the man page for this one:

    us, user   : time running un-niced user processes
    sy, system : time running kernel processes
    ni, nice   : time running niced user processes
    id, idle   : time spent in the kernel idle handler
    wa, IO-wait : time waiting for I/O completion
    hi : time spent servicing hardware interrupts
    si : time spent servicing software interrupts
    st : time stolen from this vm by the hypervisor

- **KiB Mem**: In digits, this is the amount of RAM available to your system, broken down into the total, free, used, and buffers/caches.

 Buffers/caches are memory that's in use, but which can be annexed by any program that wishes to use it in an instant. Linux likes RAM, and unused RAM is wasted RAM, so it will do everything it can to use it.

- **KiB Swap**: Also in digits, this is the amount of Swap available, broken down once more.

If you want a nicer view, cycling through the options by hitting *M* a few times will give you visual representations:

```
KiB Mem : 20.6/499428   [||||||||||||||||||||||                        ]
KiB Swap:  0.0/1572860  [                                              ]
```

Lastly, we have the ever-changing process list and information about running jobs on your system:

```
  PID USER      PR  NI    VIRT    RES    SHR S %CPU %MEM     TIME+ COMMAND
 3453 vagrant   20   0   61668   2196   1548 R  0.7  0.4   0:00.61 top
    1 root      20   0  128060   6648   4096 S  0.0  1.3   0:01.05 systemd
    2 root      20   0       0      0      0 S  0.0  0.0   0:00.00 kthreadd
    3 root      20   0       0      0      0 S  0.0  0.0   0:00.10 ksoftirqd/0
    5 root       0 -20       0      0      0 S  0.0  0.0   0:00.00 kworker/0:0H
    6 root      20   0       0      0      0 S  0.0  0.0   0:00.05 kworker/u2:0
    7 root      rt   0       0      0      0 S  0.0  0.0   0:00.00 migration/0
    8 root      20   0       0      0      0 S  0.0  0.0   0:00.00 rcu_bh
    9 root      20   0       0      0      0 S  0.0  0.0   0:00.22 rcu_sched
   10 root       0 -20       0      0      0 S  0.0  0.0   0:00.00 lru-add-drain
   11 root      rt   0       0      0      0 S  0.0  0.0   0:00.02 watchdog/0
   13 root      20   0       0      0      0 S  0.0  0.0   0:00.00 kdevtmpfs
   14 root       0 -20       0      0      0 S  0.0  0.0   0:00.00 netns
   15 root      20   0       0      0      0 S  0.0  0.0   0:00.00 khungtaskd
   16 root       0 -20       0      0      0 S  0.0  0.0   0:00.00 writeback
   17 root       0 -20       0      0      0 S  0.0  0.0   0:00.00 kintegrityd
   18 root       0 -20       0      0      0 S  0.0  0.0   0:00.00 bioset
   19 root       0 -20       0      0      0 S  0.0  0.0   0:00.00 kblockd
   20 root       0 -20       0      0      0 S  0.0  0.0   0:00.00 md
   21 root       0 -20       0      0      0 S  0.0  0.0   0:00.00 edac-poller
   30 root      20   0       0      0      0 S  0.0  0.0   0:00.00 kswapd0
   31 root      25   5       0      0      0 S  0.0  0.0   0:00.00 ksmd
   32 root       0 -20       0      0      0 S  0.0  0.0   0:00.00 crypto
   40 root       0 -20       0      0      0 S  0.0  0.0   0:00.00 kthrotld
   41 root       0 -20       0      0      0 S  0.0  0.0   0:00.00 kmpath_rdacd
   42 root       0 -20       0      0      0 S  0.0  0.0   0:00.00 kaluad
   43 root       0 -20       0      0      0 S  0.0  0.0   0:00.00 kpsmoused
```

By default, this is organized by CPU usage (%CPU) but you can adjust that if you wish.

Along the top, we have the following:

- The PID of the task in question
- The user running the process
- PR, the priority of a task (the higher the priority, the more likely it is to get prioritized)
- NI, the nice value of a task; minus values have a higher priority
- VIRT, the virtual memory being used by the task (all memory, including the likes of shared libraries)
- RES, the non-swapped physical memory being used by the task
- SHR, mostly RES, without some bits that are too technical for this book

- S, the state of the process (running, sleeping, zombie, and so on)
- %CPU, how much CPU time a task has used since the last refresh, a percentage of the total CPU time available
- %MEM, how much available physical memory a task is currently using
- TIME+, an update of TIME, it's the total CPU time the task has used since starting; the plus increases granularity
- COMMAND, the name of the task

Phew!

That's `top`, but it's so much more than that, and it might look slightly different on different systems. It can also do color, but only one distribution I know of switches it on out of the box.

It's a good idea to load `top` and hit *H* or *?* for a helpful indication of what `top` is capable of.

free

`free` is a great way to see how busy your system is at a glance; more specifically, it's the quickest way of finding out how much memory is being used on your box.

Thankfully, `free` has fewer options than `top`. Mostly, the flags are just to change the output of the command, making it more human-readable or less, if that's your thing.

 Personally, I use −m which outputs the value in mebibytes, but if your system has Gigs of memory, you might find −g more useful.

In the following, you will see `free -ht` on our `centos1` VM: −h is used for human-readable output, giving a nice mix of mebibyte and gibibyte values; −t is a flag to add a `Total` line, giving a sum of `Mem` and `Swap` values:

```
[vagrant@centos1 ~]$ free -ht
              total        used        free      shared  buff/cache   available
Mem:           487M         62M        291M        4.5M        134M        386M
Swap:          1.5G          0B        1.5G
Total:         2.0G         62M        1.8G
```

The important field is `available`, as it effectively tells you how much physical memory is available before the system starts swapping; if this is 0, you're going to be constantly reading and writing to disk, which can slow a system drastically.

htop

`htop` is like `top`, but prettier. If a box is under my control (and providing the appropriate approval has been given), you're very likely to find `htop` installed.

In a pinch, `top` is fine, and you're guaranteed to find it pre-installed on a box, but if you want something that doesn't feel like it's from the 1970s, `htop` is extremely helpful.

Here's `htop` on our `centos1` VM:

Note that we still have all the same information that `top` gives us, only now we've made use of what a modern Terminal emulator can do, giving us colors by default, and nicely aligning output into a window that also supports mouse input (try it!).

Further to `top`, we have the ability to format our output quickly and easily by changing the look of our window; the options such as `Tree` at the bottom of the screen (*F5*) can provide a very useful tree view when pressed (note it changes to read `Sorted`):

As with top, there are also options for changing what's shown in terms of columns and information, although, unlike `top`, these are under the Setup menu (*F3*) and changes are persisted to disk in the form of a configuration file, located at `~/.config/htop/htoprc`.

NetData

Popular mainly due to being able to market itself effectively, NetData is an aggregator of all the system information it can get hold of.

 This is not an advert nor an endorsement, merely an example of what third-party software can do. NetData does use a centralized server for logging some data, such as system hostnames, meaning you should check against your internal security policy if you intend to use this tool. See the NetData security page for more information:

https://docs.netdata.cloud/docs/netdata-security/

As with everything, understand what the software you're installing does, before you blindly click **Accept**.

Flipping over to our Debian VM, we're going to install NetData here, as it's available in the backports repository (software added to previously released Debian versions after the fact).

First, we need to enable the `backports` repository and then we can install our package:

```
$ echo "deb http://ftp.debian.org/debian stretch-backports main" |
sudo tee -a /etc/apt/sources.list
$ sudo apt update
$ sudo apt install netdata -y
```

As Debian typically starts services by default, after installation, NetData is now enabled and started.

By default, though, it will only listen on localhost, which is why we needed to forward that IP and port in our *Getting ready* section. If you've not done so, log off from your `debian1` VM and use the command from that section.

Now, navigating to `http://127.0.0.1:19999` in your local machine's web browser will forward that connection through to your VM, and you should see the NetData GUI:

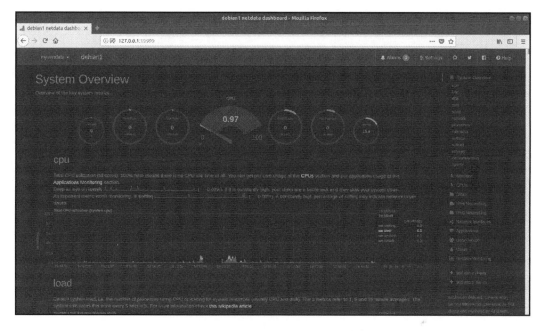

NetData Homepage

Even I've got to admit, the interface is pretty swish.

Note that, on the right, it even gives you a snippet of information about what NetData is doing, and where it's getting information from: netdata on `debian1` collects 686 metrics every second, presented as 142 charts and monitored by 41 alarms, using 11 MB of memory for 1 hour, 6 minutes and 36 seconds of real-time history.

How it works...

`top` queries the kernel to gather information about a running system, making it very fast at reflecting the nature of the box it's been run on. It's also incredibly lightweight, meaning that unless a box is extremely overloaded, there's a good chance `top` will still run (and if it is overloaded, you've got bigger issues). It's been around since the 1980s; it's tried and tested.

`free` takes a look at the values available in `/proc/meminfo`, meaning that while you can query these files yourself (and some people do), `free` provides a nicer way of looking at values (and gives you the option to refresh on a periodic basis, if that's what you're after).

`htop` queries the system in much the same way as `top` (though this isn't necessarily the same across operating systems such as macOS or the BSD family). The difference with `htop` is that it uses the `ncurses` library to display itself, and while it's not as old as `top`, it has been around for about 14 years at the time of writing.

NetData uses various sources (and can use custom plugins) to collect data every second; it then displays this data to the user.

There's more...

NetData might look cool, and, at a glance, it can be a nifty way of finding out what your server is up to (especially if you've got it on a wall in your office or something), but this isn't an advertisement, and I would advise caution when using tools such as this. Not because they're dangerous (though always check your sources), but because they can be a little frivolous, and serve as nothing more than a dashboard that management might like to see on your PC monitor occasionally.

Ooh! I've thought of another great use for NetData, maybe as some sort of background set-dressing in some cheesy DC or SciFi TV show; that'd be neat too.

What we looked at here are only a sample of the tools on offer. The defaults will always be available to you (the tops and frees of the world), but there are hundreds of others to choose from, some of which might fit your needs, and some of which might fit that wallboard in the corner of the office that no one else ever uses.

Have a look around, search the net, and try things out.

It's Linux, there are a hundred ways to accomplish the same thing.

Local monitoring tools

Like tools that keep an eye on the resources of your system here and now, there are tools for looking at the historic data on your system. NetData could be considered one of these, depending on how you use it, but there are more besides, and we'll look at a few more that can help you to debug past problems.

We're going to take a look at the following:

- atop
- sar
- vmstat

Getting ready

For this section, we're going to continue to use the Vagrantfile from the first section of this chapter.

Log on to centos1, the VM we're going to be using in this section:

```
$ vagrant ssh centos1
```

Install the tools we'll be using:

```
$ sudo yum install epel-release -y
$ sudo yum install atop sysstat -y
```

How to do it...

Once you've got all your tools installed, work through each of the following sections.

atop

atop (Advanced System and Process Monitoring)

To begin, run atop normally:

```
$ atop
```

You should see something like this:

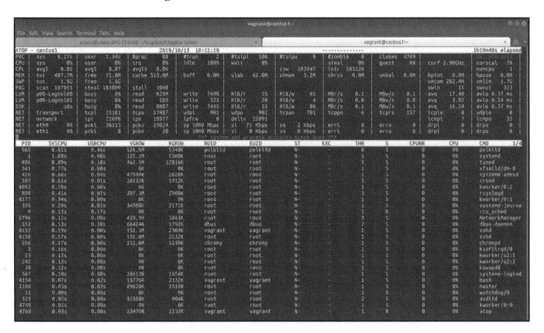

This gives us some good information, specifically the system and process activity since boot, before it rotates onto a rolling display of the activity over the previous 10 seconds. In other words, 10 seconds later, it looks like this:

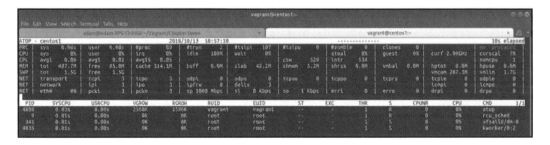

Furthermore, `atop` can be used to store data not just of the current boot, but also periodically.

Enable the `atop` service as follows:

```
$ sudo systemctl enable atop --now
```

You will now find that historic days are logged to `/var/log/atop` in a binary format and those same files can then be replayed at a future date, in case you want to know what happened to your system in the middle of the night that caused all those red alerts:

```
$ sudo ls /var/log/atop/
atop_20181013  daily.log
```

To read a file again, you can either specify the full filename, or the date you're after:

```
$ atop -r 20181013
```

Because we started the service at `18:56:14`, that's what we see when we load this file:

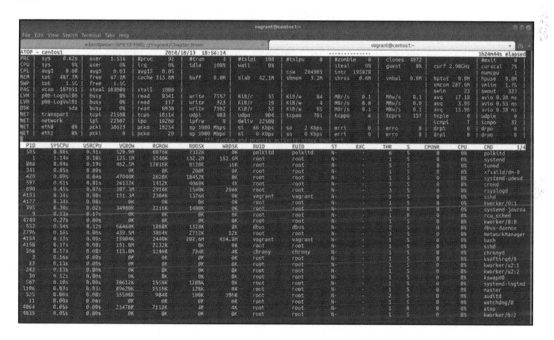

We can then adjust the samples by using *t* and *T* to move forward and backward.

`atop` is restarted at midnight by a `cron` job:

```
$ sudo cat /etc/cron.d/atop
# daily restart of atop at midnight
0 0 * * * root systemctl try-restart atop
```

sar

`sar` is a way of reading system information, but it also allows you to read historic information.

It's enabled with a `systemctl` command, which actually triggers a binary called `sa1` to start at boot:

```
$ sudo systemctl enable --now sysstat
```

Run via a `cron` job, `sar` is executed every 10 minutes to grab system information. It then has a daily summary created at 23:53:

```
$ sudo cat /etc/cron.d/sysstat
# Run system activity accounting tool every 10 minutes
*/10 * * * * root /usr/lib64/sa/sa1 1 1
# 0 * * * * root /usr/lib64/sa/sa1 600 6 &
# Generate a daily summary of process accounting at 23:53
53 23 * * * root /usr/lib64/sa/sa2 -A
```

To specify a `sar` file to open and read, use the `-f` flag:

```
$ sar -f /var/log/sa/sa13
Linux 3.10.0-862.2.3.el7.x86_64 (centos1)        13/10/18      _x86_64_
(1 CPU)
```

18:50:01 %idle	CPU	%user	%nice	%system	%iowait	%steal
19:00:01 99.76	all	0.03	0.00	0.21	0.00	0.00
Average: 99.76	all	0.03	0.00	0.21	0.00	0.00

19:07:51	LINUX RESTART					
19:10:01 %idle	CPU	%user	%nice	%system	%iowait	%steal
19:14:43 99.75	all	0.04	0.00	0.22	0.00	0.00
19:15:07 99.35	all	0.17	0.00	0.48	0.00	0.00
19:20:01 99.87	all	0.01	0.00	0.12	0.00	0.00
19:30:01 99.91	all	0.00	0.00	0.09	0.00	0.00
19:40:01 99.90	all	0.00	0.00	0.10	0.00	0.00

```
Average:        all    0.01    0.00    0.12    0.00    0.00
99.87
```

Or, if you want to be more granular, you can specify start and stop times:

```
$ sar -f /var/log/sa/sa13 -s 19:10:00 -e 19:15:08
Linux 3.10.0-862.2.3.el7.x86_64 (centos1) 13/10/18 _x86_64_ (1 CPU)

19:10:01 CPU %user %nice %system %iowait %steal %idle
19:14:43 all 0.04 0.00 0.22 0.00 0.00 99.75
19:15:07 all 0.17 0.00 0.48 0.

00 0.00 99.35
Average: all 0.05 0.00 0.24 0.00 0.00 99.72
```

vmstat

vmstat is a great way to report on memory statistics; by default, its output looks like this:

```
$ vmstat
procs -----------memory---------- ---swap-- -----io---- -system-- ----
--cpu-----
 r  b   swpd   free   buff  cache   si   so    bi    bo    in   cs us
sy id wa st
 2  0   1544  65260      0 367336    0    0    57    78    45    47  0
 0 100  0  0
```

Where vmstat excels, though, is the fact its initial report (the preceding output) is the information since boot, and you can add a digit to the end of your command, to get a rolling summary:

```
$ vmstat 5
procs -----------memory---------- ---swap-- -----io---- -system-- ----
--cpu-----
 r  b   swpd   free   buff  cache   si   so    bi    bo    in   cs us
sy id wa st
 2  0   1544  65140      0 367336    0    0    57    77    45    47  0
 0 100  0  0
 0  0   1544  65140      0 367336    0    0     0     0    49    48  0
 0 100  0  0
 0  0   1544  64768      0 367336    0    0     0     0    51    54  0
 0 100  0  0
 0  0   1544  64768      0 367336    0    0     0     0    48    48  0
 0 100  0  0
 0  0   1544  64768      0 367336    0    0     0     1    46    46  0
 0 100  0  0
```

0	0	1544	64768	0 367336	0	0	0	0	47	46	0
0	100	0	0								
0	0	1544	64588	0 367336	0	0	0	0	49	53	0
0	100	0	0								
0	0	1544	64784	0 367336	0	0	0	0	49	51	0
0	100	0	0								
0	0	1544	64784	0 367336	0	0	0	0	48	48	0
0	100	0	0								
1	0	1544	64784	0 367336	0	0	0	0	46	48	0
0	100	0	0								

Again, like NetData, vmstat could fit in either category (this or the preceding section) and, as a result, it falls to the user to decide how to do it. You could, for example, write a systemd-timer to run vmstat 10 times, every hour, and output the result to a file for you to peruse at a later date. This is a bit more manual than the out-of-the-box solutions such as sar and atop, but it would be good practice for bigger projects.

How it works...

As with our previous section, out of the box, a lot of the atop and sar setup is done for you, but further configuration changes can be made in the relevant configuration files for the processes.

Under CentOS, these live in /etc/sysconfig, as is traditional:

```
$ cat /etc/sysconfig/atop
# sysconfig atop
#

# Current Day format
CURDAY=`date +%Y%m%d`
# Log files path
LOGPATH=/var/log/atop
# Binaries path
BINPATH=/usr/bin
# PID File
PIDFILE=/var/run/atop.pid
# interval (default 10 minutes)
INTERVAL=600

$ cat /etc/sysconfig/sysstat
# sysstat-10.1.5 configuration file.
# How long to keep log files (in days).
# If value is greater than 28, then log files are kept in
# multiple directories, one for each month.
```

```
HISTORY=28
# Compress (using gzip or bzip2) sa and sar files older than (in
days):
COMPRESSAFTER=31
# Parameters for the system activity data collector (see sadc manual
page)
# which are used for the generation of log files.
SADC_OPTIONS="-S DISK"
# Compression program to use.
ZIP="bzip2"
```

When `atop` is started (using `systemd`), the `/usr/share/atop/atop.daily` script is triggered, using options from `sysconfig`.

When `sysstat` is enabled with `systemd`, it specifically tells `sar` to start with a dummy record, signifying a new boot. This is in addition to the `cron` entries we saw previously, and which are dictated by the configuration file in `/etc/sysconfig`.

It's a bit complicated using these tools, but you will soon find the data to be invaluable to you if you get good at interpreting and using the information they provide.

Remote monitoring tools

Being able to query a server locally and find out what it's doing is great, but that's rarely how things are done in the real world (outside your single box that you might maintain for personal projects). In company scenarios, it's much more likely that you'll have a monitoring solution of some sort, perhaps with agents on your boxes, which keeps an eye on the health of machines in your care.

Nagios is the undisputed king of monitoring installations the world over, not because it's the best, or the most flashy, but simply because it's one of the oldest, and once a monitoring solution is in place, you'll find teams are very hesitant about switching over to a new one.

It has caused several clones to be created, and various offshoots (some using the original source code and some not), but all of them will behave in a similar fashion.

In this part, we're going to install **Nagios** on `centos1`, and have it monitor both itself and `debian1`, while we install **Icinga2** on `centos2`, and have it monitor `debian2`.

Getting ready

For this section, the `Vagrantfile` from the first section will suffice. We will be using all four of our VMs.

We'll run through the Nagios setup first, then move on to Icinga2 afterward.

Connect to each of your boxes, or start with `centos1` and `debian1`, before moving on to `centos2` and `debian2` later.

When connecting to `centos1` for the `Nagios` installation, you will want to use the following port forward:

```
$ vagrant ssh centos1 -- -L 127.0.0.1:8080:127.0.0.1:80
```

How to do it...

As mentioned, we'll run through Nagios first, and then Icinga2.

Nagios

On `centos1`, let's install Nagios from EPEL:

```
$ sudo yum install -y epel-release
$ sudo yum install -y httpd nagios nagios-plugins-all nagios-plugins-nrpe
```

Now that's finished (which can take some time, as there are a lot of plugins), we should start and enable our service, along with `httpd`, which should be installed by default:

```
$ sudo systemctl enable --now nagios
$ sudo systemctl enable --now httpd
```

Out of the box, you will get an insecure nagios-web setup. If you've connected to your Vagrant VM as suggested previously, you should now be able to navigate to the web interface on the forwarded port (`http://127.0.0.1:8080/nagios`):

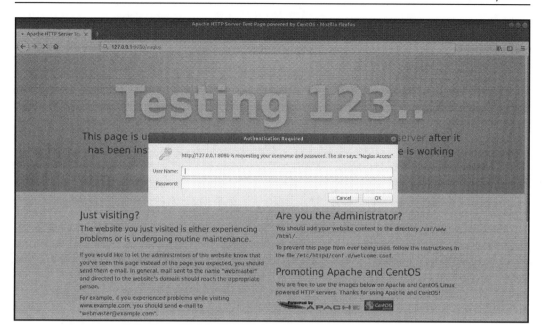

We actually haven't set our `nagiosadmin` password yet (for the basic `http auth` prompt), so let's do that now:

```
$ sudo htpasswd /etc/nagios/passwd nagiosadmin
New password:
Re-type new password:
Updating password for user nagiosadmin
```

Once your password is set, try inputting it in the prompt box:

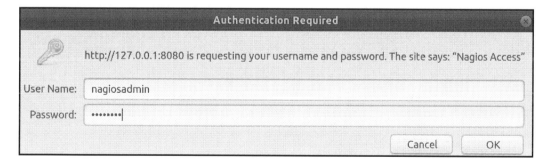

You should see the Nagios landing page:

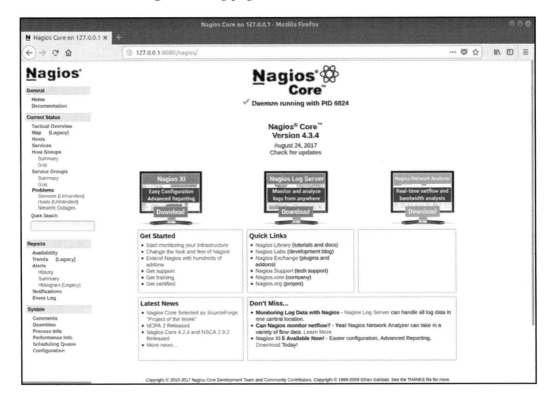

As I've mentioned in other places, I wouldn't recommend using basic HTTP authentication in this manner, as it's insecure. If you can't use HTTPS/TLS to secure the web page, you should block it so that it can only be accessed on the box locally, and use something like SSH forwarding to encrypt connections to the portal. Ideally, though, get a certificate from LetsEncrypt and make life easy for yourself.

Now click on **Services** on the left-hand side; this is where you'll mostly want to be, as it shows the hosts and services on that host that Nagios is currently monitoring:

By default, you can see that we're only monitoring our localhost, which is fine for now, but we want to add debian1 into the mix. Back on the command line, let's get to work by first pointing to our debian1 file in the Nagios configuration file:

```
$ echo "cfg_file=/etc/nagios/objects/debian1.cfg" | sudo tee -a
/etc/nagios/nagios.cfg
```

Now we need to create debian1.cfg:

```
$ sudo cp /etc/nagios/objects/localhost.cfg
/etc/nagios/objects/debian1.cfg
```

We've got all the same configuration as the localhost machine at the moment, so we're going to replace these with debian1 specific values. We're also going to create a new host group specifically for remote VMs, and we're going to change the local checks to first use check_nrpe:

```
$ sudo sed -i 's/localhost/debian1/g' /etc/nagios/objects/debian1.cfg
$ sudo sed -i 's/127.0.0.1/192.168.33.12/g'
/etc/nagios/objects/debian1.cfg
$ sudo sed -i 's/linux-servers/remote-vms/g'
/etc/nagios/objects/debian1.cfg
$ sudo sed -i 's/check_local/check_nrpe!check_client/g'
/etc/nagios/objects/debian1.cfg
```

With those in place, we have to define the `check_nrpe` command:

```
$ cat <<HERE | sudo tee -a /etc/nagios/objects/commands.cfg
define command{
        command_name    check_nrpe
        command_line    \$USER1\$/check_nrpe -H \$HOSTADDRESS\$ -c
\$ARG1\$
        }
HERE
```

Once done, we can restart our Nagios installation:

```
$ sudo systemctl restart nagios
```

Looking again at your **Services** page, you'll now see `debian1`, likely with a lot of checks failing.

This is because NRPE isn't set up on `debian1`, so let's SSH to `debian1` and do that now!

First, we need to install the various bits and pieces:

```
$ sudo apt install monitoring-plugins nagios-nrpe-server -y
```

Now, we need to allow our `centos1` box to talk to `debian1` (via port `5666`):

```
$ sudo sed -i
's/allowed_hosts=127.0.0.1/allowed_hosts=127.0.0.1,192.168.33.10/g'
/etc/nagios/nrpe.cfg
```

We also need to define the client commands that our server is going to request be run on the client:

```
$ cat <<HERE | sudo tee /etc/nagios/nrpe_local.cfg
command[check_client_load]=/usr/lib/nagios/plugins/check_load -w
5.0,4.0,3.0 -c 10.0,6.0,4.0
command[check_client_users]=/usr/lib/nagios/plugins/check_users -w 20
-c 50
command[check_client_disk]=/usr/lib/nagios/plugins/check_disk -w 20% -
c 10% -p /
command[check_client_swap]=/usr/lib/nagios/plugins/check_swap -w 20 -c
10
command[check_client_procs]=/usr/lib/nagios/plugins/check_procs -w 250
-c 400 -s RSZDT
HERE
```

Finally, we're at the point we can restart the `nrpe` service on `debian1`:

```
$ sudo systemctl restart nagios-nrpe-server
```

Now, looking back at the Nagios web interface (don't forget to SSH to the `centos1` VM again if you disconnected), we should see our services being checked correctly:

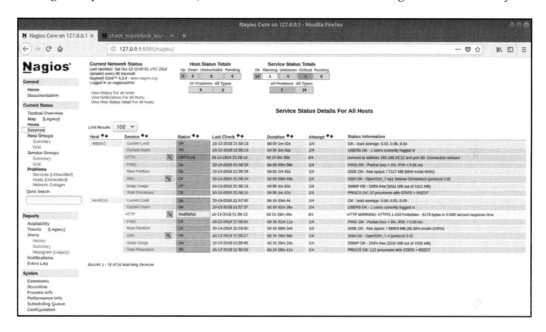

Nagios Services Page with 'debian1'

Note that we have a failing check (**HTTP**) because `debian1` doesn't have a web server installed and running.

 If your checks haven't cycled through yet, you can force all services on a host to be checked by clicking on the host's name and then selecting the **Schedule a check of all services on this host** command.

Icinga2

Like Nagios (which is where it was originally derived from), Icinga2 has the concept of a central server, with agents on other hosts that it can keep an eye on.

We're going to install `Icinga2` on our `centos2` VM, and then monitor our `debian2` VM from our first host.

To get started, jump on to `centos2` and install `Icinga2`:

```
$ vagrant ssh centos2 -- -L 127.0.0.1:8181:127.0.0.1:80
```

Note the forwarding section; this will be for the GUI setup later on (port `8181`):

```
$ sudo yum install epel-release -y
$ sudo yum install centos-release-scl -y
$ sudo yum install
https://packages.icinga.com/epel/icinga-rpm-release-7-latest.noarch.rp
m -y
$ sudo yum install httpd icinga2 icinga2-ido-mysql nagios-plugins-all
icinga2-selinux mariadb-server mariadb icingaweb2 icingacli
icingaweb2-selinux rh-php71-php-mysqlnd -y
$ sudo systemctl enable --now icinga2
$ sudo systemctl enable --now mariadb
```

Run through the `mariadb` installation script (the root password is blank by default; set it to something you'll remember):

```
$ mysql_secure_installation

NOTE: RUNNING ALL PARTS OF THIS SCRIPT IS RECOMMENDED FOR ALL MariaDB
      SERVERS IN PRODUCTION USE!  PLEASE READ EACH STEP CAREFULLY!

In order to log into MariaDB to secure it, we'll need the current
password for the root user.  If you've just installed MariaDB, and
you haven't set the root password yet, the password will be blank,
so you should just press enter here.

Enter current password for root (enter for none):
OK, successfully used password, moving on...

Setting the root password ensures that nobody can log into the MariaDB
root user without the proper authorisation.

Set root password? [Y/n] Y
New password:
Re-enter new password:
Password updated successfully!
Reloading privilege tables..
 ... Success!

By default, a MariaDB installation has an anonymous user, allowing
anyone
```

to log into MariaDB without having to have a user account created for
them. This is intended only for testing, and to make the installation
go a bit smoother. You should remove them before moving into a
production environment.

Remove anonymous users? [Y/n] **Y**
 ... Success!

Normally, root should only be allowed to connect from 'localhost'.
This
ensures that someone cannot guess at the root password from the
network.

Disallow root login remotely? [Y/n] **Y**
 ... Success!

By default, MariaDB comes with a database named 'test' that anyone can
access. This is also intended only for testing, and should be removed
before moving into a production environment.

Remove test database and access to it? [Y/n] **Y**
 - Dropping test database...
 ... Success!
 - Removing privileges on test database...
 ... Success!

Reloading the privilege tables will ensure that all changes made so
far
will take effect immediately.

Reload privilege tables now? [Y/n] **Y**
 ... Success!

Cleaning up...

All done! If you've completed all of the above steps, your MariaDB
installation should now be secure.

Thanks for using MariaDB!

Now set up `mariadb` for `icinga`. This information can be found in the Icinga2
Getting Started guide, https://icinga.com/docs/icinga2/latest/doc/02-getting-
started/#setting-up-icinga-web-2:

```
$ mysql -u root -p<The Password You Set Above>

MariaDB [(none)]> CREATE DATABASE icinga;
Query OK, 1 row affected (0.00 sec)
```

```
MariaDB [(none)]> GRANT SELECT, INSERT, UPDATE, DELETE, DROP, CREATE
VIEW, INDEX, EXECUTE ON icinga.* TO 'icinga'@'localhost' IDENTIFIED BY
'icinga';
Query OK, 0 rows affected (0.06 sec)

MariaDB [(none)]> quit
Bye
```

Finally, import the supplied schema database:

```
$ mysql -u root -p icinga < /usr/share/icinga2-ido-
mysql/schema/mysql.sql
```

Enable the actual plugin in icinga2, and restart the service:

```
$ sudo icinga2 feature enable ido-mysql
$ sudo systemctl restart icinga2
```

Once the database setup is done, we can move on to the actual web installation.

We included httpd (apache) in the installation step of this section, because it's what Icinga2 recommends, though NGINX can be used too (and indeed is the default on FreeBSD).

Begin by starting and enabling it:

```
$ sudo systemctl enable --now httpd
```

Next, enable the api feature of icinga2 and restart it:

```
$ sudo icinga2 api setup
$ sudo systemctl restart icinga2
```

A root user and random password will be added to api-users.conf:

```
$ sudo cat /etc/icinga2/conf.d/api-users.conf
/**
 * The ApiUser objects are used for authentication against the API.
 */
object ApiUser "root" {
  password = "40ebca8aaaf1eba0"
  // client_cn = ""

  permissions = [ "*" ]
}
```

Icinga2 web also needs **FastCGI Process Manager** (**FPM**) enabled, so do this:

```
$ sudo sed -i 's/;date.timezone =/date.timezone = UTC/g'
/etc/opt/rh/rh-php71/php.ini
$ sudo systemctl enable --now rh-php71-php-fpm.service
```

Once done, you should be able to hit the installed Icinga2 web setup in your browser (using our forwarded connection), `http://127.0.0.1:8181/icingaweb2/setup`:

To find your setup code, get back to your `centos2` command line and run the following:

```
$ sudo icingacli setup token create
The newly generated setup token is: 052f63696e4dc84c
```

Enter your code and click next through the installation (making sure there's no *red* on the **Requirements** page; yellow is okay for the Imagick PHP module):

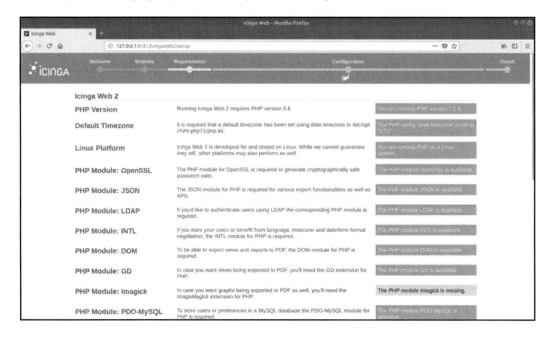

When prompted for the authentication type, choose **Database**:

On the next page, you'll be prompted to provide a database name, a database username, and a database password. Choose suitable values (don't worry if they're not created yet, we'll do that next):

Here, you can see I chose `icinga2web` for the database name and username. Click **Next**.

On the screen immediately following, you will be asked to pass in the credentials of a user who can access MariaDB to create the new database; I chose to use the MariaDB root user we set earlier:

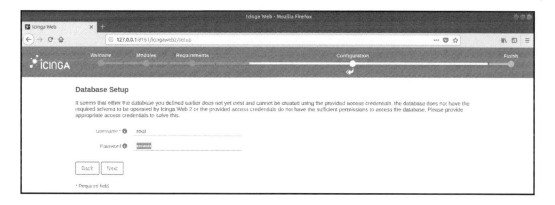

You'll be prompted to choose a **Backend Name**, which is an aesthetic decision so that you can recognise the backend later:

And you'll be asked to create a web user; I went with `icingaweb`:

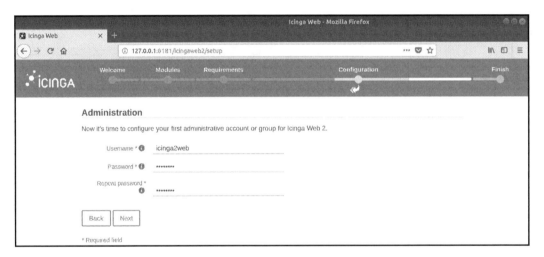

I kept the **Application Configuration** as the default:

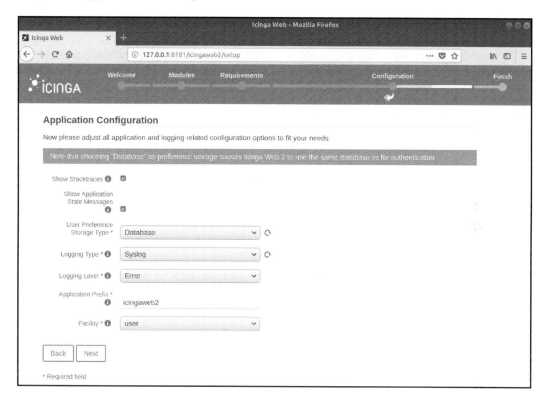

Lastly, you'll be prompted to confirm the settings you've put in; have a quick once-over before continuing.

Clicking **Next** a couple more times brings you to the **Monitoring Backend** setup (where IcingaWeb2 looks to find the monitoring database):

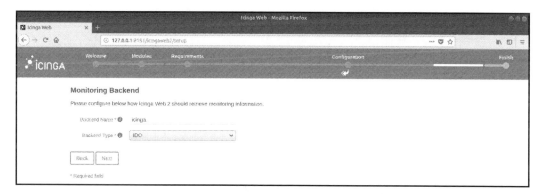

You'll be prompted to add connection details that can be used to query the icinga database (which we set up using the MariaDB CLI ealier in this chapter). We set the following defaults: username `icinga`, and password `icinga`:

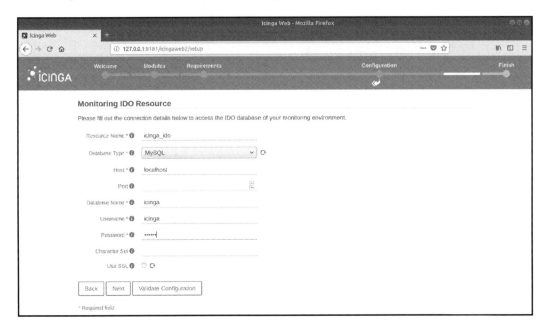

Use the **Validate Configuration** button to validate your configuration.

On the **Command Transport** screen, you'll be prompted to enter the details of the API user we created. We only added root, so let's use that for now (from the api-users.conf file earlier):

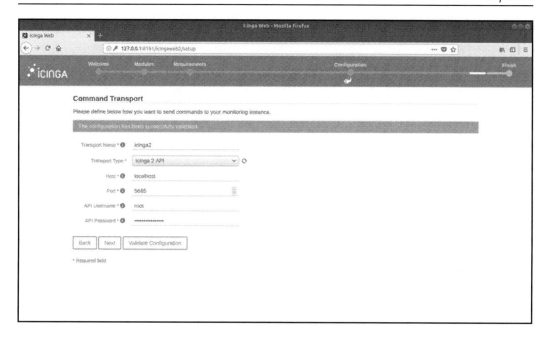

Click **Next** until you get to the end, where you should end up with a happy green banner:

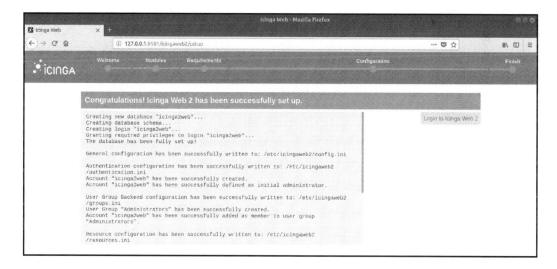

Continue to the prompted login page, and log in with the web user we created:

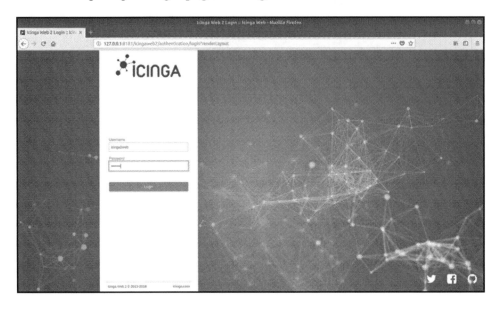

Icinga2 Login Page

The design might have changed a bit by the time you get around to reading this book, but hopefully you have something that's close to the following Icinga2 Dashboard:

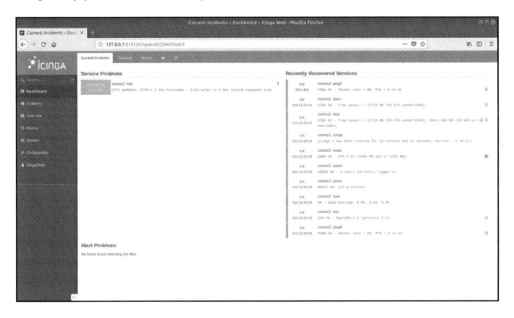

Have a poke around, before moving onto the next section, where we'll add another host.

Firstly, we have to establish our first server as the `master` before we install `icinga2` on our client.

You do this with a setup script; I've put the only change needed in bold:

```
$ sudo icinga2 node wizard
Welcome to the Icinga 2 Setup Wizard!

We will guide you through all required configuration details.

Please specify if this is a satellite/client setup ('n' installs a
master setup) [Y/n]: n

Starting the Master setup routine...

Please specify the common name (CN) [centos2]:
Reconfiguring Icinga...
Checking for existing certificates for common name 'centos2'...
Certificate '/var/lib/icinga2/certs//centos2.crt' for CN 'centos2'
already existing. Skipping certificate generation.
Generating master configuration for Icinga 2.
'api' feature already enabled.

Master zone name [master]:

Default global zones: global-templates director-global
Do you want to specify additional global zones? [y/N]:
Please specify the API bind host/port (optional):
Bind Host []:
Bind Port []:

Do you want to disable the inclusion of the conf.d directory [Y/n]:
Disabling the inclusion of the conf.d directory...
Checking if the api-users.conf file exists...

Done.

Now restart your Icinga 2 daemon to finish the installation!
```

Do as it suggests and restart `icinga2`:

```
$ sudo systemctl restart icinga2
```

Generate a token for our client to use when connecting:

```
$ sudo icinga2 pki ticket --cn debian2
8c7ecd2c04e6ca73bb0d1a6cc62ae4041bf2d5d2
```

Now SSH to your `debian2` box and install `icinga2`:

```
$ sudo apt install icinga2 -y
```

Run through the node installation, this time specifying that we're an agent, and passing in the token from earlier when prompted:

```
$ sudo icinga2 node wizard
Welcome to the Icinga 2 Setup Wizard!

We'll guide you through all required configuration details.



Please specify if this is a satellite setup ('n' installs a master
setup) [Y/n]:
Starting the Node setup routine...
Please specify the common name (CN) [debian2]:
Please specify the master endpoint(s) this node should connect to:
Master Common Name (CN from your master setup): centos2
Do you want to establish a connection to the master from this node?
[Y/n]:
Please fill out the master connection information:
Master endpoint host (Your master's IP address or FQDN): 192.168.33.11
Master endpoint port [5665]:
Add more master endpoints? [y/N]:
Please specify the master connection for CSR auto-signing (defaults to
master endpoint host):
Host [192.168.33.11]:
Port [5665]:
information/base: Writing private key to
'/etc/icinga2/pki/debian2.key'.
information/base: Writing X509 certificate to
'/etc/icinga2/pki/debian2.crt'.
information/cli: Fetching public certificate from master
(192.168.33.11, 5665):

Certificate information:

  Subject:     CN = centos2
  Issuer:      CN = Icinga CA
  Valid From:  Oct 13 22:34:30 2018 GMT
  Valid Until: Oct  9 22:34:30 2033 GMT
```

```
 Fingerprint: B5 0B 00 5D 5F 34 14 08 D7 48 8E DA E1 83 96 35 D9 0F 54
1F

Is this information correct? [y/N]: y
information/cli: Received trusted master certificate.

Please specify the request ticket generated on your Icinga 2 master.
 (Hint: # icinga2 pki ticket --cn 'debian2'):
8c7ecd2c04e6ca73bb0d1a6cc62ae4041bf2d5d2
information/cli: Requesting certificate with ticket
'8c7ecd2c04e6ca73bb0d1a6cc62ae4041bf2d5d2'.

information/cli: Created backup file
'/etc/icinga2/pki/debian2.crt.orig'.
information/cli: Writing signed certificate to file
'/etc/icinga2/pki/debian2.crt'.
information/cli: Writing CA certificate to file
'/etc/icinga2/pki/ca.crt'.
Please specify the API bind host/port (optional):
Bind Host []:
Bind Port []:
Accept config from master? [y/N]: y
Accept commands from master? [y/N]: y
information/cli: Disabling the Notification feature.
Disabling feature notification. Make sure to restart Icinga 2 for
these changes to take effect.
information/cli: Enabling the Apilistener feature.
Enabling feature api. Make sure to restart Icinga 2 for these changes
to take effect.
information/cli: Created backup file '/etc/icinga2/features-
available/api.conf.orig'.
information/cli: Generating local zones.conf.
information/cli: Dumping config items to file
'/etc/icinga2/zones.conf'.
information/cli: Created backup file '/etc/icinga2/zones.conf.orig'.
information/cli: Updating constants.conf.
information/cli: Created backup file
'/etc/icinga2/constants.conf.orig'.
information/cli: Updating constants file
'/etc/icinga2/constants.conf'.
information/cli: Updating constants file
'/etc/icinga2/constants.conf'.
Done.

Now restart your Icinga 2 daemon to finish the installation!
```

Restart `icinga2` on `debian2`:

```
$ sudo systemctl restart icinga2
```

Now, we need to configure the master to actually check the client; we've got an established connection, viewable with `ss`:

```
$ ss -t
State        Recv-Q Send-Q                                    Local
Address:Port                                                  Peer
Address:Port
ESTAB      0      0
10.0.2.15:ssh
10.0.2.2:44828
ESTAB 0 0 192.168.33.13:5665 192.168.33.11:49398
```

Now, back on `centos2`, add the following configuration:

```
$ cat <<HERE | sudo tee -a /etc/icinga2/zones.conf
object Endpoint "debian2" {
  host = "192.168.33.13"
}
object Zone "debian2" {
  endpoints = [ "debian2" ]
  parent = "master"
}
HERE
```

Create a `hosts` directory for the zone in question:

```
$ sudo mkdir -p /etc/icinga2/zones.d/master
```

And add an appropriate `hosts` configuration:

```
$ cat <<HERE | sudo tee /etc/icinga2/zones.d/master/hosts.conf
object Host "debian2" {
  check_command = "hostalive"
  address = "192.168.33.13"
  vars.client_endpoint = name
  vars.os = "Linux"
}
HERE
```

Restart `icinga2`:

```
$ sudo systemctl restart icinga2
```

At this point, you should see your client in the Icinga2 web GUI:

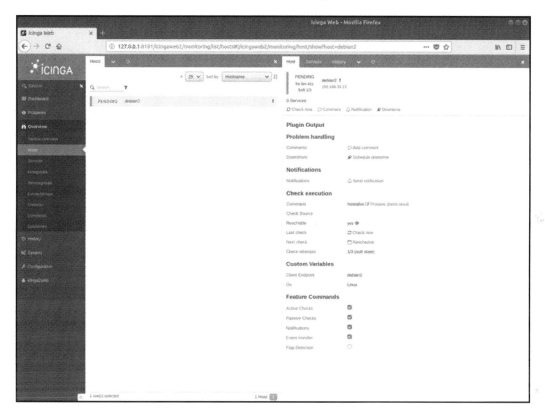

Icinga2 Hosts page with pending checks

It's a bit useless to just have ping check a host (well, mostly; ping alerts have saved me before), so let's add some of the recommended service checks too:

```
$ cat <<HERE | sudo tee /etc/icinga2/zones.d/master/services.conf
apply Service "ping4" {
 check_command = "ping4"
 assign where host.address
}
apply Service "ssh" {
 check_command = "ssh"
 assign where host.vars.os == "Linux"
}
apply Service "disk" {
 check_command = "disk"
 command_endpoint = host.vars.client_endpoint
 assign where host.vars.client_endpoint
```

```
}
apply Service "icinga" {
 check_command = "icinga"
 command_endpoint = host.vars.client_endpoint
  assign where host.vars.client_endpoint
}
apply Service "ntp_time" {
 check_command = "ntp_time"
 command_endpoint = host.vars.client_endpoint
  assign where host.vars.client_endpoint
}
HERE
```

Restart the service again.

```
$ sudo systemctl restart icinga2
```

Looking back at our GUI, this will now show our debian2 box with some services checks (where one of the five failed):

Icinga2 Hosts page with 'debian2'

How it works...

By having a master server that is capable of seeing other servers in an estate, you give yourself the visibility needed to know when problems have occurred that need your immediate attention.

Monitoring tools such as Nagios and Icinga2 usually work by interacting with a remote machine, querying its status by using either scripts on the box, or custom commands remotely, and reporting on the output of those commands. This can be done in a variety of ways, including, but not limited to, the NRPE agent, remote SSH commands, or SNMP results queried from an SNMP daemon.

By creating a single-source-of-truth on the state of your infrastructure, you can learn immediately when there's a problem with your estate, and even correlate data based on multiple symptoms seen.

Icinga2, Nagios, Zabbix, and Sensu all behave in a relatively similar fashion, and all ultimately are good tools for the job, but usually it's down to the personal preference of the implementing team (or individual) as to which is adopted.

You won't go wrong by installing Nagios and having a play around with it, as it's easily the one I've come across the most in the wild, and its children/cousins rule the scene at the moment.

There's more...

Here, we spun up a Nagios and Icinga2 installation quickly, to show what both are capable of with a few simple commands. These configurations aren't production-ready, and consideration should be given to things such as reusable patterns for monitoring checks, as well as security (for things such as TLS on the GUI, and utilizing secure communication methods between the master and the clients).

As with a lot of the software in this book, you should now have a good understanding of how to get started, but should consider all your options when implementing a solution for your own systems. If you have a relatively small pool to monitor, and it's unlikely to grow, you might considers the Nagios file-based monitoring setup suitable; if you have a larger, multi-region spanning estate, you may find Icinga2 and its zones more to your liking.

We also didn't touch on emails and alerting, only mentioning the visual alerts that Nagios and Icinga2 produce. There are multiple ways of plugging alerts into both solutions (such as SMS alerts, or flashing bulbs in the corner of the room) but, out of the box, they both handle email relatively well (assuming you've got a functional email server to pass alerts through).

Lastly, this is just a getting started guide, and there are many more ways to set up both Icinga2 and Nagios. They can be thought of more as frameworks than software in a lot of ways, being a fairly blank canvas out of the box and still enabling you to build a production system in as complex or simple a fashion as you wish.

I've come across Icinga2 installations where I've been immensely cocky and sure of myself (more so than usual), only to start scratching my head 5 minutes in as I tried to unpick the mess of hand-cranked configuration that had been left for me.

See also

The monitoring plugins we used here are interesting, because there was a bitter argument some years ago when the old `nagios-plugins.org` domain was repointed from an independently maintained server to one controlled by Nagios Enterprises.

What followed this repointing was an argument and split, which resulted in `monitoring-plugins` and `nagios-plugins` becoming seperate entities. For what it's worth, `nagios-plugins` is an alias to `monitoring-plugins` on Debian systems at the time of writing.

More information can be found in this blog post: `https://www.monitoring-plugins.org/news/new-project-name.html`.

The Debian bug report can be found here: `https://bugs.debian.org/cgi-bin/bugreport.cgi?bug=736331`.

And here's the Red Hat bug report, with added drama (don't get involved): `https://bugzilla.redhat.com/show_bug.cgi?id=1054340`.

Centralizing logging with the Elastic Stack

Earlier, we mentioned solutions to remote logging that involved forwarding our logging solutions (`syslog` and `journald`) to other hosts, running the same or similar software, so that the logs could be aggregated in one spot.

This is a nice solution, and works well in a small environment, but it's not got a lot of bells and whistles, and if there's one thing we like in IT, it's shiny things we can show to management and then never use.

Elastic Stack is one such product; in their own words:

> *Built on an open source foundation, the Elastic Stack lets you reliably and securely take data from any source, in any format, and search, analyze, and visualize it in real time.*

Bold claims, but certainly with backing. Elastic Stack is now the *de facto* aggregate logging solution for most businesses above a medium size, perhaps with a few contenders at the enterprise level.

We're going to set up a small solution on `centos1`, and forward our logs from `centos2`, `debian1`, and `debian2` to it.

 I've spent the day wrestling with X-Pack and Elastic Stack, so if anything I write sounds sarcastic or mean spirited, it's probably intentional.

Getting ready

In this section, we're going to use all our VMs, and it might be an idea to `vagrant destroy` and `vagrant up` them all first.

Please note that, for this section, we're going to be installing the version 6 release of certain Elastic Stack components. The configuration has changed historically, and may do again by the time you read this book; if anything doesn't work as you expect, refer to the Elastic documentation for your version to fill in the gaps.

For this section, we're going to run through the initial setup on `centos1`, then pop onto the other VMs and configure their logging destination.

Mostly, I don't suggest this, but it might be a good idea to reset your VMs to a fresh starting point for this bit:

```
$ vagrant destroy -f
$ vagrant up
$ vagrant ssh centos1 -- -L127.0.0.1:5601:127.0.0.1:5601
```

For convenience, and because this isn't a book on installing and configuring the Elastic Stack, we're going to run through an installation of Elasticsearch, Kibana, and Logstash in quite rapid fashion.

First, we need Java:

```
$ sudo yum install java-1.8.0-openjdk -y
```

How to do it...

On centos1, let's grab the Elastic repository:

```
$ cat <<HERE | sudo tee /etc/yum.repos.d/elasticsearch.repo
[elasticsearch-6.x]
name=Elasticsearch repository for 6.x packages
baseurl=https://artifacts.elastic.co/packages/6.x/yum
gpgcheck=1
gpgkey=https://artifacts.elastic.co/GPG-KEY-elasticsearch
enabled=1
autorefresh=1
type=rpm-md
HERE
```

Now we need to install the various components:

```
$ sudo yum install elasticsearch kibana logstash -y
```

And we need to start them, with a number of configuration tweaks:

```
$ sudo systemctl daemon-reload
$ sudo systemctl enable --now elasticsearch
$ sudo systemctl enable --now kibana
```

We're going to use the Elastic syslog example (from https://www.elastic.co/guide/en/logstash/6.4/config-examples.html#_processing_syslog_messages) to configure our Logstash setup:

```
$ cat <<HERE | sudo tee /etc/logstash/conf.d/logstash-syslog.conf
input {
```

```
    tcp {
      port => 5000
      type => syslog
    }
    udp {
      port => 5000
      type => syslog
    }
  }

  filter {
    if [type] == "syslog" {
      grok {
        match => { "message" => "%{SYSLOGTIMESTAMP:syslog_timestamp}
%{SYSLOGHOST:syslog_hostname}
%{DATA:syslog_program}(?:\[%{POSINT:syslog_pid}\])?:
%{GREEDYDATA:syslog_message}" }
        add_field => [ "received_at", "%{@timestamp}" ]
        add_field => [ "received_from", "%{host}" ]
      }
      date {
        match => [ "syslog_timestamp", "MMM  d HH:mm:ss", "MMM dd
HH:mm:ss" ]
      }
    }
  }

  output {
    elasticsearch { hosts => ["localhost:9200"] }
    stdout { codec => rubydebug }
  }
  HERE
```

 This configuration sets an input method for data, in this case `tcp` and `udp` ports `5000`. It then sets a filter up for `syslog` content, and finally sets up an output to Elasticsearch (the backend, if you will).

Now we can start `Logstash`:

```
$ sudo systemctl enable --now logstash
```

What you should see are various ports listening on your box (this may take some time, as the various components start up):

```
$ ss -tunal '( src :5601 or src :9200 or src :5000 )'
Netid  State        Recv-Q Send-Q
Local Address:Port
```

```
Peer Address:Port
udp      UNCONN     0       0
*:5000
*:*
tcp      LISTEN     0       128
127.0.0.1:5601
*:*
tcp      LISTEN     0       128
:::5000
:::*
tcp      LISTEN     0       128
::ffff:127.0.0.1:9200
:::*
tcp      LISTEN     0       128
::1:9200
:::*
```

Now, we can configure our other machines to point to `Logstash` on `centos1`.

centos2

Use the following `rsyslog` change to start forwarding `centos2` logs to `Logstash` of the `centos1` instance:

```
$ sudo sed -i 's/#*.* @@remote-host:514/*.* @192.168.33.10:5000/g'
/etc/rsyslog.conf
$ sudo systemctl restart rsyslog
```

> I recommended rebuilding the VMs earlier, but if you haven't, the preceding command may need tweaking if you followed the earlier sections about remote `syslog` configuration. Open the file and confirm the line looks as you expect.

You can test your configuration by using the following on `centos2`:

```
$ logger -p syslog.err "Digimon was better than Pokemon."
```

debian1 and debian2

For the Debian configuration, use the following lines:

```
$ echo "*.* @192.168.33.10:5000" | sudo tee -a /etc/rsyslog.conf
$ sudo systemctl restart rsyslog
$ logger -p syslog.err "Digimon was better than Pokemon."
```

Kibana

We have data in `Logstash`, but unless you've jumped the gun a bit, you won't be able to see it yet.

If you've forwarded your connection to `centos1`, as indicated at the start of this section, you should be able to navigate to `http://localhost:5601` in the browser of your choosing, and be greeted by the Kibana start page (assuming your installations have gone okay):

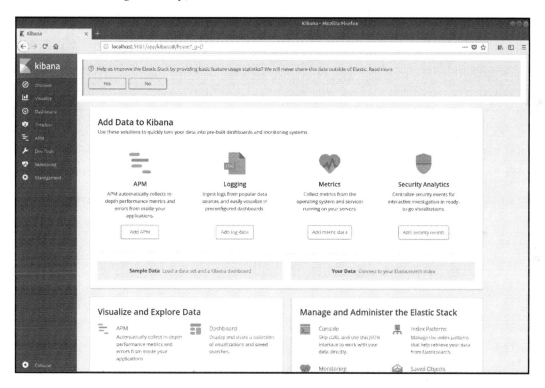

If you've used Kibana before, you might expect to click **Discover** and see your logs, but instead you get kicked over to **Management**:

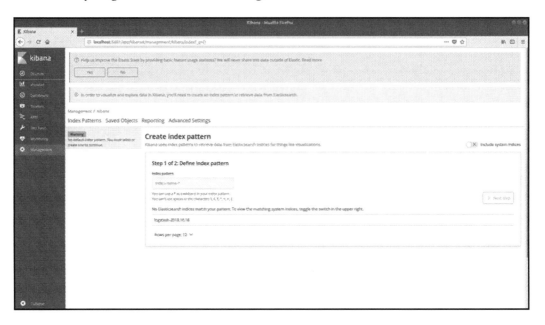

Enter * as the wildcard entry for the index pattern, and then click **Next step** on the right:

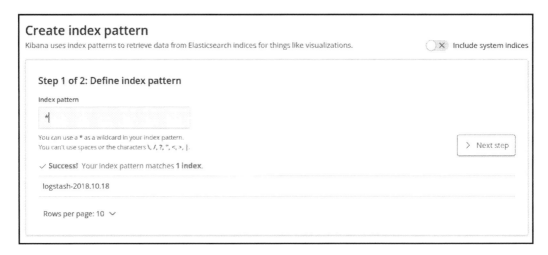

In the next section, choose **@timestamp** from the drop-down list provided and then click **Create index pattern** on the right:

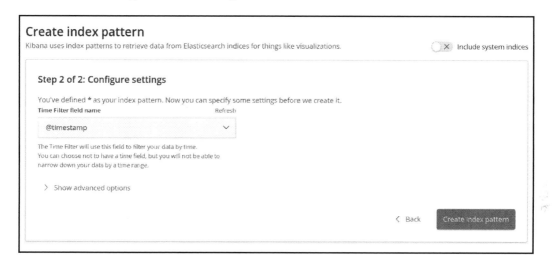

Once the index has been created, click **Discover** on the left-hand side again; this time, you should be given a proper view:

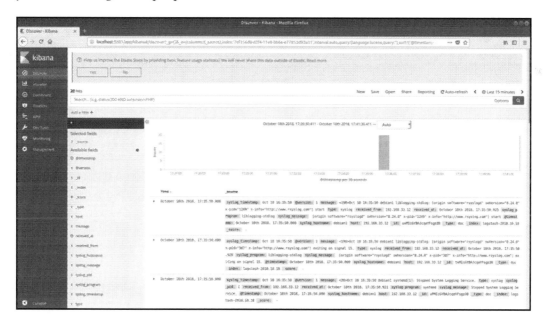

Obviously, we want to filter down, just to make sure we've got everything.

Put the following filter query in the search box at the top:

```
(host:192.168.33.13 OR host:192.168.33.12 OR host:192.168.33.11) AND
message:"Pokemon*"
```

You should see something like this:

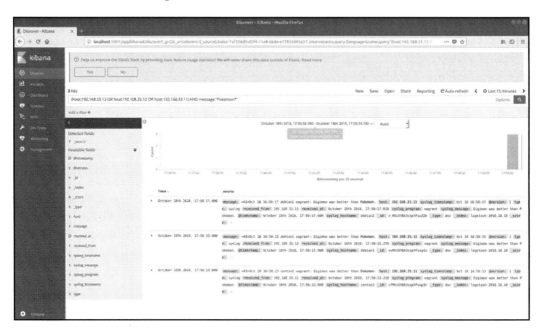

Kibana Discover Page

> If there's no data visible in Kibana, it's possible that Logstash wasn't
> fully started before you sent logs from the other hosts. Try sending
> your logs again using the `logger` commands above.

How it works...

What we're effectively doing is setting up three things:

- **Elasticsearch**: To act as the storage point for all the data we want to pipe
  into our box

- **Kibana**: To act as the frontend and dashboard to our data, meaning we can query and peruse it at our leisure
- **Logstash**: To create a listener that acts just like the `syslog` receiver we set up earlier on in this chapter

When all three of these components are enabled, they create a way to centralize any logs (or other data) that we might wish to throw at our solution.

It's basically a pretty way of making a `syslog` receiver, which also happens to be capable of a lot more besides.

One thing we didn't do here was forward our logs from `centos1` to its own `Logstash` listener; this can be done, but does require a bit of tweaking to ensure you don't accidentally create a storm of logs that grow exponentially as its own log messages are fed back into itself. I may or may not have done this once.

There's more...

The Elastic Stack isn't just Elasticsearch, Kibana, and Logstash there are also more tools and features that are completely modular and can be integrated into your installation as you wish.

They include, but aren't limited to, the following:

- Heartbeat – for uptime monitoring
- Filebeat – for sending logs from remote machines
- Machine learning capabilities

We also set up a very noddy solution here, and one I certainly wouldn't use in production. It lacks security on the transported data, streaming plain logs to our receiver, and there's also no login prompt to secure the Kibana dashboard, or TLS for security in the browser.

X-Pack is one way to solve these problems, available as a trial in the default installation, or through a license, which is going to cost you. It allows you to set up security in your installation, both node communication and login security (with things such as the Kibana user login).

The Elastic Stack is also quite a resource hungry suite of software, and you might want to architect your solution properly before diving right in and installing it on the medium-sized box in the cupboard.

Roundup – Monitoring and Logging

While it's no one's favorite subject (outside some very strange individuals I know, one of whom is a technical editor for this book), logging and monitoring is a crucial part of any installation, big or small.

You want to know when your boxes have died or, better yet, when they're about to die, and you also want to be able to retroactively work out why they conked out in the first place.

Monitoring and logging can be as complex or simple as you want it to be. Some companies hire specific individuals to deal with these components in a silo, but, in smaller organizations, it could very well be you who ends up managing and configuring everything. If this is the case, then I currently recommend setting up Icinga2 and some sort of Elastic Stack implementation, but your needs and budget may vary.

One elephant in the room that we need to talk about is on-call, and the fact that you're probably going to do it at some point in your career (unless you've got to the blessed point where you can say "I've done my time" and leave it for lesser mortals to undertake).

In general, monitoring is your friend when doing on-call, and while, in an ideal world, you'd never get called out because of a problem, you can at least set up things such as automated phone calls to wake you up, before something becomes a wider issue that someone else notices outside of your company. You don't want to be in the situation where your company website is down all weekend, and you lose thousands of pounds of sales.

Over time, logs and long-term monitoring data can also help to highlight issues that you didn't realize were recurring, because the time between events is weeks or even months; this is a good reason for setting up historic alerts and pattern matching on dashboards in Kibana.

If someone is having to clear logs on a box every 5 weeks, and it's a different person in the team each time, you might not realize that there's a bigger underlying issue that needs addressing, or you might just find you've lost hundreds of hours over an issue that could be fixed with a simple `systemd` timer.

On the whole, I hate monitoring, and I'm loath to trawl through logs, but they're necessary in our line of work, and there's a lot of clever people making very swish tools that you can use to make your life easier.

It also doesn't hurt when you have to show off a dashboard to the CEO, and they're distracted by the pretty widgets and whistles.

8
Permissions, SELinux, and AppArmor

In this chapter, we're going to cover the following topics:

- Linux file permissions
- Modifying file permissions
- Users and groups
- AppArmor and modification
- SELinux and modification
- Checking SELinux is running, and the importance of keeping it running
- Resetting SELinux permissions

Introduction

In the early days, way back in the mists of the 90s, Linux didn't have a great deal in terms of access control...then came permissions and attributes. Permissions and attributes are the elements of a file that dictate what access the system and users have to that file (or folder), and what it's capable of doing to the file in terms of interaction. At a basic level, you use `ls` to view information on permissions (more on this later), but for now, see the following example:

```
$ ls -l .
total 0
-rw-rw-r--. 1 vagrant vagrant 0 Oct 28 10:42 examplefile
```

In this chapter, we will learn about permissions from the basic Linux offerings, to SELinux and AppArmor. We'll also look at troubleshooting issues that might be caused by SELinux or AppArmor. We will also learn the importance of not disabling extended permission controls.

In terms of security, locking down your system is obviously important, and at its extreme, you could create a system where every program is ignorant of every other program (effectively having each program siloed).

While security is never a bad thing, a balance is crucial. You don't want to start stressing over the permissions of every file in an Ubuntu install, there's literally thousands and you'd go mad before you finished... unless it's literally your sole job to do this, or you want an especially dull hobby, in which case go nuts!

Technical requirements

Throughout this chapter, we're going to use the following `Vagrantfile`; note that we only use two machines: CentOS to highlight SELinux features and abilities, and an Ubuntu installation for AppArmor:

```ruby
# -*- mode: ruby -*-
# vi: set ft=ruby :

$provisionScript = <<-SCRIPT
sed -i 's/console=tty0 console=ttyS0,115200n8//g' /boot/grub2/grub.cfg
systemctl restart sshd
SCRIPT

Vagrant.configure("2") do |config|

  config.vm.define "centos7" do |centos7|
  centos7.vm.box = "centos/7"
  centos7.vm.box_version = "1804.02"
  centos7.vm.provision "shell",
  inline: $provisionScript
  end

  config.vm.define "ubuntu1804" do |ubuntu1804|
  ubuntu1804.vm.box = "ubuntu/bionic64"
  ubuntu1804.vm.box_version = "20180927.0.0"
  end

end
```

 At the time of writing, the `provisionScript` used here is to fix a slight problem with one of the sections in this chapter. If you experience issues surrounding this script, feel free to remove it from your configuration (there is a note later on about this, in the relevant section, where we talk about `.autorelabel`).

Linux file permissions

To begin, we're going to go right back to basics by taking a look at the default Linux file permissions.

In this section, we're going to use a file and a directory on our CentOS box, to highlight some important and basic knowledge that we can use going forward.

 File permissions on Unix and Unix-like systems are different from those found on Windows and other OS installations. If you connect a hard drive formatted with a Unix file-system (such as XFS) to a Windows box, it is unlikely it will be able to read the permissions on the files accurately (unless you've got software to do it for you). These lines have been blurred a bit in recent years, thanks to things like the Windows Subsystem for Linux included in Windows 10, but the principle is basically true.

Getting ready

Jump onto your CentOS box. For the sake of this section, everything we discuss is universal across Linux distributions:

```
$ vagrant ssh centos7
```

Create a file, a directory, and a file in that directory as follows:

```
$ touch examplefile
$ mkdir exampledir
$ touch exampledir/examplefile-in-exampledir
```

How to do it...

With your files from the *Getting ready* section in place, run an `ls -l` on what we've created:

```
$ ls -l
total 0
drwxrwxr-x. 2 vagrant vagrant 39 Oct 28 11:01 exampledir
-rw-rw-r--. 1 vagrant vagrant 0 Oct 28 11:00 examplefile
```

-l, used here, means using a long-listing format, and is used not just to print the files and folders found, but to give us a more complete picture.

How it works...

We'll need to break this down, because at first glance, it can appear quite confusing:

exampledir

Starting with `exampledir`, let's look at the permissions and ownership of this directory.

```
drwxrwxr-x. 2 vagrant vagrant
```

We have an array of letters, a number 2, and then two names, `vagrant` and `vagrant`.

```
drwxrwxr-x.
```

The `d` at the beginning is an easy one; it indicates that the listed item is actually a directory.

```
drwxrwxr-x.
```

Then, we have three elements that appear similar, and the first of these are the user permissions. Here, the permissions are read, write, and execute.

This means that the user will be able to `touch` (create) files in the directory, `mv` (rename) them, `ls` (list) them, `cat/less` (read) them, and even `rm` (delete) them should they wish.

```
drwxrwxr-x.
```

Next, we have the group permissions, here again as read, write, and execute.

```
drwxrwxr-x.
```

Thirdly, we have the permissions of everyone, and in this case anyone can read, or change into the directory.

They won't be able to create, rename, or delete existing files, because they don't have the write (`w`) permission.

This is something that even experienced sysadmins forget. If you're in a group that can access the contents of a file within a directory, but the directory's own permissions don't allow this, you're not going to be able to complete the action. I've heard some quite notable groans of realization related to this little tidbit.

We also have the . at the end of the block. Right now, we don't have to worry about this too much, but it indicates that the directory has a security context applied to it:

```
drwxrwxr-x. 2
```

The digit, in this case 2, refers to the number of locations pointing to the inode (the place on the disk where the data is actually stored). The reason why it's 2 in this case is because two entries are created every time a directory is made, viewable with ls -la:

```
$ ls -la exampledir/
total 0
drwxrwxr-x. 2 vagrant vagrant 39 Oct 28 11:18 .
drwx------. 4 vagrant vagrant 132 Oct 28 11:01 ..
-rw-rw-r--. 1 vagrant vagrant 0 Oct 28 11:18 examplefile-in-exampledir
```

Here, we can see two special entries, . and .., which refer to this directory, and the parent directory, respectively.

There are therefore two links to this directory; the first is from the parent (/home/vagrant/exampledir) and the second is from within the directory itself (/home/vagrant/exampledir/.). Confused yet?

Now for a much easier bit, the vagrant vagrant entries:

```
vagrant vagrant
```

These are simply the user, then the group, whose permissions are reflected in the drwxrwxr-x. block. There is no entry for everyone as that would be pointless.

examplefile

Moving on to examplefile, we have the following:.

```
-rw-rw-r--. 1 vagrant vagrant  0 Oct 28 11:00 examplefile
```

Here, we can see much the same as exampledir, with a few changes.

The d has been replaced by a—character, meaning we're dealing with an actual file.

    -rw-rw-r--.

The permissions for the user and group are read only and write, meaning the file can be read and modified, but it can't yet be executed by the user and group.

    -rw-rw-**r--**.

The permissions for everyone else are only read, meaning the file can have cat/less applied, but it can't be modified or executed.

    -rw-rw-r--. **1**

And finally, we can see a 1 for the number of links, which makes sense as the underlying inode isn't referenced from elsewhere.

There's more...

There are a few more things to mention that are useful to know, even if we don't touch on them here.

Root access to directories and files

The god/super/almighty user (root) has pretty much carte blanche access to everything on the system, meaning that a common shortcut you might see people enacting is the following, should they get frustrated at their inability to read a file:

    $ sudo cat examplefile

This would work, because root has that power, but it's a bad habit to get into using sudo for everything. Be selective with it, and think about what you're doing before you arbitrarily stick sudo in front of things because you're frustrated. (Mostly, this is a message to myself, because I'm just as guilty of this as anyone.)

Other execute characters

Instead of the humble x in the execute column, it's possible to also see other characters, the most common of which are s and t.

Take a look at these permissions for the `wall` program:

```
$ ls -l /usr/bin/wall
-r-xr-sr-x. 1 root tty 15344 Jun 9 2014 /usr/bin/wall
```

Note how the group has `s` set in place of an `x`.

This is known as the `setuid` and `setgid` bit, depending on if it's in the user or group triad, and effectively it changes the executing user's permissions to those of the owner or group, again depending on the triad. In this case, those users executing the `wall` command get the permissions of the `tty` group (allowing `wall` to output to all `tty`s).

Here, I'm using `wall` as the vagrant user:

```
$ wall There is no Hitchhikers Movie!
$
Broadcast message from vagrant@localhost.localdomain (pts/0) (Sun Oct
28 11:52:12 2018):

There is no Hitchhikers Movie!
```

The `t` entry, or sticky bit, is again quite rare, but it is set most commonly on the `/tmp` directory:

```
$ ls -la /tmp
total 0
drwxrwxrwt. 8 root root 172 Oct 28 11:54 .
<SNIP>
```

Remember that the `.` character refers to this directory.

It sets it so that only the owner of a file in `/tmp` can rename or remove that file, meaning if I create a file in `/tmp` as the `vagrant` user, another person can't come along and remove my file (except `root`). Visually, it looks like the following:

```
$ rm /tmp/test2
rm: remove write-protected regular empty file '/tmp/test2'? y
rm: cannot remove '/tmp/test2': Operation not permitted
```

There's more than these two other execute characters, but these are the most common.

Modifying file permissions

Creating files is all well and good, but eventually we'll come across a use case where the default permissions just aren't acceptable.

A good example of this is SSH, which will downright refuse to function unless some particularly rigid file permissions are in place on your public and private keys.

So, here come "The Three Musketeers", in the form of `chown`, `chmod`, and `chattr`.

If you want to be really annoying, and lose friends easily, insist on calling these by their full titles: change ownership, change mode, and change attributes.

Getting ready

In this section, we are going to again use our CentOS VM from our `Vagrantfile`, as everything we're doing is universally applicable.

SSH to your CentOS VM:

```
$ vagrant ssh centos7
```

Move into the `/home` directory (up one level) and create a file, a directory, and a file in that directory:

```
$ cd /home
$ sudo touch permissionfile
$ sudo mkdir permissiondir
$ sudo touch permissiondir/permissionfile-in-permissiondir
```

We're also going to create another dummy user that we can use to explain what we're doing in this section:

```
$ sudo adduser packt -s /bin/bash -p
'$1$2QzaOp2Q$Ke2yWZ1N2h4rk8r8P95Sv/'
```

Note the password we've set here is 'correcthorsebatterystaple'.

How to do it...

We'll run through the three commands (`chown`, `chmod`, and `chattr`) in order.

chown

Starting at the easiest bit, we're going to look at the ownership of the files in question.

Begin by listing what we have already:

```
$ ls -lha
total 0
drwxr-xr-x. 4 root    root     64 Oct 28 12:37 .
dr-xr-xr-x. 18 root   root    239 Oct 28 12:35 ..
drwxr-xr-x. 2 root    root     45 Oct 28 12:37 permissiondir
-rw-r--r--. 1 root    root      0 Oct 28 12:37 permissionfile
drwx------. 3 vagrant vagrant  74 May 12 18:54 vagrant
```

Say we wanted to make it so our vagrant user could write to the `permissionfile`, instead of its current ability to only read it. Note the following for this:

```
$ echo "RFCs are great if boring." > permissionfile
-bash: permissionfile: Permission denied
```

We would use `chown` to make this change, by passing the user and group we want to change the file to:

```
$ sudo chown vagrant:root permissionfile
```

Now, check the permissions:

```
$ ls -l permissionfile
-rw-r--r--. 1 vagrant root 0 Oct 28 12:37 permissionfile
```

This means that we, as the vagrant user, can now write to the file:

```
$ echo "RFCs are great if boring." > permissionfile
$ cat permissionfile
RFCs are great if boring.
```

But, other users (that aren't `root`) can't write to the file:

```
$ su - packt -c "echo IMPOSSIBLE > /home/permissionfile"
Password:
-bash: /home/permissionfile: Permission denied
```

Here, we're using `su` to execute a command as the Packt user, and we're showing that though we tried to `echo IMPOSSIBLE` to the file, it failed. We used the full path for `permissionfile` to make sure we didn't create the file in the Packt user's `home` directory.

chmod

We're being a bit unfair on the old Packt user here, so let's give everyone the ability to write to the file, rather than just `vagrant`:

```
$ sudo chmod 646 permissionfile
$ ls -l permissionfile
-rw-r--rw-. 1 vagrant root 26 Oct 28 12:48 permissionfile
```

Now, we should be able to write to the file as any user, instead of just vagrant:

```
$ su - packt -c "echo POSSIBLE > /home/permissionfile"
Password:
$ cat permissionfile
POSSIBLE
```

chattr

I'm starting to think we've been much too lenient here, so let's completely lock down the file so no one (even almighty `root`) can mess with it:

```
$ sudo chattr +i permissionfile
```

We've made the file immutable!

```
$ echo "RFCs are great if boring." > permissionfile
-bash: permissionfile: Permission denied
```

We can see this using the `lsattr` command:

```
$ lsattr permissionfile
----i---------- permissionfile
```

And, not even `root` is able to modify the file:

```
$ sudo echo "RFCs are great if boring." > permissionfile
-bash: permissionfile: Permission denied
```

 There are various attributes that can be applied to a file with `chattr`, but I'd put money on the immutable option being the most commonly used.

To remove the attribute, use `chattr` again:

```
$ sudo chattr -i permissionfile
```

How it works...

Running through each of the commands again, let's take a brief look at what we did.

chown

First, we changed the ownership of our file:

```
$ sudo chown vagrant:root permissionfile
```

Here, we're using chown in its most basic way, dictating which user and group the file should belong to. The values are colon-separated, though if you're backward like me, you occasionally use the deprecated and incorrect full stop (.)instead.

You can just specify a user if you want to leave the group alone:

```
$ sudo chown vagrant permissionfile
```

chmod

Next, we changed our file so that anyone could write to it:

```
$ sudo chmod 646 permissionfile
```

Here, we passed certain octal values to the permissionfile in order to change the rights for the user, group, and everyone else in turn.

I won't go into great detail on this, but effectively, the first digit indicates what values the user's triad should be, then the group's triad, then everyone else.

Our user gets the value of 6 that translates to read/write; our group can only read 4 and everyone else can read/write 6.

This is because each of the values has a numeric equivalent, as follows:

- x = 1
- w = 2
- r = 4

So, the 6 value is 4+2, or r/w, and the 4 value is only r.

You could set 777, which would mean r/w/x for everything and everyone, and it's frequently done by people who don't understand file permissions properly. It's not a good practice, and should be dissuaded outside of troubleshooting. If I find a box where someone has run chmod 777 on a file in production, that person is getting their access revoked and a quick primer on permissions plonked into their calendar.

chattr

Lastly, we changed one of the file's attributes, specifically making the file immutable to even root, before we removed the flag again.

There are many more flags than just immutable; all of them listed in the chattr main page, and some of them can be useful in niche situations:

- a: A file can only be appended to (useful for logs)
- c: To compress and uncompress transparently
- s: Results in the file's blocks are zeroed and written back to disk on file deletion

Not all attributes are honored by all file systems; check if your filesystem supports them too (hint: ext4 doesn't support quite a few).

There's more...

There are one or two more things to note, before we wrap this section.

Avoiding octal notation (if you hate it) in chmod

You don't absolutely have to use the octal format in the chmod world; it does give you other options that are easier to read:

```
$ sudo chmod uo=rw,g=r permissionfile
```

The preceding command would give the user and others the read/write rights, and the group the read rights.

Or, you might add a value to the permissions:

```
$ sudo chmod g+x permissionfile
```

This would grant the group the additional ability to execute the file:

```
$ ls -l permissionfile
-rw-r-xrw-. 1 vagrant root 26 Oct 28 13:03 permissionfile
```

Hierarchical permissions

We created a directory, and a file in that directory, so let's take a quick look at understanding directory permissions.

To start, our `permissiondir` looks like this:

```
$ ls -la permissiondir
total 0
drwxr-xr-x. 2 root root 45 Oct 28 12:37 .
drwxr-xr-x. 5 root root 77 Oct 28 12:37 ..
-rw-r--r--. 1 root root 0 Oct 28 12:37 permissionfile-in-permissiondir
```

We can't currently rename this file, despite us wanting to, as it's too long:

```
$ mv permissiondir/permissionfile-in-permissiondir
permissiondir/permissionfile2
mv: cannot move 'permissiondir/permissionfile-in-permissiondir' to
'permissiondir/permissionfile2': Permission denied
```

So, let's set the write permission on this file for everyone:

```
$ sudo chmod 646 permissiondir/permissionfile-in-permissiondir
```

And now, let's try again:

```
$ mv permissiondir/permissionfile-in-permissiondir
permissiondir/permissionfile2
mv: cannot move 'permissiondir/permissionfile-in-permissiondir' to
'permissiondir/permissionfile2': Permission denied
```

Huh.

Okay, so the reason for this is because it's actually the directory permissions stopping us from moving the file, not the file permissions. We have to modify the directory that the file is contained in, as the permissions won't let us rename (mv) a file as they are:

```
$ sudo chmod 667 permissiondir/
```

And we should be able to move the file, because our permissions are now extremely liberal:

```
$ mv permissiondir/permissionfile-in-permissiondir
permissiondir/permissionfile2
```

Success!

See also

One thing we didn't cover in this section were **access control lists** (**ACLs**) that can be used to further extend a file's permissions.

Start by putting a small command in our permissionfile to make it execute something:

```
$ echo "printf 'Fire indeed hot'" > permissionfile
```

Say we want to view our entire access control list for a file; we would use getfacl:

```
$ getfacl permissionfile
# file: permissionfile
# owner: vagrant
# group: root
user::rw-
group::r-x
other::rw-
```

Here, we can see the owner is vagrant, and the user has rw.

But, what if we wanted Packt to be able to execute the file, without impacting the other permissions? At the moment, Packt can't because it's not in the root group.

One potential solution is setfacl:

```
$ setfacl -m u:packt:rwx permissionfile
```

We can now see a little + sign with `ls`, showing us that the file has extended access controls:

```
$ ls -l permissionfile
-rw-r-xrw-+ 1 vagrant root 26 Oct 28 13:03 permissionfile
```

And, we can see those using `getfacl` again:

```
$ getfacl permissionfile
# file: permissionfile
# owner: vagrant
# group: root
user::rw-
user:packt:rwx
group::r-x
mask::rwx
other::rw-
```

This means that our `vagrant` user can't execute the file:

```
$ ./permissionfile
-bash: ./permissionfile: Permission denied
```

But, our Packt user can:

```
$ su - packt -c "/home/permissionfile"
Password:
Fire indeed hot
```

Technical requirements

For this section, we're going to jump onto both our CentOS and Ubuntu VMs, to highlight some important differences in approach to users and groups.

Users and groups

We've covered users and groups in terms of file permissions, but it's a good idea to run over what we know about users and groups in brief.

In this section, we're going to delve into a short primer on users and groups, determining which user a process is running as, how it changes to that user, and finding which users exist on your system by using /etc/passwd and similar commands.

Getting ready

Use Vagrant to connect to your Ubuntu and CentOS VMs, in different windows or one after the other:

```
$ vagrant ssh centos7
$ vagrant ssh ubuntu1804
```

How to do it...

Over a few short sections, we're going to look at different elements of users and groups.

whoami

If you ever need to know who you are, ask yourself through deep reflection and inner contemplation.

If you need to know what users are logged into a server as (or running a command as), it's a lot easier:

```
$ whoami
vagrant
$ sudo whoami
root
```

Users on a system

To show what users are in place on a system, check out /etc/passwd.

On CentOS, it'll look something like this:

```
$ cat /etc/passwd
root:x:0:0:root:/root:/bin/bash
bin:x:1:1:bin:/bin:/sbin/nologin
daemon:x:2:2:daemon:/sbin:/sbin/nologin
adm:x:3:4:adm:/var/adm:/sbin/nologin
lp:x:4:7:lp:/var/spool/lpd:/sbin/nologin
sync:x:5:0:sync:/sbin:/bin/sync
shutdown:x:6:0:shutdown:/sbin:/sbin/shutdown
halt:x:7:0:halt:/sbin:/sbin/halt
mail:x:8:12:mail:/var/spool/mail:/sbin/nologin
operator:x:11:0:operator:/root:/sbin/nologin
```

```
games:x:12:100:games:/usr/games:/sbin/nologin
ftp:x:14:50:FTP User:/var/ftp:/sbin/nologin
nobody:x:99:99:Nobody:/:/sbin/nologin
systemd-network:x:192:192:systemd Network Management:/:/sbin/nologin
dbus:x:81:81:System message bus:/:/sbin/nologin
polkitd:x:999:998:User for polkitd:/:/sbin/nologin
rpc:x:32:32:Rpcbind Daemon:/var/lib/rpcbind:/sbin/nologin
rpcuser:x:29:29:RPC Service User:/var/lib/nfs:/sbin/nologin
nfsnobody:x:65534:65534:Anonymous NFS User:/var/lib/nfs:/sbin/nologin
sshd:x:74:74:Privilege-separated SSH:/var/empty/sshd:/sbin/nologin
postfix:x:89:89::/var/spool/postfix:/sbin/nologin
chrony:x:998:996::/var/lib/chrony:/sbin/nologin
vagrant:x:1000:1000:vagrant:/home/vagrant:/bin/bash
packt:x:1001:1001::/home/packt:/bin/bash
```

And, on Ubuntu, it'll look something like this:

```
$ cat /etc/passwd
root:x:0:0:root:/root:/bin/bash
daemon:x:1:1:daemon:/usr/sbin:/usr/sbin/nologin
bin:x:2:2:bin:/bin:/usr/sbin/nologin
sys:x:3:3:sys:/dev:/usr/sbin/nologin
sync:x:4:65534:sync:/bin:/bin/sync
games:x:5:60:games:/usr/games:/usr/sbin/nologin
man:x:6:12:man:/var/cache/man:/usr/sbin/nologin
lp:x:7:7:lp:/var/spool/lpd:/usr/sbin/nologin
mail:x:8:8:mail:/var/mail:/usr/sbin/nologin
news:x:9:9:news:/var/spool/news:/usr/sbin/nologin
uucp:x:10:10:uucp:/var/spool/uucp:/usr/sbin/nologin
proxy:x:13:13:proxy:/bin:/usr/sbin/nologin
www-data:x:33:33:www-data:/var/www:/usr/sbin/nologin
backup:x:34:34:backup:/var/backups:/usr/sbin/nologin
list:x:38:38:Mailing List Manager:/var/list:/usr/sbin/nologin
irc:x:39:39:ircd:/var/run/ircd:/usr/sbin/nologin
gnats:x:41:41:Gnats Bug-Reporting System
(admin):/var/lib/gnats:/usr/sbin/nologin
nobody:x:65534:65534:nobody:/nonexistent:/usr/sbin/nologin
systemd-network:x:100:102:systemd Network
Management,,,:/run/systemd/netif:/usr/sbin/nologin
systemd-resolve:x:101:103:systemd
Resolver,,,:/run/systemd/resolve:/usr/sbin/nologin
syslog:x:102:106::/home/syslog:/usr/sbin/nologin
messagebus:x:103:107::/nonexistent:/usr/sbin/nologin
_apt:x:104:65534::/nonexistent:/usr/sbin/nologin
lxd:x:105:65534::/var/lib/lxd/:/bin/false
uuidd:x:106:110::/run/uuidd:/usr/sbin/nologin
dnsmasq:x:107:65534:dnsmasq,,,:/var/lib/misc:/usr/sbin/nologin
landscape:x:108:112::/var/lib/landscape:/usr/sbin/nologin
```

```
sshd:x:109:65534::/run/sshd:/usr/sbin/nologin
pollinate:x:110:1::/var/cache/pollinate:/bin/false
vagrant:x:1000:1000:,,,:/home/vagrant:/bin/bash
ubuntu:x:1001:1001:Ubuntu:/home/ubuntu:/bin/bash
```

Most of these users you will not have created yourself; they are system users for the most part, or bundled with software you've installed.

Groups on a system

Groups are discovered in a similar fashion to users, and again, you won't have created most of them.

For CentOS, note the following:

```
$ cat /etc/group
root:x:0:
bin:x:1:
daemon:x:2:
sys:x:3:
adm:x:4:
tty:x:5:
disk:x:6:
lp:x:7:
mem:x:8:
kmem:x:9:
wheel:x:10:
<SNIP>
postfix:x:89:
chrony:x:996:
screen:x:84:
vagrant:x:1000:vagrant
packt:x:1001:
```

And for Ubuntu, note the following:

```
$ cat /etc/group
root:x:0:
daemon:x:1:
bin:x:2:
sys:x:3:
adm:x:4:syslog,ubuntu
tty:x:5:
<SNIP>
landscape:x:112:
admin:x:113:
netdev:x:114:ubuntu
```

```
vboxsf:x:115:
vagrant:x:1000:
ubuntu:x:1001:
```

I've emboldened the first big difference between this Ubuntu and CentOS system, namely the `wheel` and `admin` groups. `wheel` doesn't exist on our Ubuntu system, because it's been replaced by the `admin` group; this means that the `visudo` file on Ubuntu references the members of the `admin` group instead of `wheel`. Something to remember.

Daemons using users

On our Ubuntu system, the `syslogd` daemon is run using the `syslog` user.

We can confirm this by locating our `rsyslogd` process and checking the user in the leftmost column:

```
$ pidof rsyslogd
917
$ ps -up 917
USER PID %CPU %MEM VSZ RSS TTY STAT START TIME COMMAND
syslog 917 0.0 0.4 263036 4416 ? Ssl 10:41 0:00 /usr/sbin/rsyslogd -n
```

And we can see why this user is found by checking out the `/etc/rsyslog.conf` configuration file:

```
$ grep PrivDrop /etc/rsyslog.conf
$PrivDropToUser syslog
$PrivDropToGroup syslog
```

If you wanted to quickly exclude processes running as `root`, you might use a quick one-liner such as the following (though it's not perfect by any means).

This is on our CentOS VM:

```
$ ps aux | grep -v root
USER PID %CPU %MEM VSZ RSS TTY STAT START TIME COMMAND
dbus 558 0.0 0.5 66428 2568 ? Ssl 12:34 0:00 /usr/bin/dbus-daemon --
system --address=systemd: --nofork --nopidfile --systemd-activation
rpc 559 0.0 0.2 69220 1060 ? Ss 12:34 0:00 /sbin/rpcbind -w
polkitd 568 0.0 1.6 538436 8020 ? Ssl 12:34 0:00
/usr/lib/polkit-1/polkitd --no-debug
chrony 581 0.0 0.3 117752 1828 ? S 12:34 0:00 /usr/sbin/chronyd
postfix 1088 0.0 0.8 89792 4080 ? S 12:35 0:00 qmgr -l -t unix -u
```

```
vagrant 3369 0.0 0.5 154904 2688 ? S 14:11 0:00 sshd: vagrant@pts/0
vagrant 3370 0.0 0.5 15776 2660 pts/0 Ss 14:11 0:00 -bash
postfix 3399 0.0 0.8 89724 4052 ? S 14:15 0:00 pickup -l -t unix -u
vagrant 3404 0.0 0.3 55140 1872 pts/0 R+ 14:32 0:00 ps aux
```

How it works...

Generally, different users and groups will have specific uses, deliberately segregated so that they're not too powerful in their own right. If you've got a multi-tenanted system (which is very rare these days) with more than one person logging on to do their day-to-day work, you want to make sure that person can't make life harder for everyone else, by doing something silly like overwriting the logs on the box.

You might solve this issue by putting all human users in one group, and while allowing them their own users with limited access, you could then give the group access to things such as shared directories and applications they might need to use.

Processes have the option to drop their privilege, though not all will do so out of the box, and if you want to go this extra mile, it's usually a lot of work to set up. Here, we saw `syslog` starting up (as `root`) then immediately lowering its own privilege level to that of the `syslog` user and group.

The reason `rsyslogd` has to start as `root` is because it binds to a port lower than `1024`, which are the restricted ports only accessible to `root` programs.

Some distributions and operating systems take this approach a lot more strictly than others, but as with everything security-related, it's like another layer to the onion of being secure.

There's more...

Take a look at this user, on your Ubuntu VM:

```
$ grep apt /etc/passwd
_apt:x:104:65534::/nonexistent:/usr/sbin/nologin
```

It's got an underscore, the only one to have one in the entirety of the `/etc/passwd` file; why might that be?

One potential reason is that it's a system account and the application maintainer or developer decided to denote this with an underscore character, as is the case with other operating systems.

AppArmor and modification

In this section, we're going to use AppArmor on Ubuntu and determine what effect it has on our system.

AppArmor is installed by default on Ubuntu. It was originally developed by SUSE, but Canonical seem to have stuck their flag firmly in the AppArmor planet, introducing it in Ubuntu 7.04 and turning it on by default in 7.10 (2007).

Like SELinux, AppArmor is a way of introducing mandatory access controls (MAC) into Linux; it has been included in the kernel since 2.6.36.

Getting ready

In this section, we're going to be using our Ubuntu VM.

SSH to your Ubuntu VM:

```
$ vagrant ssh ubuntu1804
```

How to do it...

First thing's first, let's make sure that `apparmor` is running, using our old pal, `systemctl`:

```
$ systemctl status apparmor
● apparmor.service - AppArmor initialization
   Loaded: loaded (/lib/systemd/system/apparmor.service; enabled;
vendor preset: enabled)
   Active: active (exited) since Sun 2018-10-28 10:41:23 UTC; 4h 21min
ago
     Docs: man:apparmor(7)
           http://wiki.apparmor.net/
  Process: 426 ExecStart=/etc/init.d/apparmor start (code=exited,
status=0/SUCCESS)
 Main PID: 426 (code=exited, status=0/SUCCESS)

Warning: Journal has been rotated since unit was started. Log output
is incomplete or unavailable.
```

To see what profiles are loaded, and what mode they're running in, use
`apparmor_status`:

```
$ sudo apparmor_status
apparmor module is loaded.
15 profiles are loaded.
15 profiles are in enforce mode.
   /sbin/dhclient
   /usr/bin/lxc-start
   /usr/bin/man
   /usr/lib/NetworkManager/nm-dhcp-client.action
   /usr/lib/NetworkManager/nm-dhcp-helper
   /usr/lib/connman/scripts/dhclient-script
   /usr/lib/snapd/snap-confine
   /usr/lib/snapd/snap-confine//mount-namespace-capture-helper
   /usr/sbin/tcpdump
   lxc-container-default
   lxc-container-default-cgns
   lxc-container-default-with-mounting
  lxc-container-default-with-nesting
   man_filter
   man_groff
0 profiles are in complain mode.
0 processes have profiles defined.
0 processes are in enforce mode.
0 processes are in complain mode.
0 processes are unconfined but have a profile defined.
```

To understand how AppArmor can limit applications, let's make a modification to the
`tcpdump` profile and restart AppArmor:

```
$ sudo sed -i 's/capability net_raw,/#capability net_raw,/g'
/etc/apparmor.d/usr.sbin.tcpdump
$ sudo systemctl restart apparmor
```

What we did here was remove the ability of `tcpdump` to capture, making it pretty
useless:

```
$ sudo tcpdump -i enp0s3
tcpdump: enp0s3: You don't have permission to capture on that device
(socket: Operation not permitted)
```

If we look at the kernel log, we can see the denial from us trying to run `tcpdump`:

```
$ sudo journalctl -k --since 15:34 --no-pager
-- Logs begin at Sun 2018-10-28 10:41:21 UTC, end at Sun 2018-10-28
15:39:29 UTC. --
Oct 28 15:34:34 ubuntu-bionic kernel: kauditd_printk_skb: 6 callbacks
```

```
suppressed
Oct 28 15:34:34 ubuntu-bionic kernel: audit: type=1400
audit(1540740874.554:97): apparmor="DENIED" operation="capable"
profile="/usr/sbin/tcpdump" pid=3365 comm="tcpdump" capability=13
capname="net_raw"
```

Note the capibility name, `net_raw`, that we removed with `sed` earlier.

How it works...

Profiles for AppArmor are written and loaded into the kernel using the `apparmor_parser` program. Mostly, these will be profiles located in `/etc/apparmor.d/`; though if a program doesn't have a profile, AppArmor doesn't stop it from running.

When the actual systemd unit is started, an `init.d` script is run (located at `/etc/init.d/apparmor`), which does the actual calling of `apparmor_parser`.

When profiles are run in enforcement mode, as the preceding fifteen are, they must adhere to the policy definition, or they will not be able to act outside the policy's requirements, and violations are logged. If profiles are in complain mode, the policy is not enforced, but violations are logged for later perusal.

Profiles are generally named by replacing the executable's slash location with dots:

```
/sbin/dhclient -> sbin.dhclient
/usr/sbin/tcpdump -> usr.sbin.tcpdump
```

If we take a look at the top few lines of the `tcpdump` profile, we can start to see how profiles are built up:

```
$ cat /etc/apparmor.d/usr.sbin.tcpdump
# vim:syntax=apparmor
#include <tunables/global>

/usr/sbin/tcpdump {
  #include <abstractions/base>
  #include <abstractions/nameservice>
  #include <abstractions/user-tmp>

  #capability net_raw,
  capability setuid,
  capability setgid,
  capability dac_override,
 network raw,
```

```
    network packet,

    # for -D
    @{PROC}/bus/usb/ r,
    @{PROC}/bus/usb/** r,
 <SNIP>
```

We can see first that the name of the binary is specified, then a select amount of includes (which are rules that could be used across other programs too).

Next, we have `capability`, including the one we commented out. There are a list of capabilities, viewable in the `man (7) capabilities` page where they're listed with names like `CAP_NET_RAW` and `CAP_SETGID`, but here they're lowercase.

When we removed this `capability`, `tcpdump` lost the capability to use RAW and PACKET sockets, as well as to bind to any address for transparent proxying.

Further down, we can see how the author of the file has used comments, and flags for `tcpdump`, to describe what they're allowing with what permission. In the following example, they're allowing the use of `gzip` and `bzip2` specifically, so that the `-z` option works:

```
    # for -z
    /{usr/,}bin/gzip ixr,
    /{usr/,}bin/bzip2 ixr,
```

The syntax can be compared and understood using the surprisingly detailed `apparmor.d` man page.

There's more...

While AppArmor is nice and it definitely does what it advertises, there are some caveats:

- It relies on developers to write and supply profiles (or others who contribute the time)
- Profiles have to be bulletproof before they can be included in the default installation, which could be the reason there are so few even after a decade
- It's fairly unknown and most people don't even bother with it outside of the defaults

It also goes off path, rather than inode, meaning you can do things such as create a hardlink to bypass restrictions:

```
$ sudo ln /usr/sbin/tcpdump /usr/sbin/tcpdump-clone
```

Admittedly, if you're on a box and have sudo, it's pretty much game over at that point anyway:

```
$ sudo tcpdump -i enp0s3
tcpdump: enp0s3: You don't have permission to capture on that device
(socket: Operation not permitted)
$ sudo tcpdump-clone -i enp0s3
tcpdump-clone: verbose output suppressed, use -v or -vv for full
protocol decode
listening on enp0s3, link-type EN10MB (Ethernet), capture size 262144
bytes
15:52:52.803301 IP ubuntu-bionic.ssh > _gateway.37936: Flags [P.], seq
410213354:410213518, ack 1991801602, win 36720, length 164
<SNIP>
```

You might ask why you need something like this on your system if it's so easy to tweak and bypass, but the answer is relatively simple.

If you have a web server on the public internet, there's a good chance it might get attacked at some point, and when that happens, you might be completely up to date and get hit by a zero-day exploit (however unlikely). Your web server could then be compromised, and the individual attacking you might then use it to try and set up a different process, running on a different port, or even use it to start reading files that it shouldn't.

Mandatory access controls go a long way to ensuring this doesn't happen, and life gets just that bit more frustrating for the person on the other end of the attack. They might have your web server, but that's all they've got.

SELinux and modification

Like AppArmor, **Security-Enhanced Linux (SELinux)** is a way to introduce mandatory access controls into Linux, only it has a couple of key differences:

- It's more widely used and loathed than AppArmor
- It's primarily used on Red Hat-based distributions

If you're in the enterprise world, or thinking of going there, SELinux is a great tool to add to your tool belt.

You might recall that we've already touched on SELinux previously, making a couple of small changes to allow things like SSH to run on different ports; here, we're exploring it further.

Getting ready

For this section, we're going to use our CentOS VM.

SSH to your CentOS VM, forwarding `8080` as you do:

```
$ vagrant ssh centos7 -- -L 127.0.0.1:5858:127.0.0.1:5858
```

Make sure NGINX and some utilities are installed, and that NGINX is started for this example:

```
$ sudo yum install epel-release -y
$ sudo yum install policycoreutils-python setroubleshoot -y
$ sudo yum install nginx -y
$ sudo systemctl enable --now nginx
```

How to do it...

We're going to change the port on which NGINX listens by default, to show how much of a pain SELinux can be.

First, check that NGINX is running on port `80` (the default) by using `curl` and printing the return code:

```
$ curl -I localhost:80
HTTP/1.1 200 OK
Server: nginx/1.12.2
Date: Mon, 29 Oct 2018 17:36:35 GMT
Content-Type: text/html
Content-Length: 3700
Last-Modified: Tue, 06 Mar 2018 09:26:21 GMT
Connection: keep-alive
ETag: "5a9e5ebd-e74"
Accept-Ranges: bytes
```

Using `-I` here means that we don't pull in a screen full of code, and instead we just get the pertinent information, like the return code (`200` being OK).

Cool, so that's all working normally, and SELinux isn't getting in the way.

What if we want NGINX to listen on a different port? Say the one we forwarded? Let's try it:

```
$ sudo sed -i 's/80 default_server;/5858 default_server;/g'
/etc/nginx/nginx.conf
$ sudo systemctl restart nginx
Job for nginx.service failed because the control process exited with
error code. See "systemctl status nginx.service" and "journalctl -xe"
for details.
```

Running our `curl` command again with the new port should report an error (obviously, as the service failed to start):

```
$ curl -I localhost:5858
curl: (7) Failed connect to localhost:5858; Connection refused
```

Odd…but not really.

This is because NGINX is only allowed to run on certain ports, 80 being one, 8080 being another, and so on. 5858 is obscure and weird; why would a web server want to run on it?

Because of this, we have to update SELinux to allow NGINX to run on the new port:

```
$ sudo semanage port --add --type http_port_t --proto tcp 5858
ValueError: Port tcp/5858 already defined
```

Oh damn, it looks like 5858 is already defined for something else (in this case Node.js – curse you Node.js!).

Thankfully, this isn't the end of the world, we just have to modify the port rather than add one:

```
$ sudo semanage port --modify --type http_port_t --proto tcp 5858
```

Now, we can restart NGINX, and it should work fine:

```
$ sudo systemctl restart nginx
$ curl -I localhost:5858
HTTP/1.1 200 OK
Server: nginx/1.12.2
Date: Mon, 29 Oct 2018 18:17:37 GMT
Content-Type: text/html
Content-Length: 3700
Last-Modified: Tue, 06 Mar 2018 09:26:21 GMT
```

```
Connection: keep-alive
ETag: "5a9e5ebd-e74"
Accept-Ranges: bytes
```

You can also visit it in your browser:

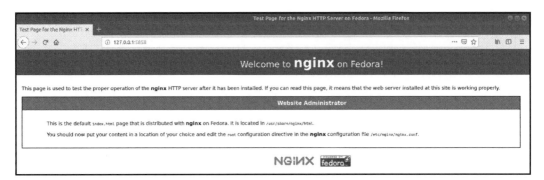

 Yep, it says Fedora, and yes, it's wrong.

So, that's the first step, but now we've decided that instead of the default NGINX welcome page, we want it to show our file in /srv/webserver/arbitrary-location/.

First, let's create this directory structure and put a simple file in there to serve:

```
$ sudo mkdir -p /srv/webserver/arbitrary-location/
$ echo "HELLO WORLD" | sudo tee /srv/webserver/arbitrary-
location/index.html
HELLO WORLD
```

Next, let's check the permissions we have on the existing page location, and make sure they're the same:

```
$ ls -lha /usr/share/nginx/html/
total 20K
drwxr-xr-x. 2 root root   99 Oct 29 17:36 .
drwxr-xr-x. 4 root root   33 Oct 29 17:36 ..
-rw-r--r--. 1 root root 3.6K Mar  6 2018 404.html
-rw-r--r--. 1 root root 3.7K Mar  6 2018 50x.html
-rw-r--r--. 1 root root 3.7K Mar  6 2018 index.html
-rw-r--r--. 1 root root  368 Mar  6 2018 nginx-logo.png
-rw-r--r--. 1 root root 2.8K Mar  6 2018 poweredby.png
```

We'll make sure ours are the same:

```
$ ls -lha /srv/webserver/arbitrary-location/
total 4.0K
drwxr-xr-x. 2 root root 24 Oct 29 18:43 .
drwxr-xr-x. 4 root root 62 Oct 29 18:40 ..
-rw-r--r--. 1 root root 12 Oct 29 18:43 index.html
```

Next, we'll update our NGINX config to log to this new location:

```
$ sudo sed -i
's/\/usr\/share\/nginx\/html/\/srv\/webserver\/arbitrary-location/g'
/etc/nginx/nginx.conf
```

And now, we restart our service:

```
$ sudo systemctl restart nginx
```

Let's give our curl a go, omitting the -I this time so we get our page back:

```
$ curl localhost:5858
<html>
<head><title>403 Forbidden</title></head>
<body bgcolor="white">
<center><h1>403 Forbidden</h1></center>
<hr><center>nginx/1.12.2</center>
</body>
</html>
```

Oops…that doesn't look right.

Unsurprisingly, SELinux is to blame, but the fix is a fairly simple set of commands that we can use to correct the fcontext of the file in question:

```
$ sudo semanage fcontext --add --type httpd_sys_content_t
/srv/webserver/arbitrary-location/index.html
$ sudo restorecon /srv/webserver/arbitrary-location/index.html
```

Trying our curl now should give us our message:

```
$ curl localhost:5858
HELLO WORLD
```

And we can view it in our browser like so:

 If this isn't worthy of Tate Modern, I don't know what is.

How it works...

When we changed the port and restarted the service, we got some errors:

```
$ sudo journalctl -e -u nginx --no-pager | tail -n 8
Oct 29 17:43:17 localhost.localdomain systemd[1]: Starting The nginx
HTTP and reverse proxy server...
Oct 29 17:43:17 localhost.localdomain nginx[4334]: nginx: the
configuration file /etc/nginx/nginx.conf syntax is ok
Oct 29 17:43:17 localhost.localdomain nginx[4334]: nginx: [emerg]
bind() to 0.0.0.0:5858 failed (13: Permission denied)
Oct 29 17:43:17 localhost.localdomain nginx[4334]: nginx:
configuration file /etc/nginx/nginx.conf test failed
Oct 29 17:43:17 localhost.localdomain systemd[1]: nginx.service:
control process exited, code=exited status=1
Oct 29 17:43:17 localhost.localdomain systemd[1]: Failed to start The
nginx HTTP and reverse proxy server.
Oct 29 17:43:17 localhost.localdomain systemd[1]: Unit nginx.service
entered failed state.
Oct 29 17:43:17 localhost.localdomain systemd[1]: nginx.service
failed.
```

Note the specific `Permission denied` entry on the `5858` port.

You can query SELinux port types and their number, using the `semanage` command we installed as part of the utilities installation earlier:

```
$ sudo semanage port -l | grep http
http_cache_port_t tcp 8080, 8118, 8123, 10001-10010
http_cache_port_t udp 3130
http_port_t tcp 80, 81, 443, 488, 8008, 8009, 8443, 9000
pegasus_http_port_t tcp 5988
pegasus_https_port_t tcp 5989
```

Here, we can see that while 80 and other ports are permitted as HTTP ports, 5858 wasn't there initially.

After we added the additional port just shown, this command looked different:

```
$ sudo semanage port -l | grep http
http_cache_port_t tcp 8080, 8118, 8123, 10001-10010
http_cache_port_t udp 3130
http_port_t tcp 5858, 80, 81, 443, 488, 8008, 8009, 8443, 9000
pegasus_http_port_t tcp 5988
pegasus_https_port_t tcp 5989
```

So, SELinux now allows this port to be used.

In terms of the file, we can check what `fcontext` NGINX needs files to have, using the `ls -Z` option.

Seen here, we run it against the default files:

```
$ ls -lhaZ /usr/share/nginx/html/
drwxr-xr-x. root root system_u:object_r:httpd_sys_content_t:s0 .
drwxr-xr-x. root root system_u:object_r:usr_t:s0 ..
-rw-r--r--. root root system_u:object_r:httpd_sys_content_t:s0
404.html
-rw-r--r--. root root system_u:object_r:httpd_sys_content_t:s0
50x.html
-rw-r--r--. root root system_u:object_r:httpd_sys_content_t:s0
index.html
-rw-r--r--. root root system_u:object_r:httpd_sys_content_t:s0 nginx-
logo.png
-rw-r--r--. root root system_u:object_r:httpd_sys_content_t:s0
poweredby.png
```

This is a good way to determine what context you need to give the new files you create.

When we applied our new policy rule and restored the policy values to the system, our file was suddenly capable of being used by NGINX.

There's more...

SELinux isn't really as bad as everyone thinks, and it's come a long way since the days when things used to silently fail for no obvious reason. Generally, there's a plethora of tools and debugging programs available to you these days when it comes to finding the correct configuration for your system and programs, though they can (and do) fill books by themselves.

If you take anything away from this section, understand that disabling SELinux isn't the answer (that is, setting it to permissive mode), and that outside of a development environment, all you're doing is making life less secure for yourself in the future.

`semanage` also isn't the only way to manage SELinux policies, but it's very easy to use and quite a neat way to introduce yourself to the wonderful world of policy files.

See also

Generally, desktop systems don't use SELinux, with the exception of Fedora, so if you really want to start messing around with it, fire up a VM with Fedora installed and take a look at tools such as `audit2allow` and `chcon`.

Checking SELinux is running, and the importance of keeping it running

In this section, we're going to look at how we check that SELinux is enabled and running on our system, and we're going to use the logs that SELinux writes to during its operation. At the same time, we're going to use `setroubleshoot` to help us in determining what might be the issue with what we're trying to do.

To again stress, there was a period when SELinux started to become a thing, and people dismissed it immediately. Most online guides would begin with the immortal words "be sure to check SELinux is disabled". Thankfully, that mentality has mostly died out now, and people have come to accept SELinux as their one-true-god.

It's extremely tempting, when you come across an issue caused by SELinux, to simply disable it. This is doubly true if the issue is on a production server, and you're under pressure to fix it. Abstain from the easy solution of disabling SELinux, as doing so will only going to come around and bit you in the future.

That said, I will now touch on how to disable SELinux (to aid with troubleshooting!).

Getting ready

For this section, we're going to use our CentOS VM.

SSH to your CentOS VM:

```
$ vagrant ssh centos7
```

If not installed from the previous section, make sure NGINX and our various tools are installed:

```
$ sudo yum install epel-release -y
$ sudo yum install policycoreutils-python setroubleshoot -y
$ sudo yum install nginx -y
$ sudo systemctl enable --now nginx
```

How to do it...

Firstly, and easily, you can check the current status of SELinux with sestatus:

```
$ sestatus
SELinux status: enabled
SELinuxfs mount: /sys/fs/selinux
SELinux root directory: /etc/selinux
Loaded policy name: targeted
Current mode: enforcing
Mode from config file: enforcing
Policy MLS status: enabled
Policy deny_unknown status: allowed
Max kernel policy version: 31
```

Here, we see that it's enabled, and the mode that it's operating in is enforcing, meaning that violations of the policy are denied.

To disable SELinux on the fly (temporarily,) there's a relatively easy command:

```
$ sudo setenforce Permissive
```

But this will change again at boot-time.

For now, let's leave it enabled:

```
$ sudo setenforce Enforcing
```

Next, we're going to change the port that we want NGINX to use (again), restart NGINX, watch it fail, and see how we'd go about determining the problem.

Changing the port can be done like so:

```
$ sudo sed -i 's/5858 default_server;/5757 default_server;/g'
/etc/nginx/nginx.conf
```

If you didn't change the port in the previous section (you're starting fresh), then you'll want to substitute the 5858 shown here for 80.

Restarting NGINX is easiest with `systemctl`:

```
$ sudo systemctl restart nginx
Job for nginx.service failed because the control process exited with
error code. See "systemctl status nginx.service" and "journalctl -xe"
for details.
```

What we can do now is determine why it failed:

```
$ sudo sealert -a /var/log/audit/audit.log
```

This might give you a lot of results, especially if you've been running the box for some time, but near to the end should be a report that looks similar to the following:

```
--------------------------------------------------------------------------
----------

SELinux is preventing /usr/sbin/nginx from name_bind access on the
tcp_socket port 5757.

***** Plugin bind_ports (92.2 confidence) suggests
************************

If you want to allow /usr/sbin/nginx to bind to network port 5757
Then you need to modify the port type.
Do
# semanage port -a -t PORT_TYPE -p tcp 5757
    where PORT_TYPE is one of the following: http_cache_port_t,
http_port_t, jboss_management_port_t, jboss_messaging_port_t,
```

ntop_port_t, puppet_port_t.

***** Plugin catchall_boolean (7.83 confidence) suggests
****

If you want to allow nis to enabled
Then you must tell SELinux about this by enabling the 'nis_enabled'
boolean.

Do
setsebool -P nis_enabled 1

***** Plugin catchall (1.41 confidence) suggests
****

If you believe that nginx should be allowed name_bind access on the
port 5757 tcp_socket by default.
Then you should report this as a bug.
You can generate a local policy module to allow this access.
Do
allow this access for now by executing:
 # ausearch -c 'nginx' --raw | audit2allow -M my-nginx
 # semodule -i my-nginx.pp

Additional Information:
Source Context system_u:system_r:httpd_t:s0
Target Context system_u:object_r:unreserved_port_t:s0
Target Objects port 5757 [tcp_socket]
Source nginx
Source Path /usr/sbin/nginx
Port 5757
Host <Unknown>
Source RPM Packages nginx-1.12.2-2.el7.x86_64
Target RPM Packages
Policy RPM selinux-policy-3.13.1-192.el7_5.3.noarch
Selinux Enabled True
Policy Type targeted
Enforcing Mode Enforcing
Host Name localhost.localdomain
Platform Linux localhost.localdomain
                              3.10.0-862.2.3.el7.x86_64 #1 SMP Wed May
9
                              18:05:47 UTC 2018 x86_64 x86_64
Alert Count 1
First Seen 2018-10-30 17:27:06 UTC
Last Seen 2018-10-30 17:27:06 UTC
Local ID 65a65b11-892c-4795-8a1f-163822aa3a0f

```
Raw Audit Messages
type=AVC msg=audit(1540920426.452:335): avc: denied { name_bind } for
pid=4551 comm="nginx" src=5757 scontext=system_u:system_r:httpd_t:s0
tcontext=system_u:object_r:unreserved_port_t:s0 tclass=tcp_socket


type=SYSCALL msg=audit(1540920426.452:335): arch=x86_64 syscall=bind
success=no exit=EACCES a0=6 a1=5580c9397668 a2=10 a3=7fff97b00870
items=0 ppid=1 pid=4551 auid=4294967295 uid=0 gid=0 euid=0 suid=0
fsuid=0 egid=0 sgid=0 fsgid=0 tty=(none) ses=4294967295 comm=nginx
exe=/usr/sbin/nginx subj=system_u:system_r:httpd_t:s0 key=(null)

Hash: nginx,httpd_t,unreserved_port_t,tcp_socket,name_bind
```

Emboldened at the top is the one-line summary of what `sealert` thinks the issue is; in this case, it's right.

It then gives you a `semanage` command, similar to what we used earlier, to modify the policy.

It also gives you two commands, `ausearch` and `semodule`, that you can use to generate a local policy, which is effectively used alongside the base policy, but which can be included with things like Ansible installation scripts.

For example, you have an Ansible role that installs NGINX on a custom port, but it's okay because you can bundle the text-based policy alongside the configuration, and load it in the Ansible configuration run.

Let's run these:

```
$ sudo ausearch -c 'nginx' --raw | audit2allow -M my-nginx
******************** IMPORTANT ***********************
To make this policy package active, execute:

semodule -i my-nginx.pp
$ sudo semodule -i my-nginx.pp
```

Now, try restarting NGINX, and `curl` our new port:

```
$ sudo systemctl restart nginx
$ curl -I localhost:5757
HTTP/1.1 200 OK
Server: nginx/1.12.2
Date: Tue, 30 Oct 2018 17:41:42 GMT
Content-Type: text/html
Content-Length: 12
Last-Modified: Mon, 29 Oct 2018 18:43:12 GMT
```

```
Connection: keep-alive
ETag: "5bd754c0-c"
Accept-Ranges: bytes
```

Woop!

How it works...

SELinux's configuration (in terms of if it's running and in what mode) is set in the /etc/selinux/config file:

```
$ cat /etc/selinux/config

# This file controls the state of SELinux on the system.
# SELINUX= can take one of these three values:
# enforcing - SELinux security policy is enforced.
# permissive - SELinux prints warnings instead of enforcing.
# disabled - No SELinux policy is loaded.
SELINUX=enforcing
# SELINUXTYPE= can take one of three two values:
# targeted - Targeted processes are protected,
# minimum - Modification of targeted policy. Only selected processes
are protected.
# mls - Multi Level Security protection.
SELINUXTYPE=targeted
```

If you want to disable SELinux permanently, this is the file that you would change, flipping enforcing to permissive or even disabled.

When it comes to the custom policy we loaded, we're looking at something a bit more complex.

This command made two files:

```
$ sudo ausearch -c 'nginx' --raw | audit2allow -M my-nginx
$ ls
my-nginx.pp my-nginx.te
```

The .pp file is a compiled policy, ready to be loaded, and the .te file is a human-readable file for your confirmation.

When we loaded the policy using the semodule -i command, we activated it.

You can see your active policies with `semodule` again:

```
$ sudo semodule -l | grep my-nginx
my-nginx 1.0
```

There's more...

`audit2allow` does its best, but it doesn't always get policy files quite right (or it creates them with too much power, effectively making SELinux useless). Always get someone to sanity-check your configuration prior to loading it, unless you're really, really confident.

See also

I said at the start that it's important to ensure SELinux is running and to make sure you keep it running.

The problems that arise from disabling it and leaving it disabled should be obvious, but just to paint you a picture, note the following.

It's the end of the day on a Friday, just before the Christmas break, and most of the staff have already left after making some final checks to make sure your e-commerce site stays up during the Christmas and Boxing Day rush of people returning unwanted presents.

You're about to clock off when you notice an issue with the site, leading customers to believe they can get three hundred points off the latest Nintendo console, and you can't be having any of that nonsense.

You go in and make a manual change, adding an extra config file to correctly load the prices, and you restart the service.

The service doesn't come back up.

Panic sets in.

Your stomach drops out.

Someone in the distance lets out a bellow.

With speed and dexterity, you disable SELinux, restarting the service and bringing everything back online. The site is up, and the console now shows the right price.

Phew—you go home and eat several mince pies to celebrate.

Then, no one notices SELinux is disabled all year, until it comes time to push another version of the software next Christmas, using your CI/CD infrastructure that also makes sure SELinux is enabled. When that happens, the site goes down.

Everyone panics and no one is sure what happened, but you don't care because you long since quit the company for making you work stupid hours, and you've decided to move to Japan to start a fruit-growing business.

Everything catches fire.

See what you did?

Leave SELinux enabled!

Resetting SELinux permissions

In this section, we're going to talk about resetting SELinux permissions, and touch upon how you might reset a `root` password on a box you've forgotten the password for, while accounting for SELinux, which will hinder you otherwise.

Getting ready

Connect to your CentOS VM:

```
$ vagrant ssh centos7
```

How to do it...

First off, it's important to understand that with SELinux, we effectively have a running-ish configuration and a saved configuration. When you're running your system, it's important that any changes you make to SELinux are saved, to be loaded in the event of an SELinux relabel.

To see this in action, let's copy some contexts around.

Start by taking a look at the context our `.bashrc` file has (because it's immediately available):

```
$ ls -lhaZ .bashrc
-rw-r--r--. vagrant vagrant unconfined_u:object_r:user_home_t:s0
.bashrc
```

There are four parts to this: we have a user (`unconfined_u`), a role (`object_r`), a type (`user_home_t`), and the sensitivity of the resource (`s0`.) The type is what's important to us here.

Say we want to change the type; we can do it on the fly by copying the type from another file (in this case, the `authorized_keys` file, which looks like this):

```
$ ls -lhaZ .ssh/authorized_keys
-rw-------. vagrant vagrant unconfined_u:object_r:ssh_home_t:s0
.ssh/authorized_keys
$ chcon --reference=.ssh/authorized_keys .bashrc
```

Note now that when we look at our `.bashrc` file, the SELinux context has changed:

```
$ ls -lhaZ .bashrc
-rw-r--r--. vagrant vagrant unconfined_u:object_r:ssh_home_t:s0
.bashrc
```

But `chcon` isn't permanent, and what we've effectively done is change the running configuration of SELinux, meaning we can reset it with a simple command:

```
$ restorecon .bashrc
$ ls -lhaZ .bashrc
-rw-r--r--. vagrant vagrant unconfined_u:object_r:user_home_t:s0
.bashrc
```

You may recall that earlier, we did this the other way around, using `semanage` to add a new context to a file, then using `restorecon` to apply that context.

Another way to go about fixing temporary context changes is to relabel your filesystem.

Let's make our change again, copying the `authorized_keys` context once more:

```
$ chcon --reference=.ssh/authorized_keys .bashrc
```

Now, let's put a very specific file in a very specific location, and reboot:

```
$ sudo touch /.autorelabel
$ sudo reboot
```

Once your machine comes back up, take a look at the file's context again:

```
$ ls -lhaZ .bashrc
-rw-r--r--. vagrant vagrant unconfined_u:object_r:user_home_t:s0
.bashrc
```

And, you'll also discover the `.autorelabel` file we added has been automatically deleted.

> The `Vagrantfile` for this chapter very specifically removes some console options as part of the bootstrap process for the CentOS VM. This is because if you don't, the `.autorelabel` function won't work. If you experience problems with this fix, try it on a physical machine or a vanilla VM (*in a development environment!*).

How it works...

What `restorecon` does is check a file's context against what it expects to be true, and if it finds anything amiss, it will correct it with the static configuration it knows about.

When we ran the `.autorelabel` function, we effectively ran the `fixfiles relabel` command across our system at boot-time, prior to our touched file being deleted. What you'll notice is that this boot may take longer as it has more of a job to do when coming up.

There's more...

By default, `restorecon` will only restore the `type` context and leave the others as it found them. This can be overridden with the `-F` flag.

We also mentioned resetting the `root` user's password, which is made oh-so-annoying by SELinux.

Let's say you've forgotten the `root` password to your box; the way to go about fixing this is to boot into single-user mode, change the password, and reboot...or at least, that used to be the way.

Now, the steps involved look like this:

1. Reboot the system.
2. Edit the GRUB entry for your installation before it times out.
3. Make sure the `linux16` line is `rw` instead of `ro`, and change the `init` to something like `/bin/bash`.
4. Continue the boot process.
5. Make sure your / directory is mounted as `rw`, and you can edit files.
6. Run `passwd` to update the `root` password.
7. Run `touch .autorelabel` in the / directory, and reboot.
8. Check you can log in.

If you skip the `touch .autorelabel` step, it won't work, and you'll have to start again.

In the grand scheme of things, it's not much, but it can be infuriating in the moment.

Roundup – permissions, SELinux, and AppArmor

At what point is it too late?

When have you exhausted every possible avenue for resolving your problem?

Do you have decent backups that you've checked and confirmed work?

Are you tearing your hair out?

Has it been three days, and have you not seen daylight since Tuesday?

Permissions can be tricky and awkward, and sometimes it's just better to say, "Screw it, this system is too far gone, I'm starting again." My general rule of thumb for this sort of thing is how many meals I have skipped trying to fix something, and if it's more than one, that's too many meals skipped.

Before now, I've done stupid things, as I think I've made painfully clear throughout this book so far. I've chmod'd entire systems to `777` recursively (which breaks a lot), I've deleted directories in an effort to free up space, only to discover that directory was actually rather important to the system's good health (I won't share which one, but it had files and non-files inside it). I've even stopped an accidental `rm` of much more than I intended to `rm` and stressed myself blue trying to work out how much of the filesystem I'd actually hosed.

In short, I've broken systems to the point where they're technically fixable, but where the time it would take outweighs the heartache of doing a recovery.

SELinux, AppArmor, and simple blanket Linux permissions can leave you scouring the internet for obscure error messages, in the hope someone else has come across the exact same problem as you, and that they've decided to share their solution (as long as it isn't "It's fine, I fixed it, closing this thread").

But all that said, the macOS systems, and even POSIX standard file permissions, are important. It can be time-consuming and annoying, but using tools such as `audit2allow` can greatly reduce your blood pressure, while adding to your awesomeness, and learning the correct `chmod` incantations can speed up your troubleshooting tenfold.

For the most part, the software you install from the official repositories is going to be set up sensibly, and as long as the third party is worth their salt, you might even find that other repositories you add later include appropriate SELinux permissions on their software. The situation is so much better than it was when SELinux first started to be a thing.

I remember when people recommended disabling SELinux as step one on their guides, and I'm glad we're beyond those days, but sometimes it can be tempting.

Those moments when you're at your wit's end, and you just want your application to work, can be the most tempting moments to disable SELinux. Hold firm, be steadfast, and tell yourself you're not going to be beaten by a computer.

It's not like you're up against HAL 9000.

Containers and Virtualization

9

In this chapter, we're going to be covering the following topics:

- What is a container?
- Installing Docker
- Running your first Docker container
- Debugging a container
- Searching for containers (and security)
- What is virtualization?
- Starting a QEMU machine with our VM
- Using virsh and virt-install
- Comparing the benefits of local installs, containers, and VMs
- Brief comparison of virtualization options (VMware, proxmox, and more)

Introduction

I'm going to be honest: containers and virtualization is one of my favorite things to talk about in relation to computers and servers. The very concept of being able to install an entirely different computer, within your computer, is a concept that just sings brilliance to me.

It's not a new idea; this principle has been around for quite some time, with even my first OS9 computer being capable of virtualization to some degree. Going back further, the root of the term is from the 1960s, though it had a slightly different meaning than it does in modern-day vernacular.

You've probably used a **virtual machine** (**VM**) already, though you might not even know you have. VMs are quick these days, with a negligible performance hit compared to running on the underlying tin, thanks to advantages in virtualization that mean that you're no longer emulating everything to do with the VM, and instead you're passing VM instructions straight through to the host computer's CPU.

VMs are undeniably a powerhouse of hosting and development, with the ability to quickly spin up and tear down machines, being a godsend when you're constantly breaking things or looking into a secure and cheap way to segment a massive workhorse of a server.

These days, containers have somewhat taken the mantle away from VMs, though they each have their advantages, and they exist in harmony rather than in constant war with each other.

Containers, unlike virtual machines, are more like a slice of a system, if you will, with a shared core.

When you're using a container on a Linux system, you're sharing the kernel of the host machine, rather than installing your own, and you've usually not bothered with the emulation of extra hardware, like disk controllers.

Again, containers and containerization aren't new concepts, with the idea having been around since the days of jails on FreeBSD, and latterly Zones on Solaris (both of which still exist in one shape or another, and which we'll look at later). They have exploded recently though (within the last few years) with the introduction of **Docker**, which made the whole idea of containers a lot easier for people to swallow (and their marketing was stellar).

In this chapter, we're going to look at containers and virtual machines, discuss the pros and cons of each, and talk about management of a virtual environment.

Technical requirements

In this section, and for this chapter, we're going to use our Ubuntu machine primarily.

Mostly, this is because Ubuntu comes with a lot of the more up-to-date elements we require out of the box, whereas CentOS has had a lot of things patched backward (back-ported) thanks to its long shelf life.

Feel free to use the following `Vagrantfile`:

```ruby
# -*- mode: ruby -*-
# vi: set ft=ruby :

Vagrant.configure("2") do |config|

  config.vm.define "ubuntu1804" do |ubuntu1804|
    ubuntu1804.vm.box = "ubuntu/bionic64"
    ubuntu1804.vm.box_version = "20180927.0.0"
  end

  config.vm.define "centos7" do |centos7|
    centos7.vm.box = "centos/7"
    centos7.vm.box_version = "1804.02"
  end

end
```

What is a container?

In this section, we're going to look at what containers actually are at a bit of a deeper level than we covered in the introduction.

We won't go into a huge amount of depth (because we'd get lost and have to call James Cameron to get us out), but we will touch on the core of what makes a container a container, and how it differs from running a full-fledged virtual machine.

Getting ready

SSH to your Ubuntu VM:

```
$ vagrant ssh ubuntu1804
```

How to do it...

We're going to create a container without using the most popular tool on the market.

Containers utilize certain kernel features (namespaces and cgroups), which means that they're not strictly portable to the Windows and Macs of the world.

First, we're going to create a storage pool for our containers to use:

```
$ sudo lxc storage create example-pool dir
```

 Directory storage pools are discouraged for production use. You're better off using a tailored solution that uses LVM or ZFS, but for testing and examples, it's fine.

Next, we're going to start a container with this pool:

```
$ sudo lxc launch ubuntu:18.04 example-container -s example-pool
Creating example
Retrieving image: rootfs: 31% (1.63MB/s)
```

 The preceding retrieval can take some time, and will depend on your network connection speed.

At the end of this process, our container should be created. We can list it by using the following:

```
$ sudo lxc list
+-------------------+---------+------+------+------------+-----------+
| NAME | STATE | IPV4 | IPV6 | TYPE | SNAPSHOTS |
+-------------------+---------+------+------+------------+-----------+
| example-container | RUNNING | | | PERSISTENT | 0 |
+-------------------+---------+------+------+------------+-----------+
```

Then, we can execute the commands inside it:

```
$ sudo lxc exec example-container hostname
example-container
```

 Here, we're running a command that, when run on our host VM, would tell us `ubuntu-bionic`. Therefore, by checking it alongside our `lxc` command, we can prove it's running in the container.

If we wanted to enter the container, we could simply start a shell:

```
$ sudo lxc exec example-container bash
root@example-container:~# hostname
example-container
```

There you have it – a very quick slice of an operating system, inside your operating system!

Once you're done, simply type `exit` or hit *Ctrl + D* to log out of the container:

```
root@example-container:~# exit
```

Then, we can destroy it with the following commands:

```
$ sudo lxc stop example-container
$ sudo lxc delete example-container
```

 One thing people frequently forget, both in the LXC world and the Docker world, is that you've got more than just the container to contend with. We've deleted the container, but if you really want to clean up shop, you will have to delete the image you downloaded and the storage pool, too.

How it works...

To elaborate somewhat on the cgroups and namespaces comment, what containers are in reality are functions of the kernel and user space tools to make things look nice. LXC is a tool that abstracts complexity away, simplifying the setup of our semi-segregated machines into a few easy-to-use commands.

cgroups (Linux control groups)

Here's an excerpt from the *Linux Programmer's Manual*:

> *"Control groups, usually referred to as cgroups, are a Linux kernel feature that allows processes to be organized into hierarchical groups whose usage of various types of resources can then be limited and monitored. The kernel's cgroup interface is provided through a pseudo-filesystem called cgroupfs. Grouping is implemented in the core cgroup kernel code, while resource tracking and limits are implemented in a set of per-resource-type subsystems (memory, CPU, and so on)."*

In practice, this means that the kernel has the ability to group processes together into a stack and that it can then control and monitor the resource usage of it.

namespaces

Without starting a trend, here's the *Linux Programmer's Manual* again:

> *"A namespace wraps a global system resource in an abstraction that makes it appear to the processes within the namespace that they have their own isolated instance of the global resource. Changes to the global resource are visible to other processes that are members of the namespace, but are invisible to other processes. One use of namespaces is to implement containers."*

In practice, this means that your singular network interface can have multiple namespaces attached to it, which the utilizing processes will believe is the sole instance of that device.

Network interfaces aren't the only example, but they're one of the more obvious candidates as every VM needs a NIC.

The breakdown of our creation

When we created the storage pool at the beginning of this section, what we were really doing was informing our system (the `lxd` daemon) that it needed to use a specific directory for container storage, namely the one below `/var/lib/lxd/storage-pools/`:

```
$ sudo ls /var/lib/lxd/storage-pools/example-pool
containers
```

When we started our container, what we first did was download a prepackaged image from a default internet location that served as the base for the container we created.

Here, it's seen as an alphanumeric string, but it's really Ubuntu 18.04 in cut-down-container form:

```
$ sudo ls -lhA /var/lib/lxd/images/
total 175M
-rw-r--r-- 1 root root 788 Nov 4 15:44
30b9f587eb6fb50566f4183240933496d7b787f719aafb4b58e6a341495a38ad
-rw-r--r-- 1 root root 175M Nov 4 15:47
30b9f587eb6fb50566f4183240933496d7b787f719aafb4b58e6a341495a38ad.rootf
s
```

Note the size of this container, `175 M`, which is one of the primary advantages that people highlight regarding containers (they're tiny, and this is actually one of the bigger examples!).

When our container is running, we can see it from the host as a collection of processes:

```
$ ps uf -p 3908 --ppid 3908 --ppid 3919
```

The output should look something like the following screenshot:

This container therefore has most of an OS inside it, which it has inherited from the image we pulled down, though it notably doesn't contain a kernel that is shared with the host VM.

Imagine a container like an orange (I also quite like oranges) where each segment can exist as its own little parcel of juicy goodness, but without the outer rind of the orange giving it structure and passing it nutrients, it's useless. This is in contrast to a virtual machine, which is more like an eternally young baby spider (hear me out) where each exist independently as living, breathing creatures, but they still ride around on their mother's back, ready to deliver a dose of eldritch horror to anyone who comes into contact with a brood.

There's more...

At the moment, you should have a container created by LXC, inside a virtual machine managed by Vagrant (and utilizing VirtualBox) atop your own laptop, desktop, or server.

This can get a bit tricky to visualize, but a lot of clever people put a lot of hours into making sure this sort of setup works without problems.

The LXD daemon

As ever, we can use `systemctl` to visualize our service:

```
$ systemctl status lxd
● lxd.service - LXD - main daemon
   Loaded: loaded (/lib/systemd/system/lxd.service; indirect; vendor
preset: enabled)
   Active: active (running) since Sun 2018-11-04 15:41:14 UTC; 33min
ago
     Docs: man:lxd(1)
  Process: 2058 ExecStartPost=/usr/bin/lxd waitready --timeout=600
(code=exited, status=0/SUCCESS)
  Process: 2036 ExecStartPre=/usr/lib/x86_64-linux-gnu/lxc/lxc-
apparmor-load (code=exited, status=0/SUCCESS)
 Main PID: 2057 (lxd)
    Tasks: 16
   CGroup: /system.slice/lxd.service
           └─2057 /usr/lib/lxd/lxd --group lxd --
logfile=/var/log/lxd/lxd.log
```

See also

At the top of this section, we ran `hostname` inside our container, but that doesn't give you a clue as to what the container is doing. One thing that I find particularly handy is the ability to check the processes running in my container, without having to dig out process IDs for my `ps` command first.

Here, I'm using the following command:

```
$ sudo lxc exec example-container top
```

This gives me the following output:

Note that it's significantly quieter than the host machine, and very few daemons are actually running in the container.

Installing Docker

By far the most popular solution to running containers on Linux (at least at the time of writing) is Docker.

Starting out as a way for Docker Inc. (then dotCloud) to better utilize containers in their **PaaS** (**Platform-as-a-Service**) company, Docker quickly gained traction in the open source world and was soon seen as the future of computing in a lot of circles (the cynical sysadmins generally came after the developers got wind of it).

Because it's effectively a simple way to use already-present kernel features, and includes the Docker Hub for people to both upload and download pre-built images, it made containers easy.

Soon, people were containerizing everything, from Firefox, to Nginx, to entire distributions, just because.

 I firmly believe that the ease with which Docker made it possible to upload and download their images contributed to its success. As I've already mentioned, the concepts of containers go back to the nineties, but there was no "jail prison" or "zones zone" for people to download pre-built collections of software from. Docker Hub provided this on an already popular platform.

Getting ready

Most distributions come with Docker in some form or another in the traditional repositories. However, this is frequently out of step with upstream or just plain old, so it's a good idea to utilize the upstream Docker repositories in your environment.

SSH to your Ubuntu VM:

```
$ vagrant ssh ubuntu1804
```

How to do it...

Docker keeps a page up to date on how to install Docker on your distribution of choice (see `https://docs.docker.com/install`). The following are the condensed instructions for Ubuntu.

Run an update to make sure you're ready to install Docker:

```
$ sudo apt update
```

Install the GPG key and then add the repository itself:

```
$ wget https://download.docker.com/linux/ubuntu/gpg
$ sudo apt-key add gpg
$ sudo apt-add-repository 'deb [arch=amd64]
https://download.docker.com/linux/ubuntu bionic stable'
```

As ever, check the GPG fingerprint against an official source.

Now, we can finally install Docker itself (this may take some time):

```
$ sudo apt install docker-ce -y
```

We can also check the status of our Docker daemon by using `systemctl`:

```
$ systemctl status docker
● docker.service - Docker Application Container Engine
   Loaded: loaded (/lib/systemd/system/docker.service; enabled; vendor
preset: enabled)
   Active: active (running) since Sun 2018-11-04 16:56:26 UTC; 52s ago
     Docs: https://docs.docker.com
 Main PID: 11257 (dockerd)
    Tasks: 23
   CGroup: /system.slice/docker.service
           ├─11257 /usr/bin/dockerd -H fd://
           └─11275 docker-containerd --config
/var/run/docker/containerd/containerd.toml
```

You may have noticed we haven't started and enabled this service. This is mostly because Debian-derived systems like to start services for you... there are a variety of reasons I don't like this approach personally, but it is what it is.

How it works...

Before we start, you may have noticed that we constantly worked with a package called `docker-ce`, and this is for a very good reason.

There are two base versions of Docker, **Community Edition (CE)** and **Enterprise Edition (EE)**. Mostly, you will only ever see CE in the wild, and it's perfectly functional for all of your needs.

All we did here was go to the writers of the software directly and add their own GPG key and repository information, alongside our Ubuntu defaults. Docker is a very dynamic program, meaning it has frequent and sizable releases. At the time of writing, we installed `18.06.1-ce`, but that might change before you know it. Docker works on a YEAR-MONTH release format:

```
$ docker --version
Docker version 18.06.1-ce, build e68fc7a
```

We also installed two primary components (alongside a lot of tools and extras), which were the Docker command-line tool and the Docker daemon.

Docker works in the same way as other user space tools, making use of the kernel functionality. What sets it apart is how user-friendly it can be.

You mostly work with Docker through the command-line tool `docker`, which, in turn, communicated with the Docker daemon. This daemon is the component that's responsible for managing the containers it's instructed to create, and maintaining the images that it pulls in from Docker Hub or other registries.

A Docker registry is a repository of images. The most popular is Docker Hub, but there's nothing stopping you from creating your own, or using an off-the-shelf solution to manage one, like Artifactory.

The last component to be aware of for now is the runtime that Docker is using, which is `runC` (the universal container runtime) out of the box.

The runtime is actually just the name given to the collection of unified systems that Docker will use to run containers (think of cgroups and namespaces bundled into one word, though there's other features, too). What this means is that while `runC` is Linux-specific, if Windows has a container runtime (Host Compute Service), then Docker can utilize this instead.

This does not make the containers universal between operating systems – you can't create a container for Linux and spin it up in the Windows-specific runtime, but it does make the Docker tooling universal.

There's more...

The easiest way to get all the information you could want to know about your Docker installation is to use the `docker info` command:

```
$ sudo docker info
Containers: 0
 Running: 0
 Paused: 0
 Stopped: 0
Images: 1
Server Version: 18.06.1-ce
Storage Driver: overlay2
 Backing Filesystem: extfs
 Supports d_type: true
 Native Overlay Diff: true
Logging Driver: json-file
Cgroup Driver: cgroupfs
Plugins:
 Volume: local
 Network: bridge host macvlan null overlay
 Log: awslogs fluentd gcplogs gelf journald json-file logentries
splunk syslog
Swarm: inactive
Runtimes: runc
Default Runtime: runc
Init Binary: docker-init
containerd version: 468a545b9edcd5932818eb9de8e72413e616e86e
runc version: 69663f0bd4b60df09991c08812a60108003fa340
init version: fec3683
Security Options:
 apparmor
 seccomp
  Profile: default
Kernel Version: 4.15.0-34-generic
Operating System: Ubuntu 18.04.1 LTS
OSType: linux
Architecture: x86_64
CPUs: 2
Total Memory: 985.3MiB
Name: ubuntu-bionic
ID: T35X:R7ZX:MYMH:3PLU:DGXP:PSBE:KQ7O:YN4O:NBTN:4BHM:XFEN:YE5W
Docker Root Dir: /var/lib/docker
Debug Mode (client): false
Debug Mode (server): false
Registry: https://index.docker.io/v1/
Labels:
```

```
Experimental: false
Insecure Registries:
 127.0.0.0/8
Live Restore Enabled: false

WARNING: No swap limit support
```

Slightly more

One thing I haven't touched on is `containerd` and the likes of `CRI-O`. If you already know these terms, then there's a good chance you understand why I haven't mentioned them, because they're far too far out of scope for what this book is trying to accomplish.

I would encourage anyone who is interested to pick up dedicated literature on Docker and its various components as you'll not be out of work for the next few years if you understand the most popular containerization tool of the day, inside and out.

See also

Did you spot `pigz` in the list of extras downloaded with Docker? This is a particularly interesting bit of software, as it's basically a parallelized version of `gzip`. When you're decompressing a file and you've got eighteen cores, it's nice to use as many of them as you can, instead of overloading one.

Running your first Docker container

We've already used a container, way back in the LXC section, but now we're going to use the more popular system for running containers.

This section will cover some basic commands, without going into a great deal of depth.

Getting ready

In this section, we're going to use our Ubuntu VM, but make sure that Docker from the previous section is set up first.

SSH to your VM, and be sure to use the previous section to set up the upstream Docker repository before installing Docker:

```
$ vagrant ssh ubuntu1804
```

How to do it...

As with the LXC section, we're going to start an Ubuntu container, and we're then going to interact with it.

Begin with the following command:

```
$ sudo docker run -itd --rm alpine /bin/ash
Unable to find image 'alpine:latest' locally
latest: Pulling from library/alpine
4fe2ade4980c: Pull complete
Digest:
sha256:621c2f39f8133acb8e64023a94dbdf0d5ca81896102b9e57c0dc184cadaf552
8
Status: Downloaded newer image for alpine:latest
5396b707087a161338b6f74862ef949d3081b83bbdcbc3693a35504e5cfbccd4
```

Now that the container is up and running, you can view it with `docker ps`:

```
$ sudo docker ps
CONTAINER ID IMAGE COMMAND CREATED STATUS PORTS NAMES
5396b707087a alpine "/bin/ash" 45 seconds ago Up 44 seconds
ecstatic_lalande
```

You can also enter it, should you wish, with `docker exec`:

```
$ sudo docker exec -it ecstatic_lalande /bin/ash
/ #
```

You could also use `docker attach`, which would accomplish the same thing on the face of it (giving you access to a shell in the container). The only problem with this method is that you would be attaching to the active process, meaning that when you closed your session, the container would stop too.

Leaving the container again (`exit`) will bring you back to your VM's prompt.

From here, you can stop your container:

```
$ sudo docker stop ecstatic_lalande
ecstatic_lalande
```

This may take a few seconds.

The container is now deleted, and we can confirm this with another `docker ps`:

```
$ sudo docker ps -a
CONTAINER ID IMAGE COMMAND CREATED STATUS PORTS NAMES
```

How it works...

Let's break down our commands.

Creating a container

Starting with the creation of our new container, this was the command we used:

```
$ sudo docker run -itd --rm alpine /bin/ash
```

Here, we're telling Docker we want to `run` a command in a new container:

```
docker run
```

We're then informing it that we want it to be interactive, to have a pseudo-TTY, and to start detached (knocking us back to the VM shell):

```
-itd
```

Next, we're telling Docker that when the container stops, we want it to automatically remove itself:

```
--rm
```

This is a relatively new feature, only introduced because people didn't realize containers linger after they stop, and people would end up with lists of hundreds of stopped containers.

Lastly, we're saying what image (from Docker Hub) we want to use, and what command to run (here, it's Alpine Linux's default shell, `ash`):

```
alpine /bin/ash
```

Listing our container

Secondly, we used the following command to list our new container:

```
$ sudo docker ps
```

This showed the CONTAINER ID, IMAGE, COMMAND, CREATED, STATUS, PORTS, and NAMES of all our containers (or, in this case, just one).

The CONTAINER ID portion is a random string allocation, and the NAMES section features the randomly generated friendly names of your containers (though this can also be defined at creation time).

When we latterly added –a to our listing command, it was to show that the container wasn't omitted from the initial list simply because it was stopped, as the –a flag will show all containers, not just running ones.

Executing commands in our container

Next, we jumped inside our container, starting another (atop the one we've already started at creation time) shell session:

```
$ sudo docker exec -it ecstatic_lalande /bin/ash
```

Here, we executed a command by using an interactive session and another pseudo-TTY within our container (denoted here by its friendly name from docker ps).

This dropped us inside the container. If we then run top, we will see both instances of the /bin/ash command we've started:

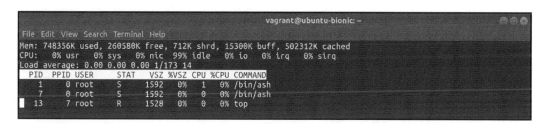

   Did you spot that one of the /bin/ash instances is PID 1?

Stopping our container

Once we'd jumped out again, we then stopped our running container:

```
$ sudo docker stop ecstatic_lalande
```

This takes a few seconds, but, once completed, the container will vanish (as we saw), though the image it used (alpine) will remain.

Because our image is still kicking around, the next time you want to use it for something, you won't have to download it!

Debugging a container

In this section, we're going to start up our container again, make a few changes, and check to see whether our changes have had any affect.

This serves to highlight the transient nature of containers, and what you can do with a running instance.

Getting ready

For this section, we're going to continue using our Ubuntu VM.

SSH to your VM, if not already connected, and start up a container:

```
$ vagrant ssh ubuntu1804
$ sudo docker run -itd --rm -p8080:8080 alpine /bin/ash
```

How to do it...

You should now have a running docker container, listed here with `docker ps`:

```
$ sudo docker ps
CONTAINER ID IMAGE COMMAND CREATED STATUS PORTS NAMES
0f649283dcaf alpine "/bin/ash" 41 seconds ago Up 39 seconds
0.0.0.0:8080->8080/tcp compassionate_boyd
```

Note that we also have a port forwarded in this example, namely port `8080`.

Port forwarding in this instance is the same as any other—we're forwarding a port from the host to a port in the container.

Try to `curl` the port:

```
$ curl localhost:8080
curl: (56) Recv failure: Connection reset by peer
```

Now, jump into the VM and let's start a web server on the specified port:

```
$ sudo docker exec -it compassionate_boyd /bin/ash
```

First, we need to install some additional busybox things:

```
# apk add busybox-extras
```

Now, we can start a small web server on port `8080` before exiting the container:

```
# touch index.html
# echo "I hated reading Shakespeare in school." > index.html
# httpd -p8080
# exit
```

Now, from your VM, you'll be able to `curl` your container's new web server:

```
$ curl localhost:8080
I hated reading Shakespeare in school.
```

Stop the container, and start a new one:

```
$ sudo docker stop compassionate_boyd
compassionate_boyd
$ sudo docker run -itd --rm -p8080:8080 alpine /bin/ash
592eceb397e7ea059c27a46e4559c3ce7ee0976ed90297f52bcbdb369e214921
```

Note that when you now `curl` your port again, it won't work, because all your previous changes to the running container have been lost, and a new one has a risen in its place:

```
$ curl localhost:8080
curl: (56) Recv failure: Connection reset by peer
```

How it works...

All we've done here is highlight that containers are ephemeral by nature, and while you can stop and start the same container (minus the `--rm` to the `docker run` command), you're running in a transient state until you tag your container and upload it to a registry somewhere.

It's generally not good practice to build a container by starting one and then installing a bunch of software inside it, before leaving it and saving it for later. The better method is to use a `Dockerfile` or some other automated and reproducible way of building containers.

What we've also done is point out that while docker containers should be a self-contained little entity, that doesn't mean you can't hop inside them to see what's going on, and even install extra software to help with your debugging, should you so wish.

There's more...

If you are interested in using a `Dockerfile` to do what we did here, it's a fairly trivial one, though it's technically outside the scope of this book.

The following would be enough to get you started:

```
FROM alpine

MAINTAINER Your Deity of Choice

RUN apk add busybox-extras
RUN touch index.html
RUN echo "I really hated reading Shakespeare in school." > index.html

EXPOSE 8080/tcp

CMD ["/usr/sbin/httpd", "-p8080", "-f"]
```

You could then build this with something like the following:

```
$ sudo docker build .
<SNIP>
Successfully built d097226c4e7c
```

Then, you could start your resulting container (detached, and forwarding the port):

```
$ sudo docker run -itd -p8080:8080 d097226c4e7c
```

We added the -f in the Dockerfile to ensure that the process remains in the foreground (and the container doesn't stop immediately):

```
$ curl localhost:8080
I really hated reading Shakespeare in school.
```

Searching for containers (and security)

In this section, you're mostly going to need access to a browser of some sort, though in a pinch, you might get away with calling up a friend and asking them to do an internet search for you (if you're a really good friend and they have literally nothing better to do).

We're also going to use our VM a bit to practice what we discover.

We're going to search for containers on Docker Hub, and we're going to touch upon the security implications of downloading and using public images.

This section is not designed to scare you, in the same way you're not supposed to be scared to run any piece of free (as in open source) software that you find – it's about doing due diligence.

Getting ready

Jump onto your Ubuntu VM (and install docker from the previous section, if you haven't already done so):

```
$ vagrant ssh ubuntu1804
```

How to do it...

From your browser of choice, which is Firefox for me, head over to https://hub.docker.com.

You'll be greeted by a page that looks like the following:

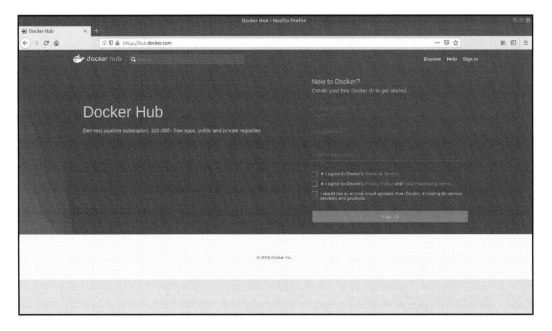

There's something of an implication here, which is the section entitled **New to Docker?**. There's no need to create a Docker ID to get started, despite what the first sentence there might suggest. You may find it handy to do so, and you may even have good reason to create an ID, but there's absolutely no need to do so initially (at least not at the time of writing…).

Instead, use the search bar at the top of the screen, and type `redis`:

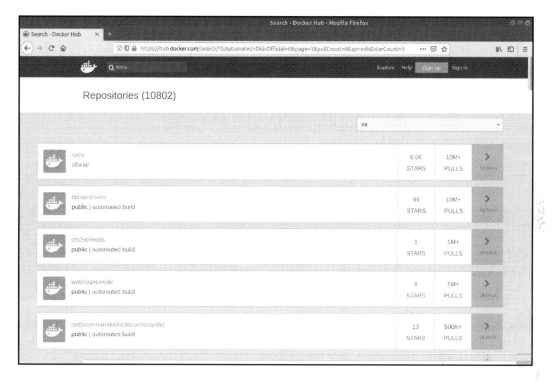

Wow! That's a lot of repositories!

Herein is the first thing it's good to know about Docker. Because it's just so easy to create images and upload them to Docker Hub (I have a few myself), there's a good chance that there's going to be multiple versions of what you want.

Here, we can see that the top result is simply titled **redis** instead of being `<username>/redis-foo` like the rest.

When an image is official, it gets the privileged honor of only having the explicit name of its software, in this case, **redis**.

Click it:

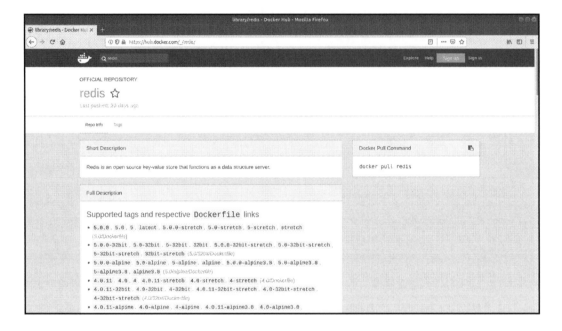

There's a few things to note here.

- Helpfully, we get a command to get started, that is, `docker pull redis` on the right.
- We get repository information, which is the default view that provides us with a short and full description. In practice, this can be as short or as long as the maintainer feels like making it.
- Finally, for this moment, we get a **Tags** section at the top. Click this now:

Tags, as with Git, are a way of denoting a specific version of the container you want to download.

The default tag is the latest and it's the image you would download if you were to run the following command (as you can see in the line immediately following our command):

```
$ sudo docker run -d redis
Unable to find image 'redis:latest' locally
latest: Pulling from library/redis
f17d81b4b692: Pull complete
b32474098757: Pull complete
<SNIP>
```

If we wanted to specifically pull in the Alpine version of Redis (as in Redis installed atop Alpine Linux), we would instead run the following:

```
$ sudo docker run -d redis:alpine
Unable to find image 'redis:alpine' locally
alpine: Pulling from library/redis
4fe2ade4980c: Already exists
fb758dc2e038: Pull complete
989f7b0c858b: Pull complete
<SNIP>
```

Note that we pulled every later except the base one, which already existed in our setup.

Et voilà! You used Docker Hub to seek out a version of everyone's favorite in-memory database!

How it works...

All we're doing here is pulling in a functional image from the global Docker Registry; this is the default, the omega, the biggest, the original, and the best (according to some people.)

Docker Hub is a repository of smaller repositories, with everyone able to put their own spin on containers they've built (or forked) and thus adding to the software soup of the world.

This obviously has disadvantages, as I alluded to in the previous sardonic line. This means that because it's so easy to punt your image onto Docker Hub, it can become increasingly frustrating to find that one image you want.

People can also be malicious, uploading containers that may very well do what they say on the tin, while at the same time using an entire core of your computer to mine bitcoin (though this sort of thing is generally found out pretty quickly when it does happen). It is up to you, as a systems administrator, DevOps person, jack-of-all-trades for your company, to work out what a container is doing, and if it's what you need.

I follow some basic principles here:

- Check whether the `Dockerfile` and source are freely available:
    - Usually, repositories on Docker Hub are triggered builds from GitLab or other source code hosting sites, meaning that you can check the code behind the container

- Check the number of downloads of the container:
    - While not an indicator of quality, since frequently the first image of a piece of software is the most popular, it's generally a good example of the thousand-eyes principle. If thousands of people are using it, there's a higher likelihood that nothing malicious is hidden in the container (though there's still a chance).

- Check to see whether it's an official project's Docker container:
    - Projects such as Redis, Kibana, and Swift all have official Docker containers, so generally I'd go with their offering above others.
    - There may also be containers from the project that aren't tagged as official and still bear the creator's moniker. Those sit firmly above Jane Bloggs containers in my books.
    - That's not to say that unofficial ones are bad, or that they don't cover a slightly different need, but, nine times out of ten, I've found this not to be the case.

- Can you just build it yourself?
    - Assuming that the `Dockerfile` is licensed freely, you could just lift it off GitLab and stick it into your build server to create an image of your own. At least that way, you know that what you see is what you get at the end of the process (assuming you're not downloading software as part of the build, from some dodgy third-party repository you've never heard of).

All that said – and it sounds like I'm being very down on homespun containers – Docker has won the war of container supremacy because of its market mind share and its ease-of-use (if it's building containers or the simplicity of finding them).

Docker Hub means that even if I have no local repositories configures, but I do have Docker installed, I can soon be running a web server on an Alpine container, that plugs into a MariaDB container, atop Gentoo.

This container could then feed logs into a containerized Elasticsearch instance, running on Slackware, on the exact same host, in about ten minutes.

There's more...

You can also search from the command line, if you feel so inclined:

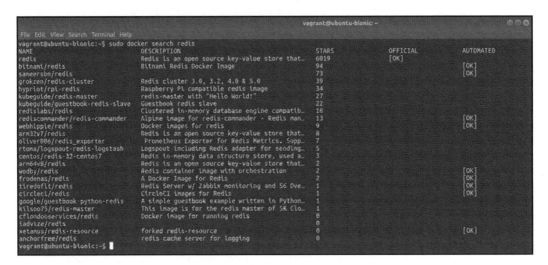

I'll be honest, I never do this, and it's mostly because everyone carries a browser around in their pocket these days. However, I know that some people out there are purists.

What is virtualization?

If you've opened this book randomly on this page, then you might now know what virtualization actually is. If you've done the normal thing, and started at the beginning, then there's an equally good chance you already understand that you've been using virtualization for almost all of this book.

Virtualization is the act of virtualizing (I know right?) one machine inside another machine. Unlike a container, though, we visualize everything from the USB controllers to the floppy drive (seriously).

This concept is not new, but the technology marches on.

For our examples, you've probably done the same thing I did and resorted to Vagrant with VirtualBox. I chose to go this route because VirtualBox is everywhere, with versions available for macOS, Linux, and Windows (along with others!). This has great advantages, but also disadvantages.

Virtualization, by its very nature, is closely tied to the software and hardware of the box it's run on. With this in mind, you might understand why enterprises generally choose to not use VirtualBox everywhere (despite having Windows and Linux machines), but instead use HyperV and KVM respectively... they're more native.

In Linux land, the virtualization software of choice is **KVM (Kernel Virtual Machine)**.

 Siderant: KVM is a terrible name for a product or piece of software. It already had a meaning before Kernel Virtual Machine was decided upon, and data center engineers the world over have been cursing this particular three letter acronym since its inception. Keyboard Video Mouse was a standard, and, in my head, I still picture a DC crash-cart when I hear those letters.

Getting ready

In this section, we're going to be looking at some basic differences between containers and virtualization.

We're going to use our Ubuntu VM, and our CentOS one, for the first time.

Log on to your CentOS and Ubuntu VMs:

```
$ vagrant ssh ubuntu1804
$ vagrant ssh centos7
```

How to do it...

In our container steps, we looked briefly at the fact that the kernel that was being run was the same on the host VM as it was inside the container.

For this step, we're going to run the same command on both of our VMs and compare the output:

```
$ uname -a
Linux ubuntu-bionic 4.15.0-36-generic #39-Ubuntu SMP Mon Sep 24
16:19:09 UTC 2018 x86_64 x86_64 x86_64 GNU/Linux
$ uname -a
Linux localhost.localdomain 3.10.0-862.2.3.el7.x86_64 #1 SMP Wed May 9
18:05:47 UTC 2018 x86_64 x86_64 x86_64 GNU/Linux
```

Our Ubuntu box is running kernel 4.15.0, and our CentOS box, version 3.10.0.

Therein is the first advantage of containers, which are able to run completely different versions of the Linux kernel.

The second advantage in this vein is the fact that virtual machines don't have to be the same operating system as their host: you can emulate a Windows, FreeBSD, or even macOS machine on a Linux box, and mostly any combination of the same.

macOS is a bit of a special case (isn't it always?) because there are license problems and you have to do it in a very specific fashion, but it can be done.

Let's look at something else that's a little bit cool.

On our CentOS VM, I've listed the disks:

```
$ lsblk
NAME MAJ:MIN RM SIZE RO TYPE MOUNTPOINT
sda 8:0 0 40G 0 disk
├─sda1 8:1 0 1M 0 part
├─sda2 8:2 0 1G 0 part /boot
└─sda3 8:3 0 39G 0 part
  ├─VolGroup00-LogVol00 253:0 0 37.5G 0 lvm /
  └─VolGroup00-LogVol01 253:1 0 1.5G 0 lvm [SWAP]
```

These aren't physical drives, they're virtual, and, as a result, you can screw up their configuration as many times as you like without damaging your host's booting potential.

This is one thing I hark on about all the time, mostly since I completely hosed the installation I had on my laptop by running a bunch of Ansible in a container. This Ansible, though I didn't know it at the time, messed around with disk partitions and layout quite forcefully, and, in the case of containers, the devices listed in /dev/ are the devices on your machine, meaning that I'd most excellently destroyed my local install. Thankfully, I worked out what had happened before I rebooted, and was able to save the work I needed before reinstalling, but I didn't do that again. I also changed the tests to use Vagrant and Virtual Machines instead...

Now, obviously, there are disadvantages too—you're basically running an entire machine, meaning that they have to boot (though you can get this down to a few seconds) and will be inherently slower than most containers to start up.

You might also only need one program to be installed (such as Steam on a Windows VM), but you get the other guff along for the ride, meaning that if you want it or not, you'll get Edge browser, Paint, and those annoying folders in the Documents section that are titled Music, Videos, and Pictures even, inexplicably, on server installations.

How it works...

It works on modern computers by taking advantage of CPU features, for the most part.

When you emulate your hardware, using either VirtualBox or KVM, what you're really doing is creating a whole separate set of instructions for the CPU to process. If we emulate VMs on top of CPUs that aren't aware of them natively, and can't deal with their instructions at near-native speeds, you have to emulate even the CPU, which can be costly and slow (more on this later).

Generally, CPUs from the last decade will have either AMD-V (in the case of AMD) or VT-x (in the case of Intel), which means that your VMs will be nearly indistinguishable from your host machine in terms of raw processing speed.

There's also **full virtualization** and **paravirtualization**, the former of which means emulating everything (like, say, emulating an aarch64 processor atop an x86_64 processor) and the latter of which means that, while the execution of processes is segregated, the actual processor being used is the same one as the host (what we talked about before in terms of CPUs being virtualization-aware).

There's more...

There's even more cool things you can do with VMs that just aren't possible with containers.

Say you're a gamer, and you really don't like using Windows, but begrudgingly admit that you really want to play Civilization with your friends, all of whom are avid Windows fanatics. You can do it (sort of) from within Linux.

Okay okay, so it's a bit disingenuous to suggest you're doing it from within Linux, but there's a method here.

You start a VM, install Windows (legally), and then connect your graphics card to your VM...

What?

Yes!

With PCI-passthrough, it's perfectly possible to give a graphics card to a virtual machine, plug a monitor in the back, and then do all your gaming on a separate screen (using the same mouse and keyboard).

Progress!

Starting a QEMU machine with our VM

In this section, we're going to start a VM inside our VM and attempt to connect to it.

Be forewarned. You will probably think that the elements of this section are slow. This is not the fault of your machine, or your own configuration—this is the fault of physics and the fact that we don't have consumer-grade quantum computing yet.

Getting ready

SSH to your Ubuntu VM:

```
$ vagrant ssh ubuntu1804
```

Install the appropriate components for running virtual machines on Ubuntu:

```
$ sudo apt install qemu -y
```

How to do it...

We're going to download an Alpine ISO and attempt an installation inside a virtual machine (inside our virtual machine):

```
$ wget
http://dl-cdn.alpinelinux.org/alpine/v3.8/releases/x86_64/alpine-virt-
3.8.1-x86_64.iso
```

 I chose Alpine for this because it's tiny, fitting into 32 MB.

Next, we need to create a virtual disk on which to install our OS:

```
$ qemu-img create example-disk 4G
Formatting 'example-disk', fmt=raw size=4294967296
```

Now, we can use QEMU to boot our ISO atop our virtual drive:

```
$ qemu-system-x86_64 -drive file=example-disk,format=raw -cdrom
alpine-virt-3.8.1-x86_64.iso -boot d -nographic
```

With any luck, you should see something like the following:

At the command-line prompt, you should be able to log in as the root user (there's no password by default):

```
localhost login: root
Welcome to Alpine!

The Alpine Wiki contains a large amount of how—to guides and general
information about administrating Alpine systems.
See <http://wiki.alpinelinux.org>.

You can setup the system with the command: setup-alpine

You may change this message by editing /etc/motd.

localhost:~#
```

Alpine functions like something approaching a live CD, so we can now go ahead and run through a quick installation to the local drive:

```
# setup-alpine
```

You'll be asked some standard questions. Mostly, you can just answer with the defaults, but for the sake of completeness, here's what I did:

- Keyboard: gb
- Keyboard variant: gb
- Hostname: [default (localhost)]
- Interface: [default (eth0)]
- IP address: [default (dhcp)]
- Manual network configuration: [default (no)]
- Password: Random
- Time zone: [default (UTC)]
- Proxy: [default (none)]
- Mirror: 3 (UK, you may find one closer to you)
- SSH server: [default (openssh)]
- Disk to use: sda
- How to use: sys
- Erase and continue: y

Once completed, you'll have an installed Alpine Linux VM inside your Ubuntu VM.

Power down the Alpine installation:

```
# poweroff
```

You'll find yourself back inside your Ubuntu VM. Now, we're going to boot Alpine again, but this time we're going to omit the ISO file and the -boot parameter:

```
$ qemu-system-x86_64 -drive file=example-disk,format=raw -nographic
```

As I said at the start, all of these steps can take a long time to complete, depending on the age of your computer.

Once booted, you'll find yourself back in your Alpine installation, this time booted from our virtual drive:

```
Welcome to Alpine Linux 3.8
Kernel 4.14.69-0-virt on an x86_64 (/dev/ttyS0)

localhost login: root
Password:
Welcome to Alpine!

The Alpine Wiki contains a large amount of how-to guides and general
information about administrating Alpine systems.
See <http://wiki.alpinelinux.org>.

You can setup the system with the command: setup-alpine

You may change this message by editing /etc/motd.

localhost:~#
```

To terminate your session, either power off the VM again or hit *Ctrl + A*, and then *X*.

How it works...

Breaking down what we're doing here step by step, we started out by downloading an ISO image from the Alpine website. This is the easiest thing to explain, as we're effectively using the ISO as a source of truth for our installation. You can also do things such as pass `/dev/cdrom` through to your VM, should you wish to use the physical drive in your machine (and you live in 2009).

Once we had our ISO image, we then created a file-based block device to install atop. This is so that we can segment one installation from another, and even move the installation from machine to machine should we wish. There are other solutions that don't involve using files – you could partition an LVM setup, giving some of the space to your VM, or you could attach a physical disk and give the entire thing to the installation.

We used `qemu-img` to create the file, but there's no reason you couldn't have used another tool such as `fallocate` to accomplish the same thing.

Next, we booted our VM using the following command:

```
$ qemu-system-x86_64 -drive file=example-disk,format=raw -cdrom
alpine-virt-3.8.1-x86_64.iso -boot d -nographic
```

Breaking this down, we have the following:

```
qemu-system-x86_64
```

This is the QEMU architecture that we want to emulate. I stuck with x86_64 for this, as it's the most common and it's the architecture that the ISO we downloaded expects to find. We could have used `qemu-system-aarch64` if we so desired, and provided we had the appropriate disc image:

```
-drive file=example-disk,format=raw
```

Here, we're passing QEMU a drive to use, specifically the `example-disk` file that we just created, and the format it was created in:

```
-cdrom alpine-virt-3.8.1-x86_64.iso
```

We specifically tell QEMU that we want to use the ISO we downloaded:

```
-boot d
```

We want to boot, specifically from the CD-ROM rather than the virtual drive:

```
-nographic
```

We're on a server here, connected over SSH, so we can't use a graphical output for our VM. This option redirects serial input and output to the console.

There's more...

There's nothing stopping you from using your QEMU-driver VM as a full-fledged machine, aside from the speed.

You can install packages, and even run things such as `htop`:

```
# apk add htop
```

```
                              vagrant@ubuntu-bionic: ~                          ● ● ⊗

 File  Edit  View  Search  Terminal  Help

   CPU[#*******                 22.1%]   Tasks: 15, 0 thr; 1 running
   Mem[|||||#**********     16.0M/112M]   Load average: 0.08 0.08 0.03
   Swp[                       0K/224M]   Uptime: 00:02:15

   PID USER      PRI  NI  VIRT   RES   SHR S CPU% MEM%   TIME+  Command
  2031 root       20   0  3540  1128   872 R  3.2  1.0  0:00.26 htop
     1 root       20   0  1516    40    32 S  0.0  0.0  0:00.77 /sbin/init
  1834 root       20   0  1516    48     0 S  0.0  0.0  0:00.01 udhcpc -b -p /var
  1894 root       20   0  1520    40     0 S  0.0  0.0  0:00.04 /sbin/syslogd -Z
  1945 root       20   0  1516    44     0 S  0.0  0.0  0:00.00 /sbin/acpid
  1971 root       20   0  1520    44     0 S  0.0  0.0  0:00.03 /usr/sbin/crond -
  2000 root       20   0  7412   364     0 S  0.0  0.3  0:00.02 /usr/sbin/sshd
  2007 root       20   0  1516     4     0 S  0.0  0.0  0:00.05 /sbin/getty 38400
  2008 root       20   0  1516     4     0 S  0.0  0.0  0:00.03 /sbin/getty 38400
  2011 root       20   0  1516     4     0 S  0.0  0.0  0:00.02 /sbin/getty 38400
  2014 root       20   0  1516     4     0 S  0.0  0.0  0:00.00 /sbin/getty 38400
  2017 root       20   0  1516     4     0 S  0.0  0.0  0:00.02 /sbin/getty 38400
  2019 root       20   0  1516     4     0 S  0.0  0.0  0:00.01 /sbin/getty 38400
  2022 root       20   0  1516     4     0 S  0.0  0.0  0:00.15 /bin/login -- roo
  2024 root       20   0  1588   972   848 S  0.0  0.8  0:00.12 -ash

F1Help   F2Setup F3Search F4Filter F5Tree   F6SortBy F7Nice - F8Nice + F9Kill   F10Quit
```

See also

You might have noticed a lot of options that we didn't use here, and QEMU's system tools are capable of quite a lot. Typically, people don't build VMs using QEMU directly – they rely on shinier and more user-friendly tools to do the job for them.

On servers, Virsh is a good choice (covered later in this chapter) and, on desktop machines, **Virtual Machine Manager (virt-manager)** is a very commonly installed package that also lets you connect to remote (headless) servers to set up VMs using clicky buttons.

Using virsh and virt-install

`virsh` and `virt-install` are good tools for individuals who are getting started with VMs on Linux. It sounds a bit old hat now, but if you can do something well on the command line, you'll wonder why you ever needed a clicky-button GUI to do the job for you.

When we talk about clients in this way, what we're referring to are frontends to the `libvirt` library, which is a C toolkit that was designed to make interacting with the kernel's virtualization functionality easier.

`virsh` and `virt-install` talk to `libvirt`, which, in turn, talks to the kernel.

Getting ready

SSH to your Ubuntu VM, and then install the `virtinst`, `libvirt-clients`, `libvirt-bin`, and `libvirt-daemon` packages:

```
$ vagrant ssh ubuntu1804
$ sudo apt update
$ sudo apt install virtinst libvirt-clients libvirt-bin libvirt-daemon
-y
```

How to do it...

First, we're going to use the `virt-install` tool that we've installed to create our VM, and then we're going to probe it with `virsh`.

Creating the VM is the simple step; it's the heartache that comes with maintaining machines that's the real drag.

virt-install

To begin, let's use the Alpine ISO we downloaded previously to spin up and install a virtual machine.

If you haven't got the ISO from the previous section, here's the command to download it again:

```
$ wget
http://dl-cdn.alpinelinux.org/alpine/v3.8/releases/x86_64/alpine-virt-
3.8.1-x86_64.iso
```

Let's use `fallocate` this time to create a block device:

```
$ fallocate -l 2G ex-alpine-2-disk
```

Now, let's use a single line to provision our domain (domain being the collective term used here for the machine and other bits):

```
$ sudo virt-install --name ex-alpine-2 --memory 512 --disk ex-
alpine-2-disk --cdrom alpine-virt-3.8.1-x86_64.iso --graphics none --
os-variant virtio26
```

We're using `virtio26` as the OS variant here because there isn't an explicit `alpine` option. Instead, this tells `virt-install` that the OS we're installing is using a kernel later than 2.6, and it supports VirtIO devices (for disks, networking, and so on). This results in us having a functioning VM, which is nice.

Assuming this goes to plan, you should again see the Alpine boot sequence.

Use the `root` user and blank password to log in, and then run through the install process, as we did in the previous section (installing to the vda device).

Disconnect from the console once the install has finished with *Ctrl +]*.

virsh

It's perfectly possible to use Virsh as a series of commands on the command line, in the traditional Unix style of `<command> <flag> <argument>` that we've seen previously.

However, it's also perfectly acceptable to use Virsh interactively, in its own mode.

Start the Virsh Terminal by using the following:

```
$ sudo virsh
Welcome to virsh, the virtualization interactive terminal.

Type:  'help' for help with commands
```

```
    'quit' to quit

virsh #
```

Now, we're going to interact with the machine we created a moment before. Start by listing it on the command line:

```
virsh # list
 Id Name State
----------------------------------------------------
 3 ex-alpine-2 running
```

By default, this command will show you running domains.

If we connect to our VM and hit *Enter* a couple of times, we can interact with our install:

```
virsh # console ex-alpine-2
Connected to domain ex-alpine-2
Escape character is ^]

localhost:~#
localhost:~#
localhost:~#
```

Hop out of the VM again with *Ctrl +]*.

Let's build on the bare-bones domain that we have, starting by taking a look at what `virt-install` has given us with `dominfo`:

```
virsh # dominfo ex-alpine-2
Id: 5
Name: ex-alpine-2
UUID: 80361635-25a3-403b-9d15-e292df27908b
OS Type: hvm
State: running
CPU(s): 1
CPU time: 81.7s
Max memory: 524288 KiB
Used memory: 524288 KiB
Persistent: yes
Autostart: disable
Managed save: no
Security model: apparmor
Security DOI: 0
Security label: libvirt-80361635-25a3-403b-9d15-e292df27908b
(enforcing)
```

Now here's the fun bit – we haven't actually rebooted our VM yet, following the install, so let's issue that using `virsh`:

```
virsh # destroy ex-alpine-2
Domain ex-alpine-2 destroyed
virsh # start ex-alpine-2
Domain ex-alpine-2 started
```

Yes, destroy is a confusing word here, but it's because the actual state of the VM is ephemeral. The data is safe on the drive. The actual configuration is part of the domain so that when we issue the `destroy` and `start` commands, we're not really deleting anything. I dislike the terminology, but it's just something you learn to live with.

Now, we can console connect to our VM, again from `virsh` (this bit, again, can take some time):

```
virsh # console ex-alpine-2
Connected to domain ex-alpine-2
Escape character is ^]

Welcome to Alpine Linux 3.8
Kernel 4.14.69-0-virt on an x86_64 (/dev/ttyS0)

localhost login:
```

And, at any time, we can disconnect using *Ctrl +]*.

Virsh is full of tricks, my favorite of which is the easy way to edit the configuration XML of your domain.

Issue an `edit` command as follows:

```
virsh # edit ex-alpine-2

Select an editor. To change later, run 'select-editor'.
  1. /bin/nano <---- easiest
  2. /usr/bin/vim.basic
  3. /usr/bin/vim.tiny
  4. /bin/ed

Choose 1-4 [1]: 2
```

You should be dropped into the editor you selected and presented with the configuration file for your VM:

```
                              vagrant@ubuntu-bionic: ~
File Edit View Search Terminal Help
<domain type='qemu'>
  <name>ex-alpine-2</name>
  <uuid>80361635-25a3-403b-9d15-e292df27908b</uuid>
  <memory unit='KiB'>524288</memory>
  <currentMemory unit='KiB'>524288</currentMemory>
  <vcpu placement='static'>1</vcpu>
  <os>
    <type arch='x86_64' machine='pc-i440fx-bionic'>hvm</type>
    <boot dev='hd'/>
  </os>
  <features>
    <acpi/>
    <apic/>
  </features>
  <clock offset='utc'>
    <timer name='rtc' tickpolicy='catchup'/>
    <timer name='pit' tickpolicy='delay'/>
    <timer name='hpet' present='no'/>
  </clock>
  <on_poweroff>destroy</on_poweroff>
  <on_reboot>restart</on_reboot>
  <on_crash>destroy</on_crash>
  <pm>
    <suspend-to-mem enabled='no'/>
    <suspend-to-disk enabled='no'/>
  </pm>
  <devices>
    <emulator>/usr/bin/qemu-system-x86_64</emulator>
    <disk type='file' device='disk'>
      <driver name='qemu' type='raw'/>
      <source file='/home/vagrant/ex-alpine-2-disk'/>
      <target dev='vda' bus='virtio'/>
      <address type='pci' domain='0x0000' bus='0x00' slot='0x04' function='0x0'/>
    </disk>
    <disk type='file' device='cdrom'>
      <driver name='qemu' type='raw'/>
      <target dev='hda' bus='ide'/>
      <readonly/>
      <address type='drive' controller='0' bus='0' target='0' unit='0'/>
    </disk>
    <controller type='usb' index='0' model='ich9-ehci1'>
      <address type='pci' domain='0x0000' bus='0x00' slot='0x03' function='0x7'/>
    </controller>
    <controller type='usb' index='0' model='ich9-uhci1'>
                                                           1,1            Top
```

This is sort of the additional way of doing things. If you're comfortable editing files directly, this might be your jam more than using the command line (and, in my experience, there are a couple of options that are just not possible to do without delving into this file).

There are also a couple more things before we leave the world of virsh, the first of which is the version command:

```
virsh # version
Compiled against library: libvirt 4.0.0
```

```
Using library: libvirt 4.0.0
Using API: QEMU 4.0.0
Running hypervisor: QEMU 2.11.1
```

It's a great way to work out the version of the hypervisor you're connected to, the libvirt library version, and the API.

You can also check the vCPU count:

```
virsh # vcpucount ex-alpine-2
maximum config 1
maximum live 1
current config 1
current live 1
```

Then, you can adjust the numbers:

```
virsh # setvcpus ex-alpine-2 2 --maximum --config --hotpluggable
```

We also know from dominfo that we gave our VM 512 MiB of memory, so let's lower that to make space for other VMs:

```
virsh # setmem ex-alpine-2 --size 400MiB
```

 We could up it too, but not beyond the max memory setting that the VM already has (in this state, at least).

How it works...

As hinted at previously, when you create a VM using virt-install, what you're actually doing is writing an initial XML file that contains the recipe for how the VM looks and acts.

This file actually exists at /etc/libvirt/qemu/ex-alpine-2.xml and can be read in the same way as any other file on the system (virsh just makes it easier, like systemctl cat).

When we use tools such as virt-install, virt-viewer, or any of the virt-* suite, we're taking a lot of typing and copying of files out of the equation. You can write a runbook that recreates an environment with just a few one-line commands. Virsh then exists to query your setup and get some basic information about the solutions you've spun up.

We can use something like `virsh autostart` to start a VM on boot, as follows:

```
virsh # autostart ex-alpine-2
Domain ex-alpine-2 marked as autostarted
```

By doing this, we're enabling the script located at `/usr/lib/libvirt/libvirt-guests.sh` to start the VM during boot.

This script, in turn, is triggered by a `systemd` unit:

```
$ systemctl cat libvirt-guests
# /lib/systemd/system/libvirt-guests.service
[Unit]
Description=Suspend/Resume Running libvirt Guests
Wants=libvirtd.service
Requires=virt-guest-shutdown.target
After=network.target
After=time-sync.target
After=libvirtd.service
After=virt-guest-shutdown.target
Documentation=man:libvirtd(8)
Documentation=https://libvirt.org

[Service]
EnvironmentFile=-/etc/default/libvirt-guests
# Hack just call traditional service until we factor
# out the code
ExecStart=/usr/lib/libvirt/libvirt-guests.sh start
ExecStop=/usr/lib/libvirt/libvirt-guests.sh stop
Type=oneshot
RemainAfterExit=yes
StandardOutput=journal+console
TimeoutStopSec=0

[Install]
WantedBy=multi-user.target
```

There's more...

Take a look at the rest of the `virt` suite:

```
$ virt-
virt-admin virt-convert virt-install virt-pki-validate virt-viewer
virt-xml-validate
virt-clone virt-host-validate virt-login-shell virt-sanlock-cleanup
virt-xml
```

There's a tool for everything, and everything's got a tool.

When you get a few minutes, take a look at `virt-clone` and `virt-viewer` – they're my favorites.

Comparing the benefits of local installs, containers, and VMs

We're going to take a look at some obvious advantages and disadvantages to local installations, containers, and VMs, as well as deciding when it might be ideal to use one or the other.

Getting ready

If you want to follow along in this section, ensure that you've got Docker installed and set up, as well as having QEMU tools enabled (both from the previous sections).

SSH to your Ubuntu VM:

```
$ vagrant ssh ubuntu1804
```

Now, you might want to install Vagrant inside our Vagrant VM (for the VM examples that follow):

```
$ sudo apt install vagrant -y
```

Once you've added yourself to the appropriate groups, log out of your VirtualBox VM and back in, prior to moving into this section.

How to do it...

From your command line, let's start an Nginx instance.

You could go about this in one of three ways.

1. Use `apt` to install Nginx from the default repositories
2. Use Docker to pull the official Nginx image from Docker Hub
3. Set up a VM and install Nginx inside it, using port forwarding from the host

These could be done in the following fashion:

```
$ sudo apt install nginx -y
$ sudo docker run -p80 -d --rm nginx
$ cat << HERE > Vagrantfile
# -*- mode: ruby -*-
# vi: set ft=ruby :

\$provisionScript = <<-SCRIPT
apt install nginx -y
SCRIPT

Vagrant.configure("2") do |config|

  config.vm.define "debian8" do |debian8|
    debian8.vm.box = "debian/jessie64"
  debian8.vm.network "forwarded_port", guest: 80, host: 8080
    debian8.vm.provision "shell",
      inline: \$provisionScript

    debian8.vm.provider "libvirt" do |lv|
      lv.driver = "qemu"
      lv.memory = 256
      lv.cpus = 1

    end

  end

end
HERE
$ sudo vagrant up
```

 I used a Vagrantfile here because it's what we've used throughout this book, but there are other ways we could go about spinning up a VM. This also might not work if there are already other VMs running inside your VM (from the previous section) and could just be far too slow to work at all.

What are the advantages and disadvantages to these different methods?

Local Nginx install

First, the local install. This is the simplest method, as we're simply installing software that is readily available from the default Ubuntu repository.

Pros:

- It comes configured in an Ubuntu fashion (that is, some Ubuntu defaults, such as start scripts) and it is pretty much guaranteed to work with your setup
- It installs extremely quickly
- It will also be kept up to date as long as the repository is kept up to date, and other software installed from the same location should interact with it in a native fashion, avoiding things like manual pointing of dependencies
- It'll obviously be fast, and thus able to utilize whatever your box grants it
- You can generally expect reasonable help with issues too, be it on the official forums, or if you have a specific support contract with Ubuntu (they may start by assuming you've installed things from their default repositories)

Cons:

- You can't install multiple versions of Nginx easily; though it's certainly possible, it's more work
- You can't easily delete all of your configuration and files without something potentially getting left behind (making a reinstall a faff)
- Nginx isn't as segregated as it could be from the rest of the system

Docker Nginx install

Moving on, we next set up an Nginx Docker container, forwarding a port as we did.

The positives here are as follows:

- It's quick to start up your instance
- Multiple instances can be started with no worry of cross contamination
- The processes are reasonably segregated from the host machine (though exploits can and do happen)
- Containers can be torn down and redeployed in a heartbeat, with no worry that lingering files might cause you problems

Some negatives are as follows:

- You have to download the container first
- Mapping ports (when not defined explicitly) results in a randomly NAT'd port, rather than port 80 by default

- You might end up with an OS in the container that isn't the same as the host OS (there can be internal security compliance issues with this)
- You've now effectively got two sources of truth for software running on your system
- Configuration within the container isn't consistent – you have to explicitly save a container's state if you modify it
- Debugging becomes slightly more awkward
- No init system (usually) if you do need one for things such as service file testing

VM Nginx install

There's a small consideration to take into account here, and that's the fact we're running a VM inside a VM, but it highlights a few problems.

Some positives are:

- It has pretty much complete OS segregation (except for some vulnerabilities like Meltdown)
- Good control over resource allocation for the VM
- Ability to tear down and spin up on a whim
- If you need to specifically make hardware changes to account for software requirements, VMs are the only way to do this easily

Some negatives are:

- VMs can be slower than containers, and there's a lot of factors you have to account for (such as if your server is already a VM)
- You're running an entirely separate OS and kernel, for the sake of one program (in this example)
- VMs usually take up more space, owing to the disk space needed for the rest of the OS
- You have to manage the updates for another machine, besides the host
- You need to keep an eye on resource segregation, which can mean extra monitoring (this is especially true if you do things such as specific CPU pinning)

How it works...

This isn't an attempt to dissuade you from choosing any particular method of installing your software, and there's plenty of reasons for choosing one method over the other.

I've worked in environments where I had to primarily use a VM, and not wanting the headache of using a VM inside a VM, I've tested software by using containers instead.

Likewise, as mentioned previously, I've screwed up host installations by making hardware configuration changes inside a Docker container, resulting in a host system that would never boot again.

Speaking from experience, you'll quickly get tired of managing different methods of installation, and having used systems where some things were installed from default repositories, some from Snaps, some from Flatpak, and some utilizing Docker containers, it gets really old, really fast.

In the example we looked at here, I would be hard pressed to not choose Docker on a web server, specifically because of the management capabilities it offers. I could easily install multiple instances of Nginx and be relatively confident they'd never know that another instance existed, without having to segregate configuration files in a weird and wonderful fashion.

It's never simple.

Also, it's worth remembering that because we used Vagrant in our VM and `libvirt` underneath, we can see our VM with Virsh:

```
virsh # list
 Id    Name                                 State
----------------------------------------------------
 22    vagrant_debian8                      running

virsh #
```

We can also see our container with docker:

```
$ sudo docker ps
CONTAINER ID         IMAGE              COMMAND
CREATED              STATUS             PORTS                      NAMES
4f610d2a6bef         nginx              "nginx -g 'daemon of..."   3
hours ago            Up 3 hours         0.0.0.0:32768->80/tcp
gallant_curie
```

Brief comparison of virtualization options (VMware, proxmox, and more)

When it comes to virtualization, everyone has their favorite solution.

You should know about two options by now, those being VirtualBox (which we've been using throughout this book) and QEMU/KVM. However, these aren't the only options available to you, should you want to run virtual machines on your server, just as containers aren't limited to Docker.

Here, we're going to run through a few other options, most of which you'll probably come across in your career at some point:

- VMware ESXi
- Proxmox
- OpenStack

Getting ready

Open your web browser of choice.

How to do it...

We're going to look at some of the options available to us, in a section dedicated to each.

VMware ESXi

One of the various offerings from VMware (now a subsidiary of Dell) ESXi isn't Linux; it's a dedicated "OS" that sits atop your hardware, and virtual machines can be configured atop ESXi.

It is a licensed product, and it isn't open source, but it fits in well with the VMware management offerings that they have alongside the hypervisor itself (for example, you can easily have several hypervisors in a pool, which are managed by a centralized box).

In terms of pros, VMware ESXi offers you the following:

- A dedicated hypervisor, designed to do one job, and do it well
- Easy setup – a few clicks and you've got a box installed
- A wide range of hardware support, including a range of servers
- Easy-to-use software and understandable menus (in this author's opinion)

In terms of cons, you might consider the following:

- VMware ESXi isn't open source; this may or may not impact your decision
- As a dedicated virtual machine server, ESXi can't do anything else of note
- It can get expensive as an offering, and while support can be bought and agreements signed, you might go for a free offering based entirely on budget

VMware is available from `https://www.vmware.com/products/esxi-and-esx.html`:

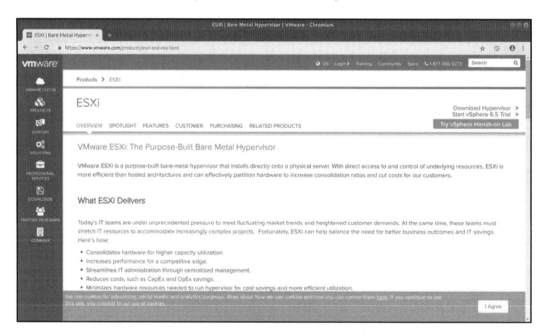

On a personal note, I admit to having used VMware products many times, for various jobs, and it does exactly what it says on the tin, with very little flourish on top. It handles things such as VM failover gracefully, in the right circumstances, and it's simple enough that anyone can be put in front of the console and navigate around easily (though I wasn't a massive fan of their first attempts at a web-based GUI).

Proxmox Virtual Environment

Another dedicated hypervisor install, Proxmox (VE), is a Linux-based (Debian, specifically) operating system that, again, has a wide range of hardware support and a friendly GUI to get you started.

This open source solution is ideal for a home-lab environment, and scales up to large installations well, meaning that you can deploy the same solution for your developers and your production rollout.

In terms of pros, you might think about the following:

- The fact it's open source, which again, may influence your decision
- The fact it's free (as in beer), with the option of paid support and training
- The knowledge that it's based on known and well-supported technologies, such as KVM and QEMU
- The fact it supports containers, as well as virtual machines

In terms of negatives, you could consider the following:

- The install base, and the fact it's not as well-known as VMware ESXi and others (though this might influence you as a positive, too)
- As a dedicated virtualization install, your Proxmox server won't do much of anything else (like ESXi)

Proxmox Virtual Environment is available at `https://www.proxmox.com/en/ downloads`:

Proxmox Virtualization Homepage

Again, speaking from personal experience, I've set up three node Proxmox clusters with automatic failover with relative ease, and everyone I've spoken to that uses Proxmox seems to appreciate what a nice solution it is in a pinch, while knowing it can extend further when needed.

OpenStack

The new kid on the block, OpenStack, is a collection of technologies that, when added together, make a solution that rivals any of the bigger virtualization environment providers.

It can be a virtual machine host, container host, file storage provider, block storage provider, and it has a rapid development cycle that keeps new features constantly coming in.

Unlike the other two solutions on this list, OpenStack is the name given to a few different software components.

For the pros, give some thought to the following:

- OpenStack has an enthusiastic and dedicated community behind it
- The components are open source and worked on by people all over the globe
- Many companies offer OpenStack solutions and offer different levels of support
- If you know OpenStack well, you won't be out of work for the next fifty years (conjecture)

In terms of cons, I might get some hate mail for this:

- OpenStack has a rapid development cycle, meaning that you generally get left behind if you don't stay on top of updates
- OpenStack sits atop whatever distribution of Linux you want it to, meaning that you have to manage the underlying OS as well in a lot of cases
- Certainly in places where I've seen OpenStack being used, it almost takes a dedicated OpenStack team to keep on top of management
- It's not easy to set up in a usable fashion, in a pinch (though development environments do exist)
- There are multiple schools of thought on what makes a good OpenStack deployment
- It's a right pain when you come to an OpenStack solution that's been neglected

If you want to give OpenStack a go (and I would encourage you to do so), the Getting Started guide can be found here: `https://wiki.openstack.org/wiki/Getting_Started`.

There's also a start page, including links to the devstack dev environment:

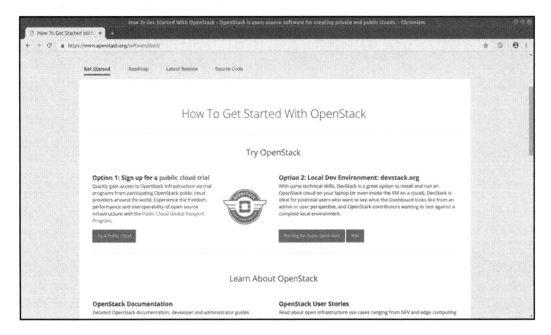

Personal thought – I know some incredibly intelligent people that love OpenStack and swear by it, but it's an area that requires a lot of love and attention, along with dedication.

How it works...

There are different ways to do the same thing. This is true for most experiences, and it's especially true in the Unix and Unix-like (Linux) world.

Here, we have three good examples of software and solutions that allow you to control virtual machine deployment in a mostly user-friendly fashion, even though you might think that all of these solutions are much more complex than you require.

I mention them here because it's good to know these options are out there, and even if you start your journey by installing VMs locally on an Ubuntu installation (using VirtualBox or KVM and Libvirt), you might wish to expand to something grander in the future.

Another option to consider is public cloud offerings, and while I'll talk about these in greater detail later, it's worth noting that there are several providers out there who'll take away the headache of managing the underlying software and let you simply install and break VMs.

If you don't have the hardware or the resources, or even the budget, you can use public cloud providers for pennies by the hour.

Take a look at Scaleway, Digital Ocean, and AWS (specifically, their Lightsail offering).

Roundup – containers and virtualization

A short few years ago, there was a movement in the Linux community. Containers were suddenly everywhere, and making fantastical promises about what was possible in an ephemeral and ever-changing world. Containers were going to solve every problem you'd ever face with software, they were going to fix every security problem you'd ever fought, and they were going to tuck you in at night while feeding your pets.

We know now that while containers are great, and they are indeed an excellent solution in a lot of circumstances, they aren't the be-all and end-all. There will still be situations where software atop a bare-metal machine will be best, or instances where a VM just makes more sense than a container, and you know what? That's okay.

If you want to, don't let me dissuade you from trying to get your own pet project working in a container – it's definitely a good learning experience, and you may find that it actually is the best way to lift and shift your installation, but don't get carried away.

VMs will always have their place too, and while a lot of testing, deployments, and dev environments have gone the way of serverless container deployments, a good local VM can still offer a nice way to work, especially if you want to understand how certain software interacts with the OS as a whole (be it a monolithic application, or lots of little applications that make up one program).

At the end of the day, it's like most things in our world. Just because you can do something in one way, doesn't necessarily mean it's the best way to do it; in the same vein, that doesn't make your proposed solution bad, and it could be perfectly functional for what you need—it's just handy to be aware of all the options.

I sincerely wish I could fit more exploration in this book, and look deeper into the different ways and means of managing and maintaining both VMs and containers, but this is not a book about either of those things – it's supposed to be a general peek into the world of Linux administration.

Remember holy wars? I've also met people who are against the very idea of containers, deeming them variously "difficult" and "pointless" solutions. If you take up this mantle and fight this corner, be prepared to lose, because the army of container proponents is bigger than the opponents at this point by a wide margin.

10
Git, Configuration Management, and Infrastructure as Code

In this chapter, we will examine the following topics:

- What is Git?
- Setting up a Git server
- Committing to our Git repository
- Branching our Git repository and committing changes
- Installing Ansible
- Using Ansible to install Java from a role
- Storing our Ansible configuration in Git
- Exploring options for IaC

Introduction

There was a time when a system administrator knew their server intimately. They could tell you every fan noise, the meaning of every beep, and what it sounded like when the metal expanded as the server got hot.

As with the hardware, the software was almost supernaturally indexed in the system administrator's head, and they could tell you at the drop of a pin what version of OpenSSL, Apache, or Midnight Commander they were running.

There's an obvious problem with this: the *hit by a bus* effect.

If a sysadmin were to be unfortunately mowed down one morning, his Walkman being thrown to the road alongside the shattered remains of his Game Boy Color, all the knowledge of the server would be lost in a singular moment. The knowledge of the strange way in which the server was set to boot, meaning it has to have the keyboard unplugged at just the right moment, will be gone forever.

You don't want one person to be intimately aware of everything to do with a server—you want multiple people, and to take it one step further, you want it written down in a format that's not only easily reproduced and modified, but also preferably so simple that even a computer could understand it.

In this chapter, we're going to look at three things that are relatively close together in the software world—a version control system, called Git; the concept of configuration management, mostly in the form of Ansible; and Infrastructure as Code, featuring everyone's favorites, Terraform and Packer.

We've actually already done a lot of this by using Vagrant as we have been doing. Vagrant is effectively a method of having infrastructure as code, though on a very small scale. The small scripts that we've put into a couple of our Vagrantfiles could easily be considered configuration management, though at a base level.

These tools are some of the best you'll come across on your journey, and Git especially is used pretty much universally, so it's good to understand.

Technical requirements

In this chapter, we're going to need a couple of **virtual machines (VMs)**.

Feel free to use the `Vagrantfile` that follows. We're mostly going to work across the private network, between the VMs:

```ruby
# -*- mode: ruby -*-
# vi: set ft=ruby :

$provisionScript = <<-SCRIPT
sed -i 's#PasswordAuthentication no#PasswordAuthentication yes#g'
/etc/ssh/sshd_config
systemctl restart sshd
SCRIPT

Vagrant.configure("2") do |config|
```

```
config.vm.provision "shell",
  inline: $provisionScript

config.vm.define "centos1" do |centos1|
  centos1.vm.box = "centos/7"
  centos1.vm.network "private_network", ip: "192.168.33.10"
  centos1.vm.hostname = "centos1"
  centos1.vm.box_version = "1804.02"
end

config.vm.define "centos2" do |centos2|
  centos2.vm.box = "centos/7"
  centos2.vm.network "private_network", ip: "192.168.33.11"
  centos2.vm.hostname = "centos2"
  centos2.vm.box_version = "1804.02"
end

end
```

What is Git?

In this section, we're going to look at the supreme overlord when it comes to **version control systems** (**VCSs**). There have been others, and there will be more to come, but right now, there's Git, and it's by far the most widely used and most popular (though not without its fair share of criticism).

Git was initially developed by Linus Torvalds—yes, that same Linus Torvalds who kick-started Linux kernel development, though these days it's primarily developed by Junio C Hamano, and many other talented hackers. It's found in software development primarily, but is increasingly used to store configuration for things like Ansible, Terraform, and any other infrastructure as code tool, enabling a historic and versioned picture of your infrastructure.

Getting ready

To understand Git, we're going to install it and start your VMs and jump onto your first CentOS box:

```
$ vagrant up
$ vagrant ssh centos1
```

How to do it...

Installing Git is simple, as it's in most default repositories (in fact, I've yet to come across a Linux distribution where it wasn't in the default repositories):

```
$ sudo yum install git -y
```

 Warning: You will most likely get Perl, and while this is not inherently a bad thing, the very mention of the word perl can make developers and sysadmins alike cringe.

We should now have Git, so let's run through some basics.

Cloning

Fundamentally, Git is a version control system that's primarily used for source code versioning (though it has other uses, too).

To demonstrate how it works, let's clone a smallish repository (in this case, Ansible):

```
$ git clone https://github.com/ansible/ansible.git
Cloning into 'ansible'...
```

This may take a couple of minutes based on your connection, but, once finished, you'll be left with an ansible folder:

```
$ ls -l
total 4
drwxrwxr-x. 14 vagrant vagrant 4096 Nov 19 18:10 ansible
```

Exploring and making changes

We now have a like-for-like copy of the devel Ansible code branch. It's devel because that's what the repository owners want the default branch to be, though frequently it will be master or develop.

Taking a look inside the folder, we'll see a lot of files with a lot of code inside:

```
$ cd ansible/
$ ls -l
total 100
drwxrwxr-x. 2 vagrant vagrant 243 Nov 19 18:10 bin
drwxrwxr-x. 3 vagrant vagrant 141 Nov 19 18:10 changelogs
-rw-rw-r--. 1 vagrant vagrant 645 Nov 19 18:10 CODING_GUIDELINES.md
drwxrwxr-x. 4 vagrant vagrant 53 Nov 19 18:10 contrib
-rw-rw-r--. 1 vagrant vagrant 35148 Nov 19 18:10 COPYING
drwxrwxr-x. 6 vagrant vagrant 60 Nov 19 18:10 docs
drwxrwxr-x. 4 vagrant vagrant 192 Nov 19 18:10 examples
drwxrwxr-x. 5 vagrant vagrant 4096 Nov 19 18:10 hacking
drwxrwxr-x. 3 vagrant vagrant 21 Nov 19 18:10 lib
drwxrwxr-x. 2 vagrant vagrant 78 Nov 19 18:10 licenses
-rw-rw-r--. 1 vagrant vagrant 13512 Nov 19 18:10 Makefile
-rw-rw-r--. 1 vagrant vagrant 852 Nov 19 18:10 MANIFEST.in
-rw-rw-r--. 1 vagrant vagrant 286 Nov 19 18:10 MODULE_GUIDELINES.md
drwxrwxr-x. 11 vagrant vagrant 133 Nov 19 18:10 packaging
-rw-rw-r--. 1 vagrant vagrant 5370 Nov 19 18:10 README.rst
-rw-rw-r--. 1 vagrant vagrant 360 Nov 19 18:10 requirements.txt
-rw-rw-r--. 1 vagrant vagrant 11028 Nov 19 18:10 setup.py
-rw-rw-r--. 1 vagrant vagrant 3389 Nov 19 18:10 shippable.yml
drwxrwxr-x. 10 vagrant vagrant 121 Nov 19 18:10 test
-rw-rw-r--. 1 vagrant vagrant 1129 Nov 19 18:10 tox.ini
```

As with any good source code, there should be a README file, which is generally a good place to start, but we're not here for Ansible right now—we're here for Git.

Run a git status:

```
$ git status
# On branch devel
nothing to commit, working directory clean
```

This tells us that we've made no changes and, as a result, our working directory is clean, given that we've done nothing yet.

Make the following change to the README file:

```
$ sed -i 's/^/The big brain am winning again. /g' README.rst
```

Now, if we apply `git status` again, we'll see our change:

```
$ git status
# On branch devel
# Changes not staged for commit:
# (use "git add <file>..." to update what will be committed)
# (use "git checkout -- <file>..." to discard changes in working
directory)
#
# modified: README.rst
#
no changes added to commit (use "git add" and/or "git commit -a")
```

As the message suggests, we could add and commit our changes, and then attempt to get them merged upstream (don't), but for now, we're going to simply revert the change we've just done that mangled the README file.

First, let's take a look at what we did:

```
$ cat README.rst
The big brain am winning again. |PyPI version| |Docs badge| |Chat
badge| |Build Status| |Code Of Conduct| |Mailing Lists| |License|
The big brain am winning again.
The big brain am winning again. *******
The big brain am winning again. Ansible
The big brain am winning again. *******
The big brain am winning again.
The big brain am winning again. Ansible is a radically simple IT
automation system. It handles
<SNIP>
```

Oh dear—let's fix that:

```
$ git checkout README.rst
$ git status
# On branch devel
nothing to commit, working directory clean
```

Note how, when we checked out the README file, we basically reset the file to its default state, meaning that git doesn't think we have anything to commit, and the file is back to normal.

Checking out is the act of overwriting our uncommitted local changes with the Git repository's version.

We can see the fact that these changes have been reverted by once again catting the file:

```
$ head -5 README.rst
|PyPI version| |Docs badge| |Chat badge| |Build Status| |Code Of
Conduct| |Mailing Lists| |License|

*******
Ansible
*******
```

Neat, eh?

It's worth remembering, though, that any changes you made prior to overwriting the file will be lost (because they weren't staged, and the repository wasn't made aware of them).

How it works...

Fundamentally, Git is a version control system, meaning that it controls the versions of the files under its care.

Most folders can theoretically be made into a Git repository, though it's usually code or configuration that gets this privilege.

When you check out a repository, you get a snapshot of where the code on the branch is at the time you check it out. If you then make changes, those changes need to be staged and either kept in a separate branch or merged into the branch you changed.

Don't worry too much about this yet—I was incredibly confused the first time someone told me about Git.

In the real world, there are a few different ways that people tend to use Git, and some relatively popular tools and practices that have been developed. The kernel method of using Git, for example, is extremely different to the GitFlow method.

We'll be going over examples of changes in the rest of this chapter, but for now, you just need to understand that if you commit and push something into a Git repository, it will have a record of that change, meaning that you can go back to an earlier version of your code at any point in the life cycle of the repository, and either copy old fixes or back-port changes into stable branches.

 Sadly, Git doesn't have the ability to import code you haven't written yet from some weird future file, but I'm still holding out hope for this feature.

Your configuration per repository is stored in the `.git` folder that's created upon a repository being imported/created:

```
$ pwd
/home/vagrant/ansible
$ ls -hla .git
total 1.5M
drwxrwxr-x. 8 vagrant vagrant 163 Nov 19 18:17 .
drwxrwxr-x. 14 vagrant vagrant 4.0K Nov 19 18:17 ..
drwxrwxr-x. 2 vagrant vagrant 6 Nov 19 18:09 branches
-rw-rw-r--. 1 vagrant vagrant 261 Nov 19 18:10 config
-rw-rw-r--. 1 vagrant vagrant 73 Nov 19 18:09 description
-rw-rw-r--. 1 vagrant vagrant 22 Nov 19 18:10 HEAD
drwxrwxr-x. 2 vagrant vagrant 242 Nov 19 18:09 hooks
-rw-rw-r--. 1 vagrant vagrant 1.4M Nov 19 18:17 index
drwxrwxr-x. 2 vagrant vagrant 21 Nov 19 18:09 info
drwxrwxr-x. 3 vagrant vagrant 30 Nov 19 18:10 logs
drwxrwxr-x. 4 vagrant vagrant 30 Nov 19 18:09 objects
-rw-rw-r--. 1 vagrant vagrant 28K Nov 19 18:10 packed-refs
drwxrwxr-x. 5 vagrant vagrant 46 Nov 19 18:10 refs
```

This folder also contains the history (in a binary format) of your repository. It is the place that's searched for when you're trying to look for changes and differences in files that aren't in your checked-out branch. Therefore, it can also be quite large.

Looking into the configuration file, we can see the defaults drawn down when we cloned the repository:

```
$ cat .git/config
[core]
  repositoryformatversion = 0
  filemode = true
  bare = false
  logallrefupdates = true
[remote "origin"]
  url = https://github.com/ansible/ansible.git
  fetch = +refs/heads/*:refs/remotes/origin/*
[branch "devel"]
  remote = origin
  merge = refs/heads/devel
```

Note the remote sections, detailing where our `origin` resides.

> There's also a `global` configuration file and a `system` file that can be used to make changes that affect every repository your user interacts with, along with every repository any user on the system interacts with.

This should give you a good indication as to why Git is so great—it allows easy collaboration because people can work on different branches or even the same branch, and there are functions in place to stop you stamping over each other's work. You can also make changes safe in the knowledge that the history of a file is there, meaning that when you inevitably break something, you can fix it with a few keystrokes.

There's more...

Git is extremely powerful, but it also has some functionality that is just plain nice.

`log`, for example, can be useful for reading commit messages:

```
$ git log --pretty=short
```

The output should look like the following screenshot:

```
                          vagrant@centos1:~/ansible
File  Edit  View  Search  Terminal  Help
commit b4542e429fcaf9f0b0edd181011a8a61859b0121
Author: Abhijeet Kasurde <akasurde@redhat.com>

    Add ckotte as VMware maintainer (#48884)

commit a32902427c8760c77623ba70873e90c3170c92ad
Author: Abhijeet Kasurde <akasurde@redhat.com>

    linode_v4: correct usage of module.fail_json (#48882)

commit 652da8255869944a99bc12389fae5cd111dc92d6
Author: Brian Coca <brian.coca+git@gmail.com>

    fix bug in config mgr

commit 87e44a7ed137d0c34b180dfb4e8ba9ed600c28e6
Author: Brian Coca <bcoca@users.noreply.github.com>

    better handling of bad type in config (#48821)

commit a7962996514eacbc95f7b245fae29556e10c240b
Author: dionben <39056321+dionben@users.noreply.github.com>

    Added support for L2 external domain association (l2dom). (#48670)

commit 2faddfc1fed4cd4c3b7084bb459a7abcc4962393
Author: Abhijeet Kasurde <akasurde@redhat.com>

    Misc typo in msc_* modules (#48716)

commit 943edb33196ca4713e9e8037721c7757740bd8e2
Author: tchernomax <maxime.deroucy@gmail.com>

    apt: add policy_rc_d option (#47191)

commit 50808ffa8fa8a2c6561035cd9c755309ffe4ea0e
Author: Chris Archibald <carchi@netapp.com>

    Add common files for ONTAP and SOLIDFIRE unit tests (#48739)

commit c7e22260355b4c08b6563fb98ebb6bf12dae5ff8
Author: Maciej Delmanowski <drybjed@gmail.com>

    Do not require TTY for 'apt-key' operations (#48580)
:
```

`tag` can be useful for listing the tags people have added to different points-in-time of the code:

```
$ git tag | head -n5
0.0.1
0.0.2
0.01
0.3
0.3.1
```

`branch` can be used to see all the different branches that Git is aware of:

```
$ git branch -a
* devel
  remotes/origin/HEAD -> origin/devel
  remotes/origin/acozine-patch-1
  remotes/origin/devel
  remotes/origin/mazer_role_loader
  remotes/origin/release1.5.0
  remotes/origin/release1.5.1
  remotes/origin/release1.5.2
<SNIP>
```

Here, we used `-a`, so remote branches are included, as well as your single local one (`devel`).

Setting up a Git server

In this section, we're going to look at setting up a small Git server, literally using what we got when we installed `git` from the CentOS repositories.

We'll create a basic repository on centos2 and work with it from centos1.

Getting ready

For this section, we're going to be using both of our machines, using centos2 as a server, and centos1 as the client.

In this instance, ensure that `git` is installed on both your machines:

```
$ sudo yum install git -y
```

How to do it...

On `centos2`, let's create our empty repository:

```
$ mkdir example.git
$ cd example.git/
$ git init --bare
Initialized empty Git repository in /home/vagrant/example.git/
```

Now, on our `centos1` machine, we can clone the repository:

```
$ git clone 192.168.33.11:example.git
Cloning into 'example'...
The authenticity of host '192.168.33.11 (192.168.33.11)' can't be
established.
ECDSA key fingerprint is
SHA256:s5NfsrM/XRuH5rXaZSaNmaUxXe3MlN2wRoJ3Q43oviU.
ECDSA key fingerprint is
MD5:ea:24:ef:b3:cf:d9:03:3d:06:da:1f:2f:d2:6b:1d:67.
Are you sure you want to continue connecting (yes/no)? yes
Warning: Permanently added '192.168.33.11' (ECDSA) to the list of
known hosts.
vagrant@192.168.33.11's password:
warning: You appear to have cloned an empty repository.
```

You'll be prompted for the `vagrant` user password (`vagrant` by default), and then you'll see a message informing you that you've cloned an empty repository.

This is fine, though, as you should now see a new `example` directory:

```
$ ls
example
$ cd example/
$ git status
# On branch master
#
# Initial commit
#
nothing to commit (create/copy files and use "git add" to track)
```

How it works...

When you initialize your repository on centos2, you're creating the first of a repository that can exist on any number of devices, and that don't necessarily have to be cloned from your central location (centos2).

If, for some reason, you're in a situation where you can't clone from the initial server (centos2), you could also clone the repository from another machine that already had the repository checked out (though you do run the risk of that repository not being up to date with the first node).

When you clone the repository, you're actually communicating over SSH with the centos2 box, and Git sends specific commands that are understood by the repository on the other side and answered.

Again, if we check out the .git repository on centos1, within the cloned repository, we can see the following:

```
$ cat .git/config
[core]
  repositoryformatversion = 0
  filemode = true
  bare = false
  logallrefupdates = true
[remote "origin"]
  url = 192.168.33.11:example.git
  fetch = +refs/heads/*:refs/remotes/origin/*
[branch "master"]
  remote = origin
  merge = refs/heads/master
```

Note the URL printed as the remote origin. Also be aware that this isn't a bare repository.

Let's take a look at the config file on the server (centos2):

```
$ cat config
[core]
  repositoryformatversion = 0
  filemode = true
  bare = true
```

It's considerably smaller, with bare set to true here.

There's more...

This is the simplest of Git repositories, and there's a bit more you can do if you want to make it a bit more interesting.

First, you might consider creating a dedicated `git` user on your system, and using this as the user that manages and owns the Git repositories. This is generally a pretty standard approach, and one shared by the off-the-shelf Git solutions, like GitLab and GitHub.

Secondly, you could think about setting up a `cgit` server, which is a small server that can be used to visualize a Git repository.

The most famous `cgit` instance is probably `git.kernel.org`:

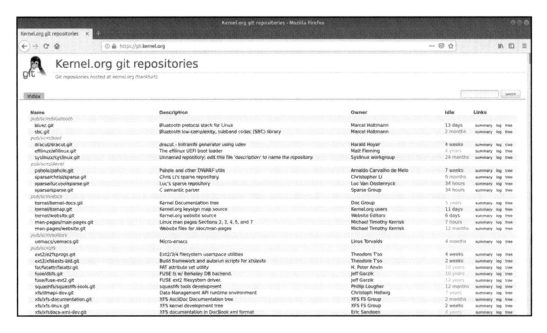

Committing to our Git repository

In this section, we're going to put together a small file, add it to the files being tracked by Git, commit our changes, and push them to the origin server.

Getting ready

If you haven't already, set up a Git server based on the previous section.

Ensure that you've checked out your repository on `centos1`.

How to do it...

Let's give our new repository a bit of information and push this to the server (proving it works):

```
$ cd example/
```

Let's start by running a git status to see where we're at:

```
$ git status
# On branch master
nothing to commit, working directory clean
```

Good—it's empty.

Now, let's echo out some text to a file, stage the file, and commit it with a message:

```
$ echo "Warcraft III was the best Warcraft game." > README
$ git add README
$ git commit -m "Adding README to repository."

*** Please tell me who you are.

Run

  git config --global user.email "you@example.com"
  git config --global user.name "Your Name"

to set your account's default identity.
Omit --global to set the identity only in this repository.

fatal: unable to auto-detect email address (got
'vagrant@centos1.(none)')
```

Ah! Now, because this is a new installation, Git prompts us to set some defaults:

```
$ git config --global user.email "you@example.com"
$ git config --global user.name "Your Name... good film."
```

Let's try that commit again:

```
$ git commit -m "Adding README to repository."
[master (root-commit) 65bf49a] Adding README to repository.
 1 file changed, 1 insertion(+)
 create mode 100644 README
```

Okay, we've committed our file, meaning that the local version of master is up to date.

However, this means that we're now out of sync with our origin repository, so we need to `push` our changes up to there, too:

```
$ git push
warning: push.default is unset; its implicit value is changing in
Git 2.0 from 'matching' to 'simple'. To squelch this message
and maintain the current behavior after the default changes, use:

  git config --global push.default matching

To squelch this message and adopt the new behavior now, use:

  git config --global push.default simple

See 'git help config' and search for 'push.default' for further
information.
(the 'simple' mode was introduced in Git 1.7.11. Use the similar mode
'current' instead of 'simple' if you sometimes use older versions of
Git)
```

Woo! Another prompt—we should set it. Personally, I chose the new behavior, because while CentOS 7 ships with an old version of Git, the march of progress continues:

```
$ git config --global push.default simple
```

Phew! Alright, let's try a push again:

```
$ git push
vagrant@192.168.33.11's password:
Counting objects: 3, done.
Writing objects: 100% (3/3), 268 bytes | 0 bytes/s, done.
Total 3 (delta 0), reused 0 (delta 0)
To 192.168.33.11:example.git
 * [new branch] master -> master
```

Here, you can see that we were prompted for our password, but once that's entered, the changes are written to the origin server.

This means that when we clone the repository from the origin again, our changes will come with it.

Try the following from your home directory to prove this:

```
$ cd ~
$ git clone 192.168.33.11:example.git example2
Cloning into 'example2'...
vagrant@192.168.33.11's password:
```

```
remote: Counting objects: 3, done.
remote: Total 3 (delta 0), reused 0 (delta 0)
Receiving objects: 100% (3/3), done.
$ ls example2
README
```

Excelsior!

How it works...

Here, we're doing a few things.

First, after we've created our foo file with some text in, we add that file:

```
$ git add README
```

In this small command, we're actually adding the README file to Git's index.

Anything we stage in this manner is added in the next commit:

```
$ git commit -m "Adding README to repository."
```

Here, we're committing (as the name suggests) our added changes to the repository. We also include a message as part of the command (with -m) instead of letting git commit drop us into whatever our default editor is set to (because every commit should have a message, since it prompts you to write one).

Lastly, we pushed our change:

```
$ git push
```

In technical terms, we're informing the remote repository (on 192.168.33.11) that some references have changed, and we tell it which ones. We also push any associated objects with these referenced changes.

Matching versus simple

A quick word on this, as we set our default in this section.

Had we set our option as matching, we would push all of our branches at once when running a git push command. This means that not only your current branch, but also master, develop, and any others you might have will also get pushed.

Simple, on the other hand, will only push the branch that you're currently working on. From a logic point of view, it's understandable that simple would be the default behavior, as it assumes that most people will only work in one branch at any one time.

Branching our Git repository and committing changes

In this section, we're going to look at branching our cloned repository and pushing those changes to our server.

Getting ready

Ensure that you've run through at least the *setup* section, but preferably the section where you committed your first file, too.

All work will be done on `centos1`, in the `example` repository.

How to do it...

Change into the `example` repository:

```
$ cd ~/example
```

Now, check that you're on `master` to start:

```
$ git branch
* master
```

Your current branch is denoted with an asterisk.

Good! Now, we're going to `branch` off from `master`, and make some changes:

```
$ git branch develop
```

Run `git branch` again:

```
$ git branch
  develop
* master
```

Note that now, we have two branches, but we're still on the `master` branch. We need to run a different command to flip to our new branch:

```
$ git checkout develop
Switched to branch 'develop'
```

Now, list what's in this branch:

```
$ ls
README
```

We've effectively made a copy of the `master` branch, meaning that all of the files committed to that branch are available in our new one.

Let's create a new file and give it some content:

```
$ echo "Keep your keys happy." > RULESFORRULERS
```

Running `git status` again informs us of our untracked changes:

```
$ git status
# On branch develop
# Untracked files:
# (use "git add <file>..." to include in what will be committed)
#
# RULESFORRULERS
nothing added to commit but untracked files present (use "git add" to
track)
```

As it says, let's `add` and `commit` this file:

```
$ git add *
$ git commit -m "Adding an extremely important file\!"
[develop 7f91f4d] Adding an extremely important file\!
 1 file changed, 1 insertion(+)
 create mode 100644 RULESFORRULERS
```

We've now got a branch locally, with a committed file that doesn't exist on the origin server at all.

Let's try to push our branch to 192.168.33.11:

```
$ git push
fatal: The current branch develop has no upstream branch.
To push the current branch and set the remote as upstream, use

    git push --set-upstream origin develop
```

Oh no!

Because our local develop branch has no upstream counterpart configured, the push fails.

However, you already knew that because you're a diligent sysadmin and you actually read the error message, along with the helpful command it gave us to rectify this problem:

```
$ git push --set-upstream origin develop
vagrant@192.168.33.11's password:
Counting objects: 4, done.
Compressing objects: 100% (2/2), done.
Writing objects: 100% (3/3), 326 bytes | 0 bytes/s, done.
Total 3 (delta 0), reused 0 (delta 0)
To 192.168.33.11:example.git
 * [new branch] develop -> develop
Branch develop set up to track remote branch develop from origin.
```

Okay, so we've now got a develop and master branch locally, as well as a copy on the upstream server.

Let's check out master to see what it looks like now:

```
$ git checkout master
Switched to branch 'master'
$ ls
README
```

What? Where's our file? It was in this directory!

Ah, but no, this is a different branch of the same directory, and, in this dark, dark timeline, our work doesn't exist.

Let's just check the differences between our two branches:

```
$ git diff develop
diff --git a/RULESFORRULERS b/RULESFORRULERS
deleted file mode 100644
```

```
index c895005..0000000
--- a/RULESFORRULERS
+++ /dev/null
@@ -1 +0,0 @@
-Keep your keys happy.
```

There's our work!

Okay, so what if we want to merge our changes in from develop?

Git does that:

```
$ git merge develop
Updating 65bf49a..7f91f4d
Fast-forward
 RULESFORRULERS | 1 +
 1 file changed, 1 insertion(+)
 create mode 100644 RULESFORRULERS
$ ls
README RULESFORRULERS
```

Boom! We're still on our master branch, but the file is back.

Confusingly, though, if we now run git status, we see a new message:

```
$ git status
# On branch master
# Your branch is ahead of 'origin/master' by 1 commit.
# (use "git push" to publish your local commits)
#
nothing to commit, working directory clean
```

Thankfully, again, the message is nice and explanatory. Our local master branch is fine, but upstream isn't yet aware of our changes.

We can prove this with another diff:

```
$ git diff origin/master
diff --git a/RULESFORRULERS b/RULESFORRULERS
new file mode 100644
index 0000000..c895005
--- /dev/null
+++ b/RULESFORRULERS
@@ -0,0 +1 @@
+Keep your keys happy.
```

Let's get our changes up there:

```
$ git push
vagrant@192.168.33.11's password:
Total 0 (delta 0), reused 0 (delta 0)
To 192.168.33.11:example.git
   65bf49a..7f91f4d master -> master
```

Magic.

How it works...

Okay, so it's not really magic, just the product of some extremely brilliant coding.

When we branched from `master` (or any branch, for that matter), we created a point-in-time clone of that branch in our new one. We then made changes to the branch, doing things like testing configuration changes, or purposefully breaking things, without affecting the `master` branch (and our known good configuration).

That much is easy to understand (I think), but the problems begin when we want to make sure that our changes are pushed to the server.

We ran `git push`, which complained. This was because we didn't have a section in our .git/config file that told git where to push our local branch.

After we run the suggested command, our `.git/config` now looks like this:

```
$ cat .git/config
[core]
  repositoryformatversion = 0
  filemode = true
  bare = false
  logallrefupdates = true
[remote "origin"]
  url = 192.168.33.11:example.git
  fetch = +refs/heads/*:refs/remotes/origin/*
[branch "master"]
  remote = origin
  merge = refs/heads/master
[branch "develop"]
  remote = origin
  merge = refs/heads/develop
```

Note the inclusion of a new branch definition.

So, the push is done, and remote looks good.

We then flipped back to `master` and performed our `git diff` command:

```
$ git diff develop
diff --git a/RULESFORRULERS b/RULESFORRULERS
deleted file mode 100644
index c895005..0000000
--- a/RULESFORRULERS
+++ /dev/null
@@ -1 +0,0 @@
-Keep your keys happy.
```

This should be reasonably self-explanatory, but we're performing a `diff` against the branch we're on right now, as well as the designated branch.

You could achieve the same thing with the following syntax, which is a bit more explicit:

```
$ git diff master..develop
```

Alternatively, you could even check the two branches you're not on:

```
$ git diff origin/master..origin/develop
```

In this way, we start to see how powerful Git can be as a development tool.

It also neatly segues me into talking about `origin` branches.

In this section, we compared our local master with `origin/master`, as follows:

```
$ git diff origin/master
diff --git a/RULESFORRULERS b/RULESFORRULERS
new file mode 100644
index 0000000..c895005
--- /dev/null
+++ b/RULESFORRULERS
@@ -0,0 +1 @@
+Keep your keys happy.
```

From our `.git/config`, we learned that `origin` is the name of the remote repository, as far as Git is concerned:

```
[remote "origin"]
  url = 192.168.33.11:example.git
  fetch = +refs/heads/*:refs/remotes/origin/*
```

Ergo, `origin/master` is the `master` branch on the `remote` server.

Our pushing to the `origin/master` (in the form of `git push`) keeps our code up to date.

There's more...

You might be wondering why you'd bother pushing to a `remote` branch if you're just going to locally merge your branch into `master` anyway.

The answer is simple: in most environments, you end up working with a lot of other people, and it's a good development tool to be able to show what you've changed and what you're working on. It also allows for things such as in-branch collaboration prior to merging, as anyone else is able to check out your branch for themselves.

It's also true that most people don't just use a Git server in their infrastructure, instead looking for solutions such as Gogs and GitLab, which are Git servers with added functionality (like user management).

You could also be thinking about the server, and appreciating that in this section, it dragged along a bit, and wasn't really needed.

Let's have a quick look at the changes to our server by first creating and checking out a new branch:

```
$ git checkout -b super-fixes
Switched to a new branch 'super-fixes'
```

I used the shorthand for creating and checking out a branch here, adding -b to the `git checkout` command. There's hundreds of little tricks with Git, and people tend to have their favorites.

In this branch, let's create a new file and push it upstream:

```
$ echo "Never look tired." > RULESFORRULERS
$ git commit -am "Another git trick, adding and committing in one
line."
[super-fixes a9b53e8] Another git trick, adding and committing in one
line.
 1 file changed, 1 insertion(+), 1 deletion(-)
$ git push --set-upstream origin super-fixes
vagrant@192.168.33.11's password:
Counting objects: 5, done.
Compressing objects: 100% (2/2), done.
Writing objects: 100% (3/3), 329 bytes | 0 bytes/s, done.
```

```
Total 3 (delta 0), reused 0 (delta 0)
To 192.168.33.11:example.git
 * [new branch] super-fixes -> super-fixes
Branch super-fixes set up to track remote branch super-fixes from
origin.
```

Next, flip on to `centos2` and nip into the repository:

```
$ cd ~/example.git/
```

By running `ls`, you won't see your actual files:

```
$ ls
branches config description gitweb HEAD hooks info objects pid refs
```

Instead, your files are in the `objects` directory, unreadable in their current format:

```
$ ls objects/
1c 29 65 7f 84 a5 a9 b0 c8 info pack
```

We can see our branches by their `ref`:

```
$ ls refs/heads/
develop master super-fixes
```

You wouldn't work in the bare repository on the server—you'd clone and adjust your repository on another machine—but it's neat to look into the inner working occasionally.

See also

You might want to install GitLab, or Gogs, or any of the other GUI-Git implementations so that you can play around with them. Personally, I find them to be reasonably intuitive, and teams of people tend to work better when they have a GUI to jointly despise than a series of console commands.

Installing Ansible

In this section, we're going to look at one of the most popular configuration management tools in the form of Ansible. Like others (such as Chef, Puppet, and Salt), Ansible is a way of codifying your server configuration, by which I mean that any changes you want to make can be written into a file and applied to a server, or a collection of servers, programatically.

The configuration files you put together can be saved to a central store, most commonly Git, and you can build things such as automatic pipelines around your configuration so that changes to that configuration are applied automatically.

In the default scenario, your Ansible is run from a designated box in your infrastructure (usually a GitLab, Jenkins, or Ansible Tower install), or in smaller environments. It's not unusual to see engineers making changes from their own machines.

 Ansible isn't just for servers with modules that cover a wide range of scenarios, such as cloud provider configuration, switch configuration, and even certificate management.

We're going to run through some small Ansible commands on centos1, applying changes to centos2.

Getting ready

Open a connection to your `centos1` machine, installing Ansible at the same time:

```
$ vagrant ssh centos1
$ sudo yum install ansible ansible-doc -y
```

How to do it...

First, we're going to just check the version of Ansible that we've got installed:

```
$ ansible --version
ansible 2.4.2.0
  config file = /etc/ansible/ansible.cfg
  configured module search path =
[u'/home/vagrant/.ansible/plugins/modules',
u'/usr/share/ansible/plugins/modules']
  ansible python module location = /usr/lib/python2.7/site-
packages/ansible
  executable location = /usr/bin/ansible
  python version = 2.7.5 (default, Apr 11 2018, 07:36:10) [GCC 4.8.5
20150623 (Red Hat 4.8.5-28)]
```

This is version `2.4.2.0`.

As with a lot of packages from the standard repositories, they tend to be a stable (older) version. If you wanted to, it's also possible to install `pip` (covered in `Chapter 11, Web Servers, Databases, and Mail Servers`) and use it to install a more recent version of Ansible. For now, we're going to stick with `2.4.2.0`.

To test whether our connectivity is there, we can use a default Ansible module called `ping` (though this isn't ICMP). You will be prompted for an `SSH password` (vagrant):

```
$ ANSIBLE_HOST_KEY_CHECKING=false ansible -k -m ping -i 192.168.33.11,
192.168.33.11
SSH password:
192.168.33.11 | SUCCESS => {
    "changed": false,
    "ping": "pong"
}
```

We add the 'ANSIBLE_HOST_KEY_CHECKING=false' variable to ensure the remote machine's SSH host key get's accepted when we run our command. Subsequent commands shouldn't require this. In a production scenario, you should always confirm you trust the remote machine's key.

Awesome! Our `centos2` box responded, and better still, our command tells us that this didn't result in a change to the remote machine (more on this later).

Next, let's try installing something using a different module. We want to install a package, but we don't know how.

For this, you could either go to the Ansible website (`https://docs.ansible.com/ansible/latest/modules/list_of_all_modules.html`) and search for `package`, or you could use `ansible-doc`:

```
$ ansible-doc -l
```

When run, you will be dropped into a pager, along with a list of all the Ansible modules available. Run a search (typing the / character, followed by the search string) for `package` and keep going until you find a module of that name:

 There's no guarantee that a module exists for the functionality you want, but there's also a good chance it does. Search for keywords that relate to what you're trying to do, and, nine times out of ten, you might be pleasantly surprised.

Assuming you've found out that the package module is called `package`, you can quit out of this pager.

Now, let's see what the syntax is for `package`:

```
$ ansible-doc -s package
- name: Generic OS package manager
  package:
        name: # (required) Package name, or package specifier with
version, like `name-1.0'. Be aware that packages are not always named
the same and this module will not 'translate' them
                                per distro.
        state: # (required) Whether to install (`present', or remove
(`absent') a package. Other states depend on the underlying package
module, i.e `latest'.
        use: # The required package manager module to use (yum, apt,
etc). The default 'auto' will use existing facts or try to autodetect
it. You should only use this field if the
                                automatic selection is not working for
some reason.
```

This looks good, and what it tells us is that the requirements are just what we need in order to `name` the package, and dictate what state it should be in.

Excellent! We can use this knowledge:

```
$ ansible -b -k -m package -a 'name=zip state=present' -i
192.168.33.11, 192.168.33.11
SSH password:
192.168.33.11 | SUCCESS => {
    "changed": true,
    "msg": "warning:
/var/cache/yum/x86_64/7/base/packages/zip-3.0-11.el7.x86_64.rpm:
Header V3 RSA/SHA256 Signature, key ID f4a80eb5: NOKEY\nImporting GPG
key 0xF4A80EB5:\n Userid : \"CentOS-7 Key (CentOS 7 Official Signing
Key) <security@centos.org>\"\n Fingerprint: 6341 ab27 53d7 8a78 a7c2
7bb1 24c6 a8a7 f4a8 0eb5\n Package : centos-
release-7-5.1804.el7.centos.x86_64 (@anaconda)\n From : /etc/pki/rpm-
gpg/RPM-GPG-KEY-CentOS-7\n",
    "rc": 0,
    "results": [
        "Loaded plugins: fastestmirror\nLoading mirror speeds from
cached hostfile\n * base: mirrors.vooservers.com\n * extras:
mirror.sov.uk.goscomb.net\n * updates:
mirror.sov.uk.goscomb.net\nResolving Dependencies\n--> Running
transaction check\n---> Package zip.x86_64 0:3.0-11.el7 will be
installed\n--> Finished Dependency Resolution\n\nDependencies
Resolved\n\n===============================================================
```

```
=====================\n Package Arch Version Repository
Size\n=================================================================
================\nInstalling:\n zip x86_64 3.0-11.el7 base 260
k\n\nTransaction
Summary\n=================================================================
===================\nInstall 1 Package\n\nTotal download size: 260
k\nInstalled size: 796 k\nDownloading packages:\nPublic key for
zip-3.0-11.el7.x86_64.rpm is not installed\nRetrieving key from
file:///etc/pki/rpm-gpg/RPM-GPG-KEY-CentOS-7\nRunning transaction
check\nRunning transaction test\nTransaction test succeeded\nRunning
transaction\n Installing : zip-3.0-11.el7.x86_64 1/1 \n Verifying :
zip-3.0-11.el7.x86_64 1/1 \n\nInstalled:\n zip.x86_64 0:3.0-11.el7
\n\nComplete!\n"
    ]
}
```

We could have also included −K if the sudo action required a password on the remote machine, ours didn't.

Cool! So we managed to use Ansible to install the `zip` package on our remote machine (I'll leave it up to the reader to guess what this package does). Let's run that command again—what's going to happen? Will it reinstall the package?

```
$ ansible -b -k -m package -a 'name=zip state=present' -i
192.168.33.11, 192.168.33.11
SSH password:
192.168.33.11 | SUCCESS => {
    "changed": false,
    "msg": "",
    "rc": 0,
    "results": [
        "zip-3.0-11.el7.x86_64 providing zip is already installed"
    ]
}
```

As it turns out, no, Ansible won't reinstall the package. This is one of the fundamental ideals, if you will, of Ansible. Jobs run against a remote host should be idempotent, that is, they shouldn't make any changes when they don't need to.

It is good practice, when writing Ansible, to ensure that the code you write is idempotent, rather than having it making a change each time it's run. The code won't be idempotent if changes are constantly made, and you can't ever guarantee the state of your systems.

Sometimes, especially when executing straight commands on a remote system, idempotence will have to be thought about carefully, and occasionally manually constructed into the logic of your Ansible runs, though this is a more advanced discipline. Even I occasionally defer to far smarter friends on the subject.

For the sake of completeness, let's do one last thing:

```
$ ansible -b -k -m yum -a 'name=zip state=present' -i 192.168.33.11,
192.168.33.11
SSH password:
192.168.33.11 | SUCCESS => {
    "changed": false,
    "msg": "",
    "rc": 0,
    "results": [
        "zip-3.0-11.el7.x86_64 providing zip is already installed"
    ]
}
```

Can you spot the difference between this command and our last?

It's yum!

Specifically, what we've now done is used the Ansible yum module in place of package, meaning that we've not made it so that our command will only work on YUM-based systems. This highlights that there's more than one way to accomplish the same goals, and we'll talk about why you might want to use either module soon.

How it works...

Now that we've had a quick look at how Ansible can be used to run jobs on remote machines, let's break down what we did, starting with the ping module:

```
$ ANSIBLE_HOST_KEY_CHECKING=false ansible -k -m ping -i 192.168.33.11,
192.168.33.11
```

Let's go over those arguments in order:

```
-k
```

Here, -k means that Ansible will know to prompt us for a password, with which we're going to connect to the remote machine (our Vagrant user's SSH password):

```
-m ping
```

Here, we're telling Ansible that we want to use the `ping` module:

```
-i 192.168.33.11,
```

Here, we're building an inventory, though admittedly an inventory of one machine.

Ansible needs to know the list of hosts it can work with—its inventory—but here, we only have one, so we're using that (being sure to end with a comma):

```
192.168.33.11
```

Finally, we end with the IP of the host we're trying to hit, which, somewhat counter-intuitively, we have to repeat.

One thing we are missing here is the `-u` flag, which we would use if we wanted to `SSH` to the remote host as a user that wasn't `vagrant`.

Since we're here, we're going to also take a look at our second `ansible-doc` command:

```
$ ansible-doc -s package
```

Here, we wanted to see a snippet of the code that we could write for use with the `package` module. This is extremely useful on a server in a pinch, or in an exam situation where you may not have access to the wider internet.

Lastly, let's break down our final command (though the same principles can be applied to the `package` example):

```
$ ansible -b -k -m yum -a 'name=zip state=present' -i 192.168.33.11,
192.168.33.11
```

Here, there are a couple of differences:

```
-b
```

We use `-b` here because we're making a change that requires us to "become" on the remote machine. This means running a command with privilege escalation (becoming root).

```
-m yum -a 'name=zip state=present'
```

Here, we've added `-a` to our list of arguments, specifically because the `yum` module requires arguments of its own, which we then place inside quotes.

These arguments can get quite long based on the module you're using, but here it's a relatively small amount.

We used `yum` the second time, specifically to highlight that while the same goals were achieved (the installation of the `zip` package), we have the option to tie our command to particular distributions.

The reason for this is simple when you look at the list of arguments available to the `package` module:

- `name`
- `state`
- `use`

You can also look at those available to the `yum` module to help with this:

- `allow_downgrade`
- `conf_file`
- `disable_gpg_check`
- `disablerepo`
- `enablerepo`
- `exclude`
- `installroot`
- `list`
- `name`
- `security`
- `skip_broken`
- `state`
- `update_cache`
- `validate_certs`

Hopefully, you can see how the `yum` module could be used to craft much more specific and detailed instructions for Ansible to follow.

In the real world, I have seen engineers write code that attempts to satisfy all use cases with one role, that is, a role can be applied and accomplish the same thing on a Debian, CentOS, or Alpine system. This is perhaps a noble goal, but it usually results in immense frustration on the part of the engineer, or the engineer who comes next, due to inflexibility. Generally, I have found it easier to simply use the distro-specific modules, and get Ansible to check what sort of distro it's running on prior to choosing which commands to execute or, better yet, just use one distribution in your infrastructure instead of a mixture.

There's more...

There's a couple more small things to be aware of.

The raw module

In this case, centos2 already had Python installed (which Ansible needs in order to run modules on remote machines). However, if it hadn't, you would have had to install it on the machine first, or use Ansible's built-in `raw` module prior to any others.

When you use `raw`, you're actually running commands directly on the remote machine. This is most commonly seen with a line similar to the following:

```
$ ansible -b -k -m raw -a 'whoami' -i 192.168.33.11, 192.168.33.11
SSH password:
192.168.33.11 | SUCCESS | rc=0 >>
root
Shared connection to 192.168.33.11 closed.
```

Note that the remote machine simply responded with SUCCESS and the resulting command.

We would use this to install `python`:

```
$ ansible -b -k -m raw -a 'yum install python -y' -i 192.168.33.11,
192.168.33.11
SSH password:
192.168.33.11 | SUCCESS | rc=0 >>
Loaded plugins: fastestmirror
Loading mirror speeds from cached hostfile
<SNIP>
Updated:
```

```
python.x86_64 0:2.7.5-69.el7_5
```

```
Dependency Updated:
  python-libs.x86_64 0:2.7.5-69.el7_5
```

```
Complete!
Shared connection to 192.168.33.11 closed.
```

It's not nicely formatted, but as we now have `python` on the `remote` machine, we will be able to use proper Ansible modules instead of relying on simple `SSH` executions.

The shell and command modules

Like `raw`, you can pass native commands to a remote machine using Ansible (in fact, you could translate an entire bash script into an Ansible role remarkably easily), though usually this type of functionality is reserved for instances where you absolutely can't achieve what you're trying to do with dedicated Ansible modules.

These two do, however, require Python to be on the remote machine.

First, let's look at the `shell` module:

```
$ ansible -b -k -m shell -a 'whoami > BUTTER; cat BUTTER | rev' -i
192.168.33.11, 192.168.33.11
SSH password:
192.168.33.11 | SUCCESS | rc=0 >>
toor
```

Note that I'm basically running a small one-liner within my Ansible command.

Next, let's use the `command` module:

```
$ ansible -b -k -m command -a 'whoami > BUTTER; cat BUTTER | rev' -i
192.168.33.11, 192.168.33.11
SSH password:
192.168.33.11 | FAILED | rc=1 >>
whoami: extra operand '>'
Try 'whoami --help' for more information.non-zero return code
```

Ah... this failed.

This is because `command` doesn't explicitly run a shell (such as Bash), so when we tried to use a bashism in the form of >, it failed. The `command` module is only really good for short commands:

```
$ ansible -b -k -m command -a 'whoami' -i 192.168.33.11, 192.168.33.11
SSH password:
192.168.33.11 | SUCCESS | rc=0 >>
root
```

See also

Here, we used an `SSH` passphrase to run remote commands on our box, but this is not usually done (especially in automated environments). Generally, SSH keys are used, with privileges being carefully controlled.

Using Ansible to install Java from a role

Ansible is great for doing what we just did, running easy-to-understand commands by using modules on remote machines.

But that isn't its bread and butter. Instead, Ansible really shines when it comes to running a whole slew of commands against a remote machine, and making vast configuration changes in seconds.

In this section, we're going to write a small Ansible Playbook to import an Ansible Role from a public repository, and apply that role to our centos2 machine.

Hang on to your hats!

Getting ready

For this section, we are again using our `Vagrantfile` and two CentOS VMs.

It would be a good idea to complete the previous section before working on this one.

`SSH` to your `centos1` machine:

```
$ vagrant ssh centos1
```

How to do it...

Let's start by creating a directory in which we're going to work and dropping into it:

```
$ mkdir ansible-example
$ cd ansible-example/
```

Now, we said we're going to use a public Ansible role for this job, so let's run a search for one:

```
$ ansible-galaxy search "java for linux" --author geerlingguy

Found 7 roles matching your search:

Name Description
---- -----------
geerlingguy.ac-solr Apache Solr container for Docker.
geerlingguy.elasticsearch Elasticsearch for Linux.
geerlingguy.java Java for Linux
geerlingguy.puppet Puppet for Linux.
geerlingguy.solr Apache Solr for Linux.
geerlingguy.sonar SonarQube for Linux
geerlingguy.tomcat6 Tomcat 6 for RHEL/CentOS and Debian/Ubuntu.
```

You could also use the `https://galaxy.ansible.com/` website:

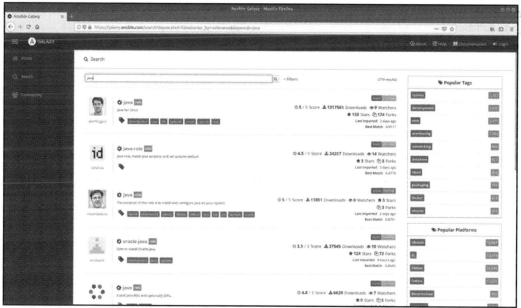

Searching for java on Ansible Galaxy

I actually tend to use the website more than the command line, simply because it gives you a good overview of role popularity at a glance. I already knew that the one written by `geerlingguy` was very popular, so I chose to explicitly include his name in the search.

Now that we know what role we want to use, let's download it:

```
$ sudo ansible-galaxy install geerlingguy.java
- downloading role 'java', owned by geerlingguy
- downloading role from
https://github.com/geerlingguy/ansible-role-java/archive/1.9.4.tar.gz
- extracting geerlingguy.java to /etc/ansible/roles/geerlingguy.java
- geerlingguy.java (1.9.4) was installed successfully
```

Awesome! We have our role.

Now how do we apply it?

With a Playbook, of course!

Run the following on your system:

```
$ cat <<HERE > playbook.yml
---
- hosts: all
  roles:
  - geerlingguy.java
HERE
```

Now, run our `playbook` against centos2:

```
$ ansible-playbook -k -b -i 192.168.33.11, playbook.yml
```

You should see a stream of information run across your screen, as the role we downloaded earlier is applied to the remote machine:

Note `ok=6` and `changed=1` at the bottom of the run. If you now run the playbook a second time, you should get `changed=0` since the role is idempotent.

And there you have it! With only three commands (realistically), you've got a Java installation on your remote machine.

How it works...

Running through what we did in this section, command by command, we'll break down what happened.

```
$ ansible-galaxy search "java for linux" --author geerlingguy
```

Initially, we needed to know whether someone had already written an Ansible role to install Java on a box. As it happens, we were able to search for Java for Linux while passing in an author's name, resulting in seven roles being found.

I have a friend who likes to write his own Ansible for a job, but I've always been of the opinion that if a solution already exists (and it's suitable), there's no harm in adopting work that others have written, providing that its license allows you to do so, and your company is fine with it. The open source community is good, and if someone's already invented the wheel, try putting down the hammer and chisel.

```
$ sudo ansible-galaxy install geerlingguy.java
```

Once we knew of the role we wanted, we ran the `install` command. Specifically, we had to use `sudo` for this, as the role in question is pulled onto your box and placed in the shared `/etc/ansible/roles/` directory, which our user doesn't have write access to.

You can see this role (and copy or tweak it required) by looking in the directory.

```
$ ls /etc/ansible/roles/geerlingguy.java/
defaults LICENSE meta molecule README.md tasks templates vars
```

The actual role starts in `tasks/main.yml`, so it's a good idea to take a look in there, too.

```
$ cat /etc/ansible/roles/geerlingguy.java/tasks/main.yml
---
- name: Include OS-specific variables for Fedora or FreeBSD.
  include_vars: "{{ ansible_distribution }}.yml"
  when: ansible_distribution == 'FreeBSD' or ansible_distribution ==
'Fedora'

- name: Include version-specific variables for CentOS/RHEL.
  include_vars: "RedHat-{{ ansible_distribution_version.split('.')[0]
}}.yml"
<SNIP>
```

Next, we created a small `playbook.yml` file to dictate which role we should install where.

```
$ cat <<HERE > playbook.yml
---
- hosts: all
  roles:
  - geerlingguy.java
HERE
```

Of note here is the fact that we listed the `hosts` as `all` rather than a specific hostname or IP, and the roles are in the form of a YAML list.

You can make a playbook into quite a complex beast by adding different variables, different rules on where to apply different roles, and a variety of other options.

```
$ ansible-playbook -k -b -i 192.168.33.11, playbook.yml
```

Finally, we used `ansible-playbook` to actually apply the contents of `playbook.yml` to `centos2`. We used the common options `-k`, `-b`, and `-i` to build up our command.

This now goes to `centos2`, and executes every line of the `geerlingguy.java` role.

There's more...

It might seem like overkill to put together a playbook for the sake of one role, but the beauty of playbooks is that they're not bound to one role. You can include as many as you want in the list within the `playbook.yml` file, and, as long as they don't conflict with each other, you should have a very smooth Ansible experience.

Take a look at this `playbook.yml` file instead:

```
$ cat <<HERE > playbook.yml
---
- hosts: all
  roles:
  - geerlingguy.java
  - geerlingguy.docker
  - geerlingguy.apache
HERE
```

We also used `galaxy` in a very specific way, using `ansible-galaxy` to install the role from the internet first. You could also include a `requirements.yml` file with your code, which `ansible-galaxy` is able to read so that it might download any listed roles it finds, prior to attempting to apply them to a remote box:

```
$ cat <<HERE > playbook-requirements.yml
---
- name: geerlingguy.java
- name: geerlingguy.docker
- name: geerlingguy.apache
HERE
```

Then, prior to your `playbook` run, you would first run `galaxy`:

```
$ sudo ansible-galaxy install -r playbook-requirements.yml
 [WARNING]: - geerlingguy.java (1.9.4) is already installed - use --
force to change version to unspecified

- downloading role 'docker', owned by geerlingguy
- downloading role from
https://github.com/geerlingguy/ansible-role-docker/archive/2.5.2.tar.g
z
- extracting geerlingguy.docker to
/etc/ansible/roles/geerlingguy.docker
- geerlingguy.docker (2.5.2) was installed successfully
- downloading role 'apache', owned by geerlingguy
- downloading role from
https://github.com/geerlingguy/ansible-role-apache/archive/3.0.3.tar.g
z
- extracting geerlingguy.apache to
/etc/ansible/roles/geerlingguy.apache
- geerlingguy.apache (3.0.3) was installed successfully
```

This means that when you do run `ansible-playbook`, you've got your roles ready:

```
$ ansible-playbook -k -b -i 192.168.33.11, playbook.yml
SSH password:

PLAY [all]
**********************************************************************
**********************************************************************
************************

TASK [Gathering Facts]
**********************************************************************
**********************************************************************
*************
ok: [192.168.33.11]

<SNIP>

RUNNING HANDLER [geerlingguy.apache : restart apache]
**********************************************************************
*************************************************
changed: [192.168.33.11]
```

```
PLAY RECAP
**********************************************************************
**********************************************************************
************************
192.168.33.11 : ok=33 changed=14 unreachable=0 failed=0
```

See also

As I mentioned in the *How to do it...* section, I was already aware of `geerlingguy.java` because the author (`geerlingguy`) is prolific in the Ansible he writes. There's a good chance you'll see the name again, regardless of the institution you end up working for.

Storing our Ansible configuration in Git

Let's combine what we've learned so far and store the Ansible configuration we wrote in the last section on our Git server.

Getting ready

In this section, we're going to primarily use `centos1`, but we're going to upload our configuration to `centos2`.

SSH to both of your virtual machines:

```
$ vagrant ssh centos1
```

```
$ vagrant ssh centos2
```

On centos2, create another bare `Git repository` from your home directory:

```
$ git init --bare ansible-example.git
Initialized empty Git repository in /home/vagrant/ansible-example.git/
```

How to do it...

On `centos1`, switch to your `ansible-example` directory:

```
$ cd ansible-example/
```

Next, initialize the directory to be a `Git repository`:

```
$ git init
```

Add the files we had in the directory already, and `commit` them to the repository:

```
$ git add *
$ git commit -m "Adding my playbook files."
```

Once done, your local repository is good, but we still want to `push` them to a remote destination.

Add your remote with the alias `origin`:

```
$ git remote add origin vagrant@192.168.33.11:ansible-example.git
```

Finally, we can `push` our changes to the `remote` repository:

```
$ git push --set-upstream origin master
vagrant@192.168.33.11's password:
Counting objects: 4, done.
Compressing objects: 100% (4/4), done.
Writing objects: 100% (4/4), 388 bytes | 0 bytes/s, done.
Total 4 (delta 0), reused 0 (delta 0)
To vagrant@192.168.33.11:ansible-example.git
 * [new branch] master -> master
Branch master set up to track remote branch master from origin.
```

How it works...

All we've done here is combine what we've done in the last few sections:

- We created a Git repository on the centos2 machine
- We took the Ansible configuration we'd written and initialized a repository around it
- We set our `remote` destination to be centos2
- We pushed our configuration to the remote machine

Now, even if centos1 were to go away, you'll have a copy of your configuration on centos2, and others can clone that information down, make changes, and push back up.

 There's a reason you traditionally see a "build server" of some description or other in the land of system administration. This is because you can claim it as a focal point for distribution configuration and managing your infrastructure. It's easy to see how out of sync you could get were five people in a team to work on one project at the same time, each in a different branch, with their own changes.

Exploring options for IaC

In this section, we'll be downloading some binaries from Hashicorp's site, and also using our centos1 VM.

Completely automating your infrastructure is beyond the scope of this book, but there's no reason we can't talk about a couple of the most popular tools on the market at the moment.

Both Terraform and Packer are made by Hashicorp, who have a reputation for making life easier for system administrators, or never releasing a version 1.0.0 of their products, depending on who you ask.

 Hashicorp are also the people who maintain Vagrant, though they did once try to replace it with a program called Otto—we don't talk about Otto.

Terraform is a way of writing your infrastructure as declarative code, with a wide range of providers to choose from, including AWS, Azure, Scaleway, Digital Ocean, and more.

Packer, on the other hand, is a way of building your base image for your provider of choice, baking all the software you think you're going to need globally into a default image, that you can then expand on with programs such as Chef, Ansible, or Puppet.

If you've ever clicked your way through a provider's online portal for provisioning VMs, object storage, or networking, you probably already appreciate why Terraform and Packer sound amazing.

Neither of these tools were the first to do what they intended to do, but they do them well, and, at the time of writing, they have a vast, vast chunk of the collective mind-share.

Getting ready

SSH to `centos1` and download both Terraform and Packer:

```
$ vagrant ssh centos1
$ curl -O
https://releases.hashicorp.com/terraform/0.11.10/terraform_0.11.10_lin
ux_amd64.zip
$ curl -O
https://releases.hashicorp.com/packer/1.3.2/packer_1.3.2_linux_amd64.z
ip
```

Now, we need to unzip these binaries, so first install the appropriate tool. Then, unzip both of our applications and move them to `/usr/local/bin/`:

```
$ sudo yum install unzip -y
$ unzip packer_1.3.2_linux_amd64.zip
$ unzip terraform_0.11.10_linux_amd64.zip
$ sudo mv terraform /usr/local/bin/
$ sudo mv packer /usr/local/bin/
```

Terraform and Packer evolve so quickly that remarkably few repositories will actually have them. The programs also complain if you use a version that's out of date, displaying a large banner every time you use them. The only repository I've come across that seems to consistently package Terraform is the FreeBSD default repo (and even that's out of date).

We're also going to be using `docker` for this, so if you haven't got it installed on your virtual machine, run the following (this was covered in more detail earlier in this book):

```
$ sudo yum install yum-utils -y
$ sudo yum-config-manager --add-repo
https://download.docker.com/linux/centos/docker-ce.repo
$ sudo yum install docker-ce -y
$ sudo systemctl enable --now docker
```

How to do it...

We'll go over our two programs in turn.

Terraform

Starting at the top, we're going to use Terraform to create a small Docker deployment locally. This is the easiest to show as we have all of the tools we need on our VM, and it doesn't mean I have to tell you to go out and start a free trial on some cloud provider.

Start by creating a directory for us to work in:

```
$ mkdir example-terraform
$ cd example-terraform
```

Next, shove the following configuration into a `main.tf` file:

```
$ cat <<HERE > main.tf
provider "docker" {
  host = "unix:///var/run/docker.sock"
}

resource "docker_image" "example-image" {
  name = "nginx"
}

resource "docker_container" "example-container" {
  name = "nginx-example"
  image = "\${docker_image.example-image.latest}"
}
HERE
```

Then, initialize Terraform:

```
$ sudo /usr/local/bin/terraform init

Initializing provider plugins...

The following providers do not have any version constraints in
configuration,
so the latest version was installed.

To prevent automatic upgrades to new major versions that may contain
breaking
changes, it is recommended to add version = "..." constraints to the
```

```
corresponding provider blocks in configuration, with the constraint
strings
suggested below.

* provider.docker: version = "~> 1.1"

Terraform has been successfully initialized!

You may now begin working with Terraform. Try running "terraform plan"
to see
any changes that are required for your infrastructure. All Terraform
commands
should now work.

If you ever set or change modules or backend configuration for
Terraform,
rerun this command to reinitialize your working directory. If you
forget, other
commands will detect it and remind you to do so if necessary.
```

 We're using sudo here because our user isn't in the group that can control Docker and, as a result, Terraform won't be able to talk to Docker either when invoked by us.

Once initialized, you should now be able to apply our configuration.

Look at docker ps first:

```
$ sudo docker ps
CONTAINER ID IMAGE COMMAND CREATED STATUS PORTS NAMES
```

Then, run terraform apply:

```
$ sudo /usr/local/bin/terraform apply

An execution plan has been generated and is shown below.
Resource actions are indicated with the following symbols:
  + create

Terraform will perform the following actions:

  + docker_container.example-container
      id: <computed>
      attach: "false"
      bridge: <computed>
      container_logs: <computed>
      exit_code: <computed>
```

```
        gateway: <computed>
        image: "${docker_image.example-image.latest}"
        ip_address: <computed>
        ip_prefix_length: <computed>
        log_driver: "json-file"
        logs: "false"
        must_run: "true"
        name: "nginx-example"
        network_data.#: <computed>
        restart: "no"
        rm: "false"
        start: "true"

    + docker_image.example-image
        id: <computed>
        latest: <computed>
        name: "nginx"


Plan: 2 to add, 0 to change, 0 to destroy.

Do you want to perform these actions?
    Terraform will perform the actions described above.
    Only 'yes' will be accepted to approve.

    Enter a value:
```

You should see a breakdown of the actions about to be taken, and a prompt to get you to type yes. Do so and hit *Enter*:

```
    Enter a value: yes

docker_image.example-image: Creating...
    latest: "" => "<computed>"
    name: "" => "nginx"
docker_image.example-image: Still creating... (10s elapsed)
docker_image.example-image: Creation complete after 18s (ID:
sha256:568c4670fa800978e08e4a51132b995a54f8d5ae83ca133ef5546d092b864ac
fnginx)
docker_container.example-container: Creating...
    attach: "" => "false"
    bridge: "" => "<computed>"
    container_logs: "" => "<computed>"
    exit_code: "" => "<computed>"
    gateway: "" => "<computed>"
    image: "" =>
"sha256:568c4670fa800978e08e4a51132b995a54f8d5ae83ca133ef5546d092b864a
cf"
```

```
    ip_address: "" => "<computed>"
    ip_prefix_length: "" => "<computed>"
    log_driver: "" => "json-file"
    logs: "" => "false"
    must_run: "" => "true"
    name: "" => "nginx-example"
    network_data.#: "" => "<computed>"
    restart: "" => "no"
    rm: "" => "false"
    start: "" => "true"
docker_container.example-container: Creation complete after 0s (ID:
4f462e164239c65605c9106378ffb260b8bb7f5d27dc1fe0e008589a1387650e)

Apply complete! Resources: 2 added, 0 changed, 0 destroyed.
```

Excellent!

Run `docker ps` again to find out what you've just created:

```
$ sudo docker ps
CONTAINER ID IMAGE COMMAND CREATED STATUS PORTS NAMES
4f462e164239 568c4670fa80 "nginx -g 'daemon of...'" 28 seconds ago Up 26
seconds 80/tcp nginx-example
```

Now, let's `destroy` our container, again using Terraform:

```
$ sudo /usr/local/bin/terraform destroy
docker_image.example-image: Refreshing state... (ID:
sha256:568c4670fa800978e08e4a51132b995a54f8d5ae83ca133ef5546d092b864ac
fnginx)
docker_container.example-container: Refreshing state... (ID:
4f462e164239c65605c9106378ffb260b8bb7f5d27dc1fe0e008589a1387650e)

An execution plan has been generated and is shown below.
Resource actions are indicated with the following symbols:
  - destroy

Terraform will perform the following actions:

  - docker_container.example-container

  - docker_image.example-image


Plan: 0 to add, 0 to change, 2 to destroy.

Do you really want to destroy all resources?
  Terraform will destroy all your managed infrastructure, as shown
```

```
above.
   There is no undo. Only 'yes' will be accepted to confirm.

   Enter a value:
```

Once again, we're prompted to type `yes` in the field provided. Do so and hit *Enter*:

```
   Enter a value: yes

docker_container.example-container: Destroying... (ID:
4f462e164239c65605c9106378ffb260b8bb7f5d27dc1fe0e008589a1387650e)
docker_container.example-container: Destruction complete after 0s
docker_image.example-image: Destroying... (ID:
sha256:568c4670fa800978e08e4a51132b995a54f8d5ae83ca133ef5546d092b864ac
fnginx)
docker_image.example-image: Destruction complete after 0s

Destroy complete! Resources: 2 destroyed.
```

Boom! Our container is gone.

Packer

Say we don't want to just use the container from Docker Hub. Say we want to tweak it slightly before we deploy it using Terraform.

This is where Packer comes in, which is a very versatile tool. Packer has builders for AWS, Scaleway, LXC, VirtualBox, QEMU, and others, but the one we're interested in is Docker.

Head back into your home directory and create an `example-packer` directory:

```
$ cd ~
$ mkdir example-packer
$ cd example-packer
```

Next, output the following to a file:

```
$ cat <<HERE > docker.json
{

  "builders":[
  {
    "type": "docker",
    "image": "nginx",
    "commit": true,
    "pull": true,
```

```
    "changes": [
      "LABEL custom=true",
      "EXPOSE 443"
    ]
  }],

  "provisioners":[
  {
    "type": "shell",
    "inline": ["echo 'Bring back Black Books!'","apt remove nginx -y"]
  }]


}
HERE
```

Once done, you should be able to run `packer` to `build` and tweak your container:

```
$ sudo /usr/local/bin/packer build docker.json
docker output will be in this color.

==> docker: Creating a temporary directory for sharing data...
==> docker: Pulling Docker image: nginx
    docker: Using default tag: latest
    docker: latest: Pulling from library/nginx
    docker: Digest:
sha256:5d32f60db294b5deb55d078cd4feb410ad88e6fe77500c87d3970eca97f54db
a
    docker: Status: Image is up to date for nginx:latest
==> docker: Starting docker container...
    docker: Run command: docker run -v /root/.packer.d/tmp/packer-
docker860052889:/packer-files -d -i -t nginx /bin/bash
    docker: Container ID:
2047e58a479904968bff162d279ac42d1e162878fb6b8e2176bb3e4551669c17
==> docker: Using docker communicator to connect: 172.17.0.2
==> docker: Provisioning with shell script: /tmp/packer-shell763812364
    docker:
    docker: WARNING: apt does not have a stable CLI interface. Use
with caution in scripts.
    docker: Bring back Black Books!
    docker:
    docker: Reading package lists...
    docker: Building dependency tree...
    docker: Reading state information...
    docker: The following packages were automatically installed and
are no longer required:
    docker: fontconfig-config fonts-dejavu-core libbsd0 libedit2
libexpat1
    docker: libfontconfig1 libfreetype6 libgd3 libgeoip1 libicu57
```

```
libjbig0
    docker: libjpeg62-turbo libpng16-16 libssl1.1 libtiff5 libwebp6
libx11-6 libx11-data
    docker: libxau6 libxcb1 libxdmcp6 libxml2 libxpm4 libxslt1.1 ucf
    docker: Use 'apt autoremove' to remove them.
    docker: The following packages will be REMOVED:
    docker: nginx nginx-module-geoip nginx-module-image-filter nginx-
module-njs
    docker: nginx-module-xslt
    docker: 0 upgraded, 0 newly installed, 5 to remove and 0 not
upgraded.
    docker: After this operation, 5336 kB disk space will be freed.
    docker: (Reading database ... 7026 files and directories currently
installed.)
    docker: Removing nginx-module-njs (1.15.7.0.2.6-1~stretch) ...
    docker: Removing nginx-module-xslt (1.15.7-1~stretch) ...
    docker: Removing nginx-module-geoip (1.15.7-1~stretch) ...
    docker: Removing nginx-module-image-filter (1.15.7-1~stretch) ...
    docker: Removing nginx (1.15.7-1~stretch) ...
    docker: invoke-rc.d: could not determine current runlevel
    docker: invoke-rc.d: policy-rc.d denied execution of stop.
==> docker: Committing the container
    docker: Image ID:
sha256:53a34cbb093015f423de89ad874afebb3b9470f3750e858729f75ed8e3f4bce
4
==> docker: Killing the container:
2047e58a479904968bff162d279ac42d1e162878fb6b8e2176bb3e4551669c17
Build 'docker' finished.

==> Builds finished. The artifacts of successful builds are:
--> docker: Imported Docker image:
sha256:53a34cbb093015f423de89ad874afebb3b9470f3750e858729f75ed8e3f4bce
4
```

Great! We've now got an image we can use elsewhere:

```
$ sudo docker image ls
REPOSITORY TAG IMAGE ID CREATED SIZE
<none> <none> 53a34cbb0930 19 seconds ago 110MB
nginx latest 568c4670fa80 19 hours ago 109MB
alpine latest 196d12cf6ab1 2 months ago 4.41MB
```

How it works...

Let's break this down a bit, starting with Terraform.

In this section, we defined what we wanted our infrastructure to look like by writing the configuration to a `main.tf` file:

```
provider "docker" {
  host = "unix:///var/run/docker.sock"
}

resource "docker_image" "example-image" {
  name = "nginx"
}

resource "docker_container" "example-container" {
  name = "nginx-example"
  image = "${docker_image.example-image.latest}"
}
```

Specifically, what we're doing here is giving Terraform its provider and the necessary information to connect with said provider (in this case, a Unix socket):

```
provider "docker" {
  host = "unix:///var/run/docker.sock"
}
```

We're then informing Terraform of the image we want to use as the base of our container:

```
resource "docker_image" "example-image" {
  name = "nginx"
}
```

Finally, we're saying that the container should be called `nginx-example` and that it should use the image that we defined previously (note the use of a referencing variable to the preceding block):

```
resource "docker_container" "example-container" {
  name = "nginx-example"
  image = "${docker_image.example-image.latest}"
}
```

Once we saved it, we ran a command to initialize the directory for Terraform use:

```
$ sudo /usr/local/bin/terraform init
```

This downloads the provider (docker) and sets up the directory for us to use it. We then applied our configuration:

```
$ sudo /usr/local/bin/terraform apply
```

Terraform looks for any files ending in .tf within the directory it's invoked from.

Afterward, we destroyed our setup:

```
$ sudo /usr/local/bin/terraform destroy
```

Your directory will end up looking something like this:

```
$ ls -lha
total 16K
drwxrwxr-x. 3 vagrant vagrant 96 Nov 28 17:05 .
drwx------. 9 vagrant vagrant 4.0K Nov 28 17:07 ..
-rw-rw-r--. 1 vagrant vagrant 251 Nov 28 17:02 main.tf
drwxr-xr-x. 3 root root 21 Nov 28 17:02 .terraform
-rw-r--r--. 1 root root 318 Nov 28 17:05 terraform.tfstate
-rw-r--r--. 1 root root 2.9K Nov 28 17:05 terraform.tfstate.backup
```

Note the state file. This is important as it contains the known state of the infrastructure you've provisioned. Looking inside, you'll see a JSON-like syntax, though this can change. The Terraform state file shouldn't be altered by hand.

I have horror stories revolving around having to manually recover the state of infrastructure, as I'm sure many others do too, and believe me when I tell you that losing a state file is not fun, nor is it going to be a quick recovery process. Needless to say, it's a good idea to keep this file backed up.

It's also worth noting that you can store the Terraform state file in a remote location. This can be configured to "lock" when in use (to avoid conflicting changes from two users trying to access the state file at once.) It also means the state file doesn't live on your local machine, or a Jenkins slave, making distributed building easier.

The preceding terraform directory contains the actual plugin that we downloaded when we initialized the repository.

On to Packer!

With Packer, things are a little different. First, we set up this configuration file:

```
{

  "builders":[
  {
    "type": "docker",
    "image": "nginx",
    "commit": true,
    "pull": true,
```

```
    "changes": [
      "LABEL custom=true",
      "EXPOSE 443"
    ]
  }],

  "provisioners":[
  {
    "type": "shell",
    "inline": ["echo 'Bring back Black Books!'","apt remove nginx -y"]
  }]

}
```

It's a very vanilla example, but it serves its purpose.

The first thing you might notice is that it's JSON formatted, rather than using HCL (as Terraform does for its configuration). Secondly, you might note that while we have a builder configured (docker), we also have a provisioner (shell).

```
  "builders":[
  {
    "type": "docker",
    "image": "nginx",
    "commit": true,
    "pull": true,
    "changes": [
      "LABEL custom=true",
      "EXPOSE 443"
    ]
  }],
```

Starting with the builder, you can see that we're using `docker` as the type so that Packer knows what builder this is, and we're also using the `nginx` image we used previously as the base.

We apply some metadata changes in the form of a label and expose a different port to the default in the image (80). We can see these in the resulting Docker image:

```
$ sudo docker inspect 53a34cbb0930 | grep "custom\|443"
                "443/tcp": {},
                "custom": "true",
```

Next, we proceed to the meat of the Packer job, the provisioning step:

```
"provisioners":[
{
  "type": "shell",
  "inline": ["echo 'Bring back Black Books!'","apt remove nginx -y"]
}]
```

This is the part in which you would make changes to the container such as here, where we used `shell` to `echo` a poignant statement to the screen, and then aggressively removed the container's sole purpose in protest.

> Packer has other provisioners, such as Ansible, Chef, and Puppet, but `shell` is the easiest to understand and implement.

Lastly, we built our image:

```
$ sudo /usr/local/bin/packer build docker.json
```

Packer pulled the designated image from Docker Hub and then proceeded to make the changes we specified to both metadata and contents, before finally packing up the image and storing it locally.

We could have introduced a post-processor step too, to variously tag and upload our new image to somewhere for safe keeping.

There's more...

Here's a small but interesting titbit. Terraform has a built-in command for making sure that all of your syntax is nicely formatted (meaning that everyone can conform to the same standard, without getting into silly arguments about spacing):

```
$ terraform fmt
main.tf
```

Honestly, I think this is one of the greatest things about Terraform, because it means that no one can have an opinion of their own, and if there's a world I want to live in, it's that one.

See also

Hashicorp make a lot of stuff, and while it's important to remember that there are several options out there when it comes to Infrastructure as Code, it's undeniable to say that at the moment, if you know their suite well, you'll be seriously bolstering your chances of getting a job.

Other tools from Hashicorp include the following:

- Vagrant, as we know and love
- Vault, for secret storage
- Consul, for service discovery

Roundup – Git, Configuration Management, and Infrastructure as Code

This is not a book on Ansible, and while I'm tempted to write one, there are already a considerable number out there (though truth be told, Ansible is so fast paced that you're better off learning as you go, and I don't usually advocate that). That said, I do like Ansible, and, along with the other tools listed in this chapter (Git, Terraform, Packer), it has made my life so much easier over the last couple of years that I've been using it.

There's something to be said for the idea that administrators are lazy, because all we really want to do is make our jobs easier, by automating away the tedious bits. We all used to joke that we'd end up automating ourselves out of a job one day, but some of the less lazy in our clan didn't like that idea, and seemingly decided that they were going to develop a new thing on an almost monthly basis, just so we could pick up the thing and decide we desperately needed to use it in our infrastructure.

Git is magical making our needs around source control and distribution seamless (except when you forget how to recover from the complete mess you've got yourself in, and decide it's easier to just delete the directory and clone it again).

Ansible is a savior, meaning that we no longer have to call up long-retired graybeards in the early hours of the morning just to find out how the heck they managed to get half of that old snowflake server running in RAM, and the rest seemingly pulling itself in from a network drive.

Don't assume that just because somewhere uses Ansible, and they claim to be fully automated, that they don't have one server kicking around somewhere that no one wants to touch because it does something silly like handle the IVR for the phone server. In these cases, you can do one of two things. Either option A: offer to automate the old and crusty snowflake, bringing it in line with the rest of the infrastructure; or option B: stick your head in the sand like everyone else, and hope it doesn't break while you're on shift (though it will... it will...).

Terraform is a headache in code form, though for all of the grievances users occasionally have with it, there's no denying that in a cloud-orientated world, having a tool that can automatically provision hundreds of boxes in your Azure subscription is a must, and if it means that you don't have to learn PowerShell—so much the better. It is worth saying, though, that I have a friend who insists Terraform isn't ready yet, and, as a result, he wraps the generation of Terraform files in an Ansible role... don't ask.

Packer removes tedium and ensures that your Ansible playbooks don't take an age to apply because you've done the sensible thing and incorporated all your sane defaults into a base image (hint, hint!).

To round off this chapter, let's talk about the age of the cloud.

All the tools we've mentioned are great in an ephemeral world, where servers can spin up for a few minutes, complete their purpose in life, and then be unceremoniously removed from existence by an omnipotent cronjob. They do have their drawbacks, though, and it's important to be careful when using tools such as Terraform to manage an estate.

There's a reason why Terraform prompts you with an effective "are you really sure" message before it'll let you delete infrastructure. I would always advise being one hundred percent confident in what you're about to do, before you do it. You don't want to be the one responsible for destroying production (make sure you have good backups).

In the old days, when I accidentally turned off a server because I got it confused with a different server of a similar name, and it was down for twelve hours before anyone noticed, the ramifications were minimal. I could simply turn the box back on while apologising profusely to the client.

Now, if you accidentally run `terraform destroy` against prod, and it also takes the data with it, you've done more than just flipped the boxes off. They're gone, kaput, Avada Kedavra'd, so be careful. We have these tools to make our lives easier, but sometimes I wonder if we're not also giving ourselves the capability for so much more accidental destruction.

 That story about me turning off a box may or may not be true......it's true.

11

Web Servers, Databases, and Mail Servers

In this chapter, we will examine the following topics:

- Installing and understanding a web server
- Basic Apache configuration
- Basic Nginx configuration
- SSL, TLS, and LetsEncrypt
- Basic MySQL or MariaDB installation
- Basic PostgreSQL installation
- Local MTA usage and configuration (Postfix)
- Local MTA usage and configuration (Exim)
- NoSQL documents (MongoDB example)
- NoSQL KV (Redis example)
- Messaging brokers and queues (RabbitMQ example)

Introduction

There's a good chance that you'll come across websites at some point in your career as a system administrator or developer.

Websites are these things that exist on the internet, where people go to find stuff (technical description). Most of the web runs on Linux, with segmented and darker corners for Windows et al.

It's typical for a lot of people to start their Linux careers working for either an ISP or a web host of some sort, meaning that a lot of newcomers to the field get thrown into the deep end of having to manage very public websites immediately. This isn't a bad thing, as you tend to learn quickly in environments with a variety of issues, and when you're surrounded by a host of other people who are all experiencing the same frustration day in, day out, it can be quite the learning experience.

 That's not to say that everyone goes the route of a web host or ISP. I started working with Linux properly when I joined a small telecoms company, meaning my exposure to web technologies was minimal, and my exposure to **private branch exchange (PBX)** phone systems was considerably greater.

Needless to say, if you do go into the route of managing websites or maintaining them for other people, you will be in good company. Most engineers you meet at various levels will have done their time in the trenches, manning the phones, and dealing with developers across the globe at all hours of the morning.

I wouldn't go so far as to say working with websites is fun, but constantly refreshing a broken web page while troubleshooting, only to have it eventually spring into life as though it'd never left, is a hell of a cathartic experience, even if it is three in the morning.

There are many different components to the web, and though the heyday of static HTML sites has been and gone (though it's looking at a bit of a resurgence recently thanks to auto-generated websites hosted in places such as Amazon's S3), there are many interesting technologies to get your teeth into.

Starting at the easiest, we're going to look at actual web servers (that serve web content), databases (that hold web content), and TLSs (that encrypt web content in transit).

We're also going to look at some other pieces of technology that you'll probably come across at some point (again, definitely if you work for a hosting provider). These are:

- (e)mail transfer agents (such as Postfix and Exim)
- NoSQL databases (such as MongoDB)
- fast **key value (KV)** stores (such as Redis)
- message brokers (such as RabbitMQ)

Don't let any of these scare you—they've just words on a page.

Technical requirements

In this section, we're going to be using both CentOS and Debian. This is because while software in the Linux world is fairly universal, some distributions choose specific defaults for things such as their web and mail servers.

Feel free to use the following `Vagrantfile` for this chapter:

```ruby
# -*- mode: ruby -*-
# vi: set ft=ruby :

Vagrant.configure("2") do |config|

  config.vm.define "centos1" do |centos1|
    centos1.vm.box = "centos/7"
    centos1.vm.network "private_network", ip: "192.168.33.10"
    centos1.vm.hostname = "centos1"
    centos1.vm.box_version = "1804.02"
  end

  config.vm.define "debian1" do |debian1|
    debian1.vm.box = "debian/stretch64"
    debian1.vm.network "private_network", ip: "192.168.33.11"
    debian1.vm.hostname = "debian1"
    debian1.vm.box_version = "9.5.0"
    debian1.vm.provider "virtualbox" do |debian1p|
      debian1p.cpus = 1
    end
  end

end
```

Installing and understanding a web server

A web server is the component you're interacting with directly when you go to a website. It traditionally listens on port `80` (for **Hypertext Transfer Protocol (HTTP)**) or `443` (for **Hypertext Transfer Protocol Secure (HTTPS)**).

When you type a URL into your browser, these ports are generally hidden unless explicitly defined; for example, hitting `https://duckduckgo.com` in Chrome or Firefox will load the website, but it won't tell you that it's connecting on port `443`. In a similar fashion, if you go to `https://duckduckgo.com:443`, the exact same page should load.

Also, if you try to go to port 80 using HTTPS (`https://duckduckgo.com:80/`), you will generally get an error saying the site can't provide a secure connection:

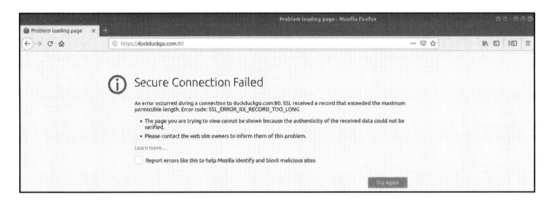

This is because you tried to talk to an insecure port (80) using a secure protocol (HTTPS).

Web servers literally serve the web, but they're usually just the frontend to other technology. Blog posts on a Wordpress install, for example, might be stored in a database behind the scenes, while they're presented to the end-user by the web server frontend.

It's the job of the web server to determine how to display the content of a page to the requesting client.

 Different clients send different "user agents," which tell the web server what type of pages it'll be able to display to you. Think of it in terms of a desktop and phone internet browser: if sites are coded to understand the different user agents of your devices, the exact same website can look completely different on different devices.

Getting ready

We're going to use both our VMs and set up a web server on each:

```
$ vagrant ssh centos1 -- -L 127.0.0.1:8080:127.0.0.1:80
$ vagrant ssh debian1 -- -L 127.0.0.1:8181:127.0.0.1:80
```

How to do it...

Starting with our CentOS box, we're going to install the default web server that's provided in the official repositories.

Installing httpd (Apache) on CentOS

As the title suggests, CentOS re-badges the Apache HTTP Server as `httpd`, I suspect to genericise the product for ease of understanding (though I've met a fair amount of system administrators who dislike this re-badge, including me).

Install `httpd` like so:

```
$ sudo yum install httpd -y
```

Now let's start it, since this is CentOS:

```
$ sudo systemctl enable --now httpd
```

As we forwarded ports when we logged into our Vagrant boxes, we should now be able to navigate to our forwarded address and port (`http://127.0.0.1:8080`) in our local browser:

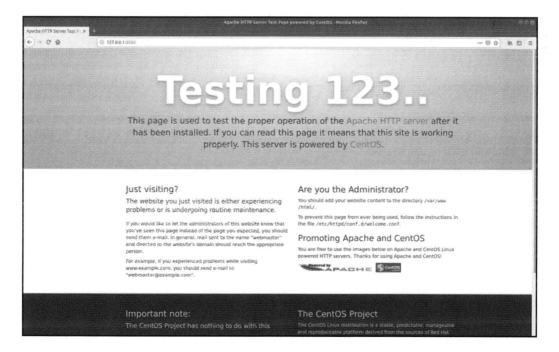

This is the default `splash` page for Apache on CentOS, configured out of the box.

Installing Nginx on Debian

Now, on our Debian box, let's install Nginx instead:

```
$ sudo apt install nginx -y
```

Once installed, as it's Debian, the service will probably start automatically:

```
$ systemctl status nginx --no-pager
● nginx.service - A high performance web server and a reverse proxy
server
   Loaded: loaded (/lib/systemd/system/nginx.service; enabled; vendor
preset: enabled)
   Active: active (running) since Sun 2018-12-02 11:54:11 GMT; 21s ago
     Docs: man:nginx(8)
  Process: 1936 ExecStart=/usr/sbin/nginx -g daemon on; master_process
on; (code=exited, status=0/SUCCESS)
  Process: 1933 ExecStartPre=/usr/sbin/nginx -t -q -g daemon on;
master_process on; (code=exited, status=0/SUCCESS)
 Main PID: 1938 (nginx)
    Tasks: 2 (limit: 4915)
   CGroup: /system.slice/nginx.service
           ├─1938 nginx: master process /usr/sbin/nginx -g daemon on;
master_process on;
           └─1939 nginx: worker process
```

As we've forwarded a different port (`http://127.0.0.1:8181`) to our Debian machine, we should be able to visit this in our browser, too:

Well, that's a lot less swish out of the box...

How it works...

What we've done here is install two different web servers, though they accomplish the same thing.

Arguably, there's no better and simultaneously worse place for standards compliance than the web, which means that, regardless of the web server you choose to use (Apache, Nginx), you should still be able to serve content in a consistent fashion.

 Standards compliance is the term we use to refer to the agreed standards for computer systems. A **Request for Comments** (RFC) might dictate anything from which IP ranges are to be used for private use, to how two systems wishing to securely communicate over HTTPS go about doing that. The **Internet Engineering Task Force** (IETF) is one of the bodies that manages RFCs.

The first server we installed was Apache, which for years was the "go to" web server and the one that is still considered "battle hardened" by a lot of the more traditional administrators out there. It's obviously the default on CentOS installations, meaning that the install base is still very large.

At the time of writing, Apache is still seen as the bigger player, but Nginx has been rising to fame in recent years, and looks set to take over (more on this later).

We then installed Nginx on our Debian box (though Apache is available too). Debian's claim to fame of having thousands of packages available comes to the fore here, as it also has a slew of different web servers you might like to try (I only chose Apache and Nginx as the two biggest).

Regardless of which one you install, both of these systems are now more than capable of serving static HTTP content to the internet (or at least your little slice of your network, as it's not publicly accessible).

If we look at the `ss` output on our Debian box, we see the following:

```
$ ss -tuna
Netid State Recv-Q Send-Q Local Address:Port Peer Address:Port
udp UNCONN 0 0 *:68 *:*
tcp LISTEN 0 128 *:80 *:*
tcp LISTEN 0 128 *:22 *:*
tcp ESTAB 0 0 10.0.2.15:22 10.0.2.2:40136
tcp ESTAB 0 0 127.0.0.1:56490 127.0.0.1:80
tcp ESTAB 0 0 127.0.0.1:80 127.0.0.1:56490
tcp LISTEN 0 128 :::80 :::*
tcp LISTEN 0 128 :::22 :::*
```

We can see port 80, listening on all available IPs, and we can see the established communication, which is actually coming from our forwarded web connection and Firefox. It's the exact same story on the CentOS box.

All of this is great, and it means that when our client (Firefox in this example) requests content from the web server (Apache), that server is able to deliver the requested content in a fashion and style that the client can understand.

Firefox can then display the content to the end user in a way they will understand, as pictures of cats, or whatever other information they might be searching on the internet (though it should always be cats).

There's more...

I mentioned other web servers, and it's true that there's quite a few.

In OpenBSD land, you'll probably find yourself installing httpd, which isn't a re-badged Apache (as is the case on CentOS), but is actually completely different software, that just happens to share the same name, and perform similar functions...

Or, you might like the idea of Tomcat, which is less of a traditional web server, as it acts as a frontend to Java servlets (usually some sort of web application).

There's lighttpd too, which is (as the name might suggest) supposed to be a lightweight web server, without the many bells and whistles of functionality that Nginx or Apache provide.

In the Windows world (a horrible place that I don't like to visit), you get IIS, which is more of a suite of internet services that's available on a Windows server.

Basic Apache configuration

We've installed httpd on our CentOS machine, meaning that we've got a web server running on port 80 and we're able to hit it from our Firefox installation on our host machine.

In this section, we're going to take a look at how our server knows what to display and what we can do to set up a site of our own so that people aren't greeted by the default Apache page when they visit our IP.

Getting ready

For this section, we're going to use the `Vagrantfile` from the previous section. If you haven't already installed Apache on the CentOS VM, do so at this point.

Connect to your CentOS box:

```
$ vagrant ssh centos1 -- -L 127.0.0.1:8080:127.0.0.1:80
```

How to do it...

First, we should have a quick look at where the default configuration is being loaded from. On the default page, we can see the following section:

> ## Are you the Administrator?
>
> You should add your website content to the directory /var/www /html/.
>
> To prevent this page from ever being used, follow the instructions in the file /etc/httpd/conf.d/welcome.conf.

It turns out that we are, in fact, the administrator. With that in mind, let's take a look at what we can do.

First, we can `ls` the directory listed in this message to see what's there already:

```
$ ls /var/www/html/
$
```

There's nothing... odd.

Let's put a basic `index.html` page in this directory, just to see what happens:

```
$ cat <<HERE | sudo tee -a /var/www/html/index.html
WE APOLOGISE FOR THE INCONVENIENCE.
HERE
```

Now let's visit our website once more:

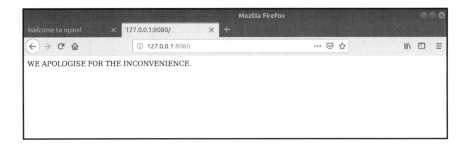

It's changed!

OK, so clearly this directory is being used for something, but it doesn't explain where the configuration on what to display lives.

Let's cat the suggested `welcome` file:

```
$ cat /etc/httpd/conf.d/welcome.conf
#
# This configuration file enables the default "Welcome" page if there
# is no default index page present for the root URL. To disable the
# Welcome page, comment out all the lines below.
#
# NOTE: if this file is removed, it will be restored on upgrades.
#
<LocationMatch "^/+$">
    Options -Indexes
    ErrorDocument 403 /.noindex.html
</LocationMatch>

<Directory /usr/share/httpd/noindex>
    AllowOverride None
    Require all granted
</Directory>

Alias /.noindex.html /usr/share/httpd/noindex/index.html
Alias /noindex/css/bootstrap.min.css
/usr/share/httpd/noindex/css/bootstrap.min.css
Alias /noindex/css/open-sans.css /usr/share/httpd/noindex/css/open-
sans.css
Alias /images/apache_pb.gif
/usr/share/httpd/noindex/images/apache_pb.gif
Alias /images/poweredby.png
/usr/share/httpd/noindex/images/poweredby.png
```

The important takeaway is as follows:

"This configuration file enables the default "Welcome" page if there is no default index page present for the root URL."

OK, so let's not worry about this for now, and instead focus on our own file.

First, because you can have a large amount of different websites on one web server (virtual hosts), let's create a small amount of segregation within our folder structure to keep different website files separate:

```
$ sudo mkdir /var/www/god-to-marvin
$ sudo mv /var/www/html/index.html /var/www/god-to-marvin/
```

> **TIP**
>
> At this point, our web server will go back to showing the default Apache page, as we've moved our only `index.html` file.

Next, add the configuration that's required for this directory to be read:

```
$ cat <<HERE | sudo tee -a /etc/httpd/conf.d/god-to-marvin.conf
<VirtualHost 127.0.0.1:80>
    ServerAdmin thebestsysadmin@example.com
    DocumentRoot "/var/www/god-to-marvin/"
    ServerName 127.0.0.1
    ServerAlias 127.0.0.1
</VirtualHost>
HERE
```

Then, we need to reload the configuration:

```
$ sudo systemctl reload httpd
```

Next, head back to our Firefox window and try to visit `http://127.0.0.1:8080/`. You should see your message again:

With this in place, while nothing on the surface has changed, it means that you can add more websites and more quotes from beloved science fiction franchises in the future.

How it works...

The reason we were able to drop a file into `/var/www/html/` and view it in our browser was because of the `DocumentRoot` setting within the main Apache configuration file, which can be seen here:

```
$ cat /etc/httpd/conf/httpd.conf | grep ^DocumentRoot
DocumentRoot "/var/www/html"
```

The reason we used `index.html` as the filename, aside from it being convention, was because of the following line:

```
$ cat /etc/httpd/conf/httpd.conf | grep "^ DirectoryIndex"
    DirectoryIndex index.html
```

This dictates which file to load when a directory is requested.

While the `/etc/httpd/conf/httpd.conf` file is the default configuration file, we're also able to add additional configuration for websites under the `/etc/httpd/conf.d/` directory, as we did in this case.

We used a very specific stanza for our own configuration, as shown here:

```
<VirtualHost 127.0.0.1:80>
    ServerAdmin thebestsysadmin@example.com
    DocumentRoot "/var/www/god-to-marvin/"
    ServerName 127.0.0.1
    ServerAlias 127.0.0.1
</VirtualHost>
```

This stanza meant that while we could continue to host the same content as we did previously on our site, we're also able to host other content too, with different `DocumentRoot`s.

When we visited our site a second time, instead of being directed to `/var/www/html` as the `DocumentRoot`, we were instead pointed to `/var/www/god-to-marvin` because the preceding configuration dictated as such.

We also have a `ServerName` and a `ServerAlias` directive, though in this case the Alias does nothing.

`ServerName` is the domain or IP address that the end user typed into their browser. The alias can be others associated with that name.

For example, you could have the following:

```
ServerName example.com
ServerAlias www.example.com fish.example.com europe.example.com
```

All of these would hit the same `DocumentRoot`.

There's more...

Virtual hosts only really come into their own when you have multiple domain names pointing at a server. In practice, you can have hundreds of different domain names pointing to one box, but because Apache is aware of the domain you're using to connect, it will only serve the exact site you've requested.

In multi-tenant situations, it's not uncommon for multiple clients to coexist on one server, only manipulating and updating their own files, oblivious to the fact they're sharing a box with other companies and users.

If it costs a hosting company a few pounds a month to set up a web server and they can charge customers of theirs to host sites with them, the company could make their money back in no time.

See also

In testing environments, you tend to see multiple websites on one box at once, because they're usually lightweight and several can run in parallel. This presents a problem for testing domain name resolution though, as it can get costly and time-consuming to use public domain name services for test and temporary websites.

One solution to this problem is to use the /etc/hosts file (on Linux and Unix systems) instead.

A default /etc/hosts file might look like this:

```
$ cat /etc/hosts
127.0.0.1 centos1 centos1
127.0.0.1 localhost localhost.localdomain localhost4
localhost4.localdomain4
::1 localhost localhost.localdomain localhost6 localhost6.localdomain6
```

You could add an additional line to this file, as follows:

```
192.168.33.11 mysupersite.com
```

Now when you go to mysupersite.com in your browser, the name will be resolved to the IP address you specified, instead of going out to an external DNS server for name resolution.

In this way, you can have multiple "virtual hosts" on your Apache web server, and because your browser is requesting named sites (even if they're all on the same IP address), you will get different content depending on the name you connected with.

The only issue with people mucking around with their /etc/hosts file is when they forget to change them back and get confused when they can't connect to the "real" site anymore.

Basic Nginx configuration

Heading on to our Debian server now, we're going to have a look at the default Nginx page that we can see when we visit http://127.0.0.1:8181/, and we're going to replace this text with our own message.

Nginx, as we stated previously, is growing in popularity. It has become the go-to web server because of its ease-of-use and flexibility when required—not that this is a marketing pitch; they're both open source and free.

Getting ready

For this section, we're going to use the `Vagrantfile` from the first section. If you haven't already installed Nginx on the Debian VM, do so at this point.

Connect to your Debian box:

```
$ vagrant ssh debian1 -- -L 127.0.0.1:8181:127.0.0.1:80
```

How to do it...

Our default Nginx page doesn't have any pointers on where to look for configuration changes, only pointing you to the official documentation (which is well worth a peruse) and a commercial support offering.

This default page actually lives in a very similar location to the one we've just been examining on CentOS:

```
$ cat /var/www/html/index.nginx-debian.html
<!DOCTYPE html>
<html>
<head>
<title>Welcome to nginx!</title>
<style>
    body {
        width: 35em;
        margin: 0 auto;
        font-family: Tahoma, Verdana, Arial, sans-serif;
    }
</style>
</head>
<body>
<h1>Welcome to nginx!</h1>
<p>If you see this page, the nginx web server is successfully
installed and
working. Further configuration is required.</p>

<p>For online documentation and support please refer to
<a href="http://nginx.org/">nginx.org</a>.<br/>
Commercial support is available at
```

```
<a href="http://nginx.com/">nginx.com</a>.</p>

<p><em>Thank you for using nginx.</em></p>
</body>
</html>
```

Note that this file is called `index.nginx-debian.html` and that it's the only file in `/var/www/html` to begin with.

Like Apache, Nginx has a concept of virtual hosts, which we're going to configure in `/etc/nginx/conf.d/`.

Let's start by creating some content:

```
$ sudo mkdir /var/www/fenchurch
$ cat <<HERE | sudo tee -a /var/www/fenchurch/index.html
How come I'm in one book, then I just disappear?
HERE
```

Now we can add to our chosen virtual hosts directory:

```
$ cat <<HERE | sudo tee /etc/nginx/conf.d/fenchurch.conf
server {
listen 80;
listen [::]:80;

root /var/www/fenchurch;
index index.html;

server_name 127.0.0.1;

location / {
try_files \$uri \$uri/ =404;
}
}
HERE
```

Then, we need to load Nginx:

```
$ sudo systemctl reload nginx
```

Now we should be able to see our question in our browser when pointing to the forwarded port we set up:

Cool!

How it works...

Our default Nginx configuration file is located at /etc/nginx/nginx.conf and it sets things like the process ID location, along with the user that Nginx will run as (www-data here), on this Debian installation:

```
$ head /etc/nginx/nginx.conf
user www-data;
worker_processes auto;
pid /run/nginx.pid;
include /etc/nginx/modules-enabled/*.conf;

events {
  worker_connections 768;
  # multi_accept on;
}
```

Within this file, there also exists the following block of configuration:

```
##
# Virtual Host Configs
##

include /etc/nginx/conf.d/*.conf;
include /etc/nginx/sites-enabled/*;
```

Note that the top directory is the one we chose to use for our configuration.

When we placed the fenchurch.conf configuration in the /etc/nginx/conf.d/ directory, we were instructing Nginx to load this configuration, along with everything else it loads at launch.

Let's look at our configuration:

```
server {
listen 80;
listen [::]:80;

root /var/www/fenchurch;
index index.html;

server_name 127.0.0.1;

location / {
try_files $uri $uri/ =404;
}
}
```

The `listen` directives are fairly straightforward, but if you had multiple IP addresses on a box, they might be expanded to include a specific entry.

Next, our `root` entry is the root location of website files. Here, it's set to the one we chose to create for our great question.

`index` is the name of the file to load when Nginx enters the directory. The standard `index.html` is used here.

And, like Apache, `server_name` is the domain name or IP address that the end user is hoping to receive content for. It could be a string of names, as seen elsewhere:

```
server_name example.com herring.example.com dwarf.example.com;
```

Lastly, the `try_files` line within the `location` block means that files of a given link will be searched for, and if they're not found, a `404` will be given instead.

You can test this by trying to go to a non-existent file in your browser, for example, `http://127.0.0.1:8181/prefect`:

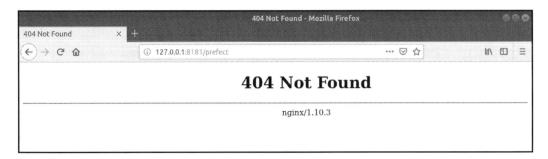

However, we could change the 404 to a 403 and reload the Nginx config:

```
$ sudo sed -i 's/404/403/g' /etc/nginx/conf.d/fenchurch.conf
$ sudo systemctl reload nginx
```

If we do this, we get a 403 Forbidden instead:

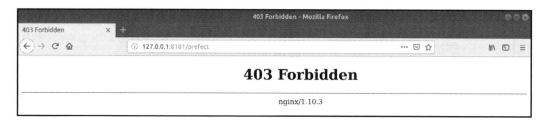

 404 is perhaps the most common code that web servers return, but you should be aware that there are more, and they do actually mean different things (provided they've been configured to return correctly). 200 is OK, 401 means unauthorized, and so on.

There's more...

You might be wondering about using systemctl reload, and why I chose to use that instead of restart.

The answer should become clearer when we cat the systemd unit file for Nginx:

```
$ systemctl cat nginx | grep Reload
ExecReload=/usr/sbin/nginx -g 'daemon on; master_process on;' -s
reload
```

There's a specific ExecReload line that runs with the -s reload flag.

This sends the reload signal to Nginx (SIGHUP); that is, it's less disruptive to the running process.

See also

In Debian and Debian-like distributions, the concept of a sites-enabled and sites-available directory has become commonplace.

Theoretically, any sites you have on your box could go in the `sites-available` directory, and once you're happy with them, you create a symlink to the `sites-enabled` directory.

Personally, I find this setup a bit confusing and somewhat outdated for an automated world, but if that's your jam, then maybe the Debian way of doing things is for you. I won't judge.

SSL, TLS, and LetsEncrypt

We haven't talked about the "S" part of the HTTP equation yet. Specifically, the S stands for security, unlike Superman's, which apparently isn't an S, and is actually the crest of the House of El.

Unlike Superman, web servers could be lying to you.

When you visit a website, you like to know that the website you're hitting is legitimately owned and operated by the company you believe it to be. If you go to Amazon, Apple, or PayPal, you want to know that they are who they say they are before you hand over your digital cash.

However, you also want the website to be able to take your credit card information in a secure fashion so that those digits and secrets don't get spread over the internet in plain text format for anyone to read.

Look out for the padlock:

Most browsers (if not all) should show a little padlock when you visit a secure site, and as long as the site isn't fraudulent, you shouldn't get a warning about potential problems.

 HTTPS is absolutely not perfect, as has been displayed previously by security researchers. It's possible to get legitimate certificates for companies you've set up that just happen to have the same or similar name to existing brands. Be absolutely sure that who you're sending your credit card information to is the real deal.

You can click on this padlock and get information about the `Certificate` that the site is using to communicate with you, detailing things such as the owner of the cert, the website in question, and the internet body that verified it:

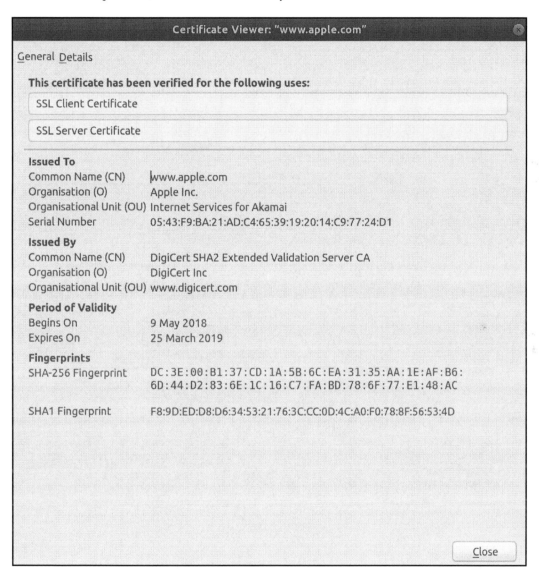

In this section, we're going to set up our site to listen for HTTPS connections instead of HTTP, and we're going to discuss a body known as `Let's Encrypt`.

Getting ready

In this section, we're going to use our Debian VM.

If you haven't already, it would be a good idea to set up Nginx as described in the previous sections, including your virtual hosts entry.

If you've not done already, set up your virtual host on your Debian VM using Nginx.

Everything we do in this section is also possible in Apache, though with a different configuration.

Ensure that you're forwarding your connection to your VM, this time using a new port:

```
$ vagrant ssh debian1 -- -L 127.0.0.1:8484:127.0.0.1:443
```

How to do it...

Assuming your site is currently up and running on port 80, inside your VM, you should be able to make the following changes to your files to enable HTTPS communication:

```
$ sudo sed -i 's/listen 80/listen 443 ssl/g'
/etc/nginx/conf.d/fenchurch.conf
$ sudo sed -i '4iinclude snippets/snakeoil.conf;'
/etc/nginx/conf.d/fenchurch.conf
```

Ensure that your file looks similar to the following by using `cat`:

```
$ cat /etc/nginx/conf.d/fenchurch.conf
server {
listen 443 ssl;
listen [::]:80;
include snippets/snakeoil.conf;

root /var/www/fenchurch;
index index.html;

server_name 127.0.0.1;

location / {
try_files $uri $uri/ =404;
}
}
```

Now ensure that the `snake oil` certificates are available by installing the `ssl-cert` package:

```
$ sudo apt install ssl-cert -y
```

Then, reload our configuration:

```
$ sudo systemctl reload nginx
```

You should now be able to visit the `https://127.0.0.1:8484` address in your browser, and hopefully see a warning such as the following:

This means that while the server is configured to listen on HTTPS and you can connect to it, the browser doesn't think the certificate is legitimate (because it isn't) and as a result it will warn you before you try to go any further:

At this point, you could press **Add Exception...** and trust the self-signed certificate, enabling you to visit the website. However, unless you're absolutely sure that you should be seeing the warning, and you're OK with it (because you're testing), it's not a good habit to get into.

How it works...

The following is a BIG SUPER WARNING:

The certificates used here are for example only, hence the name "snake oil". They should **NEVER** be used in production, by anyone, even for a joke. You should only use legitimate certificates for any servers you set up (outside of testing and development, which shouldn't be public facing anyway).

Now that that's out of the way, let's look at what we've got here:

```
server {
listen 443 ssl;
listen [::]:80;
include snippets/snakeoil.conf;

root /var/www/fenchurch;
index index.html;

server_name 127.0.0.1;

location / {
try_files $uri $uri/ =404;
}
}
```

We used a couple of sed commands to change this file, but we could have just copied the contents into the file instead if we wanted.

We changed the listen port to 443 (from 80) and added an ssl directive. We also included a snippet example file, in this case, snakeoil.conf:

```
$ cat /etc/nginx/snippets/snakeoil.conf
# Self signed certificates generated by the ssl-cert package
# Don't use them in a production server!

ssl_certificate /etc/ssl/certs/ssl-cert-snakeoil.pem;
ssl_certificate_key /etc/ssl/private/ssl-cert-snakeoil.key;
```

So, our little virtual host has access to an SSL certificate and a certificate key.

Reloading our configuration meant that these settings were applied and that we could then hit our site on 443, inside Firefox.

We then got the scary message about the cert being bogus, but we expected that to happen.

We also use the terms SSL and TLS interchangeably quite a bit in this profession (even I'm guilty of it), and that's technically incorrect (the worst kind of incorrect).

Secure Sockets Layer (SSL) is a long deprecated protocol that's been replaced by **Transport Layer Security (TLS)**, which is now the standard and usually default for providing security of data in transit.

There's been several versions of both protocols:

- SSL 1.0: Never Published
- SSL 2.0: 1995
- SSL 3.0: 1996
- TLS 1.0: 1999
- TLS 1.1: 2006
- TLS 1.2: 2008
- TLS 1.3: 2018

Realistically, you should be using only TLS 1.2 these days, and when 1.3 becomes ubiquitous, I'd recommend flipping to that too.

There's entire articles about the various attacks that can be used against some of these protocols, and I would always advise reading up on the recommendations of the day when you're setting up a web server.

Heartbleed is usually a good place to start reading up on SSL/TLS vulnerabilities.

 Some older operating systems don't support newer protocols, meaning that you sometimes get websites using long-dead and insecure protocols just to appease the XP users of the world. If your boss demands you use SSL (any version) or a TLS earlier than 1.2, I would suggest a nice sit-down over a cup of tea so that you can explain why that would be a bad idea.

There's more...

There are a couple of other things, just to make sure you've got a good jumping-off point.

Let's Encrypt

If you don't want to use your own CA, you might consider using Let's Encrypt, a certificate authority that provides free certificates.

Usually, certificates cost money—a lot of money in some cases (such as Extended Validation certificates)—so it's nice to be able to secure your sites using a free offering.

The certificates are only valid for 90 days, which is something of a drawback, but it's perfectly possible to implement auto-renewal to combat this perceived problem.

Deployment and renewal can be accomplished by various tools that are available in a lot of distributions. On Debian boxes, you might consider installing the `certbot` package and having a go at configuring a web server of your own.

Work environment certificates

It's worth noting that the only thing that makes a certificate "trusted" in the traditional sense is that you know who signed it. Some browsers and most operating systems come with a list of "trusted" **certificate authorities (CAs)** that verify that a certificate is legitimate.

The same is true for workplaces: What you tend to see (especially in bigger companies) are in-house certificate authorities whose integrity-checking certificate is installed on every laptop and desktop the company owns. The net result of this is that it's much easier for a company to sign certificates for internal use, but they'll still show a warning if any of those systems are accessed from outside (as the outside device won't have the company CA installed).

You may find that your own employer has a CA on your company laptop, installed alongside the bigwigs from America, China, and a few governments, too.

See also

It's nice to talk about security in the abstract, but the simple fact of the matter is that it's actually quite a confusing topic, and one that the general public isn't that well versed in.

You'd like to think that when an end user is presented with a big, scary banner telling them that the site they're trying to hit isn't legitimate and that they'd click away as fast as they can... but this doesn't happen in a lot of cases.

In reality, an unhealthy number of end users just get annoyed at having to click through a few warning, before they reach the site they want (or the site pretending to be the site they want).

Recent years have seen various attempts at damage limitation when it comes to users blindly accepting fake certificates, such as browsers making it mildly more annoying to add exceptions for websites, but still it happens.

This highlights a problem you will come across time and time again as a sysadmin, that of user-education, and making sure your users have a basic understanding of website security.

Basic MySQL or MariaDB Installation

Databases are great—they keep **Database Administrators** (**DBAs**) in jobs, and they provide a convenient way of storing data on a system that isn't a series of randomly sized flat files in a directory.

Traditionally, databases have been a great place to store ordered data of specific type and size, meaning that you get databases backing all sorts of things, from bank transaction records to website inventory numbers.

SQL databases are what people are most familiar with (more on NoSQL databases later), and one of the most common is MariaDB, which is a fork of MySQL.

 MariaDB was forked from MySQL after the acquisition of the latter by Oracle. This is perhaps an understandable concern, as a lot of people in the open source space view Oracle as evil, though naturally I have no strong feelings one way or the other.

If you run a Wordpress site, you may have already come across MariaDB or MySQL because they're the databases of choice for most people when setting up that particular blogging platform.

Getting ready

In this section, we're going to be using our CentOS VM.

We're leaving web servers for now, meaning that you don't have to worry about having completed the previous sections to proceed.

Let's hop on to our CentOS VM:

```
$ vagrant ssh centos1
```

How to do it...

It's considered a good practice to install software before you try to interact with it. Bearing this in mind, install mariadb-server:

```
$ sudo yum install mariadb-server -y
```

Next, ensure that it's started and configured to start at boot (this can take a few seconds):

```
$ sudo systemctl enable --now mariadb
Created symlink from /etc/systemd/system/multi-
user.target.wants/mariadb.service to
/usr/lib/systemd/system/mariadb.service.
```

Before we go any further, run the mysql_secure_installation script:

```
$ mysql_secure_installation
```

This will present you with a series of prompts. Answer them as follows:

- Enter current password for root (enter for none): <BLANK, HIT ENTER>
- Set root password? Y
- New password: examplerootpassword
- Remove anonymous users? Y
- Disallow root login remotely? Y
- Remove test database and access to it? Y
- Reload privilege tables now? Y

Remember: these are just examples for this book. There may be reasons why you need some of these settings, and you should always set a secure root password in the real world.

Next, log in to your database:

```
$ mysql -uroot -pexamplerootpassword
Welcome to the MariaDB monitor. Commands end with ; or \g.
Your MariaDB connection id is 10
Server version: 5.5.60-MariaDB MariaDB Server
Copyright (c) 2000, 2018, Oracle, MariaDB Corporation Ab and others.
Type 'help;' or '\h' for help. Type '\c' to clear the current input
statement.
MariaDB [(none)]>
```

We gave the password directly on the command line here, for display purposes, however you can omit the actual password entirely, and instead have MariaDB prompt you for the password (this way it won't show up in your Bash history).

Listing, creating, and selecting databases and tables

From inside your new prompt, you're now able to list the databases within `MariaDB` (confusing I know, but the database server (`MariaDB`) can have multiple databases that it manages):

```
MariaDB [(none)]> show databases;
+--------------------+
| Database |
+--------------------+
| information_schema |
| mysql |
| performance_schema |
+--------------------+
3 rows in set (0.00 sec)
```

We want to take a look at the built-in `mysql` database, so let's flip to that:

```
MariaDB [(none)]> use mysql;
Reading table information for completion of table and column names
You can turn off this feature to get a quicker startup with -A

Database changed
```

Once we're using this database, we can list the tables inside it:

```
MariaDB [mysql]> show tables;
+---------------------------+
| Tables_in_mysql |
+---------------------------+
| columns_priv |
| db |
| event |
| func |
| general_log |
| help_category |
| help_keyword |
| help_relation |
| help_topic |
| host |
| ndb_binlog_index |
| plugin |
| proc |
| procs_priv |
| proxies_priv |
| servers |
| slow_log |
| tables_priv |
| time_zone |
| time_zone_leap_second |
| time_zone_name |
| time_zone_transition |
| time_zone_transition_type |
| user |
+---------------------------+
24 rows in set (0.00 sec)
```

Now we can get information about specific tables. Here, we're getting the Host, User, and Password from the user table:

```
MariaDB [mysql]> select Host,User,Password from user;
+-----------+------+-------------------------------------------+
| Host | User | Password |
+-----------+------+-------------------------------------------+
| localhost | root | *F61E89B5042AB6D880D5BA79586B46BA93FABF09 |
| 127.0.0.1 | root | *F61E89B5042AB6D880D5BA79586B46BA93FABF09 |
| ::1 | root | *F61E89B5042AB6D880D5BA79586B46BA93FABF09 |
+-----------+------+-------------------------------------------+
3 rows in set (0.00 sec)
```

On top of this, we can create our own database and tables, too.

Let's create `exampledb` as a database:

```
MariaDB [mysql]> create database exampledb;
Query OK, 1 row affected (0.00 sec)
```

We can then `use` this database and add a table:

```
MariaDB [mysql]> use exampledb;
Database changed
MariaDB [exampledb]> create table exampletable (food varchar(10),
goodbad char(1));
Query OK, 0 rows affected (0.00 sec)
```

Let's `describe` the table we just created, looking at our fields:

```
MariaDB [exampledb]> describe exampletable;
+----------+-------------+------+-----+---------+-------+
| Field    | Type        | Null | Key | Default | Extra |
+----------+-------------+------+-----+---------+-------+
| food     | varchar(10) | YES  |     | NULL    |       |
| goodbad  | char(1)     | YES  |     | NULL    |       |
+----------+-------------+------+-----+---------+-------+
2 rows in set (0.00 sec)
```

Next, populate it with some data:

```
MariaDB [exampledb]> insert into exampletable values
('strawberries','b');
Query OK, 1 row affected, 1 warning (0.00 sec)
```

Now we can see what we've just put into our table by `selecting` the contents:

```
MariaDB [exampledb]> select * from exampletable;
+------------+---------+
| food       | goodbad |
+------------+---------+
| strawberri | b       |
+------------+---------+
1 row in set (0.00 sec)
```

To exit your database, type `exit` (or hit *CTRL + D*):

```
MariaDB [exampledb]> exit
Bye
$
```

How it works...

We installed MariaDB on our system and started it. As a result of that, we created several databases and associated data in the /var/lib/mysql directory:

```
$ ls /var/lib/mysql
aria_log.00000001 exampledb ib_logfile0 mysql performance_schema
aria_log_control ibdata1 ib_logfile1 mysql.sock
```

After running through the secure setup script, we then entered our database using the password we'd just set:

```
$ mysql -uroot -pexamplerootpassword
```

This dropped us into a completely different shell, one within the MariaDB program, which enabled us to manipulate the databases that MariaDB controls.

We created a database and a table inside it after a bit of poking around:

```
MariaDB [mysql]> create database exampledb;
MariaDB [exampledb]> create table exampletable (food varchar(10),
goodbad char(1));
```

The table we specifically created had the name exampletable. We gave it two fields: a food field and a goodbad field.

We then inserted some data into the database:

```
MariaDB [exampledb]> insert into exampletable values
('strawberries','b');
```

As it happens, because we set the food field to be a varchar of 10, the strawberries entry was too long, leading it to be cut off:

```
MariaDB [exampledb]> select * from exampletable;
+------------+---------+
| food       | goodbad |
+------------+---------+
| strawberri | b       |
+------------+---------+
1 row in set (0.00 sec)
```

This highlights one of the good things about traditional SQL databases, where you can be very granular about the type of data that's stored in each field and how much data you can store there.

This database now exists on our filesystem, as seen when we listed the `mysql` directory previously:

```
$ sudo ls /var/lib/mysql/exampledb/
db.opt exampletable.frm
```

When you reboot your system, the changes you made to the database will continue to exist.

There's more...

As hinted at in the opening blurb, MariaDB is a fork of MySQL, which is the reason that while we installed `MariaDB` here, we also used the `mysql` series of commands for interacting with it. This was to ensure backwards compatibility.

See also

There are also database permissions, which we haven't covered, and which are just as crucial as regular filesystem permissions. You don't want two Wordpress installations on the same host to be able to read the database of each other, so you would create a dedicated user for each and give them their own DB within Maria.

Basic PostgreSQL installation

There's another popular SQL database out there, and I'm not talking about MSSQL (which is OK, and it even works on Linux these days!).

PostgreSQL (pronounce it however you want; everyone else does) has been around since 1996, and a lot of people swear by it as a vastly superior product to MySQL or MariaDB.

Personally, I don't get all that excited about databases, so these sort of conversations usually pass me by in a haze of wondering-where-my-next-coffee-is-going-to-come-from.

Like MySQL and MariaDB, Postgres is available in a lot of default repositories, and a lot of popular software will give you the option of using Postgres as a backend instead of MariaDB.

Getting ready

In this section, we're going to use our CentOS machine once more.

Hop on to our CentOS VM (or stay on it if you're there already):

```
$ vagrant ssh centos1
```

How to do it...

Like Maria, we actually have to install the software first:

```
$ sudo yum install postgresql-server -y
```

Unlike Maria, we have to set Postgres up before we can use it:

```
$ sudo postgresql-setup initdb
Initializing database ... OK
```

However, once that's done, you can start and enable the server:

```
$ sudo systemctl enable --now postgresql
```

Now, log into your database (in a slightly different fashion than Maria):

```
$ sudo -u postgres psql
psql (9.2.24)
Type "help" for help.

postgres=#
```

Listing, creating, and selecting databases and tables

Some people find it easier to remember Postgres commands and syntax compared to MariaDB and MySQL. Personally, I always have to look them up, which results in liberal use of \?, which drops you into the `help` menu.

Starting at the basics, use \l to list all databases that Postgres manages:

```
postgres-# \l
                              List of databases
    Name  |  Owner  | Encoding | Collate | Ctype | Access privileges
----------+---------+----------+---------+-------+---------
```

```
----------------
 postgres  | postgres | UTF8 | en_GB.UTF-8 | en_GB.UTF-8 |
 template0 | postgres | UTF8 | en_GB.UTF-8 | en_GB.UTF-8 | =c/postgres
+
           | | | | | postgres=CTc/postgres
 template1 | postgres | UTF8 | en_GB.UTF-8 | en_GB.UTF-8 | =c/postgres
+
           | | | | | postgres=CTc/postgres
(3 rows)
```

To create a database, we're going to copy one of the two templates available to us:

```
postgres=# create database exampledb template template1;
CREATE DATABASE
```

To change to our new database, use \c:

```
postgres=# \c exampledb
You are now connected to database "exampledb" as user "postgres".
```

You might think that to list tables we would use \t, or perhaps \lt, but you'd be incorrect.

To list tables in the current database, use \dt:

```
exampledb=# \dt
No relations found.
```

There's none in this DB, so let's create one:

```
exampledb=# create table prime_ministers(firstname varchar(10),
lastname varchar(10));
CREATE TABLE
```

We also need to populate it:

```
exampledb=# insert into prime_ministers (firstname, lastname) values
('Lord', 'Rosebury'), ('George', 'Canning'), ('Tony', 'Blair');
INSERT 0 3
```

Then, we need to describe it:

```
exampledb=# \d prime_ministers
        Table "public.prime_ministers"
  Column   | Type | Modifiers
-----------+------------------------+-----------
 firstname | character varying(10) |
 lastname  | character varying(10) |
```

Finally, we need to select from it:

```
exampledb=# select * from prime_ministers;
 firstname | lastname
-----------+----------
 Lord | Rosebury
 George | Canning
 Tony | Blair
(3 rows)
```

Exit Postgres with \q or *CTRL + D*:

```
exampledb=# \q
$
```

How it works...

After installing Postgres, we end up with data in /var/lib/pgsql, like so:

```
$ sudo ls /var/lib/pgsql/
backups data initdb.log
```

We then logged into our database, using the user that was created for us during installation:

```
$ sudo -u postgres psql
$ cat /etc/passwd | grep postgres
postgres:x:26:26:PostgreSQL Server:/var/lib/pgsql:/bin/bash
```

Once inside, we proceeded to create a database of our own, using template1 as a template:

```
postgres=# create database exampledb template template1;
```

template1 can be modified so that you can have a consistent starting point for new systems, though, again, I find that this is easier to store in infrastructure as code repositories nowadays.

We created a table inside our database (after changing to it):

```
exampledb=# create table prime_ministers(firstname varchar(10),
lastname varchar(10));
```

Note that again we're defining specific fields, with types that are associated (`varchar` is a very flexible data type, but it's not a good idea to use it for everything. Using proper types for the sort of data you want to associate with a field is better for performance).

We populated our table with content, described, and selected from it:

```
exampledb=# insert into prime_ministers (firstname, lastname) values
('Lord', 'Rosebury'), ('George', 'Canning'), ('Tony', 'Blair');
exampledb=# \d prime_ministers
exampledb=# select * from prime_ministers;
```

Hopefully, you've noted that a lot of the syntax we used in this section is the exact same as the syntax that was used in the MariaDB installation. There's a reason for this, and it's because of the name `SQL` that both of these databases carry.

Structured Query Language is reasonably consistent, but it's not the case that a command used in one SQL DB will be copy-and-pastable into another DB. Sadly, that's a pipe dream for the most part.

Outside of the table and database manipulation commands (`\l`, `\dt`, and so on), you'd be forgiven for confusing Postgres and Maria syntax, but it's sometimes just different enough to be annoying.

We've also not added MSSQL into the mix.

 If you ever hear someone refer to SQL as seeqwel, instead of S.Q.L., there's a good chance they've picked up the name from a Windows DBA, or someone old enough to remember SQL was originally the "Structured English Query Language". It no longer has an "e" in the name, but some people insist on creating this ephemeral "e" when they pronounce the acronym.

Holy wars...

Local MTA usage and configuration (Postfix)

Email still exists, and while this is a travesty in itself, it also offers us the opportunity to look at why you might find yourself interacting with a mail server in your day-to-day job.

Traditionally, servers sometimes ran a series of checks on a nightly or weekly basis before compiling the results into a document and firing it off to the sysadmin, who could then peruse the report and pick up on anomalies or unexpected behavior. Mostly, this is a forgotten art, and very few people ever bother to configure the default mailing location on their system to be anything other than root@localhost.

It's for this reason that you occasionally see you have new mail or a similar notification when you log into a console. The mail in there is usually something that you don't care too much about, from a program that informed you it was broken in a different way five days before.

That's not to say that mail isn't important—it's still actively used by monitoring systems as a first "alert" method, and, as surprising as it sounds, some people really do still run their own mail servers (though, these days, you're more likely to find a company using an off-the-shelf solution such as ProtonMail, configured with their own domain records).

Email has issues, even when used as an alerting method in a monitoring system. I've lost count of the number of places I've been who've had a Nagios, Icinga2, or Zabbix set up, configured to email out when there's a problem, but also when the problem goes away, or when there might possibly be a problem that someone should look at. An alert email can mount up fast, resulting in alert fatigue when engineers simply pipe their email to a junk folder and never check it (except when it gets too full and they occasionally empty it out). Text messages are a much more annoying method of alerting—try those.

Getting ready

In this section, we're going to use our CentOS VM, mostly because Postfix is installed by default on CentOS boxes.

Log on to your CentOS box and make sure that Postfix is running:

```
$ vagrant ssh centos1
$ systemctl status postfix
● postfix.service - Postfix Mail Transport Agent
   Loaded: loaded (/usr/lib/systemd/system/postfix.service; enabled;
vendor preset: disabled)
   Active: active (running) since Sun 2018-12-02 11:35:12 UTC; 21h ago
 Main PID: 1125 (master)
```

```
CGroup: /system.slice/postfix.service
        ├── 1125 /usr/libexec/postfix/master -w
        ├── 1129 qmgr -l -t unix -u
        └──10453 pickup -l -t unix -u
```

If it's not installed and not running, you can simply install the postfix package:

```
$ sudo yum install postfix -y
```

How to do it...

Mostly, you'll find that Postfix is already installed and configured, so let's trawl through what we've got out of the box and look at some common utilities.

First, let's check which MTA your system is configured to use by using the alternatives command:

```
$ alternatives --list | grep mta
mta auto /usr/sbin/sendmail.postfix
```

This tells us that the system is utilizing Postfix to send mail.

Try sending some mail to an example address. For this, we first need to install a small command line, that is, mailx:

```
$ sudo yum install mailx -y
```

You can now run the following mail command, writing whatever you want into the newlines (and ending the email with a single . on the last line):

```
$ mail -s "Example Subject" packt@example.co
This is an example email.
We end emails written in this way, using the '.' symbol.
That way, the client knows when the email has come to a close.
.
EOT
$
```

If we now type mail again, we get dropped into the mail shell:

```
$ mail
Heirloom Mail version 12.5 7/5/10. Type ? for help.
"/var/spool/mail/vagrant": 1 message 1 unread
>U 1 Mail Delivery System Mon Dec 3 09:35 76/2632 "Undelivered Mail
Returned to Sender"
&
```

Note what we're informed that we have one message, one of which is unread, and below that we get the emboldened line, with the subject in quotes.

To open the message, type in the number corresponding to the message in question:

```
                                    vagrant@centos1:~                              ● ● ●
 File  Edit  View  Search  Terminal  Help
Message  1:
From MAILER-DAEMON  Mon Dec  3 09:35:43 2018
Return-Path: <>
X-Original-To: vagrant@centos1.localdomain
Delivered-To: vagrant@centos1.localdomain
Date: Mon,  3 Dec 2018 09:35:43 +0000 (UTC)
From: MAILER-DAEMON@centos1.localdomain (Mail Delivery System)
Subject: Undelivered Mail Returned to Sender
To: vagrant@centos1.localdomain
Auto-Submitted: auto-replied
Content-Type: multipart/report; report-type=delivery-status;
        boundary="8E9A1206B117.1543829743/centos1.localdomain"
Status: RO

Part 1:
Content-Description: Notification
Content-Type: text/plain; charset=us-ascii

This is the mail system at host centos1.localdomain.

I'm sorry to have to inform you that your message could not
be delivered to one or more recipients. It's attached below.

For further assistance, please send mail to postmaster.

If you do so, please include this problem report. You can
delete your own text from the attached returned message.

                    The mail system

<packt@example.co>: Host or domain name not found. Name service error for
    name=example.co type=AAAA: Host not found

Part 2:
Content-Description: Delivery report
Content-Type: message/delivery-status


Part 3:
Content-Description: Undelivered Message
Content-Type: message/rfc822

From vagrant@centos1.localdomain Mon Dec  3 09:35:43 2018
Return-Path: <vagrant@centos1.localdomain>
Date: Mon, 03 Dec 2018 09:35:43 +0000
To: packt@example.co
Subject: Example Subject
User-Agent: Heirloom mailx 12.5 7/5/10
Content-Type: text/plain; charset=us-ascii
From: vagrant@centos1.localdomain (vagrant)

This is an example email.
We end emails written in this way, using the '.' symbol.
That way, the client knows when the email has come to a close.
& █
```

You're dropped into a pager, which allows you to scroll through your message.

You can see a few important things in this message, the first of which being that the responding system is MAILER-DAEMON@centos1.localdomain (mail delivery system), which suggests that our message didn't get very far.

The email then suggests some things you can do to help alleviate your issue, the first of which is contact the postmaster, who, like the pagemaster from the film of the same name, tends to have a certain ethereal quality.

At the bottom, you get a snippet of your email.

What does this tell us? Well, first and foremost, it tells us that your mail server can't send the message you just attempted to email.

Next, it tells us that Postfix is functioning enough to process mail, because a bounce is still mail.

main.cf

Postfix uses a primary configuration file at /etc/postfix/main.cf.

This file contains a lot of configuration options, but out of the box, it's not configured to do much of anything (it won't accept incoming mail from another system, for example).

/etc/aliases

This is the database, or map, of accounts that receive certain mail.

Generally, the only configuration change made in this file is the destination for the root's mail. On a local system, you could map this to your user:

```
# Person who should get root's mail
root: vagrant
```

Then, you run newaliases to apply this change:

```
$ sudo newaliases
```

Again, it's not done frequently, but some people still like to grab emails that are intended for root just to make sure that random programs aren't dying and screaming into the void as they're claimed by the reaper.

How it works...

For more detailed output on what's going on when your message fails to send, you can usually check /var/log/maillog:

```
$ sudo cat /var/log/maillog
Dec 2 11:35:12 localhost postfix/postfix-script[1120]: starting the
Postfix mail system
Dec 2 11:35:12 localhost postfix/master[1125]: daemon started --
version 2.10.1, configuration /etc/postfix
Dec 3 09:35:43 localhost postfix/pickup[11157]: 8E9A1206B117: uid=1000
from=<vagrant>
Dec 3 09:35:43 localhost postfix/cleanup[11317]: 8E9A1206B117:
message-id=<20181203093543.8E9A1206B117@centos1.localdomain>
Dec 3 09:35:43 localhost postfix/qmgr[1129]: 8E9A1206B117:
from=<vagrant@centos1.localdomain>, size=601, nrcpt=1 (queue active)
Dec 3 09:35:43 localhost postfix/smtp[11319]: 8E9A1206B117:
to=<packt@example.co>, relay=none, delay=0.12,
delays=0.04/0.01/0.06/0, dsn=5.4.4, status=bounced (Host or domain
name not found. Name service error for name=example.co type=AAAA: Host
not found)
Dec 3 09:35:43 localhost postfix/cleanup[11317]: A88F7206B118:
message-id=<20181203093543.A88F7206B118@centos1.localdomain>
Dec 3 09:35:43 localhost postfix/qmgr[1129]: A88F7206B118: from=<>,
size=2545, nrcpt=1 (queue active)
Dec 3 09:35:43 localhost postfix/bounce[11320]: 8E9A1206B117: sender
non-delivery notification: A88F7206B118
Dec 3 09:35:43 localhost postfix/qmgr[1129]: 8E9A1206B117: removed
Dec 3 09:35:43 localhost postfix/local[11321]: A88F7206B118:
to=<vagrant@centos1.localdomain>, relay=local, delay=0.02,
delays=0/0.02/0/0, dsn=2.0.0, status=sent (delivered to mailbox)
Dec 3 09:35:43 localhost postfix/qmgr[1129]: A88F7206B118: removed
```

Here, we get a bit of detail around what happened, and if we find the message we want, we can follow the message-id through the thread of the message.

First, we can see the message being picked up by Postfix:

```
Dec 3 09:35:43 localhost postfix/pickup[11157]: 8E9A1206B117: uid=1000
from=<vagrant>
```

Next, the daemon processes the message before passing it to the mail queue:

```
Dec 3 09:35:43 localhost postfix/cleanup[11317]: 8E9A1206B117:
message-id=<20181203093543.8E9A1206B117@centos1.localdomain>
```

We learn that the message is on the queue, waiting to be sent:

```
Dec 3 09:35:43 localhost postfix/qmgr[1129]: 8E9A1206B117:
from=<vagrant@centos1.localdomain>, size=601, nrcpt=1 (queue active)
```

Finally (for this message), SMTP tries to process the mail:

```
Dec 3 09:35:43 localhost postfix/smtp[11319]: 8E9A1206B117:
to=<packt@example.co>, relay=none, delay=0.12,
delays=0.04/0.01/0.06/0, dsn=5.4.4, status=bounced (Host or domain
name not found. Name service error for name=example.co type=AAAA: Host
not found)
```

It immediately fails because the domain isn't real.

A bounce message is created, that is, A88F7206B118, and processed (while the original message, 8E9A1206B117, is removed):

```
Dec 3 09:35:43 localhost postfix/cleanup[11317]: A88F7206B118:
message-id=<20181203093543.A88F7206B118@centos1.localdomain>
Dec 3 09:35:43 localhost postfix/qmgr[1129]: A88F7206B118: from=<>,
size=2545, nrcpt=1 (queue active)
Dec 3 09:35:43 localhost postfix/bounce[11320]: 8E9A1206B117: sender
non-delivery notification: A88F7206B118
Dec 3 09:35:43 localhost postfix/qmgr[1129]: 8E9A1206B117: removed
```

This is done before being sent to the local user, who initiated the mail attempt in the first place:

```
Dec 3 09:35:43 localhost postfix/local[11321]: A88F7206B118:
to=<vagrant@centos1.localdomain>, relay=local, delay=0.02,
delays=0/0.02/0/0, dsn=2.0.0, status=sent (delivered to mailbox)
Dec 3 09:35:43 localhost postfix/qmgr[1129]: A88F7206B118: removed
```

It lands in /var/spool/mail/vagrant, as denoted by this friendly message:

```
You have mail in /var/spool/mail/vagrant
```

Each of the steps here is done by Postfix, with one master daemon being responsible for a lot of little daemons, each of which has a specific job.

If we run ps and look for the postfix daemon, you'll find something such as this:

```
1125 ? Ss 0:00 /usr/libexec/postfix/master -w
1129 ? S 0:00 \_ qmgr -l -t unix -u
11157 ? S 0:00 \_ pickup -l -t unix -u
```

`qmgr`, as the name suggests, is the queue manager, and pickup is for local mail pickup.

To view the queue, you can use the `postqueue` command:

```
$ postqueue -p
-Queue ID- --Size-- ----Arrival Time---- -Sender/Recipient-------
D71FD206B117 458 Mon Dec 3 10:04:18 vagrant@centos1.localdomain
                       (connect to nasa.com[192.64.147.150]:25: Connection
refused)
                                        contact@nasa.com

-- 0 Kbytes in 1 Request.
```

Here, you can see a message I sent to `contact@nasa.com`. This doesn't work because our connection attempt gets refused.

Also, note port `25`, a traditional mail-receiving port.

If you wanted to empty the queue, you'd use `postsuper`, like so:

```
$ sudo postsuper -d D71FD206B117
postsuper: D71FD206B117: removed
postsuper: Deleted: 1 message
```

 You can also `flush` mail queues, which attempts redelivery of the mail in them. Generally, though, unless you've fixed the problem that caused undeliverable mail in the first place, you've just caused the mail to fail again. What's more, you've probably ground your server to a halt in the process.

There's more...

Postfix is a **Mail Transport Agent (MTA)**.

Sadly, this isn't a book on configuring mail servers, because there are many, many books on this subject already. All you need to be aware of is how to interact with a default Postfix installation, should you ever come across one in the wild.

If you want to know more about Postfix, or want to run your own mail server, I would advise against it. However, if you came back and said you really, really wanted to run your own mail server, I would suggest sitting down with Postfix for a weekend, reading up on best practices (don't create an open-relay, for example), and trying not to give up immediately. All power to you.

 Really, though, most companies these days either use some form of Exchange server, or they're just using Google, ProtonMail, FastMail, and so on instead.

See also

It's worth reading up on email because there actually is a good chance that you'll find yourself opening an email one day to look at the headers. Understanding why email works in the way it does (that is, handing off a message to the next mail server in a chain, until it eventually gets to the end user) can be very valuable in this context.

I may expand this section in the future, if the notion of running your own email server sees some miraculous resurgence.

Local MTA usage and configuration (Exim)

Like Postfix, we have Exim, which is another MTA.

Where Postfix is powerful and has its focus on security, Exim is known for being extremely customizable, and with a pedigree that goes all the way back to 1995 (inching out Postfix by three years). It's been the favorite of the Debian project for years, and, as a result, a lot of the documentation on setting up a mail server references Exim.

Also, like Postfix, this won't be a long section on fully configuring Exim, as that would require something much longer than a section, chapter, or realistically a book when done right. Instead, we're going to look at some configuration, the Exim log file, and what happens when you try to send a message from your local system.

Getting ready

In this section, we're going to use our Debian machine.

To ensure that Exim is installed on your system, run the following:

```
$ sudo apt install exim4 -y
```

There's quite a few packages in the Exim suite, and it can take some time to run through them all.

Check it's running with `systemctl status`:

```
$ systemctl status exim4
● exim4.service - LSB: exim Mail Transport Agent
 Loaded: loaded (/etc/init.d/exim4; generated; vendor preset: enabled)
 Active: active (running) since Wed 2018-12-05 17:38:01 GMT; 1min 29s
ago
 Docs: man:systemd-sysv-generator(8)
 Process: 5402 ExecStart=/etc/init.d/exim4 start (code=exited,
status=0/SUCCESS)
 Tasks: 1 (limit: 4915)
 CGroup: /system.slice/exim4.service
   └─5649 /usr/sbin/exim4 -bd -q30m
```

How to do it...

Post-installation, let's quickly test what the mail server looks like out of the box.

Starting by sending an example mail:

```
$ mail -s "Example Subject" packt@example.co
Cc:
This is another piece of example mail.
In this case we need to end with Ctrl-D.
Like so!
$
```

If we now run `mail` again, we'll see our bounced message:

```
$ mail
"/var/mail/vagrant": 1 message 1 new
>N 1 Mail Delivery Syst Wed Dec 5 17:46 56/1737 Mail delivery failed:
returnin
?
```

Again, hitting 1 and *Enter* will load the first message:

```
                              vagrant@debian1: ~                                    ● ▣ ⊗
File  Edit  View  Search  Terminal  Help
Return-path: <>
Envelope-to: vagrant@debian1
Delivery-date: Wed, 05 Dec 2018 17:46:39 +0000
Received: from Debian-exim by debian1 with local (Exim 4.89)
        id 1gUbFv-0001Wz-3Q
        for vagrant@debian1; Wed, 05 Dec 2018 17:46:39 +0000
X-Failed-Recipients: packt@example.co
Auto-Submitted: auto-replied
From: Mail Delivery System <Mailer-Daemon@debian1>
To: vagrant@debian1
Content-Type: multipart/report; report-type=delivery-status; boundary=1544031999-exim
dsn-1804289383
MIME-Version: 1.0
Subject: Mail delivery failed: returning message to sender
Message-Id: <E1gUbFv-0001Wz-3Q@debian1>
Date: Wed, 05 Dec 2018 17:46:39 +0000

--1544031999-eximdsn-1804289383
Content-type: text/plain; charset=us-ascii

This message was created automatically by mail delivery software.

A message that you sent could not be delivered to one or more of its
recipients. This is a permanent error. The following address(es) failed:

  packt@example.co
    Mailing to remote domains not supported

--1544031999-eximdsn-1804289383
Content-type: message/delivery-status

Reporting-MTA: dns; debian1

Action: failed
Final-Recipient: rfc822;packt@example.co
Status: 5.0.0

--1544031999-eximdsn-1804289383
Content-type: message/rfc822

Return-path: <vagrant@debian1>
Received: from vagrant by debian1 with local (Exim 4.89)
        (envelope-from <vagrant@debian1>)
        id 1gUbFu-0001Wx-W4
--More--
```

Here, we actually get the helpful message `Mailing to remote domains not supported` as the server in question is incapable of doing so.

With Exim, you can also test how it might route mail to a given address with the `address testing mode`. When given the preceding address, it prints a familiar message:

```
$ sudo exim -bt packt@example.co
R: nonlocal for packt@example.co
packt@example.co is undeliverable: Mailing to remote domains not
supported
```

It even tells you it's non-local, whereas if we give the same command, replacing the fake email with a local user, we get the following:

```
$ sudo exim -bt vagrant@localhost
R: system_aliases for vagrant@localhost
R: userforward for vagrant@localhost
R: procmail for vagrant@localhost
R: maildrop for vagrant@localhost
R: lowuid_aliases for vagrant@localhost (UID 1000)
R: local_user for vagrant@localhost
vagrant@localhost
  router = local_user, transport = mail_spool
```

The transport used is the local `mail_spool`, and there's no messages about mail being undeliverable.

We can also use `ss` to confirm that our mail server is only listening on port 25 locally (`127.0.0.1 & ::1`):

```
$ ss -tna '( sport = :smtp )'
State Recv-Q Send-Q Local Address:Port Peer Address:Port
LISTEN 0 20 127.0.0.1:25 *:*
LISTEN 0 20 ::1:25 :::*
```

How it works...

Exim configuration is found in the `/etc/exim4` folder on our Debian host. Listing this file looks as follows:

```
$ ls /etc/exim4/
conf.d exim4.conf.template passwd.client update-exim4.conf.conf
```

The configuration file that's being actively used is the `update-exim4.conf.conf` file (yes, that's `.conf` twice).

This file looks as follows out of the box:

```
# /etc/exim4/update-exim4.conf.conf
#
# Edit this file and /etc/mailname by hand and execute update-
exim4.conf
# yourself or use 'dpkg-reconfigure exim4-config'
#
# Please note that this is _not_ a dpkg-conffile and that automatic
changes
# to this file might happen. The code handling this will honor your
local
# changes, so this is usually fine, but will break local schemes that
mess
# around with multiple versions of the file.
#
# update-exim4.conf uses this file to determine variable values to
generate
# exim configuration macros for the configuration file.
#
# Most settings found in here do have corresponding questions in the
# Debconf configuration, but not all of them.
#
# This is a Debian specific file

dc_eximconfig_configtype='local'
dc_other_hostnames='debian1'
dc_local_interfaces='127.0.0.1 ; ::1'
dc_readhost=''
dc_relay_domains=''
dc_minimaldns='false'
dc_relay_nets=''
dc_smarthost=''
CFILEMODE='644'
dc_use_split_config='false'
dc_hide_mailname=''
dc_mailname_in_oh='true'
dc_localdelivery='mail_spool'
```

It can, however, be amended, as the file suggests, by using `sudo dpkg-reconfigure exim4-config`:

```
$ sudo dpkg-reconfigure exim4-config
```

This will drop you into a TUI, which looks like this:

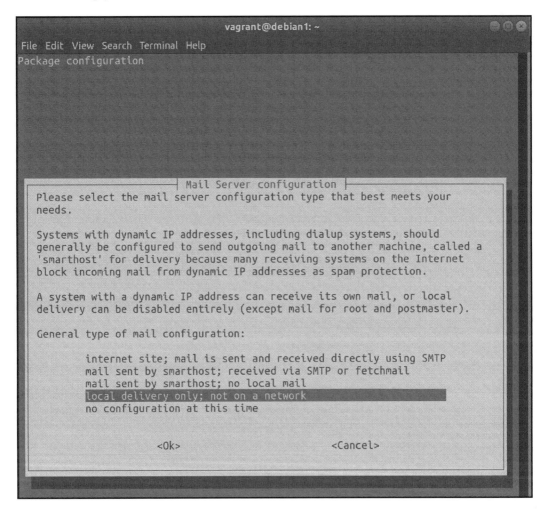

Here, you can reconfigure your mail server to your liking, including setting it up as an internet mail server.

Once done to your liking, you will find that the configuration file has been updated to reflect those settings.

If you want to know whether certain configuration settings have taken effect, you can use the `exiwhat` command, as follows:

```
$ sudo exiwhat
 3280 daemon(4.89): -q30m, listening for SMTP on [127.0.0.1]:25
[::1]:25
```

Exim, like Postfix, also supplies a helpful `maillog`, though in the case of Exim, it's called the `mainlog` and it's generally in a specific `exim` directory:

```
$ sudo ls /var/log/exim4/
mainlog
```

The contents is relatively familiar:

```
$ sudo cat /var/log/exim4/mainlog
<SNIP>
2018-12-05 19:03:15 1gUcS3-0000xe-Ps <= vagrant@debian1 U=vagrant
P=local S=466
2018-12-05 19:03:15 1gUcS3-0000xe-Ps ** packt@example.co R=nonlocal:
Mailing to remote domains not supported
2018-12-05 19:03:15 1gUcS3-0000xg-SC <= <> R=1gUcS3-0000xe-Ps
U=Debian-exim P=local S=1645
2018-12-05 19:03:15 1gUcS3-0000xe-Ps Completed
2018-12-05 19:03:15 1gUcS3-0000xg-SC => vagrant <vagrant@debian1>
R=local_user T=mail_spool
2018-12-05 19:03:15 1gUcS3-0000xg-SC Completed
```

We can see some fairly obvious lines in here that we can expand on, too:

```
2018-12-05 19:03:15 1gUcS3-0000xe-Ps <= vagrant@debian1 U=vagrant
P=local S=466
```

The following message has arrived `from vagrant@debian1` (`<=`):

```
2018-12-05 19:03:15 1gUcS3-0000xe-Ps ** packt@example.co R=nonlocal:
Mailing to remote domains not supported
```

The delivery of the message failed, as the address bounced (`**`):

```
2018-12-05 19:03:15 1gUcS3-0000xg-SC <= <> R=1gUcS3-0000xe-Ps
U=Debian-exim P=local S=1645
```

A new message has been received from Debian-exim:

```
2018-12-05 19:03:15 1gUcS3-0000xe-Ps Completed
```

The original message's journey has come to an end:

```
2018-12-05 19:03:15 1gUcS3-0000xg-SC => vagrant <vagrant@debian1>
R=local_user T=mail_spool
```

The new message has gone out to the vagrant user (=>):

```
2018-12-05 19:03:15 1gUcS3-0000xg-SC Completed
```

The new message's journey has now ended too.

There's more...

I've got to give a shout out here to an indispensable site for Exim troubleshooting: http://bradthemad.org/tech/notes/exim_cheatsheet.php.

If you ever find yourself stuck on that one thing you know Exim can do, or you're certain there's a specific query for the information you're trying to glean, check out Brad's Exim Cheatsheet—you won't be the first.

Thanks Brad, for helping administrators everywhere.

NoSQL documents (MongoDB example)

We took a look at **Structured Query Language (SQL)** services earlier, in the form of MariaDB and PostgreSQL. Now we're going to look at the "newer" way of storing data in a database, in a NoSQL fashion.

Unlike the table-based relationships of more traditional databases, NoSQL databases store data in other ways (such as key-value stores, tuple stores, or document stores). They've come to prominence in recent years due to the sudden and abrupt influx of big data products to the market, which rely on such databases for storage a lot of the time.

NoSQL databases can take a few different forms, as hinted at previously, and we'll be taking a look at an example of one in the next section (Redis).

When thinking about why you might use a NoSQL database in place of a traditional one, you might consider aspects such as scalability, flexibility, and speed, all of which can be features of good NoSQL setups.

The term **database** is perhaps more loosely and accurately applied to NoSQL setups, which can be a base for data, but that might not require the use of structured storage for the data they contain.

We're going to install MongoDB in this section, and take a look at the way data is stored in its databases.

LARGE DISCLAIMER:

MongoDB is perhaps infamous for being a target for unscrupulous members of hacking society. This is because MongoDB can be installed with default settings that let it listen on the internet, on an open port, without any sort of access requirements enabled. THIS IS BAD, and you should always consider the security implications of what you're doing, prior to doing them. As with any application, security is primarily the responsibility of the administrator doing the installation and management. I go on and on about security in certain sections of this book, but it's important to hammer the point home. Too often, I've seen lackadaisical approaches to deploying servers (of all kinds) that result in a great big hole in your network. When given free reign, I've seen some very intelligent people do very silly things without thinking about it (such as leaving default admin credentials set on a public-facing build server), and Hanlon's razor always applies:

"Never attribute to malice that is adequately explained by stupidity."

Getting ready

In this section, we're going to be using our CentOS machine, SSH to it:

```
$ vagrant ssh centos1
```

Install the EPEL repository, and then MongoDB:

```
$ sudo yum install epel-release -y
$ sudo yum install mongodb mongodb-server -y
```

We're using the EPEL repository for convenience here, but there are more ways to install MongoDB. Specifically, using the official repositories is the recommended approach for production systems.

How to do it...

Once installed, you can start and enable MongoDB with the `mongod` daemon:

```
$ sudo systemctl enable --now mongod
```

By default, MongoDB will start on localhost port 27017, but confirm this using `ss` or other tools:

```
$ ss -a '( sport = :27017 )'
State Recv-Q Send-Q Local Address:Port Peer Address:Port
LISTEN 0 128 127.0.0.1:27017 *:*
```

Once started, you can connect to your database using the `mongo` command-line tool:

```
$ mongo
```

The output of the preceding command is as follows:

Note that we connected to `test` by default. We can confirm what DB we're connected to (if we missed the notification) with the `db` command:

```
> db
test
```

We can change databases easily (and in familiar fashion) by using `use`:

```
> use local
switched to db local
```

Within our current database, we can see the collections. Because we've switched to `local`, these look as follows:

```
> show collections
startup_log
system.indexes
```

The syntax for working with collections is db.`<collection name>`.`<blah>`, so if we wanted to query everything within the startup_log collection, we could do the following:

```
> db.system.indexes.find()
{ "v" : 1, "key" : { "_id" : 1 }, "name" : "_id_", "ns" :
"local.startup_log" }
```

Obviously, this is a bit messy, so we can use .pretty() to make it nicer to read:

```
> db.system.indexes.find().pretty()
{
  "v" : 1,
  "key" : {
    "_id" : 1
  },
  "name" : "_id_",
  "ns" : "local.startup_log"
}
```

You should already be seeing similarities with SQL databases, though the syntax is wildly different in a lot of cases.

Let's flip back to our test database and create a collection of our own:

```
> use test
switched to db test
> db.distributions.insert( { name: "Ubuntu", developer: "Canonical
Ltd.", initial_year: 2004 } )
WriteResult({ "nInserted" : 1 })
```

Now, by performing a find on this collection, we should see the data we just shoved in:

```
> db.distributions.find().pretty()
{
  "_id" : ObjectId("5c081ba9832e06b5d1b64d50"),
  "name" : "Ubuntu",
  "developer" : "Canonical Ltd.",
  "initial_year" : 2004
}
```

Let's add another line, this time with some more fields:

```
> db.distributions.insert( { name: "Alpine Linux", developer: "Alpine
Linux development team", initial_year: 2010, first_version: 2.0,
forked_from: "LEAF Project" } )
WriteResult({ "nInserted" : 1 })
```

Let's perform our find again:

```
> db.distributions.find().pretty()
{
 "_id" : ObjectId("5c081ba9832e06b5d1b64d50"),
 "name" : "Ubuntu",
 "developer" : "Canonical Ltd.",
 "initial_year" : 2004
}
{
 "_id" : ObjectId("5c081c31832e06b5d1b64d51"),
 "name" : "Alpine Linux",
 "developer" : "Alpine Linux development team",
 "initial_year" : 2010,
 "first_version" : 2,
 "forked_from" : "LEAF Project"
}
```

Note that while our insert was fine, the 2.0 from the first_version field has been simplified to an integer.

If we wanted to narrow down our search, we could specifically search for entries with the name of Ubuntu:

```
> db.distributions.find({"name": "Ubuntu"}).pretty()
{
  "_id" : ObjectId("5c081ba9832e06b5d1b64d50"),
  "name" : "Ubuntu",
  "developer" : "Canonical Ltd.",
  "initial_year" : 2004
}
```

Alternatively, if we wanted to print specific values only (just the names here), we could use the following:

```
> db.distributions.find( {}, {"name": 1, "_id": 0} ).pretty()
{ "name" : "Ubuntu" }
{ "name" : "Alpine Linux" }
```

Note the odd structure of this query, where we've specified 1 to include the name, but 0 to omit the _id, which is included by default.

There's plenty of other things you can do, including searching by a specific query (in this case, looking for all entries with an initial_year greater than 2004):

```
> db.distributions.find({"initial_year": { $gt: 2004}}).pretty()
{
```

```
    "_id" : ObjectId("5c081c31832e06b5d1b64d51"),
    "name" : "Alpine Linux",
    "developer" : "Alpine Linux development team",
    "initial_year" : 2010,
    "first_version" : 2,
    "forked_from" : "LEAF Project"
}
```

Specifically, though, we're interested in differences between this method of storing data and a traditional method.

How it works...

Since we're working with `documents` and things are being created on the fly (rather than having tables that are populated with a strict dataset), our preceding commands can seem a lot more ad hoc than traditional databases would perform.

When we created our collection, we didn't have to define anything. We simply started writing data inside our test database:

```
> db.distributions.insert( { name: "Ubuntu", developer: "Canonical
Ltd.", initial_year: 2004 } )
```

From there, we were able to add more data, only to then start querying what we'd just written.

The data we added subsequently didn't really matter, and while there were correlations in the documents we wrote, such as the name, developer, and `initial_year` fields, there were some fields that were unique to our second insert. The database didn't care.

Because of this method of storing data in a database, NoSQL systems can be seen as a lot more flexible in terms of input.

This data is now stored within MongoDB, ready to be accessed quickly and easily by any program that wants to query it (commonly something such as a Node.js application).

We can see exactly where the `dbPath` value is using another query:

```
> use local
switched to db local
> db.startup_log.find( {}, {"cmdLine.storage": 1} ).pretty()
{
    "_id" : "centos1-1544033443006",
```

```
    "cmdLine" : {
      "storage" : {
        "dbPath" : "/var/lib/mongodb"
      }
    }
  }
```

This means that we can also view it on our host system:

```
$ sudo ls -l /var/lib/mongodb/
total 163844
drwxr-xr-x. 2 mongodb mongodb 29 Dec 5 18:40 journal
-rw-------. 1 mongodb mongodb 67108864 Dec 5 18:10 local.0
-rw-------. 1 mongodb mongodb 16777216 Dec 5 18:10 local.ns
-rwxr-xr-x. 1 mongodb mongodb 6 Dec 5 18:10 mongod.lock
-rw-------. 1 mongodb mongodb 67108864 Dec 5 18:42 test.0
-rw-------. 1 mongodb mongodb 16777216 Dec 5 18:42 test.ns
drwxr-xr-x. 2 mongodb mongodb 6 Dec 5 18:40 _tmp
```

There's more...

I suggested the EPEL version of MongoDB is old. At the time of writing this is true, so it's a good idea to try the most recent version from the upstream repositories, if you'd like to use MongoDB for your own systems.

Again, I would hammer the point home that enabling some sort of security on your system is also a must if you plan on using it in production.

Also, if you're still trying to think of a situation where NoSQL databases could be more useful than traditional PostgreSQL or MySQL setups, think of something such as logging.

You would hope that a log file is consistent, with the same fields, and the same type of data in each. However, log files might change, their order could be different, the types could suddenly change, and the number of fields could increase.

If you're using a traditional database as the backend for these logs (perfectly possible), you would have to add new tables in the best case, or use a different database entirely in the worst case.

Piping these same logs into a NoSQL system, one specifically designed to deal with documents, shouldn't impact the running of the system at all, as the collection will simply adapt to the new information you've provided.

NoSQL KV (Redis example)

We've had a look at one type of NoSQL database already, in the form of MongoDB (a document-specific instance). Now we're going to look at a different type of NoSQL database, specifically Redis, which is a **key-value** (**KV**) offering.

Its unique selling point is the fact it's an entirely in-memory database (with some writing out to disk periodically, if desired). This means that Redis is not only a great cache for storing the data you're manipulating or using, but it's also extremely fast.

Because of Redis's design, it is a commonly seen component in web stack setups, where speed is important for processing requests efficiently.

Of note is one criticism of NoSQL databases that is used in regard to Redis and others, where data can be lost easily under specific scenarios. Because Redis stores its data primarily in memory, writing out to disk occasionally, there is a chance that the catastrophic failure of a node can result in loss of data, even if it is only a few seconds worth.

Getting ready

In this section, we're going to use our CentOS VM again.

SSH to your CentOS machine:

```
$ vagrant ssh centos1
```

Install the EPEL repository, and then MongoDB:

```
$ sudo yum install epel-release -y
$ sudo yum install redis -y
```

> Again, we're using EPEL for convenience, but more up-to-date offerings are out there, and one of the most preferred ways of running Redis is in Docker containers.

How to do it...

Out of the box, systemd will start the redis-server binary by using the /etc/redis.conf configuration file. Let's go ahead and do that now:

```
$ sudo systemctl enable --now redis
Created symlink from /etc/systemd/system/multi-
user.target.wants/redis.service to
/usr/lib/systemd/system/redis.service.
```

The default port being used is 6379, which we can again check using ss:

```
$ ss -a '( sport = :6379 )'
State Recv-Q Send-Q Local Address:Port Peer Address:Port
LISTEN 0 128 127.0.0.1:6379 *:*
```

Here, we're listening on localhost, port 6379:

 The same warning as ever applies: If you start opening any of your installed services, make sure they're secure and aren't about to let bad actors steal your data.

Connecting to an instance is achieved using redis-cli from the command line, and simply invoking it should land you inside the Redis shell:

```
$ redis-cli
127.0.0.1:6379>
```

Redis recommends using ping to see whether Redis is responding properly:

```
127.0.0.1:6379> ping
PONG
```

Because Redis is a KV store, the syntax for interacting with it can be incredibly simple. The following example creates a key with a string value:

```
127.0.0.1:6379> set distro centos
OK
```

To retrieve that data, we use get:

```
127.0.0.1:6379> get distro
"centos"
```

If we wanted to set an integer value, we simply specify it:

```
> set number_of_linux_distros 20
OK
```

We could then increment it whenever a new Linux distribution is created:

```
127.0.0.1:6379> incr number_of_linux_distros
(integer) 21
127.0.0.1:6379> incr number_of_linux_distros
(integer) 22
127.0.0.1:6379> incr number_of_linux_distros
(integer) 23
127.0.0.1:6379> incr number_of_linux_distros
(integer) 24
127.0.0.1:6379> incr number_of_linux_distros
(integer) 25
127.0.0.1:6379> get number_of_linux_distros
"25"
```

You're not limited to one get at a time either with `mget`:

```
127.0.0.1:6379> mget distro number_of_linux_distros
1) "centos"
2) "25"
```

You might be wondering what utility this could have. I mean, sure, it's quick, but is it really so good that it becomes an indispensable part of any decent web stack?

Redis can do a lot more, including storing binary data (such as images) as the value to a key; it can create keys with a short time to live, meaning it could be used for temporary caching; and it can be clustered.

How it's used is generally up to the programmer of an application, and not up to the admin who's tasked with setting it up. However, that doesn't mean you can't suggest it if your developers are all sat around a table scratching their heads, trying to think of an in-memory key-value store that they can use as a cache for website data.

How it works...

We started Redis as a service, using `/etc/redis.conf` as the configuration file (the default).

The default settings shipped with the EPEL version, at the time of writing, mean that when it starts, it's on the localhost address (127.0.0.1) and port 6379:

```
$ sudo cat /etc/redis.conf | grep "port 6379\|^bind 127.0.0.1"
bind 127.0.0.1
port 6379~
```

The settings in here also set the mode (protected by default) that dictates how Redis can start when listening on other ports:

```
# By default protected mode is enabled. You should disable it only if
# you are sure you want clients from other hosts to connect to Redis
# even if no authentication is configured, nor a specific set of
interfaces
# are explicitly listed using the "bind" directive.
protected-mode yes
```

Sensible!

We know Redis is in-memory, but there's also that fact about it writing out to disk occasionally.

This DB dump is viewable in the given directory from the config file:

```
$ sudo ls /var/lib/redis
dump.rdb
```

Unless the appendonly value is set, this database file lags a little behind the running instance, meaning that if Redis or the server crash, you can lose a few seconds of data.

How robust you want your data to be is generally up to the application developers. If they don't mind the possibility that you might lose a second or two of data, meaning a value might not be cached or similar, then you might want to not take the performance impact of writing everything to disk as fast as you can.

Messaging brokers and queues (RabbitMQ example)

Moving on from databases of all shapes and sizes, in this section, we're going to look at something very different, in the form of a messaging software called RabbitMQ.

Like Redis, RabbitMQ is a staple of a lot of modern web applications, because of its open source and wel-documented nature.

"But what is a messaging queue?"

I knew you'd ask that, unless you already know, in which case this section might be a bit useless to you.

A **messaging queue**, usually utilizing the **Advanced Message Queuing Protocol (AMQP)**, is part of a message broker, which is software that's used to send and receive messages as part of an application stack.

These messages are usually sent from different components that can talk and listen in different ways. The messaging broker is there to facilitate the conversation between these components.

You'll commonly find that messaging brokers and queues start to come into conversations about "decoupling", which is a fancy way of suggesting different elements of an application stack shouldn't be so reliant on one another.

Think of a web server, talking to a processing application for data. In the old world, the web server would talk to the processing application directly, firing messages backward and forward while waiting for responses. This can be good in a flat design, but you run the risk of things such as the frontend website locking up, while the backend-processing application gets stuck on a tricky task.

Instead of this direct communication, message brokers can be used, and while it does rely on the web developers writing code that doesn't rely on a direct or immediate response from the backend, it effectively decouples the hard dependency of the backend application working (or being there at all).

In theory. you could rip out a database from a queue, replace it, and the frontend website would be none the wiser.

> You also tend to see RabbitMQ (and others) in designs for distributed and redundant setups, instead of one website talking to one processing the backend, several frontends, and several backends just talk to the queue, taking and processing messages as they see fit.

Getting ready

In this section, we're going to use our Debian box... just for a change.

Connect to `debian1`, like so:

```
$ vagrant ssh debian1 -- -L 127.0.0.1:15672:127.0.0.1:15672
```

Note the forwarded ports for accessing the management interface later.

 A word of warning: RabbitMQ starts on all interfaces by default in this setup, so you should ensure that you have a firewall keeping those ports inaccessible from the outside. If you're just working on the Vagrant test VM for this, then it should only be set up for a local network anyway.

Install `rabbitmq-server` from the default repositories:

```
$ sudo apt install rabbitmq-server -y
```

How to do it...

Once installed, Rabbit should start up automatically (ah, Debian). This means that we can immediately see what's running with `ps` (and the default user it runs as, `rabbitmq`):

```
$ ps -fu rabbitmq
UID PID PPID C STIME TTY TIME CMD
rabbitmq 5085 1 0 14:25 ? 00:00:00 /bin/sh /usr/sbin/rabbitmq-server
rabbitmq 5094 5085 0 14:25 ? 00:00:00 /bin/sh -e
/usr/lib/rabbitmq/bin/rabbitmq-server
rabbitmq 5244 1 0 14:25 ? 00:00:00 /usr/lib/erlang/erts-8.2.1/bin/epmd
-daemon
rabbitmq 5307 5094 0 14:25 ? 00:00:02
/usr/lib/erlang/erts-8.2.1/bin/beam -W w -A 64 -P 1048576 -t 5000000 -
stbt db -zdbbl 32000 -K true -B i -- -root /usr/lib/erlang
rabbitmq 5417 5307 0 14:25 ? 00:00:00 erl_child_setup 65536
rabbitmq 5442 5417 0 14:25 ? 00:00:00 inet_gethost 4
rabbitmq 5443 5442 0 14:25 ? 00:00:00 inet_gethost 4
```

From this, we can immediately see that RabbitMQ uses Erlang, and that
the `/usr/lib/rabbitmq/bin/rabbitmq-server` script is used to start the server.

First, let's set up the RabbitMQ management interface:

```
$ sudo rabbitmq-plugins enable rabbitmq_management
The following plugins have been enabled:
  mochiweb
  webmachine
  rabbitmq_web_dispatch
  amqp_client
  rabbitmq_management_agent
  rabbitmq_management

Applying plugin configuration to rabbit@debian1... started 6 plugins.
```

Now, you should be able to hit this interface on your local machine.

Navigate to `http://127.0.0.1:15672` and you should see something such as the
following:

The default username and password are `guest`/`guest`.

Going back to my security point from earlier, this highlights the
need to set up and configure software in a secure testing
environment, with absolutely no production data, prior to going
anywhere near a live environment.

Once logged in, you should see this:

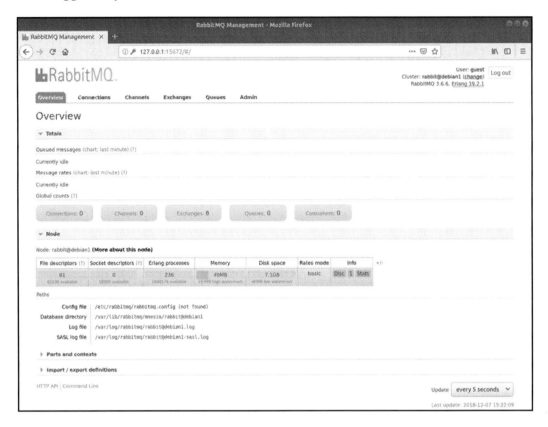

RabbitMQ overview page

Usually, I would suggest starting with the CLI, but it just so happens that this is a great way to visualize what Rabbit is, and what it's doing.

At the top of this screen, we have our **Totals**, which are a breakdown of the messages that Rabbit is currently aware of (it's idle right now).

In the **Nodes** section, we can see straight away that we have a single node, called `rabbit@debian1`, and that we have a breakdown of its usage at the moment.

We also have a list of the relevant **Paths** that Rabbit looks for, including the configuration file (currently not there) and the actual database directory. There's also information on the various log files.

Have a click around this interface (though you may find it a bit sparse).

Back on the command line, let's take a look at how you might query information on a remote server that doesn't have a web interface enabled.

Start by listing the queues:

```
$ sudo rabbitmqctl list_queues
Listing queues ...
```

This is empty, as we saw on the GUI (if you clicked on the **Queues** tab).

By default, we have one `vhost`, which is a way to segment RabbitMQ (like vhosts in Apache and Nginx):

```
$ sudo rabbitmqctl list_vhosts
Listing vhosts ...
/
```

We can take a look at the configured users:

```
$ sudo rabbitmqctl list_users
Listing users ...
guest [administrator]
```

We can also create users:

```
$ sudo rabbitmqctl add_user exampleUser examplePassword
Creating user "exampleUser" ...
```

Let's create a `vhost` to go along with that:

```
$ sudo rabbitmqctl add_vhost exampleVhost
Creating vhost "exampleVhost" ...
```

Now let's give our user access to said `vhost`:

```
$ sudo rabbitmqctl set_permissions -p exampleVhost exampleUser ".*"
".*" ".*"
Setting permissions for user "exampleUser" in vhost "exampleVhost" ...
```

How it works...

Most of what we did should be self-explanatory, with the exception of the permissions line:

```
$ sudo rabbitmqctl set_permissions -p exampleVhost exampleUser ".*"
".*" ".*"
```

Here, we're specifically granting access to `configure`, `write`, and `read` to our user, `exampleUser`. This means that within the `exampleVhost vhost`, our user will have complete access to do as they please.

 Access is granted here by way of Regex, meaning that you can have more fine-grained control over what a user can and can't access within a `vhost`.

Like Redis, RabbitMQ really doesn't do much without setup and without applications talking to it.

Various languages have ways of interfacing with RabbitMQ. It's generally up to the developers of your company to decide how they're going to write to the queues, which queues they're going to write to, how they're going to read from those queues once done, and what language they're going to use.

Sadly, from an administrator's point of view, you'll very rarely have anything to do with the actual requests and actions of RabbitMQ. Most of your job is going to centre around making sure security is in place (TLS, user authentication, and so on) and ensuring clusters remain consistent.

I would highly recommend going through the Rabbit documentation and having a go at some of their quickstart guides for interacting with Rabbit. If you have a developer mindset, or you just like hacking around with Python scripts, it could be a good way to gain a deep understanding of this messaging broker, and messaging brokers in general.

Roundup – web servers, databases, and mail servers

In this chapter, I deliberately tried to talk about some of the most popular technology on the market at the moment, including programs that I know for a fact have large minds and market share. Some of this software has been around for ages, near decades, but more of it has joined the scene recently, owed in large part to the explosion of cloud computing in the latter half of the 2010s.

When we talk about web servers, mail servers, and databases, they come in all shapes and sizes, meaning that it's hard to suggest sensible defaults that will fit absolutely all use cases. The only advice that I can give, and which is universal, is to not compromise security for simplicity. (You've probably read enough about leaks and security breaches in recent months and years that you want to make sure your name isn't tied to something catastrophic such as that.)

That's not to say this stuff can't be fun. The weird and wonderful things people are doing with NoSQL databases, messaging brokers, and even mail servers are extremely interesting to a lot of people, one of whom might be you!

I also don't want to really take you away from the notion of running any of this stuff yourself, especially now that most of this stuff is available "as a service" from various cloud providers and third parties. It can be a great learning experience and teach you the good and bad of certain programs when you install and configure this stuff yourself.

One other thing to note, and this is just like, my opinion, man.

I don't like mixing similar technologies in the same infrastructure. If you need an SQL database, and you've never used one in your infrastructure before, it's fine to think about it for a while before deciding on either MariaDB or PostgreSQL. Most modern software just wants some sort of SQL backend, and it doesn't care what software provides it.

That GitLab server you're installing? Maybe you've decided to use PostgreSQL.

Now you've got a WordPress instance to set up? Go with PostgreSQL again.

You need something to connect Icinga2 to? Try PostgreSQL.

Imagine how much of a headache you might get into if you decide to use MariaDB for one thing, MySQL for another, and PostgreSQL for a third. Unless there's an extremely good reason to use one over the other, I'm a big fan of keeping your infrastructure as simple as you can. That way, when you have to learn a bit of SQL to properly manage your databases, you only have to worry about the intricacies of a certain SQL provider, rather than three different ones.

This is across the board, too—if you've got to set up a mail server for something, I would always favor setting up Postfix on both Debian and CentOS machines, just so I know where to look in terms of logs and configuration directives, regardless of the OS I'm on.

In fact, scratch that! Take it one step further and choose a single OS to deploy, scrapping any notion of a mixed Debian, CentOS, and Ubuntu deployment.

Logically, this doesn't only save your sanity when it comes to managing components, but it drastically cuts down on the infrastructure as code you'd have to maintain, the repositories you'd have to mirror, and the security mailing lists you have to subscribe to.

But in your own time? Meh, that's up to you—go nuts, play, learn.

Super personal preference time!

If you tied me to a chair, and said I absolutely had to choose which software I prefer, I'd say the following:

- Postfix > Exim
- Nginx > Apache
- MariaDB > PostgreSQL

Note: This is tongue-in-cheek; don't take these to heart.

12

Troubleshooting and Workplace Diplomacy

In this chapter, we will examine the following topics:

- What is troubleshooting?
- Isolating the real issue
- Giving estimates and deciding on next steps
- Using `ss`, `iftop`, `tcpdump`, and others for network issues
- Using `curl`, `wget`, and `openssl` for remote web issues
- Using `itop`, `top`, and `vmstat` for local resource issues
- Using `ps`, `lsof`, `strace`, and `/proc` for service issues
- Making a copy of problems for later debugging
- Temporary solutions and when to invoke them
- Handling irate developers
- Handling irate managers
- Handling irate business owners

Introduction

In this chapter, we're going to start winding down on the technical aspects of what we've looked at. We're not going to look at new services and software too much, and the software we do use is going to be mostly those tools we've already covered in other areas (only here we will talk about when and how you might use them).

Troubleshooting is the main focus of this chapter, with a lot of emphasis on doing the communication aspect of troubleshooting too. You can be the best engineer in the world, a literal code-whisperer, and yet if you're not able to relay your findings in a way that someone else can understand, all your ability amounts to naught.

When you troubleshoot something, in extra-time or under-fire, you've got to make sure that what you learn is properly noted (even if it's on a scrap of paper initially, and in a document store such as Confluence later) so that, should it happen again, someone who isn't you will be able to work out what's going on faster, and hopefully fix the issue sooner.

While you troubleshoot, it's also worth keeping those around you informed of what's happening. I've seen this done in various ways over the years, but a more common-place solution to keeping people in the picture these days seems to be a Rocket.Chat or Slack channel that you can post announcements and information into. That way, anyone can keep abreast of the situation, even if it's only due to a passing interest.

And, yes, there will be occasions where you're troubleshooting that someone wants an update every five minutes on what's going on. This can be a client, a manager, a developer, or a business owner, but it's important to keep your cool in these situations, not get stressed, and ensure you keep your answers succinct and to the point, without too much guesswork.

Technical requirements

All of what we do in this chapter can be accomplished using a single node; in this case, I'm using a CentOS machine.

Feel free to use the `Vagrantfile` to play along:

```ruby
# -*- mode: ruby -*-
# vi: set ft=ruby :

Vagrant.configure("2") do |config|

  config.vm.define "centos1" do |centos1|
    centos1.vm.box = "centos/7"
    centos1.vm.network "private_network", ip: "192.168.33.10"
    centos1.vm.hostname = "centos1"
    centos1.vm.box_version = "1804.02"
  end

end
```

What is troubleshooting?

Troubleshooting, or **debugging** (more frequently used for specific software), is the act of trying to work out what's going wrong with a solution right now or what went wrong historically during an incident. That incident can be anything from the entire network going down in a data center, to working out why that one Docker container suddenly decided it was going to bounce itself up and down like a tennis ball.

No software is perfect. If it were, we'd all be out of jobs, and it's because of this simple statement of fact that you will almost inevitably find yourself in a situation at some point in your life where you're faced with a broken system and there's someone screaming at you to fix it.

You can do everything in your power before this point to try to ensure you never experience something such as a production outage, including using multiple environments and testing changes through a promotion pipeline. But I can guarantee that you'll never account for everything, and, as most companies will tell you, issues can and will happen in production too. You just have to hope that when issues do happen, you're not being woken up at two in the morning to fix them, because you're the on-call engineer.

How to do it...

When troubleshooting an issue, there's some important first steps to take:

1. Get a drink of your choice, or ask someone nicely to make one for you (if the incident is so serious it requires an immediate immediate response). Try to avoid this drink being alcoholic. I usually go for tea.
2. Ensure you know what raised the alert. Generally, this will be from a monitoring system, or a panicked shift engineer on the other end of the phone. This is a good jumping-off point for the next step.
3. Get the impact of the problem; for example, does it mean that the website is down and no one can do their Christmas shopping, or is the system that routes incoming support calls down? This will help you to assess the importance of the issue.

There is a difference between people not being able to call into the support desk at three in the morning, and a traffic routing system for a small municipality being down. Surprisingly, though, some people will panic the exact same amount, no matter the scale of the issue.

4. Once these things are established, move on to isolating the real issue.

Isolating the real issue

When you're troubleshooting, or you've been presented with an obvious problem and it's up to you to work out what's going on, it's important not to jump to conclusions. It can be extremely easy to see a problem, such as a website being down, and immediately think, *Ah, I've seen this before; it was that time the database had too many rows to count and the website slowed to a crawl—I'll look there.*

Lightning does strike twice in computing, especially when root causes haven't been addressed, but it's an anti-troubleshooting technique to immediately assume you know the cause of a problem, based on tentative similarities with past issues.

Getting ready

After you've got as much information about the problem, either from your own cursory glance of the symptoms (the website is down) or the support person who pestered you with it, it's time to get to the issue of isolation.

Be sure to recreate the issue for yourself. It's an important and often overlooked step that should be taken by anyone looking into an issue. If you have the means to recreate a problem, you should start by doing so, even if it's as simple as going to the company's URL in your browser and checking for yourself that the site doesn't load. This is important, as it gives you a base from which to start, and you can use the same series of steps every time you make a change, or believe you've fixed the problem. If you can confirm that the problem exists, work to fix the said problem. Then, prove it's fixed for at least you, after which you can start to engage other people in the process and ask them to confirm the same.

Stabbing around in the dark doesn't only put you at risk of losing fingers, but it also makes it incredibly hard to determine when, or if, a chance you've made has actually had an impact.

You might also find that in recreating the issue for yourself, you come across some pertinent information that hasn't been readily shared with you. "The website is down" is a vague statement, but "the website is timing out" is more informative, and if you go to a site to find it's been hijacked by someone using it to share pictures of their cat, then it might not be down, but the URL could be compromised.

How to do it...

Once the issue is recreated, you can get down to the meat of the work:

1. To begin, you need to know which boxes are likely to be connected to the problem, either directly, or by one degree of separation. For example, if the company website is down, I would immediately log on to whichever system hosted the website, while trying to find information on any systems that supplied it, such as messaging brokers or databases.

2. If you don't know what the topology of the deployment looks like off the top of your head, and you can't find a document in your internal systems that details the layout, it can be a good idea to engage others in the process of troubleshooting.

You might not feel entirely comfortable about waking someone else up in the middle of the night, or pestering someone at their desk, but if it would take you literally hours to reverse-engineer a setup, and it's definitely worth considering circumventing this effort and going to the source instead. If the other person is reasonable, they'll probably offer their knowledge, though they may be grumpy about it, and you'll have to apologise the next time you see them.

3. Once you are sure you've got all the systems you might need to check in your head, or better yet, on a notepad, you should begin the isolation. Depending on how lucky you are, this can be a quick or a slow process.

4. Using the example of web servers and websites being down, you might try to SSH to your company website boxes and find that you can't. This could mean one of two things straight away:
    - There's a network problem hampering communication
    - The box is down

4. These issues may seem wide-ranging, but they're easy to isolate. The next step here would be trying to SSH to another box, preferably in the same network, and if you can connect to it you've narrowed the field of what the issue might be. It would suggest that the first box is down, or experiencing personal network issues.

5. Assuming you can't get to another box, you should try another couple to be sure, and if you can't get to them either, it might be time to get your network team involved (or if you have the power to do so, logging on to the switches or routers yourself).

6. If you've determined that it's one or two boxes having a problem, you might have to get a data center engineer into the situation (or drive down yourself, if it's your job) and plug into the box directly. If it's a cloud solution, it'll be time to break open whatever console you have access to and check for obvious issues that way.

7. Once you're on the box, it's a good idea to check that the same issues can be recreated locally on the box itself. We'll talk about ways you might do this in a little while.

8. If you work through your troubleshooting steps and determine that the local box isn't the issue, it's time to work outwards and test the other parts of the solution that you haven't checked yet, or might not have direct control over.

 People have different techniques when it comes to troubleshooting, but I like to check the stuff I have direct access and control over first. There's a good chance for certain issues that problems are being caused by external factors (such as your distributed content delivery provider having problems), but in cases such as these, it's a good idea to try to prove external factors as much as possible before you get on the phone yourself and start blaming other people.

10. Check the next most likely candidate for the source of the issue (the load balancer in front of the web server maybe, or the database behind it) and carry on until you find something that isn't behaving as it should.

Giving estimates and deciding on next steps

While you're working through the troubleshooting process, it's a great idea to make notes as you go, and keep track of significant times during the incident:

- What time was the incident first reported?
- What time did you get into a position to start troubleshooting?
- What time did you isolate the issue?
- What time was pertinent information discovered?
- And so on

Another thing to be aware of is the **estimate**. Estimates are something that higher-ups like to hear, in a lot of cases, because it means they can pass the estimates on to their own higher-ups, or to customers.

If you have no clear idea what's causing an issue yet, you can't give a reliable estimate, and you should explain this. However, if you've managed to isolate the issue and found it to be caused by something such as a stored procedure running against a database, it may be possible to give a rough estimate in that situation. Deciding on the next steps can be tricky due to various factors, as we'll see here.

Getting ready

Using the example from the last recipe, you've discovered that the website you're looking at is going slow because of a stored procedure running against the database. You've determined that this stored procedure runs weekly, and that it ran successfully last Sunday, where it took about an hour to complete before everything went back to normal, and no alarms were triggered.

Now, though, it's been an hour and a half, with no obvious sign of the stored procedure finishing its run. You should note what you've found, make a note of the time that you found it, and inform whoever you need to that you believe you've found the source of the problem.

Try to avoid using phrases such as "it's definitely this" or "I've found the problem," because those kinds of absolutes only succeed in making you look foolish and potentially making other people angry when they turn out to be red herrings.

How to do it...

Estimates can be easy, or they can be incredibly difficult. I wouldn't advise pulling numbers out of the air, as they can make you seem incompetent when you end up waving at your self-imposed deadlines as they fly by. What you can check, though, are historical records:

1. If your stored procedure is running and taking a while, start by looking back through your logs and trying to determine how long the last few runs took. The more data the better.

   If you've got logs going back two years, and you can see that the stored procedure took a few minutes to run at the beginning of its life, when the company was small and the database was smaller, then you might start to build a picture of a job taking longer to run, the larger the database gets. You could confirm this by checking each run in a chart and seeing whether the increase in the time taken correlates with size. At this point, you might be able to pull a figure out that you know will be roughly when the job will finish.

2. If, however, those historic logs show that the stored procedure always runs at the same time, for the same amount of time, then you might start to believe something else has caused the sudden uptick in processing time. You should note this, and decide what to do next.

 It goes without saying, but checking specific process logs (if they exist) is also a must in situations such as this, as is reading through and understanding what the script or stored procedure might do. Again, if you need to get others involved, make a judgement call, but don't try and shoulder absolutely everything yourself, as this only results in more pressure and more stress.

In this situation, you have to start thinking about factors outside the database that might be affecting processing time:

- Has there been any recent work that might have changed how the stored procedure works (check Git logs)?
- Has anyone logged on to the box recently and made changes (check audit logs)?
- Is there anything else running on the database server that could be impacting performance (check top for process information)?

It's up to you to decide on the priority of these things and work through them one at a time.

3. Back to the estimates problem: if you've determined that the cause of the problem is a code change, and you need to roll back to an earlier version, then it's not impossible to again provide an estimate. You should know how long a package is going to take to build, and how soon it will be deployed to boxes before a service can be restarted.

4. Ultimately, though, the adage of *"it takes as long as it takes"* is true, though it's best not to say this to people pestering you for answers. Let them down more gently, and assure them you're working on it... show them your notes.

There's more...

A lot of places have timetables for what's supposed to happen during an incident, for example:

- If the issue is ongoing within an hour, inform only designated individuals
- If the issue is taking longer than an hour or up to two, inform stakeholders
- If the issue looks likely to leave systems offline for longer, arrange meetings every thirty minutes to keep stakeholders updated

 Though not consistent anywhere I've worked, good companies have plans in place to make sure everyone is on the same page, and better places don't invite the troubleshooting engineers to these meetings, instead designating a liaison who gets the information from the engineers while they're working.

Using ss, iftop, tcpdump, and others for network issues

In this recipe, we're going to list a few tools that can be used for isolating and debugging network issues, most of which can be found in the default repositories of common distributions.

A lot of these, if not all, where covered before in this book, but it's a good idea to repeat these tools over and over again, because 20% of what you'll find yourself doing in a troubleshooting scenario is trying to remember which tool is good for troubleshooting this particular problem.

Getting ready

In this recipe, feel free to try out some or all of the commands listed (or even go off script and have a read of the relevant man pages). We will be using the CentOS VM.

SSH to your CentOS VM:

```
$ vagrant ssh centos1
```

Install two of the tools we will be using:

```
$ sudo yum install epel-release -y
$ sudo yum install iftop tcpdump -y
```

How to do it...

We're going to run through our tools in turn.

Ping

If you think you've got a network problem, the ping command is one of the oldest tools available to you, and one of your best friends:

1. Start by making sure your networking is up, pinging your loopback address and your own node IP. We will check whether the localhost is working:

```
$ ping 127.0.0.1
PING 127.0.0.1 (127.0.0.1) 56(84) bytes of data.
64 bytes from 127.0.0.1: icmp_seq=1 ttl=64 time=0.044 ms
64 bytes from 127.0.0.1: icmp_seq=2 ttl=64 time=0.081 ms
64 bytes from 127.0.0.1: icmp_seq=3 ttl=64 time=0.086 ms
--- 127.0.0.1 ping statistics ---
3 packets transmitted, 3 received, 0% packet loss, time
1999ms
rtt min/avg/max/mdev = 0.044/0.070/0.086/0.019 ms
```

2. Then, check your `Eth1` address:

```
$ ping 192.168.33.10
PING 192.168.33.10 (192.168.33.10) 56(84) bytes of data.
64 bytes from 192.168.33.10: icmp_seq=1 ttl=64 time=0.064
ms
64 bytes from 192.168.33.10: icmp_seq=2 ttl=64 time=0.069
ms
64 bytes from 192.168.33.10: icmp_seq=3 ttl=64 time=0.098
ms
--- 192.168.33.10 ping statistics ---
3 packets transmitted, 3 received, 0% packet loss, time
2008ms
rtt min/avg/max/mdev = 0.064/0.077/0.098/0.015 ms
```

3. Now that you're sure your networking stack is up, check that you can talk to your router. If you don't know your router's IP, grab that first:

```
$ ip route | grep default
default via 10.0.2.2 dev eth0 proto dhcp metric 102
```

4. We will now ping that IP:

```
$ ping 10.0.2.2
PING 10.0.2.2 (10.0.2.2) 56(84) bytes of data.
64 bytes from 10.0.2.2: icmp_seq=1 ttl=64 time=0.473 ms
64 bytes from 10.0.2.2: icmp_seq=2 ttl=64 time=0.861 ms
64 bytes from 10.0.2.2: icmp_seq=3 ttl=64 time=0.451 ms
--- 10.0.2.2 ping statistics ---
3 packets transmitted, 3 received, 0% packet loss, time
2016ms
rtt min/avg/max/mdev = 0.451/0.595/0.861/0.188 ms
```

Awesome! We're relatively sure that our actual packet routing is fine.

5. Next, check whether your DNS works using the `ping` command:

```
$ ping bbc.co.uk
PING bbc.co.uk (151.101.192.81) 56(84) bytes of data.
64 bytes from 151.101.192.81 (151.101.192.81): icmp_seq=1
ttl=63 time=43.9 ms
64 bytes from 151.101.192.81 (151.101.192.81): icmp_seq=2
ttl=63 time=31.5 ms
64 bytes from 151.101.192.81 (151.101.192.81): icmp_seq=3
ttl=63 time=38.4 ms
--- bbc.co.uk ping statistics ---
3 packets transmitted, 3 received, 0% packet loss, time
```

```
2017ms
rtt min/avg/max/mdev = 31.545/37.973/43.910/5.059 ms
```

Cool, so we know we can resolve domain names to IPs.

Should name resolution not work for some reason, try checking that your /etc/resolv.conf actually has a nameserver entry in it, and try pinging that server to see whether you can actually reach it for communication. DNS resolution failures can have weird knock-on effects (such as slow SSH connections on some default installations).

Ping is great, and many issues that are encountered can be tracked down immediately, thanks to its simplicity.

SS

The ss is great for local port checking, as I might have made obvious for the number of times we've used it throughout this book so far:

1. If you have a web server on your machine, and you know for a fact it should be running on port 80, you might find yourself using the fish arguments first, regardless:

```
$ ss -tuna
Netid State Recv-Q Send-Q Local Address:Port Peer
Address:Port
udp UNCONN 0 0 *:733 *:*
udp UNCONN 0 0 127.0.0.1:323 *:*
udp UNCONN 0 0 *:68 *:*
udp UNCONN 0 0 *:111 *:*
udp UNCONN 0 0 :::733 :::*
udp UNCONN 0 0 ::1:323 :::*
udp UNCONN 0 0 :::111 :::*
tcp LISTEN 0 128 *:111 *:*
tcp LISTEN 0 128 *:22 *:*
tcp LISTEN 0 100 127.0.0.1:25 *:*
tcp ESTAB 0 0 10.0.2.15:22 10.0.2.2:51224
tcp LISTEN 0 128 :::111 :::*
tcp LISTEN 0 128 :::22 :::*
tcp LISTEN 0 100 ::1:25 :::*
```

We do this immediately in some situations, just to get an overview of what the box thinks it's doing in terms of IP networking.

We get to see what ports are active and listening on the box, immediately ruling out usual suspects (such as 22 and 25), and we get to see connected (ESTAB) sessions from remote connections, in this case, my machine.

You can also run ss without the -n argument, if you want to see a best-guess at service names. I call it "best-guess" because all ss will do is read the /etc/services file and match a port to a name, but there's no guarantee that SSH is really running on 22, instead of 2323 or something else.

2. You can also use ss to get a snapshot of what the machine looks like in terms of networking right now:

```
$ ss -s
Total: 194 (kernel 0)
TCP: 7 (estab 1, closed 0, orphaned 0, synrecv 0, timewait
0/0), ports 0

Transport Total IP IPv6
* 0 - -
RAW 0 0 0
UDP 7 4 3
TCP 7 4 3
INET 14 8 6
FRAG 0 0 0
```

iftop

This is the first of the tools in this recipe that's unlikely to be installed by default; we sometimes come to iftop during the troubleshooting process because it's great for visualization. Humans tend to like visualization. We're simple creatures with simple dreams, and those dreams are generally vivid in color, and feature confusing graphs and charts (if you're me).

As a result, where a computer prefers strings and structure, we tend to like a good representation of what it is we're looking at, and iftop gives us this:

```
$ sudo iftop
```

We've generated a bit of traffic here, to three different locations, to show how easy it can be to see different sources and communication:

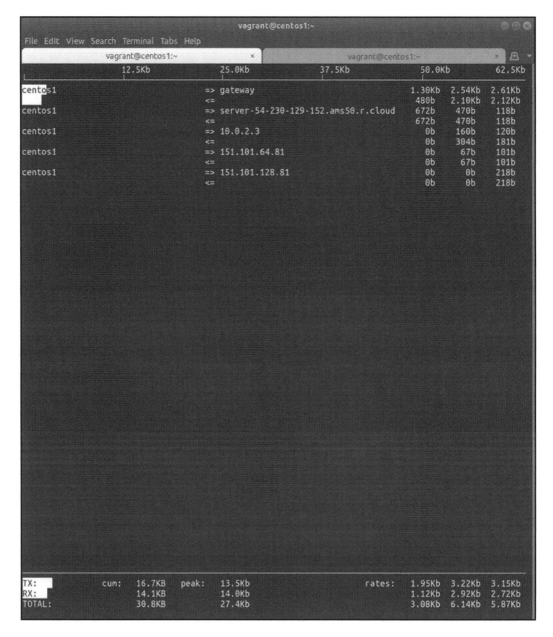

We went into `iftop` a lot earlier in this book, but remember that it exists!

tcpdump

Another tool we've used before is `tcpdump`; it prints and saves network traffic for debugging later or in the moment:

```
$ sudo tcpdump not port 22
tcpdump: verbose output suppressed, use -v or -vv for full protocol
decode
listening on eth0, link-type EN10MB (Ethernet), capture size 262144
bytes
15:26:48.864239 IP centos1 >
server-54-230-129-152.ams50.r.cloudfront.net: ICMP echo request, id
3927, seq 284, length 64
15:26:48.866009 IP centos1.46283 > 10.0.2.3.domain: 32699+ PTR?
152.129.230.54.in-addr.arpa. (45)
15:26:48.899019 IP 10.0.2.3.domain > centos1.46283: 32699 1/0/0 PTR
server-54-230-129-152.ams50.r.cloudfront.net. (103)
15:26:48.899678 IP centos1.44944 > 10.0.2.3.domain: 7093+ PTR?
15.2.0.10.in-addr.arpa. (40)
15:26:48.900853 IP 10.0.2.3.domain > centos1.44944: 7093 NXDomain
0/0/0 (40)
15:26:48.903765 IP centos1.37253 > 10.0.2.3.domain: 25988+ PTR?
3.2.0.10.in-addr.arpa. (39)
15:26:48.911352 IP server-54-230-129-152.ams50.r.cloudfront.net >
centos1: ICMP echo reply, id 3927, seq 284, length 64
15:26:48.964402 IP 10.0.2.3.domain > centos1.37253: 25988 NXDomain
0/0/0 (39)
15:26:49.869214 IP centos1 >
server-54-230-129-152.ams50.r.cloudfront.net: ICMP echo request, id
3927, seq 285, length 64
15:26:49.909387 IP server-54-230-129-152.ams50.r.cloudfront.net >
centos1: ICMP echo reply, id 3927, seq 285, length 64
15:26:50.875756 IP centos1 >
server-54-230-129-152.ams50.r.cloudfront.net: ICMP echo request, id
3927, seq 286, length 64
15:26:50.913753 IP server-54-230-129-152.ams50.r.cloudfront.net >
centos1: ICMP echo reply, id 3927, seq 286, length 64
15:26:51.881191 IP centos1 >
server-54-230-129-152.ams50.r.cloudfront.net: ICMP echo request, id
3927, seq 287, length 64
15:26:51.927357 IP server-54-230-129-152.ams50.r.cloudfront.net >
centos1: ICMP echo reply, id 3927, seq 287, length 64
^C
14 packets captured
14 packets received by filter
0 packets dropped by kernel
```

Note the preceding example, where I specifically ran `tcpdump` but excluded SSH traffic:

```
$ sudo tcpdump not port 22
```

As a result, what I got was a lot of information on the ping requests from my second session, but, crucially, I avoided the noise from the SSH traffic. (Which would be extra noisy, because every time something is printed to my session, that's SSH traffic, meaning it would grow and grow and grow.)

Though if we did want to debug SSH, this is possible and quite easy, given that `tcpdump` lets you output to a file:

```
$ sudo tcpdump port 22 -w ssh-traffic.pcap
tcpdump: listening on eth0, link-type EN10MB (Ethernet), capture size
262144 bytes
^C3 packets captured
5 packets received by filter
0 packets dropped by kernel
```

This file can then be opened and read with tools such as Wireshark: `https://www.wireshark.org/`.

Using cURL, wget, and OpenSSL for remote web issues

If you've come to the conclusion that during your immense troubleshooting session that the issue you're facing is one of the following, then some of these tools might be for you:

- Something to do with the connectivity to a remote site
- Something to do with the certificates associated with a remote site

Getting ready

SSH to your CentOS VM:

```
$ vagrant ssh centos1
```

 cURL and OpenSSL should be universal at this point, and you can expect a system to have them by default.

Wget is a bit more elusive, and is rarely part of a default install, but it's easy enough to install:

```
$ sudo yum install wget -y
```

 At the moment, OpenSSL is everywhere, but due to a string of high-profile vulnerabilities, *cough* heartbleed *cough*, it has been forked a couple of times to produce approximations, though hopefully approximations with a limited number of problems. The most famous of these is `LibreSSL` by the OpenBSD folks, and while it's the default in that particular OS, it's unlikely to be the default in CentOS or Ubuntu any time soon.

For the examples in this recipe, we're also going to break the trust of some key areas of the internet (only locally to your VM, though—don't worry). To do this, you can run the following command:

```
$ sudo mv /etc/pki/ /etc/pki-backup
```

How to do it...

We're going to run through these three programs, including examples of how you might use them as we go.

cURL

If you've ever used an open source OS, of any sort, there's a good chance that cURL has been bundled alongside it, and as a result you will find its license agreements under the license agreements page (things such as game consoles, intelligent cars, and fridges usually feature a build of cURL). However, it's generally always available to you on the command line, and, as a result, it's a favorite of a lot of admins. This is partly because cURL features an extensive (and highly detailed) list of exit codes:

1. For example, curling the BBC results in the following:

```
$ curl bbc.co.uk
$ echo $?
0
```

The `curl` command was successful, so we got a 0 exit code, which pretty much universally means OK.

We can try to `curl` an illegal URL:

```
$ curl bbc.co.uks
curl: (6) Could not resolve host: bbc.co.uks; Unknown
error
$ echo $?
6
```

Here, we get a 6 exit code. This is defined in the cURL manual, as follows:

```
        6       Couldn't resolve host. The given remote host
was not resolved.
```

2. Another popular flag, which you'll see used frequently, is `-I`:

```
$ curl -I bbc.co.uk
HTTP/1.1 301 Moved Permanently
Server: Varnish
Retry-After: 0
Content-Length: 0
Accept-Ranges: bytes
Date: Sun, 09 Dec 2018 15:25:09 GMT
Via: 1.1 varnish
Connection: close
X-Served-By: cache-lcy19221-LCY
X-Cache: MISS
X-Cache-Hits: 0
X-Timer: S1544369109.457379,VS0,VE0
```

```
Location: http://www.bbc.co.uk/
cache-control: public, max-age=3600
```

What you're looking at are the headers from the site we've tried to hit. Instantly, this tells us a couple of things:

- We're actually getting a `301`, redirecting us to a different address
- We're hitting a `varnish` server (a popular caching server)

If we instead attempt to hit the BBC on HTTPS, and with the `www` subdomain, we get the following exit code:

```
$ curl -I https://www.bbc.co.uk
curl: (77) Problem with the SSL CA cert (path? access
rights?)
```

This, crucially, is caused because cURL doesn't have access to a **Certificate Authority (CA)**, as we moved the only authority on the system, at the head of this chapter. Helpfully, it even gives you the exit code, and details of what it thinks the problem is, in the output.

3. This brings us to another cURL option, `-k`:

```
$ curl -k -I https://www.bbc.co.uk
HTTP/1.1 200 OK
Content-Type: text/html; charset=utf-8
ETag: W/"48dfc-dDZDVBqnqFbBCKLot3DWVM1tjvM"
X-Frame-Options: SAMEORIGIN
<SNIP>
X-Cache-Hits: 513
X-Cache-Age: 90
Cache-Control: private, max-age=0, must-revalidate
Vary: Accept-Encoding, X-CDN, X-BBC-Edge-Scheme
```

Here note that we've got a `200` (`OK`) response, despite not having access to a CA to validate the website as being legitimate. `-k` is used to set the insecure flag, see the following section of the cURL documentation (available at `https://curl.haxx.se/docs/manpage.html`):

-k, --insecure

(TLS) By default, every SSL connection curl makes is verified to be secure. This option allows curl to proceed and operate even for server connections otherwise considered insecure.

Obviously, using `-k` isn't advisable, ideal, or practical for everyday use. Instead, you should ensure that your CAs are up to date and the site you're trying to connect to isn't fraudulent.

4. Feel free to replace your CA certificates now:

```
$ sudo mv /etc/pki-backup/ /etc/pki/
```

5. You can also use `curl` to download remote files by using the `-o` option (after you've replaced your CA certificates, or you will get a certificate error):

```
$ curl https://www.bbc.co.uk -o index.html
  % Total % Received % Xferd Average Speed Time Time Time
Current
                                   Dload Upload Total Spent
Left Speed
100 291k 100 291k 0 0 867k 0 --:--:-- --:--:-- --:--:--
871k
$ ls -lh
total 292K
-rw-rw-r--. 1 vagrant vagrant 292K Dec 9 15:33 index.html
```

Here, we simply pulled the entire page and saved it to `index.html` locally.

cURL is also frequently used during troubleshooting and debugging to talk to REST APIs; this is because, from the command line, an engineer or admin can easily craft custom requests and see the output from the web server.

Wget

Like cURL, Wget is a tool for talking to web servers.

By default, the output is quite verbose and will tell you exactly what's happening:

```
$ wget bbc.co.uk
--2018-12-09 15:46:15-- http://bbc.co.uk/
Resolving bbc.co.uk (bbc.co.uk)... 151.101.128.81, 151.101.0.81,
151.101.64.81, ...
Connecting to bbc.co.uk (bbc.co.uk)|151.101.128.81|:80... connected.
HTTP request sent, awaiting response... 301 Moved Permanently
Location: http://www.bbc.co.uk/ [following]
--2018-12-09 15:46:15-- http://www.bbc.co.uk/
Resolving www.bbc.co.uk (www.bbc.co.uk)... 212.58.249.215,
212.58.244.27
```

```
Connecting to www.bbc.co.uk (www.bbc.co.uk)|212.58.249.215|:80...
connected.
HTTP request sent, awaiting response... 301 Moved Permanently
Location: https://www.bbc.co.uk/ [following]
--2018-12-09 15:46:15-- https://www.bbc.co.uk/
Connecting to www.bbc.co.uk (www.bbc.co.uk)|212.58.249.215|:443...
connected.
HTTP request sent, awaiting response... 200 OK
Length: 298285 (291K) [text/html]
Saving to: 'index.html.1'

100%[===========================================================>]
298,285  --.-K/s  in 0.1s

2018-12-09 15:46:15 (2.66 MB/s) - 'index.html.1' saved [298285/298285]
```

Here, we can see the following:

- wget resolving the website to an IP address
- Connecting and getting a 301 telling it the site has moved
- Following the site to http://www.bbc.co.uk
- Getting another 301 telling the client to use HTTPS
- Following the site to https://www.bbc.co.uk
- Finally, connecting, getting a 200, and immediately downloading index.html (which it saves to index.html.1 as we already have one from curl)

From this, we can deduce that the BBC could save milliseconds with each request if it just knocked out one of those redirects (pointing to HTTPS straight away), and we also learn that wget's default behaviour is to save the content locally (instead of spitting things to stdout like cURL).

 wget also features an "insecure" flag in the form of --no-check-certificate, though I don't want to bang on about skipping certificate checks in this book (because they're important).

wget is found to be ideal for downloading multiple files from websites, manipulating what we are downloading, and running checksum checks on the content. Personally, I think the flags are a little more intuitive than cURL, and it's the default behaviour of downloading files locally that I find more than useful when troubleshooting.

OpenSSL

When it comes to certificate checking, there isn't a better tool (right now) than OpenSSL.

Used to create both certificates, and entire CAs, OpenSSL can also be an excellent troubleshooting tool for your certificate problems.

For example, if you want to quickly check the certificate chain of a website, you can use `s_client`:

```
$ openssl s_client -quiet -connect bbc.co.uk:443
depth=2 C = BE, O = GlobalSign nv-sa, OU = Root CA, CN = GlobalSign
Root CA
verify return:1
depth=1 C = BE, O = GlobalSign nv-sa, CN = GlobalSign Organization
Validation CA - SHA256 - G2
verify return:1
depth=0 C = GB, ST = London, L = London, O = British Broadcasting
Corporation, CN = www.bbc.com
verify return:1
```

Here, we can see the `Root CA` (GlobalSign Root CA), followed by the `GlobalSign Organization Validation CA`, and finishing with the `British Broadcasting Corporation` certificate. It also shows us the **common name (CN)** of the site (`www.bbc.com`).

This is actually interesting, because we're not following redirects when we do this, so we're actually returning the certificates used by `bbc.co.uk` instead of `www.bbc.co.uk`, which look like this:

```
$ openssl s_client -quiet -connect www.bbc.co.uk:443
depth=2 C = BE, O = GlobalSign nv-sa, OU = Root CA, CN = GlobalSign
Root CA
verify return:1
depth=1 C = BE, O = GlobalSign nv-sa, CN = GlobalSign Organization
Validation CA - SHA256 - G2
verify return:1
depth=0 C = GB, ST = London, L = London, O = British Broadcasting
Corporation, CN = *.bbc.co.uk
verify return:1
```

If you wanted the actual text representation of certificates in the chain, you can print these:

```
$ openssl s_client -showcerts -connect www.bbc.co.uk:443
CONNECTED(00000003)
depth=2 C = BE, O = GlobalSign nv-sa, OU = Root CA, CN = GlobalSign
Root CA
verify return:1
depth=1 C = BE, O = GlobalSign nv-sa, CN = GlobalSign Organization
Validation CA - SHA256 - G2
verify return:1
depth=0 C = GB, ST = London, L = London, O = British Broadcasting
Corporation, CN = *.bbc.co.uk
verify return:1
---
Certificate chain
 0 s:/C=GB/ST=London/L=London/O=British Broadcasting
Corporation/CN=*.bbc.co.uk
   i:/C=BE/O=GlobalSign nv-sa/CN=GlobalSign Organization Validation CA
- SHA256 - G2
-----BEGIN CERTIFICATE-----
MIIHDDCCBfSgAwIBAgIMRXeRavSdIQuVZRucMA0GCSqGSIb3DQEBCwUAMGYxCzAJ
BgNVBAYTAkJFMRkwFwYDVQQKExBHbG9iYWxTaWduIG52LXNhMTwOgYDVQQDEzNH
<SNIP>
MNHQq0dFAyAa4lcxMjGe/Lfez46BoYQUoQNn8oFv5/xsSI5U3cuxPnKy0ilj1jfc
sDEmTARcxkQrFsFlt7mnmMmCVgEU6ywlqSuR7xg6RLo=
-----END CERTIFICATE-----
 1 s:/C=BE/O=GlobalSign nv-sa/CN=GlobalSign Organization Validation CA
- SHA256 - G2
   i:/C=BE/O=GlobalSign nv-sa/OU=Root CA/CN=GlobalSign Root CA
-----BEGIN CERTIFICATE-----
MIIEaTCCA1GgAwIBAgILBAAAAAABRE7wQkcwDQYJKoZIhvcNAQELBQAwVzELMAkG
A1UEBhMCQkUxGTAXBgNVBAoTEEdsb2JhbFNpZ24gbnYtc2ExEDAOBgNVBAsTB1Jv
<SNIP>
SOlCdjSXVWkkDoPWoC209fN5ikkodBpBocLTJIg1MGCUF7ThBCIxPTsvFwayuJ2G
K1pp74P1S8SqtCr4fKGxhZSM9AyHDPSsQPhZSZg=
-----END CERTIFICATE-----
---
Server certificate
subject=/C=GB/ST=London/L=London/O=British Broadcasting
Corporation/CN=*.bbc.co.uk
issuer=/C=BE/O=GlobalSign nv-sa/CN=GlobalSign Organization Validation
CA - SHA256 - G2
---
No client certificate CA names sent
Peer signing digest: SHA256
<SNIP>
---
```

First, we get the text representation of the BBC certificate, then the text representation of the intermediary CA.

If we want to test and make sure that a secure protocol is being used, we can do so with simple flags:

1. First, we'll check that the insecure `sslv3` isn't enabled:

```
$ openssl s_client -showcerts -connect bbc.co.uk:443 -ssl3
CONNECTED(00000003)
140015333689232:error:14094410:SSL
routines:ssl3_read_bytes:sslv3 alert handshake
failure:s3_pkt.c:1493:SSL alert number 40
140015333689232:error:1409E0E5:SSL
routines:ssl3_write_bytes:ssl handshake
failure:s3_pkt.c:659:
---
no peer certificate available
---
No client certificate CA names sent
---
SSL handshake has read 7 bytes and written 0 bytes
---
New, (NONE), Cipher is (NONE)
Secure Renegotiation IS NOT supported
Compression: NONE
Expansion: NONE
No ALPN negotiated
SSL-Session:
    Protocol : SSLv3
    Cipher : 0000
    Session-ID:
    Session-ID-ctx:
    Master-Key:
    Key-Arg : None
    Krb5 Principal: None
    PSK identity: None
    PSK identity hint: None
    Start Time: 1544372823
    Timeout : 7200 (sec)
    Verify return code: 0 (ok)
---
```

This doesn't work (thankfully).

2. Now, we'll check for `TLS1.2` support:

```
$ openssl s_client -showcerts -connect bbc.co.uk:443 -
tls1_2
CONNECTED(00000003)
depth=2 C = BE, O = GlobalSign nv-sa, OU = Root CA, CN =
GlobalSign Root CA
verify return:1
depth=1 C = BE, O = GlobalSign nv-sa, CN = GlobalSign
Organization Validation CA - SHA256 - G2
verify return:1
depth=0 C = GB, ST = London, L = London, O = British
Broadcasting Corporation, CN = www.bbc.com
verify return:1
---
Certificate chain
 0 s:/C=GB/ST=London/L=London/O=British Broadcasting
Corporation/CN=www.bbc.com
   i:/C=BE/O=GlobalSign nv-sa/CN=GlobalSign Organization
Validation CA - SHA256 - G2
-----BEGIN CERTIFICATE-----
MIIGnDCCBYSgAwIBAgIMIrGYrFe1HwATfmJWMA0GCSqGSIb3DQEBCwUAMG
YxCzAJ
Y2FjZXJ0OL2dzb3JnYW5pemF0aW9udmFsc2hhMmcycjEuY3J0MD8GCCsGAQ
UFBzAB
<SNIP>
J+k3TBG221H4c3ahePIfp7IzijJhdb7jZ21HHMSbJu4LN+C7Z3QuCQDnCJ
IGO31r
YT7jN6sjN7FQXGEk+P0UNg==
-----END CERTIFICATE-----
 1 s:/C=BE/O=GlobalSign nv-sa/CN=GlobalSign Organization
Validation CA - SHA256 - G2
   i:/C=BE/O=GlobalSign nv-sa/OU=Root CA/CN=GlobalSign
Root CA
-----BEGIN CERTIFICATE-----
MIIEaTCCA1GgAwIBAgILBAAAAAAABRE7wQkcwDQYJKoZIhvcNAQELBQAwVz
ELMAkG
A1UEBhMCQkUxGTAXBgNVBAoTEEdsb2JhFNpZ24gbnYtc2ExEDAOBgNVBA
sTB1Jv
<SNIP>
SOlCdjSXVWkkDoPWoC209fN5ikkodBpBocLTJIg1MGCUF7ThBCIxPTsvFw
ayuJ2G
K1pp74P1S8SqtCr4fKGxhZSM9AyHDPSsQPhZSZg=
-----END CERTIFICATE-----
---
Server certificate
subject=/C=GB/ST=London/L=London/O=British Broadcasting
Corporation/CN=www.bbc.com
```

```
issuer=/C=BE/O=GlobalSign nv-sa/CN=GlobalSign Organization
Validation CA - SHA256 - G2
---
No client certificate CA names sent
Peer signing digest: SHA512
Server Temp Key: ECDH, P-256, 256 bits
---
SSL handshake has read 3486 bytes and written 415 bytes
---
New, TLSv1/SSLv3, Cipher is ECDHE-RSA-AES128-GCM-SHA256
Server public key is 2048 bit
Secure Renegotiation IS supported
Compression: NONE
<SNIP>
---
```

Phew! So, we've established that we can talk to bbc.co.uk and that the certificates we see are functional. But what if we wanted information on those certificates?

We know that we're hitting bbc.co.uk, and yet the certificate CN is www.bbc.com; logically, this should result in a certificate error in your browser, so why doesn't it?

3. Let's check!

```
$ openssl s_client -connect bbc.co.uk:443 | openssl x509 -
text | grep DNS
depth=2 C = BE, O = GlobalSign nv-sa, OU = Root CA, CN =
GlobalSign Root CA
verify return:1
depth=1 C = BE, O = GlobalSign nv-sa, CN = GlobalSign
Organization Validation CA - SHA256 - G2
verify return:1
depth=0 C = GB, ST = London, L = London, O = British
Broadcasting Corporation, CN = www.bbc.com
verify return:1
                    DNS:www.bbc.com, DNS:fig.bbc.co.uk,
DNS:bbc.co.uk, DNS:www.bbc.co.uk, DNS:news.bbc.co.uk,
DNS:m.bbc.co.uk, DNS:m.bbc.com, DNS:bbc.com
```

Here, we're piping the output of our s_client command into OpenSSL again. We're then using the x509 (certificate management tool) to output the text information of the cert (decoded from that splodge of text seen previously), and then we're grepping out for DNS.

Specifically, DNS usually sits under this heading:

```
X509v3 Subject Alternative Name:
        DNS:www.bbc.com, DNS:fig.bbc.co.uk,
DNS:bbc.co.uk, DNS:www.bbc.co.uk, DNS:news.bbc.co.uk,
DNS:m.bbc.co.uk, DNS:m.bbc.com, DNS:bbc.com
```

Subject Alternative Names (SANs) are alternative names that this certificate can cover. One of these names is `bbc.co.uk`, and another is `www.bbc.co.uk`. There's also a `news` one and a couple of **mobile (m)** entries (presumably for historic reasons).

Isn't OpenSSL cool?

...When it's not causing mass hysteria.

Using iotop, top, and vmstat for local resource issues

Again, these are more tools that we've definitely covered before, but which can be extremely handy when it comes to troubleshooting local problems, specifically those around resources.

Getting ready

SSH to your CentOS VM:

```
$ vagrant ssh centos1
```

Install the appropriate packages:

```
$ sudo yum install iotop -y
```

How to do it...

We'll run through these tools in brief, but hopefully you've already picked up their basic usage from the rest of this book.

iotop

Invoked with the following command, `iotop` displays I/O usage on a system, by process:

```
$ sudo iotop
```

On our system, this means that we can see very little in the way of activity (because the VM isn't doing much by default):

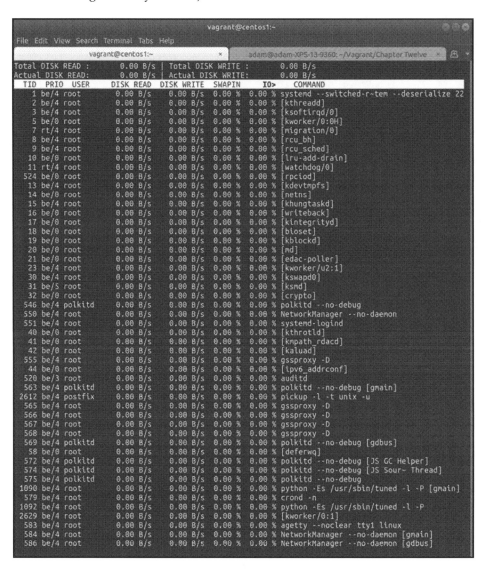

As with `ps`, the square brackets around a thread (such as "`[kthrotld]`", for example) denote kernel threads.

If we wanted to see I/O in action, we could do the following in another session:

```
$ fallocate -l 2G examplefile
$ rsync -z -P --bwlimit=2M examplefile examplefile-copied
```

> We're specifically compressing and bandwidth, limiting the transfer of the preceding file. We've also got a -P in there, but that's mostly so that you can see what's happening as it happens.

In our first session (`iotop`), we should see the rsync command in action:

```
                                    vagrant@centos1:~
File  Edit  View  Search  Terminal  Tabs  Help
              vagrant@centos1:~                 ×              vagrant@centos1:~                 ×
Total DISK READ :      0.00 B/s | Total DISK WRITE :       95.21 M/s
Actual DISK READ:      0.00 B/s | Actual DISK WRITE:       91.17 M/s
  TID  PRIO  USER      DISK READ   DISK WRITE   SWAPIN      IO>    COMMAND
 2706 be/4 vagrant     0.00 B/s    95.21 M/s   0.00 %    0.00 % rsync -z -P --bwlimi~e examplefile-copied
    1 be/4 root        0.00 B/s     0.00 B/s   0.00 %    0.00 % systemd --switched-r~tem --deserialize 22
    2 be/4 root        0.00 B/s     0.00 B/s   0.00 %    0.00 % [kthreadd]
    3 be/4 root        0.00 B/s     0.00 B/s   0.00 %    0.00 % [ksoftirqd/0]
    5 be/0 root        0.00 B/s     0.00 B/s   0.00 %    0.00 % [kworker/0:0H]
    7 rt/4 root        0.00 B/s     0.00 B/s   0.00 %    0.00 % [migration/0]
    8 be/4 root        0.00 B/s     0.00 B/s   0.00 %    0.00 % [rcu_bh]
    9 be/4 root        0.00 B/s     0.00 B/s   0.00 %    0.00 % [rcu_sched]
   10 be/0 root        0.00 B/s     0.00 B/s   0.00 %    0.00 % [lru-add-drain]
   11 rt/4 root        0.00 B/s     0.00 B/s   0.00 %    0.00 % [watchdog/0]
  524 be/0 root        0.00 B/s     0.00 B/s   0.00 %    0.00 % [rpciod]
   13 be/4 root        0.00 B/s     0.00 B/s   0.00 %    0.00 % [kdevtmpfs]
   14 be/0 root        0.00 B/s     0.00 B/s   0.00 %    0.00 % [netns]
   15 be/4 root        0.00 B/s     0.00 B/s   0.00 %    0.00 % [khungtaskd]
   16 be/0 root        0.00 B/s     0.00 B/s   0.00 %    0.00 % [writeback]
   17 be/0 root        0.00 B/s     0.00 B/s   0.00 %    0.00 % [kintegrityd]
   18 be/0 root        0.00 B/s     0.00 B/s   0.00 %    0.00 % [bioset]
   19 be/0 root        0.00 B/s     0.00 B/s   0.00 %    0.00 % [kblockd]
   20 be/0 root        0.00 B/s     0.00 B/s   0.00 %    0.00 % [md]
   21 be/0 root        0.00 B/s     0.00 B/s   0.00 %    0.00 % [edac-poller]
   23 be/4 root        0.00 B/s     0.00 B/s   0.00 %    0.00 % [kworker/u2:1]
  542 be/4 dbus        0.00 B/s     0.00 B/s   0.00 %    0.00 % dbus-daemon --system~---systemd-activation
   31 be/5 root        0.00 B/s     0.00 B/s   0.00 %    0.00 % [ksmd]
   32 be/0 root        0.00 B/s     0.00 B/s   0.00 %    0.00 % [crypto]
  546 be/4 polkitd     0.00 B/s     0.00 B/s   0.00 %    0.00 % polkitd --no-debug
  550 be/4 root        0.00 B/s     0.00 B/s   0.00 %    0.00 % NetworkManager --no-daemon
  551 be/4 root        0.00 B/s     0.00 B/s   0.00 %    0.00 % systemd-logind
   40 be/0 root        0.00 B/s     0.00 B/s   0.00 %    0.00 % [kthrotld]
   41 be/0 root        0.00 B/s     0.00 B/s   0.00 %    0.00 % [kmpath_rdacd]
   42 be/0 root        0.00 B/s     0.00 B/s   0.00 %    0.00 % [kaluad]
  555 be/4 root        0.00 B/s     0.00 B/s   0.00 %    0.00 % gssproxy -D
   44 be/0 root        0.00 B/s     0.00 B/s   0.00 %    0.00 % [ipv6_addrconf]
  520 be/3 root        0.00 B/s     0.00 B/s   0.00 %    0.00 % auditd
  563 be/4 polkitd     0.00 B/s     0.00 B/s   0.00 %    0.00 % polkitd --no-debug [gmain]
  564 be/4 root        0.00 B/s     0.00 B/s   0.00 %    0.00 % gssproxy -D
  565 be/4 root        0.00 B/s     0.00 B/s   0.00 %    0.00 % gssproxy -D
  566 be/4 root        0.00 B/s     0.00 B/s   0.00 %    0.00 % gssproxy -D
 1079 be/4 postfix     0.00 B/s     0.00 B/s   0.00 %    0.00 % qmgr -l -t unix -u
  568 be/4 root        0.00 B/s     0.00 B/s   0.00 %    0.00 % gssproxy -D
  569 be/4 polkitd     0.00 B/s     0.00 B/s   0.00 %    0.00 % polkitd --no-debug [gdbus]
   58 be/0 root        0.00 B/s     0.00 B/s   0.00 %    0.00 % [deferwq]
  572 be/4 polkitd     0.00 B/s     0.00 B/s   0.00 %    0.00 % polkitd --no-debug [JS GC Helper]
  574 be/4 polkitd     0.00 B/s     0.00 B/s   0.00 %    0.00 % polkitd --no-debug [JS Sour~ Thread]
  575 be/4 polkitd     0.00 B/s     0.00 B/s   0.00 %    0.00 % polkitd --no-debug
 1090 be/4 root        0.00 B/s     0.00 B/s   0.00 %    0.00 % python -Es /usr/sbin/tuned -l -P [gmain]
  579 be/4 root        0.00 B/s     0.00 B/s   0.00 %    0.00 % crond -n
 1092 be/4 root        0.00 B/s     0.00 B/s   0.00 %    0.00 % python -Es /usr/sbin/tuned -l -P
  583 be/4 root        0.00 B/s     0.00 B/s   0.00 %    0.00 % agetty --noclear tty1 linux
  584 be/4 root        0.00 B/s     0.00 B/s   0.00 %    0.00 % NetworkManager --no-daemon [gmain]
  586 be/4 root        0.00 B/s     0.00 B/s   0.00 %    0.00 % NetworkManager --no-daemon [gdbus]
```

Note how the very top line is our command, and shows our specific DISK WRITEs as being 95.21 M/s.

top

You've probably used top so many times now that you're sick of reading about it, and you probably know a great deal about how useful it can be, despite its simple invocation.

```
$ top
```

Pretty much universal across UNIX systems, top gives you a near-real-time representation of process usage across your system:

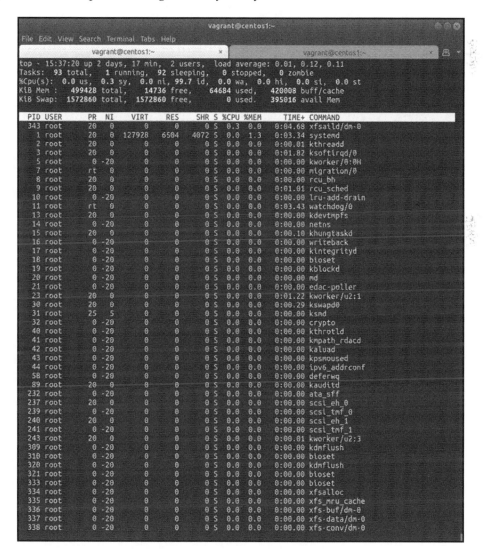

When it comes to troubleshooting, top is generally indispensable. Not only useful for seeing process, memory, and CPU information at a glance, top will work with an extremely small footprint, meaning that it's likely to work on systems that are seemingly exponentially contended.

Even if you prefer top alternatives, such as `htop` or glances, there's no guarantee that these programs will be available on each and every system you touch. Because of this, it's a good idea to become familiar with top, then fall back to alternatives once you're sure you can use it properly (or at least passably!).

vmstat

On systems that are very contended, or where you might want to output system information for later correlation and debugging, vmstat is ideal. Giving you more of a global overview of your system, it can be handy to store periodic values to a file, which you can then check later:

1. When run on its own, it can also be set to periodically print to screen:

```
$ vmstat -t 3
procs -----------memory---------- ---swap-- -----io---- -
system-- ------cpu----- -----timestamp-----
 r b swpd free buff cache si so bi bo in cs us sy id wa st
UTC
 2 0 0 15072 164 419900 0 0 1 12 11 11 0 0 100 0 0
2018-12-11 15:40:46
 0 0 0 15084 164 419900 0 0 0 0 15 12 0 0 100 0 0
2018-12-11 15:40:49
 0 0 0 15084 164 419900 0 0 0 0 11 9 0 0 100 0 0
2018-12-11 15:40:52
 0 0 0 15084 164 419900 0 0 0 0 11 10 0 0 100 0 0
2018-12-11 15:40:55
 0 0 0 15084 164 419900 0 0 0 0 10 8 0 0 100 0 0
2018-12-11 15:40:58
 0 0 0 15084 164 419900 0 0 0 0 15 12 0 0 100 0 0
2018-12-11 15:41:01
...
```

2. Outputting to a file is just as easy; simply redirect `stdout`:

```
$ vmstat -t 3 > vmstats
^C
$ cat vmstats
procs -----------memory---------- ---swap-- -----io---- -
```

```
system-- ------cpu----- -----timestamp-----
 r b swpd free buff cache si so bi bo in cs us sy id wa st
UTC
 1 0 0 11848 164 423132 0 0 1 12 11 11 0 0 100 0 0
2018-12-11 15:43:35
 0 0 0 11856 164 423136 0 0 0 17 12 0 0 100 0 0
2018-12-11 15:43:38
 0 0 0 11856 164 423136 0 0 1 15 19 0 0 100 0 0
2018-12-11 15:43:41
 0 0 0 11856 164 423136 0 0 0 14 11 0 0 100 0 0
2018-12-11 15:43:44
```

Using ps, lsof, Strace, and /proc for service issues

ps, lsof, strace, and /proc are all valuable tools when troubleshooting under fire. They can display something so obvious that you'd never have thought to look for it in a million years, and they can also work through certain tasks quicker than you'll be able to do so yourself.

strace is probably the most often overlooked of these tools, and it's easily one of the most awkward to learn well, but it should always be at the back of your mind for program debugging.

 Personally, I generally forget about strace quite a lot, that is until someone wanders over and asks me why I'm trying to debug something in the most awkward way possible, before reminding me that strace is a thing that exists.

Getting ready

SSH to your CentOS VM:

> `$ vagrant ssh centos1`

Install lsof for this section (the others should be installed already):

> `$ sudo yum install lsof -y`

How to do it...

Running through each of our commands in turn, let's make our `ps` rundown very quick!

ps

`ps`, which is used to show a `snapshot` of the current processes on a system, is a first port of call for many admins, and with good reason:

```
$ ps -ef
UID PID PPID C STIME TTY TIME CMD
root 1 0 0 Dec09 ? 00:00:03 /usr/lib/systemd/systemd --switched-root -
-system --d
root 2 0 0 Dec09 ? 00:00:00 [kthreadd]
root 3 2 0 Dec09 ? 00:00:01 [ksoftirqd/0]
root 5 2 0 Dec09 ? 00:00:00 [kworker/0:0H]
root 7 2 0 Dec09 ? 00:00:00 [migration/0]
root 8 2 0 Dec09 ? 00:00:00 [rcu_bh]
root 9 2 0 Dec09 ? 00:00:01 [rcu_sched]
<SNIP>
root 2690 2 0 15:28 ? 00:00:01 [kworker/0:1]
postfix 2756 1065 0 15:42 ? 00:00:00 pickup -l -t unix -u
root 2759 2 0 15:43 ? 00:00:00 [kworker/0:2]
root 2783 2 0 15:48 ? 00:00:00 [kworker/0:0]
vagrant 2800 2636 0 15:50 pts/0 00:00:00 ps -ef
```

As noted, `ps` also includes kernel threads by default (those in square brackets).

More frequently than carefully crafted `ps` commands I've just seen people pipe the output through other commands to accomplish what they need. It's not uncommon to see commands such as this in the wild:

```
$ ps aux | grep rsysl | grep -v grep | column -t -o, | cut -f1,9,10,11
-d","
root,Dec09,0:22,/usr/sbin/rsyslogd
```

This isn't necessarily a bad thing, and it's generally done as a quick query instead of something you'd actually put in a script.

Big tip, no one (well... nearly no one) writes commands, as they're printed in text books. More often than not, the person crafting the command will get a close approximation of what they want using the primary command, and then they'll shove it through a series of other commands to get the output they really need. We all (well... nearly all) do it.

What I'm getting at is don't worry when you can't remember exact `ps` syntax when troubleshooting; do whatever you can do quickly.

lsof

`lsof` is a great tool with a very confusing help section. In short, it's used to list open files on a system, but run raw (without arguments), that's a lot of information.

The most common way I've seen it used is like so:

```
$ lsof | head -n1; sudo lsof | grep "$(pidof rsyslogd)" | grep -v
"socket\|lib64\|dev\|rs:main\|in:imjour" | grep REG
COMMAND PID TID USER FD TYPE DEVICE SIZE/OFF NODE NAME
rsyslogd 861 root txt REG 253,0 663872 34070960 /usr/sbin/rsyslogd
rsyslogd 861 root mem REG 0,19 4194304 7276
/run/log/journal/deb74f074ec9471f91c6c5dd7370484f/system.journal
rsyslogd 861 root 4w REG 253,0 182727 100834552 /var/log/messages
rsyslogd 861 root 5r REG 0,19 4194304 7276
/run/log/journal/deb74f074ec9471f91c6c5dd7370484f/system.journal
rsyslogd 861 root 6w REG 253,0 12423 100834553 /var/log/secure
rsyslogd 861 root 7w REG 253,0 15083 100664480 /var/log/cron
rsyslogd 861 root 9w REG 253,0 392 100834554 /var/log/maillog
```

This is confusing, yes, so let's break it down a bit:

```
lsof | head -n1;
```

This is one stupid trick to make sure you have the header line in your output to screen; it does arguably waste clock cycles, as we're running `lsof` twice (once just to get the first line), but who's counting?

The semi-colon means the end of the command:

```
sudo lsof | grep "$(pidof rsyslogd)"
```

Now, we're using `lsof` again, only this time we're specifically grepping out lines that match the process ID of `rsyslogd`. The use of a dollar and parentheses here invokes a `subshell` that returns the value of the command run:

```
$ pidof rsyslogd
861
```

Lastly, we run our output through `grep -v` to return a list of strings. These are generally built up gradually by the person running the command, while they work out the entries they don't need. Finally, we grep for REG explicitly to remove other entries we're not interested in (such as DIR, for `directory`):

```
grep -v "socket\|lib64\|dev\|rs:main\|in:imjour" | grep REG
```

It looks stupid and long, but it works.

Strace

`strace`, a program that's written to specifically trace system calls (and signals), is often forgotten, but extremely powerful. If you want to find out what a program is doing in real-time, you can use `strace`.

At a glance, it can be extremely baffling:

```
$ sudo strace -p $(pidof NetworkManager)
strace: Process 550 attached
restart_syscall(<... resuming interrupted poll ...>) = 1
epoll_wait(14, [], 1, 0) = 0
poll([{fd=11, events=POLLIN}], 1, 0) = 1 ([{fd=11, revents=POLLIN}])
read(11,
"\2\0\0\0\200\0\0\0G\10\0\0\20\0\0\00054\0\0\0\0\0\0\0\0\0\0\0\0\0\0\0".
.., 2048) = 128
poll([{fd=11, events=POLLIN}], 1, 0) = 0 (Timeout)
poll([{fd=3, events=POLLIN}, {fd=6, events=POLLIN}, {fd=7,
events=POLLIN|POLLPRI}, {fd=11, events=POLLIN}, {fd=12,
events=POLLIN}, {fd=14, events=POLLIN}, {fd=15, events=POLLIN}], 7,
41395) = 1 ([{fd=11, revents=POLLIN}])
epoll_wait(14, [], 1, 0)
...
```

What we're looking at here are the events triggered by me connecting to a box (`NetworkManager` being the process we're following).

We can see that a few system calls are made, mainly `epoll_wait` and `poll`.

The man pages for these calls lists the following:

- `epoll_wait`, `epoll_pwait`: Wait for an I/O event on an `epoll` file descriptor
- `poll`, `ppoll`: Wait for some event on a file descriptor

These might not be overly helpful when you're not a C or kernel hacker, but with a perusal of the manual pages, they can point you to the source of the problems.

Generally, `strace` is a nice tool to use when a program is locking up, and you're not sure why (usually after you've checked the logs and discovered there's nothing useful in them). You can connect to the program as it's running, wait for (or cause) a lock, and then find the last few things it tried to do.

Another useful use of `strace` is finding files that a program is opening:

```
$ strace cat testfile 2>&1 | grep open
open("/etc/ld.so.cache", O_RDONLY|O_CLOEXEC) = 3
open("/lib64/libc.so.6", O_RDONLY|O_CLOEXEC) = 3
open("/usr/lib/locale/locale-archive", O_RDONLY|O_CLOEXEC) = 3
open("testfile", O_RDONLY) = -1 ENOENT (No such file or directory)
open("/usr/share/locale/locale.alias", O_RDONLY|O_CLOEXEC) = 3
open("/usr/share/locale/en_GB.UTF-8/LC_MESSAGES/libc.mo", O_RDONLY) =
-1 ENOENT (No such file or directory)
open("/usr/share/locale/en_GB.utf8/LC_MESSAGES/libc.mo", O_RDONLY) =
-1 ENOENT (No such file or directory)
open("/usr/share/locale/en_GB/LC_MESSAGES/libc.mo", O_RDONLY) = 3
open("/usr/share/locale/en.UTF-8/LC_MESSAGES/libc.mo", O_RDONLY) = -1
ENOENT (No such file or directory)
open("/usr/share/locale/en.utf8/LC_MESSAGES/libc.mo", O_RDONLY) = -1
ENOENT (No such file or directory)
open("/usr/share/locale/en/LC_MESSAGES/libc.mo", O_RDONLY) = -1 ENOENT
(No such file or directory)
```

Here, we ran `cat testfile`, but did so with `strace` as the first command.

We can then see (by grepping for `open`) the files that cat attempted to use when reading our file, and we can also see the response when it determines the file doesn't exist.

> `strace` prints to `stderr` by default, so we redirected `stderr` to `stdout` in our command using `2>&1` first.

/proc

Again, you're probably sick of reading about /proc, but here's a real-world example of how useful it can be.

VMs suck for entropy, so it's usually a good idea to work out how much random data you can generate on your system. You can find that a lack of entropy can severely hamper processes that need to do things such as encrypt files.

Using /proc, we can determine the entropy that's currently available to our system:

```
$ cat /proc/sys/kernel/random/entropy_avail
874
```

This is one great example of how useful /proc can be. But what else is it useful for?

We could use /proc to quickly count up the number of CPU cores our machine has:

```
$ cat /proc/cpuinfo | grep "core id"
core id : 0
```

We only have one CPU core in our machine. How about network statistics?

Here, we're using /proc to check the TCP statistics relating to our system, at the current point in time:

```
$ cat /proc/net/snmp | grep Tcp
Tcp: RtoAlgorithm RtoMin RtoMax MaxConn ActiveOpens PassiveOpens
AttemptFails EstabResets CurrEstab InSegs OutSegs RetransSegs InErrs
OutRsts InCsumErrors
Tcp: 1 200 120000 -1 117 5 0 5 1 19756 13690 2 0 97 0
```

Yes, there are better and faster ways of getting this information in general, but it's important to appreciate that a lot of the information you otherwise scrape is actually gained from the "process information pseudo-filesystem" in the first place.

Making a copy of problems for later debugging

In this section, we're going to talk about copying files for later debugging. Frequently, we find ourselves on systems where a problem has resulted in an outage. In these situations, the impetus among engineers can be to get the system up again, no matter what the problem is.

You might discover, during your troubleshooting steps, that /var/log has filled up, and has taken the rest of the disk with it. In these situations, it can be incredibly tempting to simply delete the offending log file(s) and restart the broken daemon.

You should do that, but not right away. First, you need to make sure you've got the file for later consumption so that the problem doesn't happen again.

Getting ready

In this example, we're going to mess around with some of the log files in /var/log/. We're going to use our CentOS VM again.

How to do it...

Take a quick look in /var/log/ at the messages file:

```
$ ls -lh /var/log/messages
-rw-------. 1 root root 179K Dec 11 16:18 /var/log/messages
```

It's not huge, but if you've got an incredibly small disk, this could be a massive problem.

Say you've completely run out of space on the /var/log partition—what happens?

Let's remind ourselves of an example VM's partition layout, noting the lack of a dedicated '/var' partition:

```
$ df -h
Filesystem Size Used Avail Use% Mounted on
/dev/mapper/VolGroup00-LogVol00 38G 4.8G 33G 13% /
devtmpfs 235M 0 235M 0% /dev
tmpfs 244M 0 244M 0% /dev/shm
tmpfs 244M 4.5M 240M 2% /run
tmpfs 244M 0 244M 0% /sys/fs/cgroup
/dev/sda2 1014M 63M 952M 7% /boot
tmpfs 49M 0 49M 0% /run/user/1000
```

The quick answers to the preceding question are as follows:

- If the /var/log partition is the same one that / is on (as it is here), you've got a problem, and might even find yourself unable to reboot a system due to a lack of space. The /var/log partition could consume all available disk space, even what's needed by critical services, such as SSH.

- If the `/var/log` partition is on its own partition (which it really should be), then you can't log anything anymore. While this might not bring the system down, it would still cause issues if you need to keep logs for debugging or auditing purposes (and don't pipe them away somewhere, such as an Elastic Stack cluster).

In the case of the first problem, you've pretty much got to resign yourself to rebooting the box using either one of several abrupt tricks (or getting the data center to take a look themselves).

In the case of the second problem, you'll have to do a few things:

1. Determine which process is running rampant, using the various other techniques we've discussed. Kill the process and stop the service if it can't be fixed immediately.
2. Copy the contents of `/var/log/messages` to another part of the system (a partition with more space) or a different system if required (using `rsync` or `scp`).
3. See if you can manually trigger `logrotate` to rotate and compress your messages log. This might fail depending on the actual space that's available.

If you can't manually compress or `logrotate` a file, it may be time to delete the original messages file and create a new one in its place (with the same permissions).

 You should make a copy of your logs prior to deleting them. Otherwise, you'll have no idea what happened to cause the issue in the first place.

Temporary solutions and when to invoke them

Temporary solutions can be great, and necessary, depending on the situation you've found yourself in.

For example, if you've found yourself being awoken by an alarm at 5:00, informing you that a disk only has about 10% of disk space left available, you might decide to invoke a temporary fix:

1. You've troubleshooted and determined that the disk is filling up at a rate of a gigabyte an hour, meaning it'll be full in an hour and a half
2. You've also determined that the LVM setup on the box has 10 GB of free space available to you, to grow your logical volume
3. You check to make sure the problem isn't caused by a more significant issue (the site being down) and realize it's just a noisy log because of Christmas sales
4. You apply 50% of the free LVM space to your logical volume, and go back to bed

This is a good temporary solution because it means that the problem can be safely investigated during daylight hours (when others might be available, and you making the problem worse won't be that much of an issue). However, you should be aware of the flaws.

Temporary solutions in IT, as in UK politics, tend to become permanent fixes faster than you can blink. In our example, this will be less of an issue, because we only have a finite amount of disk space, but I've seen it happen whereby this solution becomes the recommended "fix" and engineers proceed to continue adding virtual disks for much longer than they should, only compounding the problem further (and potentially masking other issues, too).

How to do it...

If a temporary solution buys you time, or means alarms stop going off and a website comes back online, then by all means do them, but also make a note of what you've done and log it in whatever ticketing system you use.

Be responsible for your own cludge. It's on you, and only you, to ensure that your temporary cron-job, system timer, or disk-space extension doesn't become the permanent fix for a problem.

In a similar vein, if you write a bash script to periodically check a log file, and if it's over a certain size to compress it, make sure you also write checks to ensure that the bash script is working. There's nothing more annoying than coming to a system that has a "fix" applied to it, only to discover that the bash script eventually fell over due to being unable to work with files over a certain size, and nobody noticed.

You will not be thanked if a temporary "fix" that you put in place brings down a box a few months later. This will also only be made worse if you've since left the company, and find that your name is jokingly dragged through the mud forevermore, whenever there's a similar issue to the one you've caused. If there's one thing you should avoid, it's allowing your name to become a verb in relation to something going wrong.

Handling irate developers

The systems administration life would be an awful lot easier if we never had to deal with other people (and I'd imagine those other people would say much the same about us).

So, let's talk about developers. Our developer friends are doing their job, developing. It's in the nature of computing that no software is perfect, and bugs will creep in to even the most beautiful of code; it can even pass its previous tests, run perfectly in development and preprod environments, only to bring down production.

You can think you've got a solution working perfectly, running like a dream, purring like a cat, and then one new "feature" from a developer can seemingly bring an entire solution crashing to the floor. It can be tempting to look for someone to blame in these scenarios. However, I would instead urge calm and composure, because getting annoyed at something usually only makes the situation worse (and, half of the time, it's something you did and forgot about that caused the problem anyway...). Everyone can start to blame everyone else in nightmare situations, so it's up to you (and your colleagues) to remain level-headed, working together to find the root of the problem.

If a developer comes to you to report an issue, either in a live environment or a non-live environment, and assuming they've gone through the appropriate channels before doing so (submitting a ticket, talking to team leads, and so on), you may find that they're already frustrated with what's going on.

How to do it...

It can be tempting to dismiss this sort of request out of hand because you're busy on something else, or you don't think it's your job to fix the problem. This would be bad diplomacy, and would generally only result in both parties getting annoyed with each other:

1. Instead, appreciate that the other person is only trying to do their job, and whatever they've come to report, it's probably hindering them actually carrying on with the said job. The problem could be of their own design, or because of an issue you've missed in your infrastructure, but whatever the reason, it's important to handle the situation carefully.

2. Even if you're not the point of contact for the issue in question, and you have no idea how you'd even start debugging it, consider smiling, politely explaining how much of an idiot you are with things such as that, and directing them (or better yet leading them) to someone who might be able to triage or help with their problem.

Good communication and diplomacy results in a calmer working environment, and the idea of "you scratch my back, I'll scratch yours" comes into play, if you ever need a friendly `dev` to help you debug an issue you think might be caused by an application.

This goes the other way, too; don't feel pressured to drop absolutely everything just because someone has come over to you and started screaming that "your terrible infrastructure sucks"; in these situations, it's best to first find a mediator for the problem (a manager, usually) before looking into an issue. It's not appropriate for anyone to scream at or belittle anyone else in a workplace, remember that, and if you ever find yourself getting wound up, it might be a good idea to remove yourself from a situation entirely before it escalates. I've seen good engineers get into serious trouble and put their jobs on the line, just for having a temper.

Handling irate managers

Managers, such as developers, are only doing their jobs. They are perhaps harder to talk to in some circumstances, as they sometimes just want the problem and the solution to the problem in plain English, even if you don't know what the solution (or problem) is yet. Some of the best managers understand that not every problem can be located and fixed within ten minutes, and, likewise, some of the worst expects you to have fully formed solutions in the time it takes them to stand up from their desk and march over to yours.

Should you find yourself in the situation where you're having to talk to an irate manager, perhaps because there's a production issue and someone higher than them is breathing down their neck too, try not to wind them up further by bombarding them with jargon they're unlikely to understand, or similarly giving them vague platitudes.

 I'm using the term *manager* loosely here; the same logical could be applied to delivery leads, team leads, and so on.

How to do it...

Not all managers are technical, but a lot are. It's generally a good idea to establish how technical your manager is early on so that you can gauge the exact level of information you need to pass on to them during an issue. If they're on, above, or about your level, you can probably give them everything and allow for them to distill it upstream; if they're less technically minded, it's better to summarize key points.

Remember that good managers manage and shield engineers or others from the day-to-day pressures of a workplace that aren't technical. Sure, you might get invited to the odd meeting to explain a solution, or defend a technical decision, but for the most part it's an engineer's job to engineer, an administrator's job to administrate, and a manager's job to manage (while also doing all the meetings the others don't want to).

Should an angry manager start bombarding you with questions, or asking for updates every five minutes, during a period when you're trying to concentrate, it might be time to direct them to a ticket you're keeping your logs in, and simply pasting a message in there every few minutes to update stakeholders on progress. I mentioned slack channels too, or other communication mediums, and these can be a good way of keeping people informed while allowing you time to concentrate.

Before now, I've been dragged on to conference calls with the following people on during actual problems:

- My manager
- My manager's manager
- My manager's manager's manager
- Other members of the team
- Members of the development team
- A representative of the sales team
- A representative of the client-relations team

Now, I don't know about you, but that seems like too many people for a call when there's an ongoing problem.

In my professional opinion, it is OK to say you can't join a call of that magnitude right that second, while also providing an update of where exactly you are in your troubleshooting.

Handling irate business owners

Above co-workers, managers, and even division leaders, are business owners. Again, there are good business owners, and there are bad business owners. Most of the time, you'll probably never meet them in larger companies, but it seems to be something of a universal law that you'll cross paths at some point, and sometimes, this will coincide with an actual outage, just because the universe thinks it's funny.

Business owners can lose their job and their business in one fell swoop if there's a perceived mistake in their leadership. This won't be a defense of capitalism, and I'm not about to suggest the rising up of the working classes to seize the means of production, but it's always worth bearing in mind that the person who's getting angry at you for not giving complete enough (in their mind) answers might actually be about to lose their customer base and, by extension, livelihood.

How to do it...

Tread carefully when the person you're talking to has the power to hire or fire you, depending on what you say. Where you might lose your job if you royally screw up (and frankly, it would have to be continuous and egregious screw ups), it's only your job, and you might be able to find another one while putting that particular chapter of your life behind you.

Hopefully, you won't, but if you do ever find yourself in the situation where you're dealing with an extremely irate individual with the power to let you go (off a cliff or otherwise), it's generally tread-on-eggshells time. Assure them that you're doing everything in your power to resolve the issue, point to progress made, if there is any, and reassure them that every able-bodied individual is working on the problem.

Who knows—if you impress them enough in a time of crisis, keeping your head when all around are losing theirs, you might find yourself in a favored position in the not-too-distant future.

Roundup - Troubleshooting and workplace diplomacy

This chapter was something of a mixed bag because I tried to suggest what the best courses of action can be during a production (or even a minor) problem. I included programs I thought might be useful to you in a pinch, some vague directives on what you should think about during an outage, and then concluded with a few suggestions on dealing with other people during what could be the most stressful time of your professional career.

All that said, there's time for a few more points I'd like to make.

Don't trust time

A good 70 percent of the time (random figure), I've found time to be the root cause of most of my problems. It is because of this that one of the first commands I run when I log on to a box is `date`:

```
$ date
Tue 11 Dec 17:51:33 UTC 2018
```

If the time is wrong (and not just offset because of timezones), then there's a very good chance that the weird and wonderful problems you're seeing are the direct result of two or more computer systems arguing about which of their completely arbitrary representations of time is correct.

Fix time before you fix anything else.

 Incorrect time and fixing incorrect time can cause problems of its own so, check and keep backups regularly.

Don't overlook the simple

Alongside `date`, another command I run almost as an impulse is `df -h`:

```
$ df -h
Filesystem Size Used Avail Use% Mounted on
/dev/mapper/VolGroup00-LogVol00 38G 4.8G 33G 13% /
devtmpfs 235M 0 235M 0% /dev
tmpfs 244M 0 244M 0% /dev/shm
tmpfs 244M 4.5M 240M 2% /run
tmpfs 244M 0 244M 0% /sys/fs/cgroup
/dev/sda2 1014M 63M 952M 7% /boot
tmpfs 49M 0 49M 0% /run/user/1000
```

Like time being wrong, cosmically stupid errors can occur when disk space has run out, with no actual indication as to what the real problem is. Programs rarely print *I can't write to this file, so I'm broken,* and instead usually settle on cryptic, baffling, and altogether mind-numbing errors that make no sense on the face of it.

Check disk space second.

On "cloud" deployments

Time for another small rant!

One of the most annoying things that "cloud" has done has been to introduce the "solution" of "destroy and redeploy".

In the realm of temporary fixes, I consider the most egregious temporary fix to be "Oh, just tear down the solution and let it rebuild; that error happens sometimes."

This isn't a "fix", and it annoys me immensely when I hear it. Yes, we can simply destroy and recreate environments these days, at the drop of a hat usually, but that doesn't excuse the original error that caused your systems to break in the first place. If they did it once, there's every chance that they'll do it again, and if they wake me up in the middle of the night or interrupt my holiday to Egypt, someone is getting a sternly worded email.

"Destroy and recreate" should be a means for getting a solution back online, but as we covered in this chapter, you should also have a backup of any files you might need to work out what went wrong, and you shouldn't consider the problem to be "resolved" until it stops happening.

If anyone ever tells you a solution is to destroy and recreate, tell them to fix their code.

Learn from my mistakes

In terms of handling irate people, I'm a good authority, because as many of my former colleagues will attest, I usually was that irate person.

It took me a good few years to realize that getting angry at a situation or people didn't make the situation any better, or my workplace nicer; it only made my mood worse. Thankfully, I've learned from my mistakes, and I take a very different approach to problems these days, not just flipping immediately to complain-and-blame mode (though I would always endeavour to fix the problem) and instead taking a step back from the situation first, assessing it, and then diving in with a nice cup of tea.

Being zen in a crisis is hard; I'm not going to claim otherwise, but the more people with level heads, the calmer the situation will stay. It's far too easy to jump on to random threads when you're worked up, reaching dead ends and getting more annoyed before backtracking.

Breathe.

13

BSDs, Solaris, Windows, IaaS and PaaS, and DevOps

The following topics will be covered in this chapter:

- Determining the type of system you're on
- Understanding how the BSDs differ
- Understanding how Solaris and illumos differ
- Understanding how Windows differs
- IaaS (Infrastructure as a Service)
- PaaS (Platform as a Service)
- The Ops versus DevOps Wars

Introduction

When I was approached to write this book, I was initially asked to compose twelve chapters on the Linux system and modern administration. I now wish I'd agreed to that initial pitch, but instead I brazenly suggested a thirteenth chapter. What a fool I was.

So here we are, the ultimate chapter in this slog of a read (sorry, I'm so sorry), and it's all about the other systems in the computing world that you're going to need to know, because unfortunately, modern computing and IT infrastructure is frequently a hodgepodge of trends and antiques, in the form of Windows, Linux, and the mesh that goes in between.

We're going to look at the BSDs briefly, because they're probably the closest you can get to "real" Unix in this day and age, and they're also close enough to Linux that there's BSD users out there who get viscerally angry when you use phrases like "they're close enough to Linux."

Then, we're going to discuss Solaris (again, in brief) and talk about the two forms it takes in modern infrastructure.

We'll have to discuss Windows, although I'm going to attempt to keep this section the briefest. If you're anything like me, you dislike the word "Windows" and all the connotations it brings. (We're not fooled by your semi-hippy approach to Linux in recent years, Microsoft—some of us like to be stubbornly tribal.)

Following our foray into other OSes, we're also going to look at **Infrastructure as a Service (IaaS)** and **Platform as a Service (PaaS)**, despite how stupid these anagrams are, because they're a big part of modern DevOps and platform creation. You will have to use services like AWS and Azure in any full career, so it's good to get an understanding of the way they work sooner rather than later.

Lastly, there'll be a word on DevOps (I'll save the surprises of that section, for that section).

Determining the type of system you're on

Think about this: you were blindfolded, bundled into the trunk of a car, and then unmasked at the other end of a long journey to be presented with a blinking prompt. How would you determine what sort of system you were on?

Your immediate instinct might be to assume you've been placed in front of a Linux box, but that's not a certainty. While it's true that Linux dominates the server's space, just because the instance has a black screen, white text, and a login prompt, doesn't mean that you've been placed in front of our friendly penguin OS.

It could be Linux, a BSD system, a Solaris system, or one of the many Unix derivatives from the nineties.

Assuming you've been given the credentials to log in, do so.

How to do it...

There's an easy starting point.

uname

When you've logged in successfully, determine what sort of kernel you're running:

```
$ uname
Linux
```

Well that was anti-climactic... it's just a regular Linux system.

But what if it wasn't? Imagine the following:

```
$ uname
FreeBSD
```

That's more like it! This is a FreeBSD box!

Or is it a different BSD?

```
$ uname
OpenBSD
```

An OpenBSD box, cool! But we can go one further:

```
$ uname
SunOS
```

Huh? What's a SunOS when it's at home?

 The short answer is that you can assume you've landed on either an Oracle Solaris or illumos distribution, both of which are relatively rare, but deserve a degree of respect.

The filesystem check

If you're still uncertain, you can quickly check the type of filesystem being used for slash-root, /:

```
$ mount | grep "/ "
/dev/mapper/VolGroup00-LogVol00 on / type xfs
(rw,relatime,seclabel,attr2,inode64,noquota)
```

XFS is commonly found on Linux systems, specifically RHEL and CentOS:

```
$ mount | grep "/ "
/dev/ada0s1a on / (ufs, local, journaled soft-updates)
```

The **Unix file system** (**UFS**) is usually seen on FreeBSD boxes (alongside ZFS, if you've got the RAM for it):

```
$ mount | grep "/ "
/dev/wd0a on / type ffs (local)
```

FFS? You're joking... no, it's the **fast file system** (**FFS**), and it's commonly used on OpenBSD boxes:

> FFS and UFS have the same heritage, though the code base isn't identical.

```
$ mount | grep "/ "
/ on rpool/ROOT/openindiana read/write/setuid/devices/dev=4410002 on
Thu Jan 1 00:00:00 1970
```

While we don't get an actual filesystem type here, we can see openindiana listed in the output, which we know to be an illumos distribution. We can then use zfs to determine what our filesystem design is (and confirm it's zfs):

```
$ zfs list
NAME USED AVAIL REFER MOUNTPOINT
rpool 6.82G 41.1G 31.5K /rpool
rpool/ROOT 2.70G 41.1G 23K legacy
rpool/ROOT/openindiana 2.70G 41.1G 2.46G /
rpool/ROOT/openindiana/var 203M 41.1G 202M /var
rpool/dump 2.00G 41.1G 2.00G -
rpool/export 73.5K 41.1G 23K /export
rpool/export/home 50.5K 41.1G 23K /export/home
rpool/export/home/vagrant 27.5K 41.1G 27.5K /export/home/vagrant
rpool/swap 2.13G 43.3G 12K -
```

How it works...

Though the prompts might look the same (though generally, these distributions don't set Bash as the default shell; that's a Linux thing), but the underlying system can be vastly different from the familiar GNU userland that you're used to.

When we run uname, as we've discussed previously, we output the kernel of the system we've logged on to.

Hopefully it's a Linux box, especially if you've been held against your will and asked to fix something, but even if you're somewhat good with Linux, things should be relatively familiar. Processes run, the default tools are the same, and you can read README files or man pages to understand what you don't yet.

The filesystem check we did isn't the most scientific, but you can usually guarantee that commands like mount and df will be available to you, thanks to their pedigree.

There's more...

There's a notable omission in the preceding section, and that's how you work out if you're on a Windows system or not.

The easiest way I've found to check that I'm at a Windows prompt is to measure how quickly my soul is ebbing away from my body. Failing that, I look for a Music folder somewhere on the filesystem, which seems to be inexplicably on desktop and server installs alike.

Obviously, if the preceding two methods fail you, then consider that Windows usually has a GUI (unless it's a modern Server OS with a trendy systems administrator, in which case it might just be a blue PowerShell prompt instead. Either way, I suspect you'll know).

Understanding how the BSDs differ

You might have noticed that I deliberately split up OpenBSD and FreeBSD in this chapter, but they're just different distributions of "BSD", right?

Wrong.

Unlike Linux, the different "flavors" of BSD don't share a kernel, and are more like different OSes than different distributions.

OpenBSD, FreeBSD, NetBSD, and Dragonfly BSD are all unique and distinct projects.

 NetBSD even has a Dreamcast port. Finally, that console has a use!

That's not to say there's no sharing of code and fixes between the distributions—providing porting is quicker than writing your own implementation, and the BSDs are more likely to use more "liberal" open source licenses, such as the MIT license, instead of "restrictive" open source licenses like the GPL (generally for ideological reasons).

The differences

As we've already said, the BSDs are distinct operating systems, with an estimated ranking of popularity as follows:

- FreeBSD
- OpenBSD
- NetBSD
- Other BSDs

Here, I'm going to touch on the two most popular and well-known: FreeBSD and OpenBSD.

FreeBSD

An OS with a varied focus (servers, desktops, IOT devices), FreeBSD is the most popular of the BSD derivatives.

It prides itself on having a vast array of software available, both in the form of pre-built packages (built quarterly at the time of writing) and "ports" that are built locally and are usually the most recent version of that piece of software.

 A lot of open source software is heavily Linux focused. This isn't the fault of the BSDs—it simply comes down to market share. Because of this focus, the FreeBSD project has a lot of volunteers who dedicate their time to making packages work natively on FreeBSD, having to do minor and sometimes major tweaks to software to get it to compile and run. Much of this effort is then pushed back upstream, and I've yet to see a project that isn't thankful for FreeBSD support being added.

Another element of FreeBSD that makes it a popular choice for people of the BSD mindset is the fact that it ships with ZFS as standard, and you're prompted to use ZFS for additional storage as well as the root filesystem of your device.

ZFS (specifically OpenZFS) is a filesystem, storage management, and all round wonder solution for storage desires. I've heard it being called "the last word in filesystems," and it's only the license associated with it that makes it uncommon on Linux platforms (FreeBSD has no such qualms).

 The cuddle, or **Common Development and Distribution License** (**CDDL**) is a fairly rare license in the open source world. Produced by Sun Microsystems in its heyday, the license has been called "incompatible" with the GPL.

While ZFS really is a great solution for storage, it can be confusing to newcomers, owing to the fact it doesn't follow the same patterns as traditional filesystems (even UFS—FreeBSD's simpler alternative) and blurs the lines a lot between filesystems and things like partitions. It also has some flaws. Because of its design, ZFS is memory-hungry, and given the fluctuating price of RAM in recent years, this can be prohibitive for end users.

FreeBSD also has a focus on stability, meaning that it includes features like the ability to rollback changes easily (if using ZFS) and has a very solid upgrade path (though it can be a little confusing and convoluted).

Jails are worth a mention too, since FreeBSD fans will be annoyed if I don't bring them up. Before Docker, there were jails, the ability to segment portions of your OS from each other on FreeBSD systems. Introduced in 2000, they allow FreeBSD users to segregate their software on a host system, and even install different versions of FreeBSD alongside each other so that software explicitly written for FreeBSD 9 can run on a FreeBSD 12 box.

 It's a bit unfair that jails didn't really take off, though a lot of this is down to FreeBSD market share again. They're also a lot more unwieldy than Docker and other container solutions, despite being arguably superior. I hold that Docker took off in the way it did owing in large part to places like Docker Hub, which FreeBSD lacked an equivalent of.

In short, I can sum up FreeBSD like so:

- **Pros**:
    - Ships with ZFS
    - Very up-to-date packages available
    - Stable systems

- FreeBSD jails
- Sensible segmentation of first-party packages and third-party (additional packages are normally wholly installed under `/usr/local/`)
- Very good "FreeBSD Handbook"

- **Cons**:

  - Smaller install base than Linux systems
  - Unlikely to have newer drivers (though this has improved in recent years)
  - Usually favors older solutions (X over Wayland)
  - Upgrade process can be confusing
  - Sometimes gets overlooked by vendors for patches and security disclosures (think vulnerabilities in Intel CPUs)

FreeBSD is a good choice, but I deliberately don't recommend it to Windows or macOS switchers. Instead, I point them to popular Linux distributions like Ubuntu and Fedora. FreeBSD has its place, and you can do a lot worse for a storage server, but it's not the first choice in a lot of minds.

OpenBSD

An OS with an almost legendary focus on security and stability, OpenBSD is the software that took out its "Linux compatibility layer" because of concerns around the security of keeping it.

If you've not heard of or used OpenBSD, I can guarantee that you've at least used an associated project. Some that fall under the OpenBSD realm are the following:

- LibreSSL
- OpenSMTPD
- OpenNTPD
- OpenSSH
- httpd (that's the OpenBSD-specific package, not re-badged Apache)

This means that while you've probably never SSH'd onto an OpenBSD system itself, you're still using software that's built primarily on OpenBSD systems. I know of no distribution of Linux that doesn't use OpenSSH as the default SSH client and server (though alternatives do exist).

The software aside, for as good as that software is, OpenBSD is so much more.

Being a relatively small project, and again both open source and donation-funded, OpenBSD doesn't have a very large install base, but it's extremely popular when it comes to embedded systems, firewalls, and routers. This is because while its multi-processor elements perhaps aren't as robust as some other projects, it features software such as the **packet filter (pf)** firewall, and is known for putting security first.

OpenBSD's tagline on their website is "Only two remote holes in the default install, in a heck of a long time!", which just goes to show exactly how committed to security they are. I've seen OpenBSD actively remove software because of the simple fact that it had dubious security associated with it.

 LibreSSL was born out of the frustration around OpenSSL and the fact that it was easier to fork and fix the project (in the developer's minds) than it was to argue for increased security upstream. It's easy to see how software that underpins a lot of the internet's security should be kept secure.

Famous for tweaking software to diminish the opportunity for vulnerabilities to pop up, this can sometimes backfire on OpenBSD, as they can get overlooked for vulnerability disclosure, for fear they'll fix the problem immediately (instead of waiting until the "official" date at which the vulnerability can be revealed to the public). For an interesting case study of this, see the "KRACK Attacks" vulnerability, and OpenBSD's response (https://www.krackattacks.com/#openbsd).

Because OpenBSD is a different OS to FreeBSD, it doesn't include the likes of jails nor does it have ZFS (favoring FFS). There isn't much you can do to the default installation in terms of tweaks, and the argument goes that "you shouldn't have to."

It can be used as a desktop, server (generally a firewall from what I've seen), or an embedded OS.

You could probably sum up OpenBSD as such:

- **Pros**:
    - Extremely heavy focus on security
    - Heavy focus on quality of code
    - Reasonable upgrade path (though time-consuming)
    - Frequent release cycle and fast patching
    - Pf, which is honestly great

- **Cons**:
  - Lack of packages (though its ports system has a lot)
  - Stable and secure can mean a lack of features (this depends on the individual really)
  - Very small install base
  - FFS is creaky and showing its age
  - Theo de Raadt (OpenBSD's benevolent dictator for life) is known to speak his mind (read into that what you will)

I use OpenBSD on a singular laptop, mostly for the experience of the thing, but we're on 6.4 now and it was first installed with 6.0 (that also featured some kick-ass release artwork). The laptop runs well, though it's doing very little most of the time. I have also tried using OpenBSD as a server, but for my sins I soon found it annoying when I couldn't get hold of packages I thought were pretty standard.

Understanding how Solaris and illumos differ

I've sort of been dreading this section, because it's very hard to talk about companies like Oracle without getting at least a little annoyed.

We're going to look briefly at the history of Oracle and their Sun acquisition, as well as looking at the OpenSolaris movement and the systems that spawned out of it.

Before we start, I should point out that illumos and Solaris have a very Unix background, and they're arguably the "purest" Unix derivatives available today. You might have never used either of them, but there's a good chance you've used a website or an online portal that's back-ended by either of these two OSes.

The differences

First, a bit of history.

Solaris (sort-of-previously SunOS) was released in the early nineties by Sun Microsystems, and was initially designed to work on the also-Sun SPARC line of processors, though it quickly got expanded to support x86 processors too.

For a while, Sun (and its purple behemoths in server racks everywhere) were well regarded and a fairly common sight in data centers. The company went from strength to strength, developing things such as Solaris Zones (like FreeBSD jails, as we discussed previously), ZFS, and Java.

Not really a home-user system, Solaris was popular alongside SPARC processors in enterprise environments, though as Linux gained traction and market mind-share, this and other alternative OSes, soon lost ground.

In 2005, Sun made the decision to open source Solaris under the CDDL license, creating the "OpenSolaris" project at the same time. This was an effort to build a community around Solaris that might increase uptake and mind-share.

However, when Oracle bought Sun in 2009 (completed in 2010), they almost immediately discontinued the practice of distributing public updates to the source code, and effectively reverted Solaris 11 (as it was) to being a closed source product.

They couldn't put the genie back in the bottle though, and the code had been released once already, meaning that while OpenSolaris effectively died, derivatives continued.

Confusingly, a lot of these derivatives fall under the "illumos" umbrella, which is probably the main fork of the OpenSolaris project, with some related projects such as SmartOS (from Joyent, now a Samsung company) deviating slightly.

illumos (small "i", for some reason) comprises a kernel, system libraries, system software, and device drivers.

In general, this means that when people refer to "Solaris" nowadays, they're either remembering Sun-of-old lovingly, alongside installations they may have done a decade ago, or they're using it to refer to the not-uncommon Solaris 11 that Oracle is still publishing, supporting, and allegedly actively developing. At the time of writing, the latest release was 11.4 in August of 2018.

I refer to SmartOS, OpenIndiana, and others as Solaris in casual conversation, though this is technically incorrect and probably going to get me an angry letter from Oracle one of these days.

Oracle Solaris

As we've already said, Oracle still actively publishes and supports Solaris, though a lot of the installations you'll come across these days are likely old installs that are still going. Solaris 10, first released in 2005, is technically still in support.

 Solaris 10 officially goes out of support in January 2021—though I'm willing to bet the limit to how long this support continues comes down to how deep your pockets are.

Featuring SPARC processor support and a tendency toward database installations, Solaris may be something you come across in your lifetime as an engineer, and if you do decide to become familiar with it, there's a good chance you'll join a diminishing pool of people with the knowledge of how to support it, meaning you may find yourself in demand.

 Please don't decide to learn Oracle Solaris inside and out on the gamble of having work in the future—I won't be held responsible if you find yourself an expert in a dead field.

ZFS is also a strong feature of Solaris, and while cross compatibility was attempted by the OpenZFS project, this seems to have fallen by the wayside in recent years, owing mostly to the diverging code base and a seeming unwillingness to keep parity of features by Oracle (though don't take my word on that—I'm just a consumer of rumor).

illumos

The spiritual continuation of the OpenSolaris project, illumos forms the base of a few different distributions that sought to keep the legacy of CDDL-based Solaris alive.

OpenIndiana is perhaps the most user-friendly of these distributions, and still features ongoing enhancements. It can be downloaded and tried out in a VM (which I would encourage, just for a poke around).

When you run it, though, don't be surprised to find references to Solaris and SunOS:

```
$ uname -a
SunOS openindiana 5.11 illumos-42a3762d01 i86pc i386 i86pc
```

Featuring a small package pool, you're also unlikely to find the trendier software of the day, but it will have the programming languages you're familiar with, and it's undeniably solid.

Both Oracle's Solaris and illumos have had some great minds work on them in the past, meaning that they also feature stable kernels and sensible approaches to development (if you believe some of the more vocal engineers who worked on it).

Sadly, there's a certain amount of head-butting that goes on in the Solaris, BSD, and Linux world, with everyone being very opinionated about the "correct" way to do specific things, despite all of these OSes being able to trace their legacy or inspiration back to a common core (Unix).

Personally, I like installing OSs and tinkering—I'm weird like that.

Understanding how Windows differs

You'll have to use Windows—it's a fact of life (at least at the moment).

If you're not forced to use Windows as the desktop OS of choice in your workplace, then there's a good chance there's going to be at least one Windows server you have to babysit or manage.

Windows still sees common installations for the following reasons:

- Active Directory
- Email with Exchange
- File servers

It's also used in the wider server world, with software like IIS holding a sizeable (though much smaller than open source offerings) chunk of the web.

Right from the off, and as we talked about previously, Windows and Linux differ in some key ways.

The differences

Windows is licensed. This is perhaps the most obvious difference between the open source offerings and the proprietary world. If you want to use Windows in production, you have to ensure that you're correctly licensed, or face a fine for being out of compliance.

Funnily enough, this is probably the biggest reason why Linux saw the adoption that it did. When faced with a free offering of something that can do the exact same thing you're trying to do with Windows, most admins would at least try the free version first.

The second most obvious difference, although this is slowly changing, is the fact that Windows installs a GUI by default, whereas Linux prefers a simple text prompt.

 The argument of CLI versus GUI has raged for years, and I'm not about to continue it now, but I will say that expending extra resources on graphics capabilities on an OS that's rarely—if ever—going to be logged into, seems immensely stupid and wasteful.

While it's perfectly possible to install a cut-down version of Windows now that doesn't feature a GUI (Windows Server 2016 Nano, for example), it's still not frequently seen in data centers, and a lot of functionality is still mostly driven by GUIs (especially in third-party software).

Unlike Linux, where SSH is king, Windows features **Remote Desktop Protocol** (RDP) as its connection method of choice, delivering a graphical representation of the server's desktop to your local machine.

Amusingly, RDP has also started to be replaced by the likes of remote PowerShell connections, and even SSH (which Microsoft has seemingly started to appreciate as a very nice and lightweight solution, though adoption rates are still up in the air).

Obviously, Windows also doesn't feature the Linux kernel, instead using the **NT kernel** for its own interaction with hardware and low-level work.

Anecdote time!

A few years ago, I was talking with a friend as we walked through the city after work. I was young and naive, so I casually mentioned that it might be a good idea for Linux people to use Windows more, because adoption from our side would only drive improvements on the other side of the fence.

This resulted in raucous laughter and mockery, along with my friend relaying this mad suggestion to others from our workplace once we got to the restaurant we were heading to. Everyone had a good chuckle at my expense and the matter was closed, with the general consensus from us Linux people being that Windows was always going to be garbage, and nothing could save it.

Fast forward a few years, that same friend now actively advocates PowerShell, has Windows installed on his work machine, and talks about the virtues of using Windows over Linux for select tasks.

I bring this up because I suspect he'll read this book at some point, and I just want to remind him that back in the midst of time, he dismissed Windows out of hand, just for being Windows.

Times do change, and while Microsoft still get a lot of (arguably justified) flack for their stance on things like privacy, they do seem to be making an effort to realize their OS as a cloud-world solution.

Some people reading this will be old enough to remember **embrace, extend, and extinguish (EEE)**, which is a phrase that was used internally at Microsoft to talk about its plan for manipulating open and widely adopted standards, extending them with proprietary additions before pushing the open and free alternatives out of the market, by saying their product could do everything the others could, and more. (Think AD, which is basically LDAP with more bells and whistles.)

There's a few people who believe Microsoft's recent "Microsoft loves Linux" stance is just a ploy, and we're about to see a revival of the "EEE" approach.

IaaS (Infrastructure as a Service)

In short and disingenuously, IaaS can be summed up as "cloud servers."

IaaS is the term used by cloud providers for denoting the idea that you can shift all those dusty, noisy, and expensive on-premises boxes into "the cloud."

In reality, the cloud is just the marketing term for "a bunch of servers in various data centres," and it annoys many engineers who dislike wool-filled terms that only serve to obfuscate and confuse.

The benefits of doing something like shifting your infrastructure into the cloud should be obvious, and we've discussed the idea of **Infrastructure as Code (IaC)**before.

Gone are the days when deploying a development environment means buying new servers from your distributor, racking and cabling them all, and making sure you've got a decent method of getting your OS of choice on there.

Now, infrastructure, from switches to firewalls and servers, can be deployed with only a few clicks of the mouse, or better yet, a few commands on the keyboard.

IaaS means that you can deploy thousands of boxes in seconds, and tear them down just as quickly. This scalability and ease of deployment has meant that companies who would previously need to have entire data centres, just for jobs they ran once a month, can now save the cost of power and cooling by simply spinning up those servers for one "fifteen minute job" and then removing them again.

Perhaps the biggest benefit of using a cloud solution for your infrastructure though, is the fact you don't have to worry about the underlying hardware. Someone else (the provider) is responsible for making sure that the servers you're building on top of are working, and you generally don't have to concern yourself with things like hardware alarms.

IaaS providers and features

The biggest provider of IaaS services at the moment is Amazon, with their **Amazon Web Services (AWS)** offering. It might seem a bit strange that an online retailer is also the biggest supplier of cloud solutions, but when you consider the infrastructure they would have had to design and build for their own platform, it makes sense that they would see their way to selling it as a service.

AWS is well supported by IaC tools such as Terraform and Packer, being a first class citizen, and it also features tools of its own, such as CloudFormation (like Terraform).

Amusingly, AWS also obfuscates names for some strange reason, leading to sites like `https://www.expeditedssl.com/aws-in-plain-english`, which offers a list of Amazon's names for things, and then the English equivalent.

EC2, for example, is basically Amazon's name for servers.

AWS was launched in 2006, meaning that they had a head-start on Azure, which launched in 2010.

Microsoft, with Azure, are probably the second largest supplier of cloud solutions, and they have the added advantage that if your enterprise signs up to use Office365 for email and documents, there's a good chance Microsoft will push you to use Azure for your infrastructure, too.

There's obviously other providers too, and not all IaaS has to be a remote solution. You could deploy an OpenStack installation in your data centre, and then interact with its APIs to create an IaaS platform that you use to programmatically spin up virtual infrastructure. Obviously, the caveat here is that you still have to maintain the underlying boxes, OS, and IaaS software.

Google has an IaaS offering, as do Oracle, Rackspace, and IBM. On the smaller side, you have the likes of DigitalOcean, Scaleway, and OVH. The choice is yours as to which you use, and it comes down to features that are offered more often than not.

If you have certain requirements (such as data sovereignty), you may find that you absolutely have to use an on-shore offering, meaning that you may find some of the contenders for IaaS providers are instantly ruled out, but there's usually something to fit your needs.

IaaS provides the administrator with flexibility, which means that you no longer run the risk of under-speccing a box for specific software, as you can determine if you need more resources and simply destroy the box, before creating a new one of a bigger type.

IaaS means that your firewall and load balancer rules are no longer stored in a dumped config file from the half-U box that's inconspicuously whirring near your feat. Instead, you can configure text files, which are then read and applied as the rest of your infrastructure is built.

IaaS even means that you can test your infrastructure periodically, destroying and rebuilding whole clusters on a schedule, just to make sure an OS update or a code change hasn't broken anything.

PaaS (Platform as a Service)

On the other side of IaaS, or perhaps in parallel to it, is the concept of PaaS.

Platform as a Service is almost the logical continuation of the virtualization of infrastructure, abstracting one level further and asking the question "why are we asking our users to spin up a server for PostgreSQL, when we could just spin up a PostgreSQL instance?".

Yes, there will always be a server somewhere, that's a given. These services don't just run ephemerally atop a CPU that's floating in a room full of mist somewhere (despite that being a cool mental image), but the critical part of this philosophy is the idea that you don't care.

Realistically, you don't give a damn about the OS your database is running on, as long as it's actually running and isn't about to crash. However, as an administrator in the past, you would be tasked with exactly that—keeping on top of patches and reboots just to make sure that the database itself kept going.

PaaS as a concept therefore sounds wonderful.

Why should you spin up several OS instances for hosting a website, running a database, or deploying Redis, when you could use off-the-shelf offerings that provide an endpoint to connect to, and leave the worry of the OS behind?

In the new world, you can deploy your website to a shared web segment, connect to a database you've specified, and interact with a Redis endpoint that you've no idea what version of Linux it's running on top of (if it's Linux at all!).

In theory, this also means that developers will have an easier time when writing software, as they don't have to concern themselves with specific OS quirks or minor differences that might affect their code. As long as developers target the common platform provided to them by PaaS, they need not know what OS is running underneath at all.

PaaS providers and features

As with IaaS, AWS and Azure are rife with PaaS offerings.

The most obvious offerings are databases, with AWS offering PaaS relational databases, NoSQL databases (DynamoDB), and caching systems like Amazon ElastiCache.

Azure offerings for databases include MSSQL deployments (obviously) and recently, the inclusion of PostgreSQL too.

Amazon offer domain name services in the form of Route 53 (ha-ha guys, very clever, now quit it with the stupid naming). They also offer CDN solutions, VPN setups, and Active Directory services.

Azure offer a CDN solution too, alongside Web Apps (used to host web applications and sites), Azure Blob Storage, and non-relational database offerings, such as Cosmos DB. There's even a specifically named "Redis Cache" offering to stop you having to create your own.

The list goes on and on, meaning that it's not uncommon for greenfield projects to get lost among the potentials they can use in their deployment. I would hazard that a good rule of thumb for any 21st Century sysadmin should be "if you don't have to manage it, don't try."

If you can get away with using a PaaS option, do, because in the long run it'll save you an immense amount of headaches. While the learning curve might be steep to begin with, you'll thank your lucky stars that you've gone with a PaaS offering the next time there's some major OS vulnerability and you need to start a round of critical patching.

Azure and AWS are the obvious two, but as with IaaS, other providers do exist. GCP (Google Compute Platform) is the most obvious third contender, but the smaller providers are taking their tentative first steps into the market too.

DigitalOcean have started offering things like managed Kubernetes (which is sort of PaaS, because you can deploy your own containers into a managed platform), block storage, and load balancers. Scaleway have started a public beta for Object Storage (at the time of writing).

I think the biggest problem with PaaS is the fact that a lot of work goes into it behind the scenes to make it seamless for the end users.

You consume that database offering like it's nothing, creating your schema atop a transparent fabric, but somewhere down the chain, someone is having to design and maintain the systems those PaaS offerings sit atop... I hope they get paid a lot of money to do it.

Obviously, there's negatives—when you go PaaS, there's frequently a case of WYSIWYG (what you see is what you get), and the off-the-shelf offering you're using won't always be a hundred percent suitable for what you need. If it's ninety percent suitable, though, you need to make the judgement call on if it's worth that ten percent, or if you'd rather fight a full-fat but customizable IaaS deployment instead.

The Ops versus DevOps Wars

DevOps as a word has been misunderstood, abused, and twisted by recruiters everywhere.

Go to the subreddit for DevOps (`https://old.reddit.com/r/devops`) and you'll see DevOps referred to as a "movement," which is what it was originally intended to be.

A contraction of Development and Operations, DevOps is supposed to be a methodology that combines the principles of software development with traditional IT operations.

However, we live in the real world, and while it might be fun for you to shout "DevOps isn't a job title!" at the recruiter on the other end of the phone (don't do this), it doesn't make the winds of change any weaker.

I've been called a DevOps engineer, and I know many other people who have too. I've also applied for jobs that were specifically hiring for "a DevOps person to come on-board and help us evolve." It comes down to usage, as with so much in the language world, and if the person doing the hiring says "I want a DevOps," then the recruiter is going to advertise for one.

The sector itself is only going from strength to strength, as the proven advantages of combining traditional development approaches with infrastructure and application management become more obvious, and the rise of IaaS and PaaS solutions has only succeeded in speeding this adoption up.

In short, I would say working in a DevOps environment comes down to the following:

- Appreciating infrastructure as code
- Valuing reusability of code and practices
- Assessing and adopting new technologies or practices where appropriate

Many people have different definitions of what "DevOps" is, despite those who shout until they're blue in the face that it's a black and white definition, but perhaps the worst offenders are the stuck sysadmins and operations engineers who simply don't believe in progress.

I've met people like this—those who don't believe in codification—who seem to like snowflake servers for some reason, and who always bill themselves as administrators, despite being overlooked for jobs because of it.

There's definitely value in knowing and appreciating traditional system administration, but those skills go hand in hand with modern methodologies.

More of a skirmish, really

It used to be that every sysadmin was expected to know at least a little bit of SQL, because they were usually thought of as being the DBA (Database Administrator) for the infrastructure, too. Now, it's assumed that the sysadmin will also be proficient in at least a couple of "DevOps" tools.

> "DevOps tools" also has a bit of a vague definition, but anything by Hashicorp probably applies.

Where things start to get tricky is the devolution of responsibility.

There are companies out there that have the following:

- A platform team
- An operations team
- A DevOps team
- A development team with a DevOps engineer

You tell me, based on the aforementioned list, who is responsible for making sure that the OS is up to date.

It's the platform team, surely? The platform is theirs, so they've got a responsibility to ensure that all the OSes in the environment are on the latest version.

But what about the DevOps team? They wrote the code to configure the boxes, and we know that a bit of their Ansible runs a "yum update" right at the beginning—surely they should just run that same Ansible again?

What about operations? In the past, their responsibility might have been ensuring OS changes didn't impact software, so surely they should be the ones to update the OS?

The developers are the ones who want the latest features of that OS package, and they're the ones who've asked for the update to be done—does the responsibility therefore lie with their "DevOps" team member?

It's confusing, but not uncommon, to see arguments about responsibility, or even arguments about what job title an individual is hired for.

Partly, this is the fault of the company for not defining a rigid structure, but it's also the fault of people who bill themselves a certain way and then silo themselves from anything they don't deem to be related to their job.

If you find yourself in a company like this, with warring factions who don't want to take responsibility for anything, it might be an idea to talk to your superior, or superior's superior, or even CTO, about structure.

A friend of mine once said (and I'm paraphrasing), "the job title changes, but we're just operations engineers at the end of the day." His meaning was that while new technologies and trends come and go (I'm looking at you, Node.js!), we'll still be needed in our traditional capacities to pick up the pieces when it all goes to hell.

Roundup – BSDs, Solaris, Windows, IaaS and PaaS, DevOps

I wanted this chapter to be a bit of a mixed bag that touched on various addendum elements to our existence as system administrators. Many of these concepts could fill a chapter on their own, but I've already been told by a few people that this book is too long, and I've not even finished writing it yet!

Hopefully you've got some idea about the other OSes that exist in the world, if you didn't already, and you might even have an inclination to go away from this chapter and install SmartOS, or OpenBSD, which I would highly encourage. It's good to not silo yourself, and who knows? At some point in the future, this beast we know as Linux might die, and something else could rise from the ashes to take its place. You should be ready.

Like Linux dying, traditional system administration is definitely changing, and if my somewhat sarcastic tone throughout this chapter has suggested anything, it's that you should be ready to change with it. IaaS is already commonplace, though it's increasingly losing market share to PaaS solutions, especially in the enterprise world. Learn how to deploy a website without touching an underlying OS once, and you'll be in demand (for the moment, at least).

Lastly, there's DevOps, which I've tried to keep short on purpose, because I already think I'm going to get people arguing with me about definitions. My friend is right, and our job title seems to changes every five years, but ultimately it always comes back to the same thing—do you know where to find the log file, and can you work out why the service crashed?

If you take anything away from this section, take away the fact that you'll never know everything there is to know about the systems administration world, but the more you know, the more you can earn... or the more pride you might feel in your work—something fluffy like that.

Other Books You May Enjoy

If you enjoyed this book, you may be interested in these other books by Packt:

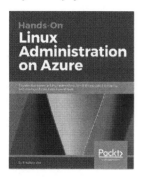

Hands-On Linux Administration on Azure
Frederik Vos

ISBN: 978-1-78913-096-6

- Understand why Azure is the ideal solution for your open source workloads
- Master essential Linux skills and learn to find your way around the Linux environment
- Deploy Linux in an Azure environment
- Use configuration management to manage Linux in Azure
- Manage containers in an Azure environment
- Enhance Linux security and use Azure's identity management systems
- Automate deployment with Azure Resource Manager (ARM) and Powershell
- Employ Ansible to manage Linux instances in an Azure cloud environment

PowerShell Core for Linux Administrators Cookbook
Prashanth Jayaram, Ram Iyer

ISBN: 978-1-78913-723-1

- Leverage the object model of the shell, which is based on .NET Core
- Administer computers locally as well as remotely using PowerShell over OpenSSH
- Get to grips with advanced concepts of PowerShell functions
- Use PowerShell for administration on the cloud
- Know the best practices pertaining to PowerShell scripts and functions
- Exploit the cross-platform capabilities of PowerShell to manage scheduled jobs, Docker containers and SQL Databases

Leave a review - let other readers know what you think

Please share your thoughts on this book with others by leaving a review on the site that you bought it from. If you purchased the book from Amazon, please leave us an honest review on this book's Amazon page. This is vital so that other potential readers can see and use your unbiased opinion to make purchasing decisions, we can understand what our customers think about our products, and our authors can see your feedback on the title that they have worked with Packt to create. It will only take a few minutes of your time, but is valuable to other potential customers, our authors, and Packt. Thank you!

Index